SYSTEMS OF PSYCHOTHERAPY

A Transtheoretical Analysis

■ SYSTEMS OF PSYCHOTHERAPY

A Transtheoretical	James O. Prochaska
Analysis	*Department of*
	Psychology
	University of
	Rhode Island

Second Edition

BROOKS/COLE PUBLISHING COMPANY
Pacific Grove, California

© THE DORSEY PRESS, 1979, and 1984

ISBN 0-534-10708-7
Former ISBN 0-256-03049-9
Library of Congress Catalog Card No. 83-51070

Printed in the United States of America

10 9 8 7

To Jan

PREFACE

IN THE PAST SEVERAL YEARS the need for integration across therapy systems has been increasingly recognized. In fact Allen Bergin, one of the editors of the *Handbook of Psychotherapy,* has called the search for synthesis the most important trend in contemporary psychotherapy. It is gratifying to know that experts such as Marvin Goldfried in his book, *Converging Themes in Psychotherapy,* have recognized *Systems of Psychotherapy* as a significant contribution toward convergence in psychotherapy.

Even more gratifying have been the many letters and comments from students, professors, and professionals who have found this book to be helpful in developing a more integrative overview of the field of psychotherapy. While the feedback has been surprisingly positive, readers have contributed some excellent suggestions for the second edition. For the most part these suggestions seem to reflect four of the most important developments in psychotherapy.

The first development is the resurgence of interest in psychoanalytic therapies. This resurgence has been led in part by the growing awareness of object relations theory. The second edition now includes an important section in Chapter 2 on the implications of object relations theory for therapy.

The second development is the increased acceptance of cognitive approaches to therapy. The expanding importance of cognitive approaches has led to the inclusion of sections on Beck's cognitive therapy in Chapter 7 and Meichenbaum's cognitive behavior modification in Chapter 10.

The third major development has been the rise of systems therapies. Systems thinking has crossed the boundaries of family therapy and is now an important part of general psychotherapy. A new chapter has been added on systems therapies, including the communications perspectives of Jackson, Haley, and Satir, the structural therapy of Minuchin, and the family systems therapy of Bowen.

The fourth major development is the movement toward integration across therapy systems. The final chapter presents the advances that have been made in building a transtheoretical model of systematic eclecticism.

With these additions this book now includes an analysis of 24 theories of psychotherapy. This means that a broader survey is provided than is available in most books on therapy. Increasing the breadth of this book, however, has been done only within the context of a comparative analysis that seeks to discover what is common to different therapy systems without blurring their essential differences.

The second edition also includes a broader survey of therapy outcome research than is available in most books on therapy. The expanding area of comparative therapy outcome research has been updated. A decision has been made, however, to emphasize studies that have focused on actual clients. Analogue studies using college students or community volunteers with circumscribed symptoms are included either when they are the only studies available on particular therapies or when they provide unique insights into therapeutic processes.

The number of people who have contributed to my appreciation for the complexities of psychotherapy continues to expand. In particular I have benefited from close collaboration with colleagues and students such as Wayne Velicer, John Norcross, Ellie McConnaughy, Nancy Wilcox, Steve Ginpil, Ed Guadagnoli, Duane Lapsanski, Peter Reid, and Bill Zwick. Special appreciation goes to my good friend, collaborator, and co-developer of the transtheoretical approach, Carlo C. DiClemente. People who have been particularly helpful from a distance include Mitchell Balter, Gerald Davison, Marvin Goldfried, and Saul Shiffman. I am also grateful to the National Cancer Institute for their generous support of our Self-Change Laboratory and our research on the transtheoretical model of change. A special thanks goes to Julie Lee and Elaine Taylor for their tireless efforts in working the word processor to make this manuscript well prepared for printing.

As with the first edition, my deepest appreciation goes to my wife, friend, and colleague, Jan, and to my children, Jason and Jodi, who enable me, even in the process of completing a book, to share in the joys of living and growing.

James O. Prochaska

PREFACE TO
THE FIRST EDITION

THIS BOOK PROVIDES a systematic survey of 18 theories of psychotherapy. It is designed to be more than just a survey since it also strives to be a synthesis both within each system and across the various systems of psychotherapy. Within a particular system of therapy, this book follows the integrative steps that flow from the system's theory of personality to its theory of psychopathology and culminates in its theory of therapeutic processes.

To begin synthesizing across systems, this book provides an integrative, eclectic framework that can highlight the many similarities of therapy systems without blurring their essential differences. The comparative analysis that emerges clearly demonstrates how much therapeutic systems agree on the processes producing change while disagreeing on the content that needs to be changed.

The goals of this book reflect in part the personal goals I have as a practitioner, teacher, researcher, and theorist of therapy.

As an eclectic therapist, I have some appreciation for the vitality and personal meaning that different therapeutic approaches can have for different clients and therapists. In this book I attempt to communicate the excitement and depth of understanding that emerges from theories constructed to help guide us through the inner and outer worlds of our clients. I try to avoid just describing each system as a detached observer, but rather try to throw myself into each system and respond to it as an advocate.

As a therapist I believe that a book on such a vital field as psychotherapy must try to come alive to do justice to the discipline. To this end I have included a wealth of case illustrations drawn from my own practice over the past 12 years. At least one reviewer of this book seemed to find it difficult to believe how many different therapies I have used in my work as an eclectic. All I can say is that the cases described reflect the actual procedures used, though some of the details about individuals have been changed at times to guarantee the confidentiality of my clients.

As a teacher of those becoming therapists I realize the complexity of the concepts underlying most major approaches to therapy. This book attempts to present the essential concepts clearly and concisely while also trying to avoid oversimplification. Some of my students have argued that theorists seem to have a knack for making things more complicated than they are. Of course, most theorists of therapy are convinced that the conditions of clients and of change are indeed more complex than common sense would lead us to believe. I hope that as students move through these systems of therapy they can gain a deeper appreciation for either how complex is the human condition or how complex are the minds of those attempting to articulate the human condition.

The theories in this book each assume that therapy has the potential for making a powerful impact on patients. Therapy is seen more as analogous to penicillin than to an aspirin. With interventions expected to produce strong rather than weak effects, we should be able to demonstrate the effectiveness of therapeutic systems even in the face of error due to measurement and control problems. This book includes, therefore, a comprehensive survey of the controlled outcome studies that have been designed to test the effectiveness of each of the systems of therapy.

As a theorist of therapy, I believe the field does not need any additional systems of therapy. What our ambiguous and amorphous discipline does need is a continuing effort to pull together the essential variables that are operating whenever any therapy system is being effective and to discard those variables that are not essential to the effective practice of therapy. From comparative analyses of the major systems of therapy, it is hoped we will have a more clear understanding of which variables need to be tested most completely in our clinics and in our research laboratories. From comparative analyses like the present book and from comparative research, the hope is that we can move toward a higher level of integration that will begin to yield a transtheoretical form of therapy.

My own endeavors in completing this book have been aided immeasurably by my students, colleagues, friends, and family. In particular I appreciate the efforts of Cora Banerjee, Val Brewer, Carlo DiClemente, Carol Heckerman, Ray Kilduff, Jeanne Lemkau, Bill Merkel, Dolph Printz, Pam Roffman, Ruth Schennum, Rick Silverman, Tim Swann, Will Wilson, and George Zachery, graduate students in our program whose work benefited this book. I would like to give special thanks to my students, Carlo DiClemente, Carol Heckerman, Bill Merkel, and Dolph Printz for their challenges and contributions to my thinking about therapy.

I am also grateful to Kenneth Heller and Lee Sechrest for their thorough reviews of the manuscript and to Gerald Davison, not only for his consistently insightful comments but also for the reinforcements that he seemed to deliver at just the right intervals; these individuals, of course, bear no responsibility for any of the book's shortcomings. I am also indebted to the typographical and cryptological skills of my manuscript secretary, Jean Parrish. Finally, my deepest appreciation to my wife, friend, and colleague, Jan, and to my children, Jason and Jodi, who were willing to sacrifice for the sake of my scholarship, available for support when I emerged from my solitude, and always ready for fun when I strayed from my study.

James O. Prochaska

CONTENTS

AN INTEGRATIVE ECLECTIC FRAMEWORK FOR COMPARING SYSTEMS OF PSYCHOTHERAPY

THE FIELD OF PSYCHOTHERAPY is fragmenting from future shock. The fragmentation comes from the unprecedented pace at which new therapies are placed on the market. In 1976 Parloff reported 130 therapies on the therapeutic marketplace. By 1979 *Time* magazine was reporting over 200 therapies. New approaches are usually presented as the best answer to treatment, with the developers of new systems usually claiming 80 to 100 percent success (e.g., Janov, 1970; Stampfl & Levis, 1967; Wolpe, 1958). Students, practitioners, and patients are faced with the dilemma of too many choices. With so many therapy systems claiming success, how do we choose which therapy, if any, to study or to use?

A book by a proponent of a particular therapy system can be quite persuasive. We may even find ourselves using the new ideas in therapy while reading the book. But when we turn to an advocate of a radically different approach, the confusion returns. Listening to proponents compare therapies does little for our confusion, except to confirm the rule that those who cannot agree on basic assumptions are often reduced to calling each other names. The author believes, however, that fragmentation in the field of psychotherapy can best be reduced by a comparative analysis of systems of psychotherapy that highlights the many similiarities across systems without blurring essential differences.

A comparative analysis requires an adequate understanding of each of the individual systems of therapy to be compared. In discussing each system, we will first introduce the developer of the system. We shall then trace the system's theory of personality as it leads to its theory of abnormal personality and concludes in its theory of therapy. Available controlled research will then be presented on the effectiveness of each system of therapy.

In comparing systems we will use an integrative eclectic model to demonstrate their similarities and differences. An eclectic model was selected in part because of the eclectic spirit of seeking what is useful and worthwhile in each system of therapy rather than looking primarily for what is most easily criticized. We also agree with an eclectic definition that views therapy as the application of psychological principles to the solution of personal problems, with the particular principles applied being determined by the particular problems to be solved. Eclecticism also seems to represent the mainstream of modern therapy, since recent research suggests that eclecticism is the most popular orientation for therapists (Norcross & Prochaska, 1982; Prochaska & Norcross, 1983).

What is lacking for most eclectics is an adequate, integrative model that can provide an intellectual framework for thinking and working across systems. Later in this chapter, an integrative model will be presented that is complex enough to do justice to the complexities of psychotherapy yet simple enough to reduce confusion in the field. In the model it is assumed that there are 5, rather than 200, basic processes of change that underlie contemporary systems of therapy. The model also demonstrates how the content of therapy can be reduced to four different levels of personal functioning rather than having to work with 200 theories of personality.

The systems of therapy will be compared on the particular process or combination of processes used to produce change and on the level of personal functioning that is to be changed. The systems will also be compared on how they would conceptualize and treat the most common problems that occur at each level of personal functioning, such as esteem, intimacy, and impulse-control problems. Since therapists are concerned primarily with the real problems of real people, we will not limit our comparative analysis to just concepts and data. Our analysis also will include a comparison of how each of the major systems would conceptualize and treat the same complex client.

We have limited our comparative analysis to 24 systems of therapy. Systems have been omitted because they seem to be dying a natural death and are best left undisturbed, because they are so poorly developed that they have no theories of personality or pathology, or because they are primarily variations on major themes that are already included in the book. The final criterion for exclusion is less open to bias, and that is that no system was excluded if more than 3 percent of surveyed therapists considered themselves to be followers of it (Norcross & Prochaska, 1982).

Before entering further into the poorly charted field of psychotherapy, let us become familiar with an integrative, eclectic model that will serve as the basis for our comparative analysis of the major systems of psychotherapy. While it is assumed that this model can do justice to the variety of therapies to be analyzed, it is by no means a closed system. As we progress from one therapy to another, we may find that additions or deletions are needed in order to build a model that more adequately fits the field of psychotherapy. With this openness in mind, let us examine the variables that at this point seem sufficient to begin synthesizing the increasingly divergent discipline of psychotherapy.

PRECONDITIONS FOR THERAPY: NONSPECIFIC VARIABLES

First we must consider the variety of nonspecific variables that are assumed to influence the outcome of therapy. The term *nonspecific* implies that these variables are not specific to any particular system of therapy. They are frequently not even specified by theories as being of central importance but nevertheless are assumed to be part of any approach to therapy.

Expectation

Expectation is one of the most widely debated and investigated of these nonspecific variables. More than 100 studies (DuPont, 1975) have been carried out to determine just how much of the variance of the therapy's success is accounted for by the particular expectations patients have toward therapy. The working hypothesis of most of these studies is that the effectiveness of therapy is influenced by the extent to which clients expect the treatment to be effective. Some critics hold that therapy is nothing but a process in which we induce an expectation in our clients that our treatment will cure them, and that any resulting improvement is a function of the client's expecting to improve. Surely many therapists wish on difficult days that the process were so simple!

The available evidence suggests no such simple answer. The studies are rather evenly divided as to whether expectations induced in clients even effect improvement, let alone determine outcome (DuPont, 1975; Wilkins, 1971). Of the studies reporting expectation effects, the vast majority demonstrate that a high, positive expectation adds to the effectiveness of such therapies as systematic desensitization. The therapies studied, however, can by no means be reduced to only expectation effects. While the evidence is not yet in, it will be our assumption that expectation is an important variable for all systems of therapy. Rather than being the central process of change, however, a positive expectation is assumed to be a critical precondition for therapy to continue. It is assumed that most clients would not participate in a process that costs them dearly in time, money, and energy if they did not expect the process to help them. In order for clients to cooperate with such processes as being desensitized, hypnotized, or analyzed, it seems reasonable that most of them would need to expect at least some improvement from their efforts.

The Hawthorne Effect

Psychologists have known for years that many people can improve in such behaviors as work output just by having special attention paid to them. In the classic Hawthorne studies (Roethlisberger & Dickson, 1939) on the effects of improved lighting on productivity in a factory, it was discovered that participants increased their output as a result of just being in a study and having special attention paid to them. Usually such improvement is assumed to be due to the increase in morale and esteem that people experience from having others attend to them.

One aspect of all therapies is that the therapist gives special attention to the client. Consequently, attention has been assumed to be one of the nonspecific variables that either affect or determine the results of therapy. Anyone who has been in therapy can appreciate the gratification that comes from having a competent professional give undivided attention for an hour. To be freely ego-centric and talk just about ourselves without worrying about someone else wanting to talk, and then to have someone truly attend to our monologues, surely can be a boost to our narcissistic esteem. This special attention may indeed affect the results of therapy, including perhaps cases in which patients do not improve because they do not want to give up such special attention.

Researchers have frequently found that attention does indeed lead to im-provement regardless of whether the attention is followed by any other thera-peutic processes. Paul (1966), for example, found that 50 percent of public-speaking phobics demonstrated marked improvement of their symptoms fol-lowing treatment with an attention placebo that was intended to control for such nonspecific variables as attention. Equally striking was his finding that a group receiving similar attention plus insight-oriented therapy demonstrated no greater improvement than the group receiving attention placebo alone, while a group receiving attention plus desensitization showed much greater improvement. While there were problems with fairness of Paul's test of insight therapy, such as being limited to only five sessions, his study does suggest that attention can be a powerful nonspecific variable in therapy.

Since special attention is inherent in the procedures of almost all therapies, it is assumed that such attention is probably one of the variables affecting outcome. To be able to conclude that any particular therapy is more than just an attention placebo, it is necessary that the research on that therapy include controls for attention effects. It is not enough to demonstrate that a particular system of therapy is better than no treatment, since the improvement from that particular therapy may be due entirely to the attention given the patients. The most popular way to control for such effects is to use attention-placebo groups, as in Paul's study where control subjects were given as much attention as clients in therapy but did not participate in processes designed to produce change. Another alternative is to examine studies that compare the effective-ness of one system of therapy with that of another, such as Freudian analysis with Adlerian therapy. If one therapeutic approach does better than another, we can conclude that its effects are due to more than just attention, since the less effective treatment included—and therefore controlled for— effects of at-tention. However, we do not know whether the less effective therapy is any-thing other than a placebo effect even if it leads to greater improvement than no treatment. Finally, in such comparative studies, if both therapies lead to significant improvement, and neither therapy does better than the other, we cannot conclude that the therapies are anything more than Hawthorne effects, unless an attention-placebo control has also been included in the study. To be considered an adequately controlled evaluation of a therapy's effectiveness, studies must include controls for such nonspecific variables as attention.

PROCESSES OF CHANGE

Rather than there being as many processes as therapies, the multitude of therapy systems are assumed by the author to be reducible to one or more of the following five basic processes of change.

Consciousness Raising

Traditionally, increasing an individual's consciousness has been one of the major processes of change in psychotherapy. Consciousness-raising programs sound so contemporary, yet therapists with a variety of persuasions have been working for decades to increase the consciousness of clients. Beginning with Freud's assumption that the basic therapeutic cure is "to make the unconscious conscious," all of the systems that London (1964) labels the "verbal psychotherapies" begin by working to raise the individual's level of awareness. It is fitting that verbal therapies work with consciousness, since traditionally consciousness has been assumed to be a human characteristic that emerged with the evolution of language.

While much about changing consciousness remains to be discovered, there are some aspects of consciousness raising that appear to be relevant to systems of psychotherapy. With language and consciousness we do not respond reflexively to the energy in a stimulus, such as the mechanical energy from a hand hitting against our back, which causes us to react with movement. Instead we respond to the information contained in stimuli, such as whether that hand touching us is a pat on the back from a friend, a robber grabbing us, or a spouse hitting us. In order to respond effectively, we must have adequate information to guide us in making a response appropriate to the stimulus. Therapies that involve increasing consciousness are assumed to increase the information available to individuals so they can make the most effective responses to the stimuli impinging on them.

As with each of the other basic processes of change, the therapist's focus can be to produce change either at the level of the individual's experience or at the level of the individual's environment. When the information given clients is contained in the stimulation generated by the individual's own actions and experiences, we call that *feedback*. An example of this process occurred with a stern and proper middle-aged woman who was unaware of just how angry she appeared to be. She could not connect her children's avoidance of her or her recent rash of automobile accidents with anger, because she kept insisting that she was not at all angry. After viewing videotapes of herself interacting with members of a therapy group, however, she was stunned. All she could say was, "My God, how angry I seem to be!"

(We should indicate at this point that in the case of this woman, as with so many clients in therapy, we cannot demonstrate that the way we conceptualize the person's problems is, in fact, the way things really are. We cannot, for example, demonstrate in an empirical manner that this woman's problems were due to angry feelings that were outside of her awareness. Nevertheless, it can still be useful in therapy to make assumptions about the origins of a client's problems. As future case illustrations are presented, they will be described in the manner that the author found most helpful for the purposes of therapy without assuming some ultimate validity of the clinical interpretations.)

When the information given in therapy is contained in stimulation generated by environmental events, we call this *education*. An example of change in therapy due to such education was an aging man who became quite depressed over the fact that his time to attain erections and reach orgasms had increased noticeably over the past few years. He was very relieved when he learned that such delay was what Masters and Johnson (1966) found to be normal in older men.

One of the most important areas for feedback is the information regarding the cognitive processes and structures that individuals use to ward off threatening information about themselves or their environments. These defensive processes and structures are like blinders, such as the "rose-colored glasses" that some people use to selectively attend to only the positive information about themselves and the world and disattend to negative input. Such cognitive blinders prevent individuals from being able to increase their consciousness without feedback or education from an outside party. For example, my wife, who is also a therapist, confronted me with the following information that made me aware of one set of blinders I was wearing. We were trying to see if we could anticipate who would be on our partner's list of sexually attractive individuals. I was absolutely sure that my first three guesses would be high on my wife's list. When I said a friend's name, my wife laughed and said that she knew I always thought that, but she wasn't attracted to him. She also said that she was now sure that his wife was on my list. My next two guesses were also wrong, but my wife was quickly able to guess that I found their wives attractive. I was amazed to realize how much I had been projecting over the years and how my projection kept me from being aware of the qualities in men that my wife found appealing.

Since our conceptualization of consciousness raising focuses on information processing, using the more current label of *cognitive* approaches to therapy might seem preferable to *consciousness-changing* approaches. The concept of changes in consciousness is used, however, partly because it has a much longer history in psychotherapy. Even more important, the term *cognitive processes* might be misleading if it implied that the information processed in therapy produced only a cognitive response in clients. Obviously, the information in therapy is usually very personal and likely to produce as strong an affective response as a cognitive response.

An illustration of this occurred during a session with a family that had come into therapy partly because the stepfather had beaten his 16-year-old stepson when he found him smoking marijuana. For several years the stepfather had lectured the boy about the dangers of drinking and of drugs, but the boy could not understand why his stepfather got so livid over the issue. Finally, the stepfather revealed that he had been an alcoholic for 10 years and had spent a year in a hospital struggling to overcome his problem. The stepfather said he had withheld the information because of the effect it might have on his stepson's feelings and actions toward him. We assume that information such as this, that is central to personal problems, always carries the potential for producing emotional and behavioral changes as well as cognitive change.

How can our awareness of such information lead to a change in our actions or experiences? Since definitive answers are not available from research, we must at times rely on analogies to further our understanding. If we think of our consciousness as a beam of light, then the information unavailable to us is like darkness containing stimuli that we can bump into, be held back by, or be directed by without knowing just what is influencing us. In the areas of darkness, we are like blind individuals, knowing that there is an array of stimuli influencing us but not having enough light on the stimuli to guide us effectively in our lives. For example, without being aware of how aging normally affects a man's sexual response, the aging man would not know whether the best direction for himself was to admit he was over the hill and give up on sex, to eat two raw eggs a day as an aphrodisiac, or to enjoy his present ability to respond without trying to live up to some stereotype of male sexuality.

As we shall see, many systems of therapy agree that individuals can change as a function of increasing consciousness. A translation of traditional terms will also demonstrate that these systems are involved in the process of making available experiential or environmental information that was previously unavailable to the individual. The disagreement among some of these consciousness-raising systems is on the concrete techniques that are most effective in helping individuals process information that can have a profound impact on them.

Catharsis

Catharsis has one of the longest traditions as a process of therapeutic change. It is well known that the ancient Greeks, for example, believed that evoking emotions was one of the best means of providing personal relief and improvement. Traditionally, catharsis has been based on a hydraulic model of emotions in which unacceptable affects, such as anger, guilt, or anxiety, are blocked from direct expression. The damming off of such emotions results in pressure from affects to be released in some manner, no matter how indirectly, such as anger being expressed through headaches. If emotions can be released more directly in therapy, then their reservoir of energy is discharged, and the person is freed from a source of symptoms.

At times the patient with blocked emotions is compared to a person with constipation, and the patient is seen as emotionally constipated. What such patients need to release the stress on their system is a good, emotional bowel movement. In this analogy, therapy serves as a psychological enema that allows patients to purge their emotions and be free from fighting such feelings. The therapeutic process is aimed at helping patients break through their emotional blocks. By expressing the dark side of themselves in the presence of another, the individuals are presumably more able to accept such emotions as natural phenomena that need not be so severely controlled in the future.

Most often this therapeutic process has been at the level of individual experience, in which the stimuli that elicit cathartic reactions come from within the individual. We shall call this form of catharsis *corrective emotional experiences*. A therapist related an experience of such catharsis a couple of years ago when he was trying to fight off a bout of depression. He hadn't been able to get in touch with the source of his depression, so he took off a mental health day from work. Alone at home, he put on some music and started to express some of his feelings in a free form of dance that he can do only when no one else is present. After some very releasing movements, he began to experience some childhood rage toward his father for always being on his back. He soon let himself express his intense anger by tearing to shreds the shirt on his back. By the time his wife got home, he felt quite relieved, although she thought he had flipped when she saw his shirt.

The belief that cathartic reactions can be evoked by observing emotional scenes in the environment dates back at least to Aristotle's writings on theater and music, so we shall call this source of catharsis *dramatic relief*. A patient suffering from headaches, insomnia, and other expressions of depression found himself weeping heavily during Bergman's *Scenes from a Marriage*. He began to experience how disappointed he was in himself for having traded the possibility of a satisfying marriage for security. He felt his depression beginning to lift because of the inspiration he felt from Bergman to leave his hopelessly devitalized marriage.

Choosing

The role of choice in producing individual change has been in the background of many systems of psychotherapy. The concept of choosing has lacked respectability in the highly deterministic world view of most scientists. Many theorists of therapy did not want to give their critics more reason to call therapists tender-minded by openly discussing the issues of freedom and choice. Consequently, we will see that many therapy systems seem to assume that clients will choose to change as a result of therapy but do not articulate the means by which clients come to use the process of choosing.

Because there has been so little open consideration of choosing as a fundamental change process, it is most difficult to suggest what choice is a function of. Some theorists suggest that choice is irreducible, since to reduce choice to other events is to suggest the paradox that such events determine our choices. Human action is seen as freely chosen, and to say that anything else determines our choice is to show bad faith in ourselves as free beings. There are few therapists, however, who accept such a radical view of human freedom for their clients, since they usually believe that many conditions limit their clients' choosing.

From a behavioral point of view, choice would be, in part, a function of the number of alternative responses available to an individual. If there is only one response available, there is no choice. From a more humanistic point of view, the number of responses available can radically increase by our becoming more conscious of alternatives that we previously had not considered. Thus for a variety of therapy systems, an increase in choice is thought to result from an increase in consciousness that would occur in therapy.

Traditionally, the freedom to choose has been seen as a uniquely human response made possible by the development of the consciousness that accompanies the acquisition of language. Responsibility is the burden that accompanies the awareness that we are the ones able to respond, to speak for ourselves. Since choice and responsibility are made possible by the emergence of language, it seems only natural that the therapeutic process of becoming freer to choose how to respond has been a verbal process.

The easiest choices in therapy follow from accurate information processing that includes an awareness of the consequences of particular alternatives. If a woman was informed, for example, that birth control pills eventually cause cancer in all women, then her best alternative is to follow the information she has just processed. The situation with the pill, however, as with so many aspects of life, is that we are not aware of all the consequences of choice. In these situations, there are no clear external guidelines to become aware of, and we are faced with the possibility of choosing an alternative that might be a terrible mistake. Then our ability to choose is more clearly a function of our ability to accept the anxiety inherent in taking responsibility for our future. An example of such anxiety was seen in a student in my class who came to see me about the anxiety attacks she was having since she told her parents that she was pregnant. They insisted that she get an abortion, but she and her husband wanted to have a baby. They were both students, however, and entirely dependent on her wealthy parents for financial support. Her parents had informed her that the consequence of having a baby at this time would be disinheritance, since they believed she would not finish college once she had a baby. In 21 years she had never openly differed with her parents, and although she was controlled by them, she had always felt protected by them as well. Now after just a few meetings, she became more aware that her anxiety attacks reflected her need to choose. Her basic choice was not whether she was going to sacrifice her fetus to her family's fortune, but whether she was going to continue to sacrifice herself.

At an experiential level then, an increase in choosing involves the individual becoming aware of new alternatives, including the conscious creation of new alternatives for living. This process also involves the individual experiencing the anxiety inherent in being responsible for which alternative is followed. We shall call this experiential level of increased choosing a move toward *self-liberation*. When changes in the environment lead to more alternatives open to individuals, such as more jobs open to gay people, we shall call this a move toward *social liberation*. Therapists working for such social changes are usually called *advocates*.

Conditional Stimuli

At the opposite extreme from changing through choosing is a process in which we change by making critical changes in the conditional stimuli that control our responses. Changes in conditional stimuli are necessitated either when the individual's behavior is elicited by classically conditioned stimuli (CS) or when stimuli are discriminable (S^D) occasions for individuals to emit responses that are instrumentally conditioned. When troublesome responses are conditioned to such stimuli, then being conscious of the stimuli will not produce change, nor can conditioning be overcome just through the process of choosing to change.

Again either we can change the way we experience or respond to particular stimuli or we can change the environment to minimize the probability of the stimuli occurring. Changing our responses to the stimuli is referred to in our model as *counter-conditioning*, while changing the environment involves *stimulus control* procedures. Counter-conditioning was used in the treatment of a new bride with a penetration phobia who responded to intercourse with involuntary muscle spasms. This condition, known as vaginismus, prevented penetration. She did not want to change her environment but rather to change her response to her husband. As in most counter-conditioning cases, the procedure involved a gradual approach to the CS of intercourse while experiencing a response, such as relaxation or sexual arousal, that is incompatible with the undesired response of anxiety and muscle spasms that had been elicited by intercourse.

Stimulus control procedures involve clients or therapists restructuring the environment so that the probability of a particular conditional stimulus occurring is significantly reduced. A high-strung college student had a variety of problems, including considerable anxiety when driving his car. Whenever the car began to shake in the slightest, the student would also begin to shake. He attributed this particular problem to a frightening episode he had had earlier in the year, when the universal joint on his car broke with a startling noise. Not only once but three times it broke before a mechanic discovered that the real problem was a bent drive shaft. Since the problem appeared to be a function of conditioning, a counter-conditioning approach was the treatment of choice. Before the treatment was under way, however, the student traded in his car for a van. Since his anxiety response did not generalize to his van, he solved his problem through his own stimulus control procedure.

Contingency Control

Almost axiomatic for many behavior therapists is that behavior is under the control of the consequences to which it leads. As most of us have learned, if a desired reinforcement is made contingent on a particular response, then the probability is increased that we will make that response; whereas if particular punishments are made contingent on particular responses, we are less likely to emit those responses. By changing the contingencies that govern our behavior, it is widely assumed that we change our behavior, including troubled behavior. The extent to which particular consequences control behavior is a function of such variables as the immediacy, saliency, and schedule of the consequences. From a more humanistic point of view and from the point of view of certain behaviorists (e.g., Rotter, 1954; 1970), the individual's valuing of particular consequences is also an important variable affecting contingency control.

If changes in an individual are made by changing the contingencies in the environment, we call this *contingency management*. For example, a student with a bashful bladder wanted to increase his ability to use public rest rooms, and he also wanted more money to improve his style of living. As a result he made a contingency contract that earned him one dollar of his fee for each time during the week he urinated in a public rest room. I'm pleased to say that I lost money on that case.

Very seldom have behavior therapists considered the alternative, but there are important means by which individuals can change their experience or response to anticipated consequences without changing the consequences themselves. Changing responses to consequences without changing contingencies will be called *reevaluation*. A very shy man continued to desire a relationship with a woman but avoided asking anyone out because of his anticipation that he might get turned down. After several intensive discussions, he began to accept that when a woman turns down a date, it is a statement about her and not about him; we don't know whether she is waiting for someone else to ask her out, whether she doesn't like mustaches, whether she is afraid of men, or whether she doesn't know him well enough; we don't know what her saying no says about him. After reevaluating how he would interpret being turned down for a date, the fellow began asking out women, even though he was turned down on his first request for a date.

INITIAL INTEGRATION OF PROCESSES OF CHANGE

An overview of the basic processes of change is presented in Table 1. The processes of consciousness raising, catharsis, and choosing represent the heart of the traditional verbal psychotherapies, including both the psychoanalytic and the humanistic traditions. These major schools have focused primarily on the subjective aspects of the individual, the processes occurring within the skin of the organism. This perspective of the individual sees greater potential for inner-directed changes that can counteract some of the external pressures from the environment.

The processes dealing with conditional stimuli and contingencies have been the major focus of the behavioral orientation to therapy. This orientation focuses on the more external environmental forces that set limits on the individual potential for inner-directed change. These are what the existentialists would call the more *objective* level of the organism.

Our more integrative model suggests that to focus only on the subjective processes of consciousness, catharsis, and choice, is to act as if inner-directedness is the whole picture and to ignore the very real limits the environment can place on individual change. On the other hand, the behavioral focus on the more objective, environmental processes selectively ignores the potential for inner, subjective change that individuals possess. An integrative model sees a combination of the two approaches as providing a more balanced view that moves along the continuous dimensions of inner to outer control, subjective to objective functioning, and self-induced to environmentally induced changes. These continuous dimensions would appear to give a more com-

TABLE 1
Therapeutic Change Processes at Experiential and Environmental Levels

Verbal Therapies	Action or Behavioral Therapies

Consciousness raising
  Experiential level—feedback
  Environmental level—education
	Conditional stimuli
	  Experiential level—counter-conditioning
	  Environmental level—stimulus control

Catharsis
  Experiential level—corrective emotional
    experiences
  Environmental level—dramatic relief
	Contingency control
	  Experiential level—reevaluation
	  Environmental level—contingency
	    management

Choosing
  Experiential level—self-liberation
  Environmental level—social liberation	

plete picture of individuals by accepting their potential for inner change while recognizing the limits that environmental conditions and contingencies can place on such change. Focusing therapeutically on change in the environmental conditions and contingencies can be seen as a more objective means of attempting to broaden or expand the current limits on inner-directed, subjective processes of change.

THEORY OF THERAPEUTIC CONTENT

The processes of change are the contributions unique to a theory of therapy. The content that is to be changed in any particular therapy is largely a carry-over from that system's theory of personality and psychopathology. Many books supposedly focusing on therapy frequently confuse content and process and end up describing primarily the content of therapy, with little explanation about the processes. As a result, they really are books on theories of personality rather than theories of therapy.

As we shall see, systems of therapy that do not contain theories of personality, like some of the behavioral therapies, are primarily process theories and have few predetermined concepts about the content of therapy. Other systems of therapy, such as Daseinanalysis, which adopt change processes from other systems of therapy, such as psychoanalysis, will primarily have things to say about the content of therapy. Many systems of therapy differ primarily in their content, or theory of personality, while agreeing on the processes, or theory of therapeutic change.

Since systems of therapy have many more differences regarding the content of therapy, it is much more difficult to bring order and integration to this area. Nevertheless, Maddi (1972) has presented a comparative model for theories of personality that is helpful in bringing some order to this fragmented field. The present book has adapted parts of Maddi's model in helping to provide greater integration for the vast array of content in the various therapy approaches.

In Maddi's terms, many systems of therapy assume a *conflict* view of personality and psychopathology. Conflict therapy systems differ on the level of personality functioning on which they focus. Some see personal problems as a result of conflicts within the individual. Maddi calls these *intrapsychic* conflicts, but we shall use the term *intrapersonal* conflicts, which indicates that the conflicts are between forces within the person, such as a conflict between a desire to be independent and fears about leaving home. Other theories focus on the interpersonal level of personality functions and are especially concerned with conflicts between persons, such as a conflict between a woman who likes to save money and her husband who likes to spend money. Another group of theories focuses primarily on the conflicts that occur between an individual and society. We shall call these *individuo-social* conflicts, such as a conflict for an individual who wants to live a homosexual life but is afraid of the ostracism that may occur because of society's lack of acceptance of homosexual individuals. Finally, there are an increasing number of therapies concerned with helping individuals go beyond such conflicts to growth and fulfillment.

In our eclectic model we assume that different groups of clients have problems due to conflicts at different levels of personal functioning. Some clients express intrapersonal conflicts, others are having interpersonal conflicts, and still others are in conflict with society. Finally, some of our clients have resolved many of their own conflicts and are turning to therapy with questions of how they can best create a more fulfilling life.

Since we assume that there are groups of patients troubled at each level of functioning, we will compare the various systems of therapy and determine how each would conceptualize and treat the problems that most commonly occur at each level of conflict and growth. At the intrapersonal level, we will examine the approach of each therapy to conflicts over anxiety and defenses, self-esteem, and personal responsibility. At the interpersonal level, we will focus on problems with intimacy and sexuality, communication, hostility, and control of others. On the individuo-social level, we will compare approaches to issues of adjustment versus transcendence, rules for living, and the control of impulses. At the level of going beyond conflicts to fulfillment, we will examine therapeutic approaches to the fundamental questions of meaning in life, values in living, and the ideal person that would emerge from successful therapy. Table 2 summarizes the most common therapeutic content that occurs at different levels of personality.

Certainly there are honest differences about whether or not particular problems, such as sexual conflicts, are best seen as intra- or interpersonal problems, and we expect disagreement over our assignment of problems to a particular level of personality functioning. We also recognize that any viable theory of personality can reduce all problems to the particular level of functioning that the theory assumes critical to personality. For example, a viable intrapersonal theory of personality can present a convincing case that sexual problems are primarily due to conflicts within the individuals, such as between sexual desires and anxieties over performance. On the other hand, a theory focusing on the individuo-social level could present a coherent argument that sexual problems are primarily due to the inherent conflicts between an individual's sexual desires and the society's prohibitions concerning sexuality. Our eclectic assumption is that a comparative analysis of therapies will demonstrate that particular systems have been especially effective in conceptualizing and treating problems related to their level of personality theory.

In comparing systems we also expect that if a theory focuses on the intrapersonal level of functioning, then the therapy is much more likely to work with just the individual, since the basic problem will be assumed to lie within the

TABLE 2
Therapeutic Content at Different Levels of Personality

1. Intrapersonal conflicts
   a. Anxieties and defenses
   b. Self-esteem problems
   c. Personal responsibility
	3. Individuo-social conflicts
	   a. Adjustment versus transcendence
	   b. Rules for living
	   c. Impulse control

2. Interpersonal conflicts
   a. Intimacy and sexuality
   b. Communication
   c. Hostility
   d. Control of others
	4. Beyond conflict to fulfillment
	   a. Meaning in life
	   b. Values
	   c. The ideal person

individual. If the therapy has an interpersonal theory of personality, it is more likely to involve two or more persons in conflict, such as a husband and wife or family members. Therapies that focus on individuo-social conflicts will work to change the individual, if the system's values are on the side of society. For example, in working with a pedophiliac who has no inner conflict over having sexual relations with children, a therapist will work to change the individual if the therapist's values agree with society's values that such sexual behavior is unacceptable. However, if the therapist's values are on the side of the individual in a particular conflict, such as with a gay person wanting to be free to be openly homosexual, the therapist is more likely to work with or support movements such as gay liberation that are working to change the society. In comparing therapies then, we will examine which level of personality functioning they focus on and whether or not such a focus leads to working primarily with individuals alone, with two or more individuals together, or with groups working to change the society.

THEORY OF THE THERAPEUTIC RELATIONSHIP

The therapeutic relationship has been saved for final consideration because it has been the area of greatest theoretical controversy. Some systems of therapy, such as some of the radical behavioral therapies, view the relationship between client and therapist as being of no theoretical importance, since the processes and content that must occur in therapy could just as readily occur with only a programmed computer and a client present and the therapist absent. For these systems a therapist is included for practical considerations, such as the fact that our technology in programming therapeutic processes and content is not developed fully enough to allow the therapist to be absent.

Other systems of therapy, such as rational-emotive therapy, see a good relationship between therapist and client as one of the preconditions necessary for therapy to proceed. From this point of view, the client must trust the therapist before being able to participate in the processes of change.

Still other systems, such as Rogerian therapy, see the relationship as the essential process that produces change. Since Rogers (1957) has been most articulate in describing what he believes are the necessary conditions for a therapeutic relationship, let us briefly outline his criteria so that we can use these for comparing systems on the nature of the therapeutic relationship.

1. Of the two people in the relationship, the therapist must be more congruent or emotionally healthy than the client.
2. The therapist must relate in a genuine manner.
3. The therapist must relate with unconditional positive regard.
4. The therapist must relate with accurate empathy.

Finally there are systems of therapy, such as psychoanalysis, that view the relationship between therapist and patient as primarily the source of content to be processed in therapy. In this view the relationship is important because it brings the content of therapy right into the consulting room. The content that needs to be changed, then, is able to occur during therapy rather than the person having to focus on content issues that occur outside of therapy.

When analyzing systems it will be necessary to determine whether the therapeutic relationship is assumed to be part of the preconditions, processes, or content of therapy, or whether the relationship is seen as superfluous for therapy.

THE CASE OF MRS. C.

Therapy systems are not just a combination of theoretical processes and contents and empirical validation studies. The systems are first and foremost concerned with the serious problems of real people. In comparing systems, it is important to present a picture of how the various therapies would conceptualize and treat the problems of a real client. The client we have selected for such comparative purposes is Mrs. C.

Mrs. C. is a 47-year-old mother of six children—Arlene, 17; Barry, 15; Charles, 13; Debra, 11; Ellen, 9; and Frederick, 7. Without reading further, an astute observer might be able to guess the type of personality Mrs. C. would most likely reveal.

The orderliness of children named alphabetically and born every two years is consistent with other obsessive-compulsive characteristics of Mrs. C. For the past 10 years she has been plagued by a compulsive washing problem. Her baseline charts, in which she recorded her washing behavior each day before therapy began, indicated that she washed her hands 25 to 30 times a day, 5 to 10 minutes at a time. Her daily morning shower lasted about two hours with rituals involving each part of her body, beginning with her rectum. If she lost track of where she was in her ritual, she would have to start all over. A couple of times this had resulted in her husband, George, going off to work with his wife in the shower only to return eight hours later with her still involved in her ritual. To avoid such lengthy showers, George had begun helping his wife keep track of her ritual, so that she at times would yell out, "Which arm, George?" and he would yell back, "Left arm, Martha." His participation in the shower ritual required George to rise at 5:00 A.M. in order to have his wife out of the shower before he left for work at 7:00 A.M. Two years of such a schedule were making George ready to explode.

George was finding himself increasingly impatient with many of his wife's other problems. She would not let anyone wear a pair of underwear more than one day and often wouldn't even let these underwear be washed. There were piles of dirty underwear in each corner of the house. When we had the husband gather up the underwear for the laundry, we had him count the underwear but he quit counting after the thousandth pair. He felt depressed over the fact that he had more than $500 invested in once-worn underwear.

Other objects were scattered around the house, since a fork or a can of food dropped on the floor could not be picked up in Mrs. C.'s presence. Mrs. C. had been doing no housework—no cooking, cleaning, or washing for two years. One of her children described the house as a state dump, and my visit to the home confirmed this impression. Mrs. C. did work part-time. What would be a likely job for her? Something to do with washing, of course; and, in fact, she was a dental assistant, which included washing all of the dentist's equipment.

As if these were not enough problems, Mrs. C. had become very unappealing in appearance. She had not purchased a dress in seven years, and her clothes were getting ragged. She had never in her life been to a beautician and now seldom set her own hair. Her incessant washing of her body and hair led to an appearance like a combination of a prune and a boiled lobster with the frizzies.

Mrs. C.'s washing ritual also included going around the house nude from the waist up as she went from her bedroom bath to the downstairs bath to complete her washing. This was especially upsetting to Mr. C. because of the embarrassment it was producing in their teenage sons. Her children were also upset over the fact that Mrs. C. was frequently nagging them to wash their hands and change their underwear, and she would not let them bring any friends into the house.

To complete the list of Mrs. C.'s problems, she was a hoarder who had two closets filled with dozens of towels and sheets, dozens of unused earrings, and most of her clothes from the past 20 years. She did not consider the hoarding a problem since it was a family characteristic which she believed was inherited from her mother and from her mother's mother.

Mrs. C. was totally frigid. She said she had never been sexually excited in her life, but at least for the first 13 years she was very willing to engage in sexual relations to satisfy her husband. However, in the past two years she had had intercourse just twice, since sex had become increasingly unpleasant for her.

Finally, Mrs. C. was currently quite depressed. She had made a suicide gesture by swallowing a bottle of aspirins because she had an inkling that her therapist was giving up on her and her husband was probably going to send her to a state hospital.

Most of Mrs. C.'s compulsive problems revolved around an obsession with pinworms. Ten years earlier her oldest daughter had come home with pinworms. That was in 1957 when a severe epidemic of Asian flu had spread across the country, and Mrs. C. had to care for a sick family while being pregnant, sick with the flu herself, and having a demanding one-year-old child in her arms. Her physician told her that to avoid having the pinworms spread throughout the family, Mrs. C. would have to be extremely careful about the children's underwear, clothes, and sheets and that she should boil all of these articles to kill any pinworm eggs. Mr. C. confirmed that they were both rather anxious about a pinworm epidemic in the home and were both preoccupied with cleanliness during this time. However, Mrs. C.'s preoccupation with cleanliness and pinworms continued even after it had been confirmed that her daughter's pinworms were gone.

Prior to 1957, the C.s reported having a relatively good marriage. They both wanted a large family, and Mr. C.'s income as a business executive allowed them to afford a large family and a large house without financial strain. During the first 13 years of their marriage, Mrs. C. demonstrated some of her obsessive-compulsive traits, but Mr. C. felt they were never to such a degree as to be considered problems. Mr. C. and the older children recalled the many happy times they had had with Mrs. C., and they seemed to have been able to keep alive the warmth and love that they onced shared with this now preoccupied person.

Mrs. C. came from a very strict and authoritarian Catholic home. She was the middle of three girls, all of whom were dominated by a father who was 6 feet 4 inches tall and weighed 250 pounds. As a teenager, Mrs. C.'s father would wait up for her after dates to question her about what she had done, and once he went so far as to follow her on a date. He tolerated absolutely no expression of anger, especially toward himself, and when she would try to explain her point of view politely, he would often tell her to shut up. Mrs. C.'s mother was a frigid, compulsive woman who told her daughters how disgusting sex was. She also frequently warned her daughters about diseases and the importance of cleanliness.

In developing a therapy program for Mrs. C., one of the serious differential diagnostic questions was whether Mrs. C. was plagued primarily with severe obsessive-compulsive problems or whether these were just covering a schizophrenic process. A full battery of testing was completed, and the projective test results were consistent with those from previous tests that had found no evidence of a thought disorder or other signs of a schizophrenic process.

Mrs. C. had had a total of six years of therapy, and throughout this time her therapists had always considered her problems to be severely neurotic in nature, since they too had seen no evidence of psychotic thinking or experiencing on Mrs. C.'s part. The only time schizophrenia was ever used as a diagnosis for Mrs. C. was following some extensive therapy that failed to lead to any improvement. The consensus in our clinic was that Mrs. C. was demonstrating a severe obsessive-compulsive neurosis that was going to be extremely difficult to treat.

At the end of each of the following chapters, we shall see how each of the major therapy systems might explain Mrs. C.'s problems and how their therapy might help her to overcome these devastating preoccupations.

PSYCHOANALYSIS

2

KAREN WAS TO BE TERMINATED from her nursing program if her problems were not resolved. She had always been a competent student who seemed to get along well with peers and patients. Now, since beginning her rotation on 3 South, a surgical ward, headaches and dizzy spells plagued her. Of more serious consequence were the two medical errors she had made when giving patients medications. She realized that such errors could be fatal and was as concerned as her nursing faculty that she understand why such problems had begun in this final year of her education. Karen knew she had many negative feelings toward the head nurse on 3 South, but she did not believe these feelings could account for her current dilemma.

After a few weeks in therapy, we realized that one of Karen's important conflicts revolved around the death of her father when she was 12 years old. Karen had just gone to live with her father after living alone with her mother for seven years. She remembered how upset she was when her father had a heart attack and had to be rushed to the hospital. For a while it looked as though her father was going to pull through, and Karen began enjoying her daily visits to see him. During one of these visits, her father clutched his chest in obvious pain and told Karen to get a nurse. She was unclear as to why, but she remembered how helpless she felt when she could not find a nurse. Her search seemed endless, and when she finally found a nurse, her father was dead.

I don't know why, but I asked Karen the name of the ward on which her father had died. She paused and thought, and then to our surprise, she blurted out, "3 South." She cried heavily as she expressed how confused she was and

how angry she felt toward the nurses on that ward for not being more available, although she thought that maybe they had been involved with another emergency. After weeping and shaking and expressing her resentment, Karen felt quite calm and relaxed for the first time in months. My psychoanalytic supervisor said her symptoms would disappear, and sure enough they did. He knew we would have to go much deeper into what earlier conflicts this adolescent experience represented, but for now, Karen's problems in the nursing program were relieved.

A SKETCH OF THE FIRST PSYCHOANALYST

Early in his career as a therapist, Sigmund Freud (1856–1939) was quite impressed by the way some of his patients seemed to recover following such cathartic recalling of an early trauma. But he soon discovered that more profound, lasting changes required changes in his own approach. Gradually, he switched from catharsis therapy to a dynamic analysis that radically increased not only the consciousness of his clients but also the consciousness of his culture.

Freud's genius has been admired by many, but he complained throughout his life about not having been given a better brain (Jones, 1955). Freud himself believed that his outstanding attribute was his courage. Certainly it took tremendous daring to descend into the uncharted depths of humanity and then to declare to such a strict Victorian culture what he had discovered. For years he struggled for success. Beginning in 1873, with his entry into the University of Vienna at age 17, to his work as a research scholar in an institute of physiology, to earning his M.D. in 1891 and his residency in neurology, he expected that his hard work and commitment would result in recognition and financial success. He had never intended to practice medicine, but he found the rewards for research to be quite restricted and the opportunities for academic advancement for a Jew to be limited. Finally, after marrying at age 30, he began to develop a rewarding private practice. Yet Freud was willing to risk his hard-earned financial success in order to communicate to his colleagues that his work with patients convinced him that the basis of neuroses was sex.

Freud's profound insights were met with professional insults, and his private practice rapidly declined. For months he received no new referrals. For years he had to rely on his inner courage to continue his lonely intellectual pursuits without a colleague to share his insights. During this same period of the 1890s, he began his lonely and painful self-analysis, in part to overcome some neurotic symptoms and in part to serve as his own subject in his studies of the unconscious. Surprisingly, Freud was not basically alienated by his professional isolation. He was able to interpret the opposition he met as part of the natural resistance to taboo ideas.

Finally, in the early 1900s, Freud's risky work began to be recognized by scholars, such as the dying William James, as the system that would shape 20th-century psychology. Shape it he did, along with the incredibly brilliant group of colleagues that joined the Vienna Psychoanalytic Society. Most of these colleagues contributed to the development of psychoanalysis, but Freud insisted that as the founder he alone had the right to decide what should be

called psychoanalysis. This led some of the best minds, such as Adler, Jung, and Rank, to leave the Psychoanalytic Society to develop their own systems. Freud's insistence may also have set a precedent for a dogmatism that relied more on authority than on evidence for the final confirmation of theory. Freud himself continued throughout his lifetime, however, to be critical of his own theories and would painfully discard his ideas if experience contradicted them.

Success did not diminish Freud's commitment to his scholarly work or to his patients. He worked an 18-hour day that began with seeing patients at 8:00 A.M. until 1:00 P.M.; a break for lunch and a walk with his family; patients again from 3:00 until 9:00 or 10:00 P.M.; a dinner and a walk with his wife; followed by writing letters and books until 1:00 or 2:00 A.M. His dedication to his work was remarkable, although it is also striking that this man, dedicated to understanding sex and its vicissitudes, left little time or energy for his own sexuality. Nevertheless, his commitment to work right up until his death from bone cancer at age 85 resulted in the most comprehensive theory of personality, psychopathology, and psychotherapy ever developed.

THEORY OF PERSONALITY

Freud's theory of personality was as complex as he was. He viewed personality from six different perspectives: the *topographic*, which involves conscious versus unconscious modes of functioning; the *dynamic*, which involves the interaction of forces, such as conflicts between instincts and defenses; the *genetic*, which is concerned with the origin and development of psychic phenomena through the oral, anal, phallic, latency, and genital stages; the *economic*, which involves the distribution, transformation, and expenditure of energy; the *structural*, which involves the persistent functional units of the id, ego, and superego; and the *adaptive* view, implied by Freud and developed by Hartmann (1958), which involves the inborn preparedness of the individual to interact with an evolving series of normal and predictable environments. We will focus primarily on his dynamic, genetic, and structural perspectives, since these are most directly related to his theories of psychopathology and psychotherapy.

Freud believed that the basic dynamic forces motivating personality were sex and aggression. These forces were assumed to be instincts that have a somatic basis but are expressed in fantasies, desires, feelings, thoughts, and—most directly—actions. The individual constantly desires immediate gratification of sexual and aggressive impulses. The demand for immediate gratification leads to inevitable conflicts with social rules that insist on some control over sex and aggression if social institutions, such as families, are to remain stable and orderly. The individual is forced to develop defense mechanisms or inner controls that can keep sex and aggression from being expressed in uncontrollable outbursts. Without such defenses, civilization would be reduced to a jungle of raping, ravaging beasts.

The development of defense mechanisms keeps individuals from becoming conscious of basic inner desires to rape and ravage. The assumption here is that if individuals are not aware of such desires, they cannot act on them—at least not directly. The defenses serve to keep the individual out of danger of punishment for breaking social rules. Defenses also keep the individual from

experiencing the anxiety and guilt that would be elicited by desires to break parental and social rules. For defenses to work adequately, the person must remain unconscious of the very mechanisms being used to keep sexual and aggressive impulses from coming into awareness. Otherwise, the individual is faced with a dilemma that is like having to keep a secret from a three-year-old child who knows you have a secret—the badgering to know what is being hidden could be overwhelming.

In Maddi's (1972) terms, the core of the Freudian personality is the unconscious conflict among the individual's sexual and aggressive impulses, the society's rules aimed at controlling such impulses, and the individual's defense mechanisms that are used to control the impulses in such a way as to keep guilt and anxiety to a minimum while allowing at least some safe, indirect gratification of the impulses. While all personalities revolve around such unconscious conflicts, people differ as to the particular impulses, rules, anxieties, and defenses that are in conflict. Such differences depend on the particular stage in life at which an individual's conflicts occur.

For Freud, the stages of life are determined primarily by the unfolding of sexuality in the oral, anal, phallic, and genital stages. Differences in experiences during each of these stages are critical in determining the variety of traits and types of personalities that develop.

Oral Stage

During the first 18 months of life, the infant's sexual desires are centered in the oral region. The child's greatest pleasure is to suck on a satisfying object, such as a breast. The instinctual urges are to passively receive oral gratification during the oral-incorporative phase and to more actively take in oral pleasure during the oral-aggressive phase. Sucking on breasts or bottles, putting toys, fingers, or toes in the mouth, and even babbling are some of the actions a child can take to get at least some oral gratification. As adults, we can appreciate oral sexuality through kissing, deep kissing, fellatio, cunnilingus, or oral caressing of breasts and other parts of the body.

The infant's oral sexual needs are intense and urgent, but the child is dependent on parental figures to provide the breasts or bottles necessary for adequate oral gratification. How the parents respond to such urgent needs can have a marked influence on the child's personality. Parents who are either too depriving or overindulgent can make it difficult for a child to mature from the oral stage to later stages of personality development. With deprivation the child can remain fixated at the oral stage, with energies directed primarily toward finding the oral gratification that was never received. With overindulgence, the child can also become fixated at the oral stage, but with energies directed toward trying to repeat and maintain such gratifying conditions. Fixation due to either deprivation or overgratification leads to the development of an oral personality that includes the following bipolar traits (Abraham, 1927; Glover, 1925): optimism-pessimism, gullibility-suspiciousness, cockiness-self-belittlement, manipulativeness-passivity, and admiration-envy.

While it is by no means a rule, it is easiest to think of overindulgence leading to preverbal images of the world and oneself that result in traits at the left end of each pole. Optimism then would come from an image that things have

always been great, so there is no reason to expect that they will not continue. Gullibility would derive from the experience of finding early in life that whatever was received from people was good, so why not swallow whatever people say now. Cockiness would relate to feelings of having been something super for parents to dote on; while manipulativeness would relate to the set that comes from being able to get parents to do whatever is wanted. Admiration would be due to feelings that other people are as good as oneself and one's parents.

Deprivation, on the other hand, is more likely to lead to pessimism, since the set from the start is that one's needs will not be met. Suspiciousness comes from a feeling that if parents cannot be trusted, who can one trust. Self-belittlement would be due to an image of having been awful, if one's folks could not care enough; while passiveness would relate to conclusions that no matter how hard one kicks or cries, parents will not care. Envy is an inner craving to have the traits that would make one lovable enough for people to provide special care.

Besides such traits, fixation at the oral stage brings a tendency to rely on more primitive defenses when threatened or frustrated. Denial derives from having to finally close one's eyes and go to sleep as a way of shutting out the oral needs that are not being met. On a cognitive level, this defense involves closing off one's attention to threatening aspects of the world or self. Projection has a bodily basis in the infant spitting up anything bad that is taken in and making the bad things part of the environment. Cognitively, projection involves perceiving in the environment those aspects of oneself that are bad or threatening. Incorporation on a bodily level includes the taking in of food and liquids and making these objects an actual part of oneself. Cognitively this defense involves making images of others part of one's own image.

In the oral stage children are inherently dependent on others to meet their needs. Therefore, individuals fixated at this stage are especially concerned with defending against separation anxiety. Oral personalities are anxious that if their loved ones really knew how selfish, demanding, and dependent they really are, their loved ones might leave or withdraw their love. With experience they learn that they had better control their intense desire to be cuddled, cared for, fed, and suckled, lest they be left alone. So they learn to deny or project such stingy, narcissistic wishes, although deep down they continually crave to passively receive without giving or to aggressively take without deserving.

The well-defended oral personality is not to be considered pathological but rather an immature person like all of the pregenital personalities we shall discuss. There certainly are many people who are overly optimistic, gullible, and cocky, who deny faults in themselves or others, without considering themselves or being considered by others as pathological. Likewise, there are many people who believe it is wisest to be suspicious, to not expect too much from this world, and to be perceptive of all the selfishness and manipulativeness in others. These people are also rarely judged to be pathological.

Anal Stage

In a society that assigned functions of the anus to the outhouse, that gagged at the sight or smell of the products of the anus, it must have been ghastly

to think that a physician, like Freud, believed that this dirty area could be the most intense source of pleasure for children of ages 18 months to three years. Even in our ultra-clean society, many people still find it difficult to imagine that their anuses can be a source of sensuous satisfaction. In the privacy of their own bathrooms, however, many people can admit to themselves that the releasing of the anus can be the real "pause that refreshes." As one of my constipated patients said, it is his most pleasurable time of the month.

Children in the anal stage are apt to learn that intense urges to play with the anus or its products brings them into conflict with society's rules of cleanliness. Even the pleasure of letting go of the anus must come under the parents' rules for bowel control. Prior to toilet training, the child was free to immediately release the sphincter muscles as soon as tension built up in the anus. But now society, as represented by the parents, demands that the child control the inherent desire for immediate tension reduction. In Erikson's (1950) terms, the child must now learn to hold on and then to let go. Not only that, but the child must also learn the proper timing of holding on and letting go. If the child lets go when it is time to hold on—trouble; and if the child holds on when it is time to let go—trouble!

The child is most likely to become conflicted and fixated at the anal stage if the parents again are either too demanding or overindulgent. The bipolar traits that develop from anal fixation have been clearly articulated by Freud (1925) and Fenichel (1945): stinginess-overgenerosity, constrictedness-expansiveness, stubbornness-acquiescence, orderliness-messiness, meticulousness-dirtiness, punctuality-tardiness, precision-vagueness.

Much of Freud's concern was with the overdemanding or overcontrolling parents who forced toilet training too quickly or too harshly. The individual from this type of experience was seen as more likely to develop an anal personality dominated by holding-on tendencies. The child's unarticulated experience appears to have been a sense of having been forced to let go when the child didn't want to let go. Then when the child did let go, what did the parents do with the present to them—just flushed it down the toilet. Now such individuals react as if they will be damned before they again let go against their will. So these personalities hold tightly to money (stinginess), hold onto their feelings (constrictedness), and hold tightly to their own way (stubbornness). In the process of harsh toilet training, however, such people also learn that they are punished if they are not really clean or meticulous, if they are not punctual and orderly about where they go, and if they do not handle their matters precisely.

Overindulgent parents who are lackadaisical about toilet training are more likely to encourage a child to just let go whenever any pressure is felt. This route to an anal personality results in people who are more likely to easily let go of money (wasteful), let go of feelings (explosiveness), and let go of their wills (acquiescent). Lack of concern with such a basic social rule as proper toilet training is assumed to also encourage a child to be generally messy, dirty, tardy, and unconcerned with details (vagueness).

Conflicts during the anal stages are also assumed to lead to the development of particular defenses. *Reaction formation,* or experiencing the opposite of what one really desires, develops first as a reaction to being very clean and neat like the parents demand rather than expressing anal desires to be messy. *Undoing,* or atoning for unacceptable desires or actions, occurs when the

child learns that it is safer to say, "I'm sorry I let go in my pants," rather than saying, "I like the warm feeling the poo in my pants gives me." *Isolation*, or not experiencing the feelings that would go with the thoughts, emerges in part when the child has to think about an anal function as if it is a mechanical act rather than an instinctual experience. *Intellectualization*, or the process of neutralizing affect-laden experiences by talking in intellectual or logical terms, is partly related to such experiences as talking about the regularity of bowel movement as being soothing to one's gastrointestinal system.

Anal characters use such defenses to control anal desires to soil wherever and whenever they want and to control their anal erotic desire to pleasure their anus by touching it, caressing it, or putting things into it. Even individuals from overindulgent families find out that they really cannot exercise their anuses whenever they want without receiving punishment from their peers or from parental figures like teachers. Both types of anal characters also use these defenses to remain unaware of the great deal of hostility and aggression that is related to conflicts over toilet training and other areas of life in which the culture insists on controlling the individual's instincts. Again, a well-defended anal character is considered immature and not pathological. Anal people are very likely to take pride in their punctuality and even to be admired by others for these traits.

Phallic Stage

The name of this stage suggests a problem that Freud had with theorizing too much about men and then generalizing to women, since this stage is named after the genitalia of the male and not the female. For both, the sexual desires during the phallic stage are thought to be focused in the genitalia. From ages three to six, both sexes are assumed to be very interested in their own genitalia and to increase their frequency of masturbation. They are also very interested in the opposite sex and engage in games of doctor and patient in which they examine each other to satisfy their sexual curiosities.

The conflict for youngsters is not with their genital desires, since theoretically other kids could satisfy these desires. The conflict is over the object of their sexual desires, which in this stage is the parent of the opposite sex. The boy's desire for his mother is explained as a natural outgrowth of the mother having been the major source of gratification for his previous needs, such as needs for sucking. Therefore, it seemed logical to assume that the son would direct his genital sexual desires initially toward his mother and would expect her to gratify him. The oedipal conflict, of course, is that the father already has the rights and privileges of enjoying the mother. The son's fear is that the father might punish his rival by removing the source of the problem—the son's penis. The dread over castration eventually causes the son to repress his desire for his mother, repress his hostile rivalry toward his father, and identify with his father's rules in the hope that if he acts as his father would have him act, maybe he can avoid castration.

Why a girl ends up desiring her father rather than her mother is more difficult to explain, since the mother was assumed to be the main source of instinc-

tual gratification for daughters as well as sons. Freud assumed that girls become hostile toward their mothers when they discover that their mothers cheated them by not giving them a penis. Why Freud assumed that females would conclude that there was something wrong with them because they did not have a penis rather than vice versa has always been something of a mystery. For example, a non-Freudian colleague tells the story of his five-year-old daughter's discovery of her three-year-old brother's penis. Rather than envying his penis, she went yelling, "Mama, Mama, Andy's 'gina fell out."

Nevertheless and in spite of understandable protest by enlightened women, many classical analysts still assume that girls initially envy penises, that they become enraged toward their mothers, and that they turn their desires to their fathers in part to be able to at least share the phallus of their father.

Again, a critical issue is how the parents respond to the genital desires of their children. Over-rejection or overindulgence can both lead to fixations at the phallic stage that result in formation of the following bipolar traits: vanity-self-hatred, pride-humility, stylishness-plainness, flirtatiousness-shyness, gregariousness-isolation, brashness-bashfulness.

Over-rejection, in which the parents give their opposite-sex children little affection, no hugs or kisses, and no appreciation of their attractiveness, is likely to lead to the following self-image: "I must be hateful if my parent wouldn't even hug or kiss me. Why flirt, dress stylishly, be outgoing or brash, or take pride in myself if the opposite sex is sure to find me undesirable." On the other hand, a person who has had an overindulgent parent, whether seductively or actually incestuous, can more readily develop feelings of vanity. They feel they must be really something if Daddy preferred them over Mommy or vice versa. The flirting, stylishness, pride, and brashness would all be based on maintaining an image of being the most desirable person in the world.

Conflicts over sexual desires toward one's parent are not just due to how the parent reacts. The child also has to defend against castration anxieties, including the female's supposed anxiety that her rivalrous mother might damage her further. The child must also defend against society's basic incest taboo. These conflicts lead to the child having to use repression as the major defense against incestuous desires. By becoming unaware of even fantasies about one's opposite-sex parent, the youngster feels safe from incest and the consequent castration or taboos that would accompany it. However, as with all conflicted desires, the impulse is always present and can be kept in control only by unconscious defenses.

Latency Stage

In the classical Freudian theory, this stage involved no new unfolding of sexuality but rather was a stage in which the pregenital desires were primarily repressed. Freud associated no new personality development with this stage, since he believed that all pregenital personality formulation was completed by age six. Latency is seen as primarily a lull between the conflicted, pregenital time and the storm that was to reemerge with adolescence—the beginning of the genital stage.

Genital Stage

In Freudian theory an individual does not develop to the genital stage without at least some conflict between instinctual desires and the rules of parents and society. Some individuals will be fixated at the oral, anal, or phallic stage and will demonstrate the related personality type. Other individuals will experience conflicts at each of the stages and will demonstrate a mixed personality that is a combination of traits and defenses of each stage. But no one becomes a fully mature, genital character without undergoing a successful analysis. Since such a personality is the ideal goal of analysis, we shall delay discussion of it until the section on this theory's ideal individual.

THEORY OF PSYCHOPATHOLOGY

Since all personalities are at least partially immature due to inevitable conflicts and fixations at pregenital stages, all of us are vulnerable to regressing into psychopathology. We are more vulnerable if our conflicts and fixations occurred earlier in life, since we would be dependent on more immature defenses for dealing with anxiety. We also are more vulnerable the more intense our pregenital conflicts are, since more of our energy will be bound up in defending against pregenital impulses, and less energy will be available for coping with adult stresses and conflicts. As indicated earlier, however, well-defended oral, anal, phallic, or mixed personalities may never break down unless placed under environmental circumstances that precipitate stress and lead to an exacerbation of defensiveness and the formation of symptoms.

Precipitating events, such as the death of a loved one, an offer of an affair, or an illness, stimulate the impulse or impulses that individuals have been controlling all their lives. They react on an unconscious level to this current event as if it were a repetition of a childhood experience, such as rejection by a parent or desire for taboo sex. Their infantile reactions make them panicky that their impulses may now get out of control and that the punishment they dreaded all their lives, such as separation or castration, will occur. Such individuals are also panicky because they feel their very personality is threatened with disintegration; their type of personality has always been a delicate balance of traits and defenses that kept impulses and anxieties at a safe level. Like children, they are terrified that their adult personality will break down and that they will become entirely dominated by infantile instincts and fears. These individuals are reexperiencing at an unconscious level the same infantile conflicts that were once the cause of their personality development and now threaten to be the cause of their personality disintegration.

In the face of such threats, the person is highly motivated to spend whatever energy is necessary to keep impulses from coming into consciousness. This may mean just an exacerbation of previous defenses to the point where they become pathological. For example, a married woman who had been offered an affair and has an intense desire for taboo sex may rely more heavily on repressing such desires. Soon she is entirely fatigued and may show other symptoms of neurasthenia, but at least she does not have the energy to act on an affair even if she wanted to. While she constantly complains about her fatigue, for her it is better to be tired than be in terror of acting out her infantile

desires. A woman who did not have such intense fixations and conflicts over taboo sex might just decline the offer or might accept if she thought it was worth the risks.

When a person overreacts to life's events to such an extent that symptoms develop, it is clear to the Freudians that such symptoms are defending against unacceptable impulses and childish anxieties. In many cases, the symptoms also serve as indirect expressions of the person's unacceptable wish. For example, Karen's symptoms of headaches, dizziness, and medical errors diverted her attention from emerging rage toward the nurse on 3 South and the anxiety that would accompany such rage. The medical errors also provided some expression of her hostile wishes without Karen being at all aware that she was even angry, to say nothing of being threatened by internal rage. When symptoms serve both as defenses against unacceptable impulses and as indirect expressions of these wishes, then the symptoms are doubly resistant to change. Other benefits from symptoms, such as special attention from loved ones or doctors, are secondary gains and make symptoms even more resistant to change.

But why does a person like Karen overreact in the first place to an event like being assigned to 3 South? Why did she respond to the current 3 South as if she were a 12-year-old again? Why didn't she just make the logical discrimination that the fact that both wards are named 3 South does not mean they are the same? Obviously, Karen was not aware of responding to 3 South as if she were a 12-year-old. If her response to 3 South was primarily on a conscious level, then she could indeed have made such logical distinctions based on her conscious, secondary thought process. But unconscious responses like Karen's follow primary-process thinking, which is alogical. Logical thinking includes reasoning from the subjects of sentences, so that we reason: (1) All men are mortals; (2) Socrates was a man; therefore (3) Socrates was mortal. In primary-process thinking, reasoning frequently follows the *predicates* of statements, so that we think: (1) The Virgin Mary was a virgin; (2) I am a virgin; therefore (3) I am the Virgin Mary. Or in Karen's case: (1) The ward where they let my father die was 3 South; (2) The ward where I am now is 3 South; therefore (3) This 3 South is where they let my father die. When people like Karen respond on an unconscious level, they do not go through any such reasoning processes, but rather their primary-process reaction is automatically alogical.

Primary-process responding is also *atemporal* with no differentiation between past, present, and future. Therefore, on an unconscious level Karen's response makes no distinctions between the 3 South of 10 years ago and the 3 South of now. On an unconscious level, all is now, and so the same impulses and anxieties are elicited that were present 10 years ago. Primary-process experiencing is also condensed so that the energies that are connected to a complex set of ideas and events are focused on one idea. Thus, for Karen 3 South elicited all of the energies that were originally attached to the sequence of father dying, running for help, no nurses available, father dead.

Displacement is another characteristic of primary-process thinking, and it involves placing the energies from highly charged ideas onto more neutral ideas. In this case Karen displaced the intense anger she felt toward her father for leaving onto her image of the more neutral people responsible for 3 South. Primary-process thinking is also *symbolic*, which means that any *pars pro toto*

or any part of an event represents the total event, such as the name 3 South being a symbol of the many feelings stirred up over the death of Karen's father. Finally, primary-process experiencing includes both *manifest and latent content*, wherein the content that is conscious or manifest is only a minor portion of the hidden or latent meaning of events. Karen was, thus, originally aware of only the manifest event of becoming upset on her new ward and wasn't even aware of the latent significance of the name 3 South until it was uncovered in therapy.

With this understanding of primary-process responding, we can more fully appreciate why Karen's unconscious response to being placed on the present 3 South appeared to be irrational or alogical. We can also appreciate why she currently was reacting in a manner more appropriate to an angry child and why her response involved much more energy and meaning than could be understood from a relatively neutral idea like 3 South.

If we went even further into the latent meaning of this event for Karen, we would probably find that her exprience at age 12 represented her original loss of her father when she was five. The rage that threatened to break out toward the nurses on 3 South may have been in part displaced from her original rage toward her mother, who Karen imagined caused her father to leave at an age when she so desired him. Being on 3 South may also have threatened to bring to awareness feelings of sexual desire for her father mixed with hostility for his leaving when she needed him so. Even the fantasy that she might wish his death could damage Karen's image of herself as the caring daughter who would have saved her father if she had been a nurse 10 years ago. To protect her image of herself, to protect herself from acting out or experiencing dangerous impulses, and to protect herself from all the anxiety and guilt such impulses would elicit can be the reasons symptoms might form as defenses of last resort.

If the essence of such pathology is fundamentally at an unconscious level and if the person has no awareness of the significance of precipitating events, the impulses that are being elicited, the anxieties that threaten panic, and the defensive yet gratifying nature of symptoms, then how is a person to be helped to overcome such pathology?

THEORY OF THERAPEUTIC PROCESSES

For Freud there was only one process that could succeed—to make the unconscious conscious. To be able to respond to environmental events in a more realistic manner, we must first be conscious of how our pathological responses to the environment have been due to the unconscious, primary-process meaning we attribute to environmental events. To remove symptoms we must become conscious of our resistance to let go of the symptoms because they both defend against and give partial release to unacceptable impulses. We must gradually realize that our impulses are not as dangerous as we thought as children and that we can use more constructive defenses to keep our impulses in control, in part by allowing more mature expressions of our instincts. Finally, to prevent future relapses we must use our conscious processes to release our pregenital fixations so that we can continue to de-

velop to mature, genital levels of functioning. Such radical increases in consciousness require considerable work on the part of both patients and analysts.

Consciousness Raising

THE PATIENT'S WORK: FREE ASSOCIATION

The patient's work sounds very simple—to just freely say whatever comes to mind, no matter how trivial the thought or association may seem. If patients could let their minds go and associate without defending, then their associations would have to be dominated by instincts. Since the instincts are the source of all energy and thereby the strongest forces in the individual, and since the instincts are always pressing to emerge into consciousness, then patients would immediately associate to thoughts, feelings, fantasies, and wishes that express instincts. But the person's earliest lessons in life were that such direct, uncontrolled expressions of instincts are most dangerous. The person also learned at the time symptoms developed that a loosening of defenses can be terrifying and can lead to pathology. Now just because the doctor has ordered the patient to lie on the couch and say everything that comes to mind does not mean that the patient can do so without considerable resistance or defensiveness. To help the patient continue to work in the face of such terror and resulting defensiveness, the analyst must form a *working alliance* with the part of the person's ego that wants relief from suffering and is rational enough to believe that the analyst's directions can bring such relief. From this alliance patients also become willing to recall in detail dreams and childhood memories even though such material brings them even closer to their threatening impulses.

THE THERAPIST'S WORK

The therapist's work begins with evaluating the patient to see if the patient is indeed a suitable candidate for psychoanalysis. As Greenson (1967, p. 34) succinctly puts it, "People who do not dare regress from reality and those who cannot return readily to reality are poor risks for psychoanalysis." This generally means that patients diagnosed as schizophrenic, manic-depressive, schizoid, or borderline personalities are considered poor risks for analysis.

If analysis does proceed, the therapist uses the following four procedures in analyzing the patient's resistance to free associating and the transference that emerges as the patient regresses and expresses instinctual desires to the analyst (Bibring, 1954; Greenson, 1967).

Confrontation and Clarification. Confrontation and clarification are fundamentally feedback procedures. In analytic confrontation the therapist makes sure patients are aware of the particular actions or expriences that are being analyzed. For example, in confronting a particular transference phenomenon, the analyst might give the patient the following feedback: "You seem to be feeling angry toward me," or "You seem to have sexual feelings toward me." Clarification frequently blends with confrontation since clarification is sharper and more detailed feedback regarding the particular phenomenon

that the patient is experiencing. Greenson (1967, p. 304) gives an example of how, after confronting a patient with his hatred for the analyst, he helped the patient clarify the exact details of his hatred: "He would like to beat me to a pulp, literally grind me up and mash me into a jelly-like mass of bloody, slimy goo. Then he'd eat me up in one big 'slurp' like the goddamned oatmeal his mother made him eat as a kid. Then he'd shit me out as a foul-smelling poison-ous shit. And when I asked him, 'And what would you do with this foul-smelling shit?' he replied, 'I'd grind you into the dirt so you could join my dear dead mother!'"

Interpretation.   Confronting and clarifying a patient's experience or action are basically preparatory steps for the most important analytic proce-dure of interpretation. Greenson (1967, p. 39) defines interpretation in such a way as to make it almost synonomous with analysis itself:

To interpret means to make an unconscious phenomenon conscious. More precisely, it means to make conscious the unconscious meaning, source, history, mode, or course of a given psychic event. The analyst uses his own unconscious, his empathy and intuition as well as his theoretical knowledge for arriving at an interpretation. By interpreting we go beyond what is readily observable and we assign meaning and causality to a psy-chological phenomenon.

Since interpretation goes beyond the experience of the patient, it is more than just feedback to the patient. The meaning and causality assigned to psy-chological phenomena are determined, at least in part, by psychoanalytic the-ory. Therefore, the information patients are given regarding the meaning and causality of their responses is in part an education on how psychoanalysis makes sense out of people and their problems. This is not to say that interpre-tations are given in theoretical terms. They certainly are personalized for the individual, and in that respect are feedback. Nevertheless, through interpreta-tions patients are taught to view their conscious experiences as caused by unconscious processes, their adult behavior as determined by childhood ex-periences, their analysts as if they were parents or other significant figures from the past, and so on.

Therapists committed to psychoanalytic theory assume that patients ac-cept such teachings because the psychoanalytic interpretations hold true for the patient. After all, it is the patient's response that verifies an interpretation. If patients gain insight, that is, if they have a cognitive and affective awakening about aspects of themselves that were previously hidden, and if they become less resistant and more able to freely associate, then analysts have some evi-dence for the validity of their interpretations. The most critical response for verifying interpretations is whether or not the interpretations eventually lead to a change in the client for the better.

The problem with improvement as the criterion for the verification of inter-pretations is that improvement in analysis is expected to be a slow, gradual process. First, the analyst and the patient must interpret the repeated resist-ance the client throws up against becoming conscious of threatening forces from within. The client misses appointments, comes late, dramatically recovers and wants to leave therapy, wants to leave because of not recovering, represses dreams, and does a million things to shore up defenses. Then as

blind resistance is gradually reduced through insightful interpretations, the client begins to release hidden instincts toward the therapist. The patient wants to satisfy impulses by displacing frustrated sexual and aggressive impulses onto the therapist, and gradually a *neurotic transference* develops in which the patient relives all of the significant human relationships from childhood. For weeks or months, the therapist is experienced as the nongiving, miserly mother who does not care about the patient; then the analyst is the lecherous father who wants to seduce the patient; or the wonderful, wise parent who can do no wrong; or the stupid fool who is always wrong. Such transference reactions serve as intense resistances—why mature further when you feel so good beating on your therapist or feel so safe with such a wise, caring parent. Painfully, through repeated interpretations, the patient must realize that such intense feelings and impulses come from within and represent the patient's pregenital conflicts and are not realistic feelings elicited by the relatively blank-screen analyst.

Working Through. The slow, gradual process of working again and again with the insights that have come from interpretations of resistance and transference is called *working through*. In this last but longest step in therapy, patients are acutely conscious of their many defensive maneuvers, including symptoms. They are undeniably aware of the impulses they have tried to defend against and the many ways they still get expressed, such as in symptoms. They realize that they need not fear their impulses to the degree they once did as children, since in transference relationships they expressed impulses in intense words and were not castrated, rejected, or overwhelmed. Gradually the person becomes aware that there are indeed new and more mature ways of controlling instincts that allow some gratification without guilt or anxiety. Gradually the patient channels impulses through these new controls or defenses and gives up immature defenses and symptoms. The use of new defenses and the radical increase in consciousness are seen by Freudians as actual structural changes in personality in which energies that were bound up in pregenital conflicts are now available to the more mature ego of the individual.

Other Processes. Most analysts accept that corrective emotional experiences can lead to temporary relief of symptoms, especially for traumatic neuroses. Catharsis, however, even if used by an analyst, is not considered part of the analytic process. There is only one fundamental change process in analysis, and that is to increase consciousness, and all the steps in analysis are part of that process.

THEORY OF THERAPEUTIC CONTENT

Intrapersonal Conflicts

Psychoanalysis obviously focuses on intrapersonal conflicts in therapy, with the individual's inner conflicts among impulses, anxiety, and defenses being of central concern. Problems may be acted out at an interpersonal level, but the origin and resolution of such problems can be derived only through an analysis of each individual's intrapsychic conflicts.

ANXIETIES AND DEFENSES

We have already discussed anxiety due to threats of separation and castration. The Freudians also postulate *primal anxiety*, which is due to the assumed birth trauma of being overwhelmed with stimulation. Primal anxiety is the bodily basis for *panic*, which is the adult threat of being overwhelmed with instinctual stimulation. *Moral anxiety* or guilt is the threat that comes with breaking the rules that have been internalized.

In therapy, anxiety is a motivator that may drive a person to seek relief because of its aversive properties. Once in therapy, however, an analyst must be careful not to uncover impulses too quickly lest the person panic and either flee therapy or have a psychotic experience of being overwhelmed. Anxiety is one of the major reasons therapy moves slowly, partly because anxiety signals the person to shore up resistance when dangerous associations are being approached and partly because analysts feel that immature egos cannot hold up under high levels of anxiety.

Defenses or *resistance*, as defenses are called when they occur in therapy, are half of the content of psychoanalysis. Pretty much any behavior in therapy can serve defensive functions—talking too fast or too slowly, too much or too little, feeling good toward the therapist or feeling hostile, focusing on details or avoiding details. So the analyst is never without material to process. It is just a matter of which defenses are most likely to be accepted by the client as resistance, such as missing appointments or not being able to recall dreams. The goal in therapy is not to remove defenses but rather to replace immature and distorting defenses with more mature, realistic, and gratifying defenses.

SELF-ESTEEM

Self-esteem has not been a major content area for psychoanalysis. It seems to be taken for granted that patients will have conflicts over self-esteem. Some will have unrealistically low esteem, such as deprived oral characters who engage in continual self-belittlement or rejected phallic characters who feel ugly and undesirable. Some patients will have unrealistically high self-esteem, such as overindulged oral characters who are cocky or overindulged phallic characters who are vain and brash. Pregenital personalities cannot feel fundamentally good about themselves as long as they are dominated by infantile desires to be selfishly taken care of, hostilely controlling, or seductively narcissistic. Lack of genuine self-esteem, however, is the result of personality problems, not the cause of such problems, and analysts do not treat esteem problems directly. Acceptance of such infantile characteristics may bring temporary relief, but what the pregenital personality really needs is a personality transplant. The best that can be done is to help patients consciously restructure their personalities into a more genital level of functioning, and only then can individuals experience a stable sense of self-esteem.

RESPONSIBILITY

In a totally deterministic system like psychoanalysis, how can we talk about individual responsibility? In practice, the analyst expects the patient to be re-

sponsible for the bill, to keep appointments three to six times a week, and to free associate as best as possible. But theoretically, there is no freedom and no choice in psychoanalysis and, therefore, no responsibility. How can we hold a person responsible for any action, whether it be murder, rape, or just not paying a bill, if all pathological and immature behavior is determined by unconscious conflicts and pregenital fixations? This inability to hold an individual responsible for his or her actions is one of the reasons why Mowrer (1961) has said that Freud freed us from a generation of neurotics and gave us a generation of psychopaths.

Interpersonal Conflicts

INTIMACY AND SEXUALITY

Intimacy, the revealing and sharing between two people as they really are, is fundamentally impossible for an immature personality. The problem of intimacy is basically a transference problem. The pregential personality cannot relate to another person as the other person really is but distorts the other according to childhood images of what people are like. In Piagetian terms, the person's earliest interpersonal experiences with parents result in internalized schemas that are primitive concepts of what people are like. Any new experience of a person is assimilated into this schema through selective attention to that person's actions.

While Piaget (1952) suggests that children's schemas of people change to accommodate new experiences, the Freudian concept of fixation suggests that pregential personalities do not continue to develop their schemas of people. Rather, immature individuals distort their experiences of people to fit internalized images. For example, if individuals develop a concept of people as untrustworthy and rejecting, then they would attend to the slightest reason for mistrust and the slightest sign of rejection as evidence that a new, potential intimate is the same as all the rejecting people they have known from the time they were born.

A thorough analysis is the only way such people can mature to a level where they can perceive individuals with the freshness and uniqueness that each deserves. It is only by being fully aware of how we have distorted our relationships in the past that we can avoid such destructive distortion in the present.

Sexual relationships for immature people are also primarily transference relationships. Two immature people can only engage in object relationships in which the other is seen as perhaps finally being the one who will satisfy ungratified pregenital instincts. So the oral character may relate sexually with a clingingness and demandingness that smothers a spouse. The anal personality may relate sexually in a very routinized manner, such as each night when the 11:00 news is over rather than when sex is spontaneously desired. The phallic character may relate as the teasing, seductive person who promises so much in bed but has so little to give. The ability to relate to another as a mature, heterosexual partner results only after a satisfying working through of one's pregenital fixations. Otherwise we are reduced to two objects bumping in the night.

COMMUNICATION

Communication between most people has been characterized not as a dialogue but as interlocking monologues. Such is definitely the nature of communication between two immature people. Such people are locked into their own egocentric worlds in which others are only objects for their own gratification. They do not respond to what the other says but rather to their own desires that they want satisfied by the other. They do not talk to each other but rather speak to their internal image of what the other is supposed to be. The messages they send have a manifest content that is also directed at hiding what the person really wants to say. If it takes an analyst years of listening with the third ear (Reik, 1948) to interpret what the person really means, how can a spouse with two blocked ears be expected to hear?

From a classical Freudian view, attempts at marriage counseling between two immature personalities will only produce absurd dialogue that is best left to modern playwrights like Pinter.

HOSTILITY

The violence in our urban era is seen by Freudians as a reflection of the hostility inherent in humans. Just as the work of ethologists like Tinbergen (1951) and Lorenz (1963) suggested that animals have instincts to release aggression, the work of Freud suggested that the human animal has aggressive instincts to strike out and destroy. But humans also desire to live in civilized societies, and the stability of social organizations, such as marriage, the family, and communities, is continuously threatened by the hostile outbursts of poorly defended personalities. With individuals such as paranoid personalities, who are barely controlling their rage, defenses must be strengthened through supportive therapy or medication rather than uncovered by analysis. With overcontrolled neurotic types, the best we can expect is to rechannel hostility into more socially acceptable outlets such as competition, assertiveness, or hunting. Otherwise, we shall all be hunters and the hunted.

CONTROL

Struggles over interpersonal control are frequently struggles over whose defenses will dominate the relationship. The more rigid the defenses, the more likely individuals will insist on others conforming to their view of the world and their ways of acting. For example, the person who repeatedly projects hostility onto the world is likely to put considerable pressure on others to see the world as a hostile place. On the other hand, if a person defends with repressive, rose-colored glasses, then interactions will be focused on only the cheery aspects of the world. If two people with incompatible defenses try to interact, there will be conflict. So, for example, an insignificant issue like deciding what movie to see can turn into a heated conflict for control when it involves a spouse with rose-colored glasses who wants to see a light comedy and a hostility-projecting spouse who wants to see a war movie.

Individuals also expect to control relationships when they experience the person they are relating to as nothing more than an object that exists to gratify their infantile desires. Each pregenital type of personality has its unique style of

controlling others: oral characters control by clinging, anal characters control through sheer stubbornness, and phallic characters through seductiveness. The most intensely controlling people seem to be anal personalities who have come from overcontrolling families. These individuals feel they were once forced to give in on the toilet and thereby lost control over their bodies. Now they act as if their commitment is to never again give in. A woman like this was raised by a governess who seemed to enjoy giving her cold-water enemas to force her to let go when she was two. She married a man who was toilet trained at 10 months of age. He was complaining that his wife could never let go and really enjoy their sexual relationship. She went along with his demands for sex but seemed unable to let go to have an orgasm. The trauma that brought them into therapy involved the wife deciding to solve her problem. She read Masters and Johnson and reserved a room in New York so they could have a sexual holiday. Once in New York, she became very aroused as she approached her husband, but he was now unable to get an erection. He was so determined to control their sexual relationship that he shut off his penis to spite his wife.

In therapy the analyst must be very aware of how a patient is trying to control. The analyst must recognize when such control is serving defensive purposes of resistance or gratifying purposes of transference. The analyst must confront and clarify the patient's attempts to control and then interpret the meaning and causality of controlling maneuvers. The analyst's most effective method of counter-control is silence, so no matter what response the patient insists on, the analyst can respond with silence. It is like trying to fight with a spouse who clams up—it can be terribly frustrating, since the quiet one is in control.

Individuo-Social Conflicts

ADJUSTMENT VERSUS TRANSCENDENCE

Freud (1930) believed there was a fundamental and unresolvable conflict between an organized society's need for rules and controls and an individual's most basic desires for immediate and continual gratification without consideration for the needs of others. Freud certainly believed that cultures did not have to be as oppressive about childhood sexuality as was his Victorian age. Without doubt, he, more than any other individual, was responsible for our modern sexual revolution. Nevertheless, that cultures must be repressive to some degree was accepted by Freud. Being the civilized individual he was, he threw his weight behind civilization and was willing to treat its discontents.

There are radical Freudians, such as Norman Brown (1959), who believe that individuals need not be repressed. All of the destructive expressions of the death instinct, such as violence and tearing nature down through scientific analysis and commercial construction, are the result of repeated frustration of the life instinct. If we adopt more childlike, spontaneous lifestyles, through which we give free expression to playing in bed and in fields, then we need not be frustrated and so aggressive because of our frustration of the life instincts. Those who assume a radical Freudian view usually accept sexuality as an instinct but see aggression as due to the frustration that comes from repres-

sion of our desires for spontaneous sexuality. Radical Freudians generally believe that individuals should be encouraged to transcend their particular culture and find fulfillment by following their own unique paths in the face of possible social ostracism. Bur Freud himself, as radical as he was in many ways, was convinced that even the most conscious of individuals must make considerable compromises to the culture and leave fantasies of transcendence to the angels.

IMPULSE CONTROL

It is obvious that Freud believed that human sexual and aggressive impulses must be controlled. We are animals covered with a thin veneer of civilization. For therapists to encourage the removal of that veneer is to eventually encourage raping and rioting in the streets. There are those who believe that Freud himself contributed to removing this thin veneer. They see sexuality and aggression as out of control in our post-Freudian society. Dependency on drugs, alcohol, and food is rampant; violence seems to dominate the streets; such deviances as homosexuality and bisexuality are accepted as healthy; and gonorrhea and other veneral diseases are epidemic. Freud, however, was one of the earliest to recognize that it is much easier for therapists to loosen the controls of neurotics than to produce controls for impulse-ridden personalities. He did not preach removal of the thin veneer of controls but rather believed that the best hope for individuals and society was to replace the rigid but shaky infantile veneer with a more mature and realistic set of controls.

RULES FOR LIVING

The rules we should live by—our governments, our churches, our families, or our own—were never directly addressed by Freud. However, Freud's view of religion as a neurosis-producing institution in which people cling to their infantile needs for a superparent would suggest that he did not see churches as the best source of rules for living. Likewise, his therapeutic work to reduce the guilty control of patients' primitive superegos suggested that one's parents are not the best source of rules, since the primitive superego is the internalized parents. Freud concluded that the ego should rule the individual. The ego is uniquely structured to have direct access to demands from the superego, the id or instincts, and the outside world. The primary rule of the ego is to maximize gratification while minimizing punishment. This rule meant that mature ego functioning would lead an individual to live primarily by the rules of society in order to avoid the punishment that would come from going against society's rules.

Beyond Conflict to Fulfillment

MEANING IN LIFE

While Freud believed we could not go beyond conflict, he did suggest that we could find meaning in life while in the midst of conflict. Meaning is found in work and in love. Just why work should bring such meaning is theoretically

unclear in psychoanalysis. Partly work is one of society's best channels for sublimating our instincts, so Freud himself could sublimate his sexual curiosity into his work of analyzing his patients' sexual desires. Freud's total acceptance of the meaning of work, however, seems to come more from his almost total involvement in his own work. His voluminous productivity could come only from a person with a passion for work.

Love is a clearer source of meaning. Love is the atmosphere that allows two people to come together. Love is the most civilized expression of sexuality and, therefore, the safest and most satisfying. Obsessive ruminating about meaning in life can come only from someone too immature to love and to work.

VALUES

What we value in life is a function of what we *cathect*, that is, invest with emotional significance. We are the ones who make objects, activities, or ideas valuable by the instinctual energy that we project or displace onto these aspects of life. If our values are based on pregenital fixations, they will seem shallow or excessive, such as the degree to which a fetishist can value boots or panties or an anal character values cleanliness. People who find the world boring or empty probably have so much energy tied up in primary narcissism that they are unable to allow anything other than themselves to come alive. The more we release our energies from internal conflict, the more vital the world can become for us, and the richer our values can be. In the next section we get an idea of the areas of life that a successfully analyzed person would cathect and value.

IDEAL INDIVIDUAL

The ideal individual for Freud, which would also be his ideal goal for therapy, is a person who has sufficiently analyzed pregenital fixations and conflicts in order to attain and maintain a genital level of functioning. The genital personality is the ideal. As Maddi (1972) points out, the genital personality loves heterosexuality without the urgent dependency of the oral character. The individual is fully potent in work without the compulsivity of the anal character. Genital people are satisfied with themselves without the vanity of the phallic character. They are altruistic and generous without the saintliness of the anal character. And they are fully socialized and adjusted without suffering greatly from being civilized.

THEORY OF THE THERAPEUTIC RELATIONSHIP

There are two parts to the patient-analyst relationship, and they serve two different functions for therapy. The *working alliance* is the relatively nonneurotic, rational, and realistic attitudes of the patient toward the analyst. This working alliance is a precondition for successful analysis to occur, since these rational attitudes allow the patient to trust and cooperate with the analyst even in the face of negative transference reactions.

The *transference* part of the relationship is one of the most important sources of content for analysis. In transference reactions the patient experi-

ences feelings toward the analyst that do not befit the analyst but actually apply to significant people from the patient's past. Through displacement, impulses, feelings, and defenses pertaining to people in the past are shifted to the analyst. These transference reactions represent the conflicts between impulses and defenses that are the core of the person's pregenital personality and pathology. By repeating these impulses and defenses in relationship to the analyst, the actual content of psychopathology is present for analysis. The person does not just talk about past conflicts but actually relives these conflicts in relationship to the analyst. Experiencing such transference reactions is not a curative process, however, since the essence of the transference is unconscious. Patients know they are having intense reactions toward the analyst but are unaware of the true meaning of their reactions. It is the analysis or making conscious the unconscious content of the transference reactions that is the therapuetic process.

The analyst's own reaction to the patient must be a delicate balance between being warm and human enough to allow a working alliance to develop and yet depriving and blank enough to stimulate the patient's tranference reactions. The stereotype has emerged that an analyst is just a blank screen and therefore cool and aloof. Even such an orthodox analyst as Fenichel (1941), however, has written that above all the analyst should be human. Fenichel was appalled at how many of his patients were surprised by his own naturalness in therapy. In order for the patient to trust the analyst and believe the analyst cares, the analyst must communicate some warmth and genuine concern.

Analysts, of course, would not agree with Rogers's (1957) assumption that it is therapeutic to be genuine throughout therapy. If analysts become too real, they will interfere with the clients' needs to transfer reactions onto them that are appropriate to people from the patients' pasts. Patients can transform a blank screen into most any object they desire, but it would take a psychotic transference to distort a three-dimensional therapist into an object from the past.

While analysts agree with Rogers's general assumption that it is best to adopt a nonjudgmental attitude toward a patient's productions in order to allow for a freer flow of associations, they do not encourage the therapist to respond with unconditional positive regard. Frequently, neutral responses such as silence are more likely to stimulate transference reactions, so an analyst's reactions to the patient's productions are best described as unconditional neutral regard.

Analysts would agree with Rogers that accurate empathy is an important part of therapy, since analysts see empathy as a source of useful interpretations. Psychoanalysts also agree that an analyst must be healthier or, in Rogers's terms, more *congruent* than patients. Analysts must be more in touch with their own unconscious processes as another source of accurate interpretations. Analysts must be conscious enough to recognize when they begin to react toward their patients on the basis of counter-transference feelings which represent the analysts' desires to make clients objects of gratification of their own infantile impulses. For example, the analyst must be able to analyze hostile withholding of any warmth or support because a patient reminds the analyst of a sibling. Likewise, an analyst must be able to recognize that giving too much of oneself to a client may represent encouragement to the patient to act out sexual desires with the analyst. Basically the analyst must be healthy enough to discriminate what is coming from the patient and what the analyst is

encouraging, since a patient in the midst of transference reactions cannot be expected to make such important discriminations.

PRACTICALITIES OF PSYCHOANALYSIS

In order for analysts to be considered competent to analyze their own counter-transference reactions, they must have been psychoanalyzed by a training analyst and must have graduated from a psychoanalytic institute, a process that takes four to six years, depending on how much time is spent per week at the institute. Most analysts are physicians and psychiatrists because traditionally it has been very difficult for nonphysicians to be admitted to analytic institutes, even though Freud (1959) supported the practice of *lay analysis*, which is analysis by a nonphysician. Apparently many of the psychoanalytic institutes have become more flexible in recent years about admitting nonmedical mental health professionals into formal psychoanalytic training.

While classical analysts prefer seeing patients five or six times per week, therapy can still be considered psychoanalysis if it occurs at least three times a week. Analysis currently costs between $60 and $100 per 45–50 minute session, with the cost varying according to the city and the reputation of the analyst. Theoretically, analysis has been considered terminable in that there is always more in the unconscious that could be made conscious, but the actual work with an analyst is completed in an average of four to six years.

In orthodox analysis, patients agree not to make any major changes if possible while in analysis, such as changes in marriage or moving. Above all, they should make no important decisions without thoroughly analyzing them. At times, patients are asked to give up psychotropic medications and such chemicals as alcohol or cigarettes. The therapy itself involves just the patient and the analyst interacting alone in a private office. The patient lies on a couch with the analyst sitting in a chair at the head of the couch. The patient does most of the talking, with the analyst frequently being silent for long periods of time when the patient is working well alone. Patients are subtly encouraged to associate primarily to their past, their dreams, or their feelings toward the analyst. The analyst keeps self-disclosures to a minimum and never socializes with patients. Needless to say, the analyst becomes a central figure in the patient's life, and during the neurotic transference time, the analyst is *the* central figure. Following termination, the analyst remains one of the most significant persons in the patient's memory.

MAJOR ALTERNATIVES TO CLASSICAL PSYCHOANALYSIS

While we have focused primarily on classical psychoanalysis in this chapter, it should be emphasized that in practice many present-day followers of Freud lean more heavily upon ego psychology concepts, object relations theory, and psychoanalytically oriented psychotherapy procedures than upon classical psychoanalysis. Furthermore, there are many therapists who consider themselves Freudians who have been trained in settings other than psychoanalytic institutes, such as those in social work, clinical psychology training programs, internships, and residencies. To appreciate the orientation of ego analysts, object relations theorists, and psychoanalytically oriented psychotherapists, we shall now turn to a discussion of these three major alternatives to classical psychoanalysis.

Ego Psychology

Classical psychoanalysis has been based primarily on an id psychology in which the instincts and conflicts over such instincts are seen as the prime movers of personality, psychopathology, and psychotherapy. While id psychology remains the theory of choice of some analysts, others have followed the lead of Hartmann, Kris, and Loewenstein (1947), Erickson (1950), and Rapaport (1958), who have helped establish an influential ego psychology. While id psychology assumes that the ego derives all of its energies from the id, ego psychology assumes that there are ego processes, such as memory, perception, and motor coordination, that are inborn as well (Rapaport, 1958) and possess energy separate from the id. While id psychology assumes that the ego serves only a defensive function in trying to find a safe and satisfying balance in the ongoing conflicts between instincts and the rules of society, ego psychology assumes that there is ego functioning that is free from such conflicts. There are *conflict-free spheres of the ego* (Hartmann et al., 1947) that involve the individual's adaptation to reality and mastery of the environment (Hendricks, 1943). The ego's striving to adapt to and master an objective reality is a primary motivation in the development of the personality. Ego analysts certainly do not deny that conflicts over impulses striving for immediate gratification are important influences on development. They just assume that the separate striving of the ego for adaptation and mastery is an equally important influence.

While development of impulse control is regarded as one of the early ego tasks (Loevinger, 1976), it is by no means the only task. The individual is also striving to be effective and competent in relating to reality (White, 1959, 1960). The emergence of *effectance* and *competence* requires the development of ego processes other than just defense mechanisms. Learning visual motor coordination, discrimination of colors, and language skills, for example, are some of the tasks that individuals can be motivated to master, independent of longings for sexual or aggressive gratification. With its own energies, then, the ego becomes a major force in the development of an adaptive and competent personality. Failure to adequately develop such ego processes as judgment and moral reasoning can just as readily lead to the development of psychopathology as can early sexual or aggressive fixations. The person with inadequate ego development is by definition poorly prepared to adapt to reality.

Once the ego is assumed to have its own energies and developmental thrust, it becomes clear that more is involved in the stages of maturation than just resolution of conflicts over sex and aggression. The psychosexual stages of Freud are no longer accurate to account for all of personality and psychopathology. Development of the conflict-free spheres of the ego during the first three stages of life is just as important as defending against the inevitable conflicts over oral, anal, and phallic impulses. Furthermore, the strivings of the ego for adaptability, competency, and mastery continue well beyond the first five years of life. As a result, later stages of life are as critical in the development of personality and psychopathology as are early stages. The latency stage, for example, is seen by Erikson (1950) as critical in the development of a sense of industry, which involves learning to master many of the skills used in work. Freud, on the other hand, saw the latency stage as a quiet time-out in which no new personality traits developed. From Erikson's point of view, there are individuals who fail to develop a sense of industry not because of unconscious conflicts but because their culture discriminates against people of particular races or religions and fails to adequately educate them in the tools of that culture's trade. Failure to develop a sense of industry leads to a sense of inadequacy and inferiority. A sense of inferiority can lead to such symptoms as depression, anxiety, or avoidance of achievement. Thus individuals can develop problems later in life even if they had developed a basically healthy personality during the first three stages of life. Of course, serious conflicts from early stages can make it more difficult for later stages to progress smoothly. A person with serious dependency conflicts from the oral stage, for example, will probably have more problems developing a sense of industry than would a person free from such conflicts.

The important point for therapy here is that ego analysts will be as concerned with later developmental stages as they are with early developmental stages. By no means are all problems reduced to repetitions of unconscious conflicts from childhood. The adolescent stage, for example, brings very real issues of developing ego identity versus ego diffusion (Erikson, 1950). Young adults must use their maturing ego processes if they are to move toward intimacy rather than lapse into isolation. Mid-adulthood involves the ego energies in creating a lifestyle that brings a sense of generativity, generating something of worth with one's life lest a sense of stagnation take over. And aging adults must look back over their lives to see if they can maintain ego integrity in the face of death—if they can look back and affirm their entire lifecycle as worth living. If not, they are drained by despair.

Issues of identity, intimacy, and ego integrity are critical concerns of ego analysts. Much of therapy is focused on such contemporary issues of clients. Therapy goes back into history only as far as necessary to analyze the unresolved childhood conflicts that might be interfering with the person's present adaptation to life.

Clearly the content of ego analysis will differ from the content of classical analysis. The process of ego analysis may, however, be very similar to the classical process, with long-term intensive therapy and utilization of free association, transference, and interpretation being the rules of some ego analysts. On the other hand, many ego analysts tend to follow the more flexible format of psychoanalytically oriented psychotherapy.

Object Relations Theory

Psychoanalysis is a continually evolving system. One of the ways that psychoanalysis evolves is by new theorists emphasizing different aspects of personal development as the core organizing principals for personality and psychopathology. Freud emphasized conflicts over gratification and control of id processes as the central organizing principal of people's lives. Anal characters, for example, organize their lives around patterns of both controlling and gratifying anal impulses. Ego analysts emphasize the ego as the central organizing principal, with the resolution of ego issues, such as basic trust, autonomy, and initiative, determining the individual's way of life. Object relations theorists, such as Fairbairn (1952), Kernberg (1975; 1976), and Kohut (1971; 1977), emphasize relationships between the self and objects as the major organizing principle in people's lives.

Object relations are intrapsychic structures, not interpersonal events (Horner, 1979). Object relations are very much affected by early interpersonal relationships and in return very much affect later interpersonal relationships. Object relations are the mental representations of self and others (the objects). *Object* is the term Freud (1923) used for others, since in id psychology others serve primarily as objects for instinctual gratification, rather than as authentic individuals with needs and wants of their own.

Object relations theorists differ on the importance of id forces in the relationship between child and parent. Kernberg (1976), for example, views object relations as partly energized by basic instincts, especially aggression. Fairbairn (1952) and Kohut (1971), on the other hand, deemphasize id impulses in early relationships. Kohut (1971) assumes that children have inherent needs to be mirrored and to idealize. These needs obviously require others who can serve as objects that reflect the developing self and as objects that the self can idealize as models for future development.

The self develops through stages that are different from the classic oral, anal, phallic, and genital stages that have been emphasized in the development of id and ego processes (Mahler, 1968). The first stage of self development is *normal autism*, which comes in the first few months of life. In this primary, undifferentiated state there is no self nor object. Fixation at this stage would result in the severe pathology of primary infantile autism, which is characterized by a failure of attachment to objects and a failure of mental organization due to a lack of self-image (Horner, 1979).

Through the process of attachment, described by Bowlby (1969; 1973), the child enters the stage of *normal symbiosis*. In this stage there is a confusion in the child's mind as to what is self and what is object, since neither is perceived as independent of the other. This stage normally lasts two to seven months.

The child then enters the *differentiation* period, during which the child practices separating and individuating from significant others (Mahler, 1968). Crawling away from parents and then crawling back; walking away from parents and then running back; and even playing peekaboo, where the child disappears for a moment and then reappears, are patterns of physical play that allow children to mentally differentiate themselves as separate from the parents to whom they are attached. A failure to differentiate can result in symbiotic psychosis reflecting a fixation at the symbiotic stage.

Under normal conditions the stages of differentiation shift at about two years of age into an *integration* stage. Through integrating processes, the self and object representations, which have become independently perceived, are now fit into relationships with each other. Parent and self are perceived as both separate and related. When all goes well, children at this stage can learn to relate without having overwhelming fears of losing their autonomy, their individuality, or their sense of self.

During the integration stage the child also begins to integrate the good and the bad self-images into a single, ambivalently experienced self. Similarly, the child needs to integrate the good and the bad object images into a single, ambivalently experienced object. Experiences that originate from within the person that were not integrated into the early self-representation, such as the image of oneself as capable of anger, continue to be split off from the sense of self. If these experiences are evoked later in life, they can produce a state of disintegration, with the person's sense of self falling apart.

According to Kernberg (1976), the task of development is not only differentiation and integration but also the emergence of a sense of identity. In the earliest stage, children vacillate between different ways of thinking and acting, expressing first one part of themselves and then another. This instability is due to splitting, a defensive attempt to deal with being overwhelmed by more powerful parents (Kernberg, 1976). If the child splits off bad self-images, such as the angry self, then there is less to fear from punitive parents. Similarly, if children can split off bad object images, such as the angry mother, then the object becomes less threatening. The next step in identity development involves *introjection*, which is the literal incorporation of objects into the mind. This tends to occur during symbiosis. Mother can be experienced as less threatening if mother and child are one. A more mature identity, however, requires the process of identification, in which objects have influence but need not be "swallowed whole." With a more mature sense of identity, individuals can value both autonomy and community, since they are open to influence from others without the fear of being overwhelmed by others.

According to Kohut (1971), the ideal type of identity is an autonomous self, characterized by self-esteem and self-confidence. Because of the security from this identity, the person is not excessively dependent upon others and is also not merely a replica of the parents. Developmentally, the ideal situation is for the child to have its needs to be mirrored and to be idealized met through interaction with the parents. Who the parents are is more important than how the parents intend to interact. If the parents have accepted their own needs to shine and succeed, then their children's exhibitionism will be accepted and mirrored. If the parents have adequate self-esteem, then they can be comfortable with their children's needs to idealize them.

If, during the stages of self development, the parents are not able to meet the child's needs to have mirroring and to idealize, the child will develop a troubled identity. Kohut (1971) focuses on different types of narcissistic personalities that develop from insufficient mirroring or idealizing. Mirror-hungry personalitites, for example, are famished for admiration and appreciation. They incessantly need to be the center of the stage. Such persons tend to shift from relationship to relationship, performance to performance, in an insatiable attempt to get attention. Ideal-hungry personalities are forever in search of others whom they can admire for their prestige or power. They feel worthwhile only as long as they can look up to someone.

From Kohut's (1977) perspective, narcissistic personalities cannot be treated by traditional psychoanalysis in which the therapist alternates between being a blank screen and raising consciousness via telling interpretations.

Psychoanalysis is successful when patients are able to project emotions for others onto the therapist via transference experiences. Persons with self disorders, however, cannot project emotions and images consistently because they are too personally preoccupied. These clients must be mirrored (appreciated and respected) and must be permitted to idealize the therapist. In order to be idealized, therapists must be willing to let themselves be known rather than remain shadows for the clients' projections. By combining Roger's emphasis on empathy and unconditional positive regard (mirroring) and the existential emphasis on being authentic (idealizing), the therapist can fill the void that clients experienced in childhood. By meeting some of the clients' unmet narcissistic needs, clients can begin to develop either a mirroring transference or an idealizing transference. After such transferences are developed, the analyst can use more traditional consciousness-raising techniques, such as interpretations, to help clients become aware of how they try to organize their lives around narcissistic relationships. Clients can then begin to participate in the development of a more autonomous self.

Kernberg (1979) would agree that traditional psychoanalysis can be effective with neurotic patients who can develop neurotic transference relationships. Patients with severe self disorders, such as borderline patients with whom Kernberg specializes, cannot be effectively treated just by interpretations of transference and resistance. Borderline patients have the potential for developing psychotic transferences and can thus experience the therapist as the split-off "bad parent." Profound fears of being overwhelmed, uninhibited, rejected, or abandoned can cause such patients to leave therapy or can prevent the development of a working alliance. Kernberg (1975) emphasizes the importance of setting limits with borderline patients. Setting limits on telephone calls, on acting out aggression toward the therapist, and on how often the therapist can be seen are critical with borderline patients. Setting limits on acting out will provoke anxiety of the sort that helps to clarify the underlying meaning of the acting out. Only by setting clear limits with such clients will the therapist maintain the opportunity for interpretations to be effective. In a therapeutic relationship that combines emotional support with clear limit setting, clients can gradually become conscious of the parts of themselves that have been split off. Without clear limits, the split-off parts of self and objects can threaten to produce disintegration within the individual or within the therapeutic relationship.

Psychoanalytically Oriented Psychotherapy

Variations in the standard operating procedures of analysis have occurred throughout the history of psychoanalysis. At times innovations in therapy resulted in the unorthodox analyst being rejected by more classical colleagues, with the innovator going on to establish a new system of psychotherapy. At other times variations in orthodox analysis were seen as a practical necessity, because particular patients lacked the ego or financial resources to undergo the stress of long-term, intensive analysis. Establishing more flexible forms of psychoanalytic therapy as truly acceptable alternatives within psychoanalysis has usually been credited to Franz Alexander (1891–1963) and his colleagues at the Chicago Institute of Psychoanalysis.

Alexander and French (1946) argued that orthodox analysis was developed by Freud to serve as a scientific means of gathering knowledge about neuroses, as well as a means for treating neuroses. Once the fundamental explanations for the development of personality and psychopathology were established, however, there was no justification to proceed with all patients as if each analyst was rediscovering the oedipal complex. With a thorough understanding of the psychoanalytic principles of psychopathology, therapists can begin to design a form of psychoanalytic therapy that fits the particular patient's needs, rather than trying to fit the patient to standard analysis.

There are patients who do indeed require classical analysis, namely, those with severe and chronic neuroses and character disorders. Patients with such problems are in the minority, however. Much more common are the milder chronic cases and the acute neurotic reactions resulting from a breakdown in ego defenses due to situational stresses. Clients with milder or more acute disorders can be successfully treated in a much more economical manner than previously thought. Alexander and French (1946), for example, reported 600 such patients who were treated with psychoanalytic therapy that lasted anywhere from I to 65 sessions. The therapeutic improvements they reported with their abbreviated therapy were previously believed to be possible only with the use of the long-term, standard psychoanalysis.

Briefer therapy requires more thorough diagnosing and planning. Calling upon all that is known about a particular client and all that is known about the dynamics of psychopathology, the therapist can plan out a more precise treatment that fits the needs of a particular client. Where standard analysis might let the therapy take its own course, the psychoanalytically oriented therapist decides whether the therapy should be primarily supportive of the ego, uncovering of the id impulses, or changing the external conditions of the client's life. Obviously not all the details of therapy can be planned, and the psychoanalytically oriented therapist will rely on a conscious use of various techniques in a flexible manner, shifting tactics to fit the particular needs of the moment. The therapist is obviously more active and directive when using psychoanalytically oriented therapy than when using standard analysis.

Following the principle of flexibility, psychoanalytic therapy becomes highly individualized. The couch may be used, or therapy may proceed face-to-face. Direct conversations may be substituted for free association. A transference neurosis may be allowed to develop, or it may be avoided. Drugs and environmental manipulations will be included when appropriate. Therapeutic advice and suggestions will be included along with dynamic interpretations.

Since daily sessions tend to encourage excessive dependency, the scheduling of therapy is usually spaced over time. Daily sessions can also lead to a sense of routine in which the client fails to work as intensely as possible because tomorrow's session is always available. Therapy is scheduled as frequently or as seldom as necessary to allow an optimal emotional intensity to continue within a client. As a rule, sessions are usually more frequent at the beginning of therapy to allow an intense emotional relationship to develop between client and therapist, and then sessions are spaced out according to what seems optimal for the individual client. After therapy has progressed it is usually desirable for the therapist to interrupt therapy to give clients a chance to test their new gains and to see how well they can function without therapy. Such interruptions also pave the way for more successful termination.

Transference is an inevitable part of therapy, although the nature of the transference relationships can be controlled. A full-blown transference neurosis, for example, is usually what accounts for the length of standard analysis, so brief therapy will frequently discourage a transference neurosis from developing. A negative transference can also complicate and extend therapy and may be discouraged with particular clients. When the transference relationship is controlled and directed and when the therapist relies on a positive transference to help influence clients, then therapy can usually proceed more rapidly. A client with a positive father transference toward the therapist, for example, is much more likely to accept the therapist's suggestions to leave a destructive marriage or change to a more constructive job than would a client involved in a negative transference.

The nature of the transference can be controlled through the proper use of interpretations. If it has been decided that a transference neurosis is unnecessary or perhaps even damaging, the interpretations will be restricted to the present situation, since interpretation of the infantile neurotic conflicts encourages regression and dependency. Regression to early stages of functioning can also be interpreted as a means of avoiding dealing with present conflicts. Attention to disturbing events in the past would be used only for illuminating the motives for irrational reactions in the present.

The therapist can also control the transference by being less of a blank screen and more the type of person that clients would expect to find when they go to someone for help with personal issues. By the therapist being more real, neurotic transference reactions will be more clearly seen as inappropriate to the present situation and will be less likely to continue to develop. Counter-transference reactions in the therapist can also help foster a more therapeutic relationship. Such reactions in the therapist need not be analyzed away, but rather the therapist must consciously decide which reactions will be helpful to therapy and must express those reactions. If a client had a very rejecting father, for example, then remaining a blank screen may just encourage a negative transference, while expressing more accepting attitudes could foster a more therapeutic relationship.

The development of a safe and trusting therapeutic relationship determines whether or not clients can express the troubling emotions and feelings that have been blocked off because of early conflicts with parents. The expression of previously defended emotions and feelings, such as anger, erotic desires, and dependency, is what leads to therapeutic success. Corrective emotional experiencing, then, is a more critical process than the consciousness raising that is stressed in orthodox analysis. Of course, a flexible attitude toward therapy does not see the process as an either/or issue. Therapy at its best should be corrective emotional experiences integrated into conscious ego functioning through intellectual insights into the history of troubled emotions.

EFFECTIVENESS OF PSYCHOANALYSIS

While psychoanalysis has been concerned with the biases and distortions that come from transferences and counter-transferences, this system has not been nearly as careful in controlling for the possible biases and distortions involved in analyzing the effectiveness of psychoanalysis. For nearly 40 years, the effectiveness of psychoanalysis was supported almost entirely by selected case studies reported by enthusiastic analysts. As Meltzoff and Kornreich (1970) point out, such case studies are the empirical starting point for all therapy systems, even though such studies are open to too much bias to establish the effectiveness of any system. Following the typical history of outcome research, psychoanalysts switched first to survey studies with subjective criteria, followed by survey studies with more objective criteria, followed finally by controlled experiments.

The best known of the psychoanalytic survey studies is that of Knight (1941), who surveyed disposition data of patients who stayed in analysis for at least six months. The data involved the analysts' judgments of whether patients were "apparently cured," much improved, improved, unchanged, or worse when analysis was terminated. This survey study had the advantage of being cross-cultural in that it included data on patients seen at psychoanalytic institutes in Berlin, London, Topeka, and Chicago.

Dividing patients by diagnostic category, Knight reported the results shown in Table 3.

While survey research is open to considerable bias, such as therapists judging the outcome of their own patients, it is a good starting point for examining more controlled experiments. In a review of controlled outcome studies, 13 studies dealing with the effectiveness of psychoanalysis and psychoanalytically oriented psychotherapy were found.

The first comparative study was reported in 1953 by Heine, who compared the effectiveness of psychoanalytically oriented psychotherapy with Adlerian and nondirective therapy. Eight patients in each of the three forms of therapy rated themselves on 60 favorable changes and 60 unfavorable changes. Although statistical analyses were not done on the self-report data, Heine did conclude that the patients had experienced improvement from each form of therapy. He further concluded that the changes reported by patients from one school of therapy were no more favorable than changes from the others.

In 1954 A. A. Harris at Maudsley Hospital in London compared what he called a Freudian, analytic type of psychotherapy with CO_2 therapy that induced relaxation. Seventy-two neurotic patients were randomly assigned to

TABLE 3

Diagnostic Category	Number	Apparently Cured or Much Improved	Improved, No Change, or Worse
Neuroses	534	63.2%	36.8%
Sexual disorders	47	48.5	51.5
Character disorders	111	56.6	43.4
Organ neurosis and organic conditions (e.g., colitis, ulcers)	55	78.1	21.9
Psychoses	151	25.0	75.0
Special symptoms (e.g., migrane, epilepsy, alcoholism, and stammering)	54	29.6	70.4

TABLE 4

Method	Considerable Improvement	Distinct Improvement	Little or No Improvement
Psychoanalysis	13%	37%	50%
Psychoanalytically oriented	18	45	37
Rational-emotive	44	46	10

two groups. At the beginning of therapy and after 12–15 months, Harris evaluated each patient on the degree to which the symptoms interfered with occupational functioning. Fifty percent of the psychoanalytic patients were judged improved after this period of therapy, compared with 40 percent of the patients treated with CO_2. The difference between the two groups was not statistically significant.

In his career as a therapist, Ellis (1957b) first worked with psychoanalysis, then switched to psychoanalytically oriented psychotherapy, and finally evolved his own rational-emotive therapy. To compare his effectiveness using each of the three methods, Ellis took closed cases from his files and juxtaposed the final ratings of improvement. He selected 16 cases from psychoanalysis, 78 from psychoanalytically oriented therapy, and 78 rational-emotive cases. His results are shown in Table 4.

While Ellis concludes that these results demonstrate the superiority of rational-emotive therapy over psychoanalysis, all he has shown is that he was more effective later in his career with his own rational-emotive therapy than he was at the beginning of his career with Freudian analysis. While Ellis's study has been considered a controlled experiment, it was not planned as an experiment with all groups being run at the same time, nor does it include a no-treatment control group. Ellis's work is more accurately seen as a comparative survey report in which Ellis was the sole judge of the outcome of his own therapy.

In 1958, Orgel interviewed 15 patients with peptic ulcers who had come to him for psychoanalysis 11 to 20 years earlier. Five of the 15 had quit analysis within seven months of starting, whereas the other 10 had completed their analysis in three to five years. Prior to analysis, people in the two groups were comparable in length and severity of symptoms, age, and diagnoses. In the follow-up interviews, the 10 who stayed in analysis reported no gastric symptoms since terminating treatment. While these results are impressive, this study was also not conducted as an experiment. Consequently, the group that quit therapy was not randomly assigned and may have differed initially from the analyzed group on personality traits, such as low frustration tolerance, that influence the course of ulcer problems.

In 1961, Barendregt, Bastians, and Vermeul-Van Mullem reported an experiment that compared the effects of two and a half years of psychoanalysis and "nonanalytic" psychotherapy. Forty-seven subjects were treated by psychoanalysis, 49 by nonanalytic therapy, and 74 were in a no-treatment group composed of some subjects waiting for analysis and some not. Both prior to treatment and two and a half years later, a test battery was given, consisting of a Wechsler-Bellevue verbal IQ; neuroticism, lie score, and introversion-extroversion measures from the Two-Part Personality Measure; TAT (thematic apperception test) scores from the Atkinson and Dymond scoring system; and Rorschach scores based on predictions made from each subject's initial record. The results were primarily negative, with neither form of therapy doing clearly better than no treatment. The severe methodological problems of this study, including the facts that most of the therapists were inexperienced, few of the analyses were completed, and the subjects were selectively assigned to groups, make this study a poor test of the efficacy of psychoanalysis.

In 1964, O'Connor, Daniels, Flood, Karush, Moses, and Stern reported an experiment on the effects of psychoanalysis and psychoanalytically oriented psychotherapy on patients with ulcerative colitis. Fifty-seven patients (19 diagnosed schizophrenic, 3 neurotics, 34 personality disorders, and 1 undiagnosed) were treated in analysis or analytically oriented therapy. Fifty-seven patients (3 schizophrenics, 3 neurotics, 14 personality disorders, and 37 undiagnosed) were not psychiatrically treated and formed a control group that was matched to the treatment group on the basis of severity of disease, sex, age at onset of colitis, and use of steroid treatment. Criteria measurements included proctoscopic ratings of the degree of inflammatory changes observed in the rectum and ratings of the severity of bowel symptoms. Both ratings were on a scale of 1 to 9, with 1 being most severe. The pretreatment proctoscopic ratings for the experiments and control groups were 2.5 and 2.2, respectively, and the mean symptomatic ratings were 2.3 and 2.6. At the end of the eighth and final year of the study, gains in the protoscopic ratings averaged 0.5 for the experimental group and 0.1 for the control group; gains in the symptomatic ratings were 1.1 for treated patients and 0 for nontreated. The experimenters concluded that the treated group showed a marked and sustained improvement, while the control group remained relatively unchanged.

The fact that patients in analysis were not compared with patients receiving analytically oriented therapy makes it impossible to determine how much of the average gain was due to classical psychoanalysis and how much was due to psychoanalytically oriented psychotherapy. Nevertheless, these results are consistent with Knight's survey data, which reported psychoanalysis to be most effective in treating organic neuroses such as ulcerative colitis.

Brill, Koegler, Epstein, and Forgy (1964) compared patients in psychoanalytically oriented therapy with patients on a waiting list who were told that therapy would be available in 4 to 12 months. The patients were 20- to 40-year-old women who were neither psychotic nor severely depressed. They were randomly assigned to the treatment conditions, and following attrition there were 30 subjects in the psychotherapy group and 20 in the waiting-list group. Therapy was provided by psychiatric residents under supervision. Improvement was measured by scores on the Minnesota Multiphasic Personality Inventory (MMPI) and by ratings from the therapist, the patient, a close relative, and a social worker. Following an average of five months of treatment, patients in psychoanalytic therapy gave themselves higher ratings than did the waiting-list control group. Relatives and therapists also rated the therapy group as more improved. Two psychologists rated the before and after MMPIs blind for both groups. The waiting-list group showed no change, whereas the patients receiving therapy were rated slightly to moderately improved.

In 1965 May and Tuma compared the effectiveness of psychoanalytically oriented therapy alone in treating schizophrenic patients with psychoanalytically oriented therapy plus drugs, drugs alone, electroconvulsive therapy, and custodial hospital care. Schizophrenic subjects were preselected by teams of psychoanalysts as patients in the middle range of prognosis for whom treatment might make an appreciable difference. Twenty patients were randomly assigned to each group, following their first hospital admission. Therapy lasted for as long as one year and was provided by psychiatric residents under the supervision of psychoanalysts. Outcome measures included rehospitalization rates during the first two years following hospital discharge, total number of days in the hospital during the three years following first admission, and post-treatment status on the Menninger Health-Sickness Rating Scale as rated by eight psychoanalysts giving consensus ratings in pairs based upon interviews with the patients and ward behavior ratings from nurses. No significant differences on any of the measures were found between the psychoanalytically oriented psychotherapy group and the custodial care group.

In 1966, Heilbrunn compared classical analysis with extended analytically oriented psychotherapy and brief analytic therapy. There were 37 patients in analysis, 54 in extended analytic therapy, and 75 in brief analytic therapy, but unfortunately there was no no-treatment group. Patients were from various diagnostic groups, with most diagnosed as personality trait disturbances. Subjects were not matched on diagnosis since 13 percent of the patients in analysis were diagnosed psychotic versus less than 3 percent of those in the brief therapy group. Heilbrunn reported no significant differences in improvement between groups: 38 percent of the psychoanalysis group, 43 percent of the extended therapy group, and 45 percent of the brief analytic group improved. None of the psychotic patients improved. This study, like Ellis's, was not designed as an experiment; it had a matched group and no control group. It is more accurately seen as a survey of Heilbrunn's effectiveness with three different types of therapy.

Riess (1967) investigated the hypothesis that psychoanalytically oriented psychotherapy increases occupational efficiency and productivity. Therapists of 414 patients obtained information from their full-time working patients regarding weekly income both prior to and following treatment. For comparative purposes information was obtained on the incomes of 145 waiting-list patients slated to begin treatment at the completion of the study and matched by occupational category to experimental subjects. The mean income of the experimental groups was $80 before treatment and $112 after treatment. The average number of treatment sessions was 57. There were no differences between initial salaries of the experimental and control groups, but following treatment, the mean salary of the therapy group was $22 more than the mean salary of controls. Department of Labor statistics showed a weekly gain of $6 for pertinent occupations during the period of the study. Unfortunately, none of these data were analyzed statistically, and no placebo or comparative treatment group was included.

In 1973, Kernberg presented a final report on the Menninger Foundation's Psychotherapy Research Project. This project began in 1959 and lasted nearly 20 years. The study included 42 adult outpatients and inpatients who were seen in psychoanalysis or psychoanalytically oriented psychotherapy. Psychoanalysis lasted an average of 835 hours, while psychotherapy lasted an average of 289 hours. The majority of patients improved on the Health-Sickness Rating Scale, and there was no difference in improvement between those in psychoanalysis and those in analytic psychotherapy.

Regardless of type of therapy, a high level of initial ego strength was found to correlate with positive change. The quality of interpersonal relationships was the aspect of ego strength most predictive of outcome. The results also tended to support the hypothesis that appropriate transference resolution enhances outcome. The results, however, cannot be shown to be better than placebo therapy or no treatment, since such controls were not included.

Malan (1976a, 1976b) summarized the series of studies on psychoanalytic psychotherapy that he and his colleagues conducted at the Tavistock Clinic in London. In the original study 21 patients and in the replication study 30 patients were treated with brief therapy lasting 10 to 40 sessions. The studies sought to discover whether brief treatment, which applied the same types of interpretations as full-scale analysis, could be effective with patients who varied considerably in degree of disturbance. Follow-up data were collected five to six years after termination to assess the enduring effects of brief therapy.

The factors that were most highly related to positive outcome in both studies were interpretative, focusing on the transference relationships and on the patient's motivation for change. Positive outcome correlated with "successful dynamic interaction," which was defined as a patient who wanted insight and accepted the interpretation of the therapist, especially interpretations linking early life relationships to current behavior patterns. As with the Menninger project, these studies lacked placebo and no-treatment control groups, limiting the conclusions that can be drawn.

In the best-designed study to date, Sloane, Staples, Cristol, Yorkston, and Whipple (1975) compared the effectiveness of short-term psychoanalytically oriented psychotherapy with short-term behavior therapy. There were 30 patients randomly assigned to each of the therapy conditions, and 34 assigned to a waiting-list control group. The patients were treated at the Temple University Hospital Outpatient Clinic. They had an average age in the early 20s, with 26 percent married, 60 percent females, an average of 14 years of education, and an average income of $5,000–$6,000. Two thirds of the patients were diagnosed as neurotics and one third as personality disorders. The therapists were matched for experience, with one having 20 + years, one 10–15 years, and one 6–8 years. Two of the psychotherapists were psychoanalysts, and the third was in personal analysis with a training analyst. All three had considerable experience using short-term psychoanalytic therapies.

Each patient was assessed initially by one of three experienced psychiatrists who were not connected with the study. Together the patient and assessor identified three major target symptoms on a five-point scale. The most frequent disorders were interpersonal, anxiety, and mood problems.

Therapy lasted for four months with an average of 14 sessions. The behavior therapists were free to use whatever techniques they believed would be most helpful. The senior therapist relied almost exclusively on counter-conditioning techniques, the second therapist emphasized cognitive restructuring techniques, and the junior therapist seemed to show no preference. The psychoanalytic therapists emphasized the importance of the therapeutic relationship, followed by the exploration and expression of feelings and insight. Free association, dream analysis, and uncovering of defenses were also apparent in their approaches.

The most striking finding of the study was that, at the end of four months of therapy, both treatment groups were significantly more improved than the no-treatment group, and neither form of therapy was more effective than the other. On symptom ratings, 80 percent of the patients in each therapy group were considered either improved or recovered, compared to 48 percent in the control group. On ratings of overall adjustment, 93 percent of the patients in behavior therapy were considered improved, compared with 77 percent of the psychoanalytic psychotherapy group, and 77 percent of the waiting list. Only two patients, one in psychotherapy and one on the waiting list, were rated as worse. It should be noted that on overall adjustment, less than 10 percent in each group was rated as recovered; and on symptoms, about 10 percent of the behavior therapy group and 20 percent of the psychoanalytic psychotherapy group were rated as recovered. The extremely high percentage of waiting-list subjects rated improved may be due to the fact that this rating could be given if patients were seen as "a little better." Of course, the same holds true for the therapy patients.

After four months of therapy all patients were free to begin or continue therapy if they so desired, so follow-up data were difficult to evaluate. A one-year follow-up after the start of therapy indicated that initial gains were maintained across groups. At two years there were no differences in the rates of improvement across groups, although by that time the waiting-list group had received as much therapy as the treatment groups.

There were a few significant differences between types of patients that improved with each type of therapy. The most striking difference was that patients highest on hysteria and psychopathy on the MMPI did worse in psychoanalytic psychotherapy, whereas patients high on hysteria and mania did better in behavior therapy. There was a tendency for behavior therapy to be helpful with a broader range of patients.

From the available research, what can we conclude about the effectiveness of psychoanalysis? The most obvious answer is that the effectiveness of psychoanalysis has not been adequately tested. However, even if we accepted each of the preceding 11 studies as adequate research, we would get the following equivocal results. On the less stringent question as to whether or not psychoanalysis is more effective than no treatment, 5 of the 11 studies are positive (Brill et al., 1964; O'Connor et al., 1964; Orgel, 1958; Riess, 1967; Sloane et al., 1975), and two are negative (Barendregt et al., 1961; May & Tuma, 1965). The other four studies (Ellis, 1957b; Harris, 1954; Heilbrunn, 1966; Heine, 1953) must be considered neutral since they did not include a no-treatment control group.

On the more stringent question as to whether or not psychoanalysis is more than just a placebo therapy, we find that all 11 studies are at best neutral. Five of the studies (Brill et al.; Harris; O'Connor et al.; Orgel; Riess) failed to include a placebo control group or a comparison therapy group that could serve as a control for placebo effects. The other six studies included at least one other form of therapy to compare with psychoanalysis and/or psychoanalytically oriented psychotherapy. If psychoanalysis had been more effective than the other forms of therapy studied, we would conclude that psychoanalysis is more than a placebo therapy because the other therapies at least control for placebo effects. However, psychoanalysis was not more effective than either extended or brief analytically oriented psychotherapy (Heilbrunn), and it was not more effective than a type of nonanalytic therapy (Barendregt et al.). Psychoanalytically oriented psychotherapy was no more effective than CO_2 therapy in treating neurotics (Harris), nor was it any more effective than nondirective or Adlerian therapy (Heine). Rational-emotive therapy was more effective when used by Ellis than was Ellis's use of either psychoanalysis or psychoanalytically oriented psychotherapy. With schizophrenic patients, psychoanalytically oriented therapy was no more effective than custodial care (May & Tuma). Finally, psychoanalytically oriented therapy was not found to be significantly more effective than behavior therapy in treating neurotics and personality disorders. In fact, to date no study has found either psychoanalysis or psychoanalytically oriented psychotherapy to be significantly more effective than either a placebo treatment or some alternative form of therapy.

CRITICISMS OF PSYCHOANALYSIS

From a Behavioral Perspective

Behavioral criticisms of psychoanalysis have been frequent and intense. One set of criticisms revolves around the view that as a theory, psychoanalysis is much too subjective and unscientific. Psychoanalytic concepts such as unconscious processes, ego, and defenses are almost entirely mentalistic and unable to be linked to observable behavior in a way that can be objectively measured and validated. All too frequently Freudians have reified rather than verified their concepts, such as the ego and the id.

Such was the thrust of many traditional behavioral criticisms. But many behavior therapists present an even more devastating reaction. They do not argue with psychoanalytic theory—they ignore it. Why bother learning how a therapy is supposed to work when there are no data to demonstrate that it does work? That there have been only eight real experiments (Barendregt et al., 1961; Brill et al., 1964; Harris, 1954; Heine, 1953; May & Tuma, 1965; O'Connor et al., 1964; Orgel, 1958; Sloane et al., 1975) designed to evaluate the effectiveness of psychoanalysis after 80 years of practice is a scientific disgrace! An average of one experiment every decade is even slower than the average analysis. Freud himself can be excused as a genius too committed to theory construction to gather controlled data, but surely not all of his followers can hide behind that excuse. Unless psychoanalytic institutes demonstrate empirically that their form of therapy is more than just a placebo therapy, most behavior therapists will continue to ignore this once-dominant system as if it were a therapeutic dinosaur, too slow to survive.

From an Existential Perspective

Contrary to behavioral biases, psychoanalysis is much too objective for existentialists. Not empirically but theoretically and practically it is too objective. Just look at the psychoanalytic concept for human relationships—they are called "object relationships." Psychoanalysis conceives of human beings as objects that are merely a bundle of instinctual and defensive energy. This psychoanalytic conception of human beings has filtered into the very core of our self-concepts and consequently has been one of the dominant forces in the dehumanization of modern human beings. Where are freedom, choice, and responsibility—the subjective experiences that allow humans the option of being different from all the objects of the universe? How can a system that has placed so much emphasis on consciousness as the process of freeing people from pathology not take freedom and choice seriously? A conscious object sounds paradoxical and absurd.

From an Eclectic Perspective

It is the essence of eclecticism to seek what is of value in any therapy system, especially one as rich and complex as psychoanalysis. Many eclectics use a dynamic approach in their work, especially in their formulation of the problems with which they are working. Psychoanalysis is one of the few theories with enough personality and psychopathology content to be the core of a diagnostic manual or the content of a Rorschach evaluation. Many eclectics will also use such concepts as defenses or transference reactions in their thinking about the content of therapy. As an overall system of therapy, however, classical psychoanalysis has become much too dogmatic for the tastes of eclectics. As with most systems, the followers or disciples of a genius like Freud are usually less creative and therefore less flexible. With Freud, theory and therapy continued to evolve, but with many of the present practitioners of psychoanalysis, it seems more important to be orthodox than to be innovative and face possible ostracism for acting out their counter-transferences.

Eclectics are much more at home with the flexibility of psychoanalytically oriented psychotherapy. Eclectics are not, however, comfortable with the fact that psychoanalytically oriented psychotherapy, like psychoanalysis, has not been demonstrated to be more effective than any other form of therapy. Certainly eclectics cannot justify recommending classical psychoanalysis to clients when it is the lengthiest and most expensive alternative. The eclectic might be tempted to recommend some shorter form of psychoanalytic therapy when the presenting problem is an organic neurosis, such as ulcers or ulcerative colitis. Further recommendations for psychoanalytic therapy would require further research from the supporters of psychoanalysis.

A PSYCHOANALYTIC APPROACH TO MRS. C.

During the early years of marriage, Mrs. C. apparently made an adequate though immature adjustment as an obsessive or anal personality. Mrs. C. expressed such traits as excessive orderliness in the alphabetical ordering of her children's names, meticulousness in her concern with cleanliness, stinginess in holding on to unused clothes while buying no new ones, and constrictedness in never being able to let go of her sexual feelings and become excited.

These traits probably developed as a result of Mrs. C.'s interactions in the anal stage with overcontrolling and overdemanding parents. We know Mrs. C.'s mother was a compulsive person who was overly concerned with cleanliness and disease. Her father overcontrolled Mrs. C.'s expression of aggression and her interest in men. We can imagine that such parents could be quite harsh in their demands on such issues as toilet training and could produce many conflicts in their daughter over holding on and letting go of her bowels and other impulses. From psychoanalytic theory, we could hypothesize that Mrs. C.'s anal characteristics developed in part at least as defenses against anal pleasures such as being dirty and messy and against impulses to express anger.

Why did the experiences surrounding her daughter's case of pinworms precipitate a breakdown in Mrs. C.'s previously adaptive traits and defenses and lead to the emergence of a full-blown neurosis? Certainly illness and fatigue from the Asian flu and from caring for so many sick children would place a stress on Mrs. C.'s defenses. But the precipitating event was also of such a nature as to elicit the very impulses that Mrs. C. had had to defend against since early childhood. First of all, how would anyone feel when a daughter brings home pinworms when the family is already down with the Asian flu, and the mother is burdened with pregnancy and a toddler in diapers? Relatively unrepressed parents would be upset even though they might not express their anger directly because the child did not intend to get pinworms. But Mrs. C. was not free to express any anger as a child and would probably have to defend against any such expression as a parent.

A case of pinworms is also characterized by anal itching, with the pinworms locating in the anus. In fact, to confirm that the problem was pinworms, Mrs. C.'s physician directed her to examine her daughter's anus with a flashlight while her daughter was sleeping. So while on one level the pinworms were painful, on another level the possibility of contracting pinworms could be a temptation to provide that secret pleasure that can come from scratching an itchy anus. With defenses weakened by illness and fatigue and with threatening impulses of aggression and anal sexuality stimulated by her daughter's contracting pinworms, the conditions were set for the emergence of neurotic symptoms that can both defend against as well as give indirect expression to Mrs. C.'s unacceptable impulses.

First, let's look at how her neurotic symptoms provided further defense against her threatening impulses. The compulsive showers and hand washing are an intensification of her long-standing preoccupation with cleanliness. If danger lies in being dirty, then wash! These compulsive symptoms are in part an intensification of her reaction-formation defenses of keeping clean in order to control desires to play with dirt and other symbols of feces. If desires to damage her daughter were also breaking through, then her washing could serve both as a means of removing Mrs. C. from interactions with her daughter in the morning and as a means of undoing any guilt over aggression by washing her hands clean of such bloody thoughts. The underwear piled in each corner literally served to isolate Mrs. C. and her family from more direct contact with anal-related objects.

How did Mrs. C.'s neurotic symptoms allow some gratification of her desires? The shower ritual is most obvious, since each time she lost her place in her ritual she had to go back to giving herself anal stimulation. In the process of isolating dirty materials like the underwear and things that dropped to the floor, Mrs. C. was also able to make a mess of her house. It does not take much of an interpretation to appreciate how Mrs. C. was expressing her aggression toward her husband by making him get up at 5:00 A.M. and toward her children by not cooking or adequately caring for them.

Why was Mrs. C. so unable to express some of her feelings and desires directly and thereby prevent the need for a neurotic resolution of her conflicts? First of all, such direct expression would be entirely contrary to the total personality she had developed around controlling such impulses. Second, the regression induced by her defenses weakening would cause Mrs. C. to react to her current situation more on a primary-process level than in a more rational, secondary-process manner. At the unconscious primary level, Mrs. C. would be terrified that loosening controls would result in her going totally out of control and being overwhelmed by her impulses. Being overwhelmed by instinctual stimulation produces its own panic, but Mrs. C. would also be panicky about facing the wrath of her overcontrolling parents for being a bad girl who soiled her pants or expressed the slightest anger. At an atemporal, unconscious level, Mrs. C. would not experience herself as the adult parent who is safe to express some anger but rather as the controlled little girl who had better not express her resentment.

In considering psychoanalysis for Mrs. C., an analyst would have to be quite confident that Mrs. C.'s problem was indeed obsessive-compulsive neurosis and not pseudoneurotic schizophrenia, in which the neurotic symptoms are masking a psychotic process. Given how much she has already regressed and how much her life is dominated by defensive symptoms, there could be a real risk in encouraging her to regress further in psychoanalysis. If the analyst felt that further evaluation confirmed previous reports that Mrs. C. did not show evidence of a psychotic process, then analysis might proceed.

When directed to lie on the couch and say whatever comes to mind, Mrs. C. would become quite anxious about having to give up some of her controls to the analyst. Obviously, she has to trust enough to believe that her analyst knows what to do and will not let her get out of control entirely. Resistance to letting her thoughts go would begin immediately. It might take the form of returning immediately to her obsession with pinworms whenever she became anxious. The analyst would have to confront and clarify her pattern of talking about pinworms whenever she became anxious and then interpret this pattern in a way that would allow Mrs. C. to become aware that she uses her obsession to defend against experiencing associations that are even more threatening than pinworms. The analyst would also have to deal with Mrs. C.'s well-established defense of isolating her affect. The analyst would have to confront her pattern of saying only what she thinks about events and not what she feels about them. The analyst would also have to be very sensitive to occasions when Mrs. C. is being excessively warm and affectionate, since such expressions would likely be reactions to her true feelings of hatred and loathing for the nongiving, controlling therapist.

As Mrs. C. very gradually became aware of the defensive nature of her symptoms and her other patterns of behavior in analysis, she would be more able to experience intensely the feelings that would be emerging toward the analyst. As she regressed she might become aware of fears that her analyst was trying to control her sex life just as her father seemed to want to control her sex life when he followed her on a date during her teens. Even more threatening would be her desires to have her father-like analyst control her sexuality and thereby satisfy his and her desires together. As she regressed further, she might become aware of desires to have her father-like therapist satisfy her by having anal intercourse or to have her mother-like analyst pleasure her by wiping her rear. Mrs. C.'s transference reactions would have to include considerable hostile feelings that would be displaced from both of her parents onto her analyst, so she would be frequently enraged that the analyst was demanding and controlling while being ungiving, as were both her mother and her father. But she could not become conscious of such hostile and sexual impulses without also becoming conscious of fears that her parent-analyst was going to destroy her or reject her by sending her to a state hospital. She would also have to become acutely aware of how frequently she would try to control both her anxiety and her impulses by expressing the opposite of what she felt, by apologizing, or in other ways undoing her reactions, or by isolating her impulses into more neutral thoughts.

As Mrs. C. worked through such neurotic transferences with her analyst, she would gradually gain insight into the meaning and causes of her neurosis. She would gradually become conscious of ways in which she could channel her dangerous impulses into more mature outlets that provide both controls and gratification for her desires, such as expressing her anger in words. Over many years Mrs. C. might be able to consciously restructure her personality enough to give her ego some flexibility in expressing hostile and sexual impulses without having to panic when situations threatened to stimulate such impulses.

EXISTENTIAL ANALYSIS

MARK HAD BEEN in psychoanalytically oriented therapy for two years, and he had become much more aware of some of the historical reasons for his homosexuality. Both he and his therapist, who was leaving town, wanted to see if Mark was now able to relate fully to a woman. For 20 years since puberty, Mark had related sexually to only men except for a petting experience with a girl when he was 17. He was currently afraid that if he went out with a woman and she wanted to go to bed with him, he would have to try lest she see him as impotent. I confronted him with the fact that he was acting as if he had no choice in determining if and when he would relate sexually to a woman. Just as he respected a woman's freedom to set her limits, so, too, was he free to set his own limits. He would just have to express his honest feelings that if a woman wanted instant intimacy, then he was not the person for her.

Mark liked this idea and went out with a woman for the first time in 20 years. She was in a hurry. Mark, however, was able to accept this fact as a statement about her and not as a put-down of himself. Later he met Leesa through a mutual friend. Leesa liked Mark and agreed with his feelings about getting to know each other gradually rather than jumping into instant intimacy. For a few months they became more comfortable with each other, including more sexually comfortable. They had not had intercourse yet when they went away to the mountains of Vermont for a New Year's weekend. Accompanying them were Mark's supervisor from work and her husband. Mark was convinced that both she and her husband believed that he was gay. Mark said their jaws hit the floor when they saw how turned on Leesa was with Mark, nibbling at his ears and caressing his body.

When I saw Mark on the Monday after the holidays, he was all smiles and related with delight that he had made love four times with Leesa, and each time it was great for both of them. From my heterocentric view, I assumed that therapy was just about over, but Mark soon discovered that he was now confronted with one of the most profound choices of his life. Previously he had never really believed that he could enjoy heterosexual relationships. Now he had, but he had also discovered that for him heterosexuality was not so radically different from some of his best homosexual relationships. Mark now believed that he had the choice of following a homo- , hetero- , or bisexual style of life. At the same time, he felt frozen by the anxiety of knowing that his future would depend on this choice and not on past conditioning or conflicts.

A SKETCH OF TWO OF THE FIRST EXISTENTIAL THERAPISTS

Ludwig Binswanger (1881–1966) was one of the first therapists to emphasize the existential nature of the type of crisis that Mark was experiencing in therapy. He believed that crises in psychotherapy usually were critical choice points for the people involved. His commitment to a person's freedom to choose in therapy went as far as his acceptance of the suicide of one of his patients, Ellen West, who found death to be her most legitimate alternative (Binswanger, 1958a). Existentialists, like Binswanger, do not run from the dark side of life. Following the example of Kierkegaard (1954a; 1954b), the Danish philosopher, existentialists are willing to face aspects of life that are awful but meaningful at the same time.

Binswanger had originally struggled to find meaning in madness by translating the experience of patients into psychoanalytic theory. After reading Heidegger's profound philosophical treatise, *Being and Time* (1962), however, Binswanger (1958b) became more existential and phenomenological in his approach to patients. The phenomenological approach enabled Binswanger to face directly the immediate experience of patients and to understand the meaning of such phenomena in the patients' terms rather than in terms of the therapist's theory.

Binswanger began applying his emerging existential ideas in the Sanatarium Bellevue in Kreuglinger, Switzerland, where he succeeded his father as chief medical director in 1911. After interning under Eugene Bleuler, from whom he learned much about the symptoms of schizophrenia, he became increasingly intrigued with understanding the actual structure of existence of the people experiencing such pathological states. He continued in his work until his retirement in 1956 and his death in 1966 at the age of 85.

Medard Boss, another major existential psychotherapist, has had a remarkably similar career to Binswanger's. Born in Switzerland in 1903, he also worked under Bleuler in Zurich. Like Binswanger, he knew Freud and was heavily influenced by his thinking. Heidegger was his most important influence, and, like Binswanger, he has been concerned with translating Heidegger's philosophical position into an effective approach to psychotherapy. Boss's particular concern has been to integrate the ideas of Heidegger with the methods of Freud, as indicated in the title of his major work, *Daseinanalysis and Psychoanalysis* (1963). Boss has worked for many years in the medical school at the University of Zurich as professor of psychoanalysis.

While most existential therapists draw upon the work of Binswanger and Boss, neither dominates existentialism the way Freud dominated psychoanalysis or Rogers reflects client-centered therapy. One reason is that neither developed a comprehensive system or theory of psychotherapy. Boss, in fact, seems even antitheoretical in a letter to Hall and Lindzey (1970), in which he writes:

I can only hope that existential psychology will never develop into a theory in its modern meaning of the natural sciences. All that existential psychology can contribute to psychology is to teach the scientists to remain with the experienced and experienceable facts and phenomena, to let these phenomena tell the scientists their meaning and their references, and so do the encountered objects justice.

Some American existentialists have been more involved, however, with pulling together the many strands of existentialism into a systematic approach, and we shall draw more heavily upon the work of such systematizers as Rollo May (1958a, 1967), James Bugental (1965), and especially Ernst Keen (1970).

THEORY OF PERSONALITY

Existentialists would be uncomfortable with the term *personality* if it implies a fixed set of traits within individuals. For them existence is an emerging, a becoming, a process of being that is not fixed or characterized by particular traits. Nor does existence occur just within the individual but rather between individuals and their world.

Existence is best understood as being-in-the-world. The use of hyphens is the best we can do in English to convey the idea that a person and the environment are a unity. Existentialists have rejected the Cartesian dualism that assumes a split between mind and body, experience and environment. Being and world are inseparable because they are both essentially created by the individual. Phenomenologically, the world we relate to is our own construction that to a greater or lesser extent reflects the construction of others, depending on how conventional we are. For example, a traditional Christian's world includes a Superior Being that can be communicated with, while the atheist's existence contains no such spiritual being. In therapy a Freudian therapist experiences dynamics in patients that a behaviorist would swear are figments of the Freudian imagination. The behaviorist might argue that eventually we will all respond to the same world once it is defined by the scientific method, but the existentialist argues that the scientific method itself is a human construction that is inadequate for understanding the very being that created it. Rather than reconciling differences in world views, the existentialist accepts that to understand a particular human being is to understand the world as that person construes it.

We exist in relationship to three levels of our world. In German these are called Umwelt, Mitwelt, and Eigenwelt (Binswanger, 1963; Boss, 1963; May, 1958b). *Umwelt* connotes ourselves in relationship to the biological and physical aspects of our world, and we shall translate it as being-in-nature. *Mitwelt* refers to the world of persons, the social world; we shall call it being-with-others. *Eigenwelt* literally means own-world and refers to the way we reflect upon, evaluate, and experience ourselves; it will be translated as being-for-oneself.

Personalities differ in their ways of existing at each of these three levels of being. For example, imagine being on a beautiful, secluded beach by the ocean. One person may be afraid to set foot into the ocean since it is the home of sharks waiting to attack, whereas another person dives in eagerly, seeking refreshment from the cool waters. One person experiences a desire for a lover in such a sensuous setting, while another feels all alone. One person walks along looking at the nearby land as a golden opportunity for a seaside housing development, whereas another feels sad about the encroachment of the houses that are already moving in nearby. Still others feel at one with the ocean from where all life has come, while someone, somewhere, wants to join the ocean to end life.

When we-are-with-others, we know that they are conscious beings who can reflect upon us, evaluate us, and judge us. This may cause us to fear others and want to run from them. We may choose to clam up or to talk only about superfluous issues like the weather, lest we reveal something about ourselves that others would dislike. Frequently we anticipate what others are thinking or feeling about us, and we guide our observable behavior in order to have a favorable impact on them. Keen (1970) seems to assume that this is the way we always are with others, and he calls this level of existence *being-for-others*. Certainly this is a common mode of existence, as reflected in Riesman's (1961) characterization of the modern personality as being other-directed. Keen's translation of *Mitwelt* into being-for-others, however, overlooks the fact that there are special times with special others in which we can let ourselves be, whether we are silly or sad, anxious or mad, without having to worry about what the other person is thinking about us.

When we are being-for-ourselves, we are the ones who are reflecting upon, evaluating, or judging our own existence. Since such self-reflection can be very painful at times, we may choose not to be introspective. Or we may choose to think about ourselves only after having a few drinks or a few joints to deaden the pain somewhat. Or we may become incessantly introspective and have difficulty with being at the other two levels of existence. For existentialists, however, the risk of pain or self-preoccupation is the price we may have to pay to achieve the considered, conscious life that is so important in creating a healthy existence.

In the process of trying to create a healthy existence, we are faced with the dilemma of choosing the best way to be in-nature, with-others, and for-ourselves. With the emergence of consciousness we realize how ambiguous the world is and how open it is to different interpretations. In this book alone we are considering 24 different interpretations that could serve as guides for interpreting the natural, social, and personal aspects of our world. What is the existential alternative for living? The best alternative is not necessarily to choose to maximize reinforcements and minimize punishments as some behaviorists would suggest, or to adapt our instinctual desires to the demands of our environment as some Freudians would suggest.

The best alternative is to be authentic. For the existentialists, authenticity is its own reward. An authentic existence brings with it an openness to nature, to others, and to ourselves, because we have decided to meet the world straight on without hiding it from us or us from it. Such openness means that authentic individuals are much more aware, because they have chosen not to hide anything from themselves. An authentic existence also brings a freedom to be spontaneous with others because we do not have to fear that we might reveal something about ourselves that contradicts what we have pretended to be. A healthy existence brings with it an awareness that any relationship we do have is authentic and that if anyone cares about us it is really us they care about and not some facade constructed on their behalf. Authentic relationships allow us to truly trust others because we know they will be honest about their experience and not tell us what they think we want to hear.

An authentic existence is healthy in part because the three levels of our being are integrated or in-joint rather than in conflict. We experience ourselves as together since the way we are in nature is the way we present ourselves to others and also the way we know who we are. We do not get caught up in idealizing images about ourselves that prevent us from being intimate with others lest they tell us what we do not want to hear. Nor do we get so preoccupied with ourselves that we cannot get involved in the world around us. A healthy existence, then, involves a simultaneous and harmonious relationship to each level of being without emphasizing one level at the expense of others, such as sacrificing our evaluation of ourselves for the approval of others.

With authenticity promising so much, why don't we all choose to be authentic? Why do so many of us seem to have the inner terror that if other people really knew us they wouldn't want to be with us? Why does the other-directed personality seem to be the stereotype of our time? Why do so many people commit intellectual suicide at a young age? What is the dread that comes with being more fully aware of ourselves and our world?

Tillich (1952) has suggested that there are certain conditions inherent in existence that will tempt us to run from too much awareness. These conditions fill us with a dread called *existential anxiety*. The first source of anxiety comes with our acute awarness that at some unknown time we must die. Death may be denied by our culture, including psychology, as being particularly relevant to life, yet the fact that our total existence will end in nothingness can make us shudder. When we are honest we are also aware that our most significant others can die at any time, ending not only their existence but also the part of our being that was intimately connected with them.

A few summers ago my wife and I were swimming with our three-year-old son and one-year-old daughter in a salt pond near the ocean. A woman came over to borrow a paper cup, and when she turned around she immediately realized that her four-year-old son was missing. She was convinced he was in the water, so we began diving and diving and diving. The more we dove the more anxious we became, hoping we would find him, then gradually hoping that we wouldn't. Two hours later, when the fire department pulled him out of the deepest waters where no one expected him to be, all we could do was shudder and hold each other close.

Existential anxiety also comes from our awareness that we can be helpless against chance factors that control us without our assent. Some of these accidents, such as our genetic makeup, which affects our looks, intelligence, and physical abilities, have already set limits on who we can become without our having any choice in the matter. Then when we hear of accidents that occur daily and profoundly reverse a life, such as a vigorous 30-year-old man who recently slipped by his swimming pool, breaking his neck and becoming a quadriplegic, we anxiously are aware that a similar accident could suddenly knock us down.

Once we become conscious beings, we are aware that inherent in existence is a necessity-to-act. We must make decisions that will profoundly affect the rest of our lives, such as where we go to school, what career we choose, if and whom we choose to marry, and whether or not we have children. We must act, and yet in modern times we are less and less certain about the basis for deciding. We cannot know beforehand with any degree of certainty how our decisions will turn out, and so we are continually under the threat of being profoundly guilty. We must make decisions in relative ignorance of their ramifications, knowing that we will hurt people regularly without intending to. In critical choices we alone are responsible, and inherent in our responsibility is the anxiety of knowing that we will make serious mistakes but not knowing whether this choice is one of those mistakes. For example, when I was deciding whether or not to spend a year of my life writing this book, I was quite anxious that such a decision might be a miserable mistake. Some of you may now believe that I had good reason to be anxious.

Tillich (1952) also pointed out that the threat of meaninglessness is another contingency of human existence that produces anxiety. In our orientation to life we want to see what we do as meaningful. The particular meaning may vary from love for one person, to sex for another, to faith for still another. But when we honestly reflect on ourselves and begin to question the signficance of our existence, the issue becomes whether life itself means anything. We can rarely go to the theater or a modern museum or read a current novel without being confronted with this issue. For many of us, what we once believed in—our former religions, our former politics, or our former therapies—no longer seem as significant as they once did. This suggests that our current source of meaning may also disappear. All therapists see formerly vital marriages that have become entirely devitalized with nothing left but deadly boredom. We see people trapped in previously gratifying jobs that are now nothing more than a means of structuring time, ruts that lead nowhere. Our clients become anxious, and so do we. Part of our anxiety comes from knowing that we are the ones who created the meaning in our lives and that we are the ones who let it die. Therefore, we must be the ones to continue to create a life worth living.

The prospect that existence has no significance whatsoever can be terrifying. The conclusion that one's existence is totally absurd can be immobilizing. Such immobilization is exemplified by the main character in John Barth's *The End of the Road* (1967). Since there is no meaning in life, there is no basis on which to make a decision, so he could not act. His therapist had the ingenious solution that since nothing mattered, he could do just as well by using arbitrary principles when faced with the necessity to act. His principles for living included alphabeticity and sinistrality, which meant that when confronted with a choice in life he would choose the option that begins with the first letter of the alphabet or the option on the left.

Bugental (1965) has suggested that isolation of the individual is another condition of life that brings anxiety. Regardless of how intimate I am with others, I can never be them nor can they be me. We share experiences, but we are always under the threat of never totally understanding each other. Furthermore, we know that choosing to follow our unique direction and create our own meaning in life may lead to others not wanting to be with us. The possibility of such rejection brings forth the anxiety of being literally alone.

These sources of existential anxiety are all related to the fact that a defining characteristic of the human condition is finiteness. Death reflects the finiteness of our time; accidents, the finiteness of our power; anxiety over decisions, the finiteness of our knowledge; the threat of meaninglessness, the finiteness of our values; isolation, the finiteness of our empathy; and rejection, the finiteness of our control over another human being.

These contingencies of life have also been called the realm of *nonbeing*. These givens are matters of necessity—we must die, we must act—and hence are a negation of being, which is by definition open-ended and in the realm of possibility. Nonbeing is the ground against which the figure of being is created. Death is the ground that accents the figure of life in bold relief. Chance is the ground that determines the limits of our choice. Meaninglessness is the ground against which meaning can be seen. And isolation is the ground from which intimacy emerges. The figure of our being is conscious, chosen, and free, whereas the realm of nonbeing is without light, closed, and necessary. In daily living we experience being as our "subjectness" in which we are the active subject or agent in directing our own lives; nonbeing is experienced as our "objectness" in which we are objects determined by forces other than our will.

Authentic being survives to the extent that it takes nonbeing into itself. It perishes to the extent that it attempts to affirm itself by avoiding nonbeing. Our self as a conscious, choosing, and open subject can *be* only through confronting and surviving the anxiety of existence. To avoid existential anxiety is to avoid nonbeing in its various forms. To avoid choice and its anxiety, for example, is to fail to be a choosing subject. An authentic personality is aware that existence is a constant flow from nonbeing into being and back into nonbeing again. This is most clear throughout our total existence as we come from the darkness of having never been, live in the light of consciousness, and then return to the darkness of death. Our daily cycle is similar as our present existence emerges from the yesterday that no longer exists into the being of the present and thrusts into the unconscious nonbeing of tomorrow. This is why authentic being is said to occur only in the present. So too do we flow from aloneness into intimacy and back into aloneness, and from the necessity to act into choice and back to futher necessity to act, experiencing anxiety in each encounter with nonbeing but recognizing it as necessary for being to emerge.

THEORY OF PSYCHOPATHOLOGY

Lying is the foundation of psychopathology. Lying is the only way we can flee from nonbeing, to not allow existential anxiety into our experience. When confronted with nonbeing, such as the drowning of the four-year-old boy, we have two choices: to be anxious or to lie. We may choose to lie by telling ourselves that if we keep a constant eye on our family we can prevent accidents. We hold close our children and our spouse, and when they are in sight we feel relaxed. The lie has worked. We have avoided an encounter with the existential anxiety of accidents, but nonbeing is always there, threatening to emerge into our consciousness. Lying always leads to a closing off of part of our world, so in this case we must close off any thoughts about the man who slipped right in front of his family and broke his neck. Consciousness of such events not only brings existential anxiety but it also threatens to expose our lie.

Lying also leads to neurotic anxiety. If we become anxious, for example, just because our children are momentarily out of sight, we are experiencing neurotic anxiety. Neurotic anxiety is an inauthentic response to being, whereas existential anxiety is an honest response to nonbeing. Our children leaving our sight is essential to many expressions of their own being. They do not exist to shore up our lies. We decided that they need to be in sight in order for us to be more comfortable; they decide to be away from us in order to exist more fully and freely. We choose our lies, however, and are stuck with the consequences. The consequence now is that unless we are aware of our family at all times, we are anxious. Like a mother I saw in therapy, we may have to have our children play in the living room at all times. We may choose to walk them to and from school, to go see them at recess and lunch time, or to be anxious. We may call our spouse repeatedly on the phone, pretending to have something to say but wanting only to be reassured that our spouse is well. If we try not to call, the anxiety may become extremely intense, and we tell ourselves we have no choice—we must call.

When neurotic anxiety leads to the decision that we must act on that anxiety, we develop symptoms of psychopathology, such as a compulsion to check on our family. By saying that we must check on our family, we have become an object that no longer has the choice to let our family be. Symptoms of psychopathology are, in fact, objectifications of ourselves. In the area of our pathology, we experience ourselves as objects without will. This can be terrifying, like the nightmares in which we are being chased by someone and we want to run but, no matter how hard we will it, we cannot run. We are trapped as a consequence of our own lies.

Psychopathology is also characterized by the overemphasis of one level of being at the expense of other levels of being. In this case, there is an overemphasis on being-with-others, namely our family, at the expense of being-in-nature or being-for-ourself. We must be-with-others lest we become filled with neurotic anxiety.

Lying can occur at any level of existence. There are many examples of lying-in-nature. Many people pretend that their biological drives control their lives rather than accept the responsibility for finding healthy expressions for their natural desires. These people tell themselves they must eat and eat and eat or they must drink, must smoke, must rape. There are some theories of therapy, such as psychoanalysis, that support such a biological objectification of humanity. However, we are the ones who choose to believe such a myth about ourselves.

Hypochondriacs lie about the nature of illness and healing. They fabricate a theory that diseases of nature can be avoided if only they see the doctor often enough and fast enough. Their bodies are constant sources of anxiety that send them scurrying to a doctor with every ache and twitch. "If only I run soon enough I can outsmart nature at her games of chance," they lie. After convincing themselves they must run, trying not to run fills their being with neurotic anxiety. They have given up their will to their aches and their medicine man. "You take over, doctor," they seem to say. "This business of living is too scary for me." Lying-in-nature drastically reduces their freedom to be-with-others or to be-for-themselves, since all they can talk about or think about is their most recent attack of this or that.

Some people of a paranoid persuasion decide that nature is filled with evil forces out to destroy them. There is poison in the food, in the water, or in the air, so we must constantly beware. Others of a more manic mood can make nature into an all-loving universe. They thrust themselves into space, seeking a universal orgasm. Some people fighting off depression can conclude that it is the world that is falling apart, the world that is going to the dogs. The good old days are gone forever, and it is only downhill from here on in.

Perhaps the most common level of lying is for others. Early in life we learn that we can misrepresent ourselves to others with some success. As children we are smart enough to see that the option to lie can be a tremendous source of power. How to influence others by faking sad or mad or innocent, depending on their weak spot, is a lesson not missed by many. But, of course, every lie is accompanied by fear of discovery and the shame of being caught in a lie by others. Over the years the impending shame builds and leaves us feeling that if people really knew what we are they would leave us alone. So we spend much of our time lying-for-others, seldom free to be-with-others.

Some slaves brag of their ability to lie-to-others. Selling themselves, they call it—the royal road to success. People want them to smile, they smile; people want their egos built up, they build. They are the customer, the boss, or the professor—same difference. They have the tokens, and if they buy one's act everyone is happy. Happy to sell themselves, a small price for success, they think. The lie up their sleeves, of course, is that someday they will be free to be themselves. They promised themselves that when they get their Ph.D., then they will really live their own lives, or maybe they had better wait until they get their first job, or tenure, or that final promotion, or that new position.

But can this be pathological, we ask. It is so common, so natural. The ability to delay gratification, even the gratification of being ourselves, is a necessary part of succeeding in society. The ability to play roles is essential for making it in the academic or mental health marketplaces. Those elitist European existentialists would reserve health for only the authentic few. But what they really ask is that we not become so alienated that we equate statistically normal self-estrangement with health. If we are going to compromise ourselves away for others, then let us at least remain healthy enough to hurt about it, rather than hide behind the data that show we all do it to some extent.

Lying-for-ourselves is more complicated. First, we must consciously choose to lie; and then at some point, usually beginning when we are children, we come to believe our own lies. For years I believed that I never got angry. I became depressed alright, but never angry. When I finally got tired of getting depressed, I became aware in therapy that I could indeed get angry. To protect my idealized image of myself as a character who never lost his cool, I had to close off most of my feelings and be cold and depressed but never angry.

The Freudians would say that I was unconsciously repressing my anger. But the existentialists argue that in order to close off the "bad" parts of ourselves like anger, we have to first know that the anger is "bad." Otherwise, we have an image of an ego that is like a conscious person within a person, and the ego decides that the anger is bad and must be repressed. Sartre (1956) argues that all we need to assume is one conscious person who uses self-deception and chooses what aspects of the self to turn away from. Once we act on such bad faith in ourselves, we are faced with impending guilt of knowing who we really are, and so our lying snowballs into symptoms, such as having to get depressed in order to never be angry.

Lying-for-oneself can occur in a wide range of pathologies. Some individuals can flee the anxieties of finitude by deceiving themselves into believing they are God. One man was so convinced that he was Christ that he persuaded his six-year-old son that he must die during his 33d year. So on Good Friday of that year his son shot him.

Many people are convinced they can attain perfection, be beyond criticism, and therefore free from rejection if they only work harder. So they become workaholics. Others protect their saintly self-concepts by turning their backs on their sexuality, modeling the Virgin Mary. Still others are convinced they are the perfect spouse and yet are afraid to come in for marriage counseling. They send their partner, and once the doctor straightens out their spouse, their marriage can be perfect again.

In the process of lying, people construct a phenomenal world that may seem to be built out of a deck of cards but is very real to them nonetheless. Understanding their pathology involves an empathy for their world, including the basic psychological categories of time, space, and causality. Keen (1970) cites several forms of time that occur quite frequently in pathological reactions. A *deteriorating future* is the future of a person who feels life and the world are on a downhill course. Deterioration is the eventual outcome for all objects, and the phenomenon of their own future filled with deterioration reflects how much of an object they have become. A *status-striving future* is characteristic of people who promise themselves that someday they will really live. In the process of saving their money, their time, or their being for the future, they are unable to exist in any authentic way. They act as if meaning will come from objects outside themselves, such as material possessions, degrees, or status positions, rather than from the scary but free decisions that emerge from within. A *fantastic future* involves wishing that someday things will be different; a rich spouse will come along and endow us with wealth, or a terrific therapist will reawaken us with a magic wand. Such fantasy negates the continuous flow of time in which our present grows out of our past decisions and actions and our future emerges out of commitments we make right now. Keen does not mention the pathological pasts that many patients live in, but certainly the *ever-present past* is one of the most common time zones for troubled people. Such living in the past frequently reflects the dreaded regrets that people have over mistakes they have made. They hold onto the past as if they believe the childhood rule that slips-go-over, that they can take back a previous decision rather than accept that their errors have hurt but need not halt their personal development.

Spatial relations differ not only for brain-damaged patients but for all people. Some patients always keep their distance, which reflects how far away they feel from most everyone. In some marriages, we find spouses so egocentric that they fill the vital space of their home with little room for their partner's identity to emerge. Other people find that the object closest to them is the bar or the refrigerator, which is just a sigh away. Still others live in a clouded space, darkened by depression or distorted by drugs. This notion of a personal space has drifted into lay language, where people may declare what "bad space" they're in today or may check with their friends on where they are "at" today.

Concepts of causality also vary on a personal basis. What we believe causes our future is very critical in effecting how we act today. If we are overly objective, we may lose any basis from which to choose and may experience ourselves as being tossed and turned by the wind. Through lying we may lose contact with the source of our personal direction, our intentionality. Our intentionality involves taking a stand in life. Our stance determines what we attend to or disattend to, such as one person attending to the beauty of a beach while another person attends to the potential business from a beach. The posture or orientation we choose in life is the source of what our lives mean and the source of the meaning we attribute to a beach. Lying, however, may convince us that our life is determined by a pathology that is caused like any physical illness, an accident over which we have no control.

THEORY OF THERAPEUTIC PROCESSES

Since lying is the source of psychopathology, honesty is the solution for dissolving symptoms. With authenticity as the goal of therapy, increasing consciousness becomes one of the critical processes through which people become aware of the aspects of the world and of themselves that have been closed off by lying. Since lying also leads to an objectification of oneself in which the ability to choose is no longer experienced, therapy must involve processes through which individuals can again come to experience themselves as subjects or agents capable of directing their own lives through an increase in choosing.

Techniques are not emphasized in existential therapy because technology is an objectifying process in which the therapist as subject decides the best means by which to change the patient as object. While many patients want their doctors to fix them as a mechanic repairs a car, such emphasis on techniques can only add to patients experiencing themselves as mechanical objects. The emphasis in existentialism is to encourage clients to enter into an authentic relationship with a therapist and thereby become increasingly aware of themselves as subjects free to differ with the therapist, even to the point of choosing at any time when therapy shall end. While technique is deemphasized, we shall see that in practice the classical existentialists, such as Binswanger (1963), Boss (1963), Bugental (1965), and even May (1958a), draw heavily upon psychoanalytic techniques, especially in the early stages of therapy.

Consciousness Raising

THE CLIENT'S WORK

If the explicit direction in psychoanalysis is to say whatever comes to mind, the implicit direction in existentialism is to be whatever you want to be. Patients are allowed to present themselves as they typically would relate to the world, with little intervention from the therapist early in therapy. Existentialists share the analytic assumption that patients will repeat their previous patterns of relating and will begin to form transference relationships. While psychoanalysts assume that such transference relationships are due to instinctual fixations, existentialists see transference as a result of the patients' objectifications of themselves which keep them from being flexible and open to new and more authentic ways of being-in-the-world-of-therapy. Patients will impose their psychological categories onto therapy, so that if their experience of space with-others, for example, is a distant space, they will keep their distance from the therapist. If a patient's time is the *ever-present past*, then the patient will talk in therapy primarily about the past.

Gradually patients are encouraged to engage in a process similar to free association but perhaps most appropriately called *free experiencing*. Here patients are encouraged to express freely and honestly whatever they are experiencing in the present, although traditionally such "free" expression has in fact been limited to expression through language and not action. In trying to freely experience, patients can become increasingly conscious that they are repeating the same patterns of being, such as being-in-the-past or in the fantastic future. They can become aware that there are parts of themselves and their world that they are not open to experiencing or expressing, such as their angry self or the reality of the therapist. They usually will try to maneuver the therapist into agreeing with their reasons for closing off such experiences, but since the reasons are lies, they will run into disagreement with authenticity of the therapist. For example, in saying, "Don't you agree that it is immature to get angry?" the patient is pressuring the therapist for validation but may instead meet with an honest response such as, "No, I get angry at times, and I don't feel like a baby."

Eventually the patient is encouraged to change from a more egocentric experiencing of therapy and the therapist to a more authentic dialogue with the therapist. By the time the patient is able to enter into an ongoing dialogue, however, therapy is ready for termination.

THE THERAPIST'S WORK

Unfortunately, classical existentialists have not made clear the methods they use to increase the consciousness of clients. As with personality, many existentialists view existentialism as the stance they take in therapy and not as a system they use. As a result many existentialists would oppose a systematic approach to therapy as contrary to an authentic encounter between patient and therapist.

From the writings of Binswanger (1963), Boss (1963), Bugental (1965), Keen (1970), and May (1958a), however, we do get some idea of the variety of approaches that traditional existentialists use in therapy. They seem to agree that the therapist's work begins with understanding the phenomenal world of the patient. The phenomenological method is intended to be pretheoretical, and the therapist attempts to experience the patient's unique construal of the world without imposing any preconceptions onto the patient's experience. In understanding the patient's phenomenenal world, most existentialists seem to use a *clarification* type of feedback, through which they more fully illuminate the patient's experience, using the patient's own language rather than any theoretical language. Such illuminating feedback helps patients to become more conscious of their being, including some aspects that have been closed off.

Once the therapist has gained a phenomenal understanding of the patient, the therapist chooses what techniques to follow. As May (1958a) states, therapeutic technique follows understanding rather than the more common reverse order in which a therapist tries to understand a patient via the therapist's preferred theory and techniques. Existentialists vary most at this step. Some, such as Boss (1963) and Bugental (1965), rely mainly on interpretation to analyze or make conscious the patient's transference reactions or repeated patterns of being. While Boss and Bugental will use psychoanalytic explanations of the patient's reactions when they fit, they will also rely heavily on existential explanations, such as pointing out how the patient repeatedly runs from experiences related to death, decisions, or other aspects of nonbeing.

Other traditional existentialists, such as Keen (1970), seem to prefer a type of *confrontation* in which the information they provide the patient is generated by the therapist's genuine reaction to the patient. Existential confrontation differs from psychoanalytic confrontation in that existentialists reveal their own experience of the patient and do not just reflect the patient's experience. The existentialist is by no means concerned with remaining a blank screen as is the analyst, since the honest feedback from the existentialist's experience is seen as most able to grate up against and eventually break through the patient's closed world.

An example of such confrontation occurred when my wife, Jan, and I were dong conjoint therapy with a couple in which the husband was complaining that his wife was refusing to have sex with him. At one intense point in which the man insisted on dominating and degrading his wife, Jan told him, "You make me want to vomit." He was beside himself; he did not respond. He just fumed and the next morning came to see me individually, declaring that no woman had ever responded to him like that before. He couldn't imagine why, especially when the woman is a therapist. As I encouraged him to consider that maybe at times he stirred up similar experiences in his wife but she was afraid to express it because of his anger, he began to think that maybe, just maybe, he had something to do with his wife feeling sick when he approached her sexually. His idealized image of himself had been shaken by Jan's intense confrontation, and he tried to shore up his lies by pressuring me into agreeing that a responsible therapist doesn't talk like that. When I encouraged him to face Jan's honest feedback, his lying-for-himself began to come into the open, and he began to see himself as the not-so-perfect-man that perhaps had real trouble in being-with-women and not just with his "selfish" wife.

While a therapist may start out with interpretations, in order for therapy to become existential, the therapist must eventually confront the patient with the therapist's own authentic being. If the therapist cannot be authentic, the patient may remain in a transference relationship, and this may be the reason psychoanalysis seems interminable. How can a patient be-authentic-with-the-therapist if the analyst remains an object such as a blank screen?

As Ellenberger (1958) points out, by being authentic the therapist allows an encounter to develop, which is a new relationship that opens up new horizons rather than a transference relationship that repeats the past. Patients may continually try to freeze the therapist into the categories of their pathological world, such as to keep the therapist distant or to make the therapist the controlling authority figure that causes things to happen. By being authentic the therapist refuses to be frozen. By remaining authentic in the face of the patient's demands, the therapist confronts the patient, both verbally and experientially, with the patient's attempts at freezing the therapist and thereby keeping the patient frozen as a role or a symptom. Gradually the patient becomes aware of the therapist taking risks to be honest and sees that the therapist can remain authentic in the face of such existential anxieties as being rejected by the patient or making mistakes. The patient becomes aware of a new alternative for being and is confronted then with the choice of changing his or her existence.

Choosing

THE CLIENT'S WORK

Clients are confronted with the burden of choosing from the very beginning of therapy, when they must decide if they will commit themselves to working with this particular therapist. Patients are also confronted with having to decide what they will talk about in therapy and how they will be in therapy. The therapist will encourage clients to consider new alternatives for being, such as new alternatives for relating to a sexually turned-off wife, but the clients are expected to carry the burden of creating new alternatives in order for them to experience themselves as subjects capable of finding new directions for living. Once conscious of new alternatives, it is the client who must experience and exist with the anxiety of being responsible for which alternative to follow. The burden of choosing then is clearly on the client.

This burden is perhaps most clear when clients are faced with what Ellenberger (1958) calls kairos, which are the critical choice points in therapy in which a client is faced with deciding whether to risk changing a fundamental aspect of existence, such as being homo- or heterosexual, to be separate or married, to remain in the security of symptoms or to enter the anxiety of authenticity. The clients are the ones who must look deep into themselves to see if they can muster up the courage to leap into the unknown future, knowing there is no guarantee that they will not fall flat on their faces. As an existential friend (Atayas, 1977) puts it, once clients become conscious that at least one person can be authentic, then they no longer have the choice of being a slave who is blind to better alternatives. The patient must now choose between being a coward and becoming a free person.

THE THERAPIST'S WORK

The existential therapist takes every opportunity to clarify the choices that patients are continually faced with in therapy, whether it has to do with what they should talk about each hour, how they should structure their relationship to the therapist, or whether they will return for further therapy. With such clarification the patient becomes acutely conscious of being a subject in spite of frequent protestations about being a patient, a helpless victim of psychopathology. The therapist also encourages patients to use their uniquely human processes of consciousness, their imagination, intellect, and judgment to create rational alternatives to an apparently irrational way of being.

The therapist will remain with patients throughout their small choices and their kairos, empathizing with their anxiety and their turmoil but knowing that the road to being an authentic subject rather than an objective symptom is basically a lonely one in which the patient alone must take responsibility for the choices that are made. To jump in and rescue the patient, no matter how much the patient pulls on the therapist's rescue fantasies, would be to reinforce the lie that patients by definition are inadequate to direct their own lives.

Keen (1970, p. 200) gives the following excellent example of an existential therapist confronting a patient both with the responsibility she has for choosing to change and with the boring way that she is being.

Patient: I don't know why I keep coming here. All I do is tell you the same thing over and over. I'm not getting anywhere. [Patient complaining that therapist isn't curing her; maintenance of self-as-therapist's-object.]

Doctor: I'm getting tired of hearing the same thing over and over, too. [Doctor refusing to take responsibility for the progress of therapy and refusing to fulfill patient's expectations that he cure her; refusal of patient-as-therapist's object.]

Patient: Maybe I'll stop coming. [Patient threatening therapist; fighting to maintain role as therapist's object.]

Doctor: It's certainly your choice. [Therapist refusing to be intimidated; forcing patient-as-subject.]

Patient: What do you think I should do? [Attempt to seduce therapist into role of subject who objectifies patient.]

Doctor: What do you want to do? [Forcing again.]

Patient: I want to get better. [Plea for therapist to cure her.]

Doctor: I don't blame you. [Refusing role of subject curer and supporting desire on part of patient-as-subject.]

Patient: If you think I should stay, ok, I will. [Refusing role of subject-who-decides.]

Doctor: You want me to tell you to stay? [Confrontation with patient's evasion of the decision and calling attention to how patient is construing the therapy.]

Patient: You know what's best; you're the doctor. [Patient's confirmation of her construing therapy.]

Doctor: Do I act like a doctor?

Keen does not mention it, but if in fact the therapist acts like a doctor or some other authority figure who will cure the patient, then the therapist is lost. The patient's construal of therapy as a doctor-object relationship would be accurate rather than a lie that allows her to run from her necessity-to-act as a responsible subject. With the therapist being authentic, however, this is neither a game nor a form of combat. This is an honest confrontation between one person who experiences the potential of the other to choose and the other's desire to shore up the lie that she is not really capable of choosing.

THEORY OF THERAPEUTIC CONTENT

Existentialism is a relatively comprehensive theory of existence that is concerned with the individual at all four levels of personal functioning. Being-for-oneself is focused on intrapersonal functioning; being-with-others is the existential concept for interpersonal functioning; being-in-the-world includes but is more than the individual's relationship to society; and the search for authenticity reflects the goal of existentialists to go beyond conflict to fulfillment.

Intrapersonal Conflicts

ANXIETY AND DEFENSES

In practice, most traditional existentialists work with the individual alone. Much of the focus on therapy is on the conflicts within the individual between the existential anxieties that are inherent in being and the lies that individuals use as defenses against such anxieties. As with psychoanalysis, anxiety is a central concept in existential therapy, but anxiety is not seen as a result of punishment from the environment but rather as a natural consequence of becoming conscious of nonbeing. Rather than gradually approach anxiety in therapy, existentialists seem to frequently confront it head on, especially during the periods of kairos. The only solution to existential anxiety is that suggested by Tillich in *The Courage To Be* (1952): we must find courage within ourselves to accept existential anxiety as part of the price we pay for being uniquely human. In return we can gain the excitement of being a unique human being.

Since existential anxiety is a consequence of consciousness, the only defense against it is conscious lying, through which we turn our attention away from threats of nonbeing by pretending to be something we are not, such as immortal, omnipotent, omniscient, or anything other than finite humans. We can give different names to different forms of lying if we prefer. Projection would be the lie that the responsibility for particular experiences belongs outside of us. Denial would be the lie of insisting that either we or the world are not what we honestly know them to be. Over time such defenses can become an unconscious and habitual part of our objectified selves. But defenses can remain frozen only if we continue to run from the anguish of being more open and authentic. Lying-for-others can succeed, for example, only when our lies are hidden from others. Choosing to let others, such as a therapist, become aware of our pretenses removes the power inherent in lying. Likewise, for lies to work on ourselves, we must continue to pretend that we are not lying. To confront or to be confronted with our lying-for-ourselves frees us from a need to be something we are not.

SELF-ESTEEM

In spite of what many social scientists might say, self-esteem is not a function of how much other people value us. That is social esteem. Certainly we value being held in esteem by others. If we make the same mistake as many social scientists, however, and base our self-esteem on what others think of us, then we are reduced to being-for-others, which usually includes lying-for-others in order to win or keep their approval. The fact that social scientists report high correlations between how we value ourselves and how others value us may just support Riesman's (1961) theory that we have indeed become an other-directed society.

An inner-directed person accepts that self-esteem occurs at the level of being-for-oneself and is a function of how we evaluate ourself. An authentic person accepts that approval by oneself must come above approval by others. To strive to be free from what others think of us is romantic nonsense. We can be free, however, by caring more about what we think of ourselves than about what others think of us. When we are honest with ourselves, we know that we can feel genuinely good about ourselves only when we are genuine.

An existential therapist is not concerned with boosting a patient's shaky self-esteem. If a patient becomes depressed, for example, over living an empty life, the therapist may say, "I'm glad you're depressed. I would be worried about you if you could feel good about the way you've been living." The existentialist knows that all a therapist can do is boost a patient's social esteem through such measures as unconditional positive regard and positive reinforcements such as approval. In doing so, however, the therapist risks reinforcing the patient to remain a pigeon of other people, in this case the therapist's pigeon. Self-esteem is the hard-earned, natural response that patients can make only to themselves after struggling to be authentic.

RESPONSIBILITY

Much has already been said about the centrality of responsibility in existential therapy. We have seen how in the process of choosing to be authentic, individuals are faced with the existential anxiety of being responsible for who they become. We should also point out that to choose against authenticity, to lie, to conform, to cop out, makes us responsible for missing an opportunity to be ourselves, and we are faced with existential guilt (May, 1958a). Existential guilt is a consequence of having sinned against ourselves. If our lives become essentially inauthentic, whether it is obviously pathological such as the neurotic or psychotic or normally pathological such as the conventional conformist, we may at some time find ourselves faced with an overwhelming neurotic guilt. Neurotic guilt is a more total self-condemnation for having abdicated our responsibility to become a genuine human being and not just a ghost of a person. Such self-condemnation can be so intense that some individuals may want to destroy their lives without having really existed.

Guilt if we choose against ourselves; anxiety if we choose for ourselves; with no guarantee that we will create something of value in our one short life—no wonder Sartre has said that we are "condemned to be free." Here patients come to turn over some of the burden of such a lie to a therapist, and the existentialist insists that the patient be strong enough to become more responsible and hence freer and more authentic.

Interpersonal Conflicts

INTIMACY AND SEXUALITY

Being-intimate-with-others is an integral part of being human. The existential ideal for intimacy is poetically expressed in Buber's (1958) book, *I and Thou*. Such relationships involve the caring and sharing of what is most central and most essential in the lives of two authentic people. While this is the ideal, the reality is that all too many people feel safe to relate only to objectified others and are able to enter only I-it relationships. Perhaps even more frequently the interactions of two objectified people result in it-it relationships, which are at best two human objects relating as roles with each other. Such relationships are safe, predictable, and most efficient but include no giving or receiving of anything that is unique to the two people involved. Any two people or even two robots could fill the roles, and it would make no essential difference to the relationship.

While traditional existentialists are very concerned with intimacy, they usually do not work with two people together who are struggling to be-intimate-with-each-other. Existentialists seem to assume that the best way to solve intimacy problems is to encourage an individual to enter into an intimate relationship with a therapist. Once individuals have become unfrozen in therapy, they are assumed to be free to find someone in life who can relate in an intimate manner. The therapist plays no role in helping a person experience intimacy in therapy but rather helps by just playing no role, by being authentic.

Sexuality is less of an issue for existentialists than is intimacy. Frequently the assumption seems to be that if individuals are free to be intimate, they will be free to be sexual if that is what they choose. Sexual conflicts are dealt with to the extent that it is the person's sexuality that has been disowned or idealized in the process of self-objectification. In contrast to what psychoanalysts believe, sexuality is certainly not seen as the essence of humanity. It is bad faith to say either that we must be sexual or that we cannot be sexual. We can be sexually free, which means the freedom to say yes to our own sexuality when we believe it is best to say yes, and the freedom to say no to our sexuality when it is best for us to say no. It is only in response to our highly repressive culture, which has traditionally said no to sexuality, that we have adopted a perverted notion that sexual freedom means saying only yes. Existential sexual therapy would include helping people to be free to say no in sexual relationships regardless of whether one's spouse demands it or one's internal calendar says you are falling behind the national average of three times a week. Existential sexual therapy would better be called *sensual therapy,* where clients are encouraged to experience their whole body as sensual beings that enjoy touching and being touched from head to toe and not just genital to genital.

COMMUNICATION

Existentialists suggest that conflicts in communication are almost inherent in our isolation. Since we can never enter directly the experience of the other, we can never know fully what the other is attempting to communicate. Our own perspective is bound to do some violence to what the other is communicating, and, therefore, we again experience some existential guilt over our inability to fully be-with-others. Such guilt need not lead to withdrawal from others but can motivate us to be more sensitive so that we do the least damage as possible to another's experience. Such guilt can also help us to be authentically humble as we recognize that no matter how hard we try, we can never be smart enough or sensitive enough to know just what the other is experiencing. We cannot sit back smugly as we listen and say, "I know, I know, the same thing happened to me," because it never did.

Problems in communication are inevitable also because of the meager way in which language reflects experience. Experience is so much richer than the abstraction that words usually communicate. It is no wonder that existentialists almost seem to be poets when they attempt to communicate the most significant experience of themselves or their clients. The meagerness of words and the isolation of persons are no excuses, however, for a therapy or a science of humans to try to omit experience from the realm of understanding. Communciation through the medium of words can still present a rich enough picture of an individual's experience if the receiver drops theoretical decoders and listens with the openness of a trained phenomenologist. Experience is too much at the center of humanity for us not to have the communication of our experiences as the essence of our therapy and our science.

HOSTILITY

To experience hostility is to experience the threat of nonbeing, since our hostility is one of the quickest and surest means to end the being of ourself or another. This hostility can elicit existential anxiety and can motivate us to lie and tell ourselves or others we never get angry. The repression that follows can lead to our being unwilling to enter into intense relationships with others because such relationships are always potentially frustrating and thus may lead to hostility. To close off our aggression can also lead to feelings of depression and emptinesss as we close off one of our body's sources of vital assertions.

Just as we lie if we say we cannot get angry, so too we lie if we say we cannot control our hostility. Some choose to be hostile in order to deny their finitude so they can be God and decide who shall live and who shall die. Once they tell themselves such a lie, they are free to be possessed by the power of violence, the power to end an existence. The people they choose to destroy will be people who threaten to remind them of their nonbeing, such as by rejecting them. So the killer says, "You cannot reject me if you no longer exist." Other favorite targets for violence are people like Christ, John Kennedy, Martin Luther King, and Malcolm X, who are threats because they remind some individuals of how empty and inauthentic their own lives are in comparison.

Violence is not always a pathological act, however, for existentialists. As Camus and Sartre learned from their most meaningful days in the French underground, one of their most authentic acts was to help in the violent destruction of the Nazis. Camus (1956) later suggested in his beautiful book *The Rebel*, that the first question of existence is suicide; to be or not to be is what we decide each day we go on living. The second issue is the equally violent question of homicide, to let another be or not. The power to kill, whether it be ourself or another, tells us just how free we can be. If freedom is our first principle, then nihilism is justified, and we are free to destroy others out of the faith that something better may emerge. But if we are to control our freedom to kill, then our first principle is the affirmation of life, not freedom. Camus concludes that we can be free to kill if revolution is the only means available to remove the oppression that prevents others from being free to exist.

CONTROL

For Sartre the attempt to control another person is psychologically the most violent thing we can do to the other. Since freedom is the essence of existence for Sartre, to control other human beings is to essentially destroy them. Sartre (1955) is well aware, however, that most people have a strong desire to control others; this is one of the reasons for his saying, "Hell is other people." To control another person is to objectify that person, to deny that individual the freedom to be able to leave us, or to hurt us, or to remind us that we are not as special as we pretend to be. The desire to control others is in part to pretend that our basic security comes from being on top of things, including human things, rather than to accept that any genuine security, no matter how limited or fleeting, can come only from accepting oneself as a very special person.

By remaining unwilling to be controlled, the existential therapist teaches patients the futility of attempting to control others. No matter if the patient threatens to quit therapy, not pay a bill, go crazy, or commit suicide, the existentialist is supposed to respond only out of honesty and never out of a patient's desire to find false security through controlling others.

Individuo-Social Conflicts

ADJUSTMENT VERSUS TRANSCENDENCE

The only way a life based on adjustment might be healthy is if the society a person is adjusting to is basically honest. Few observers of our age of Vietnam and Watergate would argue that our society is a hallmark of honesty. Report after report is presented about the FBI, the CIA, and major police departments, such as the New York police lying or being on the take for the good of the gang or just for greed; a majority of business managers admit to having surreptitiously broken the law in order to succeed; and a large percentage of college students say they will cheat if given the chance.

How can you be sane in a society that seems unable or unwilling to discriminate between what is truth and what is delusion? Day after day we are bombarded via our public airwaves: "Buick, something to believe in"; "Coke is the real thing"; "Get back to basics, get back to Ford"; "You've got a lot to live"; and "Pepsi's got your life in a bottle." "I can't believe I ate the whole thing! Yes, Ralph, you ate the whole thing! I can't believe I ate the whole thing! Yes, Ralph, you ate the whole thing! I can't believe I ate the whole thing! Take an Alka-Seltzer, Ralph." No, Ralph, you klutz, don't eat the whole thing next time. Truth in advertising is another hypocritical slogan that removes only the most blatant lies but none of the subtle ones that bombard our senses.

The only way to rise above such nonsense is to become conscious of how the forces of socialization and industrialization prefer to make us automatons that are easily controlled and manipulated. Once we become conscious of the pressures to sacrifice ourselves for success or security, we must take responsibility for becoming our own person rather than someone else's pigeon. Consciousness and choice are our uniquely human characteristics through which we can become uniquely human. We can still be-with-others and be-in-the-world without having to be owned by others or bought out by the world.

We must not delude ourselves into thinking we can in any way transcend all that we have been thrown into. The givens of our life, such as our time in history, our native language, and our genetic makeup, put real limits on our freedom. As Camus (1956) has suggested, transcendence begins with choosing that which is necessary. To fight against our bodies, for example, such as trying to fly to the sun, can only destroy the limited freedom we do have for rising above our society. In spite of Kris Kristofferson, freedom is not just another word for nothing left to lose; it is a commitment to the core of our being that nothing our society can give us is worth more than losing our one chance at creating ourselves.

RULES FOR LIVING

To transcend our society to become authentic does not mean to imply that we must be antisocial. It does mean that we are the final deciders of which rules we shall say yes to and which rules we shall choose to break if necessary. In *Crime and Punishment*, Dostoevski (1963) presented a powerful portrait of Roskolnokov, who believed that to be a Great Man, an Authentic Person, meant that he had to be free to break any rule. To prove his specialness, he proceeded to kill. But Dostoevski, who is frequently cited as a forerunner of existentialism, suggests that Roskolnokov's most honest sense of decency rebelled against his act of killing the old woman as if she were an object, a sacrificial lamb in his quest to be great.

The issue for existentialism is neither rules nor antirules. The issue is who rules our life. The one who creates our rules is our ruler. Therefore, an authentic person cannot delegate the rules for living to a body of representatives, a church, an ethics committee, or a judge or jury. The individual must choose which rules to live by. If individuals happen to agree that certain rules of society, such as the Bill of Rights, are just and honest, then their own inner humanity confirms the honesty of those who originally wrote such rules. Truth then becomes shared honesty. The hope that we can be authentic and free and still social beings is based on the faith that acting from the honesty of our own being will allow us to live in harmony with the honesty but not the hypocrisy of humanity.

IMPULSE CONTROL

Unlike psychoanalysts, existentialists do not fear that by encouraging freedom to choose one's own rules, people will lose control over their impulses because of a weakening of social controls. Some people may indeed choose a hedonistic lifestyle if that is most authentic for them. Other authentic individuals, such as Gandhi, may choose to control even such a basic impulse as hunger for 40 days in order to express a stand for freedom. To say we must eat too much, drink too much, have sex too much, or get angry too much is bad faith in our potential for being self-directed individuals. People with impulse-control problems lie daily, "I'll just have one beer, or one potato chip"; or "Now that I've started I may as well eat the whole thing"; or "You made me get angry." They tell themselves lies such as that they cannot help eating rather than the honest response that they prefer to eat or drink rather than to feel bored, anxious, or depressed. Impulses are not the dominant forces of human beings, although many people let them become dominant. The processes of consciousness and choice are what direct a mature person, so that being freer does not mean becoming a beast or a Dionysion irrationalist who is authentic only when expressing every spontaneous desire.

Beyond Conflict to Fulfillment

MEANING IN LIFE

The issue is not to discover meaning in life but rather to create meaning out of our lives. The question is not what is the answer to life; the answer is that life is not a question, it is an ongoing process to be experienced, not a problem to be solved. The meaning of our existence emerges out of what we choose to stand for. Since individuals can choose to take quite different but nevertheless authentic stances in their existences, we find that a multitude of meanings have emerged throughout history. Thus we have people like Christ standing for love, Marx standing for justice, Sartre standing for freedom, Galileo standing for truth, Picasso standing for creativity, Martin Luther King standing for faith, Hitler standing for power, and Richard Nixon standing for "pettiness that plays too rough." To know what the meaning of our existence is we must ask ourselves: What do we stand for? Do we take a stand? What do we intend the essence of our existence to be? Are we in the process of becoming someone rather special who stands for something rather noble, or are we repeating a pattern that can fit most anyone? Is what we are to become worth the price we pay, worth all the other possibilities we give up in choosing to be this particular person? These are questions of meaning that can haunt us but can also motivate us in times of kairos to break out of the safe or successful route if what we see emerging is not significant enough to spend our existence on. If we do not break out during these critical periods of life, then we may at some later date break down because of the overwhelming depression, terror, or nausea that can come with the awareness that we can no longer stand what we stand for. Many such breakdowns are the result of breakthroughs of the sense of meaninglessness; but rather than being just symptoms of an inadequate existence, they can be seen as fresh opportunities to begin a more meaningful life.

VALUES

We no longer choose on the basis of our values—our choices now are the basis of our values. It was not so long ago that most people believed that there were transcendent values given by God as objective guidelines for directing their lives. For these people, choices were based on the values they learned in their families or churches, but such choices really come from outside them and their values. To choose was to seek information from a parent, a priest, a minister, or the Bible as to what was the correct value for a particular situation, such as whether or not to have an abortion in the face of an unwanted pregnancy. Their choice was basically to follow the information given to them by the authority that represented their religious source of ethics.

As more people have become aware of how culturally relative religions are and of how there are many viable alternatives to religion, they are confronted with the choice of whether they will keep the values they were taught or will choose to affirm new values. At this point the values can no longer be the source of their choice, because their very choice is what values to affirm.

In our modern times we are confronted with many situations in which there are no external guidelines, no outside values to direct us. It is no longer clear, for example, whether divorce is better than remaining married, whether having children is better than being childless, or whether having an abortion is better than keeping a fetus alive. The only criterion in such ambiguous situations can be an internal choice through which we decide to make one alternative more valuable for us. As with meaning, we do not discover moral standards; we create them by the stands we take.

IDEAL

The ideal for living and therefore for therapy is to make oneself authentic by making the choices in life that create meaning and value out of our existence. To make these choices requires considerable courage to be responsible for acting in the face of such limited information on how our life may turn out. An authentic peron must also find the courage to exist in face of the fact that the very meaning we intend in our life can be negated at any time by the forms of nonbeing, such as death or isolation. The only value a person *must* follow to become authentic is to be honest, even in the face of nothingness. Once a patient finds the courage to be basically honest, then we can no longer predict what that person will be. We can only predict what a conventional person will be, a reflection of the norms and expectations of the society, or what a pathological person will be, a reflection of the frozen past. To attempt to further define authentic individuals is to attempt to freeze them in the limits of our ideal, while authentic people refuse to be frozen even by the ideals of their therapists.

THEORY OF THE THERAPEUTIC RELATIONSHIP

The therapeutic relationship is both part of the processes of change and the best source of content for existential analysis. In attempting to engage a patient in an authentic encounter, the therapist helps the patient become aware of the ways in which the patient avoids an encounter, such as insisting on remaining a patient rather than a person. The therapeutic relationship provides one of the best opportunities for patients to choose to enter into such an authentic encounter, since the existential therapist is committed to responding authentically. If a patient has the courage to choose to be-authentic-with-the-therapist, then the patient has radically changed from lying-for-others or for-self to being-with-another.

As a source of content, the therapeutic relationship brings into the here and now the patient's pathological styles of being and lying especially for others. For psychoanalytically inspired existentialists like Boss (1963) and Bugental (1965), these lies and objectifications result in a transference relationship that is the first content to be analyzed or made conscious in order for a patient to be free to enter an encounter. For other existentialists, the fact that the patient's lying-for-others or for-self is occurring right in therapy allows patients to be confronted their pathological ways of being. Patients cannot hide the pathological content of their existence, since it is occurring in their immediate relationship to the existential analyst. Patients, for example, will eventually be forced to become conscious of their running from the existential anxiety of responsibility by the therapist remaining unwilling to take over for the patient.

In Rogerian terms, existentialists would agree that the therapist initially must be more *congruent* or *together* than the patient. Such congruency on the therapist's part is necessary for the therapist to be genuine in therapy. If the patient was equally congruent and genuine, the two could have a rewarding encounter, but then there would really be no need for therapy. Existentialists also agree with Rogers's requirement of accurate empathy being necessary for the therapist to experience the world as the patient experiences it. Existentialists do not agree, however, that a therapist must maintain unconditional positive regard toward the patient. In order to be authentic, the therapist can respond with positive regard only toward the patient's honesty and authenticity but never toward the patient's lying and pathology. That the therapist at first allows such lying and objectification to occur without overt judgment is accepted in order for the therapist to experience the patient's phenomenal world. But an authentic therapist can hold no positive regard for a patient's lying.

PRACTICALITIES OF EXISTENTIAL ANALYSIS

Existential analysts seem too unconcerned with mundane practicalities to write about them. The impression one gathers from the literature is that much of existential analysis is similar to psychoanalysis, except during times of kairos. That is, a regular appointment seems to last 50 minutes and is scheduled a few times a week. When a patient is in one of the critical crises, however, the existentialist seems to become much more flexible and may spend extended hours with the patient, such as Boss's (1963) report of spending four days at the bedside of an obsessive-compulsive patient, as the patient lived through a psychotic experience brought on by his repulsion at his own existence.

Existentialists are unconcerned with details of the office setting, since it is the authenticity of the therapist that matters. The traditional existentialists, however, have had no formalized criteria for judging the preparedness of someone to be an existential therapist. While most early existentialists had been analyzed, this does not seem to be a prerequisite, although therapists are certainly expected to be very aware of themselves and their world. Existentialists have been quite flexible about the formal backgrounds of their colleagues, with medicine, psychology, education, theology, and philosophy being just some of the disciplines represented in the background of existential analysts. Existentialists do seem to be less open to the use of medication as an adjunct to therapy. They prefer to have patients experience the authentic though acutely painful emotions like anxiety and guilt rather than to have patients pop a pill and thereby deaden the hurt but also risk deadening themselves by continuing to treat themselves as objects that can be free from existential anxiety and guilt.

MAJOR ALTERNATIVES TO CLASSICAL EXISTENTIAL ANALYSIS

Therapists committed to an existential stance have been free to choose a variety of therapeutic approaches that are compatible with the major tenets of existential psychology. While the traditional practice has been to follow the format of psychoanalysis, there are those who prefer a client-centered approach, and others (e.g., Denes-Radomisli, 1976; Dublin, 1975) who see gestalt therapy as most consistent with an existential philosophy. We examine these latter therapies in future chapters and shall now focus on logotherapy and reality therapy as two additional alternatives to existential analysis.

Logotherapy

Of the four forms of nonbeing, logotherapy is most concerned with meaninglessness (logo = meaning). After suffering through three years in Nazi concentration camps in which his mother, father, brother, and wife perished, Victor Frankl (1905–) became convinced that a will-to-meaning is the basic sustenance of existence. Stripped to a bare existence, he experienced the truth of Nietzsche's dictum: "He who has a why to live for can bear with almost any how." But facing the horror of World War II and the madness of a possible final war, more and more people find their lives becoming existential vacuums. Patients come in greater numbers doubting the meaning of work, of love, of death, of life. Psychotherapies may be adequate for resolving psychological conflicts such as conflicts between drives and defenses. But a modern therapy must also be a philosophical therapy, a therapy of meaning for those confronted with the existential frustration of being unable to find a "why to live for."

"Why don't you kill yourself?" can be a threatening but effective question for beginning therapy with some clients. After the initial startle, the person can begin to realize that the reasons given for not committing suicide contain the seeds of a meaning that can blossom into a profound purpose for living. By facing each form of nonbeing, clients can become aware of a meaning for living. The accidents of one's unique genetic composition and family heritage place limits on who one can become but can also help form the contours of one's unique identity. Death is seen as a negation of being that also brings a responsibility for acting, since if life was endless, decisions could be postponed indefinitely. Even in the face of fate, a person is responsible for the attitude that is assumed toward fate. The victims of concentration camps, for example, could choose to die for the sake of a fellow prisoner, to collaborate with the enemy for the sake of survival, or to give meaning to the future by struggling to hold on for a better day.

The meaning of life is not an abstraction. People who are preoccupied with asking what is the meaning of life should realize that life asks us what meaning we give to our existence. We can respond to life only by being responsible. We accept our responsibility when we accept the categorical imperative of logotherapy: "So live as if you were living already for the second time and as if you had acted the first time as wrongly as you are about to act now" (Frankl, 1963). Facing each moment with such acute awareness and with such responsibility enables us to find the meaning of life that is unique to us at this unique moment in our life.

Logotherapy is obviously quite similar in content to classical existential analysis, although Frankl gives meaning an even more central position in therapy. Whereas existential analysis relies on a form of therapy that is very similar to psychoanalysis, logotherapy is closer in form to some of the briefer therapies such as Adlerian. While philosophical issues will often be discussed in a warm, accepting manner, logotherapists will also confront, instruct, reason, and in a variety of ways work to convince a client to take a more conscious and responsible look at the existential vacuum that life has become. Therapy transcripts (Frankl, 1963, 1967) indicate that therapeutic techniques include interpretations and confrontations but also rely on persuasion and reasoning to a considerable extent. Logotherapy appears to be a form of consciousness raising that relies upon a combination of personal feedback and persuasive education in a philosophy of existence.

Just as existential analysis is often combined with psychoanalysis, so too is logotherapy frequently combined with psychoanalytic or Adlerian psychotherapy. For use with more traditional psychological problems, Frankl has developed two special techniques. Clients with anxiety neuroses and phobic conditions are plagued by anticipatory anxiety. They anticipate dreadful consequences from feared encounters and struggle to avoid such encounters. In struggling to avoid, however, they only increase their anxious anticipation of what will happen if they are forced into a feared encounter. Frankl calls their avoidance and withdrawal from dreaded areas of life "wrong passivity." To reverse this neurotic pattern, clients are encouraged to adopt an attitude of self-detachment and humor toward themselves and to intend to do the very thing they are dreading. With such *paradoxical intention* clients find that the way they anticipated acting is not the way they in fact will act. A student who was afraid that he would vomit if he went into the student union was instructed by me to go into the union and vomit intentionally. We joked about how he could explain his vomiting, and with sufficient self-detachment he entered the union only to discover that when he intended that which he feared, he actually ended up having much more control over his anxiety than he had anticipated. With obsessive-compulsive patients "wrong activity" is used as they strive to fight off obsessive ideas or compulsive acts. Instead of excessively attending and intending to control obsessive-compulsive behaviors, clients are instructed in "de-reflection." In de-reflection clients are instructed to ignore that which they are obsessed with by directing their awareness toward more positive aspects of life. By attending to a life full of potential meaning and value, clients substitute the "right activity" of actualizing personal potentials for the "wrong activity" of trying to fight off psychopathology.

Reality Therapy

Where logotherapy emphasizes a lack of meaning as the central concern in therapy, reality therapy emphasizes a lack of responsibility. Some readers may be surprised to find reality therapy presented as an alternative to classical existential therapy. However, the developer of reality therapy, William Glasser (1925–   ), did in fact derive many of his principles of therapy from Helmuth Kaisar, one of the first existential therapists in America. Furthermore, many of the central concerns of reality therapy parallel an existential approach toward personality and psychopathology. Glasser's (1965) approach to therapy, however, appears to be a unique blend of existential philosophy and behavioral techniques similar to the self-control procedures of behavior therapists.

Across all cultures, establishing an identity is the one basic requirement for being fully human. Identity is based on the uniquely human awareness that we are somehow separate and distinct from every other human being on the face of the earth. Our awareness of unique being brings with it a profound sense of responsibility concerning what we are going to make out of our existence. We strive to give meaning to our identity by the actions we take. The fundamental meaning of identity can best be expressed as a success identity or a failure identity. Creating a success identity involves the conviction that we are succeeding toward our personal goals because we have been willing to take responsibility for our actions and to respond to reality as it is, not as we wish it to be.

Success is not judged in terms of social recognition or social status but rather in terms of our feelings that we are progressing toward our life's goals. A success identity involves a sense of being worthwhile, in part because we are in fact responsible for the constructive actions we take. A success identity also includes the ability to love and be loved, in part because the individual is willing to accept the social responsibility that comes with caring about how one's actions help or hurt others.

A failure identity is likely to develop when a child has received inadequate love or has been made to feel worthless. Regardless of how cruel or unusual our early childhood has been, however, that is no excuse to avoid taking responsibility for our present behavior. In fact the only way we can transcend an early failure identity is to begin taking responsibility for what we do now. Obviously the past cannot be changed. The past is closed and fixed, a part of nonbeing. The present and future are open to us, however, and can come more under our control if we will take responsibility for our present actions.

Troubled people are those who maintain a failure identity because they are unwilling to accept responsibility and face reality honestly. Mental illness is the name we give to the variety of strategies that people use to ignore or deny reality and responsibility. People with grandiose delusions, who believe they are God or Napoleon, are attempting to deny failure by creating a false identity. Other patients attempt to develop a sense of being worthwhile by becoming preoccupied with how special their symptoms are. Psychopathic patients believe they can ignore reality and succeed by breaking the rules, laws, and other realistic limits set by society. Once people begin to ignore or deny reality, they are more likely to repeat their failures. A person who has failed to gain adequate love, for example, might deny the need for love and withdraw from others, and by this very withdrawal fail to find the love that could produce a sense of being worthwhile.

Therapy begins with helping clients become aware of what they are doing in the present to make themselves disturbed. The question for a depressed patient, for example, is not "What's making you depressed?" but rather "What are you doing to make yourself depressed?" If past difficulties are focused on by patients, the question is not why the person got into such difficulties, but rather why they didn't get into even more difficulty. Such a focus helps clients to become aware that even in the process of making difficulties for themselves, they still maintained some strengths and some sense of responsibility that kept them from totally destroying their own lives or the lives of others. Clients are taught to focus on the strengths they have, not on the failures they have had. With increasing awareness of their strengths, clients can begin to realize that they have abilities that they can use to succeed without denying or ignoring reality.

Therapy is primarily present-centered. The past is important only as it relates to present actions. Obviously the present is where clients can choose to change. Blaming present problems on past abuses is one of the common cop-outs of clients that unfortunately has been reinforced all too often by traditional therapists. Reality therapists do not, however, point a cold, blaming finger at patients. Clients have already had enough coldness and condemnation. Therapy needs to be personal, with a warm, real, and caring therapist providing some of the love and confirmation that were missing in the client's early life.

The personal nature of reality therapy does not imply an all-accepting therapist. Value judgments must be made, but it is the judgment of clients that is critical. Having the therapist make the value judgments only serves to take responsibility away from clients. If clients are to succeed they must come to judge their behavior as acceptable when it is responsible, which means good for the client and for those with whom the client is meaningfully related. If what clients are doing is hurting themselves or others, then their hurtful actions are irresponsible and should be changed. Effective change comes only after there is a responsible awareness of how one's actions are destructive to self or to others.

The patient decides whether present actions are irresponsible or not. Choice is really the main process of change. Therapeutic change is the result of responsible choice based on the awarenesss of the hurt that one has been creating. One of the therapist's tasks is to call clients on their cop-outs. Certainly therapists should not engage in the irresponsible activity of excusing clients' misbehavior through theoretical interpretations that blame personal problems on the past actions of parents or on the present conditions of society. Successful people know they can work within the reality of society without being swallowed up by the immorality that exists. The starting point for changing any immoral aspect of society is to accept responsibility for one's own actions.

Once a client chooses to change irresponsible behavior, the therapist is present to help the person create specific plans for changing specific behaviors. The therapist is assumed to have more of a success identity and is thus more aware of how to succeed in society. The therapist serves as a guide for people who are failing to progress in reality. Plans are made that have a chance of succeeding from week to week. If clients are taking on more than they can realistically accomplish within their present limits, then the therapist's task is to give feedback and to help the clients design more realistic plans for the week. What clients need are experiences of success, not more experiences of failure. Reality therapists seem to encourage a behavioral form of successive approximation, in which a success identity is gradually established through weekly plans that bring increasing consequences of success. Success comes, however, not through the therapist's management of contingencies, but rather through the client's self-management of behavior.

Weekly plans are put in writing, frequently in the form of a contract. Putting a plan in writing is a much clearer commitment to change. Written contracts also avoid the cop-outs of forgetting or distorting what was said. The therapist asks for details of the plan to see how realisitc it is and how much chance it has for succeeding. Obviously plans, even written plans, are not absolutes. If a plan does not succeed, then it can be changed as a function of feedback from reality. No excuses are accepted, however, if a plan does not work. The client takes responsibility, including the responsibility for choosing to change the plan. Most of us realize that things go wrong usually because people do not do what they said they were going to do. Blaming or deprecating does not help. The critical question is: Are you going to fulfill your commitment or not? If so, when? Or the therapist might say, "The plan didn't work. Let's change it."

Part of accepting reality is accepting limits, including the limits that life sets on our ability to succeed at our goals. Failure comes in not reaching our limits. Failure comes in not assuming the responsibility for succeeding to the very limits of our capacity and our reality.

RESEARCH ON THE EFFECTIVENESS OF EXISTENTIAL ANALYSIS, LOGOTHERAPY, AND REALITY THERAPY

A comprehensive review of the existential literature has revealed no controlled reseach to evaluate the effectiveness of existential analysis. Furthermore, there were not even any case survey reports in the literature since apparently no existential analyst has tallied a success rate, whether based on subjective or objective outcome criteria. This is not particularly surprising in view of the traditional existential position on controlled research. Objective therapeutic research is seen as adding to the dehumanization of patients by reducing the experience of patients to a number on a test or a score on a scale. The abstraction of people into measures attempts to further objectify patients, whereas existential analysis is committed to helping people experience their unique subjectiveness while giving up their escapes into self-objectification. Existentialists have on the basis of phenomenological principles been opposed to contributing to the myth that the usual objective methods of science can do justice to the study of humanity.

Existential analysts have been open to publishing phenomenological case analyses of various types of patients such as obsessive-compulsives (von Gebsattez, 1958), schizophrenics (Binswanger, 1958c), and psychopaths (Keen, 1970). While such reports can help us more deeply appreciate the world of such patients, they are no help in evaluating whether existential analysis is effective in its stated purpose of helping people become more authentic.

The literature review did reveal one study testing the effectiveness of logotherapy. Crumbaugh (1972) hypothesized that various forms of therapy will reduce the existential vacuum that results from the absence of meaning and purpose in life. He further hypothesized that logotherapy will reduce the existential vacuum to a greater degree than will other types of therapy. There were three unmatched treatment groups: (1) 30 subjects in logotherapy, (2) 51 patients participating in a special alcoholic treatment program, and (3) 14 students and a supervising priest in a marathon therapy program. Based on change scores from the Purpose in Life Test, all therapy groups showed predicted improvement on his operational measure of existential vacuum. The greatest reduction in existential vacuum was in the logotherapy group.

Glasser and Zunin (1973) report that there have been no long-term significant studies on the effectiveness of reality therapy. They argue (p. 308) that "evaluations of effectiveness of treatment are generally not considered to be meaningful. We do not believe that we have advanced to a sufficient degree of sophistication to be able to measure such items as happiness, fulfillment, and creativity in society, let alone in an individual." Nevertheless the authors do go on to report two studies demonstrating the effectiveness of reality therapy programs in a school setting.

Hawes (1971) assessed the effects of a Schools Without Failure program on the black child's belief in self-responsibility versus powerlessness, self-concept, and classroom behavior. Schools Without Failure are an exciting innovation of Glasser (1969), in which he applies reality therapy principles to create school programs that help youngsters develop a success identity rather than a failure identity. Hawes compared the effects of such a school with the effects of a regular public school over a 16-week period. There were 340 black pupils from the third and sixth grades in the two schools.

Results indicated that the Schools Without Failure program did significantly increase the belief in internal locus of control for success and failure in the black pupils. Students in both the third and sixth grades showed significant increases in (1) processing and seeking information, (2) time spent on school tasks, (3) peer interactions, and (4) student-teacher interactions, and a decrease in behavior characterized by compliance. Sixth-grade students from the control school showed significant changes only in decreasing compliant behavior.

Glasser and Zunin (1973) summarize an unpublished study of J. English (1970), who also assessed the impact of reality therapy on a school. Reality therapy was demonstrated to be an effective technique in reducing disciplinary problems, increasing school performance, and enhancing teacher involvement with each other, with students, and with the school system.

CRITICISMS OF EXISTENTIALISM

From a Behavioral Perspective

With no case surveys and no controlled outcome studies, we can see why some existentialists prefer to consider their approach a stance toward therapy and not a theory of therapy. But what kind of honest stance would be unwilling to fall or stand on the basis of its effectiveness in helping patients overcome their pathologies? Let the existentialists use phenomenological analyses if they prefer, but let them also demonstrate that such approaches result in greater authenticity than alternative approaches, including just the placebo effect of expecting patients to be more open and honest.

As a theory, existentialism attempts to take a giant step backward with such romantic-sounding ideas as love and will (May, 1969), which held back a science of humanity for so long. Not only is such philosophizing damaging to the human sciences, it is also, as Skinner (1971) has so cogently argued, damaging to human societies. The continued emphasis on such myths as freedom and dignity can do nothing more than lead to the continued disintegration of our society. If existentialists are truly concerned with such alienating phenomena as the fragmentation of our communities, then let them use their eloquence in support of well-designed communities in which the contingencies are sane and the consequences of breaking rules severe. To sacrifice society in the name of the elitist authentic individual is a luxury we can no longer afford.

From a Psychoanalytic Perspective

How can a therapy system like existentialism borrow so much of psychoanalytic technique and yet reject so much of psychoanalytic theory? How can existentialists be both authentic and still be so much like psychoanalysts in therapy? Doesn't that violate their own principles and doesn't it also show that effective therapy necessitates a relationship in which transference can be developed?

As a theory, existentialism does serious injustice to patients in the midst of unconscious conflicts to insist that patients are responsible and even choose the very pathologies from which they are trying to become free. Can the existentialist really believe that patients with severe compulsions to wash repeatedly or psychotic delusions of persecution have any choice over what they are driven to do? The logical consequence of such a theory can be seen in Binswanger's (1958a) analysis of the phenomenological meaning of his patient's suicide rather than taking control over the situation in an attempt to prevent her from taking the irrational step of directing her hostility toward herself.

Mowrer blamed Freud for giving us a generation of psychopaths, but with existentialism emerging as the philosophy of our modern times, with emphasis on the freedom to chose our own rules for living, is it not much more responsible for the breakdown of social order in the name of freedom?

From a Humanistic Perspective

Just to make it clear that not all humanists are sympathetic with traditional existentialism, let us look at a quote from Maslow (1960, p. 57) on the existentialist's emphasis on nonbeing:

I do not think we need take too seriously the European existentialists' harping on dread, on anguish, on despair, and the like, for which their only remedy seems to be to keep a stiff upper lip. This (is) high I.Q. whimpering on a cosmic scale.

From an Eclectic Perspective

Existentialism is rich in its appreciation of the human condition yet meager in its theory of therapy. For example, the traditional existential analyst focuses on the existential anxiety of responsibility at the expense of the other equally important forms of nonbeing. The existential analysts provide little insight into their therapeutic procedures other than repeating much of psychoanalysis combined with a few slogans about the therapist being authentic. Because of this lack of an adequate development of therapeutic procedures, May's (1958a) fear that existentialism might degenerate into an anything-goes anarchy has proven true in the case of such existential approaches as encounter groups.

The existential rejection of scientific evaluation of therapy has also encouraged an irrationalism in which many therapists feel no responsibility to evaluate the effectiveness of their therapy. What criteria are we going to use to judge the honesty of different therapists? Are we left with a solipsism in which one person's truth is another person's lie? Existentialists would do well to recognize the truth in Bronowski's (1959) book, *Science and Human Values*, that honesty is the fundamental value of science and that the scientific method is the most honest method we have. There is nothing inherent in the scientific method that says we cannot compare the phenomenological description of patients following different forms of therapy. Existentialists need to participate in the shared honesty of such comparisons, which can lead to the truth as to which approaches are most effective with which problems.

AN EXISTENTIAL ANALYSIS OF MRS. C.

An existential analysis of Mrs. C. is restricted by the case description containing just the facts and little of the phenomena of Mrs. C.'s existence. From the facts it looks as if Mrs. C.'s pre-pinworm existence was already heavily objectified. In sexual relations she was unable to be-in-nature, since she was always nonorgasmic and thus unable to just let herself be free to fully enjoy the natural joys of sexuality. Since her mother had lied about sex being disgusting, Mrs. C. at some point probably began to tell herself that she was not sexual in order to close off anything about herself that would be experienced as disgusting. The original existential anxiety connected to being sexual would probably have been the possibility of isolation in the form of rejection for being disgusting. Mrs. C. had also objectified herself by being so orderly, as exemplified by cataloging her children alphabetically and scheduling them exactly two years apart. This suggests that she reduced her anxiety over the responsibility of having and naming children by placing the responsibility outside of herself onto an alphabet and a calendar. In spite of considerable objectification, Mrs. C. was seen as no more pathological than most conventional people who try to control the anxieties of life through arbitrary rather than authentic principles.

A critical crisis occurred when Mrs. C. was burdened with the unfortunate accident of Asian flu infecting her family at a time when she was tired from caring for five children, with a sixth on the way. When the accident of the pinworms infested her daughter, an authentic response for Mrs. C. would have been to experience the intense anxiety that no matter how hard she had cleaned and cared for her children, they were still infected and were now faced with the possibility of additional infestation. Mrs. C. had never been good at facing such threats of nonbeing, and now with the additional stress of her own illness, she chose to lie to escape the anxiety over the prospect of further diseases. The lie was ready-made in the form of the doctor's orders for her to boil the clothes and wash intensely. At this point she was not particularly responsible for the orders, but she was responsible for telling herself, "If I but wash enough I can keep the nonbeing of diseases away from my children and myself." So wash she did. With her washing based on this lying-about-nature, she now was faced with the experience of neurotic anxiety over not washing. Her conclusion then was that she must wash, and such bad faith resulted in the objectification of herself into a human washing machine.

With such self-objectification, Mrs. C. experienced herself as unable to keep from washing. Causality in her life was no longer intentional but was rather a compulsive drivenness, like a motor that automatically switched on in the presence of dirt or other threats of diseases. With so much of her time and energy dedicated to washing, Mrs. C. was bound to be faced with existential guilt over the many opportunities she was missing to be-for-herself and to be-intimate-with-her-family. Her washing would also serve as an attempt to cleanse herself of such existential guilt. But the longer she continued her washing compulsion, the less she was guilty over what she was doing and the more she was faced with the possibility of experiencing neurotic guilt for what she was becoming—a washing machine in human clothes, unable to care for or share with her family and unable to let herself be spontaneous in the world.

After years of preoccupation with washing, to be confronted with the choice not to wash would also be to confront the tremendous existential anxiety over how meaningless her past decade had been. To face the choice of not washing would also be to face self-condemnation for having wasted such precious years of her life and having hurt her family by not sharing in the critical years of their development. Better to hold onto the lie that she must wash! At least that way she is not responsible, and she has not failed in life, but rather it is her doctors who have failed her. When her therapist said he was washing his hands of her case, she made a suicide gesture to force him to remain responsible for her by arranging for someone else to cure her. We can further see Mrs. C.'s desire to run from responsibility by the way she pressured her husband into taking responsibility not only for the family but even for her very compulsion. "You tell me, George, what to wash next because I am so mechanical I cannot remember or decide what to wash next" seems to be her message to her husband.

The reason for Mrs. C. beginning her washing ritual with her anus is that the anus was the locus of pinworms and may well have been seen as a source of disease, as it is with many compulsive people. So while Mrs. C. could not control all the sources of illness in the universe, she could keep her own anus clean and pretend that no germs could possibly penetrate her immaculate body. Mrs. C. lived in the vigilant future, where she keeps an ever-watchful eye open for any signs of disease, such as dirt or a child scratching. Her space was surrounded by germs and worms, her symbols of nonbeing. She could be secure in such a dreaded world only if she remained clean, not only of dirt but also of any responsibility and, therefore, any guilt for having let her family down. In effect, she was attempting to literally wash her hands clean of the whole mess.

As with many compulsive patients who have spent much of their life making themselves into objects, it could be extremely difficult to engage Mrs. C. in an authentic encounter, but it would be one of the few ways we would have to keep her from becoming totally washed up as a human being. To help Mrs. C. experience her own subjectiveness, an existentialist would look for every possibility of confronting her with choices in therapy. For example, when we went to my office for our first meeting, Mrs. C. stopped at my door and waited for me to open it so that she could avoid any possible contact with germs. Right at that point the existentialist would confront Mrs. C. with the choice of getting help by opening a new door to therapy or returning to her secure but deadening patterns from the past.

Given the choice of what to talk about in therapy, Mrs. C. would probably go on endlessly about her preoccupation with pinworms and the details of her washing. As some point her obsessive preoccupations would have to be interpreted as her means of remaining a patient so that she would not have to face her therapist as a person. The therapist might also choose to confront Mrs. C. with the therapist's own feelings, such as, "I am sick and tired of hearing the endless details about pinworms and washing. I want to see if you still exist within that laundromat you call a life. I know it will be scary and hurt like hell to open yourself up, but look, my hands are not clean either." If Mrs. C. could respond and open herself up to the therapist, there would be kairos, during which Mrs. C. would feel overwhelmed with guilt and anxiety. Both she and her therapist might fear that her compulsive symptoms did indeed cover a psychosis, but they would have to recognize that one cannot face a decade of waste without being overwhelmed with the existential anxiety and guilt that are the authentic responses to such absurd waste. The therapist would do Mrs. C. an injustice to try to minimize her anxiety and guilt as only *feelings* of anxiety and guilt; she would *be* anxious and guilty, and the only route to health is to live through her confrontation of having not been. The therapist can no more cleanse Mrs. C. of her guilt and anxiety than she could cleanse herself. By remaining with her, however, through such crises, the therapist can communicate that new options do exist for the future and that she can choose not to waste her options, including the chance to be-authentic-with-the-therapist.

CLIENT-CENTERED THERAPY

AS CARL ROGERS spoke, it became apparent that we were in the presence of a great man. The air and aura about him were warm and gentle though his words were strong and poignant. He was willing to field any question and respond to even the most critical comments. When asked how he as a therapist could be both genuine and nondisclosing, he surprised us with his candor. He said that over the past several years of working first with psychiatric clients and then with growth-oriented groups, he had come to see that his model of a therapist as reflective and nondirective had been very comfortable for a person like him. For most of his life he had been basically rather shy and nondisclosing. In the sunny climate of California with its emphasis on openness in groups, he had come to recognize that too much of his former style was a convenient role that had protected him from having to reveal much of himself. It was clear that in therapy, as in his life, he was realizing more fully the genuineness he had always valued but never really actualized. In the 70th year of his life, when lesser indivudals might be expected to cling to their cherished ways as therapists and theorists, Rogers continued to reflect an openness to new experiences even when it meant having to reject a way of being that had previously seemed so genuine.

A SKETCH OF CARL ROGERS

Carl Rogers (1902–   ) has revealed a profound openness to change, beginning with his movement away from the almost fundamentalist Protestantism of his Wisconsin farm family to the very contemporary religion of Union Seminary in Manhattan. After two years of preparation for the ministry, Rogers made a move common to a number of actual or potential clergy, and that was to turn to training in psychotherapy. He received his Ph.D. in clinical psychology in 1931 from Columbia in a highly Freudian atmosphere.

Beginning as an intern in 1927–28, Rogers spent 12 years as a psychologist at a child guidance clinic in Rochester, New York. During this time, he let his own clinical experience be the basis for his theorizing and therapy. In the midst of a very busy but apparently fertile schedule, he found time to put together his first book, *The Clinical Treatment of the Problem Child*, published in 1939. Rogers found both inspiration and confirmation of his view in the work of Otto Rank (1936), who was emphasizing the importance of the humanity of therapists and not their technical skills in remedying human problems.

In 1940, Rogers moved to Ohio State University to train students in therapy. As is so true of students, they taught Rogers several important lessons. One of these lessons was that his ideas were in fact a new view of the nature of effective therapy and not a distillation of generally accepted principles, as Rogers originally had thought. They also convinced him that if his new theory was going to be accepted by scientifically minded students, he would have to demonstrate its effectiveness through controlled research. Since Rogers himself had a strong commitment to the scientific methods of gathering knowledge, he began an extended series of outcome studies with his students both at Ohio State and later at the University of Chicago, where he moved in 1945.

The clarity of Rogers's clinical and theoretical writings in such books as *Counseling and Psychotherapy* (1942) and *Client-Centered Therapy* (1951) and the controls in his scientific research brought widespread professional and academic recognition. For such a humanistic psychologist, Rogers was tremendously successful in the traditional academic world, and in 1957 he returned to his home state at the University of Wisconsin. Here he was willing to make the acid test of any therapy, to see if his system could be effective in producing profound change in schizophrenic clients. During the five-year study, Rogers and the other therapists found themselves becoming more actively genuine, disclosing more of their inner experiencing, which seemed to lead to greater improvement in such clients.

In 1964, Rogers moved to Western Behavioral Sciences Institute in La Jolla, California, and began working with groups of normal individuals struggling to improve their human relations abilities. In 1968, Rogers and some of his research colleagues established their own Center for the Studies of the Person in La Jolla. As a world figure in humanistic approaches to therapy, Rogers has become as much involved in trying to inspire humanistic changes in education, business, and marriage, as he has been in helping individuals to more fully realize their basic humanity.

THEORY OF PERSONALITY

All humanity has but one basic motivational force, a tendency toward actualization. Rogers (1959, p. 196) defines the actualizing tendency as "the inherent tendency of the organism to develop all its capacities in ways which serve to maintain or enhance the organism." This includes not only the tendency to meet physiological needs for air, food, and water and the tendency to reduce tensions, but also the tendency to expand ourselves through growth, to enhance ouselves through relating and reproducing, to expand our effectiveness through the mastery of cultural tools, as well as to create and to move from control by external forces to control from within.

We are also born with an organismic valuing process that allows us to value positively those experiences perceived as maintaining or enhancing our lives and to value negatively those experiences that would negate our growth. We are born then with actualizing forces that motivate us and with valuing processes that regulate us; what's more, we can trust that these basic organismic processes will serve us well.

In relating to the world to realize some of our actualization tendencies, we respond not to some "real" or "pure" reality, but rather to reality as we experience it. Our world is our experienced or phenomenal world. If others wish to understand our particular actions, they must try to place themselves as much as possible into our internal frame of reference and become conscious of the world as it exists within our subjective awareness. Our reality is certainly in part shaped by the environment, but we also actively participate in the creation of our subjective world, our internal frame of reference.

As part of our actualizing tendency, we also begin to actively differentiate, to see the difference between experiences that are part of our own personal being and functioning and those that belong to others. The special experiences that we come to own are self-experiences. We are able to become consicous of self-experiences by symbolically representing these experiences in language or other symbols. This representation in awareness of being alive and functioning becomes further elaborated through interaction with significant others into a concept of self. Our concept of self includes our perceptions of what is characteristic of "I" or "me," our perceptions of our relationships to others and to the world, and the values attached to these perceptions (Rogers, 1959, p. 200).

As our consciousness of self emerges, we develop a need for positive regard for ourselves. While this need is universal in human beings, Rogers (1959) seems to agree with his student, Standal (1954), that we actually learn to need love. This need for positive regard, this need to be prized, to be accepted, to be loved, is so addictive that it becomes the most potent need of the developing person. "She loves me, she loves me not" is the endless puzzle of the emerging individual who looks to mother's face, gestures, and other ambiguous signs to see if she holds the child in positive regard. While mother's love has been emphasized, the positive regard from all others, especially significant others, becomes compelling.

Whenever another person, such as a parent, responds to a particular behavior with positive regard, our total image of how positively we are prized by the other is strengthened. On the other hand, let a parent respond to a behavior with a frown or another expression of negative regard and our total perception of how much we are loved by our parent is weakened. Consequently, the expression of positive regard by significant others is so powerful that it can become more compelling than the organismic valuing process. The individual becomes more attracted to the positive regard of others than to experiences that are of positive value in actualizing the organism. When the need for such love becomes dominant, individuals begin to guide their behavior not by the degree to which an experience maintains or enhances the organism, but by the likelihood of receiving love.

Soon individuals learn to regard themselves in much the same way as they experience regard from others, liking or disliking themselves as a total configuration for a particular behavior or experience. This self-regard that has been learned leads to individuals viewing themselves and their behavior in the same way significant others have viewed them, even when some behaviors are regarded positively that are not actually experienced organismically as satisfying, such as feeling good about ourselves for getting an A after spending many dull hours memorizing tedious material. Other behaviors are regarded negatively that are not actually experienced as unsatisfying, such as feeling badly about masturbating.

When individuals begin to act in accordance with the introjected or internalized values of others, they have acquired conditions of worth. They cannot regard themselves positively as having worth unless they live according to these conditions. For some, this means they can feel good about themselves, feel lovable and worthy, only when achieving, no matter what the cost to their organism; others feel good about themselves only when they are nice and agreeable and never say no to anyone. Once such conditions of worth have been acquired, the person has been transformed from an individual guided by values generated from organismic experiencing to a personality controlled by the values of other people. At a very early age we learn to exchange our basic tendency for actualization for the conditional love of others and ourselves.

Theoretically, such a trade need not be made. As Rogers (1959, p. 227) states so clearly, "If an individual should experience only unconditional positive regard, then no conditions of worth would develop, self-regard would be unconditional, the needs for positive regard and self-regard would never be at variance with organismic evaluation, and the individual would continue to be psychologically adjusted and would be fully functioning." Unfortunately, such hypothetical events do not appear to occur in actuality, except perhaps in therapy.

THEORY OF PSYCHOPATHOLOGY

The more conditional the love of parents the more pathology is likely to develop. Because of the need for self-regard, individuals begin to perceive their experiences selectively, in terms of their parents' conditions of worth, which have been internalized. Experiences and behaviors that are consistent with such conditions of worth are allowed accurate representation in awareness. Individuals whose parents insisted on achievement, for example, should be able to perceive and accurately recall experiences in which they were indeed doing well. Experiences and behaviors that conflict with conditions of worth, however, are distorted in order to fit the conditions of worth, or they may even be excluded from awareness. People who must achieve in order to feel good about themselves may, for example, distort their vacations into being achievement times, as they count the number of historical sites, museums, or states they visit. Some workaholics may deny entirely that they have any desire to play or just lounge around. Fun is for fools is their motto.

As some experiences are distorted or denied into consciousness, the situation arises where there is an incongruence between what is being experienced and what is symbolized as part of a person's self-concept. An example of such incongruence was suggested earlier when I indicated that I could not allow myself to experience anger and still feel good about myself. I perceived myself as one of those rare individuals who never gets angry. My wife has since told me that in situations where I would be expected to get angry, I would first begin to pucker my lips. If the frustration continued, I would then begin to whistle. I never allowed myself to become aware of such bodily experiences of anger even though I was going around like a whistling teapot ready to explode. For Rogers, the core of psychological maladjustment is the incongruity between the organism's total experience and what is accurately symbolized as part of the self-concept.

Such incongruence between self and experience is the basic estrangement in human beings. Because of conditions of worth, there are now organismic experiences that are threatening to oneself. The person can no longer live as a unified whole, which is the birthright of every human being. Instead we allow ourselves to become only part of who we really are. Our inherent tendencies for full actualization do not die, however, and we become like a house divided against itself. Sometimes our behavior is directed by the self we like to believe we are, and at other times behavior can be driven by those aspects of our organism that we have tried to disown. Psychopathology reflects a divided personality, with the tensions, defenses, and inadequate functioning that accompany such lack of wholeness.

Psychological maladjustment is a result of this basic estrangement of human beings. For the sake of maintaining the positive regard of others, we no longer remain true to who we really are, to our own natural organismic valuing of experience. At a very early age we begin to distort or to deny some of the values we experience and to perceive them only in terms of their value to others. Such falsification of ourselves and our experience is not the result of conscious choices to lie, as the existentialists would hold, but rather a natural, though tragic, development in infancy (Rogers, 1959).

As individuals live in such a state of estrangement, experiences that are incongruent with the self are *subceived* as threatening. Subception is the ability of the organism to discriminate stimuli at a level below what is required for conscious recognition. By subceiving particular experiences as threatening, the organism can use perceptual distortions, such as rationalizations, projections, or denial, to keep from becoming aware of experiences like anger, which would violate conditions of worth. If individuals were to become aware of unworthy experiences, their concepts of themselves would be threatened, their needs for self-regard would be frustrated, and they would be in a state of anxiety.

Defensive reactions, including symptoms, are developed in order to prevent threatening experiences from being accurately represented in awareness. People who feel unlovable for getting angry, for example, may deny their anger and end up with headaches. The headaches may not feel good organismically, but at least most other people can love someone who is sick. Those who have self-regard only for success may develop compulsions to work. They may drive themselves into the late hours of the night with the aid of stimulants, feeling good about each success while their body experiences tremendous stress. Some people are so threatened by experiencing sexual desires that they distort their perceptions to the point where they believe that they are pure and innocent and godlike, while others are trying to make them think dirty, rotten thoughts. One of the first patients I tested at Worcester State Hospital looked at the first Rorschach card I gave him, threw it down, and shouted, "Why the hell don't you go show these pictures to the goddamned communists? They're the ones that are perverting our kids with all of their sex education."

All human beings are threatened by some experiences that are incongruent with their self-concepts. To a lesser or greater degree, then, we all use some defenses or symptoms to preserve our self-regard and to keep from becoming anxious. While defenses help preserve positive self-regard, they do so only at a price. Defenses result in an inaccurate perception of reality due to distortion and selective omission of information. A few years ago a 45-year-old man walked into my office and said, "Oh, you're younger. You must be in favor of open marriages. I won't be able to work with you." He requested a referral to another therapist without even asking about my views on open marriage. In rigidly trying to defend their views of the world and of themselves, people end up becoming quite rigid and inadequate in their styles of perceiving and processing information. The more defensive and pathological the person, the more rigid and inadequate are their perceptual and informational processes.

There are some individuals who have such a large or significant degree of incongruence between self and experience that particular events can prevent their rigid defenses from functioning successfully and can lead to breakdowns and disorganization of their personalities. If the event threatens to demonstrate the degree of incongruence between self and experience, and if the experience occurs suddenly or with a high degree of obviousness, then such individuals are flooded with anxiety and can experience panic because their very concepts of themselves are threatened. Since their defenses are not working successfully, previously disowned experiences are now symbolized accurately in awareness. For such individuals, the organized self-images are shattered by unacceptable experiences. Since their lives have been organized around their self-concepts, they become disorganized. Such panic and disorganization were described by a sophomore who came to see me following a bad trip with LSD. Prior to the experience, he had been convinced that he was a true follower of Jesus. He had seen himself as basically loving and kind and working for the well-being of others through a radical Christian movement. During the recent experience with acid, he saw himself as an egomaniac, who was using his leadership role in his Christian group to win a following of female admirers and to see his picture in the news. He said he kept running in a circle, trying to catch his picture of himself from the papers, but he had this eery feeling that the picture was a stranger. He could not rationalize these perceptions of himself as being due to acid. He was so panicky and disorganized that he thought he might jump off the Newport Bridge to destroy his life in order to save his self. Fortunately, with the aid of crisis intervention from the counseling center and the support of some friends, he decided to enter counseling to begin the arduous process of reintegrating a sense of self that was more complete and less idealized.

Whether a person goes into therapy because of a breakdown, because of inadequate functioning due to perceptual distortions, because defensive symptoms are hurting too much, or because of a desire for greater actualization, the goal is the same—to increase the congruence between self and experience through a process of integration. Since Rogers (1957; 1959) sees the reintegration of self and experience as emerging from the therapeutic relationship, we will break with our standard format and present Rogers's theory of the therapeutic relationship before examining client-centered therapy in terms of our categories of therapeutic processes.

THEORY OF THE THERAPEUTIC RELATIONSHIP

Rogers (1957; 1959) has stated very explicitly that the necessary and sufficient conditions for therapy are contained within the therapeutic relationship. Six conditions are necessary for a relationship to result in constructive personality change. Taken together, these conditions are sufficient to account for any therapeutic change.

1. Obviously two persons must be in a relationship in which each makes some perceived difference to the other.

2. The client in the relationship is in a state of incongruence and is therefore vulnerable to anxiety because of the potential for subceiving experiences that are threatening to the self or is, in fact, anxious because such subception is already occurring. The vulnerability to anxiety or the actual anxiety is what motivates a client to seek and to stay in the therapeutic relationship.

3. The therapist is congruent, integrated, and genuine in the relationship, which means that within a therapeutic relationship therapists are freely and deeply themselves, with the actual experiences of the therapists being accurately represented in their awareness of themselves. It is the opposite of presenting a facade. This does not mean that therapists are always genuine and congruent in all aspects of life, but it is necessary when entering a therapeutic relationship. Rogers (1957, 1959) originally believed that within this condition there was no necessity for therapists to overtly disclose their genuine experiences to clients. It seemed necessary only that therapists not deceive clients or themselves. Following client-centered work with schizophrenic clients (Rogers, Gendlin, Kiesler, & Truax, 1967) and work in human relations groups, Rogers (1970) came to the conclusion that genuineness in therapists includes self-expression by therapists. The degree of such self-disclosure by Rogers himself actually seems rather minimal when compared with the extensive, spontaneous disclosure that is characteristic of many leaders of encounter groups. The following excerpt from a session with a schizophrenic client is an example that Rogers uses to demonstrate his greater willingness to express his own feeling of the moment.

Client: I think I'm beyond help.

Rogers: Huh? Feeling as though your're beyond help. I know. You feel completely hopeless about yourself. I can understand that. I don't feel hopeless, but I realize you do. (Meador & Rogers, 1973, p. 142)

We shall see that other client-centered therapists go considerably further in expressing their own immediate feelings.

4. The therapist must experience unconditional positive regard for the client. Since the client's incongruence is due to conditions of worth that have been internalized from the parents' conditional positive regard, in order for the client to be able to accept experiences that have been distorted or denied to awareness, there must be a decrease in the client's conditions of worth. There must be an increase in the client's unconditional self-regard. If the therapist can demonstrate unconditional positive regard for the client, then the client can begin to become accurately aware of experiences that were previously distorted or denied because they threatened a loss of positive regard from significant others. When clients perceive such unconditional positive regard, existing conditions of worth are weakened or dissolved and are replaced by a stronger unconditional positive self-regard. If the therapist who matters is able to prize and consistently care about clients, no matter what the clients are experiencing or expressing, then the clients become free to accept all that they are with love and caring.

5. The therapist experiences an accurate empathic understanding of the client's inner world and endeavors to communicate this understanding to the client. Through empathy we sense the client's private world as if it were our own, without our own anger, fear, or confusion getting bound up in the experience. With this clear sense of the client's world, we can communicate our understanding, including our awareness of the meanings in the client's experience of which the client is scarcely aware.

Without such deep empathic understanding, clients could not trust the therapist's unconditional positive regard. Clients would feel threatened that once the therapist came to know them more fully there would be aspects of the client that the therapist could not accept with positive regard. With accurate empathy and unconditional positive regard, clients come close to being fully known and fully accepted (Rogers, 1959).

6. The client perceives, at least to a minimal degree, the acceptance and understanding of the therapist. In order for the client to trust the caring and empathy of the therapist, the therapist must be seen as genuine and not one who is demonstrating these concerns as just a part of a role.

THEORY OF THERAPEUTIC PROCESSES

While Rogers has written extensively about the conditions of the client-therapist relationship that allow for therapeutic change, he has had much less to say about the actual processes that occur in the interactions between client and therapist to produce such change. Throughout the 1950s it seemed adequate to postulate that the therapist's orientation, such as unconditional positive regard, was all that was necessary to release a client's inherent tendency toward actualization. During the 1960s, Rogers and his colleagues (Rogers et al., 1967) began to theorize that the curative process involved the direct and intense expression of feelings leading to corrective emotional experiences. Most recently, client-centered theorists such as Anderson (1974), Wexler (1974), and Zimring (1974) have begun to view client-centered therapy as a process of expanding consciousness or awareness through therapists helping to bring about more effective information processing in clients. Currently, then, the processes of change in client-centered therapy are most accurately conceptualized as a combination of consciousness raising and corrective emotional experiencing that occurs within the context of a genuine empathic relationship characterized by unconditional positive regard.

Consciousness Raising

THE CLIENT'S WORK

Given an atmosphere of unconditional positive regard, clients are free to discuss whatever they wish in therapy. Clients, rather than therapists, direct the flow of therapy. This is the reason Rogers (1942) originally used the label *nondirective* to describe his therapy. Since clients come to therapy out of distress, however, they can be expected to express information related to personal experiences that are troubling them. The responsibility of clients, then, is to take the initiative to inform the therapist about their personal experiences and to be available for feedback from the therapist.

THE THERAPIST'S WORK

Traditionally the therapist's work in increasing the client's consciousness was seen as being almost entirely a function of feedback. As a mirror or a reflector of the client's feelings, the therapist would essentially communicate to the client messages that said, "You really feel . . . " The specifics might be, "You really feel disappointed in your father for leaning on alcohol," or "You really feel envious of your roommate's special boyfriend and you wish you didn't." Through a commitment to understand the client with accurate empathy, the therapist is not dogmatically, authoritatively, or interpretatively telling the client how or what to feel. The therapist is instead able to sensitively and exquisitely capture the essence of the experiences the client is expressing. The therapist can reflect so empathically and accurately in part because there is no distortion from having to be interpretative or self-expressive. The therapist is free to actively listen and accurately reflect the essential feelings of the client.

With such a caring and congruent mirror available, clients are able to become more fully conscious of experiences that previously were partly distorted or denied. These experiences, of course, included their feelings, more important, their *real* feelings. Perhaps of even more significance, clients begin to be more fully aware of the *You* the therapist is reflecting. The *You* with increasing richness; the *You* who produced experiences once judged to be unworthy of self-regard which are now prized and shared by a significant other. Gradually the *You* that clients become aware of through empathic feedback from the therapist is a richer and more congruent human being.

Current theorizing on client-centered therapy suggests that the therapist's work in raising consciousness involves more than just a feedback function. Anderson (1974) indicates that part of the work of a client-centered therapist is to help clients reallocate their attention so that they can make greater use of the richness that exists in the information generated by their feelings. By more flexibly and fully attending to the client's feelings, the therapist helps clients to break through some of their perceptual rigidities and distortions in order to attend to the personal meaning of experiences that previously have not been processed into awareness.

Wexler (1974) goes even further and elaborates on how the client-centered therapist serves as a surrogate information processor. In compensating for the client's more rigid and deficient style of information processing, the therapist first serves an attentional function by which experiences of clients, especially threatening experiences, can be held in awareness for further processing. If the therapist did not reflect some of the client's threatening experiences, the client's selective attentional processes would cause such information to be lost in short-term memory by being crowded out by other information that is receiving attention. For example, in talking about her roommate's boyfriend, a shy sophomore was expressing a variety of feelings, including her close relationship to her roommate, her admiration of the boyfriend, and some vague feelings of envy. Because envy was not a feeling she could accept, this client would have focused her attention on her admiration or her sense of closeness and would have lost the opportunity to become aware of feelings of envy that might be the source of her recent arguments with her roommate. Since there is always more information impinging on a client than the client can attend to, information from threatening experiences is most likely to be lost unless empathetically reflected by the therapist and thereby kept available for further processing. By selecting out such threatening information to process into awareness, the client-centered therapist is, in fact, quite directive but in a subtle and noncoercive style, and only by responding to information that is already in process in the client.

As a surrogate information processor for the client, the therapist also helps the client to adopt a more optimal mode of organizing information. As clients approach feelings that threaten self-regard, they can become anxious, confused, or defensive, and may be unable to find the exact words or adequate symbols for organizing and integrating such feelings into conscious experience. Some clients may anxiously search for words to organize their previously unacceptable feelings of anger or envy, while other clients will give up quickly and go on to something else. The effectiveness of client-centered therapists is found in the ability to empathically and accurately organize the information from a client's experience in a concise and exquisite manner. Such organized information is then more fully available to awareness. An example of such helpful organization occurred with a 55-year-old woman who was expressing a variety of upsetting feelings toward her husband. She was angry because he wouldn't spend money to fix up the house for their daughter's wedding; she was depressed over how many years she had worked to make their restaurant a success but now that they had money she still wasn't happy. She was trying to understand her husband's view that it would be better to remodel the house after they saved up the money rather than cash in one of their bonds. She said she just felt torn and confused. When I told her, "You really feel impatient with his promises that someday the two of you are really going to live," she broke into tears and said, "Yes, that's it, that's it, that's what he's always been holding out in front of me."

Wexler (1974) also argues that a more actualizing style of experiencing includes a style of information processing that organizes information using structures, symbols, or schemas that evoke richer, more intense, and more conscious expressions of life. Therapists help clients develop such evocative structures for processing information by using symbols or words that are active, vivid, potent, and poignant. All too frequently the language and symbols of clients are conventional, repetitive, dull, and safe, reflecting the defensive ways in which clients process their experiences into awareness. Evocative symbols threaten to bring experiences into awareness that have previously been damaging to the client's self-regard. As clients become aware of how therapists can capture the client's own feelings in more vital and enriched language, they have the opportunity to begin to use symbols that allow them to be conscious of how vital their lives can really be. Through the help of enhancing therapists, clients begin to use the language of actualization in place of the distorting and denying symbolization of maladjustment.

Zimring (1974) uses the philosophy of Wittgenstein (1953, 1958) to explain that as clients become aware of more vital, enhancing, and actualizing modes of expressing themselves, their experiences, in fact, become more vital, more enhancing, and more actualizing. Expression and experience are a unity in Wittgenstein's view. There are not experiences existing somewhere in the organism that are waiting to be expressed into awareness. Experiences are created by expression. Thus, the richer, the more potent, and the fuller the symbols that clients learn to use in expressing themselves, the richer, the more potent, and the fuller human beings they become.

Catharsis

In the process of increasing consciousness, client-centered therapists have emphasized the primacy of the client's feelings. The therapist's continual focus on "You really feel . . . " helps clients to become more aware of feelings but also to release, express, and own their most powerful feelings, including feelings that were once experienced as being unworthy of expression. For Rogers (1959), feelings have both emotional and personal meaning components. In the previous section we examined the expression, organization, and integration of the personal meaning, informational, or cognitive component of feelings. Now we shall examine the cathartic release of the emotional component of feelings, which is equally important in the curative process of clients. While Rogers considers the expression of emotional and cognitive components of feelings as inseparable, we have taken the liberty of discussing them separately while recognizing their experiential unity.

THE CLIENT'S WORK

In the process of expressing themselves, clients usually begin by avoiding emotionally laden experiences. When feelings are talked about early in therapy, they are described as past experiences that are external to self (Rogers & Rablen, 1958). Clients will talk about emotional problems but describe such problems as coming from outside of themselves. "My roommate is really driving me up a wall"; "My folks are really on my back"; and "My studies are really giving me a bad time" are some examples of early communications. Gradually, in response to the therapist's accurate empathy and unconditional positive regard, clients begin to describe their feelings, but they are still primarily past emotions and thus lack intensity. As clients experience themselves as accepted even with having had some negative emotions in the past, they can begin to more freely describe present feelings, but they are not yet fully living and expressing their emotional experiences. Part of the work of clients involves staying with such emerging emotions even though anxiety is aroused and their defensive responses are mobilized to selectively disattend to such threatening emotions.

Eventually clients begin to fully express their feelings of the moment. Such feelings are owned and accepted as coming from within the person and being worthy of positive regard. At the same time emotional experiences that were previously denied are bubbling up. Rather than continue to deny all such feelings, the client is gaining more confidence that such emotions can be valued and valuable. Clients are discovering that experiencing feelings with immediacy and intensity is a possible guide for living. They begin to trust their feelings and base more of their valuing on what they like or dislike, what makes them happy or sad, what produces joy or anger. With the release and owning of such emotional experiences, clients begin to once again be in touch with their inherent organismic basis for valuing their genuine feelings. Such emotional experiences need not be denied, distorted, or feared but rather should be valued. The release and acceptance of such feelings are frequently vivid, intense, and dramatic for the clients as they discover an internal basis for directing their own lives rather than having to be dominated, distorted, and threatened by the internalized values of others.

THE THERAPIST'S WORK

Originally the therapist's work seemed to be simply to allow clients to get in touch with their most basic feelings by demonstrating an attitude of unconditional prizing of all the feelings a client was releasing. Now it is recognized that therapists help clients get in touch with and express threatening emotional experiences by continually redirecting the client's attention to the feeling aspect of whatever is being discussed. As the therapist empathically reflects back to the client the essence of what the client is feeling implicitly, the client eventually becomes able to attend to and explicitly feel the emotion and the meaning of experiences.

More recently many client-centered therapists have begun to follow Rogers's lead of directly expressing some of the emotion and meaning of their own feelings (Barton, 1974). Especially in group work, therapists might express such emotions as "I feel angry about the way you're attacking Tom," or "I feel deeply moved and saddened by what you've expressed," or "I really do care about you." The theoretical justification for client-centered therapists expressing their own emotional experiences of the moment is that such expression allows for greater genuineness or congruence of the therapist. Furthermore, if therapists use nondirectiveness as an excuse to suppress their own annoyance because the poor, weak client could not take it, an attitude of fundamental disrespect for the client's powers will be communicated (Barton, 1974).

The empirical justification for therapist self-expression is the discovery (Rogers et al., 1967) that therapists who speak genuinely out of their strong feelings tend to evoke and liberate clients to release and express their own emotional experiences. Zimring (1974) and Wexler (1974) would argue that the self-expressing therapist actually creates emotional experiences in clients through such transactions rather than releasing some feelings that are implicitly existing within the client. The traditional view in client-centered therapy, however, is that threatening emotions are implicitly present in clients and are not being released because of the client's defensiveness. Through the therapist's self-expression of emotions and, still most important, through the therapist's empathic reflection of feelings, clients are gradually freed from having to deny or distort their emotions and can begin to speak and live out their strongest feelings.

THEORY OF THERAPEUTIC CONTENT

Intrapersonal Conflicts

While client-centered therapy is a theory more of process than content (Zimring, 1974), it has had important things to say about many of the most common content issues in therapy. As we have seen, client-centered theory has been especially concerned with intrapersonal conflict between the client's concept of self and the total experience of the client, which includes feelings that are threatening to the person's self-concept. Even in the movement toward group therapy and institutional consultation, client-centered therapists are still concerned with establishing an atmosphere of unconditional positive regard to help individuals overcome personal incongruence in order to be more fully functioning.

ANXIETY AND DEFENSES

Anxiety is not the cause of people's problems but rather a troubling result of a divided life. While anxiety is frequently what drives people into therapy, our task is not to desensitize anxiety but rather to sensitively listen to the client's expression of anxiety in order to more fully discover what organismic experiences are threatening to enter awareness. In practice client-centered therapists respect the potentially disorganizing effects of anxiety, and thus do not flood a client with threatening emotional experiences, but rather allow a more gradual corrective emotional experiencing to occur. The client-centered style of catharsis may be slower and less dramatic than some of the emotional flooding therapies, but it is also seen as less risky because of the belief that anxiety can and does cause incongruent people to be disorganized or broken down.

The defense against anxiety-arousing experiences is to either deny the experiences from awareness entirely or to use a whole range of distorting perceptions, such as projection or rationalization, that process experiences in a manner slanted in favor of maintaining the person's self-concept. In Piaget's terms, distorting defenses involve new experiences being assimilated into the schema of the self with no accommodation of the self-concept to what is new. The self is left unthreatened but only at the loss of opportunity to grow.

SELF-ESTEEM

Rogers placed the need for self-esteem at the center of intrapersonal problems, only he called it *self-regard*. People are more vulnerable to self-esteem problems the greater the distance between who they think they are and who they really are. The problem is not that they have too great a concept of themselves and cannot live up to it. The problem is that their concepts of themselves are too meager to let them really be all that they are born to be. Striving for self-esteem is a trap that keeps us locked into trying to actualize a concept of self that was created out of the confining conditions of our parents' prizing. The more restrictive the striving, the more we can feel good about ourselves only when we do not allow ourselves to feel much at all. The solution lies not in increasing self-esteem but rather in expanding our conditions of worth so that we can prize all that we can be and not only who we believe we are supposed to be.

RESPONSIBILITY

Being the scientist that he is and having been educated in a time in which the sciences of humanity assumed complete determinism, Rogers has not included freedom and responsibility as core constructs in his theory. The troubled person is the victim needing parental regard that was all too conditional. The therapist is responsible for providing four of the six conditions necessary for effective therapy; clients provide only themselves and a willingness to relate to the therapist. Even within this seemingly deterministic system we can imagine that freedom would be experienced in the process of releasing a safe but restrictive self-concept in order to actualize the inherent tendencies to be all that we can be. Becoming responsible would mean learning again to respond to our natural organismic valuing process rather than to the internalized values of others. The responsible person is the actualizing person who moves from heteronomy, or control by others and the environment, to autonomy, or inner control.

Interpersonal Conflicts

INTIMACY AND SEXUALITY

Intimacy is therapeutic, and therapy is intimate. In defining the necessary conditions for a therapeutic relationship, Rogers presents an excellent ideal for an intimate relationship: unconditional caring, accurate empathy, and genuineness. The major difference is that in an ongoing intimate relationship both partners are, or at least become, relatively equal in their levels of congruency in order for the relationship to truly progress, whereas therapy is ready for termination when such a level of intimacy is reached, often to the sadness of both therapist and client.

Since there is such similarity between therapy and intimacy, it is clear that some incongruent people can make major strides toward actualization without entering therapy. Unfortunately, truly intimate relationships are rare, in part because it is so difficult for us to grant to others what we withhold from ourselves, and that is our love of our humanness, including our blemishes, our defects, our imperfections. To love and to feel intimate, most people must distort their perceptions of their partners to fit their conditions of what is worthy of love, just as they distort their perceptions of themselves. Eventually, when they discover who they are really related to, they are likely to believe that the faults and the gaps in their relationship are due to their partner's incompleteness rather than to the narrow conditions of their own love.

Certainly our society has traditionally placed much too narrow conditions on our sexual worth. Such restrictive conditions have led to too many people disowning much of the fullness of their sexuality in order to hold themselves in high regard. In reacting to the many prohibitions against being sexual, we may have gone to the opposite extreme of believing that to feel worthy we have to be sexually successful, to be routinely orgasmic or even multiply orgasmic, to always be aroused and maintain lubrication or erections, to never ejaculate too quickly but to always ejaculate. Much of the performance anxiety that Masters and Johnson (1970) describe so well may indeed be a reflection of restrictive conditions of worth that say we must be sexually successful rather than sexually natural in our relationships.

A more natural sexuality that is neither goal-oriented nor performance-oriented is most likely to occur within an intimate relationship. It is in such intimate relationships that we are least likely to place either overly restrictive or overly demanding conditions of worth on either our own or our partner's style of sexual relating. When things go wrong sexually, as they will at times for nearly everyone, there is little threat of rejection or criticism in an intimate relationship. The atmosphere is present for the couple to work through their own sexual difficulties. Rogers (1972) himself revealed a very intimate experience of how his wife's unconditional regard allowed her to remain available to help him work through a period of impotence. If therapists focus only on sexual dysfunctions without helping to develop more intimate relationships, they are liable to leave couples in relationships that will continue to need therapy when things go wrong.

COMMUNICATION

Communication problems were once believed inevitable, given the inadequacy of words to express feelings. With our greater awareness of accurate empathy, however, we now know that we can indeed understand the fullness of what another is communicating if we truly care to listen. The problem of communication is no longer a language problem; it is a problem in caring. The testimony of clients from many forms of effective therapy indicate how fully people feel they can communicate and be understood when someone really cares to listen. Just as we can train therapists (Truax & Carkhuff, 1967) and paraprofessionals (Carkhuff, 1969) to increase their ability to actively listen, so too are we learning how to train parents (Gordon, 1970) and teachers (Gordon, 1974) to actively listen and effectively communicate.

HOSTILITY

From his humanistic view, Rogers sees the natural actualizing tendency as bringing people toward each other rather than driving them against each other. Hostility is not an inherent drive that must be controlled. It is in part a reaction to being overcontrolled by the restrictive conditions of parental regard. Hostility is at times our organismic way of rebelling against having to disown parts of our lives in order to be prized by others. It can also build up as a problem when people cannot express angry feelings without feeling guilty or unworthy. There are, of course, individuals who use hostility against others with little caring, but such hostile individuals were most likely raised in dehumanizing atmospheres in which they themselves experienced all too little caring.

CONTROL

Control is a problem in interpersonal relationships when individuals attempt to impose their conditions of worth on others. In subtle or not-so-subtle ways, such individuals communicate that they can continue to care only if others live up to their image of a lovable human being. Be nice, be a winner, be assertive, be deferent, be witty, be quiet, be sexy, and behave are just a few of the conditions that people can place on their partners or their children. We let ourselves be controlled by others because we value more the maintenance of their regard than what is organismically pleasing. So we in turn act in restricted ways to control the positive regard of others. As long as our conditions of worth coincide, we tend to go on controlling each other without feeling conflict. Issues of control become acute when conditions of worth conflict, such as when some people can feel worthy only when they keep others waiting. To give up being controlled and to give up controlling, people must work hard in therapy at giving up their restrictive conditions of worth.

Individuo-Social Conflicts

ADJUSTMENT VERSUS TRANSCENDENCE

Going beyond one's internalized conditions of worth to become a whole person suggests some need to transcend one's personal enculturation process. But once a person is in the process of becoming more congruent, there is no inherent conflict between being an actualizer and being part of a society. Rogers's (1959) view of the natural actualizing tendencies includes being part of a society in order to relate, to create, and to grow through the mastery of cultural tools. Rogers is certainly in favor of humanizing social institutions, such as marriages, families, schools, universities, and businesses. Such humanization would make individuo-social conflicts minimal, but it is not necessary for people to become fully functioning individuals. Since so much of Rogers's professional life has been spent in universities and growth-oriented centers, perhaps two of the most humane institutions of society, he does seem confident that autonomous clients can go out into society, be fully functioning, and still be at home in the world.

IMPULSE CONTROL

The natural organismic valuing process provides inherent regulation over impulses. A person raised in a humanistic atmosphere will eat, drink, or relate sexually in a manner that is organismically enhancing and not organismically destructive. Attempts at bringing particular impulses under control through fancy techniques or faddish diets may produce short-term gain but little long-term maintenance, since they fail to focus on enhancing natural abilities for self-regulation. Once people feel good about who they really are and are not under constant stress to be what others want, they will not need to resort to overeating, drinking, or smoking in order to feel good for the moment or to reduce stress.

RULES FOR LIVING

Humanistic rules for living can be expected to emerge from people who are centered in their natural organismic valuing process. While most specific rules, such as those governing the distribution of work in a family, would be somewhat unique to each relationship, the general atmosphere for making rules can be expected to be democratic, in which each person is held in unconditional regard, is listened to with empathy, and is able to communicate genuinely.

Beyond Conflict to Fulfillment

MEANING

Meaning emerges from the process of actualizing our tendencies to become all that we are by nature intended to be. Those who are obsessed with the belief that there must be something more to life than natural living have probably not owned all that there is to their lives. The haunting notion that there must be something more to life represents a subception in most people that there is indeed a good deal more to life than what they are experiencing, but what's missing is to be found within them and not outside them. There is no feeling of needing more to give life meaning for those in the process of living a congruent life, for those living the complete life.

VALUES

It is clear by now that the locus of evaluation, the source of evidence for values, is found within the individual. The person should be the center of the valuing process, rather than values being imposed by others. The evidence for judging values comes through the individual's senses as long as the person's perceptions are not distorted or blinded by incongruencies. The criterion for values is the actualizing tendency—does this action or experience enhance or maintain the organism? Full trust is placed in the developing individual to value what is best for growth, whether it be a particular diet, a schedule for sleep, a choice of intellectual activities, or special relationships. The fact that so few individuals seem to select activities that are most enhancing is not evidence against a centered valuing process but rather a reflection of how few people are raised to trust in their own natural valuing process.

IDEAL INDIVIDUAL

Rogers's (1961) ideal for the good life is found in a fully functioning person. This ideal type of individual would, of course, demonstrate organismic trusting. Being open to each new experience, the person would let all of the significant information in a present situation flow in and through and would trust in the course of action that would emerge as the best response to the current event. The person would not have to ruminate about decisions but would find the best decision emerging as a result of not distorting or denying any information that is relevant to current living. The openness to experiencing indicates a person who is living primarily in the present, who is neither processing information that belongs to the past nor omitting information that belongs to the present. The fully functioning person does not process experience through a rigid or structured set of categories, through a rigid concept of self, for example. Instead, in what Rogers (1961) calls *existential living*, people let the self and the personality emerge from experience; they discover a sense of structure in experience which results in a flowing, changing organization of self and personality. Self is now experienced as a process, a rich, exciting, challenging, and rewarding process rather than a constricted structure that can process only what is consistent with internalized conditions of worth.

The organismic trusting, the openness to experiencing, and the existential living in the present result in an experiential freedom in which people have freedom to choose and direct their lives from within, regardless of the sad fact that actions may indeed be somewhat predictable on the basis of past experiences. The greatest sense of freedom comes in being creative, in being able to produce new and effective thoughts, actions, and entities because the person is in touch with the spring of life.

PRACTICALITIES OF CLIENT-CENTERED THERAPY

Since the person doing the therapy is more important than formal training, client-centered therapists are welcomed from a diversity of backgrounds. Counseling psychology, counseling education, and pastoral counseling have been especially well represented in the Rogerian approach. Rogers also has had considerable influence on many programs in clinical psychology and some programs of social work, especially those that followed a Rankian tradition. Client-centered therapists and counselors have been among the most active in developing training approaches for paraprofessionals, such as students participating in self-help groups (Carkhuff, 1969). Through methods developed by Truax and Carkhuff (1967), those training to do client-centered therapy are helped via role playing and tape recording to recognize when they need to be more empathic, genuine, or unconditional in their regard. Therapy for training therapists was seen as desirable though not essential; however, currently aspiring client-centered therapists would frequently be encouraged to participate in growth-oriented group experiences from a client-centered approach.

Since clients are seen as having inherent tendencies toward actualization, client-centered therapy has traditionally believed that extensive therapy is unnecessary. The most common practice has been to see clients individually once a week for 6 to 12 months. Fees seem to follow the going rate for other forms of therapy in a given locale. Since therapy is based on a more genuine relationship, client and therapist meet face-to-face, with no intervening desk. As the emphasis on the genuine aspect of relating has received more emphasis, more client-centered therapists have gone toward working in groups in a somewhat more participant-leader model.

EFFECTIVENESS OF CLIENT-CENTERED THERAPY

Rogers has consistently stood for an unusual combination of a phenomenological understanding of clients and an empirical evaluation of therapy. He and his followers have demonstrated that a humanistic approach to doing therapy and a scientific approach to evaluating therapy need not be incompatible. Strupp (1971, p. 44) has concluded that "the impetus given research by client-centered therapy is at least equal in importance to Rogers's theoretical contributions or the effectiveness of his form of psychotherapy." Since Meador and Rogers (1973, p. 154) indicate that "client-centered therapy is probably the most extensively researched method of psychotherapy in existence," we will not be able to present a complete survey of related research but will present a fully representative review of the best-controlled outcome research on client-centered therapy.

The classic evaluation of client-centered therapy was a coordinated series of 11 projects reported in a book edited by Rogers and Dymond (1954). Each of the separate projects was part of an overall comparison of 29 clients receiving at least six sessions of therapy, and 23 subjects receiving no therapy. The treated subjects were a representative sample of students and nonstudents coming for help to the University of Chicago Counseling Center who were assigned to one of two groups, an immediate therapy group and a group waiting two months before beginning therapy. The control subjects, unfortunately, were not applicants for therapy, were better adjusted than the therapy subjects, and were volunteers being paid to participate in research on personality.

No significant gains were found while subjects were waiting. Significantly greater congruence in real and ideal self-concepts was found in patients after therapy and at a 6–12-month follow-up than was initially reported in the treated groups. The changes were significantly greater than the "equivalent controls" who had shown much greater congruence on initial testing. On an emotional adjustment score, treated subjects showed improvement from pre- to posttherapy that was sustained on follow-up. Untreated controls started at a much higher adjustment level and did not change. On a TAT adjustment score, controls were better than clients before therapy but not after treatment. Clients showed no greater acceptance of and respect for others as a consequence of therapy when compared with controls. Finally, friends of the clients did not rate them as more mature following therapy than before, nor did clients rate their own maturity as significantly increased after therapy.

Baehr (1954) compared group and individual nondirective therapy in 66 hospitalized male VA patients. Clients receiving equal amounts of group and individual therapy reported less discontentment with life following discharge and at follow-up than did clients receiving predominantly group therapy or predominantly individual therapy. This study lacked a no-treatment control group.

Ends and Page (1957) compared three forms of group therapy: client-centered, psychoanalytic, and a therapy based on two-factor learning theory with an attention placebo group of institutionalized alcoholics. Subjects were assigned to groups based on sociometric scores in order to assure group cohesiveness. Four therapists with at least two years of experience were extensively trained in each of the group therapies for a year prior to the study. A latin square design was used with a total of 16 groups. There were initially six patients in each group, but early termination left a total of 63 patients, with about four subjects in each group, leaving the design relatively intact. The control subjects met with the therapists for social discussions but not for therapy. Each group completed 15 sions in five weeks.

Following therapy the client-centered group showed improvement at the $p < .10$ level on four Q-sorts, a method of describing one's real and ideal self-concepts by sorting personality statements according to how accurately they reflect one's own perceptions of self (Stephenson, 1953): (1) their self-concepts moved closer to a self-concept described by five clinical psychologists as the healthiest possible one, (2) the discrepancy between real self and ideal self was reduced, (3) their self-concepts moved closer to posttherapy ideal, and (4) their ideal self-concepts became closer to their posttherapy real self-concepts. At follow-up the client-centered group was the only one showing a lower recidivism rate ($p < .02$) than the control group, with only a 33 percent recidivism rate compared with 53 percent of the control group being rehospitalized.

In 1959, Ends and Page reported the effects of Rogerian group therapy on another population of institutionalized alcoholics who were free from psychoses. Twenty-eight clients received 30 sessions of group therapy over six weeks, and 289 received no therapy. Both the ideal and the real self-concepts of the therapy group changed in a healthy direction at the end of 30 sessions when compared with the no-treatment group. A fascinating pattern was found during therapy in which the therapy subjects showed a "flight into health" pattern of change at the end of 10 sessions, a disintegration at the end of 20 sessions, and a reintegration at the end of 30 sessions. Such a pattern reflects the peaks-and-valleys or up-and-down pattern of progress in therapy that is experienced by many types of therapists. One wonders how the clients would have been after 40 sessions of therapy. Unfortunately, in this study a follow-up recidivism rate was not used as an outcome measure.

Semon and Goldstein (1957) compared the effects of group-centered versus leader-centered group therapy on hospitalized chronic schizophrenics.

posttherapy measures of hospital adjustment were small but significant at the .10 level. The group-centered therapy group was rated as showing somewhat better communication and interpersonal relations and somewhat better care of self and social responsibility but no differences in work or recreation.

Dorfman (1958) studied the effects of individual client-centered therapy with 9- to 12-year-olds referred by teachers as maladjusted. Seventeen students were seen for an average of 28 weeks with a range of 11 to 33 sessions. The nontreated controls were not referred for therapy but were matched on the basis of the dependent test measures. Significant improvement in the therapy group was reported on the Rogers Test of Personality Adjustment ($p < .10$), on the Social Maladjustment Scale of the Rogers test ($p < .05$), and on Sentence Completion Adjustment scores. There was no measure of actual classroom adjustment following therapy.

Cartwright (1961) studied the effects of individual client-centered therapy on the stability or consistency of identity. Nineteen clients were matched for age, sex, and student-nonstudent status with 20 controls who, unfortunately, had no intention of seeking therapy. Both the therapy and the control groups showed an increase in consistency of self and self-in-relationship-to-others on posttherapy Q sorts. Cartwright then divided the therapy subjects into 9 successes and 10 failures and compared them with 10 control subjects.

Both groups of clients were found to enter therapy with poorer adjustment than controls when they compared their self-images with the images they had of their mothers. Controls were as poorly adjusted as clients in their comparison of self-images with their images of their fathers. Successful clients improved their self-concepts in relation to their mothers but showed no improvement in comparing themselves with their fathers. Cartwright concluded that client-centered therapy seems to be effective in resolving mother problems but does not appear to change the self-in-relation-to-father image.

Cartwright and Vogel (1960) used 19 clients from the previous study, added 3 more, and used an own-control design to compare waiting-period change with therapy change, length of therapy with change, and experience of therapist with change. While the authors report significant changes in therapy compared with the waiting period, Meltzoff and Kornreich (1970, pp. 160–162) reanalyzed their data, taking the direction of Q sorts into account. They found an almost identical 50–50 improvement for both waiting and in-therapy periods. No suppport was found for greater improvement due to longer therapy, and there was equivocal support for the effects of therapists' experience, with greater experience being slightly favored.

Arbuckle and Boy (1961) investigated the effectiveness of individual client-centered therapy with junior high school boys classified as behavioral problems by the school. Thirty-six boys were divided into three groups that were extremely well matched on many relevant variables. The therapy subjects were released from detention on the conditions that for 12 weeks they report weekly to a school counselor for an hour and that they could use this time however they wished, such as talking about anything on their minds, doing homework, going to the library, or returning to class. One control group was given the traditional treatment of after-school detention, while the other was released from detention and served as a no-treatment control.

Therapy subjects showed significantly greater congruence on ideal-real

Therapy subjects showed significantly greater congruence on ideal-real self-concepts than either of the control groups; their behavior was rated as better by teachers; fewer students rejected them following treatment; and from a posttherapy interview, they were rated as having more definite educational and vocational objectives. Neither of the other two groups improved on any of these measures. The therapy group also received only two disciplinary referrals, compared with eight in the detention group and five in the no-treatment group. While there was no long-term follow-up, 11 of the 12 therapy subjects made a total of 55 visits to their counselors in the six weeks following the end of their mandatory visits.

In the study described more fully in Chapter 6 on Adlerian psychotherapy, Shlien, Mosak, and Driekurs (1962) reported the effects of time limits on Rogerian versus Adlerian therapy. Clients in both therapies significantly improved on self-ideal correlations compared with no-treatment controls. There were no differences between the therapies. Neither time-limited nor unlimited therapy was more effective, but time-limited was more efficient, since the same gains were made in half the number of sessions.

Satz and Baraff (1962) failed to find client-centered group therapy effective in treating hospitalized nonchronic, paranoid schizophrenics. The four therapy clients received both 13 hours a week of occupational therapy and 2 hours a week of group therapy. One control group of four patients received only the occupational therapy, while eight other controls received neither therapy. On Q-sort measures of congruency of ideal and actual self-concepts, the only changes were in favor of the untreated controls, whose positive change approached signficance ($p < .09$) when compared with the other two groups.

Truax, Wargo, and Silber (1966) demonstrated the effectiveness of client-centered therapy on institutionalized female delinquents. They first selected 2 therapists who were the highest of 16 therapists on measures of accurate empathy and nonpossessive warmth, since they felt that findings of no change in therapy result from using therapists who are low on these variables. Forty girls were randomly assigned to a no-therapy control group. On their most rigorous outcome measure, the therapy group was found to spend significantly more time ($p < .001$) outside of institutions during a three-year posttherapy period. The therapy group also reported less conformity on the Minnesota Counseling Inventory, but their overall inventory scores suggested that they were still prone to delinquency. Other improvements in the therapy group included a significant improvement in family relationships and a self-concept closer to a healthy concept as defined by psychologists. The control group failed to improve on any of the dependent measures.

Truax (1970) also examined the long-term effects of client-centered therapy on schizophrenic patients. Previous comparisons of the 16 therapy subjects and the 16 untreated controls had been disappointing (Martin, 1972, p. 7), so Truax divided the therapy subjects into two groups: one half received therapy highest in accurate empathy, nonpossessive warmth, and genuineness; and the other half received therapy lowest in these qualities. Raters of the types of therapy were unaware of the hypotheses of the study, the identity of the clients or the therapists, or the previous outcome of research.

The outcome criterion was the number of days spent by the patients outside a hospital in a nine-year posttherapy period. The three groups did not differ on this measure prior to therapy, nor did they differ on the mean number of days spent out of the hospital. Complicated analyses of trends did indicate, however, that therapy subjects reached their maximum level of being outside the hospital quicker than did controls; that patients receiving therapy high in empathy, nonpossessive warmth, and genuineness had a greater tendency to get out of and stay out of the hospital over time than patients receiving therapy low in these qualities; and that the high group was able to get out of and stay out of the hospital quicker than control patients. The patients receiving therapy low in accurate empathy, nonpossessive warmth, and genuineness had the lowest rate of recovery over time, even lower than the untreated controls, suggesting that such therapy actually hampered the normal process of recovery. This study suggests, then, that the effectiveness of client-centered therapy on schizophrenics does not have to do with the label given the therapy but rather with the presence or absence in therapists of such essential characteristics as accurate empathy, nonpossessive warmth, and genuineness.

Warren and Rice (1972) were concerned with the process of teaching clients to be productive in therapy in order to reduce attrition and improve outcome. Fifty-five clients with low prognoses for therapy were seen at the University of Chicago Counseling Center and were randomly assigned to three groups. Each group was offered a block of 20 sessions of client-centered therapy at the rate of 2 sessions per week. The control group of 36 subjects received only the therapy. A semicontrol group of 10 subjects also received an extra therapy-stabilizing treatment, which was designed to eliminate snags in therapy by an experimenter encouraging clients to discuss any problems they were having with the therapy or the therapist. The intent was for the client to clarify any concerns and take them into the actual therapy sessions. The nine experimental subjects received the stabilizing treatment and also a structuring treatment, in which they were carefully taught how a client can most productively participate in the process of therapy.

Clients in the combined experimental and semicontrol groups stayed in therapy significantly longer than did control clients, but only the clients in the experimental group completed the full block of interviews significantly more often than did the control subjects. Furthermore, therapists rated clients in the experimental group as more improved, and clients in the experimental group perceived more positive change than the control group but not significantly more than the semicontrol group. The posttherapy correlations between actual and ideal self-sortings were not significantly different between groups. This study suggests, then, that naive clients who may feel confused about how to behave in therapy might really benefit from outside-of-therapy instructions.

CRITICISMS OF CLIENT-CENTERED THERAPY

From a Behavioral Perspective

Rogerians should be praised for their willingness to place client-centered therapy under scientific scrutiny. They must realize, however, that they are open to devastating criticisms for the many methodological errors found in almost all of their experiments. Fatal flaws in their studies include (1) using control subjects who are not candidates for therapy (Cartwright, 1961; Dorfman, 1958; Rogers & Dymond, 1954); (2) failing to use an untreated control group (Baehr, 1954; Cartwright & Vogel, 1960; Ends & Page, 1957; Warren & Rice, 1972); (3) failing to control for placebo effects (Rogers & Dymond, 1954; Shlien et al., 1962; Truax, 1970; Truax et al., 1966); (4) relying on only self-report measures which are so open to demands to please the therapist or experimenter (Baehr, 1954; Cartwright, 1961; Cartwright & Vogel, 1960; Dorfman, 1958; Ends & Page, 1959; Rogers & Dymond, 1954; Satz & Baraff, 1962); and (5) using inappropriate statistics, such as multiple t tests or probability levels of .10 even with one-tailed tests (Cartwright & Vogel, 1960; Dorfman, 1958; Ends & Page, 1957; Semon & Goldstein, 1957). Before we enthusiastically conclude that client-centered therapy has indeed been demonstrated to be effective with a wide range of problems, we had better make a much more intensive and sophisticated analysis of the available research. Such an analysis using more rigorously scientific standards leaves the issue of the general effectiveness of client-centered therapy still an open question.

From a theoretical perspective, client-centered therapy is also open to serious question. Beneath all the rhetoric, Rogers is advocating a treatment that is apparently based on a fuzzy form of extinction. Theoretically, troubled responses are assumed to have been conditioned by the contingent love and regard of parents. The therapist is supposed to reverse the process by establishing a social learning environment in which there are no contingencies, no conditions for positive regard. The client is allowed to talk on and on about troubled behavior without being reinforced or punished. Eventually the absence of contingencies leads to an extinction of talking about troubles. Of course, we cannot determine from the verbal extinction paradigm alone whether the client's troubled behavior itself has changed or whether the client has just quit talking about such problems.

But why rely upon extinction when it is necessarily lengthy and can lead to complications, such as spontaneous recovery of the extinguished responses? Furthermore, when only extinction is used, there is no way of telling which new behaviors will be be learned in place of the maladaptive responses that are being extinguished. Rogers advocates trusting in some mysterious organismic actualizing tendency. This tendency sounds so reminiscent of the ancient belief in teleology, which assumed an acorn would grow straight and tall if we only kept our foot off it. Of course, we now know that the manner in which even an acorn develops is in part a function of how it is nourished by its ongoing environment.

From a Psychoanalytic Perspective

Rogerian theory is an example of how our perceptions can be distorted by the people we are most likely to see in therapy. Client-centered therapy is an inspirational theory of humanity that has had great appeal to college students because it was based primarily on work with students. It is a theory and therapy for ambitious individuals whose typically American drive to achieve is mistaken for some inherent tendency to actualize. Where was such a driving tendency to actualize in the chronic schizophrenics that Rogers and his colleagues (1967) failed to make into fully functioning individuals?

What client-centered therapy provides is a transference relationship that has all the elements of an idealized maternal love. Clients are promised a rose garden in which all that they are, their worst as well as their best, will be met with unconditional love. The fact is that research has demonstrated (Truax, 1966) that even Carl Rogers made his responses to clients highly conditional upon the clients expressing feelings. When clients expressed particular feelings, Rogers was much more likely to show interest or express empathy. To pretend to be unconditional in our love is to do our clients a disservice, since the real world is, in fact, conditional with love. Such pretense can encourage clients to believe that, compared to the rest of the world, only a therapist could really love such a person.

From an Eclectic Perspective

Rogers can be praised for the outstanding contributions he has made in articulating what constitutes a therapeutic relationship. The problem is, however, that he seems to have gone too far and concluded that what may be necessary conditions for therapy to proceed are also sufficient conditions for therapy to succeed. His promise of therapy sounds like a Hollywood melodrama in which one unconditional love relationship comes along and emancipates a fully functioning person who lives happily ever after. What power he attributes to one caring relationship that usually meets only one hour per week! We are asked to believe that one such relationship alone is powerful enough to overcome the crippling effects of the conditional relationships that characterize the past and present lives of clients.

Rogers's overemphasis on relationship variables can also encourage the fantasy that being an effective therapist is just a matter of feeling and relating and not of knowing much. His system suggests that anyone who is congruent, whether it be a peer counselor or a paraprofessional, can do effective therapy without necessarily having any knowledge about personality, psychopathology, and psychology.

Knowledge in Rogers's system is of little consequence—it certainly is not a necessary condition for effective therapy. Yet one wonders if it is sheer coincidence that master therapists, such as Freud, Adler, May, and Rogers himself, have been individuals with intense intellectual commitments as well as individuals capable of intense caring.

A CLIENT-CENTERED ANALYSIS OF MRS. C.

Mrs. C. was raised in an extremely rigid atmosphere in which her parents' conditions of worth included being clean, being free from germs, being asexual, and being meek and nonaggressive. From her present compulsive pattern of existence, we can imagine that her own internalized conditions of worth are just as rigid as her parents'. The only experiences she lets herself possess are those in which she is obsessed with proving how clean and free from disease she is.

Apparently in her early years of marriage she had felt loved and regarded highly enough to be more flexible and better adjusted. Just what went wrong is open to speculation. Her family being struck with a severe flu and then the possibility of a pinworm epidemic might have threatened her self-regard by confronting her with not having been clean enough and careful enough with her family. At an even more central level she may have been threatened by a subception that she could not really love her children when they were sick or dirty. Mrs. C. may well have been experiencing the rigid limits of her love in relationship to her sick children and been threatened by doubts about the kind of mother she is if she cannot really love her children when they need her the most. But she had internalized the lesson from her parents that love is really contingent, that love is much too scarce to waste on the dirty or the diseased.

While we do not know the exact experiences that were threatening to emerge into awareness, we do get the impression of a person who panicked, who was confronted with intense and undeniable experiences of being unworthy and unlovable. Much of her life became disorganized as she struggled to hold onto what little self-regard she could maintain by organizing her life around washing and avoiding germs. If we empathize with the communications contained in her symptoms, we may hear how desperately she cries out: "I am worthy. I am lovable. Look how clean I am. I am not diseased. Don't send me away. I will make myself more lovable, more worthy of of your regard. I will work harder, be cleaner."

If she could open up her feelings she might go on: "My therapist and my family can love me only if I stop washing; I can love myself only if I am clean and pure. I am in an inevitable trap where I gain their regard at the loss of my own, or hold on to what little sense of self-worth I have left by continuing to clean and risk losing the few people who have any regard left for me. Suicide seems like the only alternative in this no-win situation."

Is Mrs. C.'s view just the distorted perception of a very troubled person? Do we not cast aside the dirty and the diseased? In our society, in which every major religious group that was sampled reported valuing cleanliness more than mature love (Rokeach, 1970), should we be surprised that some people like Mrs. C. base their existence on such social values and sacrifice their own organismic experiencing, which would tell them that love is clearly more valuable than cleanliness? Mrs. C. is a tragic prototype of a culture that is so enamored with social values like cleanliness as to be estranged from organismic values like love.

Mrs. C.'s family and therapist have indeed made their caring as rigidly conditional as has she. They say don't wash and we will care about you, she says only when I wash can I care about myself. An effective therapist must establish an atmosphere in which Mrs. C. is held in high regard when she washes as well as when she doesn't, when she talks about washing as well as when she doesn't. When we appreciate that we are talking with a woman who is obsessed with maintaining what little self-regard and self-love she has left, we would not feel a need to have her give up her one remaining source of esteem—her washing.

First she needs to experience the genuine esteem of a caring other who cares whether she washes or doesn't, whether she is obsessed or not, and then she can begin to experience that being positively regarded is not contingent on either washing or not washing. Only then can she begin to gradually become a little freer to consider that maybe she, too, can love herself whether she washes or does not wash. Caring is the fundamental issue, not cleaning. Mrs. C. has been providing unconditional cleaning, cleaning whether it is warranted or not, when what she really wants is unconditional caring, caring whether she at this moment warrants it or not.

GESTALT THERAPY

AS LONG AS SEX was going well for Howard, all was well with the world. From ages 17 to 27 he had been very active sexually, with most of his time and energy spent in erotic adventures or in fantasizing about such adventures. Sexual relating was by far the most significant and satisfying activity in his life. No wonder he was so puzzled at the onset of his impotence. Except for his first experience with a prostitute at age 17, he had never had any difficulty performing in bed. In fact, Howard loved to perform and prided himself on what a great lover he was. But now, no matter how hard he tried, he just could not succeed. Needless to say, he was quite depressed and anxious over the fact that his impotence had not disappeared after months of trying to prove he was going to be fine.

Since Howard had a special partner named Ginny, whom he cared about and trusted and who wanted to be with him sexually in spite of his impotence, we began therapy with a Masters and Johnson type of sensate focusing. The results were not encouraging because of the amount of depression and anxiety Howard continued to experience in the nondemanding, pleasuring exercises. Since his erections remained basically inhibited when he was with Ginny, we decided to try systematic desensitization and then come back to sensate focusing. While Howard progressed to the point of imagining intercourse without anxiety, he did not show much generalization to the actual sensate-focusing situation.

Finally I decided to resort to a gestalt exercise to help Howard discover the significance of the intense pressure he was having over his sexual drive. I asked Howard to imagine as vividly as he could that he was his penis and that his penis had something to say. As he got into the fantasy, I encouraged him to just let the mouth of his penis say whatever it spontaneously desired, and here is what came out: "You're asking too much of me, Howard. You've been asking me to carry the whole meaning of your life on my back and that's just too big a load for any one penis to carry. I'm bound to bend under such weight."

SKETCH OF THE FIRST GESTALT THERAPIST

Frederich (Fritz) Perls (1893–1970) was the developer of gestalt therapy and the master at knowing just how to use gestalt exercises to assist people striving to become more deeply aware of themselves. Perls did not start out with such an action-oriented approach, however. Like so many developers of therapy systems, his early therapeutic career was heavily influenced by his studies of psychoanalysis with Freud. After receiving his M.D. in Berlin, where he had been born, he studied at the Berlin and the Vienna Institutes of Psychoanalysis. He was analyzed by Wilhelm Reich, who had a profound influence on his development. Perls (1969b) said that if it had not been for the advent of Hitler, he probably would have spent his total professional career doing psychoanalysis with a few select clients.

As an aware individual, however, he anticipated the horrors of Hitler; and in 1934 when Ernst Jones announced a psychoanalytic position in Johannesburg, South Africa, Perls accepted. Besides establishing a practice, he also began the South African Institute for Psychoanalysis. Over the next dozen years he developed what he first considered a revision of the Freudian method of therapy. In 1947 he published his first book, *Ego, Hunger and Aggression: A Revision of Freud's Theory and Method*. At that time he was still committed to an instinct theory but argued for the acceptance of hunger as an instinct as critical to the survival of the individual as the sexual instinct is to the survival of the species. In the face of the many other revisions that Perls was suggesting for psychoanalysis, it became obvious that he was really beginning a new system, and when he republished his first book in 1969 he subtitled it *The Beginning of Gestalt Therapy*.

With the death of Jan Smuts in South Africa and the rise of apartheid, Perls again chose to leave a country heading toward unacceptable oppression. He came to the United States in 1946, and with his therapist wife, Laura, began the New York Institute for Gestalt Therapy. In 1951, with Ralph Hefferline and Paul Goodman, he published *Gestalt Therapy: Excitement and Growth in Personality*, a book that is exciting because of its engaging presentations of gestalt exercises.

As a person Perls was very much like his writings, both vital and perplexing. It was probably his many workshops with therapists more than his writings that had such an impact on the psychotherapy profession. People saw him as keenly perceptive, provocative, manipulative, evocative, hostile, and inspiring. Many professionals came away from an encounter with Perls feeling more alive and more complete. Those that went out to spread the gestalt gospel talked affectionately and almost worshipfully of Fritz. He certainly did not discourage such a cult. Believing that modesty is for modest people, Perls (1969b) wrote in his autobiography: "I believe that I am the best therapist for any type of neurosis in the States, maybe in the world. How is this for megalomania. At the same time I have to admit that I cannot work successfully with everybody."

Such unabashed egotism was fashionable in the 1960s, and many people flocked to Esalen in Big Sur, California, where Perls held court. If it was uniqueness, honesty, and spontaneity they sought in Fritz, they were not disappointed; if it was a grandfatherly, unconditional positive regard they desired, they were frustrated. As a result of his personal impact and his professional writings, the gestalt movement became a very significant force in the last decade of Perls's life. He wanted to close out his life by building a Gestalt Training Center and Community in British Columbia, so he moved there just before his death in 1970.

With the death of Fritz, gestalt therapists lost their touchstone of just what gestalt therapy can and should be. As one would expect from such a dynamic and spontaneous force as Fritz, there were many changes in his approach over the years. Consistency was not one of his concerns. Most gestaltists, however, point to the publication in 1969 of *Gestalt Therapy Verbatim* as the best representation of Perls's latest approach to gestalt theory and therapy, and so this book serves as the main source for the following presentation of gestalt therapy.

THEORY OF PERSONALITY

In spite of our centuries-old wish to disown our bodies, we humans must accept that we are basically biological organisms. Our daily goals, or *end-goals* as Perls (1969a) prefers, are based on our biological needs and are limited to hunger, sex, survival, shelter, and breathing. The social roles we adopt are the *means-whereby* we fulfill our end-goals. Such roles as being a therapist are means-whereby we earn a living, which is a means-whereby we fulfill such end-goals as hunger and shelter. As healthy beings, our daily living centers around the particular end-goals that are emerging into awareness in order to be fulfilled. If we listen to our body the most urgent end-goal emerges, and we respond to it like to an emergency; that is, without any obsessive doubt that the most important action we can take at this moment is to fulfill the particular end-goal that has emerged into awareness. We then interact with the environment to select the substances we need to satisfy that end-goal. End-goals are experienced as pressing needs as long as they are not completed, and they are quiescent once they are given closure through an adequate exchange with the environment. If we are thirsty, for example, we experience a need to bring completeness to our thirst by responding to our need with an adequate supply of water from our environment. It is this continual process of bringing completeness to our needs, the process of forming wholes or *gestalts*, that Perls sees as the one constant law of the world that maintains the integrity of organisms.

The really serious concerns in living then are with the completion of these organismic needs, as is well known by the millions of starving poor in the world. In a spoiled society like the United States, we spend little of our time or energy in completing our natural needs. Instead we preoccupy ourselves with social games that are best seen as nothing more than social means to natural ends. Once we experience these social means as end-goals, we identify with them as essential parts of our ego, so that we act as if we must put almost all our energy into playing such roles as students or therapists. Much of our thinking is involved with practicing how we can better act out our roles in order to more effectively manipulate our social environment and convince ourselves and others of the inherent value of our roles. As we repeatedly practice our roles they become habits, rigid behavioral patterns that we experience as the essence of our character. Once we develop our social character and have a fixed personality, we have transformed our basic natural existence into a pseudosocial existence.

In a healthy, natural existence our daily life cycle would be an open, flowing process of organismic needs emerging into awareness, accompanied by a means-whereby we bring closure to the most pressing need of the moment, followed by another end-goal emerging into awareness. As long as we remain centered on what is going on within us right now, we can trust in our wisdom as organisms to select the best means-whereby we adequately complete the most pressing need of the moment.

In a healthy existence, our entire life cycle involves a natural process of maturation in which we develop from children dependent on environmental support into adults who can rely on self-support for our own existence. Our development begins as unborn children who are entirely dependent on our mothers for support—for food, oxygen, shelter, everything. As soon as we are born we have to do our own breathing, at least. Gradually we have to learn to stand on our own two feet, to crawl, to walk, to use our own muscles, our senses, our wit. Eventually we have to accept that wherever we go, whatever we do, whatever we experience, is our own responsibility and only ours. As healthy adults we are aware that we possess the ability to respond, to have thoughts, reactions, and emotions in situations that are uniquely ours. This mature responsibility is fundamentally the ability to be what one is. For Perls (1969a), "Responsibility means simply to be willing to say 'I am I' and 'I am what I am.'"

As healthy adults we also are aware that other maturing organisms are equally able to respond for themselves, and the maturation process includes shedding responsibility for anyone else. We give up our childish feelings of omnipotence and omniscience and accept that others know themselves better than we can ever know them and can better direct their own lives than we can direct them. We allow others to be self-supporting, and we give up our need to interfere in the lives of others. Others do not exist to live up to our expectations, nor do we exist to live up to the expectations of others.

The healthy personality does not become preoccupied with social roles, since these roles are nothing more than a set of social expectations that we and others have for ourselves. The mature person does not adjust to society, certainly not to an insane society like ours. Healthy individuals do not repeat the same old, tired habit patterns that are so safe and so deadly. In taking responsibility for being all that they can be, such people accept Perls's attitude of living and reviewing every second afresh. They discover that there are always new and fresh means-whereby they can complete their end-goals. This freshness is what the creative cook discovers, what the joyful sex partner knows, and what the vital therapist thrives on.

With such attractive possibilities emerging from the natural process of maturation, how is it that most people remain stuck in the immature, childish patterns of dependency? There are several childhood experiences that can interfere with the development of a healthy personality. In some families parents withdraw needed environmental support before children have developed the capacity for inner support. The child can no longer rely on the safe, secure environmental support, nor can the child rely on self-support. The child is at an *impasse*. Perls's (1970) prototype of an impasse is a blue baby that has had the placenta severed and cannot rely on oxygen from the mother but is not yet prepared to breathe on its own—a very scary situation. Another example of an impasse occurs when parents demand that a child stand without support before the child's muscles and balance are adequately developed. All the child can experience is the fear of falling. The experience of such impasses can lead to individuals becoming stuck in the maturation process.

A more frequent source of interference comes from parents who are convinced that they know what is best for their children in all situations. In such families children may fear the stick, which is some form of punishment for following their own independent direction when it differs from what the parents believe is best. The child develops *catastrophic expectations* over independent behavior, such as, "If I take the risk on my own, I won't be loved anymore or my parents won't approve of me." Perls (1969a) suggests that such catastrophic expectations are frequently projections of the child's own fears of the consequences of independence onto the parents and not usually memories of how parents actually responded to the child's display of more mature behavior.

The fact is that as we become more aware, we realize that marching to a different drummer can indeed be risky. If we are different from our parents or peers, we may risk losing their love or approval. But they are not responsible if we choose to avoid the risks of being our own person. There are even more serious risks in our society if we refuse to play roles or to adjust to social expectations. We can lose jobs, close friends, and even face the possibility of crucifixion for being outside the boundaries of society. But we still cannot blame society if we refuse to take the risks of being healthy.

Fear of negative consequences over being independent is a major factor that interferes with maturation, but it is not the most common interference. More people get stuck because they have been spoiled by parents who overindulged them as children. Perls believes that too many parents want to give their children everything they never had. As a result the children prefer to remain spoiled and to let their parents do everything for them. Many parents are also afraid to frustrate their children, yet it is only through frustration that we are motivated to rely on our own resources to overcome what is frustrating us. With giving too much and not frustrating enough, parents establish an environment that is so secure and satisfying that the children become stuck with a desire to maintain such environmental support. Perls's emphasis on being stuck by being spoiled is reminiscent of Freud's emphasis on overindulgence as one source of infantile fixations.

Perls does not blame the parents, however, for the spoiled child remaining stuck! Such children are still responsible for using all of their resources to manipulate the parents and others in the environment to take care of them. Such children develop a whole repertoire of manipulations, such as crying if that is what it takes to get support or being the nice little child if that is the role that gets others to respond. To allow immature personalities to blame their parents for their problems is to allow them to avoid responsibility for their lives, which is such a critical part of the maturation process.

THEORY OF PSYCHOPATHOLOGY

The pathological personality is the person who has become stuck in the natural process of growth or maturation. No wonder that Perls preferred the term *growth disorders* rather than *neurosis* to refer to the most common personality disorders, although he frequently still relied on the more traditional term *neurosis* when talking about psychopathology.

For Perls (1970) there are five different layers or levels of psychopathology: (1) the phony, (2) the phobic, (3) the impasse, (4) the implosive, and (5) the explosive. The phony layer is the level of existence in which we play games and play roles. At this level we behave *as if* we are big shots, *as if* we are ignorant, *as if* we are ladies, or *as if* we are he-men. Our *as if* attitudes require that we live up to a concept, live up to a fantasy that we or others have created whether it comes out as a curse or an ideal. We may think it is an ideal to act *as if* we were Christ, for example, but Perls would see it as a curse, since it is still an attempt to get away from who we really are. The result is that neurotic people have given up living in a way in which they could actualize themselves, but rather they live in order to actualize a concept. Perls (1970) compares such pathology to an elephant that would rather be a rosebush and a rosebush that tries to be a kangaroo. We remain stuck on such childhood fantasies because we do not want to be what we are. We want to be something else because we are dissatisfied with what we are. We believe we could get more approval, more love, more environmental support if we were something else.

What we create in place of our authentic selves is a fantasy life that Perls (1969a) calls *maya*. Maya is part of the phony level of existence that we construct between our real selves and the real world, so we live as if our maya is reality. Our maya serves a defensive purpose since it protects us from the threatening aspects of ourselves or our world, such as the possibility of rejection. Much of our mental life is involved with making us better prepared to live in maya. Thinking, for example, is seen as rehearsing for acting, for role playing, and this is one of the reasons that Perls says he disesteems thinking. We become so preoccupied with our concepts, our ideals, and our rehearsals, that soon we no longer have any sense of our real nature.

In the struggle to be something we are not, we disown those aspects of ourselves that may lead to disapproval or rejection. If our eyes cause us to sin, we cast out our eyes. If our genitals make us human, we disown our genitals. We become alienated from the properties of ourselves that we and significant others frown upon, and we create the holes, the void, the nothingness where something should exist. Where the voids are, we build up phony artifacts. If we disown our genitals, for example, then we can act as if we are by nature pious and saintly. We try to create the characteristics that are demanded by our society for approval and that are eventually demanded by the part of ourselves that Freud called the superego.

In the process we create our phony characters, phony because they at best represent only half of who we are. If the character we construct is mean and demanding, for example, then we can be sure that below the surface is the opposite polarity of wanting to be kind and yielding. Our phony characters attempt to shield us from the fact that authentic existence involves each individual facing a continuing sequence of personal polarities (Polster & Polster, 1973). We may rigidly adhere to being pious and saintly, for example, to keep from experiencing our opposite desires to be devilish and sexual. The healthy person attempts to find wholeness in life by accepting and expressing the opposite poles of life. Pathological individuals attempt to hide unacceptable opposites by pretending that their characters are all there is to their lives.

Perls called the most famous of the gestalt polarities Top Dog and Under Dog. We at times experience Top Dog as our conscience, the righteous part of us that insists on always being right. Top Dog attempts to be master by commanding, demanding, insisting, and scolding. Under Dog is the slavish part of us that appears to go along with the bullying demands of Top Dog's ideals but in fact attempts to control through passive resistance. Under Dog is the part of us that acts stupid, lazy, or inept as a means of trying to keep from successfully completing the orders of Top Dog. As long as people avoid accepting that they are also the opposite of what they pretend to be, that they are strong as well as weak, cruel as well as kind, and master as well as slave, they are unable to complete the gestalt of life, to experience the whole life.

To try to face all that we really are, to try to be whole, would lead us to confront the phobic layer of our pathology. At this layer we are phobic about the pain that would come in facing how dissatisfied we are with parts of ourselves. We avoid and run from emotional pain, even though such pain is a natural signal that something is wrong and needs to be changed. The phobic layer includes all of our childish catastrophic expectations that if we confront who we really are our parents will not love us, or if we act the way we really want to act our society will ostracize us. Because of such phobic responses that frequently lead to avoiding what is really hurting, most people are seen as coming to therapy not to be cured but to have their neuroses improved.

Below the phobic layer is the most critical level of psychopathology, the impasse. The impasse is the very point at which we are stuck in our own maturation. It is what the Russians call the sick point. The impasse is the point at which we are convinced that we have no chance of survival because we cannot find the means within ourselves to move ahead in the face of withdrawal of environmental support. People will not move beyond this point of being stuck because of terrors that they might die or fall apart because they cannot stand on their own feet. But neurotics also refuse to move beyond this point because it is still easier for them to manipulate and control their environment for support. So they continue to play helpless or stupid or crazy or enraged in order to get others to take care of them, including their therapists. It is easier to continue such control since so much of the developmental time and energy of the neurotic went into creating and refining effective manipulative roles and skills rather than developing self-reliance. No wonder the neurotic is both afraid and unwilling to move through the impasse to the implosive layer of neurosis.

To experience the implosive layer is to experience deadness, the deadness of parts of ourselves that we have disowned. So neurotics would experience the deadness of their ears, or of their heart, or of their genitals, or of their very soul, depending on what fundamental processes of living they have run from. Perls (1970) compares the implosive layer to a state of catatonia in which the person is frozen like a corpse. The catatonia is due to the investment of energy in the development of a rigid, habitual character that seems safe and secure but oh so dead. To go through the implosive level the person must be willing to shed the very character that has served as a sense of identity. The person is threatened with experiencing his or her own death in order to be reborn, and that is not easy, says Fritz (1969a).

To let go of one's roles, of one's habits and very character, is to release a tremendous amount of energy that has been invested in holding back from being a responsible and fully alive human being. The person is now confronted with the explosive layer of neuroses, which can involve a tremendous release of life's energies, depending on how much energy is bound up in the implosive layer. In order to become fully alive the person must be able to explode into orgasm, into anger, into grief, and into joy. With such explosions the neurotic has moved well beyond the impasse and the implosive and has taken a giant stride into the joy and sorrow of maturity.

THEORY OF THERAPEUTIC PROCESSES

Explosively breaking out of a neurotic life sounds like an exciting cathartic experience. The powerful release of the emotions of anger, orgasm, joy, and grief promises to bring a profound sense of wholeness and humanness. No wonder so many people sought out Fitz Perls as he wandered throughout the country. But Fritz quickly let people know that such a cathartic explosion could be attained only if people are first willing to struggle to increase their consciousness of the phony games and roles they play and of the parts of themselves they have disowned. They have to become aware of how they are stuck in childish fantasies because of all the energy they invest in trying to be something they are not, until what they really are is little more than a walking corpse.

Consciousness Raising

Consciousness raising in gestalt therapy is aimed at liberating people from maya, from the phony, fantasy layer of existence. Since maya is a mental world, a world of concepts, ideals, fantasies, and intellectual rehearsals, Perls says the way for us to become free from maya is to lose more and more of our mind and get back to our senses. This loss of mind is actually a radical change in consciousness from future-oriented thinking and theorizing to a present-oriented sensory awareness. At this phenomenological level of consciousness we can experience with all of our senses the reality of ourselves and the world rather than just experiencing our theoretical or idealistic conceptions of how things are supposed to be. We can have an experience of *satori* or waking up. Suddenly the world is there again, right in front of our eyes. We wake up from an intellectual trance as we wake up from a dream. And with our senses we are again able to be in touch with all that we are.

THE CLIENT'S WORK

The client's work actually sounds quite simple—to stay in the *here and now*. Awareness of the moment would allow clients to work on the healthy gestalt principle: that the most important unfinished situation will always emerge into consciousness and can be dealt with. But clients soon discover that staying in the here and now is not so simple. As soon as clients enter the "hot seat" to indicate that they are ready to be the focus of the gestalt therapist, they can be expected to repeat the phony layer of their neurosis. Some clients will play the helpless role, unable to proceed without more encouragement or direction from the therapist; others will play stupid, unable to understand just what the therapist means; others will strive to be the "perfect patient," with their Top Dog insisting that they should be able to do just what is expected of them. Clients will then be asked to participate in gestalt exercises designed to help them become more aware of the phony roles or games they are playing. They may, for example, act out the Top Dog/Under Dog exercise in which they sit in one chair as Top Dog, shouting out the "shoulds" at Under Dog, and then switch to Under Dog's chair to give all of their excuses for not being perfect.

As clients stuggle to participate in the gestalt exercises, they can also become more deeply aware of their phobic layer, of what they run from in the here and now, and the catastrophic expectations that they use as excuses to run. They might, for example, feel extremely angry at the therapist for not being supportive but refuse to express their anger for fear that the therapist might want nothing more to do with them. The clients may then be asked to own the projection of rejection and to role play who is actually threatening to reject, such as their parents or their conscience. At each step in the exercises the clients do not talk about what is entering their awareness. Clients are asked to express their conscious experiences in action by taking the chair, for example, that represents their parents or their Top Dog and expressing just what that person would say. With such active expression they become much more profoundly aware of what is interfering with their ability to exist in the here and now.

THE THERAPIST'S WORK

The therapist's work in consciousness raising is first and foremost to frustrate the client. The therapist must especially frustrate the client's attempts to manipulate the therapist into taking responsibility for the client's well-being. If the therapist is committed to helping the client, the therapist is lost from the start. Such a helping attitude is paternalistic, and the client will be determined to make the therapist feel inadequate as compensation for needing the therapist. Early in therapy the gestalt therapist instructs clients on just how responsible they are for what they do in therapy. Perls (1969a, p. 79) used the following type of instructions in beginning a workshop:

So if you want to go crazy, commit suicide, improve, get 'turned-on', or get an experience that will change your life, that's up to you. I do my thing and you do your thing. Anybody who does not want to take the responsibility for this, please do not attend this seminar. You come here out of your own free will, I don't know how grown up you are, but the essence of a grown-up person is to be able to take responsibility for himself—his thoughts, feelings, and so on. Any objections? . . . OK.

And he begins.

Gestalt therapists are aware, of course, that such instructions alone will not keep clients from trying to turn their lives over to therapists. Ultimately the only way therapists can keep from being manipulated is to be mature individuals who take responsibility for their own lives and give up trying to be responsible for others. Such individuals have adequate inner support so that they are not dependent on clients liking or needing them, nor are they afraid of colleagues condemning them for being in therapy what they want to be and not what clients or other professionals believe they should be. Perls (1969a) was not afraid, for example, to write that if a client rattled on in a meaningless monologue, he would take a snooze if he felt sleepy, even though such a response would be frowned upon by traditional therapists and clients alike. Such an honest response would, however, be sure to frustrate a client who was trying to make Perls responsible for making therapy an exciting adventure.

Part of the gestalt therapist's responsibility is to be in the here and now, just as clients are invited to be in the present. Being present-centered means that gestalt therapists cannot use any predetermined pattern of exercises in therapy. An exercise is selected because at that moment the gestalt therapist believes that it can allow the client to become more aware of what is keeping the client from remaining in the here and now. If clients continue to drift back into the resentment of the past by blaming their parents for their problems, for example, the gestalt therapist can suggest that they imagine that the parent is present in the empty chair and that they are now free to express to the parent what they always held back from saying. Such expression in the present of unfinished resentments can begin to allow clients to bring closure to their blaming game with their parents.

While the pattern of exercises cannot be predetermined, the gestalt therapist does have a wealth of exercises that can be called upon at any time to increase awareness. In *Gestalt Therapy* (Perls et al., 1951), a variety of these exercises are systematically presented so that readers can experience their own blocks of awareness. Theoretically the exercises that can be used to stimulate awareness are limited only by the creativity of the therapist. In practice, however, most gestalt therapists seem to fall back on the classical exercises of Perls (1947; 1969a; Perls et al., 1951). Most recently Levitsky and Perls (1970) have articulated the most commonly used gestalt exercises or games. The exercises that are most involved in consciousness raising include:

1. *Games of dialogue*, in which patients carry on a dialogue between polarities of their personality, such as a repressed masculine polarity confronting a dominant feminine polarity.
2. *I take responsibility*, in which clients are asked to end every statement about themselves with "and I take responsibility for it."
3. *Playing the projection*, in which clients play the role of the person involved

in any of their projections, such as playing their parents when they blame their parents.

4. *Reversals*, in which patients are to act out the very opposite of the way they usually are in order to experience some hidden polarity of themselves.

5. *Rehearsals*, in which patients reveal to the group the thinking or rehearsal they most commonly do in preparation for playing social roles, including the role of patient.

6. *Marriage counseling games*, in which spouses take turns revealing their most positive and negative feelings about each other to each other.

7. *May I feed you a sentence?*, in which the therapist asks permission to repeat and try on for size a statement that the therapist feels is particularly significant for the patient.

Gestalt therapists do not interpret what clients have to say while participating in gestalt exercises. Interpretation is seen as a representation of the traditional therapist's maya, the therapist's fantasy that the real meaning of a client and the client's world can be found in the therapist's favorite theory rather than in the client's present experience. Interpretation is just another form of one-upmanship. Interpretation is a way for therapists to convince clients that they should listen to the magnificent mind of the therapist rather than to their own senses. In practice, however, the use of the "May I feed you a sentence?" game comes awfully close to straight interpretations, although gestaltists prefer to see this exercise as feedback in which the client is free to actively spit out the therapist's message if it doesn't fit.

Gestalt therapists increase the consciousness of their clients by allowing their own eyes and ears to serve as a source of feedback that provides clients with information about themselves that has not been in their awareness. Clients are already aware of the sentences they have spoken, so gestalt therapists do not reflect on their clients' words, as would Rogerian therapists. Gestalt therapists are much more in touch with the nonverbal expressions of clients, the quality of their voices, their posture, and their movements. Gestalt therapists feed back what they see or hear, especially what they see as bodily blocks to greater awareness. They ask clients not only to attend to their nonverbal expressions, such as their arms folded across their chest, but also to become their arms in order to express how they are tensing up the muscles to keep from opening up the feelings in their hearts. With such action-oriented exercises derived from the therapist's awareness, clients begin to experience a deeper awareness that emerges from the depths of their bodies rather than off the top of their heads.

Catharsis

As clients become increasingly aware of their phony games and roles, as they become more aware of their phobic avoidance of the here and now, including their bodily blocks to the present, they are less and less able to run from themselves. The fear of being themselves, however, can bring them to an impasse. They will want to communicate to the therapist that they are unable to continue on their own, that the therapist must take over for them or they will go crazy, panic, or leave therapy. They try to convince therapists that their catastrophic expectations are real and not just leftover childhood fantasies. By pressing ahead, therapists communicate through their actions that they believe that clients do indeed have the inner strength to continue on past the impasse into their areas of deadness. With sensitively selected exercises clients can begin to reown the aspects of their personality that were sacrificed in the name of roles and games. Clients can begin to release all of the emotions that have been held back because of the catastrophic expectations that others will not love or approve of them if they are truly human.

THE CLIENT'S WORK

In order to attain such cathartic release clients must take responsibility for continuing in therapy when they most want to run. The therapist will not try to talk them into staying in the "hot seat" if they feel it is getting too hot—they can and often do leave before the explosive fireworks begin. If clients do stay in the hot seat, then they must also be responsible for really throwing themselves into the suggested exercises and not just passively play at going along with therapy. If clients are prepared to own back what has been dead within, then they must be willing to participate in gestalt dream work. Dreams are used in gestalt therapy because they are seen as the most spontaneous part of one's personality. Dreams are the time and place in which people can express all parts of themselves that have been disowned in the rat race to succeed at daily roles. For dreams to be cathartic, however, clients cannot just talk about their dreams, they must act out their dreams. Clients are encouraged to become each detail of a dream, no matter how insignificant it may seem, in order to give expression to the richness of their personality. When we become as rich and as spontaneous as our dreams, then we can be healthy and whole again.

At a time when I was preoccupied with my promotion and my tenure I found myself unable to experience any joy, not even the joy of sex. I went to a friend who is a gestalt therapist, and he asked me to conjure up a daydream rather than a dream. The daydream that emerged spontaneously was of skiing. He asked me to be the mountains, and I began to experience how warm I was when I was at my base. As I got closer to the top, what looked so beautiful was also very cold and frozen. He asked me to be the snow, and I expressed how hard and icy I could be near the top. People tripped over me there and were unable to cut through me because of how hard I was. But near the bottom people ran over me easily and wore me out. When we finished I did not feel like crying or like shouting. I felt like skiing. So I went, leaving my articles and books behind. In the sparkle of the snow and the sun I realized again what Goethe had suggested through Faust; that our joy in living emerges through deeds and not through words. In my rush to succeed I was committing one of the cardinal sins against myself, the sin of not being active enough.

Since catharsis in gestalt therapy occurs primarily as a result of clients expressing their inner experiences, such as their dreams, we can talk about the process as a form of *corrective emotional experiencing*. Gestalt therapy is also a *dramatic* therapy, however, inasmuch as it is often done in groups or workshops, and the corrective emotional experiences of the person on the hot seat serve as cathartic releases for the people who are actively observing what is occurring there.

THE THERAPIST'S WORK

Since catharsis in gestalt therapy can be very dramatic, we can conceive of the therapist's work as beginning by setting the stage for the event. The group waits with anticipation for someone to step forward to fill the emotionally charged hot seat. The therapist's attention is then focused on the client like a spotlight. The therapist suggests that the best scene for now is some particular exercise, such as dream work. The script is created mostly by the client, who decides what dream to act out. Once the client enters the scene, the therapist is like a director who is prepared to help the client live rather than just play a part in the dramatic exercise.

Gestalt therapists must be aware of when clients are trying to avoid the pain and fear of taking off their masks. Therapists try to block such avoidances by giving feedback and directing the client's attention to maneuvers that are being used to avoid, such as expressing important parts of a dream in a soft voice. If feedback alone does not produce change, then the gestalt therapist will challenge clients to put more of themselves into the exercises, like a famous director challenging actors to give their best performance. Challenging clients to be more intense is especially effective in our competitive society where people are so geared to meet any challenge. "OK, let's try it again with a fuller voice!" the gestalt therapist might yell out. Such challenges also communicate the therapist's belief that clients do indeed have the inner resources to throw themselves more fully into therapy, even when they are facing frightening or embarrassing scenes.

The gestalt therapist can use other techniques of the theater to intensify the situation. Clients may be challenged to use the repetition or exaggeration game (Levitsky & Perls, 1970) until the true affect is expressed. Such exaggeration or repetition is exemplified in the following excerpt from Perls (1969a, p. 293):

Fritz: Now talk to your Top Dog! Stop nagging.

Jane [*loud, pained*]**:** Leave me alone.

Fritz: Yah, again.

Jane: Leave me alone.

Fritz: Again.

Jane [*screaming it and crying*]**:** Leave me alone!

Fritz: Again.

Jane [*she screams it, a real blast*]**:** Leave me alone! I don't have to do what you say! [*Still crying*] I don't have to be that good! I don't have to be in this chair! I don't have to. You make me. You make me come here! [*Screams*] Aarhh! You make me pick my face [*crying*], that's what you do. [*Screams and cries*] Aarhh! I'd like to kill you.

Fritz: Say this again.

Jane: I'd like to kill you.

Fritz: Again.

Jane: I'd like to *kill* you.

Gestalt therapists will also direct clients to change their lines somewhat toward a more emotional and responsible direction, following the rule of using

"I" language (Levitsky & Perls, 1970). Fritz (1969a, p. 115) demonstrates this direction with Max.

Max: I feel the tenseness in my stomach and in my hands.

Fritz: *The* tenseness. Here we've got a noun. Now *the* tenseness is a noun. Now change the noun, the thing, into a verb.

Max: I am tense. My hands are tense.

Fritz: Your hands are tense. They have nothing to do with you.

Max: I am tense.

Fritz: You are tense. How are you tense? What are you doing?

Max: I am tensing myself.

Fritz: That's it.

An outstanding therapist like Perls is also able to use comic relief to reduce tension and humor to release joy. Fritz was admired for his spontaneity, including his humor, which emerged in his workshops. It is perhaps in the use of humor where it is most obvious that a gestalt therapist cannot plan effective therapy. For humor to be effective the therapist must be free to be spontaneous, to capture the moment in creative humor. Cathartic experiences, including the joy of humor, appear to be the dramatic results of clients who are struggling to be spontaneous interacting with therapists who are able to be spontaneous.

THEORY OF THERAPEUTIC CONTENT

Intrapersonal Conflicts

The most important problems for gestalt therapy are conflicts within the individual, such as conflicts between Top Dog and Under Dog, or between the person's social self and natural self, or between the disowned parts of the person and the catastrophic expectations that keep the person from expressing polarities that may meet with disapproval or rejection. While Perls did gestalt therapy in groups, his therapy was not really a group therapy in which the important content is the relationship between people in the group. Perls's therapy was really an individual therapy occurring in a group setting. The important content occurs within the individual as the client acts out gestalt exercises that bring an increasing awareness and a cathartic release of the disowned parts of the personality. Other individuals in the workshop relate to the person on the hot seat vicariously rather than directly. Such vicarious relating can produce cathartic effects, but the presence of people other than the therapist is not essential to the work that is going on with the person in the hot seat.

ANXIETY AND DEFENSES

For Perls (1969a) anxiety is the gap between the now and then, the here and there. Whenever we leave the reality of now and become preoccupied with the future, we experience anxiety. If we are anticipating future performances, such as exams, lectures, or therapy sessions, then our anxiety is nothing more than stage fright. How will I perform on the exam? How will my lecture go over? What will I do with that difficult client? We can also experience anxious anticipation over wonderful things that will happen—I just can't wait for that vacation to come. Many people fill this gap between the now and the future with all types of planned activities, repetitive jobs, and insurance policies to make the future predictable. These people try to replace anxiety with the security of sameness, but in the process they lose the richness of future possibilities. The problem is that in a rapidly changing society the people who try to hold onto the sameness of the status quo can become more and more panicky about the changing future.

For Perls the solution to anxiety is obvious—live in the here and now and not in the gap. By learning to be fully in the present, clients can transform anxiety into excitement. Rather than ruminating anxiously about aging, for example, people can experience the excitement of making fresh contact each day with an ever-changing environment.

Most people, however, avoid direct and immediate contact with the here and now through a variety of defensive maneuvers (Perls et al., 1951; Polster & Polster, 1973). Projectors distort experiences of themselves and their world by attributing the disowned parts of themselves to others in the environment. They avoid the excitement of their own sexuality, for example, by perceiving others, such as therapists, as being preoccupied with sex. Introjectors appear to take in the world but in a passive and nondiscriminating manner. They never really integrate and assimilate new experiences into their personal identity. They are like the gullible oral characters who swallow anything others tell them.

Retroflectors withdraw from the environment by turning back upon themselves what they would like to do to someone else or by doing to themselves what they would like someone else to do to them. A woman who would have loved to chew out her mother, for example, avoided the risk of explosion by chronically grinding her teeth. An introverted man avoided reaching out for sensual strokes from others by becoming preoccupied with masturbation.

Deflectors avoid direct contact by having their actions or reactions be chronically off-target. They may go off on tangents when talking, talk in generalities to avoid more emotion-laden specifics, or in other ways fail to get to the point of an interaction. Deflectors can avoid an impact from others, including therapists, by experiencing themselves as bored, confused, or in the wrong place.

Confluence is a means whereby individuals avoid the excitement of novelty and difference by emphasizing the superficial similarities of any new contacts. Confluence frequently involves an agreement not to disagree. Confluence ultimately leads to phony conformity because of the security that is gained by going along with the crowd rather than acting from the center of oneself.

Perls (1969a) also emphasized how often thinking is used as a means of avoiding the here and now. Perls agreed with Freud's statement that "Denken ist Probearbeit"—thinking is trial work or, as Perls prefers, thinking is rehearsing. Thinking is a means whereby we prepare ourselves for social role playing.

Perls (1969a) suggests that most people play two kinds of intellectual games as part of social role playing. The comparing game or "more than" game is a form of one-upmanship in which intellect is used to convince others that "My house is better than yours," or "I'm greater than you," or "I'm more miserable than you," or "My therapy is better than yours," or "My theory is more valid than yours." The other intellectualizing game is the fitting game in which we try to fit other people or other therapies into our favorite concepts or theories of how the world is supposed to be. Or even worse, we may struggle to fit ourselves into our favorite concept or theory of what we are supposed to be.

SELF-ESTEEM

Shaky self-esteem is not the source of neuroses but one of the results of remaining immature and dependent. As long as our esteem remains dependent on the approval and evaluation of others, we will remain preoccupied with what others think of us and with trying to meet their expectations. A solid sense of esteem seems to be one of the natural rewards of discovering that we indeed have the inner strength to be self-supportive. Therapists who do supportive therapy, which includes trying to shore up their patient's shaky esteem, in the long run can just add to the patients' esteem problems by implictly telling them that they do not have the inner resources to support themselves. On the other hand, the tough stance of the gestalt therapist, who refuses to give unnecessary support even when the patient is crying for it, is implicitly saying to patients that they have the inner strength to stand on their own. By tapping into that inner strength, clients will find a solid basis on which to feel good about themselves.

RESPONSIBILITY

We have already seen that accepting responsibility for one's life is a critical part of being a healthy, mature human being. Developmentally, people avoid taking responsibility either because they were spoiled and just find it easier to manipulate others into taking care of them or because they fear parental disapproval or rejection if they respond in a manner that is too different from what their parents expect. Unlike traditional existentialists, Perls does not see responsibility as being avoided because of existential anxiety and guilt that are inherently part of having to make decisions without knowing whether or not one's decisions will work or fail. For Perls, decisions about end-goals emerge naturally when one is centered as a natural organism. Problems with decisions occur only when people are not centered.

With a source of direction that is so natural, there is little need for existential guilt in the gestalt system. Perls (1969a) suggests that most of what people call guilt is really unexpressed resentment. Guilt over premarital sex, for example, is frequently unexpressed resentment toward one's parents or church for trying to keep a person from satisfying the natural sexual end-goals that emerge when the person is truly present-centered. Express the resentment either directly or in an empty-chair exercise in therapy, and the guilt will soon be gone.

Perls does not address the difficult aspect of responsibility that involves an obligation to live up to a commitment that one has made. He does make it clear that when he talks about responsibility he is not talking about obligations. Since a mature person does not accept responsibility for others, perhaps there are no obligations for a person who lives in the now other than to be true to oneself. For people living in the now it may be clear that making commitments is future-oriented and foolish since we cannot predict that at some future point it will be most important to act on a commitment that was made in the past.

Interpersonal Conflicts

INTIMACY AND SEXUALITY

Luthman (1972) gives an exciting picture of what intimacy is like from a gestalt approach. Contrary to convention, intimate relationships begin with a commitment to ourselves, not to another. We are committed to presenting ourselves as we are, not pretending to be something the other expects or prefers. If who we really are is not liked by another, then it is best for us to learn that early rather than waste our time on a relationship that is bound to fail no matter how much we pretend otherwise.

As we relate, we accept differences as opportunities for growth, not as reasons for conflict. Differences are bound to bring frustration, but for gestaltists frustration is welcome as a stimulus for further maturation. As we relate, we also accept that what we like and dislike is a statement about us and not a put-down of our partner. If we don't like our partner's cooking, for example, that is a statement about our taste and not a reason for saying that our partner is a lousy cook.

As differences emerge we have to be willing to stay with an issue until all of our feelings are out in the open. We then can make compromises up to the limits or boundaries of who we are as individuals. We cannot compromise ourselves away just to keep a relationship going because such compromises will lead to smoldering resentment that will eventually poison the relationship. Our limits should not be seen as attempts to control the other person, but rather as the contours of who we are. We may find that once all of our feelings are out in the open, neither of us can compromise far enough to allow the relationship to continue. Such a discovery is not a reason to blame or to hate but rather to accept that we just cannot make it together. On the other hand, if we do make it together we can love even more because we are with a person who is strong enough to be authentic first and our partner second.

While Perls has written little about sex, others such as Rosenberg (1973) and Otto and Otto (1972) have presented a series of exercises directed at helping sex to be a more total or holistic experience. The gestalt emphases on being in touch with our bodies, on getting back to our senses, and on breaking out of old habits and responding spontaneously with our whole organism are critical in freeing people to experience how sex can be so much more than genital orgasm. Learning more integrated breathing, more natural pelvic movements, how to make fantasies reality, how to enjoy the humor in sex, and how to explode into orgasm are part of making sex a more total experience.

COMMUNICATION

Since Perls worked mainly with individuals and not with ongoing relationships, he had little to say about communication conflicts. He does seem to suggest, however, that most communication is just part of social role playing. People chatter away about how great they are, how important or miserable or meager their roles in life are. As an action-oriented therapist, Perls prefers to get away from so much talk and to let real feelings be expressed in action, such as dancing to communicate joy or weeping to express sorrow. Perls was certainly astute at helping people become aware of their nonverbal communication, of what their body was attempting to say in its various postures and movements.

When we must resort to words, conflicts can be kept to a minimum by following several rules of gestalt therapy. First of all, we should try to communicate as much as possible in the imperative form, since the demand is the only real form of communication, according to Perls (1970). When we ask someone a question, for example, we are really placing a demand on that person. Instead of saying, "Would you like to go to the movies tonight?", we should be direct and say, "Let's go to the movies tonight!" With such direct demands the person with whom we are communicating knows exactly where we are at and what we want. That person then can choose to respond directly to our demands rather than respond to a question. Since what we have to say is really a statement about us and not about the other, we should own our statements by talking mainly in "I" language. Rather than say, "You really make me angry because of how rotten you treat me," we would say, "I am angry because I let you treat me so rotten. From now on treat me with more consideration!"

HOSTILITY

Problems with hostility are boundary problems. Those aspects of the world that we identify with and that we include within our ego boundaries are experienced as friendly, lovable, and open to our kindness. Those parts of the world that we experience as outside of our boundaries are alien, threatening, and subject to our hostility. If white individuals identify with white supremacy, for example, and exclude blacks from their ego boundaries, they feel free to direct hostility toward blacks and be at war with them. If white individuals, however, identify with the goals of blacks and support their efforts for wholeness in our society, then their enemy becomes racists who are outside their ego boundaries and fair game for their hostility.

In intimate relationships we expand our boundaries to include the other within our identity and create an experience of "we-ness." But even in such close relationships we usually cannot accept all aspects of another because we do not own all the aspects of ourselves. What we are most likely to be hostile toward in our intimates are the qualities in them that remind us of what we have disowned and projected outside of our boundaries into an alien world. If we are hostile toward the tardiness of a friend, we should look within to see if we have disowned certain desires to not have to live our lives by a clock.

If we do not express our resentments toward our intimates, we will begin to close off communication with them out of fear that openness might lead to our hostility being released. We have failed to bring closure to an issue, and the resentment remains an important signal that a gestalt is pressing for completion. In therapy clients are encouraged to express intensely the hostility and resentment toward the empty chair that represents intimates with whom they are having trouble communicating. After releasing their hostility, clients need to begin to forgive their intimates for not being perfect so that they can begin to forgive themselves for not being perfect.

CONTROL

Immature people are constantly involved in battles over interpersonal control. They either play a helpless, sick role in trying to manipulate others to take care of them, or they play a perfectionist Top Dog role in which they assume the responsibility for trying to get others to see the light and be more like them. They are acting out on an interpersonal level their intrapersonal pathology in which there is a constant struggle for control between Top Dog and Under Dog. Only with maturation and integration can people give up the constant struggle for control and live by the gestalt creed (Perls, 1970, p. 1):

I do my own thing and you do your thing.
I am not in this world to live up to your expectations,
And you are not in this world to live up to mine.
You are you, and I am I,
And if by chance we find each other, it's beautiful.
If not, it can't be helped.

Individuo-Social Conflicts

ADJUSTMENT VERSUS TRANSCENDENCE

Gestalt therapy is clearly a therapy of transcendence. Adjustment to society might have been an acceptable goal for therapy at some time in the past when society was more stable and healthy. But, like many critics of modern society, Perls (1970, p. 23) says: "I believe we are living in an insane society and that you only have the choice either to participate in this collective psychosis or to take risks and become healthy and perhaps also crucified."

To some extent all healthy individuals will experience themselves as outside the boundaries of society. They will experience themselves as aliens, always potential targets for the violence of society. Alienation then is the condition of the mature person, of the fully aware person, as long as society remains insane.

As Denes-Radomisli (1976) points out, to adjust to a brutalizing society means to give up more and more of yourself. To adjust to riding in the New York subways, for example, we have to give up our sense of being human, deserving of some courtesy, and have to be willing to be jostled and shoved and to shove and jostle in return. In order to be relatively comfortable in such a situation, we have to give up our awareness of being mistreated and of mistreating others. With successful adjustment we can soon be unable to feel human at all and get along just fine as a role or a robot.

Unfortunately, the alternatives for most people are alienation from society, in which the healthy person is one of the strangers in a strange land, and alienation from oneself, in which the unhealthy person is self-estranged. The final resolution for Perls was to seek transcendence by creating a gestalt community in Canada in which a limited number of healthy individuals could both be themselves and be integrated in a community of whole people.

IMPULSE CONTROL

Organismic impulses need not be controlled but need to be completed. Organismic impulses, such as seeking food when hungry or sex when aroused, are not dangerous to the individual, but rather the completion of such needs is what helps create an individual. These organismic impulses are a biological source of motivation and direction that allows individuals to rise above being just a social role. These biological sources of self-direction are relatively culture-free, and individuals can trust in their bodies to lead them to a healthy life rather than having to follow the cultural pressures to conform to an insane society. If people were raised to trust the messages from within their body, we could have a society of free and fulfilled people who let each other be rather than a society of rapers and ravagers.

RULES FOR LIVING

Rules for living sounds like a much too rigid, habitual, and determined approach to life. The only healthy organismic rule is to live in the here and now, which is a spontaneous style of life. It is a less predictable style also, and in that respect healthy individuals can be threatening to those who are ruled by society and need predictability in order to be comfortable.

Beyond Conflict to Fulfillment

MEANING

The meaning that comes from living in the now is found in the awareness that every second in our one existence is being lived afresh. No fuller life can be imagined. No regrets occur among those who jump into the stream of the present, since regrets are the plague of those stuck in the past. There are no preoccupations about the future, since we trust that our healthiest future emerges out of a present in which we attend to and complete our most urgent gestalts. There is only one authentic goal for the future, and that is to actualize ourselves as responsible and whole human beings. If that is not meaningful enough, then why not try to be a kangaroo or a king?

VALUES

What we most value at any particular time is determined by the particular organismic end-goal that is emerging into our awareness. If we are hungry right now, then food will be most valued; if we are really thirsty, than a refreshing liquid is more valuable than words, money, status, or approval. As natural beings we possess a natural intelligence that tells us what to value each moment if we have sense enough to listen. Trouble comes when we listen to our social intellect and believe that one particular value is always most important, whether it be love, success, or security. With such social values in our mind we can be willing to sacrifice what is most valuable in living—our ability to be a natural, spontaneous human being.

IDEAL INDIVIDUAL

The ideal outcome for gestalt therapy is to have people discover that they do not and never really did need a therapist. Ideal clients accept that in spite of all their manipulations to the contrary, they have the inner strength to stand on their own and be themselves. Such individuals have discovered the center of their lives, the awareness of being grounded in oneself. In being centered they take full responsibility for the direction of their lives and do not blame anything on their parents or their past. From their core they find the strength to take the risks of being spontaneous and unpredictable, including the risks of being ostracized or crucified if that is the ultimate consequence for being themselves. In return for such risks the ideal individual earns the freedom to be creative, to be truly funny, to dance with joy and to be overwhelmed with grief, to be outraged with anger, and to be totally engaged in orgasm.

THEORY OF THE THERAPEUTIC RELATIONSHIP

In Rogerian terms, Perls certainly indicated that an effective gestalt therapist needed to be more congruent or, as he would prefer, more mature, than the clients. If therapists are to be self-supporting enough to resist the patients' pressures to match their expectations, the therapists must have developed adequate maturity in their own lives.

It is also a rule of gestalt therapy (Levitsky & Perls, 1970) that the relationship should be an I-thou relationship, or what Rogers would call a *genuine encounter*. In practice, however, Perls has been criticized by such colleagues as Kempler (1973) for always playing the Top Dog and thereby forcing the client into an Under Dog or patient role. Kempler is certainly correct that in the available transcripts of Perls's work, the personal Perls or Perls as an "I" is missing. The very format of the hot seat puts clients in an Under Dog position in which they would be directed in exercises by the Top Dog therapist. If clients confronted Perls to look at his own behavior, he would counter with a psycho-analytic type of move that forced the clients to look at their own motives for making such suggestions.

Both in theory and in practice Perls seemed to agree with Rogers on the therapist's need to be able to respond with accurate empathy to what was going on in clients. Therapists need, for example, to be able to experience the projections that clients are placing on them or the parts of the clients' personalities that are being disowned and to feed back accurately these blind spots. Neither in theory nor in practice did Perls accept the Rogerian concept of unconditional positive regard. For Perls such behavior on the therapist's part would encourage the infantilization of clients, since whatever they do is fine with the therapist. Clients must learn from therapists that if they act in immature or irresponsible ways, mature people, including therapists, will react with anger, impatience, boredom, or any number of negative responses.

At its best the gestalt therapeutic relationship is part of both the process and the content of therapy. As part of the process of being in the here and now, the therapist insists on remaining present-centered regardless of the patient's attempts to flee from the now. The therapist frustrates the client's immature attempts to make the therapist take over the client's life by playing helpless, crazy, suicidal, or seductive. Through such frustrations in the relationship the client is forced to grow, to become more aware of the games being played to remain unaware and immature. Gestalt therapists use their own awareness to realize when patients are attempting to avoid parts of who they are and to block such avoidance by introducing exercises or exhortations designed to break through the patient's blocks. The relationship between the therapist's greater awareness, greater maturity, and ability to be in the now and the client's inability to stay in the now and to accept responsibility for avoiding being natural is an important part of the gestalt therapeutic process.

The clients' projections of disowned parts of their personalities onto therapists are an important part of the content of gestalt therapy. Also to the extent that gestalt therapists do indeed encourage a Top Dog/Under Dog relationship, they provide a present battleground for clients to fight out their conflicts with authority and with their conscience or internalized parent.

To the extent that gestalt books such as Perls et al.'s *Gestalt Therapy* (1951) or Rosenberg's *Total Orgasm* (1973) suggest that people can radically expand their consciousness and cathartically release their energies by participating in the exercises presented, the suggestion is made that a therapeutic relationship is not a necessary part of gestalt therapy. Certainly there is no disputing that such a relationship can enhance the effectiveness of therapy, but the relationship may in fact not be essential for healthy growth to occur through gestalt exercises. As Kempler (1973) points out, Perls himself became concerned late in his life that all too many proteges were attempting to only learn techniques instead of letting their work be a natural consequence of who they were and letting their responses to clients be a natural consequence of an authentic relationship with clients. But Perls had already set the example both in his writings and in his workshops that the gestalt exercises seem to be more essential parts of the content and process of gestalt therapy than is an authentic relationship.

PRACTICALITIES OF GESTALT THERAPY

Perls said that to do his therapy all he needed was a chair for the hot seat, an empty chair for the client's role playing, a client willing to enter the hot seat, and an audience or group willing to participate in the work going on between therapist and client. Perls seldom saw clients in an office, especially in his most famous years, since most of his therapy was done in workshops, lectures, or seminars under the sun at Esalen. Many of his clients had only one therapeutic encounter with Perls, and yet the number of people that believed Perls had an impact on them is amazing—apparently just watching Perls work with another person could produce a dramatic impact.

Gestalt therapists still prefer to do therapy in a group setting even though their work occurs primarily between the therapist and the person in the hot seat and not between group members. Most gestalt therapists also tend to see their clients weekly, although they seem to prefer at least two hours with a group and frequently longer, including marathon sessions. In Perls's workshops clients did not pay extra for the therapy they received while in the hot seat but rather just paid the entrance fee to the workshop or lecture. Most gestalt therapists charge a more standard group therapy fee of $15–$25 per session.

In terms of professional disciplines, gestalt therapists include psychologists, social workers, psychiatrists, pastoral counselors, and educators. While many tend to be more informal about their gestalt training, the more respectable route includes a minimum of one year of intensive training at one of the gestalt training institutes. Gestalt therapists also tend to be more informal about screening and follow-up in therapy, following Perls's precedent that it is the client's responsibility to decide to enter or terminate treatment. Length of treatment seems to vary considerably from one workshop session, to a marathon, to weekly meetings for six months to a year,or longer.

EFFECTIVENESS OF GESTALT THERAPY

Since gestalt therapy is seen as a growth-oriented therapy, it is not surprising that almost all of the controlled research on the effectiveness of gestalt therapy has been done with relatively normal subjects seeking growth experiences. In the earliest study, Foulds (1971) tested the hypothesis that a gestalt group of normal college students would attain an increased self-actualization as measured by the Personal Orientation Inventory (POI). Following eight four-and-a-half-hour sessions, the members of the gestalt group reported significant growth on 8 of the 12 POI scales, whereas the matched no-treatment controls reported no significant change. The author suggests that the scale changes for the gestalt group indicate reduction in compulsivity and dogmatism, greater awareness of one's needs and feelings, self-acceptance, and greater ability to develop meaningful relationships. No placebo control group was run.

Goodstein (1972) compared gestalt therapy with transactional analysis in treatment marathons with normal psychology students randomly assigned to treatment and control groups. It was predicted and confirmed that authoritarianism would decrease most and creativity would increase most in the gestalt group, whereas the prediction was confirmed that anxiety would decrease most in the transactional analysis group. Neither self-esteem nor personal adjustment improved significantly for either treatment group as compared with the controls.

Salmon (1972) researched the effectiveness of gestalt self-awareness exercises in increasing counseling effectiveness. Subjects were normal students drawn from courses for individuals preparing for helping professions. The gestalt subjects were given two group sessions plus written gestalt homework. Only one significant improvement was found for the gestalt group when compared with the no-treatment control group on the six measures used, and the author concluded that the exercises were not effective with the samples used.

In their work on encounter groups, Lieberman, Yalom, and Miles (1973) included gestalt groups among the 10 types of therapy groups run with normal college students from Stanford. None of the therapy groups was more effective in producing immediate or six-month changes than were the control groups. On the basis of self-reports, the therapy and control groups saw themselves as changing positively regardless of special experiences.

In the only controlled study with a somewhat troubled population, Gannon (1972) investigated the effects of gestalt therapy groups on the interpersonal attitudes of problem high school students. Sixty subjects were selected on the basis of negative school behaviors, high absenteeism, and police reports. The subjects were randomly assigned to one of three groups: (1) gestalt groups run by trained leaders, (2) placebo groups that had special team teaching, discussions, and field trips, and (3) a no-treatment control group. From a variety of measures, including a Semantic Differential of Attitudes and Behavior and two measures of feedback from participants and teachers, it was concluded that the gestalt group did move in the direction of improved openness and contact as a result of therapy. Unfortunately the subjects were not tested on changes in the problem behaviors that were used as the criterion for participation in the study.

The results of the studies on the growth-oriented effectiveness of gestalt therapy are at best mixed, with one study (Goodstein, 1972) finding increased growth when compared with an alternative treatment; one study (Lieberman et al., 1973) finding no advantage for gestalt therapy when compared with alternative treatments or no treatments; one study (Foulds, 1971) reporting greater growth compared with no treatment; and one study (Salmon, 1972) finding no growth in counseling effectiveness when compared with no treatment. In the one study (Gannon, 1972) thus far reported with a more troubled population, gestalt therapy did seem to produce greater growth with problem high school students than did either a special classroom experience or no treatment.

CRITICISMS OF GESTALT THERAPY

From a Behavioral Perspective

We must recognize that at a societal level the ultimate outcome of gestalt therapy would be anarchy. "You do your thing and I do my thing" may sound romantic to some, but it is a shallow slogan that reinforces the development of narcissistic and egocentric individuals who have little reason to be concerned with others. Perls states directly that his ideal individual would not take responsibility for anyone else. What happens then to the socializing responsibility of parents? Is there any evidence that human beings can live in relatively harmonious and secure societies if social expectations and approval are rejected as significant stimuli and consequences for helping to direct human behavior? Perls seems to forget that his therapy at Esalen was appealing to those who already have gone through a socialization process and tend to reject violence or force as means-whereby they satisfy such organismic end-goals as sex. Let the gestaltists test their therapy with undersocialized individuals such as psychopathic types of prisoners to see what type of community they would create.

From a Psychoanalytic Perspective

Where ego was, let there be id! The naive gestaltist would like to deny that there are indeed biological impulses that can be overwhelming to both the individual's mental well-being and the social order. What would gestaltists do with such patients as paranoids whose ego processes are in danger of being overwhelmed by rage? Encourage more rage? So much talk about responsibility and yet the gestaltists encourage professional irresponsibility by suggesting to potential patients that if they want to go crazy or commit suicide that's up to them. Such a philosophy may work fine in workshops filled with growth-seeking normals. But it is certainly dangerous as an approach to a typical caseload of patients that includes people barely able to hold onto their sanity, let alone able to be mature, self-supporting, whole human beings.

From an Eclectic Perspective

While Perls believed that he was following the existential heritage, which includes the rejection of Cartesian dualism that overvalues mind at the expense of body, what Perls in fact left us is a reverse dualism that overvalues body at the expense of mind. Perls's disesteeming of thinking encourages an irrational anti-intellectualism that could result in empty-headed organisms that are no more whole than are the disembodied products from the Cartesian tradition. Gestalt therapy is obviously in need of a cognitive theory to balance its overemphasis on biology. Some eclectics, such as James and Jongeward (1971), have suggested an integration of gestalt with the cognitive aspects of transactional analysis, while others, such as Dublin (1975) and Denes-Radomisli (1976), encourage an integration of gestalt exercises within a more classical existentialism. Until some integration is made giving equal weight to the cognitive capacities of human beings, gestalt therapy will remain a movement that attempted to balance Descartes by speaking for the body but unfortunately ended up flipping the philosophical cart, with the body now the Top Dog.

A GESTALT ANALYSIS OF MRS. C.

Like so many people in our society, Mrs. C. was raised to disown the socially unacceptable aspects of her body. For most of her life she seems to have succeeded in disowning the sources of her sexual desires and the bodily basis for her angry feelings. Since the onset of her full-blown neurosis, Mrs. C. has been engaged in trying to disown her entire body by washing it away. Fortunately the biological basis of her existence will not just lie down and die; her body keeps sending out messages that remind her that she is human and therefore subject to diseases, anger, and sexual desires. Mrs. C. refuses to listen to her body and instead keeps repeating obsessively in her mind and compulsively in her actions," Wash away body, wash away," until she is now little more than a washed-out dishrag.

Mrs. C. reports that her childhood disowning of sex and anger was due to catastrophic expectations that her parents would punish or even disown her if she did not play the role of a good, clean little girl. How much these catastrophic expectations were based on reality and how much on fantastic projections cannot be told from the record. The important point is that these fears were part of the phobic layer that motivated Mrs. C. to spend most of her existence in the phony layer of playing the model child, model mother, and now model neurotic.

At the same time her symptoms began, Mrs. C. was probably becoming increasingly dissatisfied with how responsible she had to be for everyone else, with no time or energy to realize who she really was. Five kids and a pregnancy, diapers, dishes, disease, and pinworms on top of it all! Who wouldn't want to yell out in anger and in despair? But Mrs. C. never had the guts to stand up for herself, to do what she really wanted to do, so why would we expect her to do it now? Instead she projected the responsibility for her problems onto the pinworms and then proceeded to spend her life trying to wash away the pinworms and herself. If she had confronted who she really was, a person able to get very angry, a person desiring to be free, and a person more egocentric than she ever dared to be, her childish catastrophic expectations would tell her that she would be rejected and hurt. So don't think about who you really are; think only about the pinworms and the washing!

The reason the pinworm episode represented an impasse, a sick point, was that Mrs. C. had never become a mature person, responsible to only herself. Now there were clearly too many kids, too much illness, and too many demands for Mrs. C. to move ahead on her own. With the development of such dramatic neurotic symptoms, Mrs. C. could get others, including her therapists, to try to take care of her. It was also apparent that Mrs. C. was using her symptoms to manipulate others, such as getting George to attend to her by keeping track of her shower ritual. Apparently Mrs. C. was finding it easier to remain sick and manipulative than to become healthier and stand on her own.

To work through her impasse, Mrs. C. would have to face the implosive layer of her neurosis. She would have to experience the deadness of her genitals, the total emptiness of her past 10 years, and the loss of her very center. Since she had projected the responsibility for her miserable life onto pinworms, it is no wonder that her life now centered around pinworms. Mrs. C. had no energy left to feel alive, since her organismic energy was all tied up in the rigid, neurotic patterns that had become her life.

With almost all of her energy invested in neurosis, Mrs. C. would have to go through some tremendous explosions to be born again. She would have to explode into grief over the loss of a whole decade of her life. She would have to let out all of her anger toward her daughter, her husband, her parents, and herself for letting her play the role of such a good daughter and such a good mother. Mrs. C. would also have to reach way back into the earliest years of her life to see if she could discover the bodily basis for her sexuality so that she could for the first time in her life explode with orgasm. Only with such potentially violent explosions could Mrs. C. ever again hope to experience the joy of living.

To face the fears of her catastrophic expectations, to have to cross the impasse and become responsible again, to have to face the pain of having been dead so long, and then to face the tremors of emotional explosions and shed her totally clean character that had been the source of her identity, would perhaps be too much for Mrs. C. She probably would be more than willing to accept a therapy that promised to improve her neurosis by letting her go back to being Mrs. Clean without having to wash all the time.

If Mrs. C. wanted more from therapy than to just return to her former immature adjustment to life, then a gestalt therapist would ask her to begin by staying in the here and now. Of course, she couldn't do it. She probably would continuously return to talking about pinworms or washing. She would insist on playing the helpless patient role and would let the therapist know how grateful she would be if the therapist could pull her out of her misery. Such maneuvers would be aimed at turning the responsibility for her miserable life over to the therapist. One of the most effective gestalt exercises could be to have her end all of her statements about her problems and her life with "and I take responsibility for it." If she could be encouraged and directed into really experiencing the possibility of being responsible for her neurosis, Mrs. C. might begin to experience some of the grief she must face over her wasted life.

A gestalt therapist might also encourage Mrs. C. to use the empty-chair technique to role play her relationship to pinworms. She would first speak for the pinworms, which might well come on like Top Dog, and then respond with her present feelings toward the pinworms. As they yell out at her, "You must wash or we'll eat you up," she might be able to begin to experience her rage toward the pinworms for dominating her life. As she began to let more anger seep out, she would probably want to avoid, lest she be punished or rejected for being a naughty, angry person. She might begin to become more conscious of how childish her catastrophic expectations are. She might also become increasingly more aware of just how much she has projected the responsibility for her problems onto the pinworms. It would also be important for the therapist to give Mrs. C. feedback about the variety of maneuvers she uses in order to get her therapist to take more direct control of her life.

As the gestalt therapist refused to be manipulated into rushing in to help Mrs. C., she might begin to experience increasing anger toward the therapist, which would be a breakthrough from preoccupation with pinworms to feeling angry in the here and now. As she stayed with her fears over being angry, she would begin to realize that her catastrophic expectations were indeed her projections—her therapist would not hurt or reject her, and she would not get pinworms.

To own back so much of disowned personality, Mrs. C. would probably have to participate in gestalt dream work. Since almost all of her waking hours have been rigidly spent in obsessions and washing, her sleeping hours would be the only time in which her disowned self could be spontaneously expressed. While it would be difficult to force Mrs. C. to vividly attend to her dreams because of all the pain and grief that would come with awaking to memories of having once been a real person, the breakthroughs could be tremendous if she began to face how much she had given up for the security of washing. Probably only through such dream work could such an absolutely rigid, habitual character like Mrs. C. begin the cathartic process of reawakening to and reowning all the vital organismic aspects of her existence.

ADLERIAN THERAPY

MAX WAS PREOCCUPIED with trying to get into Harvard Medical School. He was convinced that acceptance at such a superior school was his only chance of being able to demonstrate to others that he was not a clod. His own deep-seated feelings of inferiority were attributed to the fact that his younger brother had been favored at home and superior at school. Max himself had always been a good student but never outstanding. He believed that his college performance was handicapped by his concern that other students were spreading rumors about his being homosexual. Max was afraid that he might someday reach out and grab the penis of one of his fellow students in his all-male Catholic college.

In spite of what others might think, Max was sure that he was not homosexual. He said he had never desired sex with a male and had had two fairly satisfying relationships with females. Max believed that his obsession to reach out and grab his fellow students was a hostile desire to strike back at those who were bothering him. His goal in therapy was to extinguish his obsession with penises and with what his fellow students thought, so that he could succeed in his quest for Harvard. One of his previous therapists, himself a Harvard M.D., had assured Max that he was Harvard material. In spite of a glowing letter from the therapist, Max had failed to get into Harvard or into any other medical school, for that matter.

When I suggested to Max that his goals might be unrealistically and unnecessarily high, he didn't want to hear it. He was zealously doing postgraduate work to improve his scores on the premed tests, and there was no holding him back. As our relationship developed, I indicated to Max that I admired his ambition but felt he was too preoccupied with himself. He agreed but countered that if he received his M.D. from Harvard, then he could really do something for others. Taking a lead from Adler, I challenged Max to prove that he really cared about others. I challenged him to find a way to make at least one person a little happier each day for the next week.

That particular week the staff of our state hospital happened to be on strike. Max met my challenge by volunteering each day to help care for some of the most troubled patients. Then he went even further. He became quite upset over the way the patients were treated in the hospital and began organizing some of the other volunteers and some of the patients to form a citizens group for patients' rights. When he learned that such an organization already existed, he combined forces and was elected to the citizens advisory board.

As his concern for others increased, Max's preoccupation with penises and his peers' opinions decreased. He began an intense relationship with a female volunteer who was a strong advocate for patients' rights. His goal to get into Harvard, however, became even stronger as he decided to eventually go into psychiatry in order to make a real impact on the state hospital system.

A SKETCH OF ALFRED ADLER

Alfred Adler (1870–1937) was the first person to formulate how feelings of inferiority could stimulate the striving for superiority evidenced by Max. Adler himself had striven to be an outstanding physician, in part to compensate for the frailty he had experienced as a youngster with rickets. As the second son in a family of six children, he was also spurred to stand out by his rivalry with his older brother and his somewhat unhappy relationship with his mother. His strongest support, both emotionally and financially, came from his grain-merchant father, who encouraged him to complete his M.D. at Vienna University.

In 1895 Adler began to practice as an ophthalmologist and then switched to a general practice, which he maintained long after he became known as a psychiatrist. As a psychiatrist in Vienna, he could not help but consider the theories of Freud, which were creating such a stir and so much criticism. Adler was quick to appreciate the importance of Freud's ideas, and he had the courage to defend such a controversial system. Freud responded by inviting Adler to join his select Wednesday evening discussion circle.

While frequently cited as a student of Freud, Adler was a strong-minded colleague who was in harmony with Freud on some issues and in conflict on others. Adler's book, *Study of Organ Inferiority* (1917), was highly praised by Freud. On the other hand, when Adler introduced the concept of the aggression instinct in 1908, Freud disapproved. It was not until long after Adler had rejected his own aggression instinct theory that Freud incorporated it into psychoanalysis in 1923.

In 1911 the differences between Adler and Freud were becoming irreconcilable. Adler criticized Freud for an overemphasis on sexuality, while Freud condemned Adler's emphasis on conscious processes. At a tense series of meetings, Adler discussed his criticisms of Freud and faced heckling and jeering from the most ardent of Freud's followers. Following the third meeting,

Adler resigned as president of the Vienna Psychoanalytic Society and soon resigned as editor of the society's journal. Later that year Freud indicated that no one could support Adlerian concepts and remain in good standing as a psychoanalyst. Freud thus pressured other members to leave the society, while at the same time setting an unfortunate precedent of stifling serious dissent.

Adler quickly established himself as the leader of an important emerging approach to therapy. He called his system *individual psychology* to underscore the importance he placed on studying the total individual in therapy. His theoretical productivity was interrupted by service as a physician in the Austrian army during World War I. Following the war he expressed his interest in children by establishing the first of 30 child guidance clinics in the Viennese school system. Adler expressed his social interest by speaking out strongly for school reforms, improvements in child-rearing practices, and the rejection of archaic prejudices that persistently led to interpersonal conflict.

Adler's interest in common people was expressed in part in his commitment to avoid technical jargon and to speak and write in a language readily understood by nonprofessionals. Unlike many intellectuals he was very willing to speak and write for the public, and his influence among the public probably spread further than his professional influence. As an indefatigable writer and speaker, he traveled extensively to bring his message to a wide public. His influence seemed to peak just prior to the advent of Hitler, when 39 separate Adlerian societies were established.

There is currently a strong resurgence of interest in Adler's ideas, especially in the United States. Adler himself had seen the United States as a place of great potential for his ideas. In 1925, at a relatively late age, he was struggling to learn English so he could speak to American professionals and to the public in their own language. He became a professor of psychiatry at the Long Island School of Medicine and settled in New York in 1935. Two years later at the age of 67, he ignored the urgings of his friends to slow down and died from a heart attack while on a speaking tour in Scotland.

Adler's influence on others was as much personal as intellectual. Besides his serious compassion for those suffering from social ills, Adler also had a light side that loved good food, music, and the company of others. He entertained both his guests and his audiences with his excellent humor. In spite of his own fame, he abhorred pomposity. He was a man committed both professionally and personally to expressing his commonality with his fellow human beings.

THEORY OF PERSONALITY

Striving for superiority is the core motive of the human personality. To be superior is to rise above what we currently are. To be superior does not necessarily mean to attain social distinction, dominance, or leadership in society. Striving for superiority means striving to live a more perfect and complete life. It is the prepotent dynamic principle of life. There are no separate drives in life, for each drive receives its power from the striving for completion.

Striving for superiority can be expressed in many ways. Ideals for the perfect life vary from "peace and happiness throughout the land," to "honesty is the best policy," and to "Deutchland uber Alles." Perfection is an ideal created in the minds of humans who then live as if they can make their ideals real. Individuals create their own fictional goals for living and act as if their personal goals are the final purpose for life. This fictional finalism reflects the fact that psychological events are determined not so much by historical circumstances as by present expectations of how one's future life can be completed. If a person believes that a perfect life is found in heaven as the reward for being virtuous, then that person's life will be greatly influenced by striving for that goal, independent of whether heaven exists or not. Such fictional goals represent the subjective cause of psychological events. Humanity is not just a historically determined accident, an objective consequence of past external conditions. Human beings evolve as self-determined subjects that influence their futures by striving for internally created ideals.

What are the sources of this striving for superior ideals? Striving to be superior is the natural reaction to the feelings of inferiority that are subjectively experienced in the process of living. Subjective feelings of inferiority may be based on such objective facts as organ inferiorities, which are physical weaknesses of the body that predispose us toward such ailments as heart, kidney, stomach, bladder, and lung problems. An organ inferiority is a stimulus to compensate by striving to be superior. The classic case is that of Demosthenes, who compensated for his early stuttering by becoming one of the great orators of the world.

Feelings of inferiority can arise from subjectively felt psychological or social weaknesses as well as from actual bodily impairments. Young children, for example, are aware of being less intelligent and less adept than older siblings, and they strive to a higher level of development. To feel inferior is not abnormal. To feel inferior is to be aware that we are finite beings who are never wise enough, fast enough, or able enough to handle all the contingencies of life. Feelings of inferiority have been the stimulus for every improvement that has been made in humanity's ability to deal more effectively with the world.

The particular feeling of inferiority a person experiences can influence the style of life that person chooses for becoming superior. A person who felt intellectually inadequate as a child, for example, may choose to become a superior intellectual. An intellectual style of life then becomes the integrating principle of the person's life. An intellectual arranges a daily routine, develops a set of reading and thinking habits, and relates to family and friends in accordance with the goal of intellectual superiority. An intellectual style of life is a more solitary and sedentary existence than is the active life of a politician, for example.

A style of life is not the same as the behavioral patterns of a person's existence. All of a person's behavior springs from that individual's unique style of life. A style of life is a cognitive construction, an ideal representation of what a person is in the process of becoming.

People construct their lifestyles partly on the basis of early childhood experiences. The child's position in the family constellation is an especially important influence on his or her lifestyle. A second or middle child, for example, is more likely to choose an ambitious style of life as a striving to surpass the older sibling. The oldest child faces the inevitable experience of being dethroned by a new center of attention. Having to give up the position of undisputed attention and affection produces feelings of resentment and hatred that are part of sibling rivalry. The oldest child enjoys looking at the past when there was no rival and is likely to develop a more conservative style of life. The youngest child has older siblings who serve as pacemakers to goad development. Youngest children never have the experience of losing attention to a successor and are more likely to expect to live the life of a prince or princess.

While such objective facts as organ inferiorities and birth order can affect the lifestyle a person constructs, they do not ultimately determine how a person lives. The prime mover of the lifestyle is the creative self. As such, the creative self is not easily defined. It is a subjective power that gives humans the unique ability to transform objective facts into personally meaningful events. The creative self keeps a person from becoming just a product of biological and social circumstances by acting upon these circumstances to give them personal meaning. The creative self is an active process that interprets the hereditary and environmental facts of a person's life and integrates them into a unified personality that is dynamic, subjective, and unique. From all the forces impinging on a person, the creative self produces a personal goal for living that moves that person toward a more personal and perfect future.

While each style of life is a unique creation, each must take into account the society that is the background from which the figure of the person emerges. Every style of life must come to grips with the fact that humans are social beings born into a system of interpersonal relationships. A healthy style of life reflects the social interest that is an inherent potential for all human beings. A healthy personality is aware that a complete life is possible only within the context of a more perfect society. A healthy personality identifies with the inferiorities that are common to us all. The areas of ignorance that we all share, such as how to have peace in the world or how to be free from dreaded diseases, spur the healthy personality to help humanity transcend these weaknesses. As Adler (1929, p. 31) wrote, "Social interest is the true and inevitable compensation for all the natural weaknesses of individual human beings."

While social interest is an inherent potential that can capture the commitment of any person, it will not develop on its own. Social interest must be nourished and encouraged within a healthy family atmosphere that fosters cooperation, mutual respect, trust, support, and understanding. The values, attitudes, and action patterns of family members, especially the parents, make up a family atmosphere that can, if healthy, encourage children to reject purely selfish interests in favor of the greater social interests of all humanity. Healthy personalities are those who are encouraged by the prospect of living a more complete life by contributing to the construction of a more perfect world.

THEORY OF PSYCHOPATHOLOGY

Pathological personalities are those who have become discouraged from being able to attain superiority in a socially constructive style. Pathological personalities tend to emerge from family atmospheres of competition and distrust, neglect, domination, abuse, or pampering, which discourage social interests. Children from such families are more likely to strive for a more complete life at the expense of others. Children discouraged from social interests tend to choose from one of four selfish goals for attaining superiority: attention seeking, power seeking, revenge taking, and declaring deficiency or defeat (Dreikurs, 1947, 1948). While Dreikurs saw these selfish goals as the immediate strivings of children who misbehave, they can also become the final traits that lead to pathological lifestyles (Maddi, 1972).

A pampered lifestyle is encouraged when parents dote on their children, doing tasks for the children that are well within the children's abilities to do themselves (Adler, 1936). The message the children receive is that they are not capable of doing things for themselves. If children conclude that they are inadequate, they develop an inferior complex that is more than just inferiority feelings but is also a more total self-concept of being basically inadequate. Inferiority complexes lead pampered personalities to avoid tackling the basic *life* tasks of learning to work, relating to the opposite sex effectively, and being a constructive part of society. Lacking adequate social interest, they attempt to compensate through constant attention seeking. The world view of people with pampered lifestyles suggests that the world should continue to take care of them and attend to them even when they are noncontributing adults.

In striving to be the center of attention, the pampered person can become a nuisance who disrupts satisfying social interactions. The more passive, pampered lifestyle results in a laziness where the clear message is a dependent desire to be taken care of. Lazy adolescents or adults actually receive considerable negative attention from family and friends trying to goad them into a more constructive style of life. If being a nuisance or being lazy fails to bring sufficient attention or sufficient nurturance, the pampered person is likely to withdraw further from society into angry pouting.

Children reared under parental domination will also tend to develop an inferiority complex based on a profound sense of being powerless to direct their own lives. Feeling powerless as children, they will shun life's basic tasks in favor of a more destructive goal. The consuming goal of those who have been constantly dominated is to attain power so that they never again will have to experience the acute inferiority that comes from being dominated. The active power seeker may become a rebel who opposes the authority of society in order to justify seeking personal power over others. Rebels may hide behind a variety of social slogans, but their final goal is to seize enough power to never again be dominated by another person. The more passive power seeker may strive for control over others by being stubborn and unwilling to compromise for even the smallest wishes of others.

One of the most common neurotic styles to emerge from parental domination is the compulsive lifestyle (Adler, 1931). The constant nagging, scolding, deriding, and faultfinding of dominating parents can lead to an inferiority complex in which the compulsive person feels powerless to solve life's problems. Afraid of ultimate failure in life's tasks, compulsives move into the future in a hesitating manner. When feeling powerless to handle their futures, they will hesitate, using indecision and doubt to try to hold back time. They may also resort to rituals to keep dreaded time from moving ahead. Besides giving a sense of timelessness by repeating the same act over and over, rituals serve as a safeguard against further loss of self-esteem. The compulsive can always say, "If it weren't for my compulsiveness, look how much I could have done with my life."

Compulsions are even more important as a compensatory means by which compulsives can develop an almost godlike sense of power. The compulsive ritual is experienced as the arena for a tremendous struggle between the good and the evil forces of the universe that only the compulsive has the power to control. Compulsives act as if they have the power to save the world from hostile forces, from death or dreaded diseases, if they only carry out their rituals. So they check and recheck to see if the gas is off; they put knives on the table at just the proper angle; or they drive back around the block to make sure that no one has been hurt. To fail to repeat their compulsions is to risk evil consequences for the world. If compulsives feel they cannot succeed in the stages of life, they can at least create their own secondary theater of operations, their own dramatic rituals, that are under their power and control. The compulsive can ultimately declare a superior triumph, "See, I have succeeded in controlling my own urges."

Children who have been abused, beaten, and battered are more likely to want to take revenge on society rather than to help society. As adolescents and adults such individuals can develop a vicious style of life that actively seeks superiority by aggressing against a society that seems so cold and cruel. More passive revenge can be taken by those who adopt a passive-aggressive style of life and hurt others through constant inconsideration.

People raised with neglect and indifferences are apt to declare defeat. They cannot expect to succeed in a society that does not care. They wish to demonstrate their personal superiority over society by withdrawal and isolation. The message in their withdrawal is that they are above needing others. To shore up their shaky sense of superiority, such isolates may actively denigrate others and convince themselves that they really have not lost anything of value. The more passive isolates despair and declare that because of such overwhelming personal deficiencies there is no way they can be of interest or service to others.

The destructive goals of pathological personalities may be understandable given the family atmospheres that encourage such goals. Though understandable, these goals are mistakes, nonetheless. Pathological personalities construct such troubling goals by making such basic mistakes as generalizing about the nature of all of society on the basis of a very small sample they have experienced. Particular parents or sibs may be cruel or indifferent and encourage revenge or withdrawal. If it weren't for distorted perceptions, however, such troubled persons could find evidence of kindness and caring from more constructive relationships. Pathological personalities also make the basic mistake of forming conclusions about themselves based on distorted feedback from just a few people. Neglected children, for example, may erroneously conclude that they are unloved because one or both of their parents were unable to truly care for them.

The final fictions that troubled persons strive to make real will also be seen, at least by others, as basic mistakes. Over the course of their lives, it will become apparent that the pathological syles of life that have been constructed to fulfill a destructive goal do not lead to a more perfect life. The neurotic nuisance, for example, may ultimately realize that rather than becoming a perfect person he or she has become a perfect nuisance. The vicious revengers may discover that in the end they traded criminality for superiority. And the passive drinkers who have withdrawn into being high above it all via alcohol may find complete happiness only through complete drunkenness.

THEORY OF THERAPEUTIC PROCESSES

With their lifestyle having been created at a young age, most patients are too preoccupied with trying to follow the details of their cognitive maps to be fully aware of the overall pattern of their lifestyles and the goals toward which they are directed. Many clients do not even want to think about the fact that their troubled lives are the result of their self-created styles of life. They would prefer to experience themselves as the unfortunate victims of external circumstances. As a result, therapy must involve an analysis of the cognitive lifestyles of patients in order to help them become more fully conscious of how they are directing their own lives toward destructive goals.

Consciousness Raising

THE CLIENT'S WORK

Since the lifestyle is expressed in all that an individual does, clients really cannot help but reveal the general nature of their styles of life. Their styles of behaving, speaking, sitting, writing, responding, asking questions, and paying bills all have the personalized stamp of a unique style of life. If the cognitive lifestyles are to be brought into bold relief and clear consciousness, however, clients must be willing to reveal special phenomena in therapy, including their dreams, earliest memories, and family constellation. Besides revealing such important information, clients are encouraged to actively participate in the analysis of their lifestyles and the goals toward which those styles are directed.

THE THERAPIST'S WORK

In raising consciousness Adlerian therapists rely a great deal on interpreting the important information that clients present. Adlerian interpretations are not concerned with making causal connections between past events and present problems. The past is connected to the present only to demonstrate the continuity of a client's style of life. Interpretations are concerned mainly with connecting the past and the present to the future. Interpretations help clients become aware of the purposive nature of their lives, of how their past and present experiences are directed toward fulfilling future goals or purposes. Clients become aware of how all their behaviors, including their pathological behaviors, serve the goal of making real the fictional finalisms that were created early in life.

To help clients become aware of the overall pattern and purpose of their lives, therapists must present a fairly complete analysis of the client's lifestyle. A lifestyle analysis includes a summary of the client's family constellation. The order of birth, the gender of siblings, the absence of a parent, and the feelings of which child was favored are all important factors in a family constellation that can be interpreted as influencing the lifestyle a client decided to follow. An interpretation of the client's earliest recollections will give a picture of whether the client felt encouraged or discouraged to compensate for inferiority feelings in a socially constructive style.

A lifestyle analysis will also include an interpretation of the *basic mistakes* the client made in constructing a view about the nature of the world. The most common cognitive mistakes include: (1) overgeneralizations, such as "nobody cares," (2) distortions of life's demands, such as "you can't win at life," (3) minimization of one's worth, such as "I'm really inadequate" or "I'm only a housewife," (4) unrealistic goals to be secure, such as "I must please everyone," and (5) faulty values, such as "get ahead, no matter whose it is" (Mosak & Dreikurs, 1973).

Unlike many therapists, Adlerians do not stop by just analyzing the problems of clients. They are just as concerned with giving clients feedback about their personal assets. Thus, a summary of a client's strengths is included as part of an analysis of lifestyle.

After completing an analysis of the client's lifestyle as part of the early assessment phase of therapy, therapists present a summary of the lifestyle to the clients in a teacher-to-student fashion. The *lifestyle summary* is presented in therapy as if the therapist is presenting at a case conference, although here the client has a chance to cooperate in the analysis. Clients can thus indicate when they agree or disagree with the therapist's summary. Therapists can make necessary changes in their view of the client's lifestyle, or they can interpret the client's resistance to a more complete view of the lifestyle if clients are indeed resisting seeing themselves more completely.

The interpretations and presentation of a lifestyle summary include both feedback and education. Individual clients are given personal feedback about their unique family constellation, their personal feelings of inferiority, and their particular assets and basic mistakes. At the same time clients are educated to a theory of lifestyle construction that gives emphasis to such concepts as the creative self, social interest, and the striving for superiority. In interpreting life goals and demonstrating the basic mistakes in living for selfish values instead of social interests, Adlerians teach clients a new philosophy of life. In fact, Adlerians believe that a therapy is incomplete if it does not include an adequate philosophy of life (Mosak & Dreikurs, 1973).

Whether or not clients are changing their basic styles of completing life's tasks is best determined by an analysis of dreams. Dreams are a means of solving future problems, and a person's manner of dreaming will indicate how a person is currently attempting to resolve the problems of everyday life. Dreams are a rehearsal of possible alternatives for future action. Thus, if clients wish to postpone action, they will tend to forget dreams. If they wish to convince themselves to avoid particular actions, they will frighten themselves with nightmares. Clients who are making little movement in therapy may have brief dreams with little action. Clients who are ready to tackle their problems head on will throw themselves into creative analysis of their dreams. By helping clients interpret dreams, therapists are helping them become aware of new and creative alternatives for completing life's tasks.

Contingency Control

THE CLIENT'S WORK

As a cognitive approach to change, Adlerian therapy is directed at weakening the effects of present contingencies by having clients reevaluate their future goals. By reevaluating such goals as power, revenge, and attention, clients are decreasing the reinforcing effects of such consequences as being the center of attention or controlling others. In the process of reevaluating selfish goals, clients may experiment with behaviors directed toward a social interest in order to experience the consequences that result from striving for social interest. After experiencing such consequences as the good feelings that come from helping another person, clients are in a better position to realistically compare and reevaluate the consequences that they had been receiving from a self-centered life.

THE THERAPIST'S WORK

One of the techniques that therapists use to help clients reevaluate the consequences of their selfish goals is to *create images* that capture the essence of the client's goals. Clients who are constantly striving to be the center of attention may be asked to imagine themselves as Bozo the Clown, who becomes the center of attention by having people throw things at him, such as insults or sarcastic remarks. When such clients find themselves playing the buffoon, they can imagine that they are like Bozo the Clown sitting on a stool over a pool of water just egging people to knock him down. Such images encourage clients to laugh at their styles rather than to condemn themselves. Once clients can laugh about playing Bozo the Clown or Caesar the Conqueror, they can devalue the desire for attention or control by no longer taking such consequences seriously.

Therapists will also *assign tasks* to clients designed to help them experiment with expressing a social interest. Therapists might, for example, assign clients the task of doing something each day that gives pleasure to another person. In the process of completing such tasks, clients are able to experience for themselves the valuable consequences that come from doing something for someone other than themselves.

As values are changing, therapists may still have to provide techniques that help clients avoid slipping back into old habits of responding to selfish goals. *Catching oneself* is a technique that encourages clients to think about catching themselves with their hands in the cookie jar. They should try to actually catch themselves while in the process of acting out a destructive behavior, such as overeating or overdrinking. With practice, including the internal practice of anticipating putting a hand in a cookie jar, clients can learn to anticipate a situation and to turn their attention to more constructive consequences rather than automatically responding for destructive goals.

Choosing

THE CLIENT'S WORK

Just as clients originally chose particular lifestyles as children, so too are they capable of choosing to radically change their lifestyles at a later age. Once they are more fully conscious of the fictional finalisms that they are trying to make real, and once they have evaluated selfish goals in comparison with social goals, clients are freer to choose to stay with their old styles or to create a new life. Such goals as having power over others or being the center of attention are highly valued by many people, and there is no assurance that clients will choose to give up such goals in the name of social interest. Besides the value of such goals, clients may choose to stay with the security of a style of life that may not be particularly satisfying but is at least a known quantity. To consider choosing a radically new lifestyle can threaten a loss of security, and clients may opt to reaffirm their long-standing lifestyles.

THE THERAPIST'S WORK

Rather than have clients face a sudden and dramatic decision to throw themselves into the darkness of a new and unknown style of life, therapists can use techniques that encourage clients to experiment with new alternatives for living. For example, a 35-year-old widow had decided that now she valued the idea of developing an intimate relationship with a man after having known the security of six years of relying on only herself. She had met a man at her Parents Without Partners group to whom she was attracted, but he hadn't asked her out. Since she had not been making any progress in pursuing her goal for more intimacy, I suggested that she ask him if he would like to go for coffee after the meeting. She said she really found that alternative exciting but insisted that she was not the kind of person who could do such a thing. Using an Adlerian technique, I suggested that she only *act as if* she were a liberated woman rather than worrying about becoming such a person. With considerable courage she was able to *act as if* she were more liberated and was able to get closer to the man. At the same time she discovered that if she acted as if she were more liberated, she could soon make such fiction into a reality. For clients who insist that they would change if they could only choose to control overpowering emotions, a *push-button* technique is used to demonstrate to clients that they can indeed choose to control their emotions. Using fantasy, clients are instructed to close their eyes and imagine very happy incidents in their pasts. They are to become aware of the feelings that accompany such a scene. Then clients are instructed to imagine a humiliating, frustrating, or hurtful incident and note the accompanying feelings. Following this the pleasant scene is imagined again. By pushing the button on particular thoughts, clients are taught that they can indeed create whatever feelings they wish by deciding what they will think about. By practicing such cognitive control of emotions, clients are impressed with the ability they have to determine their own emotions. With an increased ability to choose whether to be angry or not, or depressed or not, clients are in the process of liberating their lifestyles from emotions that once seemed overwhelming.

THEORY OF THERAPEUTIC CONTENT

Intrapersonal Conflicts

Psychological problems are primarily intrapersonal in origin, reflecting the destructive lifestyle that was constructed by the individual at an early age. With the focus on the lifestyle of the individual, Adlerian therapy was traditionally carried out in an individual format. Nevertheless, Dreikurs (1959), a prominent student of Adler, is credited with being the first to use group therapy in private practice. Since destructive lifestyles are acted out interpersonally, a group setting does allow for firsthand information of how patients create problems in relating to others.

ANXIETY AND DEFENSES

Regardless of how self-defeating or destructive a lifestyle might be, it at least provides a sense of security. When a therapist questions or threatens lifestyle convictions, anxiety is aroused and the client is ready to resist further treatment. Anxiety can be used to frighten the therapist from pushing ahead, as when the patient threatens to go into a panic if the therapist continues to probe. Anxiety serves a primary purpose, then, of keeping the client from having to take action and move ahead into the future. Anxiety can also serve as a secondary theater of operations, allowing clients to turn their attention from solving life's tasks to trying to solve the considerable anxiety they are creating by their constant self-preoccupation. Anxiety-ridden clients can develop a sense of superiority for just being able to continue living in the face of such overwhelming anxiety. Therapists need not worry about treating anxiety directly. Therapists must, however, be aware of tendencies to avoid being direct in analyzing a self-aborted lifestyle because the therapists are so impressed or so threatened by the amount of anxiety clients can create as an excuse for holding on to a secure but unsuccessful style of life.

The most common and important defense mechanism is compensation. Compensation serves not as a defense against anxiety per se but rather as a defense against the aversive feelings of inferiority. Compensation itself does not produce problems. It is the goal toward which a person strives to be superior that determines whether or not compensation leads to problems. A person, for example, who has intense feelings of organ inferiority might compensate and strive for superiority by becoming the community's most plagued hypochondriac. On the other hand, the same person could have been encouraged to compensate by becoming the community's best physician. The issue in therapy is not to remove feelings of inferiority or to replace compensation with more effective coping mechanisms. Therapy is intended to help clients redirect their compensatory strivings from selfish and thus self-absorbing goals toward socially useful and thus self-enhancing values.

SELF-ESTEEM

Enough has been said about feelings of inferiority to indicate that problems with self-esteem are central in Adlerian therapy. The secret to solving problems of esteem is not to reassure maladjusted people that they are indeed well. Nor is self-esteem particularly enhanced through encouraging self-absorption by having clients analyze all the intricate details of their early years. The paradox of self-esteem is that it vanishes as a problem when people are encouraged to forget themselves and begin living for others. A solid sense of self-esteem can be created only by creating a style of life that is of value to the world. Live a life that affirms the value of fellow human beings, and the unintended consequence will be the creation of a self that is worthy of the highest esteem.

RESPONSIBILITY

Those who would be free from pathology must have the strength to carry the double burden of both personal and social responsibility. In becoming aware that one's own creative self is ultimately responsible for transforming the objective facts of life into personally meaningful events, a person is confronted with the ultimate responsibility of choosing in the present the goals that will allow the most perfect future to unfold. Once individuals accept responsibility for shaping their own lives, they must also accept that they are responsible for the impact that their lifestyles have on society. Will they, for example, attempt to live a more complete life by helping to create a more perfect personality while at the same time producing a more polluted place to live? The person who can hope to attain a condition of wholeness is one who can respond to the hopes of humanity.

Interpersonal Conflicts

INTIMACY AND SEXUALITY

People who are committed to selfish interests should not be surprised that their self-centeredness prevents them from experiencing intimacy. Intimacy includes being able to place the concern for a valued other above one's own immediate interests. Intimacy also requires the ability to truly cooperate with others in commonly shared goals. The selfishness that is inherent in psychopathology preempts such intimate cooperation. Yet so many people are surprised that they cannot have life both ways, that they cannot dedicate themselves to a life of selfish competitiveness, for example, without such competitiveness eventually tearing apart their marriages or their families. People would like to pretend that a lifestyle can be fragmented into convenient parts, with competition, domination, and ruthlessness at work and cooperation, equality, and caring at home. Such pretense may work for awhile, but eventually the goals of selfish success will take their toll on intimate relationships.

While sexuality was rejected by Adler as being the prime mover of life, sexuality was accepted as one of the important tasks of life. The biological fact of life is that we exist in two sexes. A task of life is to learn how to relate to that fact in a manner that allows both sexes to find mutual pleasure and significance in sexual and intimate relating. Defining our sex roles in part on the basis of cultural definitions and stereotypes, we must strive to relate to the other sex, not the opposite sex (Mosak & Dreikurs, 1973). Other people of either sex need not be transformed into the enemy. Thinking in terms of the opposite sex tends to encourage competition and conflict rather than the cooperation that comes from being fellow human beings. Without such cooperation, partners cannot expect to teach each other what is needed for sex to be a mutually rewarding experience.

COMMUNICATION

The inherent preparedness for language acquisition indicates that humans are born to be social beings. Language alone, however, does not guarantee effective communication. Problems with cornmunication are fundamentally problems with cooperation. Effective communication is by its very nature a cooperative endeavor. If one person is holding back information out of self-interest, or if another is sending misleading messages to gain a competitive advantage, then communication is bound to be conflicted. Couples with conflicts over competition, such as sex role competition, will frequently complain of problems in communicating with each other, even though each is able to communicate effectively with a friend of the same sex. The task in therapy is not to correct communication patterns but rather to help the couples reorient their values toward common goals so that their communications can be for shared rather than selfish interests.

HOSTILITY

The aggressive instinct was originally thought by Adler to be the most important human drive. He later elaborated his position to include hostility as one expression of basic *will to power*. Now we can understand hostility as perhaps the worst of many mistaken paths of striving for superiority. For those discouraged from being able to attain perfection through social contributions, there is always violence to provide a sense of superiority. To beat up someone, to hold another person at gunpoint, or to threaten someone's very life can transform the most inferior-feeling individual into a giant who is almost godlike in the ability to destroy another person's existence. To resort to hostility is, of course, to deny the value of another human being. Hostility is the worst expression of the belief that self-interest can be of higher value than social interest. Tragically the continual rise in violence in modern society may well be testimony to the prevalence of believing that only the self and never the society is really sacred.

CONTROL

All people have a need to be able to control, to master certain situations and exercise restraint over others. Pathological personalities, however, are frequently preoccupied with dominating others. The most blatant controller is the person who was once dominated by parents and has made a conviction to seek power over others in order to never again feel the intense inferiority that comes from being under another person's domination. The pampered personality is a more subtle despot, using neurotic symptoms such as anxiety, depression, or hypochondria to get others to satisfy every whim. Pampered people are trained to use the services of others for solutions to problems rather than to become self-reliant. As adults, pampered people rely on symptoms to control others, including therapists, in order to get others to care for them.

Control over others brings a sense of security, a position of superiority, and an exaggerated conviction of self-value. With such gains from control, many clients can be expected to rely on subtle and not so subtle maneuvers to control therapy. Effective therapists will be aware of when clients are trying to control, and they can respond with counter-control techniques. Clients that try to control therapy, for example, by insisting on how bad off they are and how unable they are to progress, may cry out in exaggerated self-worth, "I bet you've never had such a tough case like me before." The therapist may refuse to be impressed by responding, "No, not since last hour." The therapist is not attempting to win some control game but rather to communicate to the client that the therapist is unwilling to cooperate with the client's maneuvers.

Individuo-Social Conflicts

ADJUSTMENT VERSUS TRANSCENDENCE

The issue of adjustment versus transcendence should not pit the individual against society. Striving for transcendence is a synonym for striving for superiority and involves finding fulfillment by continuing to transcend a present level of personal adjustment by attaining a higher and more complete level of life. Healthy people will resist notions that fulfillment requires placing oneself against the system. Healthy people do not place self-esteem over social esteem in an attempt to rise above the society to which they are integrally related. Such social transcendence is for snobs and elitists who can feel superior only at the expense of the commoners that surround them. Healthy people are committed to helping the entire society transcend its present level of functioning in order to become a more perfect social system.

IMPULSE CONTROL

The civilizing roles of parents and therapists is not to inhibit bad impulses but to strengthen social interest. Children are not primarily biological beasts that must have controls imposed on destructive drives. Children are social beings who are prepared to cooperate if encouraged by parents and teachers. The issue with impulses is not that they must be inhibited but rather that they must be directed toward prosocial goals as part of the total lifestyle. Drives do not have inherent direction, such as to destroy or to dominate. Drives are just an expression of the primary thrust toward completion. Thus impulses, like sex and aggression, can be brought to completion for higher social interests, such as to provide a pleasure bond between spouses or to aid in the defense of a society against aggressors. Impulses become a problem for society only when the overall direction of a lifestyle is antisocial rather than prosocial in nature. Impulses threaten to break out of control not because of an excess of civilization but rather because some individuals lack a full appreciation and dedication to civilization.

RULES FOR LIVING

Rules are an essential part of social living, and unless we are all to be alienated isolates, it is important that we have a healthy respect for rules. To respect social rules is to affirm the importance of social interest being of higher value than anyone's particular self-interests. Rules made in an autocratic atmosphere will not encourage respect because the very process of rule making is based on the domination, power, and self-interest of the autocrat, including the autocratic parent or therapist. A democratic process encourages social cooperation and participation. Rules made through a democratic process will win respect because each of the individuals involved has had a voice in shaping the rules of the group. Thus, in an Adlerian marital workshop, the therapists were earnest antismokers. They did not feel justified, however, to unilaterally impose a rule of no smoking. Their approach was to have all participants in the workshop discuss the issue, and after each person had a chance to speak, the group as a whole decided on the smoking rules that were to govern the workshop.

Beyond Conflict to Fulfillment

MEANING

We create meaning out of our lives by the lives we create. We are not born with intrinsic meaning in our existence, but we are born with a creative self that can fashion intrinsic meaning from our existence. From the raw materials of our genetic endowment and our childhood experiences, we shape and mold the goals and the means to the goals that will give significance to our existence. If our vision is good enough and our goals are noble enough, then the lifestyles we create may be truly valued works of art that are dedicated to the best in humanity. If, out of discouragement and distortion, we dedicate our lives to banal goals, then our lifestyle may reflect more basic mistakes than basic meaning. A basic mistake that has resulted in the alienation of many contemporary individuals is the belief that existence can have meaning if it is dedicated to becoming a shrine to the self. The creative self seeks completion not by turning inward and drawing away from the world, but by reaching out to become connected to the greatest needs and the highest aspirations of humanity.

VALUES

Adler was one of the first to admit that psychotherapy is not just part of the science of what *is* but also an extension of the study of what *ought to be*.

Values have always been of central importance to a therapy that would help people find not only solutions to symptoms but also answers to the ultimate problems of living. As a philosophy of life, Adlerian therapy is a humanistic philosophy that affirms the ultimate value of individual human beings—other human beings as well as oneself. The greatest value is *Gemeinschaftsgefuhl*, the social interest that allows us to contribute to the common welfare of humanity. Social interest is not just an idealistic value that provides inspiration for life, it is also a pragmatic goal that produces mental health in life. The very enterprise of psychotherapy is a testimony to both the ideal and the real value of social interest. Certainly the highest value of any person worthy of the special position of being a therapist should be to work for the well-being of fellow human beings.

IDEAL PERSON

Inspired by goals that transcend any immediate wants or worries, the superior person is drawn to life with excitement and anticipation. Esteem is granted in knowing that the world really needs people who care. Energies are not wasted on evasive defenses or on neurotic patterns that provide ready-made excuses for failing to add to the world. The healthy person is at home in the world. The interests of the self and the interests of others are not experienced as being in basic conflict by those who care enough to find completion through cooperation. The all too common social values of security and success are rejected in favor of the even higher social value of the common good. Healthy people do not place themselves against, above, or below others. They are egalitarians who experience profound relatedness with others by identifying with the imperfections that we all share and with the aspirations of those who truly care.

THEORY OF THE THERAPEUTIC RELATIONSHIP

The therapeutic relationship is a central part of the process of helping clients overcome their long-standing discouragement so that they can be freer to reorient themselves toward a healthy social interest. Therapists help draw clients toward a genuine social interest by showing the personal interest they have for the well-being of their clients. In many ways the therapeutic relationship is a prototype of social interest. The classical values of love, faith, and hope for the human condition are essential to both social interest and an effective therapeutic relationship.

The therapist's positive regard for the client, for example, reflects the love and caring of an individual dedicated to the well-being of human beings. The therapist's willingness to relate as a genuine equal communicates a faith in the client's ability to actively contribute to finding solutions to serious problems. The therapist is not the doctor who acts upon the client, no matter how much pampered clients may act helpless in order to persuade the doctor-therapist to take over their lives. The therapist is more like a teacher who has faith in the unused potential of the student-client to create a fulfilling style of life. The genuineness of the therapist also reveals a willingness to make mistakes, to be perfectly human, which communicates a faith that imperfect human beings have the power to enhance life. Clients who are well aware of being imperfect need not look to a perfect healer for help but share the faith of the therapist that the imperfect client is capable of striving for a more complete life.

The faith and love that the client experiences through the therapeutic relationship give the client hope that can counteract the discouragement that prevents meeting life head on. Experiencing the genuine love, faith, and hope from the empathic therapist is an undeniable event that makes clients profoundly aware of the intrinsic value that social interest from one human being can have for another. With renewed hope and a vital awareness of the value of social interest, clients are provided fresh opportunities to break out of a self-centered existence and begin caring and living for others.

PRACTICALITIES OF ADLERIAN THERAPY

Adlerians have been rather flexible in the formal apsects of therapy. Approaches have varied from a traditional individual style, to a multiple-therapist approach with two therapists working together with one client, to group approaches with multiple therapists as well as clients. The multiple-therapist approach was originated by Dreikurs (1950) as a means of preventing serious transference or counter-transference problems from interfering with the progress of therapy. The presence of two therapists also allows clients to become aware of how two individuals can really differ and still cooperate.

As part of an educational approach to solving or preventing mental health problems, Adlerian workshops have become a popular technique for teaching parents how to raise children to cooperate, to care, and to be striving individuals while living in the context of a warm, supportive social group that still insists on clear limits through democratic rules. Similar workshops are available for marital couples, who can attend the educational sessions and either just sit back and learn from others or come to center stage and discuss issues in their marriage, with the audience giving considerable support and positive suggestions for solving problems. Adlerians have also established social clubs to help foster social interest both within and outside of mental hospitals. Within the social clubs the strengths of individuals are stressed, as they are encouraged to enjoy the social aspects of the clubs rather than focusing on their weaknesses through therapy.

Adlerian approaches to therapy are also flexible in regard to such issues as fees and time limits. As a reflection of their own social interests, therapists are encouraged to provide a significant contribution to the community without fees. Such social service may be done through free Friday evening marital workshops, free workshops for parents, or some private therapy hours for clients unable to pay. The course of therapy is expected to be relatively short term, with Adlerians being among the first to advocate time-limited therapy.

While Adlerians have traditionally worked with a full range of clients, they have become especially active in working with delinquents, criminal populations, marriages, and families. The resurgence of Adlerian activity in these problem areas reflects a concern with social relationships that are in danger of disintegrating because of excessive self-interest. Following Adler's original example, an increasing impact is also being made within school settings, especially with guidance counselors eager to help students clarify their values in order to find constructive goals for their energies.

The resurgence of Adlerian interventions has led to an increase in Adlerian institutes. Becoming an Adlerian therapist is more a matter of the individual's social values and potential as a helping agent rather than a function of formal credentials. Thus, Adlerian institutes have been open to educators, clergy, and even paraprofessionals, as well as to traditional mental health professionals.

EFFECTIVENESS OF ADLERIAN THERAPY

Four controlled studies on the effectiveness of Adlerian interventions were located in a review of the Adlerian literature. The earliest outcome study was carried out by Heine (1953), who compared Adlerian therapy to psychoanalytic and Rogerian approaches. Eight patients from each approach were asked to judge how much change they had experienced as a result of therapy. Although statistical analyses were not done on the self-report data, Heine did conclude that the patients had experienced improvement from each form of therapy. He further concluded that there were no important differences in outcome between the three therapies. A no-treatment control group was lacking in this study.

The best-known study of Adlerian therapy was carried out by Shlien, Mosak, and Dreikurs (1962), who compared Adlerian therapy with client-centered therapy. They also examined the effectiveness of time-limited approaches of each therapy compared with an unlimited, voluntarily terminated approach. Clients applying for therapy were tested and then placed on a three-month waiting list. The waiting period was designed to control for changes that would occur just as the result of passing time. The correlation between the client's real self-concepts and ideal self-concepts was the criterion measure for the study. The self-ideal correlations were an average of zero both before and after the three months of waiting, indicating no improvement with time alone.

Both the Adlerian and Rogerian therapies led to significant improvements in the self-ideal correlations, but there was no difference in effectiveness between the therapies. The limited and unlimited approaches produced the same amount of change, but the time-limited therapy was twice as efficient, with an average of 18 interviews compared with an average of 37 interviews in the unlimited approach.

Nelson and Haberer (1966) tested the effects of Adlerian counseling on remedial education. Prior to beginning their freshman year in college, 195 students with low grades and low aptitude scores were given seven weeks of remedial courses in English, math, and learning techniques. Three groups of 50 students each were also assigned to three Adlerian counselors for participation in lifestyle analyses. A control group of 45 students was assigned to a counselor using a causal diagnostic approach to counseling. Interestingly, the results showed an initial effect in which the Adlerian groups achieved significantly better results at the end of the remedial courses. During the first semester of college, however, the initial effect disappeared. By the end of the second semester, the Adlerian group was virtually identical with the control group.

A more recent study by Walker (1973) has found some support for using Adlerian counseling with black disadvantaged clients. Eight black clients (four men and four women) were seen by two white male counselors using Adlerian procedures, while a matched group was seen by two white counselors using a self-emergent approach. The Adlerian procedures were found to be more effective in eliciting longer client responses, more client participation, and a greater client receptivity to counseling. Walker did not, however, report whether Adlerian counseling led to greater improvement in clients' lives.

Four experiments, each with a different focus, are hardly enough to draw any firm conclusions about Adlerian therapy. Perhaps the most we can say at this time is that when Adlerian therapy has been compared with alternative treatments, it has been found to be at least as effective as such alternatives as client-centered therapy (Heine; Schlien et al.); psychoanalytic therapy (Heine); a causal diagnostic approach (Nelson & Haberer); and a self-emergent technique (Walker). The most provocative finding to emerge from the Adlerian therapy research is the suggestion that time-limited therapy may be twice as efficient as unlimited therapy. Replications of these studies are needed, however, before any final conclusions are made. With the resurgence in interest in Adlerian therapy, the hope is that more intensive and extensive outcome studies will be completed in the near future.

CRITICISMS OF ADLERIAN THERAPY

From a Behavioral Perspective

Adlerians have been unable to decide whether they are social learning theorists who attribute maladaptive behavior to such conditions as family constellations or mystics who attribute distorted lifestyles to a creative self that sounds much like a soul. Why Adlerians feel the need to resort to such concepts as choice and a creative self when concepts such as parents' pampering, abusing, ignoring, and dominating would serve as explanations is unclear. It is clear, however, that theoretical propositions concerning the effects of birth order can be defined and tested, while such concepts as striving for superiority and the creative self are vague and totally unamenable to scientific investigation. Perhaps Adlerians hold to such concepts in order to place the responsibility for changing on the clients, because the system has been unable to generate techniques powerful enough to produce adequate change in the behavior of clients. Whatever the reasons, the Adlerian school remains a strange combination of a theory that could attain scientific respectability and a religion that dedicates the soul to social interest.

From a Psychoanalytic Perspective

Freud anticipated that Adler's break with psychoanalysis would lead to the development of a superficial and sterile theory (Colby, 1951). In rejecting psychoanalysis, Adler acted as if he had rejected half of the human personality. The result is a one-dimensional theory that emphasizes the ego or self at the expense of the id, consciousness at the expense of the unconscious, social strivings at the expense of biological drives, compensation at the expense of other defenses, and the perfectable at the expense of the imperfectable. Here we have a ying without a yang, half of the person presented as if it were the whole.

As a result of the holes in Adler's holism, there emerges a naive therapy that suggests that people can be truly helped with all types of cute gimmicks. Just have a frightened, submissive woman *act as if* she is liberated and she will be liberated. Just *push a button* and an embittered recluse can change his fantasies and feelings as fast as he can change the TV station. The power of positive thinking has been peddled as a lasting cure for centuries, when in fact it is nothing but a temporary pep talk. Patients are not really emotionally crippled; they are only mistaken. People are not really locked into unconscious conflicts; they are only discouraged. Just have hope, faith, and charity, and that is the way to live successfully. Adler does indeed promise a rose garden to those who are willing to share his rose-colored glasses that filter out the truly dark side of life.

From an Eclectic Perspective

Adlerian theory seems willing to accept therapy as being an extension of the socialization process. Be more socialized and civilized, and you will be free from pathology. Such a system may be helpful with those in need of socialization or resocialization, such as children, delinquents, criminals, and psychotics. But what of the many clients who are troubled because they are oversocialized? The client with colitis and frigidity who was always the polite and proper child will not be freed by striving to be more perfect. She needs to express her anger and resentment over having to always stifle herself for the sake of social harmony. The self-sacrificing spouse who experiences an existential crisis of having no sense of self because he has always lived for others doesn't need to be encouraged to just make someone else happy once a day. He needs to know how to own himself and to assert himself for his own interests when necessary.

It is ironic that Adler called his approach *individual psychology* when in fact he ultimately values social interests over the interests of the individual. Adler attempts to resolve the inherent conflicts between society and the individual by suggesting that the individual's best interests are really served by subjugating self-interests to the interests of society. Adlerian theory may indeed help balance therapeutic approaches that worship only the self at the expense of others. Nevertheless, it would be a mistake to conclude that a complete life can be found only in living for social interests and never for pure self-interest.

AN ADLERIAN ANALYSIS OF MRS. C.

Mrs. C. is a person almost entirely preoccupied with herself. Other people are mere shadows, minor characters who just move in and out of her dramatic rituals. Her life has become a parody of a great epic. She is in a mortal struggle with the dreaded evil of pinworms, and only she can be powerful enough and perfect enough to prevent the pinworms from becoming the victors. She has obviously switched her striving for superiority from solving the primary tasks of life to a secondary theater of operations in which she can be the heroine, the star in her own style of life.

Mrs. C.'s dramatic dilemma is common to those with a compulsive personality. Having been raised under the constant castigation and derision of dominating parents, Mrs. C. was discouraged from believing that she was capable of facing life's tasks successfully. She had indeed failed at the task of coming to grips with her own sexuality. She was in the process of failing at the work of caring for five children with a sixth on the way. The intense inferiority complex that she had accepted early in life was in danger of proving to be all too true. What she decided as a child was becoming a self-fulfilling prophecy: she was too inferior to find completion through life's tasks. Her solution was to switch the arena to a neurotic struggle that was more of her own making and more under her control.

Quickly Mrs. C. became the perfect compulsive, the most complete washer others had ever known. What a special person she was, how unusual! She had already stumped several therapists and a prominent mental hospital. Yet she continued to insist that she could really live, could really care for her children and husband, if it weren't for her neurosis. Her compulsive lifestyle serves then as a compensation for her inferiority complex of being unable to solve life's tasks, as a built-in excuse for not doing more with her life, as a means of freezing time by repeating the same rituals that seem to keep life from moving ahead, and as a dramatic struggle that proves how superior she in fact is at holding back the evil forces of the world.

Progress in therapy would be a real threat to Mrs. C. She has judged herself as too inferior to progress in life. She has made a basic mistake of evaluating herself on the basis of early recollections of how her parents perceived her as an inferior being, requiring constant control and domination. What distortions she may have added to these recollections may never be known. Did her parents never support her strengths or her strivings for independence? Did she encourage their domination because she found security in being protected from sex, disease, or boys? Were there not adults in her life, such as some teachers, who encouraged her, even if her folks were in fact such tyrants? Again, answers to such questions might never be known. But what must be known by Mrs. C. is that she continues in her neurotic patterns because she concluded early in life that she was ultimately unable to succeed in life. She must become aware of the fact that she is not special or disturbed because she has intense feelings of inferiority. She shares such feelings with all human beings. Her disturbance is the result of striving to be special by trying to compensate for her inferiorities by investing all her energies in a completely self-centered life.

If Mrs. C. continues to withdraw from living with and for others, she is indeed in high risk of becoming psychotic. Her thinking and communication are of little social interest. They are almost entirely directed toward pinworms, toward her fears, and toward convincing others how special are her life circumstances. The social ties that connect thinking with social reality can break down if others continue to be of no interest to Mrs. C.

Given Mrs. C.'s almost total self-preoccupation, it will be difficult to get her engaged with a therapist. Since she has had considerable individual therapy, and since she seems only to have convinced herself of how special she is, it would be better to start her out in an Adlerian group. While she probably would resist group therapy on the grounds that she is too troubled and too in need of individual attention, being placed in a group would give the direct message that she in fact is not so special. She would have the opportunity to discover that others also have serious problems and serious feelings of inferiori and yet some of them are moving ahead in life. Finding herself unable to really care about others, Mrs. C. might insist that if she weren't so preoccupied with her own problems, then she could care about the others. The therapist or group members could correct such mistaken thinking by indicating that the reverse idea is really true: if she can begin to learn to care about others in the group she can begin to forget about herself for awhile.

Mrs. C. would also be encouraged to participate in a full analysis of her life script, including such basic mistakes as judging herself inadequate because she felt dominated by her parents. Her earliest recollections would be interpreted, as would her perceptions of her position in her family constellation. The group could be especially supportive in helping Mrs. C. to become more fully conscious of her inferiority complex. Finding that others share intense feelings of inferiority can give Mrs. C. the opportunity to rediscover a genuine interest in others.

Experiencing the caring of her therapist and of special group members can begin to reorient Mrs. C. from sheer self-interest to an emerging social interest. Tasks would be assigned to encourage interest in others, such as assigning Mrs. C. to call certain group members who are in a crisis to see how they are doing each evening. Mrs. C. would be encouraged to step further out of her special drama back into the world of others by being assigned simple tasks to add pleasure to her children's lives, such as baking them a pie. Any excuses for avoiding such tasks would be interpreted as excuses. In the process of experimenting with such tasks, Mrs. C. can become aware of the healing value that caring for others can have on self-preoccupation.

Assigning tasks can help Mrs. C. to begin reevaluating the consequences of living for others versus living to ward off pinworms. *Acting as if* she is free for the moment, at least, to create something of value for others, even a simple pie, can demonstrate that she indeed has some choice in how she is going to continue living. Ultimately she will have to confront the choice of whether to come off the stage of her limited theater of operations to reengage the world. After so many years of living for her own drama, Mrs. C. may choose to hold onto the security and esteem of being the world's greatest container of pinworms, rather than risk creating a life that might be more useful to others, even if it is a bit more mundane.

RATIONAL-EMOTIVE
THERAPY

"THE PURPOSE OF LIFE is to have a fucking good time," said Albert Ellis (1973a) as he opened a two-day workshop. As a directive therapist he believes in going right to the heart of an issue without mincing his words because someone might get anxious or upset. That is the other person's problem. Ellis' problem is to convince people to use their rational processes to create a life that maximizes the pleasure and minimizes the pain of existence. Ellis is a long-term hedonist, however, and not an irrational, short-term hedonist who indulges every momentary desire like smoking or excessive drinking at the expense of long-term suffering. Nevertheless, pleasure is still the purpose of life, and Ellis was available to help the public and professionals alike understand how their commitments to irrational philosophies and psychologies keep them from getting the most out of life.

Knowing that he stirs up considerable controversy, Ellis is most willing to be confronted by anyone in the audience, whether they want to challenge his concepts or question how he personally lives his own philosophy. So I asked him, "If the purpose of life is to have a fucking good time, why is it that you haven't taken a vacation in 15 years?" Believing that Ellis was caught in an irrational contradiction between his philosophy and his life, I was surprised with how quickly he responded, "What is wrong with me really enjoying my work? I never said we all have to have a good time in the same way." Watching Ellis in action does indeed reveal a person who finds great pleasure in his profession.

A BRIEF SKETCH OF ALBERT ELLIS

Albert Ellis (1913–   ) has been enthusiastically presenting and defending his rational approach to therapy since 1957, when he first demonstrated his innovative system at the annual convention of the American Psychological Association. Prior to that time he had practiced the psychoanalytic approaches to therapy, which he had learned while earning his Ph.D. in clinical psychology from Columbia. From the late 1940s to the early 1950s, Ellis became increasingly dissatisfied with the effectiveness and efficiency of both classical analysis and psychoanalytically oriented psychotherapy. He believed Freud was correct that irrational forces keep neurotics troubled, but he was coming to believe that the irrational forces were not unconscious conflicts from early childhood. Ellis had seen too many patients with incredible insights into their childhood and their unconscious processes who continued to keep themselves troubled. That something that Ellis saw was a continual reindoctrination of themselves in an irrational philosophy of life.

Ellis found free association to be too passive and past-oriented to seriously challenge patients' contemporary ideas about themselves and the world. He began to attack the clients' belief systems directly and pushed clients to actively work against their own irrational premises. Ellis found himself well suited to his rational approach to therapy. With his quickness of mind, clear and concrete articulation of abstract ideas, love of intellectual debate, hardheaded faith in the power of rational discourse, and excellent sense of humor for dissipating irrational anger or anxiety, Ellis (1957b) was able to demonstrate significantly greater effectiveness with his new approach than with his older psychoanalytic approaches.

In 1959, Ellis established the Institute for Rational Living in New York City as a nonprofit organization for providing adult education courses in rational living and a moderate-cost clinic for patients. In 1968, Ellis opened the Institute for Advanced Study in Rational Psychotherapy to provide professionals with extensive training in rational-emotive therapy and to offer special workshops and seminars throughout the country. Carrying 80 patients a week, running a workshop or seminar nearly every weekend, and writing more than 400 articles and books, Ellis has been a tireless advocate for a rational-emotive approach to therapy and to life.

THEORY OF PERSONALITY

A rational explanation of personality is almost as easy as ABC (Ellis, 1973b). At point A are the Activating Events of life, such as rejection by a lover or failure to get into a graduate program. Point B represents the Belief Systems that individuals use to process the Activating Events in their lives. The Beliefs can be rational (rB), such as believing that the rejection was unfortunate and regretful or that the failure was annoying and unpleasant. The Beliefs can also be irrational (iB), such as thinking, "It was awful that I was rejected," "My lover shouldn't have left me," "I will never be loved again," or "How terrible it is that I didn't get into graduate school. They should have admitted me. They have prevented me from being able to succeed."

At point C, the person experiences the personal and emotional Consequences of what has just occurred. Most people and many therapists have traditionally assumed that the critical emotional Consequences of personality development are a function of the nature of the Activating Events to which an individual has been subjected. The more benign the Agents and Activities have been in early life, the healthier the personality will be; the more aversive the Activating Events, the more emotionally troubled the person. In traditional behavioral language, this is the stimulus-response (S-R) theory of personality development, which assumes that particular Stimulus conditions produce particular Responses in the organism. But a cognitive theory like rational-emotive therapy points to processes in the Organism as the critical determinants of personality functioning. In an S-O-R model the way the Organism processes Stimulus events is critical in determining what Responses are produced. In rational-emotive theory, it is not the stimuli or Activating Events that are crucial but rather the person's perceptions and interpretations of the events. So a person who processes a rejection or a failure through a rational Belief System may feel the appropriate Consequences of sorrow, regret, annoyance, displeasure, and a determination to change whatever can be changed to prevent a recurrence of the unfortunate events. Another person confronting very similar events but processing the Actions through an irrational Belief System can produce such inappropriate Consequences as depression, hostility, anxiety, or a sense of futility and worthlessness. The point is that individuals make themselves emotionally healthy or emotionally upset by the way they process the many Activating Events of their lives. As the stoics held 2,500 years ago (Ellis, 1973c), there are virtually no legitimate reasons for rational people to make themselves terribly upset, hysterical, or emotionally disturbed.

People can avoid emotional disturbances if they base their lives on their inherent tendencies to be logical and empirical. Look at the progress we have made in the physical and biological sciences by keeping our assumptions about the world natural rather than supernatural or mystical and by using empiricism and logic to test our assumptions and develop a more effective construction to the nature of reality. How much more effective our relationship to ourselves and to others could be if we would rely on reason as our guide for living. Certainly reason is not godlike, and its limitations can at times disturb us, but there is no better basis for minimizing emotional disorders than to use rationality to process the personal and interpersonal events of our lives.

As rational human beings, we recognize that the world is not always fair, that unfortunate events will occur in all of our lives to a lesser or greater extent. We will at times, then, experience such valid emotions as sorrow, regret, displeasure, and annoyance. Realistically we know we are imperfect and will always have our failures and faults, but we will rebel at the irrational idea that anyone can ever treat us as worthless just because we are imperfect. Accepting our tendencies to put our self-interests first, we will nevertheless be determined to change unpleasant social conditions along more rational lines, because we recognize that in the long run, it is in our own self-interest to live in a more rational world.

In a more rational world, we would accept our natural predispositions to be self-preserving and pleasure-producing. We would be less likely to engage in such self-defeating events as the short-term hedonism of smoking or overeating, which provides immediate gratification at the expense of lessening our aliveness. We would actualize more of our desires to be creative, to use language effectively, to be sensuous and sexual, to love and be loved (Ellis, 1973b). We would not fall into the irrational trap, however, of thinking of these natural desires as dire necessities. Being respected and valued by others, for example, would make life happier, but we would not conclude therefore that we must be approved by others. The emotionally healthy person can live in the delicate balance between caring enough about others to be effectively related but not caring so much about others to become a prisoner of their approval.

THEORY OF PSYCHOPATHOLOGY

Just as human beings have a natural propensity to be uniquely rational and straight thinking, so too humans have an exceptionally potent propensity to be crooked-thinking creatures (Ellis, 1973c). Individuals differ in their inherent tendencies toward irrationality and so in their tendencies to be more or less irrationally disturbed. Societies and families within societies also differ in their tendencies to encourage straight or crooked thinking, although unfortunately most societies rear their children in a manner that exacerbates their strong propensities to disturb themselves. But even the best of inheritances and the best of socialization cannot remove our susceptibility to being self-defeating and self-destructive. There are no gods among us. In spite of perfectionistic and grandiose wishes to be gods, any of us at any time can fall victim to propensities to procrastinate, to make the same mistakes over rather than think things through anew, to engage in wishful thinking rather than responsible action, to be dogmatic and intolerant rather than probabilistic and open, to rely on superstition and supernaturalism rather than logic and empiricism, and to indulge in greedy, short-range hedonism that mistakes immediate gratification for a pleasurable life. The only difference between those labeled psychopathological and the majority of people is the frequency with which each group emotionally upsets itself by relying on such irrational components of personality.

The clinical pathologies and emotional pathologies of everyday life can both be explained by the ABC formula of human functioning. In emotional disturbances, Activating Events are always processed through some irrational Belief. The most common irrational Beliefs are: (1) that basic human desires, such as to be sensual and sexual, are in fact needs because we define them as needs, even though we know that priests and nuns, for example, can survive without being sexual, (2) that we cannot stand certain events, whether it be having to wait in line, face criticism, or be rejected, when in fact we can stand such events no matter how unpleasant they may be, (3) that our worth as a person is determined by our successes and failures or by particular traits, such as intelligence, as if the worth of a human being can be rated like performance traits, (4) that we must maintain the approval of parents or authority figures, as if our existence is dependent on them,(5) that the world should treat us fairly, as if the world can conform to our wishes,(6) that certain people are wicked or villainous and should be punished for their villainy, as if we can rate the lack of worth of a human being,(7) that it is awful or terrible when things do not turn out the way we would like them to be, as if an idea like *awful* is a definable term with any empirical referents, (8) that we would fail to act if we did not think things were awful or if we were not emotionally upset by anger or anxiety, as if we need to be emotionally disturbed in order to make rational actions that would make the world a more pleasant place, (9) that harmful things like cigarettes or drugs can add to happiness in life or that such harmful things are needed just because going without them may be unpleasant for awhile, (10) that human happiness is externally caused and that people have little or no ability to control their feelings, (11) that one's past history is the all-important determinant of present behavior, as if something that once strongly affected one's life should affect it indefinitely, and (12) that beliefs learned as a child, whether religious, moral, or political, should serve as adequate guides for adulthood, even though the beliefs may be purely prejudices or myths (Ellis, 1972).

What is common to these irrational Beliefs is a demanding and absolute mode of thinking that is characteristic of young children. Translating desires into needs, for example, is a style of thinking that makes a want into a must, a wish into a command. Preferences can be denied, but needs demand gratification. Needs are also more absolute and are assumed to be true for all people in all places. That we must succeed, must have approval, should be treated fairly, and must smoke or drink are all forms of immature demands. That there are people who are absolutely bad, events that are absolutely awful, and religious or moral teachings that are absolutely true reflects an authoritarian mode of absolutism that leaves no room for quibbling. Such absolute beliefs have a demanding quality about them, as if they are commands from God and are not open to question.

Processing current Activating Events through such demanding and absolute Beliefs will inevitably produce inapppropriate or emotional Consequences. These irrational Beliefs can produce such excessive upsetting consequences as anger over having to wait in line, self-pity over an unfair world, depression over parental disapproval, hostility toward wicked people, guilt over breaking a rule from a dogmatic morality, or futility over changing one's life. Just because such emotional upsets occur daily in the lives of millions of people is no reason to accept the irrational illusion that such emotional disturbances are in any way healthy or necessary. Does anxiety over final exams, for example, add anything to the education or happiness of students? Are the fitful sleep, the constant worry, the sweaty palms and armpits, and the diarrhea and stomach upset appropriate to facing a final, or are these symptoms more appropriate to someone going to war? Is the insistence that one must do well on an exam the voice of a rational adult or the thinking of a child afraid of losing the approval of parents?

Not only are emotional upsets, such as anxiety over an exam, unhealthy and unnecessary, but such emotions frequently interfere with better performance by draining energy from learning and by producing emotional noise in the cognitive system that can interfere with thinking. Many students believe that it would be better to not be so anxious about exams, but they blame their anxieties on external events like the exam or a competitive society. They fail to examine their internal beliefs about their own worth, the probable consequences of doing poorly on one exam, or the possibility of parental disapproval. Some students become enraged over grading and testing systems. They insist that tests are unfair and that grades should be dropped. Until the educational world adapts to their demands, they refuse to compromise, either flunking out or getting by with the minimum. Other students become anxious about their test anxiety. They know anxiety frequently meets with social disapproval, so they become more anxious that people will know how anxious they are. They may condemn themselves for being so anxious over an exam and end up feeling worthless and depressed.

When anxiety leads to more anxiety or depression leads to more depression, the original, inappropriate emotional Consequence becomes an Activating Event that is evaluated by further irrational Beliefs as being awful or terrible, and this produces further disturbing emotional Consequences. The vicious cycle of emotional disturbance can continue as people condemn themselves for being emotionally upset, then condemn themselves for not stopping the condemning, then condemn themselves for having to go to therapy for help, then condemn themselves for not getting better, then conclude that they are hopelessly neurotic and that nothing can be done (Ellis, 1973c).

THEORY OF THERAPEUTIC PROCESSES

As long as clients or therapists continue to focus on either the Activating Events or the disturbing emotional Consequences, little in the way of lasting help can be found. Yet traditionally all too many therapists have focused on historical Activating Events, going from point A_1 to A_2 to A_3, further and further back in the patient's history, as if anything in the past can be changed. Or therapists have focused on getting out the feelings, having clients express how anxious they are about being anxious or how angry, guilty, or depressed they are, as if such emotional Consequences will dissipate into thin air just because they have been expressed. Once the ABCs of psychopathology are understood, it becomes clear that point D will involve the client and the therapist working together to Dispute the irrational Beliefs that are producing disturbing emotional Consequences. Clients and therapists work together to raise the clients' level of consciousness from a childish, demanding, and absolute style of thinking to a logical, empirical, and probabilistic style of processing information, which characterizes the mature adult and the responsible scientist.

Consciousness Raising

THE CLIENT'S WORK

Since much of the consciousness raising in rational-emotive therapy is an *educational* process, the work of clients frequently resembles that of students. In the process of explaining their problems, clients are very quickly challenged to defend the Beliefs that underlie their emotional upsets. They are challenged to give evidence, for example, for the Belief that they must be popular in order to be happy. Clients soon learn that their favorite Beliefs and biases are not accepted by the teacher-therapist just because the client presents the belief in an absolute or demanding way. "Show me where it is written that you must be a success in order to feel good about yourself" is a common challenge to the dogmatism of clients. Clients soon become aware that they have important irrational beliefs that they cannot defend logically or empirically. They become aware that they are indeed upsetting themselves emotionally by insisting on such nonsense as the belief that just because they are the king of their family as children, they must be king of their companies in order to be happy. Such foolishness is met with impatience in rational-emotive institutes. And like honest and humble students, they have a lot to learn about this business of living, but at the same time they are encouraged to maintain the appropriate belief that they have the human potential to be as rational and as clear-headed as their teacher-therapist.

One hour a week in therapy, however, is more like the tutorials of the British universities, and if clients are to progress with any efficiency, they will have to do the homework that is assigned to them. Homework will frequently include reading some well-reasoned books, including some of those by Ellis, such as *Sex Without Guilt* (1958), *A Guide to Successful Marriage* (Ellis & Harper, 1972), and *How to Live with a Neurotic* (1957a). Homework will also include listening to and criticizing tapes of their therapy sessions, so that clients can come to recognize their own absolute or demanding Beliefs. Clients work to become aware of when they are making "should" or "must" statements when statements of preference or desire would be more accurate.

If clients say they cannot stand to be rejected by the opposite sex, they will be given behavioral assignments to ask three different people out on dates to test the hypothesis that they can indeed stand rejection. Such assignments are also helpful in providing evidence to refute the belief that a particular client is too much of a worm to have any woman go out with him. With such homework assignments, clients beome irrefutably aware that their irrational Beliefs are not grounded in fact.

As clients become more skilled in consciously catching their own slips into childish cognitions, they can take turns teaching others in rational-emotive groups and seminars. One client will be called upon to analyze the underlying Beliefs that another client is using to produce emotional upset or to criticize a fellow client's conclusion that failure to get a date this week proves that the client is a worthless worm. As many graduate students have discovered when they begin to teach, there is no better way to learn.

THE THERAPIST'S WORK

Since the propensities of clients and students to engage in crooked thinking are so profound, the rational-emotive therapist is prepared to use a multitude of didactic and feedback techniques to teach clients to distinguish between mature logical-empirical thought and the trouble-making foolishness that frequently passes for reason. The therapist begins in the first session to interpret the irrational Beliefs that are producing the clients' emotional complaints. The active therapist does not have to wait for clients to articulate all of their irrational premises. Being educated in rational-emotive theory and experienced with a variety of clients, the therapist can anticipate the nature of the underlying Beliefs by an awareness of the Activating Events and of the inappropriate emotional Consequences. To have a rejection by a husband (point A) be followed by a profound, incapacitating depression (point C) is most likely to involve the following irrational Beliefs: (1) The rejection is awful, (2) The wife can't stand it, (3) She should not be rejected, (4) She will never be accepted by any desirable partner, (5) She is a worthless worm because he rejected her, and (6) She deserves to be condemned for being so worthless (Ellis, 1973c).

Therapists need not be obsessive about the timing of interpretations. When they are confident they understand the nature of the underlying Beliefs, then they should present the information to the clients directly and forcefully. Rational-emotive therapists are under no illusions that one well-timed interpretation will produce lasting insights. Interpretations and confrontations will be made over and over until clients become undeniably aware of their irrationalities.

Interpretations do not involve making conscious connections between present upsets and past events but rather connect the present complaints to the current Beliefs that clients are using to upset themselves. In the process of giving clients feedback about the specific irrational Beliefs being used, therapists also are teaching the ABCs of rational-emotive therapy. Therapists also provide explicit information about the nature of scientific reasoning and how it can be used to solve personal problems. Through books, tapes, seminars, and frequent mini-lectures in therapy, clients are taught the essentials of rational-emotive theory. Of course, as with any theory, students tend to understand and accept rational-emotive theory more when it is made relevant to the explanation and solution of their personal problems.

Besides interpretations and confrontations, therapists also raise the consciousness of clients to a more mature, rational level through *refutations*. As effective debaters, therapists can point out inherent contradictions between the clients' Beliefs or between Beliefs and actions, such as showing clients that they can stand to be criticized even though it is uncomfortable. They do not die or go crazy or run out of the room just because the therapist has criticized one of their demanding Beliefs. If clients are deathly afraid of any homosexual desires, for example, and insist that homosexuals are bad, the therapist may counter with objective information about homosexuals. More frequently the therapist puts *refutations* in the form of the common questions "What evidence do you have . . . ?" or "Where is it written that you must . . . ?"

Believing in active learning, therapists direct their clients to do various homework assignments designed either to give evidence to refute irrational hypotheses or to practice their developing ability to rely on more rational thinking. Writing a paper on more effective means of finding a job can help a patient practice a more rational consciousness. Encouraging patients to go to a massage parlor can begin to refute the belief that they are not sensuous or that they cannot enjoy pleasure without guilt. Assigning perfectionists to wear two different colored socks or wrinkled slacks can help them to blow their own images and in the process practice their new insights that life can be a pleasure without having to be perfect.

Rational-emotive therapists use many other techniques to encourage their clients to become more rational in their emotions and behavior. Humor is one of the safest ways to get clients to become aware of some of their foolishness. Self-disclosure of the therapist's foibles can keep clients from falling back into the wishful thinking that anyone, including the therapist, can be godlike or can demonstrate to clients that the therapist can feel worthwhile while being imperfect. Encouraging the direct expression of embarrassing emotions is done not for the sake of emoting, but as the first step in clients becoming fully aware of the emotional Consequences of their irrational Beliefs. The rational-emotive therapist is in many ways eclectic in technique while maintaining a consistent and comprehensive theory of personality, pathology, and therapy.

Contingency Control

Recognizing no absolutes, including his own theory, Ellis (1973b; 1973c) is willing to rely on other therapy systems when his own approach reaches its limits. He is especially willing to use behavior therapy approaches to supplement his own therapy. Ellis has even at times characterized himself as a behavior therapist with a strong cognitive orientation. As we shall see in Chapter 10 on behavior therapy, as behavior therapists move in a more cognitive direction, they in turn frequently include the principles of rational-emotive therapy as an important part of a contemporary behavioral approach (Goldfried & Davison, 1976; Rimm & Masters, 1974).

THE CLIENT'S WORK

If the client is failing to follow through on homework assignments in spite of interpretations or exhortations from the therapist, the client might be asked to make a contingency contract that seems workable for the client. A Nixon-hater, for example, may be required to give the therapist $100 and sign a contract that states for each week the client fails to go on a date, the therapist will send a $25 check from the client to Nixon with best wishes for a successful return to the public scene.

THE THERAPIST'S WORK

Rational-emotive therapists also attempt to reduce the effects of contingencies by having clients *reevaluate* particular consequences. "What is the worst thing that can happen to you if you take a risk?" the therapist asks frequently, and "Is that consequence really awful or catastrophic or is it just inconvenient or unpleasant?" Consequences such as being laughed at, being turned down for a date, and not getting an A on an exam can be "deawfulized" and as a result defused as controlling Consequences. The therapist can deawfulize Consequences by having the group laugh at the client's foolishness, or having a female client assert herself by trying to convince a male in the group to kiss her. The therapist has clients confront the very Consequences that seem terrible so that they can reevaluate the Consequences in order to no longer be controlled by them. Similarly the therapist can assign the client to imagine 10 times a day an expected Consequence until the imagined outcome no longer elicits much emotion, which again can reduce the probable effects of contingencies. Finally, contingency controls are changed by having the client continue to ask, "But what is the objective probability that what I expect will really happen?" With a reevaluation of the objective probabilities of a particular consequence occurring, the client becomes more able to take the risks required to produce more pleasure in life.

THEORY OF THERAPEUTIC CONTENT

Intrapersonal Conflicts

Psychological problems are intrapersonal in origin, since individuals produce emotional problems within themselves by processing events through irrational belief systems. Therapy usually begins then with individual sessions focusing on the client's demanding thinking rather than on the relationship between client and therapist. Once clients are more conscious of their inappropriate cognitions, they are usually placed in groups. Therapy groups can serve as a microcosm of the larger world and clients can practice reacting to criticism, rejection, or pleasure in more rational ways. In the groups clients can practice new behaviors, such as assertion, that follow from more logical attitudes toward life. And in the groups clients can practice teaching others to be more rational. Regardless of how much of the therapy is done in a group setting, however, the focus is not on the relationships between group members but on the rational quality of thinking, emoting, or behaving that is being revealed by particular individuals.

ANXIETY AND DEFENSES

Anxiety is an inappropriate irrational consequence of inappropriate cognitions. When we examine the myriad of events about which people make themselves anxious, we see how widespread are irrational cognitions. Divorce is labeled by some as terrible, and the prospect of divorce inevitably brings anxiety. An unwanted pregnancy can be catastrophic, and parents become unduly upset about their children's sexuality. Homosexuals are believed to be horrible, and communities become threatened by having a homosexual teacher in the schools. People tell themselves they must be perfect, and they become anxious when they are confronted by criticism. They tell themselves they should be liked by everyone, and they get tense when someone is angry with them. They tell themselves they must be married to be happy, and they panic if they do not have a potential partner in their senior year. Such anxieties cannot be extinguished by desensitizing a person to a particular stimulus but rather by disputing the irrational thoughts that a person has about stimulus events. Effectively disputing the inappropriate use of labels, such as terrible or horrible, or the childish demands, such as having to be perfect, will lead to the emotional Effect of removing anxiety.

Defense mechanisms are examples of the irrational propensities of people. Projection is a clear example of people thinking that emotional upset is caused by external events. Repression is a reflection of the irrational belief that it is best to not think about unpleasant events. Rationalization is perhaps the most common defense that people use as they reflect a desire to convince the world that they are in fact reasonable human beings who have good reasons for behaving or feeling foolishly. Defenses are not to be protected. They are to be attacked. Confrontations, interpretations, and refutations can weaken these irrational forces and allow patients to become more rational and emotionally healthy people.

SELF-ESTEEM

There is no way that we can prove our worth as human beings. To base our esteem on an ability to achieve, to love, to be approved, to be honest, or even to be rational is to say that the value of the whole person is defined by the value of only a part of what that person is (Ellis, 1973b). To rate our worth by totaling the value of all our separate traits, such as intelligence, looks and competency, and our performances, such as our school grades, tennis scores, and academic degrees, is a futile irrational need for a global report card that indicates where we stand in relationship to the rest of the universe. We act as if the universe truly cares whether we are what we are supposed to be, whatever that might be. Any grand conclusion about our worth or lack of worth is a self-defined definition or devilification that declares us on the team of the deity or the devil.

If we must have self-esteem, then it is best to assume that we are good because we are alive. But even that is an inelegant solution to self-esteem because it is a tautology that defines good as alive and alive as good. We could just as readily define being alive as worthless and argue that we are bad because we exist. The elegant solution to self-esteem is to recognize the question of our worth as a meaningless and unnecessary distraction. The question is logically and empirically meaningless because there is no empirical referent for self-worth, no objective criterion in the universe that we can point to as a measure of our worth. In fact, any preoccupation with proving our worth can be a major interference in enjoying life. If self-esteem is based on performances such as grades, for example, we can cause our moods to rise and fall with the latest exam rather than enjoy our education to the fullest. If we base our esteem on competency or on looks, then we may make ourselves worried about aging and the possibility of declining competency or deteriorating looks. To give up the elusive search for self-esteem can free up energy for the meaningful question of how we can most enjoy our entire life.

RESPONSIBILITY

Clients can be held truly responsible for troubled lives only if they have been instrumental in creating their personal problems. They cannot be responsible for how others treated them in childhood; they can be responsible only for how they currently construe their childhood. They cannot be responsible for their genetic makeup; they can be responsible only if they choose to rely on their propensities for reason over their propensities to be unreasonable. Clients can insist that their parents or their genes determined all that they are and can even bolster their beliefs with a variety of psychological theories. With such insistence they can feel temporary relief, the relief that comes with shirking any weighty responsibility, including the responsibility for creating a better life.

Accepting responsibility for one's own problems does not involve blaming oneself. Blame is just another expression of the tyranny of the should: "You shouldn't have been so foolish; you shouldn't have been so demanding." The fact is, patient, you have been foolish, demanding, and dogmatic, and you continue to be as long as you engage in the irrational guilt that comes with blaming yourself and insisting that you should have been different in the past. The question is: Are you willing to be mature and responsible enough right now to use your reason to find better alternatives for living? Or will you wallow in the guilt of self-blame or the resentment of blaming your parents? Feel regret and sadness if you will, but even more feel the excitement that can come with accepting the responsibility for a more reasonable and pleasurable life.

Interpersonal Conflicts

INTIMACY AND SEXUALITY

Surely love and intimacy can add to the good life. Not being islands, nearly all individuals find it enjoyable to love and be loved by significant others. It is reasonable to want to be able to relate well in interpersonal encounters. In fact the evidence suggests that the better their interpersonal relationships, the happier people are likely to be. That is not to say, however, that love or intimacy is necessary for human existence. As soon as we define love as an absolute necessity, we become anxious, demanding, or dependent lovers. If we must have love, we become prone to being possessive of those who provide essential nourishment, jealous if they turn their love toward others, and threatened that someone will come along and take away the love we cannot live without. The clinging-vine wife, the jealous husband, the possessive partner, and the insecure spouse are examples of people defining love as a necessity. To care too much about having good personal relationships can make us as desperate as the distant ones who care too little. In spite of some very popular religious beliefs, we need not deify love in order to appreciate it. Love is a human phenomenon that adds to the pleasure and joy of living, not an absolute that can justify our existence or sanctify ourselves.

Sex also requires no sanctification. Sex is not some dirty desire that can be justified only by procreation, marriage, or love. As an outspoken advocate of *Sex Without Guilt* (1958), Ellis was a rare rational voice for sexual freedom well before the sexual revolution was rolling in the 1960s. Recognizing that sex may be more enjoyable for many people when it occurs within an intimate relationship, it is still reasonable to ask, "Where is the evidence that sex and love must go together?" To insist that sex needs love to be good is apparently a human teaching that is really a moral wolf in sheep's clothing, a form of the old repressive morality that demands that sex be justified by some higher value than the purely intrinsic pleasure it produces. Too many couples lose the joy of sex because they believe that they are always supposed to make love in an atmosphere that resembles a chapel with bells ringing. Sex can be just for fun. Sex can be the clearest expression of the natural propensity of people to be pleasure-producing. To be free to enjoy this profound pleasure is to ignore the irrational prohibitions of an antisexual society or the equally irrational demands of an achievement-oriented society that would judge the worth of individuals by the number of orgasms they achieve or the number of partners they have. Sex without guilt and without anxiety comes to those who are rational enough to express their natural sexual desires without concern for parental or performance demands.

COMMUNICATION

Most of what are labeled communication problems are, in fact, thinking problems. People who comunicate vague, boring, bizarre, repetitive, or contradictory messages are just revealing the vague, boring, bizarre, repetitive, or contradictory character of their cognitions. Effective dialogue is rare because people who can think effectively are rare. If people are helped to become more rational in their style of thinking, they will generally also become more effective in their style of communicating. There are exceptions to this rule, of course, but they are relatively rare. Many stutterers, for example, may think straight but have such desires to be perfect speakers that they are horrified at making the normal disfluencies of everyday speech. They cannot accept the hesitations, "you knows," "ohs," and "ahs" of us mortal mouths. They end up self-consciously selecting the words over which they are least likely to stumble. As a result, they stop and stammer, recycle their sentences, and do a number of other things that result in even more disastrous disfluencies. They have to quit making demands on themselves to be ultrafluent and just start stumbling along like the rest of us. There are also people who have fairly clear ideas about what they want but are nontalkers because of anxiety that others will dislike or reject what they have to say. These nonassertive speakers have to quit awfulizing about what others might think and begin taking the risks that come with directly communicating one's thoughts and desires.

HOSTILITY

Hostility is the irrational consequence of: (1) an inborn, biological tendency to become aggressive, (2) some unpleasant or frustrating event, and (3) a tendency to think crookedly about the event and a persistent refusal to work against this crooked tendency (Ellis, 1973b). All three of these variables must be present for hostility to occur. Human beings are not just reflexive animals that react to frustration with aggression, otherwise most of us would be hostile most of the time. Frustrating events are almost always available to us, since the world we live in obviously is a frequently depriving, restraining, unfair place. In order for us to erupt into rage, we have to focus on the frustrations around us; exaggerate the meanings of these events into something awful, horrendous, or villainous; and insist that such frustrations should not exist and that we can no longer stand their existence. The hostile person demands the removal of all injustices, unfairnesses, and frustrations immediately. With such impossible demands, hostile persons upset themselves unnecessarily. They are like children throwing temper tantrums because their demands are not being met immediately. There is no law that says such people have to continue with such unrealistic, immature demands. Since we cannot remove inborn tendencies to become aggressive or prevent all frustrations from occurring, our best alternative is to help hostile people think of frustrations as unfortunate events that are an unpleasant part of all our lives.

CONTROL

A need to control others is merely one expression of irrational individuals demanding that the world conform to their wishes. The tactics for gaining compliance from others include imposing the tyranny of the should onto others, followed by trying to make them feel guilty if they do not act as we believe they should. This is a favorite tactic of parents, as they insist that their children should be polite, should not speak up, should be a success, and by all means should never disgrace the family's name. Threatening to follow demands with anger is a less subtle controlling technique but works especially well with people who believe it is terrible to have someone angry at them. Most controls work only if people being controlled cooperate by allowing their irrational beliefs to respond, such as "You're right, I should feel guilty for not being polite." If the person responds rationally by saying, "Don't make guilt. I have enough trouble disputing my own internal tyrannical shoulds without having to fight yours as well." Then the person attempting to control is having subtle irrational communications exposed by the light of clear thinking. The most effective counter-control method is to dispute the irrational demands of others by asserting one's own rationality.

Individuo-Social Conflicts

ADJUSTMENT VERSUS TRANSCENDENCE

People who believe that they can in any real way transcend the restraints, injustices, limitations, and frustrations of society will inevitably make themselves emotionally upset. Fighting the inevitable is one of the foolish ways of creating high blood pressure, ulcers, anxiety, anger, or depression, and it is inevitable that we are dependent on a society filled with irrational institutions. Look at the example of the radicals of the 1960s who insisted that they were above the sanctions of the society—some were jailed, others were ostracized to foreign countries, and many are now depressed as they struggle to make it back into the mainstream of society. The fantasy to fly like Icarus far above the world represents the grandiose beliefs of irrational people that they can somehow be more than mere mortals. Like Icarus, such superhuman people eventually fall on their foolish faces.

Before we take on irrational forces in society, we had better first fight the irrational forces in ourselves. We have to first get our own heads on straight before we worry about setting straight the heads of state. To substitute one set of irrational beliefs with demands that are equally irrational may be the history of much of the world, but it certainly is not progress. If we are to make significant strides toward making our communities more pleasant places to live, we will require a substantial number of people who are committed to solving social problems through logical and empirical methods rather than through the tired, old dogmatic demands that society must be more just and decent.

IMPULSE CONTROL

Human beings are unique creatures who can make almost any desire into a seemingly uncontrollable impulse. The common desire to gain large sums of money without working can lead to a demand that the person must gamble. The desire for tasty foods can become an irresistible impulse to eat excessively, even though overeaters know obesity can be the consequence. Impulses to steal, smoke, and exhibit one's genitals are just some of the many examples of people turning desires into self-destructive demands. Such short-term hedonists ignore the realistic long-term consequences of their actions by insisting, "I should be able to eat all I want and not gain weight"; "I should be able to gamble against the odds and be a winner"; "I should be able to take what I want and not be punished." In reacting to such demands, most forces in society, including many systems of therapy, foolishly attack the impulsive behavior rather than the stinking thinking that creates such impulse-ridden characters.

Society also can define certain human desires as uncontrollable impulses and then use social forces to overcontrol individuals. Sex is a prime example. Western society has traditionally defined human sexuality as an uncontrollable irrational impulse that must be repressed lest people become possessed by a demon that brings disease, unwanted pregnancies, and a loss of decency. In fact, the irrational forces are the antisexual voices in society that have possessed the power to repress the open and free dissemination of sex information, the full availability of birth control devices, and access to humane health care that treats venereal infections like any other disease transmitted by people in close contact, not like a social disease or disgrace. That there are people who express their sexuality in irrational and irresponsible ways is not surprising in a society that has been so irrational and irresponsible in helping children to understand their sexuality as a natural desire that can be enjoyed fully within the context of a rational life. If we want to help create a less impulsive and more human world, then the one impulse we want to attack is the tendency to engage in irrational thinking, whether that tendency is occurring on an individual or a social level.

RULES FOR LIVING

Rational people accept that living in social groups involves limits that we call rules. Human beings in their pure organismic state are not noble savages with just and decent inherent tendencies. Individuals possess too powerful propensities to follow irrational beliefs for there not to be rules. All that healthy people ask is that the rules be reasonable. This means that the rules be flexible and open to change when evidence or logic indicates that different rules would allow a more pleasant life for the individuals involved. A reasonable family, for example, would set rules in a manner that allows each person affected by the rules to have a right to use rational discourse to dispute a particular limit in order to convince the rest of the family to accept a change in an unnecessary or foolish regulation.

Beyond Conflict to Fulfillment

MEANING

If we are searching for some absolute meaning to life, we are bound to be disappointed. There are no absolutes except those we create. If by meaning we seek a belief that can justify our existence, forget it. The universe does not care that we exist; we do. If by meaning, however, we are looking for that which makes life more enjoyable, then we may be able to agree that it is best to maximize our pleasures and minimize our pains, since by definition pleasure is what we enjoy. The particular pleasure that we seek is a somewhat individual matter discovered by each person in the process of living. The important thing is that our pleasures come from desires, not demands. There surely is more joy in doing what we want to do rather than what we must do. If we can keep from defining life as a demand and learn to desire life for its pleasures, then we can know life at its best. The rational person, however, does not expect life to be a rose garden. The rational person knows that there are painful thorns in each person's life but refuses to make the unfortunate events of life any more upsetting or unpleasant than they already are.

VALUES

Since all psychotherapy is, at bottom, a value system, effective therapists would do well to have a good philosophy of life (Ellis, 1973b). Effective therapists should be prepared to discuss deeply philosophic questions with clients, if they expect to get very far. Questions of values may masquerade as purely practical questions of how to become less anxious or depressed. But as London (1964) has shown, behind such clinical requests are value judgments that it is better to be less anxious or depressed. There are those who believe that the best life requires suffering and deprivation. A therapist with such values might try to convince clients to cherish their depression rather than to extinguish it. Clients are looking for a better life, if only free from symptoms, and effective therapists are prepared to present at least one alternative that has worked well for themselves.

Rational therapists do not pretend to give *the* answer to what is a better life. They only give *an* answer to a better life. It is up to clients to decide whether the rational answer is valuable for them. In many ways rational therapists are less concerned with *what* clients value and more concerned with *how* clients value. If clients base their values on absolute beliefs, then they are stuck with the tyranny of the should (they should succeed, they must have love) and the emotional upset that accompanies such demands. Believing in no universal shoulds and no tyrannical gods telling us what we must value, the rational-emotive therapist warns us to beware of the tyrant that is within us. By recognizing the relative nature of values, we can guide our lives by what would be better, what would be preferable. Given that we are human beings, we will at times act contrary to our values. But at no time can we give reason for condemning ourselves, for judging ourselves as creeps or worms because we committed an unethical act. There is at least one thing in life that is beyond good and evil, and that is ourselves.

IDEAL PERSON

It is unfortunate that many people in our society are becoming disenchanted with science because it has not been able to solve all the problems of the universe. It is unfortunate because in many ways the scientist is an excellent ideal for humanity. As an ideal, scientists are committed to the rational life, a life of applying logic and empiricism to solving problems. As Bronowski (1959) so elegantly argues, honesty and open communication are values inherent in science. Science welcomes rational criticism of ideas and methods rather than believing that criticism is awful or terrible. While scientists prefer to be correct, they surely want to know quickly if they're heading down the wrong track. They do not believe it is catastrophic if their favorite theories are eventually rejected for more elegant or effective explanations.

Scientists are fascinated, not frustrated, by what is inevitable. They recognize their own limits and do not expect that science can answer all the philosophical questions of life. At their best, scientists are hedonists who enjoy immensely their research into the unknown rather than puritans driven by demands that they must succeed. What other group of human beings can point to such accomplishments as a vaccine against the crippling of polio or the wonder of a man on the moon. The revolutionary discoveries of science are evidence for the value of a philosophy based on logic and empiricism.

THEORY OF THE THERAPEUTIC RELATIONSHIP

Being practically a polar opposite of Rogerian therapy, rational-emotive therapy agrees only with the idea that the therapist demonstrates unconditional acceptance of clients, even while atacking many of the clients' irrational beliefs and self-destructive behaviors. Full acceptance of the client as a human does not mean that the therapist must demonstrate warmth or liking toward the client. Such warmth may feel good, but it is not necessary for effective therapy to occur. Therapists demonstrate their full tolerance of clients by never evaluating the client as a person. Only some of the client's beliefs or behaviors are evaluated but never that which the client would call the self.

Rational-emotive therapists are not particularly sympathetic with patients weeping or being angry but rather use such visible indications of upset to try to prove to patients that they are believing in irrational ideas. Nor is accurate empathy with emotions particularly helpful, since such empathy is frequently a form of commiseration that only encourages the person to continue feeling bad, sad, or upset. Rational therapists are quite empathic in the sense of listening very hard to understand what clients are probably telling themselves to produce their upsetting emotions. Clients report feeling understood, not because the therapist is emoting with them but because the therapist is bringing into awareness the cause of the client's problems.

Rational-emotive therapists are frequently genuine and open, directly revealing their own ideas, beliefs, and philosophy of life. Such therapists are also willing to reveal some of their own foibles in order to dispute the client's foolish belief that anyone, even a therapist, can be more than human. Transference feelings are attacked, not encouraged, since such irrational feelings are just more examples of clients trying to demand that the world be something other than what it is.

Working as a combination of philosopher-teacher-scientist, the rational-emotive therapist views the therapeutic relationship as primarily a precondition for effective education. As long as the client remains willing to relate, the therapist can use hard-headed reasoning to teach the client how to actively dispute the irrational beliefs that are the root of emotional problems.

PRACTICALITIES OF RATIONAL-EMOTIVE THERAPY

As a no-nonsense approach in which active and direct intervention begins in the opening intake interview, rational-emotive therapy is designed to be a short-term therapy that can teach the ABCs of emotional problems in 1 to 10 sessions. Once patients have the basic ABCs down, they are most often put in group therapy to further refine and practice the rational philosophy of living that they are applying to their problems. While rational-emotive therapy can be effective with a wide range of clinical problems, Ellis (1957a) does admit that, as with almost all therapies, rational-emotive therapy is most effective in treating mildly disturbed individuals or those with a single major symptom. Patients with greater inborn tendencies toward irrational thinking, such as borderline or psychotic individuals, can be helped, but therapy is longer term, running from at least six months to a year.

A unique feature of Ellis's institutes in New York is the free weekly meetings on Friday evenings that are open to present, past, or prospective clients or to people just interested in getting a more firsthand knowledge of rational-emotive therapy. The institutes also run a private elementary school, the Living School, for normal children, which includes preventative education in how to avoid unnecessary emotional upsets.

In form, rational-emotive therapy is like most other therapies, with one-hour weekly individual sessions or two-hour group sessions being the norm. At the institutes, attempts are made to keep fees moderate, but in regular private practice fees seem to follow the going rates in the community. While many eclectics are reported to use some of the ideas or techniques of rational-emotive therapy (Ellis, 1973c), there are only about 150 registered rational-emotive therapists. A one- or two-year postgraduate internship at one of the institutes is recommended for therapists from any helping profession who want to be fully prepared to do rational-emotive therapy.

A MAJOR ALTERNATIVE TO RATIONAL-EMOTIVE THERAPY: BECK'S COGNITIVE THERAPY

Although Beck (1970, 1976) developed his cognitive therapy independently from Ellis, there are major similarities to their approaches. Beck and Ellis share the goal of helping clients to become conscious of maladaptive cognitions, to recognize the disruptive impact of such cognitions, and to replace them with more appropriate and adaptive thought patterns. According to Beck (1976), the successful client passes through several stages in correcting faulty cognitions:

"First he has to become aware of what he is thinking. Second, he needs to recognize what thoughts are awry. Then he has to substitute accurate for inaccurate judgments. Finally, he needs feedback to inform him whether his changes are correct" (p. 217).

While this sounds like a quote from Ellis, there are subtle but important differences between Beck's cognitive therapy and rational-emotive therapy. In contrast to Ellis's direct confrontational style, Beck emphasizes more of a Socratic dialogue. Therapeutic interactions are structured so that clients discover for themselves those thoughts that are inaccurate. In cognitive therapy clients are led to make personal discoveries by a tactful progression of questions.

Cognitive therapy is generally more structured than rational emotive therapy. With depression, for example, Beck limits therapy to 20 hours. Such structure discourages both therapists and clients from wasting time, while providing the client with a much needed sense of order and discipline.

Beck also distinguishes between therapeutic strategies designed to eliminate overt symptoms and those directed toward changing cognitions. As a leading authority on depressive disorders, Beck (1967, 1970, 1976) recognizes the need to first reduce such severe symptoms as suicidal impulses, insomnia, and weight loss. For symptom relief Beck relies more on contingency management, by structuring assignments in such a way that clients will succeed and be reinforced for their efforts. The first assignment might be to simply boil an egg. As the client begins to feel better, a more challenging assignment is given that can bring greater reinforcement, such as cooking a meal for the family. Often interventions introduced early in therapy include activity schedule making, in which specific daily activities are selected and evaluated strictly on the basis of how effectively they elevate mood. These activities are also rated by clients in terms of mastery and pleasure. Depressed clients who characteristically report that they can master nothing and enjoy nothing are thus confronted with feedback to the contrary. After symptoms begin to lift, then the focus of treatment shifts to underlying cognitions.

In cognitive therapy the underlying cognitions are assumed to vary with the psychiatric diagnosis of clients. Different pathologies are related to different cognitive styles. Depression, for example, is related to a different pattern of ideas than is mania, hysteria, phobias, or obsessive compulsive disorders. The basic ideation in depression has three themes or what Beck (1970) terms the *cognitive triad*: (1) Events are interpreted negatively, (2) Depressed individuals dislike themselves, and (3) The future is appraised negatively. These fundamental ideas are referred to by Beck as *rules*. In contrast to Ellis, he does not view them as necessarily irrational. Instead they are characterized as too absolute, too broad or extreme, or too arbitrary.

Basic rules give rise to maladaptive self-verbalizations or possibly visual images, which are experienced as automatic thoughts by clients. Much of therapy involves assisting clients in ferreting out automatic thinking and, ultimately, the basic rules and reevaluating those rules by testing them both logically and empirically. For example, a female client who thinks men will reject her if she expresses her positive feelings about women's liberation might be encouraged to test this hypothesis out on her date.

With practice clients learn "distancing." They learn to deal with upsetting thoughts objectively, reevaluating them rather than automatically accepting them. By using disattribution, for example, clients disabuse themselves of the belief that they are entirely responsible for their problems. Therapists also help clients reconceptualize seemingly insolvable problems so that they have workable solutions, which is particularly valuable with suicidal clients. Clients are also helped to change their expectations about themselves, their environments, and their futures. By identifying basic rules or assumptions they can become aware of how such rules lead them to expect to be depressed. Rules that predispose people to depression include:

1. In order to be happy, I have to be successful in whatever I undertake.
2. To be happy, I must be accepted by all people.
3. If I make a mistake, it means that I'm inept.
4. I can't live without love.

By becoming conscious of such basic assumptions about themselves and by reevaluating these rules for living, clients begin to free themselves from debilitating expectations that they are doomed to depression or other forms of pathology.

THE EFFECTIVENESS OF RATIONAL-EMOTIVE THERAPY

Ellis (1973c) and Murphy and Ellis (1976) cite an impressive list of studies supporting the effectiveness of rational-emotive therapy. However, these lists include many studies that are either case studies or case surveys, studies with experimentally induced anxieties, or studies with college student volunteers with nonclinical problems such as snake phobias. The present review will be limited to the appropriately controlled experiments testing the outcome of rational-emotive therapy, including some of the work with college students, since these are the best-controlled experiments available.

The first outcome research was the study by Ellis (1957b) reported in Chapter 2. As already indicated, Ellis was more effective with rational-emotive therapy than with either psychoanalysis or psychoanalytically oriented psychotherapy.

Krippner (1964) added rational-emotive therapy to a five-week reading clinic program for children to increase the effectiveness of the clinic. He also added bibliotherapy and nondirective play therapy. He compared the improvement rates of the 30 children (26 boys and 4 girls) who were in the 1962 program with the rates of 40 children (37 boys and 3 girls) who were in the program in 1963 when the three therapies were included. The age range of the children was 7 to 16, and 12 percent attended the 1962 clinic. There was no placebo or no-treatment control group.

While Krippner stated that the therapies were effective, an examination of the data reported does not support such a claim. The overall improvement score was a mean of 0.88 in 1962 and 0.89 in 1963. Rational-emotive therapy, then, along with the other two therapies, did not appear to add significantly to the effectiveness of the reading clinic.

Karst and Trexler (1970) compared the effectiveness of rational-emotive therapy with that of fixed-role therapy, a cognitive approach based on Kelly's cognitive theory of personality. The subjects were 22 college students with public speaking anxiety. Since there were not enough volunteers, a planned placebo group was dropped, and eight subjects were placed in each therapy group, leaving six in a no-treatment control group. The therapy groups were run in two sections, with four students in each section. One of the authors was trained in rational-emotive therapy and one in fixed-role therapy, and they worked together as co-therapists for each of the groups.

Of the five self-report measures of public speaking anxiety, three showed significant improvement in both therapy groups when compared with the no-treatment group. The two therapies did not differ significantly in effectiveness. A behavioral measure of disruptions in a four-minute speech following treatment indicated no significant differences among the three groups.

DiLoreto (1971) compared the effectiveness of rational-emotive therapy, client-centered therapy, systematic desensitization, and an attention placebo treatment with college students experiencing high interpersonal anxiety. One hundred freshmen and sophomores (58 women and 42 men) volunteered for nine hours of treatment. There were 20 subjects in each of the four treatments and 20 in a no-contact control group. The groups were matched for sex of the subject and included 10 students reporting a more extroverted personality and 10 with a more introverted personality. There were two therapists for each form of treatment. The therapists were advanced doctoral students in clinical and counseling psychology at Michigan State University. Each of the therapists was assigned to his or her preferred form of treatment and ran one group of five introverts and another group of five extroverts.

Interpersonal anxiety, as measured by self-report scales and behavioral ratings, was reduced significantly more in the three therapy groups than in either the placebo or the no-contact group. Systematic desensitization was significantly more effective than either rational-emotive or client-centered therapy. There was no overall difference between rational-emotive and client-centered therapy results. These two therapies did differ, however, inasmuch as rational-emotive therapy was three times more effective with introverts than with extroverts, whereas client-centered therapy was two and a half times more effective with extroverts than with introverts. Systematic desensitization was equally effective with both introverts and extroverts.

Straatmeyer and Watkins (1974) evaluated the effectiveness of two forms of rational-emotive therapy in reducing public speaking anxiety in college students. The first form was basically conventional rational-emotive therapy, while the second form left the disputing of irrational beliefs up to the students rather than the therapists actively disputing or exhorting the students to dispute their beliefs. Fifteen students were assigned to each form of therapy, 14 were assigned to an attention placebo group that discussed anxiety in general with no reference to rational-emotive concepts, and 13 were assigned to a no-treatment control group. The therapy and placebo groups each received five hours of treatment.

The four groups were compared on a self-rating of speech anxiety, a self-report measure of confidence in speaking, and two behavioral ratings of anxiety during a three-minute speech. An analysis of covariance failed to yield any significant differences among the four groups on any of the measures.

Keller, Brookling, and Croake (1975) applied rational-emotive therapy to help the aged deal with anxieties concerning getting old. Twenty-eight women and two men, 60 years of age and older, were assigned to either a rational-emotive therapy group or a waiting-list, no-treatment control group. The therapy group met for two hours a week for four weeks. The two dependent measures were the Adult Irrational Ideas Inventory and the Trait Anxiety Scale of the State Trait Anxiety Inventory. The control group showed no significant improvement on these measures, while the aged treated with rational-emotive therapy reported quite significant decreases in both anxiety and irrational thinking.

Kanter (1975) tested a form of rational-emotive therapy using imaginal processes against a form of desensitization and against desensitization combined with imaginal rational therapy for reducing interpersonal anxiety. The relatively large sample was made up of 68 community residents (18 men and 50 women) with a mean age of 35. The study was run in two parts, with the second part ($n = 33$) being an exact replication of the first part ($n = 35$). Therapy was run in groups of 8 to 10 people for seven weekly sessions lasting one and a half hours.

Each of the three treatment groups demonstrated reductions on self-report measures of interpersonal anxiety when compared with the waiting-list control group. The rational restructuring group reported greater gains in therapy than did the desensitization group, and these gains were maintained at a nine-week follow-up. The desensitization plus rational restructuring treatment was superior to desensitization alone but was not as effective as rational therapy alone. This study provides fairly strong support for the superiority of rational-emotive therapy over desensitization in the treatment of interpersonal anxiety in a noncollege population.

Moleski and Tosi (1976) compared rational-emotive therapy with systematic desensitization in the treatment of stuttering. Twenty subjects (15 men and 5 women) with a mean age of 28 and a mean educational level of 10th grade were patients in a university speech and hearing clinic. Stuttering was measured by an Oral Reading Passage test and by a disfluency index in telling a five-minute story on the TAT. Self-report measures were also taken on attiutdes toward stuttering and anxiety over speaking.

Subjects received eight intensive therapy sessions lasting 45 minutes each. Half the subjects in each therapy were given in vivo tasks involving (1) five telephone calls to significant others and (2) five spontaneous discussions with strangers.

Rational-emotive therapy, with or without in vivo tasks, was superior to systematic desensitization in reducing disfluenices and anxiety and negative attitudes about stuttering. Systematic desensitization was more effective than no treatment in reducing stuttering. The in vivo homework tasks did not have consistent effects across all criterion measures but did strengthen both therapies in reducing speech disfluencies and negative attitudes toward stuttering.

Lipsky, Kassinove, and Miller (1980) compared three variations of RET, relaxation and support, and no treatment with adult outpatients. The 37 females and 13 males had a mean age of 33, average IQs, and were multisymptomatic. They were randomly assigned to one of the following groups: (1) Standard RET using ABC methods for a minimum of 12 events, bibliotherapy, and behavioral homework assignments, (2) RET plus rational role reversal in which the client and therapist switched roles for 15 minutes of each session and the client practiced taking the therapist through the ABC approach, (3) RET plus rational-emotive imagery in which the client spent 15 minutes of each session imagining getting upset and then imagining using rational methods to reduce the upset, (4) Alternate treatment group controlling for attention placebo effect as well as providing relaxation training and support, and (5) A no-contact group. Each group received 12 sessions of therapy.

At posttreatment each of these variations of RET were found to be significantly more effective than the alternate treatment group and the no-contact group on measures of rational thinking, anxiety, depression, and neuroticism. The authors conclude that this study is important because it is the first to demonstrate the efficacy of RET with multisymptomatic clients suffering from a variety of common neurotic disturbances.

What can we conclude from these studies about the effectiveness of rational-emotive therapy? Unfortunately, the obvious conclusion is that rational-emotive therapy has not been adequately tested. Only two (Ellis, 1957a; Moleski & Tosi, 1976; Lipsky et al., 1980) of the eight studies actually used clinical patients as subjects, while the others used basically normal subjects from colleges or the surrounding community. Even if we accept all of the studies as adequate, we still find equivocal results. On the less stringent issue of rational-emotive therapy versus no treatment, five of the six studies using a no-treatment group (Kanter, 1975; Karst & Trexler, 1969; Keller et al., 1975; Moleski & Tosi, 1976; Lipsky et al., 1980) found rational-emotive therapy to be more effective.

On the more stringent question as to whether rational-emotive therapy is more effective than placebo or comparison treatments, we find that only four of seven studies supported rational-emotive therapy over alternative treatments (Ellis, 1957a; Kanter, 1975; Moleski & Tosi, 1976; Lipsky et al., 1980). At this time the most favorable conclusion we can make is that rational-emotive therapy is particularly helpful in reducing common anxieties concerning aging, public speaking, and interpersonal relating.

THE EFFECTIVENESS OF BECK'S COGNITIVE THERAPY

Rush, Beck, Kovacs, and Hallan (1977) compared the effectiveness of cognitive therapy to antidepressant chemotherapy with a group of neurotic depressives. The patients were randomly assigned to one of the two treatments. The therapists were primarily psychiatric residents who were experienced in the use of drugs with depression but not psychotherapy. Cognitive therapy lasted for a maximum of 20 sessions and a mean of 15 sessions over 11 weeks. Drug treatment averaged 11 weeks, with one 20 minute session per week.

Results indicated that both treatments reduced the symptoms of depression; but the Beck Depression Inventory and clinicians' judgments of improvement indicated that cognitive therapy patients improved significantly more at termination and at three- and six-month follow-up. In addition, 13 of 19 chemotherapy patients reentered treatment for depression following the time-limited treatment, while only 3 of 19 cognitive therapy patients sought additional treatment. The authors contrast the results of this study with the traditional findings that drug treatments for depression outperform psychotherapy.

Shaw (1977) compared the effectiveness of Beck's cognitive therapy to behavior therapy, client-centered therapy, and no-treatment with 32 depressed college students. Eight subjects were randomly assigned to each of the following groups: (1) Cognitive therapy, (2) Behavior therapy based on Lewinsohn's (1974) model of depression including the use of activity schedules, verbal contracts, and behavior rehearsal techniques to teach communication and social reinforcement skills, (3) Client-centered or nondirective therapy that was used as an attention-placebo contact group, and (4) no-treatment. Therapy sessions were held in a group setting of eight subjects and the therapist. Each group met for two hours per week for four weeks.

Cognitive therapy was most effective at posttreatment in alleviating depression as measured by Beck's Inventory and clinicians' ratings. Behavior therapy and client-centered therapy were more effective than no-treatment but did not differ significantly from each other.

Comes-Diaz (1981) tested the effectiveness of cognitive therapy and behavior therapy on depression in Puerto Rican women. The treatments were almost identical to those used in Shaw's (1977) study, except that there were five one-and-one-half-hour group sessions over four weeks, and the sessions were conducted in Spanish. The clients were 26 depressed, low socioeconomic status, unemployed, and unmarried women receiving government aid. They had a mean of 6 years of education, a mean age of 38 years, and an average of 5 years of residence in the United States. There were 8 women randomly assigned to each treatment, and 10 assigned to a waiting-list control group.

Results showed a significant reduction in depression for both therapy groups at posttreatment. There were no significant differences between cognitive therapy and behavior therapy at the end of treatment. At five-week follow-up, however, the cognitive therapy group had deteriorated somewhat on the clinicians' ratings of depression but not in the Beck Inventory or other measures of depression. The behavior therapy group showed no such signs of beginning to relapse.

LaPointe and Rimm (1980) compared a cognitive training package derived from Beck to assertive training for depression in adult females. The women responded to newspaper ads and were seen in two-hour group sessions for six weeks. Significant decreases in self-rated depression were obtained in both treatments but not in an insight therapy designed to serve as a placebo control. On subjective mood ratings 90 percent of the assertive training subjects reported improvement, compared with 83 percent of those receiving cognitive therapy, and only 76 percent in the placebo treatment. At two-month follow-up, however, the placebo group was doing as well as the two therapy groups.

CRITICISMS OF RATIONAL-EMOTIVE THERAPY

From a Behavioral Perspective

While Ellis appropriately supports the scientist as an ideal, he acts primarily as a rationalist and a philosopher. Of 400 articles and books on rational-emotive therapy, for example, only one is an empirical report on its effectiveness. Even that study was not a planned, controlled experiment but rather a retrospective survey comparing Ellis's effectiveness using rational-emotive therapy when he was an older, more experienced therapist with his earlier work using psychoanalysis and psychoanalytically oriented psychotherapy. With institutes available that include large numbers of both patients and therapists, it is difficult to rationalize how a therapist advocating empirical solutions to problems has produced so much dialogue and so little data. Perhaps Ellis is really more of an ethical philosopher preaching a set of hedonistic values based on belief rather than an empiricist teaching a theory tested by rigorous research.

What data are there, for example, to support the central assumption that behavior disorders are primarily a function of a person's beliefs about antecedent events rather than a function of the events themselves? Are we to believe that such traumatic events as being beaten by one's mother, molested by one's father, bereaved of both parents, rejected by peers, and judged a failure by teachers are less significant in producing emotional disturbances in children than are the beliefs that children have about such events? Are we to believe that emotionally disturbed people are primarily victims of their own inherent tendencies to indulge in irrational thinking rather than products of irrational environments that stimulate and reinforce not only irrational thoughts but also irrational behaviors and emotions? Because of a theoretical preference for placing the responsibility for emotional disorders on the individual, rational-emotive therapy ends up as another example of the all too common tendency in our society to blame the victim.

From a Psychoanalytic Perspective

Rational-emotive therapy replaces the irrational demands of a primitive and parental superego with demands from an attacking and authoritative therapist who teaches submissive patients to accept a questionable philosophy of life. Clients come to be cured, and instead they are converted. Using some of the oldest forms of brainwashing, of converting people to a new faith, rational-emotive therapists immediately begin to attack and tear apart the patient's world view. With the therapist being well trained in debate, patients are made even more confused and anxious as their own explanations for their problems are characterized as foolish, irrational, and immature. As patients are made to feel defenseless by the relentless onslaught of the therapist ramming away at their ego processes, they become more vulnerable to whatever the therapist is selling. In place of old defenses, the rational-emotive therapist offers intellectualization and rationalization. The therapist offers a philosophical system that is glamorized as rational, logical, and empirical but is in reality a grand word game.

Patients are taught, for example, to tell themselves that such events as having an infant cry every night from 4:00 P.M. until 3:00 A.M. does not produce *anger* but just irritation. They are told that the fact that their teenage daughter just committed suicide is not *terrible*; it is only *regretful*. It would not be *awful* if the patient had a breakdown and had to go into the state hospital; *unfortunate* is the word. Let the therapist seriously face the prospect of psychosis followed by institutionalization in one of our state hospitals and see if that prospect is just unfortunate.

From a Humanistic Perspective

Where has Ellis been in the last half of the 20th century to not recognize that the problem for all too many people is that they cannot feel enough, not that they feel too much? Alienation is the syndrome of our age, not emotional upsets. Alienation includes the inability of many people to experience the strong emotions that are part of being human. Emotions, like horror, awe, terror, and anger, may be unpleasant, but they are not inherently irrational. Yes, it may be irrational to feel awful about getting a C in a course rather than a B. But it is not inappropriate, irrational, or immature to feel awful, for example, about the proliferation of nuclear weapons throughout the world. Too many people have forgotten that nuclear explosions can indeed instill awe and terror. It may be irrational to become enraged over missing a bus, but it is not inappropriate to be outraged over the continuing destruction of our natural environment. Too many people have lost the ability to be outraged over the continuing injustices of society, such as the discrimination against blacks and Hispanics.

Rational-emotive therapy would have us desire a world that would be as emotionally bland as is the food produced by the hundreds of fast-food chains in our culture. Irritable, unpleasant, and regretful feelings may be appropriate emotions for some of the unfortunate occurrences of everyday life. But an unjust and inhumane world calls for people who can feel outrage over indecencies, horror over cruelties, and awe in the face of the awesome problems confronting our times.

From an Eclectic Perspective

Rational-emotive therapy makes the same irrational mistake that is characteristic of many clients and many true believers—overgeneralization. Rather than assume a reasonable position that some patients upset themselves emotionally by thinking in demanding or absolute terms, such as by "awfulizing" or "terribleizing," rational-emotive therapy makes the absolute generalization that nothing is awful or terrible. This overgeneralization negates the tragic side of life and places a patient profoundly depressed by the death of a wife and three children in the same category with a patient depressed over the loss of a promotion. Reason can be used to help patients discriminate between truly tragic events in life that are emotionally disturbing and unfortunate events that need not lead to emotional upsets. Likewise, rational-emotive therapy overgeneralizes about certain emotions, such as insisting that all anxiety is neurotic and self-induced. Such an absolute generalization can encourage people to be anxious about being anxious rather than accepting some anxiety as healthy and authentic, such as anxiety over major decisions or death. In the areas of values and morality, rational-emotive therapy insists that all shoulds, oughts, and musts are immature and inappropriate. A value judgment that holds that a person must be clean and orderly to be decent may indeed be destructive. The generalization, however, that any judgment that is a moral imperative is foolish could be even more destructive of human morale. For example, a rational-emotive moral judgment that reasoned that Nazism was an unfortunate movement would have been less likely to inspire people to put their lives on the line than was the absolute belief that all that is decent in human nature demanded an end to the evil of Nazism.

A RATIONAL-EMOTIVE ANALYSIS OF MRS. C.

With her compulsive desire for order, Mrs. C. could appreciate an explanation of her problems that is as simple as ABC. She already is keenly aware of

A, the Activating Event, which was the case of pinworms contracted by her daughter. She is equally aware of the personal and emotional Consequences of that event, namely, her morbid dread of pinworms and her compulsive need to wash. Like most patients and all too many therapists, however, Mrs. C. is much less aware of how her irrational Belief system transformed an irritating and unfortunate case of pinworms into a catastrophe.

Mrs. C. might have difficulty accepting that she has actively produced and maintained her own miserable world. She has convinced herself that pinworms are in fact a terrible and awful event. She might, however, be more able to appreciate how totally she has condemned herself for having allowed such diseases as the Asian flu and pinworms to infect her family. Mrs. C. might be able to agree that she does believe not only that the pinworms were terrible, but also that she was horrible for letting them occur. What a worm she is for being such a careless mother: An ideal mother, a perfect mother would never let such a terrible thing happen. But Mrs. C. failed to adequately protect her children from disease, and she believes she deserves to be condemned like a worthless worm. What a deserving target she is for pinworms—lowly, lousy, and loathesome. No wonder she feels so vulnerable to being infested by worms.

Mrs. C. has probably always had a strong propensity to think in absolutes, such as to believe that she must be perfect in order to be worthwhile. Of course, her parents encouraged such irrational beliefs by their own absolutistic demands that she be clean and free from disease or desires. Nevertheless, Mrs. C. took to such teachings as if they were truth because of her innate predisposition to think that perfection is possible. Such beliefs were evidenced in her desire for perfect order as reflected in the alphabetical naming of her children and in her need to be clean even before her full-blown compulsions developed. Irrational thinking was clearly present throughout her life, and all it took to produce undeniable pathology was a stressful Activating Event like a series of illnesses to set off her absolute, awfulizing tendencies.

Once Mrs. C. processed the pinworm event through such irrational categories as horrible, terrible, and catastrophic, she frightened herself into believing that she must do everything within her power to prevent a recurrence. She must work compulsively lest she or her family become recontaminated. We can predict, however, that she also frequently engages in self-condemnation for having to be so terribly compulsive. What a worm she is for always washing and never cooking or caring for her children! What a wife she is for always showering and never loving! The vicious cycle of self-condemnation would probably progress to condemning herself as a failure for not improving after years of therapy, for wanting to kill herself, and for letting her family and her therapist down. What better evidence for her lack of worth than the fact that her husband and her therapist are prepared to condemn her to a life in the state hospital.

A closer look would probably reveal that Mrs. C. may well be psychotic and a probable candidate for hospitalization if effective therapy is not forthcoming. Like most patients diagnosed as severe neurotics (Ellis, 1973b), Mrs. C. has many of the signs of a thinking disorder that is more characteristic of borderline or blatantly schizophrenic patients. For example, Mrs. C. has problems in focusing on a realistic solution to her problems because she is overfocused on pinworms. She perseverates, as she thinks over and over and over again about pinworms. She also magnifies the dangers of pinworms entirely out of realistic proportions, becoming almost delusional in her belief that she is constantly surrounded by pinworms wanting to infest her.

A more accurate diagnosis of Mrs. C. as a borderline psychotic would only serve as a warning to not expect any therapy to make her entirely free of pathology. Nevertheless, she and her family would be quite satisfied with having her return to her pre-pinworm level of compulsive adjustment. To make such a return, Mrs. C. will need to learn to dispute her intensely irrational belief system. She will have to learn that the pinworm event was catastrophic only because she defined it as such. As a therapist challenges her to think about the worst thing that could happen as the result of pinworms, she could begin to see that while such consequences are irritating and unpleasant, they are by no means terrible or horrible.

Nor is Mrs. C. a worm because her daughter once had pinworms. Mrs. C.'s self-condemnation will need to be attacked repeatedly by the therapist until she can begin to recognize that nothing she has done or failed to do is deserving of such condemnation. She can go on condemning herself to a compulsive existence if she continues to engage in such demanding, absolutistic thinking. Or she can begin to rely more on what rational powers she possesses to work against the irrational beliefs that distort her world into a place possessed by pinworms.

With such propensities toward irrational thinking, Mrs. C. would have to work hard at disputing her emotionally disturbing beliefs. A variety of homework assignments would be in order, such as going over her therapy tapes to learn to identify her frequent use of such demanding concepts as "must," "should," "necessary," "have to," and "ought to." She would be assigned to practice substituting more rational terms such as "want to," "prefer to," and "it would be better" for many demanding things she tells herself. A paper on the probabilities of getting pinworms and the real risks from pinworms might help her to more accurately process new information about the nature of pinworms. She could also be assigned a paper on describing where it is written that a mother must keep her children free from any disease in order to be a worthwhile human being, as a means of challenging her self-condemnation. Her husband would also be assigned important homework assignments, such as reading *How to Live with a Neurotic* (Ellis, 1957b), so that he could begin to deal with her rationally rather than give in to her irrational demands.

Eventually Mrs. C. might begin to deawfulize and thus defuse the possible consequences of pinworms. She may become more fully conscious of the fact that pinworms may be a pain, but they are not the worst of all possible fates. They may be unpleasant but not catastrophic. The therapist would interpret how such foolish beliefs lead Mrs. C. to continue to emotionally upset herself. Mrs. C. needs to become aware that the source of her problem is not pinworms or the possibility of pinworms, but rather the way in which she thinks about pinworms. Her problem is not her imperfections as a wife and mother but rather what she believes such imperfections mean for her worth as a human being. Only if Mrs. C. can learn to actively dispute such irrational beliefs (and that is a big *if*) can she become free to enjoy some of life rather than waste herself away on foolish washing. Mrs. C. could find some joy in life if she learns to quit insisting on more order than the universe provides or on perfection, when the best we can do is accept ourselves as imperfect beings who can live happily in an imprecise world if we accept life on probabilistic rather than absolutistic terms.

TRANSACTIONAL
ANALYSIS

"DADDY SURE HAS BEEN A LOT NICER since you've been going to see that man," said Sara, the 12-year-old daughter. "Do you think I could go with you one week to talk with him, too?"

When Sara came in with her father she was eager to tell me how much better things were at home. She used to hide when her dad came home from work to avoid his anger, but now she enjoyed being with him. Her father had always been extremely strict and stern and would use such put-downs as "stupid" and "dummy" when he corrected his daughter. Not only had such treatment led to problems with self-esteem and with school for the daughter, but it had also been one of the major causes of arguments between the parents.

Conditions had, however, improved markedly since the father began reading *I'm OK—You're OK* (Harris, 1967) and especially since the parents had come home from therapy and decided to play a game at dinner in which Sara and her seven-year-old sister would be the parents and the parents would play the role of the children. At first Sara was afraid to be her father, but once she got into the role she found herself imitating his angry silence and his stern reprimands, such as "Close your mouth when you're eating, stupid" or "Sit up in your chair, dummy." While such reversals of roles allowed each of the family members to see themselves more clearly, it also provided some hearty laughs together, including the normally somber father.

In our session together the father was able to tell Sara how strict his own mother and grandmother had been when he was growing up. He did not have a father at home, and he grew up believing that it was natural for all parents to be very rigid disciplinarians. He indicated to Sara that as she was getting more mature he wanted to be able to relate more as an adult with her and less as a strict parent. Sara said that one of the things she had learned was that even when her father at times acted very strict, she could help by not responding as an angry child.

Sara went on to say that she really liked the *I'm OK—You're OK* ideas and the Parent-Adult-Child concepts but could not understand how a 12-year-old like herself could be a parent. Her mother quickly asked, "Do you think the way you boss your sister around all the time is your way of being a strict parent?" Sara laughed.

A SKETCH OF THE FIRST TRANSACTIONAL ANALYST

Eric Berne (1910–1970) first came upon the phenomenon of people relating as Parent, Child, or Adult when he decided to listen to his clients and not his teachers (Berne, Steiner, & Dusay, 1973). For 10 years he had been practicing psychoanalysis and had learned to translate whatever clients were saying into the theoretical language he had gained from his teachers. Thus when a client remarked, "I feel as though I had a little boy inside of me," Berne would typically have interpreted the little boy to mean an introjected penis, as Otto Fenichel did in a similar case. But instead of asking himself, "What would Otto Fenichel say in this case?", he asked the client what he really thought about it. As it turned out the client really did feel like a little boy, and this feeling was the most significant clinical fact in determining the course of the client's life. As therapy proceeded, Berne at an appropriate time asked, "Which part of you is talking, the little boy or the grown-up man?" (Berne et al., 1973, p. 371). With the asking of this question, transactional analysis was born.

Actually Berne had been moving away from orthodox analysis for quite some time. After receiving his M.D. at McGill in 1935, he did his psychiatric residency at Yale from 1936 to 1941. He immediately began his training as a psychoanalytic candidate in New York, but this training was interrupted by service in the army from 1943 to 1946. It was during his military duty that he began working with groups and became very excited about the possibilities of group therapy, thus moving away from the strict one-to-one format of orthodox analysis.

After the war he settled in Carmel, California, and resumed his psychoanalytic studies in San Francisco with Erik Erickson as his analyst. When he applied for membership in the psychoanalytic institute in 1956, he was turned down on the basis that he was not doing psychoanalysis. Since Berne readily agreed with the accusation, he dissociated himself from psychoanalysis and in 1957 presented his first paper on transactional analysis (TA). While this paper marked the formal beginning of transactional analysis, Berne had actually developed his system during the previous decade. Beginning in the early 1950s, he had established a seminar group in Carmel in which he began to present his emerging theory and have it critiqued by the seven professionals who attended. By the time he published his first paper in 1958, the essence of his theory was already well developed.

In many ways, Berne was rather an unlikely candidate for establishing a new and popular system of psychotherapy. He was indeed creative and articulate, but he was also rather shy and lacking in the charisma that characterizes many leaders. Berne was also very modest in his initial attempts to influence the thinking of other therapists, as indicated by the small size of his initial seminar and the relatively slow pace at which he presented and published his theory.

Nevertheless, his influence increased markedly from 40 members in his San Francisco seminars in 1958 to an international association six years later. Even the popularity of *Games People Play* (1964) was a surprise, since Berne had written it primarily for professionals who were already manifesting an advanced interest in TA. Berne was actually afraid that the public success of his book might undermine his professional credibility. Instead it continued to attract a growing number of professional advocates.

Berne's work, especially his writings and clients, formed the essence of his adult life. He spent every Tuesday and Wednesday with his private practice, consultations, and seminars in San Francisco and then flew back to Carmel, where he wrote and had a second practice. His greatest fun seemed to come from going to the beach and dancing at the parties that typically followed the weekly seminars. For the most part, however, Berne seemed to prefer to be independent and relatively self-sufficient. Steiner (1974) believes that Berne had a life script that involved very strong injunctions against loving others and accepting the love of others. Like his father, a doctor, Berne had chosen early in life a script involved with curing others. For Berne this meant that his personal life was sacrificed for his professional life, with his loving relationships being relatively short-lived. Steiner speculates that when Berne died from a heart attack in 1970, he actually died from a broken heart because he was unable to let in enough of the strokes and love that others felt for him.

THEORY OF PERSONALITY

Everything in transactional analysis stems from the premise that human personality is structured into three separate ego states—Parent, Adult, and Child (PAC). These ego states are not theoretical constructs; they are phenomenological realities that are amenable to direct observation. When people are in the Child ego state, for example, they sit, stand, speak, think, perceive, and feel like they did in childhood. Behavior of the Child is impulsive and stimulus bound rather than mediated and delayed by reason. Throwing temper tantrums, being irresponsible or irrational, and engaging in wishful thinking or daydreams are some of the expressions of the Child. At the same time, the Child is the source of spontaneity, creativity, humor, and fun and is thought to be the best part of the personality, since it is the only part that can truly enjoy life.

The Child ego state is essentially preserved intact from childhood. It is as if the Child has been recorded on a nonreusable tape in the brain and can be turned on live at any time. The Child is at most eight years old and can be as young as a newborn infant. The Child can be further differentiated into the Natural Child, which is the most emotional, spontaneous, and powerful expression of a child; the Adapted Child, which is the more obedient child molded to parental demands; and the little Professor, which is the inquisitive and intuitive child who acts like a precocious adult.

The Parent ego state is also carried over essentially intact from childhood. The Parent is basically made up of behavior and attitudes that are copied from parents or authority figures. While much of the Parent is based on videotape-like recordings from childhood, the Parent can be modified throughout life as the person models new parental figures or changes from actual experiences with parenting. When the Parent is in control, people use the language of parents, with controlling words, like "should," "ought," "must," "better not," or "you'll be sorry," predominating. Gestures like pointing a finger or standing impatiently with hands on the hips are other common expressions of the Parent.

The Parent is the controlling, automatic, limit-setting, and rigid rule maker of the personality. The Parent is the nurturing and comforting part of the personality. The Parent is also the repository of traditions and values and is therefore vital for the survival of civilization. In ambiguous or unknown situations, when adequate information is unavailable to the Adult, then the Parent is the best basis for decision making.

In a second-order structural analysis of the Parent, Steiner (1974) also differentiates between the Nurturing and the Pig Parent. The Nurturing Parent acts out of genuine concern for others and provides support or protection when needed. This type of parent is potent and effective because of the respect that is engendered in others. The warm, fatherly, but firm policeman is an example of such a Parent. The Pig Parent, on the other hand, is oppressive, acting not on the basis of what is best for others but out of anger and fear of others and an irrational need to control. This type of parent makes others feel not OK, engenders fear and hatred in others, and is thus at times called the Witch or the Ogre. The Pig Parent rules not out of respect but only because it has actual power over others in particular situations. Sara's father was an example of a person acting out this more derogatory and oppressive type of Parent.

The Adult ego state is essentially a computer, an unfeeling organ of the personality that gathers and processes data for making predictions and decisions. The Adult is a gradually developed ego state that emerges as the person interacts with the physical and social environment over many years. The Adult acts more clearly on the basis of logic and reason and is the best evaluator of reality since it is not clouded by emotion. The Adult can realistically evaluate not only the environment but also the emotions and demands of the Child or the Parent.

Since each ego state is a substructure of the ego, and since, as Hartmann (1958) has suggested, the ego is the adaptive function of the personality, each ego state is adaptive when used in the appropriate situation. The Parent, for example, is ideally suited when control is necessary, such as control of children, fears, the unknown, the Child, and undesirable impulses. The Child is ideally suited when creation is desired, such as the creation of new ideas or new life. The Child is also most adaptive for fun situations, such as parties or celebrations. The Adult is best for situations where accurate prediction is necessary, such as deciding on a marriage, career, or budget.

The well-adapted personality, then, switches from one ego state to another depending upon what the present situation calls for. Only one ego state can be in operation at a time. When a particular ego state is in control of the personality, it is called the *executive* and is said to be cathected or imbued with the psychic energy necessary to activate muscles involved in behavior. The process of being able to easily and voluntarily change from one ego state to another is called *stabilization* and is the sign of a healthy or stable personality.

Ego states provide the structure of the personality but not the motivation. Motivation for behaving comes from biogenetic drives for survival, such as hunger for food, but also from psychological drives, which Berne (1966) labels *stimulus* hunger, *recognition* hunger, *structure* hunger, and *excitement* hunger. As studies on stimulus deprivation have demonstrated (Hebb, Held, Riesent, & Teuber, 1961; Solomon, Kubzansky, Leiderman, Menderson, Trumbull, & Wexler, 1961), human beings can become highly disturbed if they are deprived of adequate amounts of incoming physical stimulation. One of the most important forms of stimulation needed for a healthy personality is stroking. In young children stroking needs to be in the form of direct physical contact that comes through being held, soothed, and cuddled if they are to survive emotionally and physically (Spitz, 1945).

While direct physical contact is the most nourishing form of stroking, adults can learn to get by with just the stimulation that comes from recognition. The needs at times to be the center of another person's attention and to have our existence recognized by another human being are especially obvious in children, who will even settle for negative attention if that is the only way they can gain recognition. While positive strokes, such as smiles, greetings, applause, approval, and cheers are most valued; negative strokes such as frowns, cold looks, criticism, and disapproval at least satisfy the human hunger for recognition.

Structural hunger is the motive that develops out of the common human dilemma of deciding what to do with 8,760 hours a year. In some societies all of this time is required to meet the needs of survival, to provide adequate sleep, food, and shelter. In most societies, however, people have surplus time and would have to be constantly deciding how to structure their time if social institutions were not designed in part to help them order their lives. Religion, education, recreation, the arts, politics, marriage, and families are all designed in part to help people structure the time at their disposal. Social leaders are those individuals who have special skills to help others structure their time. The most valued leaders are those who help to structure time in the most interesting and exciting ways, since the desire to avoid boredom, to have interesting and exciting hours, seems to be part of the human condition.

One of the most exciting ways to spend time is to exchange strokes with others. An exchange of strokes is what defines a *transaction,* and the hunger for strokes and for excitement makes human beings inherently social animals that are highly motivated to participate in social transactions. Transactions that are entirely spontaneous and direct, intimate, transactions can be exciting, threatening, and overwhelming. Such free and unstructured exchanges of strokes are generally avoided, especially in short-term social interactions, in favor of more structured and safer exchanges of strokes.

The safest form of transaction is a *ritual,* which is a highly stylized interchange. There are informal rituals, such as greetings like "Hello, how are you? Fine, thank you, and how are you?" There are also formal rituals that become established as traditional ceremonies, such as weddings or funerals, which are entirely structured and predictable. Rituals convey very little information and are basically signs of mutual recognition.

The next safest form of social interaction is a work activity. Most work activities are highly programmed, not so much by tradition and custom as are rituals, but by the intrinsic nature of the material with which the individuals are working. If the individuals are working together to build a car, then the most efficient structure for such work is the assembly line. Participation in such work activities is typically geared to the Adult ego state of the workers.

Much of leisure time is safely structured through pastimes. Pastime sharers are those with mutual interests, such as horse-owners, Shriners, or people at weekend workshops. While transactions in pastimes are more informal and individualized than rituals, pastimes are nevertheless designed to minimize the possibility of incidents that are too emotional and exciting. Pastimes allow people to structure their time in fairly interesting but not too threatening transactions.

The riskiest and most exciting transactions that are still structured are the games that people play. A game is a complex series of ulterior transactions that progress to a psychological payoff, the payoff being a feeling such as guilt, depression, or anger. In an ulterior transaction, communication appears to have not just an overt, social meaning but also a covert, psychological meaning. For example, if a woman asks a man, "Why don't you come by my place to see my collection of sculpture?" and the man responds, "I'd love to. I'm really interested in art," they may be having a simple, candid interchange between two Adults beginning to share a pastime. In a game, however, both players are also communicating a message at a different level, such as Child-to-Child messages like "Boy, I'd really like to get you alone in my apartment" and "I'd sure love to look at your curves."

A game is able to progress because one player is pulling a con; that is, doing something other than what is on the surface, such as inviting the man to risk being alone in her apartment. For a con to work, the respondent has to present some type of weakness that gets hooked, such as vanity, greed, sentimentality, guilt, or fear. In this case the man's vanity is hooked, and he goes off to the apartment with great expectations.

For the payoff to occur, one of the players has to pull a switch. In this case, after fixing drinks and sitting close on the couch examining a reproduction of Rodin's The Kiss, the woman still seems to be sending a seductive communication. The man's vanity convinces him to proceed, and he puts his hand on her leg, only to be rebuffed by a slap on the face and an irate "What kind of woman do you think I am?"

The couple has just completed a heavy hand of RAPO. Besides gaining mutual recognition, excitement, and some structured time together, there is also a strong emotional payoff for each. The woman is able to profoundly affirm her position in life that she is OK, while feeling angry toward men for not being OK, just as her mother always said. The payoff for the man is to feel depressed and thereby reaffirm his conviction that he is not OK. People like these, who repeatedly seek payoffs of anger or depression, can be characterized as collecting "stamps," like the trading stamps that people save. The color of the stamps depends on the feelings that are collected, such as "red stamps" for anger and "brown stamps" for depression. Collecting such stamps allows people to eventually trade in all of their stamps on a major emotional release, such as a hostile explosion or a depressing suicide attempt.

Games also serve to reaffirm the *life position* that a person chooses very early in life. Based upon experiences from the first few years of life, children make a precocious decision of how they are in life compared with others around them. The four possible life positions are: (1) I'm OK—you're OK, (2) I'm OK—you're not OK, (3) I'm not OK—you're OK, and (4) I'm not OK—you're not OK. The first and universal position of children is to be OK unless the civilizing process helps to convince them that they are not OK. Or, as Berne believed, children are born princes and princesses, until their parents turn them into frogs (Steiner, 1974).

To adopt a position at age six or seven about being OK or not OK is bound to be a critical determinant in the *life script* that a person chooses. The decision that one is *Born to Win* (James & Jongeward, 1971), to act out a successful life plan, a get-on-with-it script, is consistent with a decision that one is indeed OK. Scripts calling for chronic failure or futility, getting-nowhere-with-it scripts, are much more likely to be selected by people who are convinced that they are not OK. The general tenor, then, of a script is made consistent with the life position a person chooses.

Many details of a life script are supplied by parental prohibitions, suggestions, and encouragements. "She argues like a lawyer," "He's such a helpful boy," "She definitely wants to be the queen bee," "You're sure going to go to hell" are parental statements that have been quite influential in the development of particular scripts. Fairy tales and children's stories are also important sources of suggestions for a life script. A person's favorite myth or fairy tale, for example, is thought to reflect the person's original life script. A 27-year-old mother of two who was prepared to leave her third husband for a more exciting life on a lover's sailboat had always had Cinderella as her favorite childhood story of how a man comes along to rescue a woman from a miserable life. While parental statements and childhood stories are important influences, the life script is still the creation of a young child who decides how to best act out a life position and to fulfill particular human hungers.

THEORY OF PSYCHOPATHOLOGY

Theoretically psychopathology can occur either at the intrapersonal level of personality, involving problems with the person's ego states, life position, or life script, or at the interpersonal level, involving transactional conflicts between the ego states of two or more people. In practice, however, psychopathology is almost always a multilevel phenomenon involving problems both within the personality and between personalities.

Problems within a person's ego states are structural problems of the personality. The most elementary structural problem is confusion, in which people are not capable of discerning their three separate ego states and in a confused manner slip from one state to another. A father, for example, who was removed from his home for almost killing his son, was talking in an Adult manner about the realistic problems he was having with his teenage son. As he was talking rationally about how the son at times talks back to his mother, he quickly became enraged and with a beet-red face expressed how he thinks the best solution is to beat his son to a pulp. The father had no idea of how he was switching from his rational Adult to his self-righteous and irate Parent who demands total respect.

Contamination is another structural problem that exists when part of one ego state intrudes into another. The Adult is the ego state most likely to be contaminated by prejudices of the Parent or myths and fantasies of the Child. A man cannot deal effectively with the realities of work, for example, if his Adult takes as fact his Child's fantasy that he is destined to marry a rich woman who will rescue him from a lowly position. One such client bolstered his arguments for his belief by going to a tealeaf reader who insisted that he would soon be engaged to a wealthy woman.

Exclusion is the structural problem of people who rigidly hold to one ego state and shut out the other two. A husband who was almost always working and continually preached to his wife about how she should take care of the house and the kids was unable to find any fun or joy in life because his rigid Parent had successfully excluded both his Child and Adult from being expressed. On the other hand, the constant Clown, the prankster who is the life of the party but disgusts his wife because he can never be serious, exhibits a dominant Child that avoids the serious aspects of life by not giving expression to his Adult or Parent ego states.

Adoption of an unhealthy life position will obviously predispose people to live troubled lives. People who decide "I'm OK—you're not OK," for example, predispose themselves to live psychopathic or criminal lives. To exploit others, rob others, beat others, cheat others, or succeed at the expense of others is just further confirmation that the person was entirely correct in deciding "I'm OK and you're not." Who needs a conscience when convinced that all I do is OK and anything that goes wrong must be the responsibility of those who aren't OK? This type of person need not be a criminal to act out this life position but can be the ruthless business executive who exploits others or the destructive lover who loves them and leaves them because that is all others are good for.

People who decide "I'm not OK—you're OK" are plagued with constant feelings of inferiority in the presence of those they judge as OK. Such a life position can lead to a life script that calls for withdrawal from others, because it is too painful to remain in their presence and be constantly reminded of not being OK. Withdrawal reaffirms the not-OK position but is even more self-defeating because it deprives the person of any chance of getting the adequate strokes from others that could lead to a belief of being OK. Withdrawn people may develop an elaborate fantasy life centering around wishes that if they become holy enough, wise enough, rich enough, or irresistible enough, then they will be OK. Failure to realize such unrealistic fantasies can ultimately lead to the tragic resolution of institutionalization or suicide.

Withdrawal is not the only alternative that can follow from assuming "I'm not OK—you're OK." The person can write a counterscript based on lines borrowed from the Parent: "You can be OK if . . . " The person is then driven to achieve whatever contingencies the Parent demands in return for strokes. Be charming enough, submissive enough, helpful enough, entertaining enough, demands the Parent. The person is constantly looking to the Parent in others for strokes and approval, and such strokes can at least ease the pain of not being OK enough.

People who conclude "I'm not OK and neither are you" are the most difficult to reach. Why should they respond to others who aren't OK? What hope is there in life when neither oneself nor others are OK? These people simply survive, if they do not commit suicide or destroy others and themselves. The extreme withdrawal of schizophrenia or psychotic depression is their most common fate. They may regress to an infantile state in the primitive hope that they may once again receive the strokes of being held and fed. Without intervention from caring others, these individuals will live out a self-destructive life of institutionalization, irreversible alcoholism, senseless homicide, or suicide.

Just as there are three basically unhealthy life positions, so too there are three basic life scripts that lead to self-destruction: (1) Depression or No Love Script, (2) Madness or No Mind Script, and (3) Addiction or No Joy Script (Steiner, 1974). The intensity of the No Love Script varies in degree from the many lonely people who are in a constant, unsuccessful quest for a loving relationship to profoundly depressed people who are ready to call it quits because they are convinced they are unloved and unlovable. Basic training in lovelessness is provided early in childhood when parents give injunctions against the free exchange of loving strokes. Strokes are controlled by a strict economy, as if love is a scarce commodity that can readily be depleted. Parental injunctions include (1) don't give yourself strokes, (2) don't give your strokes away—trade your love for something valuable, (3) don't ask for strokes when you need them since love is not worthwhile if you have to ask for it, and (4) don't reject strokes when you don't want them, even if the kisses, hugs, or compliments from some people seem oppressive and unhealthy. Acting out such injunctions from the Parent can result in such pathologies as the hypochondriac who can ask for strokes only by being sick; the neurotically modest people who can never say anything good about themselves; the miserably married people who exchange their love for money, security, or status; and the easy make who never says no to the advances of anyone.

The No Mind Script not only is the plague of those called mad but is constantly in the background of those who live in fear that someday they might go crazy. Mindlessness is also reflected in the lives of those who feel unable to cope with the world, those who get easily confused and have trouble concentrating, those who feel stupid or lazy, and those who have no willpower or mind of their own. Basic training in mindlessness comes from parental injunctions against thinking too much. Many women, for example, were traditionally discouraged from being logical, rational beings, in order to eventually become nonquestioning wives.

Parents give injunctions against thinking to protect themselves from feelings of being not OK. Children who would think clearly might see the undeniable bigotry of their parents; children with accurate intuition might sense that their parents do not really love each other; children who are logical and empirical might challenge some of the sacred-cow teachings of their parents, and the parents may look foolish. To keep their children from seeing them accurately, parents discourage children from using their minds through such techniques as directly lying about the truth the child sees. For example, a mother brought her 12-year-old daughter in to see me because the girl was quite upset over the belief that she was going crazy. The mother told me privately that the girl had been sure the mother was having an affair with the carpenter, but the mother had convincingly lied to protect herself and the carpenter. Here the girl was afraid she was becoming paranoid, when her problem was that she was intuiting things too accurately. The mother was amazed at how a dose of truth could so quickly remedy the daughter's emerging madness.

The No Joy Script is the basic plan of those who decided early in life that it was better for them to shut out the joys and pleasures of their bodies. As adults these people range in severity from those in need of a pill to sleep or caffeine or nicotine to wake up, to those who need constant aspirins or antacids to shut out bubbling messages from within, to those who can enjoy only their addiction to shopping or to TV, to those who can no longer keep going in life unless they have a fix or a fifth.

In view of Western culture's long history of deciding that the body is not OK, it is understandable that many parents continue to give injunctions to their children against experiencing and enjoying their bodies. In the process of shutting out their ability to spontaneously and freely experience their bodies, people also shut out one of the primary centers of joy in life. People lose one of the natural centers of living; that is, the birthright of the Natural Child. What seems to be one of the pleasures of drugs is that initially they shut out the Pig Parent that prohibits the pleasure of being body-centered. The catch is that as more drugs are needed to inhibit the Pig Parent, the person feels less joy and is more confronted by the sickness that comes from introducing foreign substances into the natural body. Again, the body is experienced as not OK, and the person takes even more drugs to more fully close out the body. The payoff of feeling depressed from being hung-over or having withdrawal symptoms serves in part as a reaffirmation of the belief that the body and the person are indeed not OK.

The drama of tragic life scripts is heightened by the fact that patients eventually play each of the three roles that are part of the triangle of all drama: the victim, the persecutor, and the rescuer (Karpman, 1968). The script of the spouse of an alcoholic, for example, begins with the spouse trying to rescue the poor drunk from self-destruction. Drama and excitement increase as the spouse becomes angry when rescue is not accepted and then turns to persecuting the drunk for not reforming. Eventually, the spouse's self-destructive script becomes apparent as the spouse ends up as a victim of the drunk's social, economic, and personal inadequacies.

To advance pathological scripts to their inevitably tragic conclusions, patients begin to play even heavier-handed versions of their typical games. An alcoholic who played "kick me," for example, may progress from playing "Kick me, I'm late again for dinner because I stopped at the bar" to "Kick me, I spent the check at the bar" to "Kick me, I lost my job." The payoff for the alcoholic comes in collecting brown stamps for depression and in reaffirming a position of not being OK. When enough feelings of depression are collected, the alcoholic can trade in his stamps and feel justified in killing himself, which is the action called for to conclude his tragic life script.

THEORY OF THERAPEUTIC PROCESSES

Therapy usually begins with structural analysis through which patients become more fully conscious of their ego states that were previously confused, contaminated, or excluded. Therapy then proceeds to transactional analysis, in which self-defeating transactions are made conscious, beginning with self-destructive games and commencing with full awareness of the unhealthy life positions and life scripts that have been plaguing patients. With a curative increase in consciousness, clients are then able to choose which ego states to cathect at any particular time. With heightened awareness they can also decide whether or not they will go on acting out tragic games, positions, and scripts or whether they will use their volition to choose more constructive patterns of meeting their basic human hungers.

Consciousness Raising

THE CLIENT'S WORK

Consciousness raising begins as an educational process. Clients are expected to become well informed about the language and concepts of TA, usually through bibliotherapy involving the books of Berne (1964; 1970; 1972), T. A. Harris (1967), James and Jongeward (1971), and Steiner (1974). If TA classes are available in the client's community, then the client may be instructed to take a course in TA before beginning therapy. Education continues, of course, in therapy as clients are taught to apply the concepts of TA to their own lives, beginning with becoming aware of which ego state is currently being expressed. As clients analyze their own lives in TA terms, they will frequently look to the therapist or group members for feedback regarding the accuracy of their own self-interpretations. As clients become better educated in TA and more aware of their own ego states, they are able to use their own Adults to teach others how to analyze themselves. The client's work is usually a pattern of going from student to self-analyzer to teacher of others.

As clients become more conscious of their own ego states, they can better analyze the complex transactions they enter into with others. They use their Adults to reflect upon repeated patterns of conflict so to realize whether the conflicts are due to their own games or scripts or whether they are letting themselves get caught up in the games and scripts of others. While the early stages of structural analysis depend more on the competence and assurance of the therapist informing clients about which ego states the therapist is currently observing, the later stages of transactional analysis depend more on the work of clients. Clients have almost all the relevant information regarding the overall patterns of their lives, and they must use their Adults to inform the therapist about their personal games or scripts. For example, clients must provide accurate information to complete a script checklist (Steiner, 1967), including (1) the overall course of their lives, (2) whether their lives are to be OK or not, (3) when they decided on their life courses, (4) the fairy tale hero or heroine that the life course is intended to emulate, (5) their counterscripts that allow them periods free from self-destruction, (6) the Parental injunctions against loving, thinking, or feeling joy, (7) the games that advance their courses, (8) the pastimes they use to structure their scripts, (9) the payoffs they seek in life, and (10) the tragic ending they expect from life. Clients must also use their Adults to confirm or disconfirm any hypothetical formulation the therapist may make about the client's scripts or games.

THE THERAPIST'S WORK

Since psychiatric patients are above all confused, the therapist's first task is to reduce confusion by providing patients an accurate structural diagnosis of their problems. By analyzing emotional upsets in terms of conflicts between the Parent, Child, and Adult ego states, therapists provide clients with a clear and concise framework for understanding their problems. The structural diagnosis is both education, in that it teaches patients the basic concepts of TA, and feedback since it informs clients about the personal ways in which they express their own Parent, Child, and Adult. Besides reducing confusion, the structural diagnosis can be the starting point in reducing contamination, since the diagnosis will provide clarification and interpretation about which ego states are being contaminated by which other ego states.

To encourage clients to reduce their own confusion and contamination, the therapist frequently asks clients such questions as, "What ego state are you in?", "Which part of you is talking now?", and "Which part of you said that or made that gesture?" The clients then respond in terms of their own subjective awareness, which they can check against feedback from the therapist or other members in group therapy. If clients have doubts about the therapist's or group's diagnosis, the therapist will play back audio or videotape recordings to help the client see or hear the behavior to which the therapist or group was responding. With such additional data, clients are usually able to become more clearly aware of each ego state.

Since the Adult is the least biased processor of information, the therapist attempts to reduce confusion and contamination by *hooking the Adult* of the client into playing a central role in the analysis of ego states. Therapists hook the Adult of clients by communicating from their own Adult ego state to the Adult ego state of clients. Asking for information, for example, is a request from the therapist's Adult to the Adult of the client. Since it is a principle of TA that the social response of a transactional stimulus (the request for information) is most apt to come from an ego state complementary to that from which the stimulus originated, clients are most likely to respond with communication from their own Adult. If therapists want clients to act as Adults, then the best way is for the therapists to be Adults and communicate to the clients as Adults. If therapists act as Parents and treat their patients as helpless children, then they should not be surprised if their clients have trouble responding from an objective Adult state.

Exclusion can be counteracted by the therapist giving clients *permission* to become aware of and express an ego state that typically has been excluded. A therapist might give permission to express the Child, for example, by giving a client the homework assignment of going to a folk music festival over the weekend and joining in the singing. Or the therapist may give permission for the Child to be expressed by encouraging the client to accept warm strokes from the group member toward whom the client feels closest. Since an ego state is usually excluded because of fear of injury or criticism, the client can feel freer to become aware of the risky Child once the therapist has provided a more protective and permissive setting.

Just as therapists can draw on complementary transactions to help clients, so too will they at times *cross* clients in order to help them become conscious of their reactions when crossed. A crossed transaction occurs when the ego state addressed by a comunication is not the ego state that responds to the communication. If a client addresses a message to the therapist's Adult and the therapist responds from the Parent ego state, then the Adult-to-Adult communication is crossed by a Parent-to-Child response. For example, a client may ask for information, an Adult-to-Adult transaction, such as, "Do you know if next month's TA lecture is open to the public? I have a few friends who would like to go." A complementary response would be an Adult's sharing of the information about the lecture. To cross the client, however, the therapist might respond from Parent to Child by asking, "Can't you ever find out things for yourself?"

By crossing the client deliberately, the therapist can help the client become aware of whether crossed transactions are met with anger, such as "Well, the hell with you," or withdrawal, such as a silent "Guess I'll never ask a question here again," or guilt, such as "I'm sorry for bothering you with my petty concerns." The therapist can encourage clients to become aware of constructive responses that need not threaten a relationship. The Adult seeking more information from the therapist, for example, would learn to respond to the angry therapist by asking, "Is there something bothering you today that I don't know about?" Before a therapist would use a deliberate crossed transaction to increase the awareness of a client, however, the therapist must be very confident that the therapeutic relationship is strong enough to weather it.

Becoming aware of the emotional impact of crossed transactions is part of the analysis of games patients play, since the switch in a game includes a crossed transaction. In the RAPO game, for example, the repartee that is occurring between Child and Child, who are attracted to each other, is crossed when the woman switches to her Parent and accusingly asks, "What kind of woman do you think I am?" Since the emotional impact of such a switch is the key payoff of a game, it is all important that clients become conscious of how they can cross transactions in order to elicit feelings. Much of the therapist's work in analyzing games involves confronting clients with the repetitious nature of their games and then interpreting the payoff of the games and how they help advance the client's life script.

Clients can become fully aware of the meaning of their games only after becoming conscious of how their lives are following self-selected scripts. To help clients in the difficult task of script analysis, therapists can rely on the "20 questions" that Steiner (1967) uses in completing the script checklist. Asking clients to describe their favorite fairy tale or childhood story, for example, can help clients become more fully aware of when they decided on their life script and what mythical heroes they used as models for their lives.

Therapists can also increase the client's consciousness of scripts through the technique of *script rehearsal* (Dusay, 1970). The therapist serves as director and is active in setting the stage for a critical scene from a client's script. The "star" of the rehearsal is a patient with a pressing problem. The star is seated face-to-face with the costar, a group member who plays the other person most importantly involved in the scene, such as a spouse or sibling. Two other patients stand behind the star and represent the Parent ego states. Other patients sit around representing Child ego states, while one patient serves as the observing, computing Adult. The star and costar are directed to enact the scene involving the problem the star is working on and the other patients are directed to simultaneoulsy express the ego states that they are assigned. For 10 minutes the script rehearsal is enacted, followed by a 10-minute Adult-to-Adult discussion of the multilevel meaning of the scene that just occurred.

Choosing

THE CLIENT'S WORK

In the process of becoming more fully conscious of their ego states, games, life positions, and life scripts, clients also become aware of an increase in volition. With a reduction in confusion or contamination, for example, clients are more able to choose which ego state to cathect at any particular time. After expressing a previously excluded ego state in therapy, clients can choose to express the same ego state outside of therapy. Once they become aware that their self-defeating life positions and scripts were originally decisions in childhood based on inadequate information, they can make more informed choices as Adults to live constructive, self-fulfilling lives.

Choices to radically change their lives need not, however, be sudden, all-or-none decisions. Clients can, if they choose, use the therapeutic situation to try out new alternatives. They might, for example, risk giving up games in therapy in order to experience more intimacy with the therapist or group members. Clients can choose to try out new transactions, such as directly and honestly asking for strokes when needed rather than using games to gain negative attention. Given the degree of freedom inherent in choosing, no one can predict the pace or place that clients will use to decide just how they will get on with the exciting process of life.

THE THERAPIST'S WORK

Therapists actually encourage the volitional powers of patients right from the start of therapy by making it a contractual arrangement. In the contract the patient chooses which goals to work toward, and the therapist decides whether or not such goals fit within the therapist's value system. The therapist also lets clients know that they are free to renegotiate the contract at any time or to terminate therapy once the present contract is completed.

Later in therapy, therapists aid the process of choosing by giving clients permission to use therapy to practice new alternatives. Therapists are also willing to provide strokes for clients risking more constructive lifestyles. For the most part, however, therapists recognize that choosing is a process that must fall mainly on the shoulders of clients who are accepting responsibility for both the past and future courses of their lives.

THEORY OF THERAPEUTIC CONTENT

While psychopathology is usually intrapersonal in origin, it is always, in part at least, interpersonal in expression. To allow the interpersonal aspect of personal problems to become undeniably apparent, TA is most often carried out in groups. Even in a group setting, however, the focus of TA moves back and forth between problems occurring between group members and problems that are more clearly intrapersonal in nature.

Intrapersonal Conflicts

ANXIETY AND DEFENSES

Anxiety is a reaction of the Child ego state to a possibility that the person may break an injunction of the Parent. Anxiety can be as overwhelming as the myriad terrors that children have experienced in the face of parental disapproval; terrors of being beaten, abandoned, ignored, or insulted. The anticipation that parents might withhold all strokes, for example, can make the Child feel that psychological starvation is imminent. No wonder then that patients can panic when their Child ego state reacts to a breach of injunctions from the Parent. The Parent, of course, is loaded with injunctions: "Don't laugh loudly," "Don't eat too much," "Don't leave any food in your dish," "Don't talk," "Don't show anger," "Don't enjoy sex," "Don't give strokes," "Don't be happy," "Don't be such a child," and "Don't accept strokes." Many people live in constant danger, then, that if they act directly on the basis of their human hungers, they will be overwhelmed by the panic of having broken at least one parental injunction.

Defenses have traditionally been analyzed as intrapsychic mechanisms used to keep forbidden and thus dangerous desires from being expressed. Such intrapersonal defenses are certainly important in doing therapy, but equally important are the interpersonal defenses that people use to avoid such dangerous desires as the wish to freely exchange strokes. The games people play frequently serve such defensive functions. People who are locked into mutual games have made unconscious deals to use games to avoid the risks of being intimate. A couple who find themselves arguing and bickering whenever one or the other feels like making love or feels like talking intimately is locked into the game of "uproar." As long as they are fighting there is no risk of becoming truly intimate. What's more, neither person has to admit being terrified over being intimate; their only problem is that they cannot stop fighting. While the analysis and thus the removal of game playing are important parts of TA for many clients, it should be recognized that games, like any other defenses, may serve as the final barrier to psychosis and should not be attacked too quickly. A borderline couple, for example, may need to continue playing "uproar" until each spouse's Adult ego state is decontaminated from a suspicious, paranoid Parent. Certainly the analysis of games should not become just another game engaged in at cocktail parties.

SELF-ESTEEM

Enough has been said about the importance of life positions to recognize that one's sense of being OK is central to a healthy existence. What has not been mentioned is that transactional analysts disagree as to whether the original and universal life position is to be OK or not OK. While Berne believed that children are born OK and should have a solid sense of esteem as their birthright, Harris (1967) suggests that people are born frogs until they transform themselves into princes or princesses. For Harris, "I'm not OK" is the original life position and developing a sense of esteem, a belief in being OK, is a central task of life for all people. Whether people are born with defects akin to original sin or whether parental injunctions help produce decisions about not being OK is an ongoing debate even within TA circles (Steiner, 1974). What is agreed upon, however, is that a majority of people in our society do emerge from childhood in a position of feeling not OK. Witness how quickly *I'm OK— You're OK* (Harris, 1967) became a best seller.

People may be misled into believing that because their present problem with self-esteem, their not-OK position, was originally a decision in childhood, all they have to do to become OK is to decide as an Adult that they are indeed OK. Unfortunately, it is not that easy. Even with therapy, the changing of a life position comes only after considerable struggle to become aware of the ego states involved in the original decision about a life position, the games played to enhance a life position, and the script to which that position is intimately connected. To increase one's self-esteem by declining to be OK involves a radical change in one's life script and one's transactions with the world. Feelings of genuine esteem and of being fundamentally OK accompany the awareness of having decided to live a more effective life.

RESPONSIBILITY

Patients come to therapy confused as to why their lives seem to be out of control. They are confused by their inability to sleep, to concentrate, to relax. They come confused by their own behavior, by why they so often seem unable to do what they really want to do: to exercise, to stop smoking or drinking, to quit arguing, overeating, or procrastinating. They are confused about their inability to communicate, even after 25 years of marriage. They are confused as to why their relationships seem too distant or conflicted, why their lives seem so empty. Most of all, they are confused about what to do with the mess they call their lives.

As long as systems of therapy continue to excuse people from accepting responsibility for the deficiencies in their lifestyles, patients will continue to be confused over why their lives are a mess and what they can do about it. Transactional analysis gives people permission to experiment with a variety of new behaviors; but one thing TA will not accept is the old cop-outs that people use to avoid taking responsibility for their lives. Games such as "If it weren't for you . . ." and "Look what you made me do . . ." are examples of such cop-outs. The most common, however, is the "wooden leg" game in which patients beseech others not to expect too much from them because they have a wooden leg. Wooden legs vary from being schizophrenic to being stupid, from being depressed to being lazy. Clients cry out to be excused because of countless deformities that they insist were externally imposed fates rather than self-selected destinies. The fact that clients choose their fates while still children is still no excuse from responsibility. At the same time the fact that life positions and life scripts were chosen precociously can keep clients from totally condemning themselves for having lived a self-destructive existence. The hope is that once clients accept that their basic lifestyles were self-selected, they will be free to choose a more constructive existence. But freedom means that some clients will continue to cop out and live out a destructive script to its tragic end. In such situations, therapists must be aware of their desires to get caught up in the drama as a rescuer. To take responsibility for the client and insist on being a rescuer is to risk eventually becoming a victim of the client's destructive drama.

Interpersonal Conflicts

INTIMACY AND SEXUALITY

Lifetimes pass and intimacy is rarely known. We are among the fortunate few if we experience even 15 minutes of intimacy in a lifetime (Steiner, 1974). As a candid, game-free, mutual exchange of strokes without structure and without exploitation, intimacy may well be unattainable in the structured life scripts of most people. Certainly those who have chosen early in life to demonstrate that either they or others are not OK have given up the option to be intimate. To let ourselves respond freely with others is to trust that they and we are OK.

Intimacy itself seems to be not OK for many people. The threat of intimacy comes in part from the many injunctions of the Parent to avoid freely taking or giving strokes. Free love continues to be taboo to the Parent in most people. There may, however, be an even more basic reason why intimacy seems so threatening. Intimacy brings with it the threat of being too stimulating and too exciting because it is too unstructured. Intimacy may be overwhelming because it threatens to bring chaos into the lives of people used to the security of continual structure. People who hunger to structure their lives will settle for the strokes that come with rituals, pastimes, and games rather than risk the chaos that could occur in free encounters.

Sexuality can be as free from intimacy as is the rest of life. Society in the form of the Parent strives to impose structure on human sexuality by limiting sexual encounters to patterned relationships, such as engagement and marriage. Even within patterned relationships like marriage, where sexuality is permitted, people structure much of their sexuality into rituals, work activities, pastimes, or games (Berne, 1970). The ceremony of having sex three times a week following the 11:00 P.M. news, with five minutes of foreplay and five minutes of intercourse, is a pattern of lovemaking well known by many couples. Such patterns certainly can be pleasant and pleasurable, but they are seldom intimate. There are couples who still insist on structuring the "marital act" so that the man is always on top and the woman on the bottom—to do otherwise is to be abnormal or un-American.

Other couples accept sexuality as being all part of a day's work. These individuals see sexuality as a marital duty and work to make sex as pleasant an activity as possible. Less rigid couples will accept their sexuality as part of the great, all-American pastime. They share a mutual interest in each other and enjoy the chit-chat that is part of lovemaking. They can't imagine a better pastime for a rainy day, but prefer not to risk the stormy emotions that could come with more adventuresome sexuality.

Some of the people who see their sexual lives as most intense and exciting are those whose sexual activities are just more games to play. These individuals enjoy the drama and emotional exploitations that come from such games as "They'll be glad they knew me," "Ain't it wonderful," "Look how hard I tried," and even "Now I've got you, you son of a bitch." Sexual games can advance a person's life position by proving, for example, that the opposite sex is really not OK or that one is irresistably OK.

More spontaneous sexuality and greater intimacy are for those who choose to break out of structured life scripts and risk security for excitement. The fact is, however, that many people do not need such intimacy and sexuality to be OK, and a disservice is done if the suggestion is made that people are not OK unless they are sexual Olympiads or emotional intimates. The quest for intimacy and freer sexuality may well be a luxury in a world in which all too many relationships are plagued by destructive games and self-defeating scripts.

COMMUNICATION

Communication proceeds smoothly and satisfactorily as long as the transactions between two people are complementary. A complementary transaction exists if the response to a previous message is addressed to the ego state that was the source of the message and is emitted from the ego state to which that source addressed itself. A series of Adult-to-Adult, Parent-to-Parent, or Child-to-Child transactions are clearly complementary and lead to communications that result in a satisfying sense of being mutually understood. A mutual exchange of jokes or the kidding between the Child ego states of two people is an example of smooth and satisfying communication.

Crossed transactions occur when the ego state addressed is not the ego state that responds or when the ego state addressed responds back to an ego state different from the one that sent the message. A husband joking with his wife's Child is crossed when her Adult responds with the information that his kidding wasn't funny at all. Similarly, the transaction is crossed if the Child of the wife responds back to the husband's Parent rather than his Child, such as with a tearful response about how the husband is always picking on her.

The secret in helping couples with communication problems is to help them become aware of their own ego states and how their ego states are crossing rather than complementing each other. If couples can learn to identify the ego state that was invovled in a crossed transaction and can get back into the ego state that was being addressed, they can learn to participate in complementary transactions that, in principle, at least, can lead to communication that proceeds indefinitely.

HOSTILITY

Hostility is embedded not within the individual's inherent impulses to destroy but rather in the ulterior transactions between individuals who have decided that they or others are not OK. The ongoing hostility between people playing such repetitive games as "uproar" is aimed not so much at destroying or hurting the other but at keeping the other from getting too close. Such hostility avoids the risks of intimacy while providing a more structured excitement of games. Hostility is especially exciting for those who collect red stamps to trade in on a big blow-up. Besides the cathartic release of emotion, they also have the pleasure of reaffirming how right they are to decide that others are not OK.

People in the racket of collecting angry feelings can also use their red stamps to enhance their life scripts. It they collect enough grudges, they can eventually have a hostile blow-up big enough to justify a divorce or even a homicide, without having to feel any guilt or responsibility. Responsibility for hostility can begin only when angry people are willing to use the Adult within them to consider that maybe, just maybe, they were wrong to decide that others are not OK. Hostile people, however, tend to be self-righteous people who would rather attack others than attack the painful task of considering that their basic positions in life are dead wrong.

CONTROL

Control is an issue for parents and for the Parent in people. People with a continual need to control are people with a Parent that dominates their personality and their relationships. Such perennial Parents will have less problems in their relationships if the nurturant Parent is dominant and they are indeed concerned with the best interests of those they are attempting to control. A benign dictator is certainly easier to take than a Pig Parent, but even the protective Parent will wear thin with a partner who chooses to live life as an autonomous Adult. Crossed transactions will be frequent as the Adult responds rather than the Child who is continually being addressed by the perennial Parent.

The perennial Parent is not the only source of control problems. People with little control over their own Child stimulate the Parents of others and urge others to step in to provide the controls that their own Adult and Parent are unable to provide. When others do respond as Parents, however, the Child is likely to rebel and have nothing to do with controls. If people are to break out of relationships being destroyed by control conflicts, it is clear that both the Parent and the Child in the relationship will have to begin to take responsibility for the part each plays in making control a central concern. In spite of what the self-righteous Parent or the naive Child might say, in control conflicts there are no innocent victims.

Individuo-Social Conflicts

ADJUSTMENT VERSUS TRANSCENDENCE

The only fate that can possibly be transcended is a fate that is self-imposed. The forces of self-defeating and self-destructive life scripts must be transcended, not the forces of society. People prefer to believe and are encouraged to believe by social scientists, however, that if they are losers it is only because the forces of society have been stacked against them. There is no doubt that the forces of society urge many people to resign themselves to be losers in life. Nevertheless, it is when people take a stand against themselves, when they decide that society is right and that they are not OK, that they begin to follow a loser's life. While our protective Parent would like to prevent people from the pain of recognizing that they have stacked the deck against themselves, that they are the joker in their own games, it is only through such painful self-confrontation that people can regain control over the scripted fates of their lives.

If patients decide to choose a winner's script, they need not be in constant conflict with society. They will be aware that it is only their rebellious Child who wants to be free from all restraints. The Parent within will understand the wisdom of traditions and conventions, will speak the language of control, and will help them adjust amicably to many of the authoritative forces of society. While their Adult may work to help make a more democratic and just society, the Adult is also unbiased enough to recognize that people can be winners even with the odds against them—as long as they do not continue to be against themselves.

IMPULSE CONTROL

People do in fact experience being overwhelmed at times by certain feelings, such as rage, lust, or a longing for food. They find themselves unable to keep from acting on such overwhelming feelngs, even though it is not in their best interests to be controlled by such impulses. Such people need to first track down and identify the feeling carefully and exactly (Holland, 1973). They can then become aware of the ego state that is cathected when the impulsive feeling occurs. They also can become aware that other structures of the personality are not engulfed by the impulsive feeling, and thus the feeling need not be overwhelming. Since the Child ego state is typically associated with such impulsive feelings, the person can learn to control such impulses by cathecting the Adult or Parent ego state when the impulsive feeling is threatening to get out of control.

RULES FOR LIVING

Human beings are beautifully structured to be able to live a life of flexible rules. The Adult is prepared to create rational rules for living in those areas of life that are best left to the autonomy of the individual. The Parent is structured to appreciate the necessity of traditional rules for those areas of social life that are best constrained by social rules for all. The Child, meanwhile, is able to respond freely and spontaneously in the areas of life, such as humor, that need not have any standing rules other than what mutual joy provides. The solution for conflict over rules is to help people regain the flexibility to cathect one ego state or another, depending on the social situation they are in.

Beyond Conflict to Fulfillment

MEANING

Meaninglessness is a symptom of psychological starvation. The loss of meaning is one of the major complaints associated with stroke deprivation, along with a feeling of emptiness, a lack of deep feeling, a feeling of being unloved, a sense of life not being worth living, and a chronic case of boredom. Meaning is lost when people structure their lives with rituals, pastimes, and work activities low in stroke. Pastimes, such as TV, that structure so much of a modern family's leisure just pass the time with few strokes for the spectators. Much of modern work provides little excitement or recognition for the workers. When life's activities lack any nourishment other than structure, a person is left with a deep sense of being in a rut. Breaking out of a rut and finding more meaning in life involve choosing to restructure life with activities that satisfy the hunger for human strokes.

VALUES

The fundamental value judgment in life is one's position regarding the worth of oneself and one's fellow human beings. The healthiest and most humane value system follows from the judgment "I'm OK—you're OK." The fundamental evil in life is to deny the value and worth of any human being, including oneself. Those judged to be not OK can be treated in immoral, not-OK ways. Lives of destruction and of defeat demonstrate not only the pathology but also the immorality of deciding that any part of humanity is basically not OK.

Therapy is inherently connected to positions of value. Since life positions are value positions, therapists must be prepared to throw their moral weight behind the healthiest value position that reaffirms the belief "I'm OK—you're OK." Therapists can appeal to the best in each ego state to help clients appreciate the value of being human. The Adult in clients will be aware that we are social beings who require relationships with others in order to satisfy our human hungers. The nurturing Parent in clients can appreciate the need to care about others who are hurting or in need of support. And the Child in clients can find wonder and joy in the uniqueness that is expressed when any human being is free to be spontaneous. To help clients develop healthy relationships with others and with themselves is in part to help them appreciate the value inherent in being human.

IDEAL INDIVIDUAL

An ideal individual is a stable individual who has the freedom and flexibility to shift from one ego state to another, depending on the demands of a particular situation. A stable person is realistic, rational, and responsible, avoiding games that are designed to shift the responsibility for life's problems onto others. As Parent, the stable person is a caring and cultured individual, who is committed to maintaining the most valuable traditions of the past. As Child, the stable person is spontaneous, joyful, and humorous, a delightful individual who is able to bring out the best in others.

Ideally, an aware person with the volition to act as Parent, Child, and Adult could dodge all of the destructive games that people play. Ideally, a stable person could go through life without a commitment to any rigid life script. In practice, however, the best we should expect from structural and transactional analysis is people who can keep game playing to a minimum and who can choose to live constructive and caring scripts rather than the scripts of losers.

THEORY OF THE THERAPEUTIC RELATIONSHIP

The therapeutic relationship is part of both the content and the process of therapy. The games that clients attempt to play with therapists, for example, are a critical part of the content that is to be analyzed. Clients who are consistently late or who fail to pay their bills may be playing "kick me" with the therapist. The naive therapist may indeed relate with a kick rather than an analysis of the client's self-defeating games. At the same time the relationship can be part of the process of therapy, such as when the therapist relates as an Adult in order to hook and to strengthen the Adult of the client.

The Adult of the therapist is the ego state most often involved in transactions with the client. Since the process of consciousness raising is a rational process, the therapist relies on the Adult's rational abilities for processing stimulation from the client. Therapy is said to be underway when clients are willing to switch control of their lives from their own Parent to the Adult of the therapist. The clients will at first experience such rational control from the therapist as being a function of the therapist's Parent. Eventually, clients will come to appreciate that the influence of the therapist is not the demanding, dominating force of a Parent, but rather the influence that is inherent in an Adult's ability to deal effectively with the world. Once clients decide that the Adult within them is as effective in interacting with the world as is the Adult of the therapist, then the client is ready to terminate.

In Rogerian terms, the therapeutic relationship is indeed unconditional in regard. The therapist is convinced that clients are indeed OK unconditionally rather than being OK only if they act in particular ways. Transactional analysts rely more on rational processes for analyzing ego states, games, and scripts than on empathy for processing the critical information in therapy. Certainly therapists must be able to cathect their own Child or Parent to appreciate the feelings of the client's Child or Parent. Nevertheless, the cognitive process of the rational Adult is most effective in understanding the troubled structures and transactions of clients.

To be effective, transactional analysts must be able to be genuine in therapy, since it is impossible to fake being an effective Adult, a humorous Child, or a caring Parent. Effective therapists are free to be genuinely spontaneous when they respond with the Child within them, but they certainly do not believe that the spontaneous reactions of the Child are the only genuine part of the human personality. Transactional analysts also believe in relating as equals with clients. The insistence on a therapeutic contract is an indication of the belief that therapist and client can relate as equals. The Adult of every individual is assumed to be equally effective in relating to the world, and one of the goals of therapy is to have the client relate on an Adult-to-Adult level as quickly as possible.

PRACTICALITIES OF TRANSACTIONAL ANALYSIS

Group therapy is preferred in part because a group allows a greater number of transactions, including more troubled transactions than might typically occur with an individual therapist relating primarily as Adult. A typical group is made up of eight members who meet once a week for two hours. Crisp beginnings and endings were preferred by Berne, so meetings traditionally begin and end promptly. Clients should be able to see the whole body of other members in order to pick up bodily cues that reveal Parent or Child ego states. Preferably a videotape recorder is present to help clients analyze their ego structures or transactions, although an audio recorder can serve some of the same purpose. A blackboard for diagraming ego states or crossed transactions is also recommended. The fees for TA groups follow the going fees in an area, usually ranging from $15 to $30 per session.

Transactional analysts come from the full range of helping professions. Regular membership in the International Transactional Analysis Association (ITAA) requires completion of a basic course in the principle of TA, including an examination based on the course (Holland, 1973). Clinical membership in the association requires supervision of clinical work, plus creative contributions to TA, and completion of written and oral exams. In addition, there are teaching members, who have been clinical members for two years and who have been supervised in teaching two introductory courses.

EFFECTIVENESS OF TRANSACTIONAL ANALYSIS

A review of the literature located five controlled studies on the effectiveness of transactional analysis. The first was a dissertation by Goodstein (1972) comparing the effectiveness of a 12-hour TA marathon with that of a 12-hour gestalt marathon. Sixty junior college students from psychology classes were randomly assigned to five groups: a control group, two TA groups, and two gestalt groups. The results indicated that the TA groups reported greater reductions in manifest anxiety than the gestalt groups or the control group; the gestalt groups reduced authoritarianism and increased creativity significantly more than did the TA groups; the two groups did not differ on risk taking; and neither therapy increased self-esteem or personal adjustment more than in the control subjects.

Liberman, Yalom, and Miles (1973) included two TA groups in their investigation into the encounter process. As with all the forms of therapy studied, the two TA leaders were markedly different in their leadership styles and abilities, although both were firm advocates of a TA approach. The effectiveness of the two TA groups was markedly different, with one of the groups being the most productive of the 17 groups studied and the other group the next to last in effectiveness. With such differences in outcome of the two TA groups, no real conclusions can be drawn from this study regarding the effectiveness of TA.

Jesness (1975) reported the results of the Youth Center Research Project, which compared the effectiveness of transactional analysis and behavior modification programs for delinquents. The project involved 983 adjudicated delinquents, aged 15 to 17 years, who were randomly assigned to either the Close School, based on TA or the Holton School, based on behavior therapy principles. The most comon offenses were burglary and auto theft, though almost all of the youths had fairly extensive prior records. A third of the youths had been previously institutionalized. Only youths who spent three months or more in the programs were included in the results.

Improvements on psychological measures, such as insight, value orientation, alienation, withdrawal, and mood and social anxiety, favored the transactional analysis program. Improvement on behavior ratings, such as calmness, communication and independence, slightly favored the behavior therapy program, which was based heavily on contingency contracting. Parole follow-up at six month intervals for two years showed no differences between the programs in parole violations. Approximately one third of the youths had been returned to an institution by 12 months and one half by 2 years. The parole violation rates for the two programs were significantly less, however, than baseline rates for both institutions in the two years prior to the staffs being trained in either TA or behavior therapy. The violation rates were also lower than the rates for two comparable institutions for delinquents in California. Jesness (1975) concluded that institutions for delinquents can be run so that most residents change for the better. As Jesness points out, however, to label the two programs *successful* is to use the term loosely, since only 23 percent of subjects released on parole had records clear of arrest after two years.

Olson, Ganley, Devine, and Dorsey (1981) compared the long-term effects of transactional analysis and behavior therapy with inpatient alcoholics. There were 113 patients (77 males and 36 females) ranging in age from 21 to 73, with a mean age of 44 years. They were a middle-class group and 71 percent were married and 12 percent divorced. They averaged 2.6 ounces of absolute alcohol per day or about 3½ drinks per day. Half of the group had never been in therapy before, and 33 percent were in therapy once before. The patients were randomly assigned to one of four groups: (1) mileau treatment involving two or three lectures daily, group therapy, daily AA meetings, two or three individual psychiatric consultations weekly, recreational and physical therapy; (2) mileau therapy plus three one-hour sessions of group TA; (3) mileau therapy plus two one-hour sessions of covert sensitization and two one-hour sessions of relaxation; and (4) mileau plus TA and behavior therapy combined. Treatment lasted an average of 33 days.

The four treatment groups were compared at five intervals: 6, 18, 32, 42, and 48 months. There were no significant differences between the treatment groups in terms of percentage of patients abstinent at each follow-up period. Over 50 percent of the patients were abstinent for each of the five follow-ups, and 36.3 percent were abstinent for the entire four years. All four groups had relatively low quantity and frequency rates of alcohol consumption across all follow-up periods, averaging less than two beers per day. There were no significant differences between treatment groups on the combined quantity/frequency measure.

Although the authors suggested that the TA treatment was less effective than the behavioral treatment, the statistical comparisons were not significant at the $p = .05$ level. In fact, the addition of three to four hours of TA or behavior therapy appeared to add little to the mileau therapy that was available full-time, six days per week.

Cross, Sheehan and Khan (1982) compared short-term insight therapy and behavior therapy with outpatient psychiatric subjects. The insight therapy was a combination of TA and gestalt therapy. There were 30 nonpsychiatric patients between the ages of 18 and 55, who were randomly assigned to 12 sessions of either TA/gestalt or behavior therapy. Twelve wait-list control subjects of comparable age and severity of symptoms were recruited via newspaper ads, because the clinic staff found it unacceptable to refuse treatment to anyone requesting it.

Both therapy groups reported significant improvements at posttreatment on four target symptoms: adjustment to work, family, and marriage; sexual and leisure activities; the Personal Orientation Inventory; and the Current Adjustment Scale. There were no significant differences between the therapy groups. Improvements were maintained at four-month and one-year follow-ups.

Transactional analysis has been found, then, to lead to significant improvements in delinquents, alcoholics, and neurotic outpatients. Futhermore, TA was found to produce results that were comparable to the effectiveness of behavior therapy.

CRITICISMS OF TRANSACTIONAL ANALYSIS

From a Behavioral Perspective

As an approach to theory and therapy construction, TA continues in the worst heritage of the clinical tradition. Concepts are carried over from clinical observations with total disregard to testing their scientific validity. Theoretical postulates are stated in totally untestable terms. Berne (1972, p. 415) was aware of this when he wrote: "Experimental validation of script theory is not possible with human beings." Is it possible with lower animals? Yet Berne and his followers (Holland, 1973; Steiner, 1974) continue to write about script theory as if it were verified, let alone verifiable.

Like most therapies, TA is presented as a universal treatment, appropriate for just about any problem the clinician might encounter. Universality is characteristic of therapies based on arm-chair philosophizing and theorizing. Specificity is more characteristic of therapies that are based on scientific data. As therapy becomes a more scientific endeavor, we need to be able to specify which treatments work best with which problems under which conditions. TA may work best with hypothetical constraints like scripts, games, and ego states, but what about concrete clinical problems like phobias, obsessions, and depressions. To become scientifically respectable TA needs to specify how constructs like Parent, Child, and Adult can be experimentally tested. To become clinically acceptable TA needs to specify with which problems it works best and under what conditions. Otherwise, TA remains just another in a long line of therapies for all seasons and all reasons.

From a Psychoanalytic Perspective

Transactional analysis attempts to translate the fundamental concepts of ego, superego, and id into the commonsense concepts of Adult, Parent, and Child. In the translation, TA loses the basic driving force of the personality, the instinctual drives of the id. The Child in TA becomes a neutralized concept, the innocent child of common sense, lacking the overwhelming hostility or sexuality that could account for why so many people end up with lives of destruction or defeat. On the one hand, TA would have us reject historical determinism and believe that people self-determine a loser's life through mistaken decisions at an early age. Their miserable lives are merely a mistake that can be readily reversed with a new decision. At the same time, TA would have us believe that it is parents who transform children into frogs, which is a theory of historical determinism. But if it is parents who destroy the OKness of children, what destructive driving force is there in the parents that would lead them to transform their own children from prized princes and princesses into despicable frogs? Somewhere along the line a destructive force that sounds like the id raises its ugly head in spite of TA's repeated attempts to convince us that we are really OK. The fact is there is something within us, either as children or as parents, that is not OK, and we had better come to grips with that force, lest we go on reproducing lives of destruction and defeat.

From a Humanistic Perspective

Transactional analysis is faced with the Humpty-Dumpty problem. Once you assume that human beings are broken into three separate parts, then all the king's horses and all the king's men will never put humanity back together again. Instead of the traditional dualism of Western thought, TA threatens to divide us into a tripartite personality that can never know the beauty of being whole. And it could get worse. If second-order structural analysis becomes established, the human personality will be fragmented even further, with 27 separate Ego states currently the record (Steiner, 1974). In an era when human beings come to clinics in increasing numbers because of a sense of being fragmented by the demands of modern role playing, TA would support such fragmentation by reassuring people that their personality does indeed come in separate parts. Rather than recognize the phenomena of Parent, Child, and Adult for the social roles they are, TA would have us believe that these roles are the fundamental reality of human personality. Once stuck with the assumption of fundamental fragmentation, we can never hope to find the holism that is essential to health.

From an Eclectic Perspective

Presenting a theory of therapy in common terms has the decided advantage of allowing nonprofessionals to appreciate and use the theory on their own. The popularity of TA would suggest that people are taking advantage of its simple language and trying to use it in their lives. At the same time, formulating a theory of personality, pathology, and psychotherapy in the language of everyday life brings with it the risk of producing a system lacking depth. TA does indeed come through as a commonsense theory lacking the depth required to articulate the mysteries of the human condition. TA comes through as a theory too typically American in language to capture the breadth of human experience. In fact, all too often TA sounds like a system of slick Madison Avenue slogans. "I'm OK—you're OK" sounds like a rating from an OK used-car lot. "Green stamps, red stamps, and brown stamps" suggest that our deepest human feelings occur while waiting in a supermarket to collect our favorite stamps. "Games people play" is a catch phrase more appropriate for daytime TV than for the tortured human transactions that are being analyzed.

Everyday language is best suited for articulating everyday events. If we are attempting to explain the best and the worst of human personality and human pathology, then everyday language can leave us cold. If we are attempting to affirm our humanness and the best we can say is that we are OK, then we condemn ourselves to a devitalized existence. "How did you like your date?" "Oh, he's OK." "How did you like the movie?" "It's OK." Affirming ourselves by stating that we are OK is about as strong a stance as someone who says a person is interesting or different. Saying OK is barely a position of commitment, let alone a life position on which we should base our sole existence. The problem with the language and the theory of TA is that they are too common and too cognitive, too free from the emotion and the passion that make existence exciting.

A TRANSACTIONAL ANALYSIS OF MRS. C.

Mrs. C. is locked into a mindless script that will result in madness and institutionalization unless an antidote is forthcoming. Her worst fear is that she has already gone mad. Her world threatens to go out of control. In a desperate attempt to maintain structure in her life, Mrs. C. routinizes whatever she can until her life is nothing but a repetitive series of compulsive rituals. With mindlessness lurking in the background, Mrs. C. clings to her compulsions as if they represent sanity itself. She confuses structure with sanity, ritual with rationality.

The origins of Mrs. C.'s mindless script can be found in her parental injunctions against thinking. "Shut up and do as I say," was her father's frequent injunction against any attempt of Mrs. C. to speak or know her own mind. We can imagine that her mother discounted any attempts of Mrs. C. to be reasonable about dirt, disease, or sexuality, until Mrs. C. was left with a mindless terror of these natural phenomena. With such oppressive parents, Mrs. C. at some point made the critical decision in life that her parents knew better than she; they were right and she was wrong; they were OK and she was not OK.

From her loser's life position, Mrs. C. decided on a course in life that was a variation of the "poor little me" script. She was the helpless child, the victim of awful forces like disease and dirt, and she was desperately in need of a rescuer. Cinderella-type stories would be her favorite fantasies. With the exclusion of her rational Adult ego state, she felt totally incapable of salvaging her own life. Her life was dominated by her helpless Child, who was terrified of relatively harmless parts of the world, and by her Pig Parent, who demanded total cleanliness, sexual nonresponsivenss, and nonassertiveness.

Apparently Mrs. C.'s counterscript had worked well for a while after her husband had rescued her from her tyrannical parents. For several years she seemed to lose herself in the role of parent, having one child after another, leaving herself little time to think. But early in life she had selected a script that was destined to leave her mindless. Chaos was bound to overwhelm her. Five children and a sixth on the way, an epidemic of Asian flu, and a threatening case of pinworms were enough to produce a sense of chaos that confirmed what she had decided long ago—that she indeed was not OK. Mrs. C.'s helpless Child took over, and she began again to cry out to the adults around her to rescue her from her fate.

In the "poor little me" script, however, the star cannot allow any permanent rescue unless the script is analyzed and rewritten. Mrs. C.'s first therapists probably responded to her dramatic pleas to be rescued. As she failed to respond, however, her therapists most likely began to feel victimized by Mrs. C.'s mindlessness and became persecutors who labeled the ungrateful Mrs. C. as schizophrenic and suggested that she be hospitalized. Mr. C. had also joined in the dramatic triangle as a rescuer who valiantly awoke at 5:00 A.M. to rescue Mrs. C. from her morning shower. As Mrs. C. failed to be rescued over time, Mr. C. began to feel victimized by her relentless rituals until he too wanted to persecute her by having her institutionalized. Obviously Mrs. C.'s tragic life script was rapidly approaching the inevitable climax in which she would collapse into craziness. With obvious mindlessness, poor little Mrs. C. would be entirely helpless and in need of constant parenting from others.

Mrs. C.'s mindless script included a series of self-defeating games. She played a heavy hand of "ain't it awful"—"ain't the pinworms awful," "ain't my washing awful," and "ain't my life awful." "Look how hard I tried," she would lament. "I washed, and washed, and washed, and I went to therapy for years, and I'm still a hopeless case." Her "wooden leg" game would keep others from asking too much of her. In one way or another, she would say, "I'm a helpless, obsessive-compulsive handwasher on my way to becoming a mindless schizophrenic, so don't expect me to be an adequate Adult, a warm wife, a caring mother, or a successful client."

Mrs. C. has probably received most of her strokes from her family and therapist only when she is not OK. The hunger for recognition of six children could place a serious strain on the stroke economy of the C. household. As with so many traditional wives and mothers, abundant strokes would come only when they are on the edge of being in desperate trouble. Look at the special attention and care Mrs. C. received once she became a helpless neurotic. She could be sick with flu, pregnant, and caring for five other children and never receive much special attention. But Mrs. C. had decided as a child that strokes would come freely if she adopted a helpless, not-OK position in life.

Mrs. C.'s self-destructive life course would not be moving so smoothly and rapidly toward its ultimate end if Mr. C. was not so willing to play his part so well. He appears to be locked into a script that calls for a superhuman effort at being a heroic rescuer until he finally sacrifices himself in a sense of self-righteous martyrdom. He's OK—she's not. "I it weren't for her" is a convincing game he plays to advance his self-martyred script. Without involving Mr. C. in intensive TA, we can expect that he would in subtle and not-so-subtle ways continue to encourage Mrs. C. along her mindless course in life. His is a joyless script that is perfectly matched to a spouse who has chosen a life of mindlessness.

If the C.s are to be helped from self-destructing, intensive structural analysis must be directed at the almost total lack of Adult functioning in their lives. The Adult of the therapist would need to hook Mrs. C.'s excluded Adult if therapy is to have a chance of succeeding. At the same time, Mr. C. must be made aware that even his Nurturant Parent, who intends to help Mrs. C. through her compulsions, is in fact destructive to her because it stimulates her helpless Child. Mr. C. must do all he can to cease and desist from any further rescue mission on his wife's behalf. She may threaten suicide or appear to be out of control, and yet he must not fall back into his pattern of rescuing his poor little wife. He should be encouraged to use his own Adult in times of stress to try to hook his wife's Adult to keep her Child from becoming overwhelmed by irrational fears.

Mrs. C. also needs permission to ask for strokes when she feels OK rather than having to act not OK in order to receive recognition or attention from her family. The therapist must give special attention to Mrs. C.'s strengths and let her know that strokes will be forthcoming even if she improves and not only if she deteriorates. With feedback and interpretations, Mrs. C. can be helped to become aware of how she felt the need to choose a mindless script early in life but need not continue on such a self-destructive course. Encouraging her to read books by Berne and Harris, for example, will encourage her to use her mind to help herself. Having Mrs. C. in a TA group can help her discover not only that can she use her mind to help herself, but that she also has the rational ability to be of help to others.

If Mrs. C.'s Adult can be hooked in therapy and if she can become aware of the pressures early in life that encouraged her to decide on a mindless script, then she has a chance to reverse the pathological direction of her life. If she and her husband can both become aware of how involved they have been in a dramatic rescuer-victim-persecutor triangle, then they both can realize that rescuing Mrs. C. is about as helpful as giving heroin to an addict. Mrs. C. must learn to reject all attempts from others to rescue her, even if those others are mental health professionals. Her strokes can come from discovering that with difficulty she can direct her own life. She has to learn that in spite of what her Pig Parents seemed to suggest and in spite of what she decided early in life, she has the ability to be OK. She must decide that she will no longer be the helpless child. At the same time, she needs to be aware that regardless of what some mental health professionals might say, she is not a hopeless neurotic or an incurable psychotic. In the face of such professional and parental pressures, Mrs. C. must learn that regardless of how troubled her past may have been, she can still proudly affirm herself as being fundamentally OK.

EMOTIONAL FLOODING THERAPIES

MEGAN WAS AFRAID that Roger had lost all tolerance for her sarcasm and criticism. He wanted a separation. He had tried to be patient while she struggled in intensive therapy to understand the source of her hostility. He had tried to accommodate himself to her demands but was coming to believe that his efforts were futile. For a while it had helped to understand that much of her bitterness began in puberty when her alcoholic father threatened her if she refused to play with his penis and let him fondle her body. He understood her determination to never again submit to such degrading demands. But he now was feeling degraded by her constant cutting and unwarranted attacks. They both were seeking some relief from bitterness. Megan's marital therapist thought that implosive therapy might reduce enough of her hostility to allow her marriage and her therapy to continue.

When I asked Megan to imagine as vividly as possible her experiences with her father, she had no problem picturing him staggering into her room with a bottle in his hand and a sick smirk on his face. As he began grabbing at her breasts, she could feel the revulsion and the rage welling up inside herself. But instead of passively giving in, this time I had her imagine reaching for the bottle on the bed. As he bent over to take off his shoes, she used all of her strength to crack the bottle against his skull. Sinking to the floor, he was too dazed and too drunk to keep her from hitting him again.

When she saw his penis sticking out of his pants, she felt an urge to stand on her bed and jump feet first onto his penis, smashing it against the floor. As she became more engrossed in the scene, she leaped from her chair and began jumping, stamping her shoes against the floor, shouting, "I'll crush your cock, you filthy bastard. I'll squish you into slivers, you son of a bitch. You made me feel that all men are creeps. You made me feel like a creep if I let a man near me."

A NOTE ON THE EMOTIONAL FLOODING THERAPIES

Directly stimulating, intense emotional responses, such as the rage in Megan, are characteristic of a variety of therapeutic approaches that have been classified as the *emotional flooding therapies* (Olsen, 1976). In recent years there has been a dramatic increase in the attention given to these therapies (e.g., Brown, 1973; Nichols & Zax, 1977; Olsen, 1976). In this chapter we shall examine four of the most evocative and provocative of these therapies.

As we shall see, these therapies vary considerably in the procedures used to directly stimulate strong emotions: Reich emphasizes manipulation of the body; bioenergetics relies more on bodily exercises; primal therapy involves the reliving of painful childhood memories; and implosive therapy presents a fantastic form of imagery. These approaches also vary considerably in their theoretical explanations of psychopathology and psychotherapy. Nevertheless, they share a common assumption that emotional disorders can best be treated by encouraging the direct release of blocked emotions.

In order to keep this chapter to a manageable size, the sections on personality theory and the theory of therapeutic content have been omitted. Furthermore, criticisms of each of the four therapies shall be primarily from one perspective, such as Reichian therapy being criticized primarily from a psychoanalytic perspective.

Some critics might suggest that Reichian therapy should have been omitted entirely because there are few pure Reichians practicing today. As shall soon be apparent, however, a variety of common therapeutic practices, such as analyzing resistance before transference, treating character problems and not just symptoms, focusing on nonverbal communications of patients, and working with bodily actions and not just words, are lasting contributions of Reich. Furthermore, Reich is to many of the emotional flooding therapies what Freud is to many of the insight oriented therapies—the seminal thinker who continued to spawn new approaches to treatment. Reich is, for example, a continuing influence on gestalt therapy, bioenergetics, and structural-integration, a deep-massage therapy developed by Ida Rolf (Schutz, 1971). For these reasons we now turn our attention to the life and work of Wilhelm Reich.

CHARACTER ANALYSIS OF REICH AND VEGETOTHERAPY

Wilhelm Reich (1897–1957) was one of the most controversial figures of the 20th century. Praised by Freud as a brilliant and effective therapist, he was later condemned by many Freudians as a very dangerous and grandiose paranoid. Said to be caustic, suspicious, and irrational by some, he was praised by others, such as Neill (1958) of Summerhill, as one of their warmest, most relaxed, sincere, and capable friends. As a source of inspiration for many important innovations in psychotherapy, he unfortunately is remembered by all too many for only his mistaken notions that people could be cured of such illnesses as cancer and schizophrenia by lying in an orgone box, a metallic container surrounded by wood that was assumed to accumulate the healing and life-sustaining orgone energy from the universe.

This complex man was born into a simple farming life in the German-Ukranian part of the Austrian Empire. Working in harmony with nature, he came to believe and trust in what was natural. Serving in the Austrian army in the First World War, however, he came to know the dark side of life as well. While still a medical student at the University of Vienna, he became a member of the Vienna Psychoanalytic Society in 1920, a rare honor for so young a person. Reich soon established himself as an expert on psychoanalytic technique. From 1924 to 1930, he headed an official seminar that focused on thorough systematic case studies of patients who were failures with traditional analysis. Freud was sufficiently impressed wth Reich's early contributions to include him in the inner circle of friends who met once a month in his home (Jones, 1957).

Gradually Reich's personal idiosyncracies and theoretical positions brought him into increasing conflict with the elders of psychoanalysis. His first wife was a former patient, whom he later divorced to take up residence with another woman. His later admissions (Reich, 1967) to having had affairs with some of his patients confirmed the rumors that were being spread in the analytic societies. Reich's continued commitment to a theory of complete sexual fulfillment, even for adolescents, became a source of anxiety to analysts, who were then finally attaining social respectability.

Reich himself could not accept Freud's emerging emphasis on a death instinct. Freud's hypothesis of a death instinct reflected a characteristic modern uncertainty about human nature (Robinson, 1969). Reich could not accept that nature had burdened humanity with such an evil, destructive force. For Reich the destructive forces in people were the result of the frustrations imposed by an oppressive society that prevented the full and free release of the life-giving and life-supporting orgasmic energies. Reich looked to a combination of Freudian analyses of personal repression and a Marxian analysis of social oppression as the solution to the human dilemma.

Reich's personal and professional unorthodoxies, however, soon led to his being rejected from the International Psychoanalytic Society in 1934. His book, *The Mass Psychology of Fascism* (1970), led to his being unwelcome in the Communist Party because he suggested that the authoritarian character of the working class was a major reason for Hitler's rise to power. In a matter of months he lost most of his friends (Reich, 1953). He fled Germany in 1933 to escape from Nazism only to be expelled from Denmark, Sweden, and Norway.

Coming to the United States in 1939, he believed he was finally free to continue his commitment to the personal and social liberation of humanity. Some say it was too late, that he had already sunk into madness and was preoccupied with paranoid delusions that included being able to see and capture the very energy source of life, the orgone (Cattier, 1971). Others, such as Bordella (1973), believe that paranoid ideas, such as that the atmosphere was being poisoned by flying saucers, had become a part of Reich's world view only after years of rejection, ostracism, and persecution for his life's work. Certainly there was reason for Reich to feel persecuted when he was ordered to stand trial for violation of the Federal Drug Administration's (FDA) injunction against the selling of orgone accumulators across state lines. Refusing to co-operate with the courts, Reich was found in contempt of federal court and guilty of FDA violations. His orgone boxes were ordered destroyed, with some justification. The destruction of all of his writings, however, was a totally unconstitutional penalty that lends support to those who saw Reich's trial as, at least in part, motivated by a repressive system, which had fired 200 FDA agents in one month for being alleged subversives (Bordella, 1973). In 1957 Reich was totally ostracized from society when he was sent to Lewisburg Penitentiary for two years. He died in prison eight months later.

Theory of Psychopathology

Psychopathology can be prevented only through a sexual revolution that grants people their inherent right to be sexually free and fulfilled. Sexual repression is the core of psychopathology and must be attacked. There are, however, many forces both within and outside of people that resist the natural desire for sexual happiness and health. Outside individuals there is an authoritarian social system that facilitates the unjust exploitation of humanity. An oppressive society, however, cannot rule by social controls alone. Such a society requires the cooperation of its people. The biggest threat to an oppressive society is sexually free people who, in the process of expressing their sexuality, experience a sensitivity and sociability toward others that would not allow them to tolerate the brutalization and degradation of the poor and the powerless. Those who will tenderly embrace humanity are those who have known the tenderness of a loving genital embrace.

At first Reich (1953) could not understand how the 400,000 ragged and starving unemployed in Vienna could walk by wealthy shops and privileged citizens without attacking either the shops or the privileged ones. Social controls, such as the police, were not numerous or powerful enough to prevent a revolution of people in touch with the energy and the decency that would come from living out their natural sensuality. Authoritarian societies needed authoritarian personalities, he concluded. Pathological societies need pathological personalities. Inhuman oppression is internalized into neurotic repression through the social institution of the family.

The family's social purpose is to repress sexuality. The family believes its purpose is to develop moral character in its children. The result is that families use parental power to build characters that are essentially antisexual and sick, When people are raised to automatically repress their own basic sexual humanity, they are preprogrammed to be cooperative robots that particpate in their own oppression and that of others.

Built into the person is a pathological character structure that exists to maintain sexual repression and social oppression. To attack repression, then, is to attack a patient's very character. Since a patient's character represents a total lifestyle that determines not only symptoms but also work and family relationships, a patient can be expected to be highly resistant to efforts to analyze and liberate a total lifestyle. Reich (1945) identified six typical character structures that are seen most often in therapy and that present the most difficult challenge to successful analysis: (1) the phallic-narcissistic male, who uses emotional lameness and intellectualization to repress strong emotions; (2) passive-feminine male, who uses submission and an apparent cooperative "nice guy" facade to fight off the effects of therapy; (3) the masculine-aggressive female, who uses apparent toughness and rigidity to ward off feelings; (4) the hysterical female, who uses flirtatiousness and seductiveness to avoid real commitment to a profound sexual relationship; (5) the compulsive character in both sexes, who hides behind pride in self-control and perfectionism to avoid change; and (6) the masochist character, who uses martyrdom and suffering as a way of repressing and investing sadism, and who resists health as another way of continuing to suffer.

Such rigid character structures are a form of armor that binds frozen energy and prevents the instincts from being expressed. To analyze and begin to liberate a patient's character threatens to release the emotional impulses that Freud had described so often—rage and a perverted, compulsive, and dominating sexuality. Most patients agree with Freud that such impulses represent who they really are and thus resist any attempt to analyze and release such emotions. Reich, however, believed that such destrucutive impulses result from repression of life's liberating libido. There is a monster below the social character; it results not from nature but from the unnatural process of authoritarian socialization that intends to destroy what is best in people—their life-giving and life-supporting sexuality.

These are the forces that Reich (1945) first found to be the causes and maintainers of psychopathology: (1) an oppressive, authoritarian society; (2) a repressive style of life, called *character;* and (3) a threatening group of hostile and perverted sexual impulses that result from the repression of the child's naturally tender and loving sexuality. Later Reich (1951) came to believe that parents used their power to make repression part of the child's very body. If it is indeed the body the parents want to control, then the best method is to use power and fear to make children tense their muscles so much that their bodies become suits of armor that are too tight and too controlled to allow for the sheer abandonment needed for total orgasmic release.

To attack a patient's repression involves attacking the patient's muscular tension. Reich (1951) contended that there are seven rings of muscular armor that serve as repressive forces against full genital release. Therapy then becomes a matter of releasing each of these rings of muscular armor, beginning with the muscles at the top half of the head and moving down through each ring until the muscles circling the pelvis and genitals can be liberated. Only patients who have undergone the liberation of their bodies can be truly free from neuroses and pathological character structures and become free to experience the full delights and values of being natural human beings.

Theory of Therapeutic Processes

As a Marxist, Reich (1953) was convinced that psychopathology could be prevented only with a revolution that established a nonoppressive, communist society. As a therapist, however, he was not content to let people suffer until the revolution came. In 1929 he became one of the first community mental health workers by establishing several sex information and counseling clinics in Vienna. How far ahead of his time Reich was! Even in 1972 the opening of a sex information service in Newport, Rhode Island, was thought to be radical enough to be reported in the international press (Janice Prochaska, 1972). Yet, in 1929 Reich was providing the young and unmarried with the latest birth control measures. As a feminist, he was advocating the right of women to own their bodies and was willing to risk his career by approving an abortion for any female who found it in her best interests to terminate a pregnancy. Reich worked many hours without pay to raise the consciousness of the young and the poor regarding their sexuality and how they might attain greater sexual fulfillment. This work was primarily *educational*, providing the latest information that Reich and others had gathered in their therapy work.

CONSCIOUSNESS RAISING

In terms of formal therapy, Reich's (1945) first major contribution involved character analysis. He was extremely influential in establishing the rule in psychoanalysis that resistance must be analyzed first, and for Reich the first line of resistance was the character structure of clients.

The Client's Work. Reich originally followed the standard free association rule that the patient's job is to say everything that comes to mind without censoring any feeling or fantasy. Patients provided information for analysis not only by what they said but, even more significant, by how they said it and by how they acted in therapy. Reich (1953) was one of the first to sensitize therapists to the significance of nonverbal communication. Patients could not help but provide information regarding their characteristic defenses. They might be too cooperative, appear to associate too smoothly, speak softly, smile frequently, or be submissive, stubborn, or seductive. Over time their pattern of behaving in therapy became established as the first problem to be analyzed, since the real message behind such patterns is a determination to resist changing a style of life. The hardest work of patients is to stay with therapy even when they experience their very characters as being under attack.

The Therapist's Work. Reich (1945) originally saw character analysis as a necessary preparation for psychoanalysis. Until patients are fully aware of how they use their typical patterns of responding as defenses, they are unable to ease up on such defenses and truly cooperate in the analysis of infantile conflicts. To help patients gain such awareness, the therapist must use frequent and persistent confrontations and interpretations to provide patients with *feedback* about their most characteristic and pervasive forms of resistance. For example, in treating a 25-year-old man with a few minor symptoms, Reich (1951) became aware that the patient assumed a self-confident, cool, and ironic being toward the world that communicated an attitude of being above it all and therefore unthreatened by others. In therapy this ironic and superior being came out most frequently as a smile that was neither warm nor friendly but rather a message of mockery. Reich continually confronted the young man with information concerning when the smile was occurring and how it was being used to keep therapy from having any real impact. He repeatedly interpreted the mockery that the smile was communicating toward the analyst and the analysis. Reich told his patient that he had no need to be afraid of laughing heartily and loudly at the analysis. From then on the young man began to bring out his irony and mockery much more clearly. As his character defenses became more conscious, they also became less effective and allowed more infantile memories and emotions to surface. With such infantile material closer to the surface, Reich could then resort to the more passive role of the psychoanalyst engaged in interpreting the meaning of infantile conflicts.

CATHARSIS

It is not enough to just make the unconscious conscious, to just interpret the meaning of memories and dreams into conscious language. Patients must also experience and release the intense emotions contained in dynamic conflicts. With the analysis of character armor, such emotions are inevitably expressed as the character structure is loosened and the frozen energy released. The emotions that are most likely to be experienced first are fear and rage toward the analyst for having attacked a character structure that has served as the source of security and esteem in the patient's life. As such negative emotions are cathected and the patient undergoes a corrective emotional experience, the more intense sensual and sexual instincts begin to emerge. As the infantile sexual fixations are analyzed and released, patients are free to develop relationships in which they can express to the fullest this core of life, their genital sexuality.

As Reich (1951) developed into an even more independent theorist and therapist, he became convinced that character analysis must be accompanied by a more direct liberation of the body. Repression is tied up not only in one's characteristic patterns of behavior but also in the very muscular knots of one's body. Body armor itself must be attacked with a manipulation that allows for the cathartic release of repression and emotion so that the energy of life can flow more freely through the body. With the addition of direct body work, Reich labeled his approach with the unusual name, *vegetotherapy*, referring to the use of *vegetal* to reflect the series of vital energies common to both plants and animals.

The Client's Work.   Since the body is both focus and locus of repression, the task of clients is to make their bodies available for therapeutic intervention. Clients disrobe and lie outstretched on a couch or bed to allow the therapist access to the rings of muscular armor that need to be attacked. Clients no longer free associate or even speak unless they find at times that language is the best expression they can give to the emotions that are emerging as their muscular armor begins to dissolve. Otherwise clients are free to scream out, kick the couch, curse the therapist, cry, or give any other ventilation to the overwhelming emotions that have been frozen in their muscular tensions. As each ring of armor and repression is liberated and the accompanying affects evoked, clients are able to own more fully the life that is their body.

The Therapist's Work.   The Reichian therapist is not concerned with providing a relaxing massage or a sensational physical manipulation. The therapist's work on the tense muscle knots is guided at all times by the emotional functions of the muscle tensions. Using both theoretical training and their clinical empathy, therapists recognize which emotions are locked into which muscles, such as murderous rage locked into the ocular muscles in the tense, glaring stare of the paranoid personality.

Usually the therapist attacks the rings of muscular armor in sequence, beginning at the top of the head and working down to the pelvic muscles. The therapist will stay with a muscle group until patients can express the tremendous rage that accompanies the pressure of parents having been on their backs. Besides the release of such muscle tension and the accompanying emotions, the therapist also teaches patients a method of deep breathing that both reduces tension and refreshes the body. As patients come to breathe more freely and as they shed their body armor, they gain the capacity to abandon themselves to spontaneous and involuntary movements in therapy. Little by little the various sensations of warmth, of prickling in the skin, and of shuddering movements in the limbs and trunk begin to integrate into convulsive reflex movements of the whole body. Looked at as a whole, the body appears to be expanding and contracting in a pulsating manner. The client has become free to give total and involuntary release to the most pleasurable and energizing expression of life—the orgasmic reflex.

Theory of the Therapeutic Relationship

Human beings are to be held in the highest regard, but it is the natural, genital human that is godlike, not the charade commmonly known as character. The character structure of clients represents what an oppressive society has demanded as the price of acceptance. We can no more love the oppressive defenses of neurotic individuals than we can prize the oppressive forces of an authoritarian society. We must care enough about real human beings to dedicate ourselves to the removal of both repression and oppression. Character and body armor must be attacked so that the whole human being, who is so worthy of our highest regard, can emerge. Clients can and will direct their lives effectively and responsibly, but only after effective therapists have responsibly directed them in the therapeutic process of shedding characterological and bodily blinders. Similarly, a therapist should be available to enter into a genuine relationship with clients, but only after the clients have become free to be genuine.

Empathic relating has a special meaning in vegetotherapy. Empathy is a bodily experience that is sensed in the liberated bodies of therapists who are in physical contact with the tensions and emotions locked into the muscular armor of clients. Therapists must trust in their own bodies to guide them in their physical work with clients.

Practicalities of Reichian Therapy

While Reich would have preferred therapists to be well trained in anatomy and physiology as well as in psychoanalysis, he would be much more concerned with their therapeutic experiences. A Reichian should undergo both a personal character analysis and vegetotherapy to assure a person liberated both in behavioral patterns and in body. Reich (1951) also believed the use of intensive care seminars with supervison to be essential to effective therapeutic training.

In practice Reich seemed to follow much of his psychoanalytic training, doing individual therapy with several sessions weekly. He claimed to be especially effective in treating neurotics and character disorders that were highly resistant to traditional analysis. Unlike classical analysts, he did not believe that therapy works best with verbal, intelligent, well-educated individuals but rather believed that such individuals frequently use their verbosity as an effective defense. As we have seen, he was willing to work with the poor and the oppressed.

Contemporary Reichians generally avoid the most controversial practices of Reich. They generally would, for example, have patients wear bathing suits or their underwear, rather than be nude. They reject the notion that sex with clients can be justified but rather focus on helping clients become free to develop their own fulfilling sexual and intimate relationships outside of therapy.

Effectiveness of Reichian Therapy

An historical survey of Reichian research failed to produce any controlled outcome studies on its effectiveness. Reich followed the Freudian example of intensive case studies as the means of validating his therapy. During the last two decades of his life, he turned his attention to doing research on the discovery and application of what he called *orgone energy*, the primordial, cosmic energy that is the source of all forms of matter. He believed that this cosmic energy produced the biological effect of changing living substances and could have amazing healing properties if accumulated. Orgone energy was also assumed to be the tremendous energy released during the orgasmic reflex, thus its name was intended to reflect its organic and orgasmic importance. Since his research into orgone energy took Reich primarily into the areas of biology and astrophysics, and since it has been rejected or ignored by investigators in these fields, we shall not pursue it further.

BIOENERGETICS

Alexander Lowen (1910–   ) is the therapist and theorist most responsible for the survival, revival, and advancement of Reichian therapy. Trained as a physician and psychoanalyst, Lowen underwent analysis and supervised training with Reich. Lowen's concern has been with the strictly therapeutic aspects of Reich's work, avoiding the political ramifications in part because he believed that it was Reich's political commitments that led to his destruction in a world preoccupied with the work ethic at the expense of the life and pleasure of the body (Keleman, 1973). Lowen also rejected the notion of the attainment of orgastic potency as the exclusive goal of therapy. Pleasure is the goal of therapy, with sexual pleasure being just one expression of the enjoyment of living. The freedom to enjoy life can come only in a body that is fully alive, a body that allows the full and free flow of life's energy, *bio energy*. Lowen has been a strong voice against the antipleasure, antibody, and antilife forces of society in his extensive private practice, his Bio-Energetics Institute in New York, his nationwide workshops, and his books on bioenergetics (Lowen, 1958; 1965; 1967).

Theory of Psychopathology

Psychopathology involves the repression and rigidification of life. For every rigidity of psychic functioning there is a corresponding rigidity of metabolic organismic functioning. All psychopathology embodies an arrest of the fullness of energy flow on both the psychological level of subject-world perceptions and the physiological level of purely internal channels of metabolic interaction (Brown, 1973). Such rigidifications of the body and the self certainly originate in the early conflicts between parent and child. The rigidifications eventually become the neurotic character structure and the muscular armor that Reich (1942, 1945) has described.

Reich overlooked, however, two very common clinical characters: the oral characters, who have trouble standing on their own two feet and who use dependency on the therapist to resist change; and the schizoid characters, who have a restricted inspiration in their breathing and in their living and who use their dissociation and detachment from their bodies as defensive means of remaining detached from therapy. The schizoid character has been especially difficult to treat in the past because of the risk that penetrating the detachment could result in a more pathological dissociation from reality, resulting in schizophrenia. Nevertheless, Lowen (1967) has worked extensively with such patients, helping them to put breath and life back into their bodies and their selves.

All pathological characters, and especially schizoid characters, lack an adequate *grounding* in reality. Since character structure is established in childhood, it leads to an incomplete maturation of the ego, which represents the principle that effective living must be grounded in reality (Bellis, 1976). In more Freudian terms, patients have trouble with both the pleasure principle of finding adequate fulfillment for bodily desires and the reality principle of being well integrated into the world. While Reich emphasized giving free and full energizing to the autonomic part of the nervous system that controls sexual pleasure, Lowen gives equal emphasis to the cerebral cortex being fully energized.

Inadequate grounding in reality is expressed through problems in such ego functions as judgmentally not being able to take a stand or motorically being poorly coordinated, with fears of falling, being a pushover, or walking like a duck (Bellis, 1976). Perceptually, poor grounding can be expressed in such problems as myopia, the near-sighted syndrome of intellectuals who are insensitive emotionally to people and to threats at a distance. Patients are those proverbial people who have eyes but cannot see and ears but cannot hear, at least not clearly. People well grounded in the reality that is their bodies can give voice to their feelings and their thoughts, whereas immature characters have weak, irritating, affectless, hesitating, or unimaginative voices. To have a voice in the community is an essential part of being maturely grounded in society.

Our fundamental grounding is in our bodies. "Apart from the body, life is an illusion" (Lowen, 1967, p. 758). We, as body, are the life process. To be well integrated in our living reality is to have a well-integrated body. But, as Reich discovered, the bodies of troubled individuals are knotted layers of muscular armor that prevent the smooth, integrated flow of life's energy, bio energy. Muscular defenses also prevent the smooth, integrated flow of living in the world.

Theory of the Therapeutic Processes

To just encourage the immediate release of the emotions frozen in body armor is to encourage living only by the pleasure principle. Such emotional flooding may be exciting or temporarily relieving, but it can also be dangerously overwhelming. The release of anger, for example, can be experienced as an anxiety attack unless patients are also helped to consciously analyze the origin and meaning of such anger. The freedom to express anger can also lead to unrealistic angry outbursts unless the anger is grounded in a more realistic and conscious connection to reality. Bioenergetics then includes the cathartic release of the body within the context of an analysis of the patient's infantile character structure.

CONSCIOUSNESS RAISING

The Client's Work.   Before there can be a free and full flow of feelings, clients must become aware of the chronic characterological and bodily tensions used to control feelings (Lowen, 1972). To become free of their infantile characters, they must connect their present inhibitions with the past and become aware of the bodily impulses they were forced to repress by their behavioral and bodily inhibitions. In undergoing such character analysis, the main work of clients is to struggle to unblock their ears and hear clearly the interpretations of the therapist. At times the cathartic release of certain feelings or a flood of repressed engergy will bring with it clear insight if the patients will just listen to their bodies. Most of the work of raising the consciousness of clients, however, belongs to the well-trained analyst.

The Therapist's Work.   From the initial diagnostic reading of the body's behavioral performance, the bioenergetic analyst is trained to come to quick and decisive conclusions about the precise nature of the patient's psychological weaknesses. The analyst is highly didactic, informing patients that they have a particular character structure that is revealed by an analysis of the particular rigidities in their muscular armor. Patients are told, for example, that they have a tight jaw to hold back biting impulses or tense shoulders to hold back from hitting people. Once interpretations are presented it is the responsibility of the patients to sense the tension in their jaws and their impulses to bite and be sarcastic. While interpretations are in part based on feedback about a specific patient's experience, the interpretations are in large measure based on analytic and bioenergetic theory. In many ways, then, the bioenergetic raising of consciousness involves educating patients about information that is assumed to be valid by bioenergetic analysts.

CATHARSIS

The Client's Work. In bioenergetic body work, patients are more active than in vegetotherapy. They do not just lie back and have their muscles manipulated. This occurs at times, but just as frequently patients are asked to perform exercises designed to evoke intense emotions. Patients may be asked, for example, to pit themselves against the world's field of gravity in such a way as to intensify their negative feelings against giving in or collapsing. They may be encouraged to arch their bodies off the ground by making contact with the floor with only their hands, head, and feet. After considerable struggle to stay up, they can experience the feeling of their bodies giving in to the inevitable, to the reality of life, as they tire and collapse to the floor. They can experience the fear or anger connected to giving in, and through analysis they can become aware that such negative emotions may be the result of early conflicts with parents who insisted on submission. Gradually patients may recognize that fears over giving in to reality may keep them from falling asleep or falling in love or surrendering to orgasmic reflex.

Patients are also asked to practice exercises such as yelling or kicking and hitting the couch to both release anger and experience the inner ability to focus energy on the world. Such exercises may also evoke childhood memories of wanting to strike out against parents but dreading the thought. Such exercises also help patients to experience a sense of bodily grounding, that they can express their anger intensely and yet not go entirely out of control and attack the therapist as they might have fantasized. Patients also practice proper breathing through exercises designed to release energy through a more natural breathing process.

The Therapist's Work. In bioenergetics body work the therapist does not work as systematically as in vegetotherapy. Muscular armor, for example, is not necessarily manipulated by beginning from the top of the head and moving toward the pelvis. The bioenergetic therapist works more spontaneously, working on the muscles that are currently providing the greatest resistance or those that contain the most emotions and energy. Or the therapist may not directly attack the body at any given moment but may turn to an exercise if it could be more successful in releasing emotions and energy. The therapist encourages patients to surrender to the body, to let emotion and energy flow, and to trust the body as their direct link to reality (Keleman, 1973). The highly energized therapist is tuned to energy blocks and removes such resistances to life through movements, muscular manipulations, or mental interpretations. As patients surrender to the life that is their body, they will encounter pain, sadness, tenderness, anger, and anxiety. But these are at least real feelings, which can be experienced and expressed. With the release of such emotions, patients also discover a tremendous increase in bio energy, the energy of life that flows within them and outside them. The release of such emotions and energy is then grounded in the person's expanding awareness of reality, the reality they are willing to support and help create through the investment of their new-found energy.

Theory of the Therapeutic Relationship

Lowen is similar to Reich in his view of the therapeutic relationship. He supports a doctor-patient relationship in which the doctor is the expert trained to perform the therapeutic operations necessary to heal the patient. Keleman (1971, 1973), a more radical bioenergetics theorist, goes beyond the doctor-patient view of therapy. He rejects the notion of therapy as primarily healing or fixing the unhealthy. For him bioenergetics is a practical and profound philosophy of life, the life of the body and the living earth. Therapy releases the life within us and allows us to be grounded in the living earth. Keleman sees bioenergetics as the yoga of the West, and thus the therapist relates as the yoga master to help students discover life.

Practicalities of Bioenergetics

While similar in practice to Reich's approach, Lowen does differ in allowing patients to remain clothed or work in the nude, depending on their preference. Besides individual therapy, he is also willing to do bioenergetics with groups, especially in weekend workshops.

Effectiveness of Bioenergetics

As with Reich, neither Lowen nor any of his students have carried out controlled outcome research on bioenergetics.

PRIMAL THERAPY

For 17 years Arthur Janov (1924–　) had been practicing psychoanalytic psychotherapy as a psychiatric social worker and a clinical psychologist. Then one night in group therapy a 22-year-old college student let out an eerie scream, a primal scream, that changed the course of Janov's professional life. The young man, a poor student who was withdrawn and shy, had become fascinated by an act on the London stage in which a performer paraded around in diapers, drinking milk from a bottle and shouting, "Mommy, Daddy!" At the end of the act, the performer vomited. After plastic bags were handed out, the audience was encouraged to do likewise.

The student's fascination with the act encouraged Janov to push him to call out, "Mommy, Daddy!" Though neither patient nor therapist really saw the point, the patient cooperated. To their surprise, he began writhing on the floor in agony. He appeared to be in a hypnotic trance; his breathing was rapid and spasmodic; and he began to screech "Mommy, Daddy!" in a piercing, death-like scream.

For months Janov remained fascinated by this event. The patient had improved remarkably, though no one knew why. When the proper occasion arose in therapy, Janov encouraged a 30-year-old man to call out to his parents. After considerable resistance, the patient let himself go and he, too, revealed an involuntary act in which he began breathing rapidly and deeply, writhing in near convulsions, until he finally emitted a series of curdling screams. Flooded with a stream of insights, he believed that his life had suddenly opened up and that he was becoming transformed into a healthy human being.

With the two therapeutic events too similar to be coincidental, Janov began experimenting with various means of helping patients regress into the type of profoundly cathartic experiences that led to apparently curative changes in consciousness. Janov was now into primal therapy. With the help of his wife, Vivian, as director of training of their Primal Institute in Los Angeles, Janov (1970; 1971; Janov & Holden, 1975) has continued to expand on what he claims to be the only cure for neurosis.

Theory of Psychopathology

The essence of neurosis is the encapsulation of pain within both the psyche and the body. This pool of pain, the primal pain, is the natural consequence of a child's inherent needs being unmet by significant others. The primal needs—to be fed when hungry, to be held and stimulated, to be kept warm, to have privacy, and to be allowed to develop inherited potentials—will result in pain if denied. If these needs are denied repeatedly, the child eventually comes to face primal trauma, the terribly painful trauma of being unloved (Janov & Holden, 1975). The child concludes: "If I go on striving to be who I am meant to be, my essential needs will be denied. I will be in constant pain. To remain in pain is to risk insanity or death. Let me then repress my painful memories of being unloved. Let me twist and turn to contort myself into whatever distorted being it is that my parents can love. If I must be clean or constantly achieve, if I must be submissive or sick or asexual, then I will be, since the pain of being me is intolerable."

The psychic need to repress pain is accompanied by biological mechanisms that provide for repression. These are the gating mechanisms of the brain. Three pain gates are postulated: (1) a somatosensory gate in the brainstem, (2) an affective gate in the limbic midbrain, and (3) a cognitive gate in the orbitofrontal-hypothalamic area of the brain (Janov & Holden, 1975). These three lines of defense keep the pain from being dissipated. The primal pool of pain remains as pristine, vivid, and hurtful as when it began. To be oneself is to risk reactivating this pool of pain. So the child not only continues to repress pain but also closes off much of who the child really is.

The pressure of primal pain being disconnected from awareness results in neurotic tension. Tension is channeled into increased heart rate, body temperature, and brain activation. The body works harder to keep the pain repressed. Eventually the heart may give way or ulcers, colitis, or stroke may occur. The tension leads to a myriad of symptoms designed to prevent the reactivation of pain, such as phobias of crowds, phobias of enclosed spaces that threaten to stimulate painful memories of being all alone, or homosexuality designed to gain the love of many men in order to deny the lack of love from one's father. While such symptoms are intended to provide freedom from pain, they work only for the moment to reduce tension, and then they must be repeated when the pool of pain threatens to break through the repressive gates. Neurotics cannot change because they cannot let themselves confront the pain that would have been devastating for the fragile child but need not cripple the mature adult. Liberation from neuroses requires liberation from the primal pains of childhood.

Theory of Therapeutic Processes

Primal therapy is designed to liberate people from primal pain. Lifting the gates of pain, however, results in a flood of painful emotions and memories. The patient must suffer through the humiliations, indifferences, and insults of childhood to the most unbearable of hurts. The process of reliving childhood hurts results in a cathartic release of pain and a curative increase in consciousness as present events are reconnected to previously repressed memories of pain.

CONSCIOUSNESS RAISING

The Client's Work.   In order to regain consciousness of childhood traumas, clients must be willing to work to give up everyday defenses against tension and pain. Cigarettes, tranquilizers, alcohol, TV, sex, and socializing are avoided as the client is isolated in a hotel room during the first week of therapy. Not only does such sensory deprivation weaken defenses, but it also removes external distractions and allows internal stimulation to emerge into the center of attention. Beginning with the first therapy session, clients are to focus on experiences from only the first 12–15 years of life. They are to talk about these memories in the present tense, as if the events are occurring right now. As clients let themselves regress, they discover that changes in consciousness occur so that they in fact begin to experience memories as if they are occurring right now. At first there are only flashes of the past, like fleeting dreams, but soon whole scenes run through present consciousness, like the patients of Penfield (1958) who relived memories when specific neurons in their brains were stimulated electrically during surgery. Struggling to get into this altered state of consciousness, where the past is relived in the present, is the first stage of therapy, and it places a great strain on patients as they begin to reach a new level and then slide back from fear, fatigue, or frustration.

As therapy progresses, however, clients are confronted with undeniable memories of rejection, deprivation, frustration, and humiliation. They cannot help but see the connections between their neurotic needs for approval and their past rejections, between their excesses in eating or drinking and their past deprivations, between their current expressions of rage or rivalry and their past frustrations, and between their fears of being honest and open and their past humiliations.

The Therapist's Work.   The therapist's task in raising consciousness is to help disarm the defenses so that altered states of consciousness can occur. The insistence on sensual and social isolation during the first days of therapy aids in disarming defenses. So too does the therapist's encouragement of the client to speak in the present tense, to focus on the past, and to stay with terrible memories even when the client fears that insanity may ensue. To disarm defenses and have a client experience terrifying changes in consciousness would be cruel and dangerous if the therapist was not available whenever the client needed someone during the first three weeks of therapy. The therapist, therefore, makes a commitment to only one client at a time and is available by phone 24 hours a day.

With the defenses disarmed, the therapist need not rely on intellectual interpretations to produce changes in consciousness. Feedback from the client's past is abundantly clear as the repressive gates of the brain are lifted. Clients can make their own connections between present feelings and past memories once their biological and psychological blinders are removed.

CATHARSIS

The Client's Work. As painful memories emerge into consciousness, clients also experience intense emotions. They seem to go through several stages of emotional release (Rose, 1976), beginning with an expression of anger and revenge toward parents. "I hate you! I'll kill you!" they shout. As they get into primal experiences, they externalize their images of their parents, striking or kicking the couch that represents a parent in their altered state of consciousness. As they release their childhood emotions in the present, their actual voices become more childlike, as do their words and actions. They cry and sob like children as they realize the futility of a lifetime of trying to win the love and approval of parents who are hopelessly committed to their own comfort rather than to the well-being of their children. As patients come to feel directly the raw pain of the primal trauma that was a culmination of years of indifference or insults, the involuntary release of emotion is frequently characterized by the spasmodic writhing on the floor and the shrieking of a primal scream.

The primal screams, however, are only the most dramatic release of painful emotions and have perhaps been overemphasized (Janov, 1970; Janov & Holden, 1975). The kicking, shouting, crying, cursing, and other cathartic releases are just as important in dissipating the primal pool of pain. Unfortunately, the pain is not released all at once. In the third stage of therapy, clients have numerous primal experiences, draining off more and more pain as they work first through one of the repressive gates and then through another, going further back in their history and in their hurt.

Once clients have discovered key traumatic memories, they must continually reexperience the episodes, releasing more and more of the painful emotions connected to them. This repeated cathartic confronting of critical memories is the longest stage of primal therapy and may take six months to a year or more. The client's work during this stage is done partly at home and partly in a group of other primal patients who use the group time to do their own catharting rather than to socialize or interact.

This stage is also the most uncomfortable for clients since they can no longer rely on defenses to block off feelings, and when the feelings surface it is not always possible for clients to stop and have a primal. With tension building rapidly, clients often feel disconnected as they consciously try to close off their bodily feelings as they used to do automatically. But clients also are becoming new, more authentic individuals who are learning to trust their feelings and reown their bodies. During this stage clients will use their groups and their therapists for support until they become free enough from pain to stand on their own.

During the fifth stage of therapy (Rose, 1976) clients begin to synthesize their corrective emotional experiences and their increases in consciousness. They understand with a sadness of mind and body, of total self, what it was like to give an open, innocent love to parents and not to have it returned for its own sake. They understand the deep anger that runs through them for having to have closed off so much of their authentic responses to the world in order to survive. They feel with a profound awareness the terrible void as they realize that their original openness to life was crushed. But with fear and trembling they begin again to open themselves up to life.

With the final stage of therapy, clients become more authentic human beings. They can follow their own feelings without the terrible fear and pain of losing the parents' love and approval. They have given up the fruitless battle of trying to please parents. With a calmness they have never known, they begin to give up most of their neurotic ambitions, frequently turning to nondemanding jobs that provide for their primal needs. They give up long-term goals and projects that are the result of the disciplined pain and tension of neurotics. They become independent, no longer needing the approval of others, and their independence from the world is reflected in an apolitical stance toward the world. They discover a self-sufficiency they never believed they could know.

The Therapist's Work.   To allow the painful emotions to flow, all the therapist must do is continue to disarm the patient's defenses. The patient is asked to lie on a couch in a spread-eagle position in order to be as physically defenseless as possible. No talk about the therapy is allowed. Talk of theory or content is just an intellectual defense, and the focus is to remain on early emotional events. If the patient presents a bright, humble, or hostile front, then the front is forbidden in order to get the patient beyond such defenses. If patients figet, they are told to lie still. If they giggle or yawn as feelings emerge, they are given feedback about such defenses. Whatever resistance is used, it is confronted and attacked directly.

Once patients begin to show some feelings from the past, the therapist may encourage them to breathe deeply and hard from the belly. "Open your mouth as wide as possible and keep it that way! Now pull, pull that feeling from your belly!" urges the therapist (Janov, 1971, p. 82). As patients begin to breathe deeply, writhing and shaking, the therapist encourages them to express the emerging feeling, such as "Tell Daddy you're scared." When patients resist, such as saying they won't tell the bastard anything, they are urged to say it, say it, don't hold back.

As patients get into more intense primal experiences, they may be afraid their wrenching feelings will cause them to vomit or go crazy, and the therapist's task is to reassure them that they are feeling and not vomiting, coming alive again and not going crazy. As the defenses are chipped away, patients are continually encouraged to regress fully into the past. Once they begin to enter a primal experience, they become engulfed by it. The release of emotion now becomes involuntary, as the patient may scream, "My God! He's going to kill me. Daddy hates me. He wants me out of the way. Stop, Daddy, stop!" (Janov, 1971, p. 86). And the patient may then begin to roll on the floor screaming, gagging, retching, and finally yelling out, "I'll be good, Daddy. I won't talk back again." During such painful primal experiences, the therapist remains silent, allowing affect to flow. The therapist may help in small ways, such as moving the couch to allow the patient to roll more freely or providing a cushion to be beaten. Once the patient can let go of all controls and be engulfed in primal experiences, most of the therapist's work has been done.

With the patient free to regress into primal releases, the therapist now transfers the patient to a group. In the group patients spend two hours in their own separate parts of the room catharting, as painful memories and feelings emerge, without having to worry about what others in the group will think since they are doing the same thing. If patients like, they can stay after and discuss their insights with others, but that is not an inherent part of the therapy. What is important is that patients are free to continue to drain the pool of primal pain whenever it presses to the surface, whether in the group, at home, or out in the world.

Theory of the Therapeutic Relationship

Patient and therapist have a very special relationship during the first three weeks of primal therapy. The patient knows there are no other individuals vying for the therapist's concern during that time. The therapist is available 24 hours a day just for this particular client, and the therapist's attention is almost totally on this patient, since the groups are available to help other clients. Yet the relationship between patient and therapist is not the critical content of therapy. It is the patient's past relationship to parents that is critical. Nor is this special therapeutic relationship the critical process of therapy. The cathartic release of primal pain and the accompanying increases in consciousness are assumed to be crucial. The therapeutic relationship is only a necessary precondition for effective therapy to occur. The relationship allows for enough trust so that patients can allow therapists to attack their defenses and lead them into a journey that is a painful, emotional hell. They must trust that this journey is the route to a cure from neuroses and not a regression into psychoses.

The therapist shows an unconditional caring for the clients, but not in the Rogerian style. Clients are allowed to direct the flow of therapy only after the therapist has torn down their defenses and their facades and helped them regress into the most painful of past experiences. Once patients are free to be primal, however, the therapist allows more unconditional expression of emotion than does the traditional Rogerian. Patients can roll on the floor, tear apart the couch, and even take off their clothes and masturbate without having to fear any interference from the therapist.

Empathy is used early in therapy to help appreciate the exact nature of an emerging feeling in clients and to help articulate the feeling for clients, such as by telling the clients to say, "I'm afraid of you, Daddy," or "I hate you, Mommy." Once primal experiences occur, the therapist need not use any subtle empathy to help clarify feelings. Patients become painfully aware of their emotions from head to toe. Since clients are engulfed by their emotions, there is no way a therapist's reflection could intensify the feelings of clients. During these times the therapist relates best by sitting silently until the patient's emotion is drained.

The primal therapist makes no pretense of being genuine in therapy other than being a genuinely good primal therapist. The primal therapist does need to be congruent, having undergone primal therapy, so the therapist can genuinely trust in the process and allow it to continue when more tender-hearted therapists might press the panic button and short-circuit a truly cathartic experience. The primal therapist has no concern with forming an I-thou relationship with clients. The therapist should be self-sufficient enough to not need such a relationship from clients and should trust enough in the eventual self-sufficiency of clients to not encourage them to depend on a relationship with a therapist to meet their needs.

Practicalities of Primal Therapy

Janov (1971) states emphatically that no one should do primal therapy without formal training in a primal therapy institute. The therapy is believed to be too dangerous in the hands of an inadequately trained therapist, and for this reason Janov will not reveal in writing the full procedure of his therapy. Since there are few therapists available who have been trained by the Janovs or by one of their certified trainers, there is little accessibility to what Janov would call *primal therapy*. There are other therapists, however, such as Rose (1976), who practice what they, out of deference to Janov, call *intensive feeling therapy*. For all practical purposes this is primal therapy.

The first three weeks of primal therapy cost a minimum of $2,000. While theoretically patients can have as much daily therapy time as needed during the first three weeks, in practice sessions almost always run between two and three and a half hours. Usually within this time patients have had primals of sufficient intensity to drain most of their energy or they are still too defensive to allow for a breakthrough that day. If resistance is the problem, the therapist may order them to not sleep that night in order to allow the physiological gates to fatigue and weaken.

After the initial three weeks of therapy, patients spend from six months to a year or even longer in a primal therapy gorup. The patients can, if they choose, follow their two-hour therapy groups with a more traditional rap session in which they interact with each other about insights from their primal or their everyday lives.

Effectiveness of Primal Therapy

In his initial case survey of his first 68 patients, Janov (1971) claimed that l00 percent of his patients were cured of their neuroses. While he did not give an exact breakdown of his sample, in other reports Janov (1970) indicates that they ranged in age from 17 to 48, with the largest percentage in their mid-20s. Their occupations varied from an ex-monk to many psychologists and people in the arts. Most of his clients have been in previous therapy. Most are single, since the older, married person can be the most resistant because so much of life is already invested in neurotic patterns. If both spouses enter therapy, however, they find that their marriages improve, with no separations reported among the couples.

Janov and Holden (1975) are not specific about the types of problems Janov has treated. Examples, however, include compulsions, drug addictions, homosexuality, neurotic depressions, and psychopaths. Only psychotics and brain-damaged individuals are excluded. Intellectuality is not a prerequisite since, unlike insight-oriented therapies, the less verbal patients do as well in primal therapy as the verbal.

Postprimal patients are described (Janov, 1971) as less driven, often changing from high-status but unreal work to more real work such as carpentry. The psychologists who were treated found themselves unwilling to work 30 or 40 therapy hours a week, preferring to treat one individual client at a time. The most common activity is to sit around listening to music and relaxing, compared with the tense ambition of having to be accomplishing something, which characterized their neurotic lives. Sex becomes less frequent but more enjoyable. Postprimal patients are not moody, experiencing neither enthusiastic highs nor empty lows but rather a steady calmness that comes with letting themselves and others be. Parents tend to be avoided since postprimal people have given up on the myth of winning parental approval and are no longer willing to engage in a neurotic distortion of themselves in order to please parents. Similarly, neurotic spouses or friends may be left behind if they insist on having others meet their neurotic needs. The patients also become apolitical and nonmaterialistic as they refuse to invest themselves in futile or meaningless endeavors.

Surprisingly, many of the patients report actual physical changes, including loss of physical symptoms and even an increase in the size of their breasts, hands, or feet that were assumed to have been stunted by inadequate hormonal flow. Changes in perceived temperature occur as postprimal patients become comfortable with themselves rather than being constantly cool or hot. Premenstrual cramps disappear. Postprimal patients find themselves no longer craving tobacco, alcohol, food, or tranquilizers as physical means of trying to reduce tension.

In 1973 a team of independent researchers reported on psychophysiological changes in primal therapy patients. Karle, Corriere, and Hart (1973) compared 29 patients entering primal therapy with an active control group of 10 subjects who performed a daily one-and-a-half-hour physical exercise program and an inactive control group of 10 subjects who simply read for one and a half hours. Subjects from each group had daily pre- and postsession measurements taken on blood pressure, pulse, rectal temperature, and electroencephalogram (EEG) activity. Subjects were also compared on a three-day baseline average on these measures and on a three-day posttreatment average following three weeks of therapy, exercise, or reading.

Changes in blood pressure were not significant. A greater percentage of primal subjects showed significant decreases in pulse rate compared wih the activity group but not with the inactive group. Rectal temperature changes were considered highly significant, with 82 percent of the primal patients showing decreases compared with none of the activity subjects and 18 percent of the inactive group. On EEG measures both control groups showed no change, whereas the primal patients showed a decrease in alpha waves and a general pattern of EEG changes similar to people in a relaxed physiological state even though they were awake and alert at the time of testing. While primal patients were apparently more relaxed and showed a slower metabolism, the authors of the study are careful to point out that their data do not support Janov's (1970) claim that primal therapy is the cure for neuroses. They indicate that data from other cathartic therapies, such as autogenic therapy (Luthe, 1969), show similar short-term physiological changes. Nevertheless, Janov (1971; Janov & Holden, 1975) uses the Karle et al. (1973) data to support the primacy of his therapy.

McInerny (1975) conducted a longer-term research project on pulse and core body temperature in primal patients, but he did not include control groups. With 22 patients he reported that the mean baseline on pulse was 74 beats per minute and was reduced to a mean of 70 beats per minute following three weeks of therapy and to a mean of 66 after six months of therapy. Similarly core body temperature changed from a baseline mean of 99.2° to 98.8° after three weeks and 98.7° after six months. McInerny concluded that these vital sign changes correspond to the patients' claims of reduction in neurotic tension. The physiological changes, however, were not directly correlated to reported changes in neurotic tension.

In a more recent survey of postprimal patients, Holden (1975) does not report the percentage of patients who were cured by primal therapy. From his inadequate data, however, it is clear that even after two years of primal therapy, there are patients who are not free from neurotic symptoms, which is contrary to the original claims of 100 percent effectiveness. From a survey of 83 men and women between the ages of 25 and 50 who had completed at least three months of primal therapy, Holden cites individual case reports of changes in weight, height, sleeping, eating, and other signs. He summarizes his data by claiming that a majority of the primal patients showed the following patterns of changes: straightening of posture; clearing of sinuses and nose; fuller, deeper respiration; normalization of appetite and food intake; marked decreases in sex urge with increased enjoyment of sex; marked decreases in muscle tension; and insight into the relationship between symptoms of illness and primal pain. A closer examination of the patients' reports, however, does indicate that some patients have increased fear of sex, increased muscle tension, more sleeping problems, and an increase in a variety of other symptoms following three months of primal therapy.

IMPLOSIVE THERAPY

While Thomas Stampfl (1923–   ), the developer of implosive therapy, frequently asks his clients to imagine horrible scenes such as chopping up a child, having lunch in a cesspool, or being eaten alive by rats, personally he is a very friendly and warm individual. Early in his career he became convinced that avoidance is at the heart of psychopathology, and he developed his therapy in order to help people face their most frightening and upsetting memories, feelings, and thoughts. Trained at Loyola of Chicago as a clinical psychologist, he was inspired by both the psychoanalytic content of patholgy and the learning theory processes of avoidance conditioning and extinction.

While teaching at John Carroll University in Cleveland, his purpose was to provide therapy that would be an integration of psychoanalytic and behavioral therapy. Since moving to the University of Wisconsin at Milwaukee as director of clinical psychology, he has concerned himself with documenting the behavioral foundation of implosive therapy.

Theory of Psychopathology

The symptoms and defense mechanisms that characterize psychopathology are learned avoidance responses that serve to reduce or minimize anxiety. Phobics avoid stimuli such as dogs, elevators, or heights; obsessive-compulsives may avoid dirt, disorder, or anger; many schizophrenics avoid close contact with people; some sexual deviants avoid all heterosexual relations; and hypochondriacs attempt to avoid disease. If troubled individuals did not use their symptoms or defenses to avoid such stimuli, they would be confronted with anxiety that they fear could take on panic proportions. To understand how such anxiety and avoidance responses are learned, we will do best to examine the challenging research on animal avoidance behavior. Such animal research may at first seem irrelevant to human problems, but we shall see how these studies serve as excellent analogues of human pathology and therapy (Stampfl & Levis, 1973).

A dog can be conditioned to fear and flee from a buzzer that previously had been neutral. If the dog is placed in a training cage and the buzzer is turned on, the dog will at first orient to the buzzer and then learn to ignore it. However, if the buzzer is followed by a painful or frightening stimulus, such as an electric shock or a startling, loud noise, a different pattern of responding occurs. When the buzzer and shock are both on, the animal will soon learn how to escape the shock, such as by jumping over a barrier to the other side of the cage. After several trials of the buzzer and the shock being paired together, the animal soon learns to jump over the barrier as soon as the buzzer comes on in order to avoid the shock. Following several trials of avoidance learning, the traumatic shock can be terminated and the animal continues to avoid as soon as the buzzer begins. Solomon and Wynne (1954) reported that their dogs would avoid a buzzer for hundreds of trials even though there was no chance of receiving another shock. Their dogs were behaving as if they were buzzer phobics.

Mowrer (1947) uses a two-factor theory of learning to explain avoidance conditioning. The first factor is classical or respondent conditioning, through which the animal learns to fear the buzzer because it has been paired with shock. Such conditioned fear is labeled *anxiety*. The buzzer becomes a conditioned stimulus capable of eliciting an automatic and autonomic conditioned response similar to fear. If the dog remains near the buzzer, the aversive anxiety increases in intensity. If the dog jumps over the barrier, the anxiety is reduced and the dog's avoidance response is reinforced by the powerful consequence of anxiety reduction. This second factor in learning, the actual jumping or avoiding, is called *instrumental learning*, since it is instrumental in reducing and minimizing the dog's anxiety. The classically conditioned anxiety serves as the motivating or drive stimulus that activates the avoidance response, while the anxiety reduction provides the consequence necessary for reinforcement of the instrumental avoidance response.

Applying this animal analogue to human problems, we can understand how people can learn to avoid particular stimuli. For example, a 24-year-old man entered therapy in order to overcome his dread of getting close to people, especially women. He described a childhood that was quite traumatic, with a mother who had hostile impulses and an alcoholic father who was abusive. He recalled memories such as talking jubilantly at breakfast about a field trip at school, when suddenly his mother grabbed his hair and pushed his face into the hot cereal because he was talking too loudly. He could never predict when he might get smacked in the back of the head or screamed at for showing anger, enthusiasm, or sadness. All he could predict was that when people were around, especially his parents, he was more likely to face a frightening encounter. The stimuli that were conditioned to elicit anxiety were his parents specifically and, through the process of generalization, almost any person with whom he became emotionally involved. If he would start to get close to someone, his classically conditioned anxiety would be elicited. If he then backed off and avoided such closeness, his anxiety would be reduced and his avoidance of people reinforced. Even though the new people he might approach would not shove his face into hot cereal or scream unpredictably, he was responding with anxiety and avoidance as if a shock were present in his environment.

This human example also illustrates that conditioning of problems is often a more complex phenomenon than illustrated in the more simplified animal analogue. For one thing, when children are punished or frightened in their natural environment, there is not just one stimulus, such as a buzzer, being conditioned to elicit anxiety but rather a complex series of stimuli. This young man was conditioned to experience anxiety not only in the presence of people but also when he experienced intense emotions and when he openly expressed enthusiasm or disappointment. As a result he had also learned to avoid intense emotions and lively expression of his experiences. Stampfl and Levis (Levis, 1966; Levis, Bouska, Eron, & McIlhon, 1970; Levis & Stampfl, 1972; Stampfl & Levis, 1973) have actually gone back into the laboratory to test the effects of conditioning animals to avoid a complex series of stimuli, such as dark walls, followed by a tone, followed by a flashing light. They have found that such a complex series of conditioned stimuli actually lead to more effective avoidance conditioning that is learned more readily and is remarkably more resistant to extinction than when shock is paired with a single stimulus.

The conditioning of the shy young man reveals another important difference between human and animal conditioning. As in the animal analogue, the man was conditioned to fear and avoid stimuli that were present in the environment at the time of punishment, namely, people. However, he was conditioned also to be anxious about what he was imagining or feeling at the time his parents hit him or yelled at him. Consequently, he became anxious even when he imagined exciting or emotional events, and he had learned to avoid imagining or fantasizing such experiences. Traditionally we have called this type of avoidance *repression*. Defenses then can be seen to involve the cognitive avoidance of threatening thoughts, feelings, or fantasies by avoiding attending to the internal stimuli that elicit anxiety. When the young man repressed or avoided attending to his anger, for example, he was reinforced by the reduction of anxiety that would be elicited by angry feelings.

Theory of Therapeutic Processes

If the cause of psychopathology is conditioned anxiety and avoidance, then the solution is to apply the most effective methods of extinguishing both avoidance and anxiety responses. Implosive therapy was developed in response to the single question of what therapy would be like if it reflected as faithfully as possible the operations of experimental psychologists when they subject lower animals to extinction procedures in the laboratory (Stampfl, 1976). Many studies (Baum, 1970; Black, 1958; Solomon, Kamin, & Wynne, 1953) have documented that avoidance can be effectively extinguished if the animal is blocked from performing avoidance responses in the presence of anxiety-eliciting stimuli. We found (Schiff, Smith, & Prochaska, 1972) in our lab that as little as two minutes of blocking would lead to almost total extinction of avoidance responding in rats. While extinction of the classically conditioned anxiety response takes longer (Spring, Prochaska, & Smith, 1974), such anxiety could also be effectively extinguished by preventing the animal from avoiding.

When the animal is blocked in the presence of anxiety-eliciting stimuli, intense emotional reactions are evoked. The animal will scramble about the cage, climbing the walls or attacking the barrier, freezing in the corner, shaking, followed by more scrambling. Soon the classically conditioned anxiety extinguishes, since there is no longer any shock or other unconditioned stimulus presented to reinforce the learned anxiety response. In the absence of anticipated punishment, such as shock, the animal learns to discriminate that the buzzer is not a painful stimulus, and it need not be avoided. On an animal level, this method of extinguishing anxiety by forcing the animal to remain in the presence of the conditioned stimuli is called *response prevention*. On a human level, the task for implosive therapy is to extinguish pathological anxiety by presenting clients with anxiety-eliciting conditioned stimuli while working to prevent them from avoiding such emotionally evoking stimuli (Stampfl, 1970; Stampfl & Levis, 1967, 1973).

CATHARSIS

The Client'sWork. The client's task is to imagine as vividly as possible whatever stimulus scenes the therapist describes; to experience as fully as possible the intense anxiety and any other aversive emotions, such as guilt or anger, that are elicited by the scenes; to stay with the scenes even when they most want to run or avoid; and to continue to come back to therapy, knowing what frightened scenes and emotions they are likely to experience. What keeps the clients coming back is the marked reduction in anxiety they experience even by the end of the first session.

The clients' work also involves putting themselves through the implosive scenes after the therapist has presented the scenes the first time. Clients are to make the scenes even more anxiety and emotion evoking if possible. And in between sessions clients are to complete the extinction process at home by continuing to imagine any parts of the implosive scenes that are eliciting anxiety. Clearly this cathartic therapy demands a great deal of effort and cooperation from clients.

The Therapist's Work.   Implosive therapy may demand even more effort from the therapist. It is definitely one of the most emotionally draining therapies to do. Following two or three evaluation sessions, the implosive therapist must construct stimulus scenes that evoke the maximum conditioned anxiety. Stimuli most directly related to the client's symptoms will be first in the series of anxiety-eliciting cues, such as bugs for a person with a morbid dread of bugs. When implosive therapists ask clients to imagine as vividly as possible scenes about bugs, they have the person imagine the bugs as close to them as possible, crawling on their arms, in their hair, sleeping with them in bed, under the covers, all over their bodies, with their bug eyes popping out, their antennas touching the client's lips, as they come mouth-to-mouth with each other.

More challenging for the implosive therapist is to construct scenes that have been repressed or cognitively avoided. These repressed stimuli are similar to what psychoanalytic theory refers to as the *dynamics of psychopathology*, such as repressed feelings of rage. These dynamic cues, or *hypthesized avoidance cues* as they are also called, are assumed to be the conditioned stimuli that elicit the most anxiety in clients. Dynamic cues are based on psychodynamic theories of psychopathology and on the therapist's clinical interpretations. Such cues include fears of losing control over hostile or sexual urges, anal impulses, fears of responsibility and facing one's conscience, and anxiety over anxiety itself. Implosive therapists use their full imaginations to create the most involving and evoking scenes possible.

The therapist instructs the client not to worry about whether the scenes are realistic or whether they make sense or even apply to the client. Clients are asked to imagine the scenes as if they were occurring in the present and to let themselves feel as fully as they can all the anxiety, anger, guilt, or other emotions that might be elicited by the stimuli being described.

As implosive scenes are presented, clients are observed for overt signs of anxiety, such as rapid breathing, sweaty palms or foreheads, crying, gripping the chair, or curling up and covering their faces. When signs of anxiety are observed, the therapist uses this feedback to intensify or continue to repeat the stimuli in order to elicit and thereby extinguish more anxiety. Therapists also watch for signs that the client is trying to defend against or avoid anxiety and attempt to block such avoidances or break through defenses by pushing the client even harder. An example of this occurred when one of my clients was being asked to watch her children die a slow, painful, but preventable death. They pleaded for her to save them. I originally had had her imagine that she was yelling angrily at the children, "I won't help you. I don't want to help you. I want you to die." This evoked considerable anxiety and crying. When she was putting herself through the scene by overtly describing what was going on, she changed the scene and said, "I can't help you. You will have to die. " At that point I interrupted to break through her denial of her angry wish by saying, "No, tell them you *won't* help them. You really want them to die." When she no longer used her denial, her anxiety quickly intensified, as measured by increases in her blood pressure and rate of heartbeat (Prochaska, 1968).

The therapist's work also includes staying with a scene until the anxiety has been noticeably reduced and at least partly extinguished. If a session or scene were terminated while the client was highly anxious, the client could become even more sensitized to the conditioned stimuli and might strive even more to avoid such stimuli once the session is ended. The client could also have anxiety conditioned to the therapy setting and might avoid returning to therapy. Consequently, implosive therapists are trained to stay with scenes until the client is drained of most of the emotion connected with a particlar scene.

Theory of the Therapeutic Relationship

Theoretically, a relationship need not be developed, since anxiety-eliciting stimuli could be presented on tapes or films. Horror movies, for example, can be used for children and adults to confront some of their worst anxieties of death, violence, or the unknown, and to release aversive emotions through the dramatic effects of such scenes. However, such films can produce the opposite effects of increasing anxiety because the imagery is not repeated long enough or frequently enough for anxiety to be extinguished. Observers of such films may also defend against the emotional impact of the scenes when anxiety becomes intense and may end up sensitizing themselves to particular stimuli.

A therapeutic relationship is important then in order for therapists to help clients stay with the threatening stimuli when they most want to run and to make sure the most aversive stimuli are repeated and repeated until anxiety is markedly reduced. Obviously, the therapist must be able to engender trust in the client in order for the client to continue to cooperate in therapy. Trust building is started at the beginning of the first evaluative session, as the therapist communicates a desire to understand and to help the client deal with unsettling problems.

Implosive therapists are not concerned with being genuine in therapy; they are concerned with being effective. They use empathy only during the evaluation sessions to help formulate clinical interpretations that lead to the development of effective scenes. During therapy itself it does not take empathy to observe the anxiety that clients experience during implosive scenes. Considerable regard is communicated to clients through the therapist's belief that clients are much stronger than they are usually given credit for being. Clients can have the strength and courage to confront the worst fantasies and fears imaginable as long as they know that their intense anxiety is being elicited by therapy and not by some unknown and uncontrollable inner source.

Practicalities of Implosive Therapy

Implosive therapists must be trained to overcome their own socialized tendencies to avoid producing anxiety in other people. Their own conditioned anxieties must be extinguished so that they can effectively present very aversive stimuli. In my own experience I found I had to implode myself three times on every scene before I could effectively present and stay with the scene with a client.

In the past most implosive therapists were trained to appreciate and use both psychoanalytic theory and learning theory. Since more emphasis is now placed on the learning theory foundations of implosive therapy, the psychoanalytic content is at times minimized in the training of some therapists. If a therapist works with only symptom stimuli and assumes that dynamic cues are irrelevant or nonexistent, that therapist is technically doing what is called *flooding therapy* (Malleson, 1959; Rimm & Masters, 1974) rather than traditional implosive therapy. (The use of the name *flooding therapy* to refer to treatment using only symptom stimuli is unfortunate, since there is a wide range of therapies classified as *emotional flooding therapies*, only one of which is the behavior therapy called *flooding*.)

Implosive therapists work primarily on a one-to-one basis, since avoidance problems are assumed to be primarily intrapersonal. For the most part, implosive therapy lasts only from 1 to 15 sessions. The sessions must at times run longer than the standard 50 minutes, since a therapist could do damage to clients by stopping a session on the hour when they are in the midst of experiencing intense anxiety. Implosive therapists need relatively soundproof rooms in order to let their clients emote fully and would do well to be on the first floor, since people in an office below do not always appreciate a client stamping up and down on the floor above.

Effectiveness of Implosive Therapy

Stampfl (1976) cites four controlled studies on the effectiveness of implosive therapy with clinical patients. The first study was carried out by Hogan (1966), who compared the effects of implosive therapy on 26 state hospital inpatients with a similar group of 24 patients who were assigned to "traditional" verbal therapists. All of the patients received one hour of individual therapy per week, group therapy, and medication. The implosive group had an average of 4.8 months of treatment compared with 8.2 months for the traditional treatment group. There were no no-treatment subjects.

Results indicated no significant changes on the Minnesota Multiphasic Personality Inventory (MMPI) for the nonimplosive group, whereas the group treated with implosive therapy showed significant shifts away from pathology on five MMPI scales. As a further measure of success, 18 of the 26 imploded patients had been discharged from the hospital at a one-year follow-up, while only 8 of the 24 control subjects had left.

Levis and Carrera (1967) randomly assigned 40 psychiatric outpatients to one of four groups: (1) an implosive therapy group, receiving 10 one-hour sessions of therapy following one to two hours of standard diagnostic evaluations; (2) a "conventional" therapy group, receiving 10 hours of supportive and insight-oriented therapy; (3) a similar "conventional" therapy group that received an average of 37 hours of individual therapy; and (4) a no-treatment waiting-list group. Results indicated that the imploded patients had significantly greater decreases on 9 out of 10 scales of the MMPI than did any of the control groups. The implosive group, however, had higher pretest scores on seven of the nine scales prior to treatment and thus, from a statistical point of view, had more chance to show improvement toward the norm. When all groups were compared on their posttreatment MMPI scores, there were no significant differences among the groups.

Boudewyns and Wilson (1972) assigned 32 VA inpatients of mixed diagnoses (8 psychiatric, 17 neurotic, 3 personality disorders, 3 alcoholic, and 1 situational reaction) to implosive therapy, a special form of desensitization, or a no-treatment control group. Treatment involved 2 evaluation interviews and 12 sessions of therapy. The imploded patients showed signficantly greater reduction on the depression and psychosthenia scales of the MMPI compared with the no-treatment patients and significantly greater reduction of the Mooney Problem Checklist. No significant differences were found between the imploded and desensitized patients on either of these measures. On self-rated personal goals, both the implosive and the desensitization groups improved more than the no-treatment group but did not differ from each other. Finally, on personal goals as rated by others, only the implosive and no-treatment groups differed from each other.

The fourth study cited by Stampfl was actually a test of the effectiveness of *flooding therapy*, since the therapists presented only symptom-specific stimuli and did not use dynamic cues. In this study, Boulougouris, Marks, and Marset (1971) compared flooding to desensitization in the treatment of clinical phobias. Eight patients received six sessions of flooding followed by six sessions of desensitization, while eight phobic patients received the reverse order of treatment. Results demonstrated that both therapies produced significant improvements on phobias as rated by the patients, the therapists, and an independent medical tester. Flooding yielded significantly greater improvement on the independent doctor's ratings of 70 phobics than did desensitization and significantly greater improvement on physiological measures taken while the patients imagined their phobic stimuli.

Gelder, Bancroft, Gath, Johnston, Mathews, and Shaw (1973) also compared flooding with desensitization in the treatment of 36 patients suffering from clinical phobias. A nonspecific treatment for phobias, using free association, was used as a placebo control group. Each patient was seen in three history-taking and rapport-forming sessions, followed by eight sessions of standard therapy, and then four sessions of in vivo therapy in which real rather than imagined stimuli were presented to the flooding and desensitization patients. Both the flooding and the desensitization treatments led to significant improvements on clinical ratings and behavioral approach tests when compared with the placebo treatment. There were no differences in results between the flooding and the desensitization treatments.

Prochaska (1971) compared the effects of flooding with symptom-specific cues to imploding with dynamic cues in the treatment of debilitative test anxiety in 51 college students. Both the symptom and the dynamic cue groups improved on an intelligence test compared with a no-treatment group. Only the symptom-cue group improved on the intelligence test more than a placebo control or a control group treated with a set of general anxiety cues assumed to be unrelated to testing. Subjects in both the symptom-cue and the dynamic-cue treatment groups showed slight increases in their grades and reported significantly less anxiety on their final exams. The group flooded with symptom cues and the group imploded with dynamic cues did not differ from each other on any of the measures of test anxiety. The effectiveness of the treatments was probably limited by the fact that the implosive scenes were presented with tape recorders.

Morganstern (1973) presented a comprehensive and critical review of the research on both implosive therapy and flooding therapy not only with clinical populations but also with college students having such problems as public-speaking phobias, snake and rat phobias, and test anxiety. Basically his review indicates that the studies using flooding seem to produce results that are quite similar to results with studies using implosive therapy in which dynamic cues are included in the treatment. The reviews further indicate that when implosive therapy and flooding are compared with systematic desensitization, there are no consistent differences in the effectiveness of these treatments.

CRITICISMS OF EMOTIONAL FLOODING THERAPIES

From a Behavioral Perspective

The emotional flooding therapies evoke emotion all right—disgust and fear; disgust over the fact that in the latter part of the 20th century some therapists continue to spin their yarns with total disregard for validating evidence, and fear that some unsuspecting student may mistake nonsensical notions, such as seven rings of armor or primal pains, as fact rather than fantasy. Only implosive therapy is based on any respectable concepts and evidence regarding the extinction process. But even implosive therapy is old wine in new bottles—a warmed-over version of Dollard and Miller's (1950) translation of psychoanalytic theory into learning terms. Since Stampfl has not demonstrated the validity of dynamic or hypothesized avoidance cues, he would do well to drop such unnecessary hypothetical notions and focus on only the stimuli that are clearly eliciting anxiety, namely, symptom stimuli.

Implosive therapists will have to do more than make their treatment into a more dramatic form of flooding. As Morganstern (1973) points out, implosive therapy is a high-risk treatment that has at times sensitized patients to greater anxiety in the very attempt to extinguish anxiety. Since desensitization is at least as effective in treating anxiety and avoidance reponses and since it has even more empirical support, it behooves implosive therapists to justify why their high-risk therapy should be used instead of the safer desensitization.

From a Psychoanalytic Perspective

Unfortunately, Reich became fixated at an early stage of psychoanalysis. The mainstream of analysis matured into a discipline that recognized the central importance of ego processes in the production and treatment of psychopathology. Reich remained obsessed with the orgasm. Rather than inhibition of orgasm being only one form that psychopathology can take, Reich continued to believe that the attainment of orgasm is the sine qua non of mental health. Even though analysts demonstrated in the 1930s that many neurotics and even some psychotics could attain orgasms and still be disturbed, Reich was never one to let his cherished theories be disturbed by facts.

As Brown (1973) points out, Reich idolized the autonomic nervous system and reduced humanity to a sexual energy machine. With the denigration of the cortical aspects of the nervous system, Reichian therapy degenerated into a total body manipulation aimed at releasing a reflex. Cognitive integration became less and less important. It is perhaps fitting that Reich's final form of treatment became so mechanical that the human sex machine was placed into a metal and wooden box in order to be energized by some fantastic orgone energy.

From a Humanistic Perspective

While Lowen rejected Reich's obsession with the orgasm, he developed his own obsession with energy. Charge and discharge became the goal, as if humanity is a giant metabolic battery. The sheer quantitative mobilization of energy is assumed to be possessed with some intrinsic, magic healing power. In this energy-happy system, what is considered a successful outcome in therapy was once considered to be a clinical entity—hypomania. If we combine emotional outbursts, high energy, rapid metabolism, and questionable judgment because the rational processes of humanity are not given weight equal to the "bodily battery," we have a hypomania patient who is considered cured.

Even the eruption of emotion does not come from some intrinsically meaningful struggle within the person, but rather the emotions are evoked from outside the person by artificial exercises and attacks on the body. Nor does the person play a central role in giving meaning to character or to the body. The bioenergetic therapist is blessed with a godlike sovereignty of informed opinion (Brown, 1973). The therapist imposes authoritarian interpretations upon the clients, who are expected to bow to the sovereignty of the therapist. Unfortunately, the tyranny of all-knowing parents comes awfully close to being replaced by the tyranny of all-knowing therapists.

From an Eclectic Perspective

If concepts cannot be documented, they can always be deified by being capitalized. Fill a book with Primal Pains, Primal Memories, Primal Screams, Pre-Primals, and Post-Primals, and a mythical Primal Man is created. Then claim a 100 percent cure rate and take advantage of a naive public that believes there can be one cure for the multitude of emotional and psychological problems plaguing the world. If that is not convincing enough for experienced therapists, then embed the Pool of Primal Pain in the brain, locked in by physiological gating mechanisms. Such physiologizing is bound to lend scientific respectability to a system.

But a system of therapy will never attain scientific respectability when the developer of the system refuses to describe in detail the procedures necessary to replicate the treatment. Such unwillingness to make the treatment available to the scientific community prevents the therapy from being tested by independent investigators and protects it from potential invalidation. Of course, keeping the supposed cure-all secret also protects Janov from any serious competition and provides him with a monopoly for those gullible or desperate enough to put down $2,000 on an untested treatment. The irony is that such protection for the founder of primal therapy is done in the name of protecting the public from unqualified practitioners.

Even if primal therapy turns out to be powerful enough to produce the results it claims, do we want such results? The ideal Primal Man sounds more like an adulated three-year-old with no long-term goals, no disciplined commitments, and little drive or ambition other than to be free from pain and tension. The Primal Man becomes withdrawn from the world, lying around listening to music and relaxing, contented with the myth that anyone can be self-sufficient and independent in a totally interdependent world. The Primal Man reflects a sexist machismo of strength and toughness that sees love as only letting each other be. A caring love, however, includes a dependency upon each other's willingness to reciprocate, to remain open, and to be vulnerable to the hurt that can come from letting someone into the core of one's being. In a world with so few meaningful ties between lovers, families, and responsible members of a community, Janov (1970; Janov & Holden, 1975) advocates a humanity that is only strong enough to stand alone and not strong enough to risk the true intimacy that includes counting on each other.

Extolling the virtues of primordial emotions violently felt and expressed as the only authenticity can leave us with a screaming adult unable to cope with the demands of the real world. Witness the complaint of a spouse writing to *Psychology Today* (1972) about her husband, who was one of Janov's original 68 successes. When the postprimal husband goes to a restaurant and has to wait, he screams. When his children frustrate him, he screams as if he is the child. If primal therapy can cure us of neuroses, what will cure us of primal therapy?

EMOTIONAL FLOODING WITH MRS. C.

Implosive therapy will be applied to Mrs. C. to illustrate how one of the emotional flooding therapies would conceptualize and treat her problems. From this perspective Mrs. C. is actively avoiding such conditioned stimuli as dirt and pinworms. Dirty underwear, dirt from the floors, and even thoughts of dirt or pinworms are stimuli that elicit anxiety. Since washing removes Mrs. C. from the presence of dirt or the possibility of pinworms, the washing results in a reduction of anxiety. Her compulsive hand washing is clearly an operant response that is instrumental in producing the powerful reinforcement of anxiety reduction.

Mrs. C. was originally classically conditioned to fear dirt and disease by a fairly compulsive mother. While details of her conditioning history are not given, we can imagine that dirt on her hands or clothes was probably paired with threats, castigations, slaps, or spanks, until the dirt automatically elicited anxiety. When punishment was administered, Mrs. C. would most likely be thinking about the dirt that got her in trouble, so that even thoughts of dirt were conditioned to elicit anxiety. In order to avoid further painful punishment from her parents, she learned to quickly wash her hands or clean her clothes. Such washing or cleaning would result in a rapid reduction in anxiety, and Mrs. C. was thus becoming conditioned to be clean.

In an environment that emphasizes cleanliness, Mrs. C.'s rate of washing apparently remained within a normal range until the trauma of the pinworms. As far as Mrs. C. knew, her daughter's pinworms were an unconditioned aversive stimulus—something to be realistically feared. Her physician frightened her into boiling the family's clothes and bedding in order to avoid a pinworm plague. When Mrs. C. was told about the frightening aspects of pinworms, she would have been thinking about pinworms, so the very thoughts of pinworms were conditioned to elicit anxiety. Mrs. C. was especially vulnerable at this time to further conditioning. She was already anxious about her own health and the health of her family since they all had the Asian flu. Plague upon plague could raise her anxiety to intolerable levels. She would be eagerly seeking a response that could reduce her anxiety and avoid further disease. So when the doctors said washing was the answer, washing was her response.

The washing continued, however, even after the realistic threat was gone. The shock was off and the pinworms were gone, but her anxiety was not extinguished. Both her childhood anxieties and her recently conditioned fear of pinworms remained. Her hand washing was both stimulated by her anxiety over dirt and disease and reinforced by the reduction of anxiety. If she would try to remain in the presence of dirt or a scratching child without washing, her anxiety would increase markedly to almost panic proportions. When her anxiety level became unbearable, she would rush to wash, and her washing response would be even more strongly reinforced by the reduction of panic proportions of anxiety. Even thoughts of dirt or pinworms could elicit intense anxiety. Mrs. C. was now like a conditioned animal making avoidance trial after avoidance trial with no voluntary control over her conditioned anxiety or her conditioned avoidance.

From implosive theory we would expect that dirt and pinworms are only part of a complex series of stimuli that elicit anxiety and produce avoidance. The nature of other avoidance cues can only be hypothesized. From her history we certainly see that she was conditioned to be anxious over any expression of anger, especially toward her father. She learned to repress or to avoid all expressions of anger. We might hypothesize then that piles of dirty underwear or the sight of her daughter scratching her rear could lead to aggressive thoughts or feelings. Angry fantasies have, however, already been conditioned to elicit anxiety. The avoidance of symptom stimuli, such as dirty underwear, could also serve as a means of avoiding such dynamic stimuli as anger toward her daughter.

Mrs. C.'s compulsive washing is probably controlled then by a complex series of anxiety-eliciting stimuli, such as dirt, disease, and aggressive fantasies. The method of extinguishing her compulsive avoidance of these stimuli is to have her remain in the presence of each of the anxiety-eliciting stimuli. This method would, of course, evoke high levels of aversive emotion, and Mrs. C.'s natural response would be to want to avoid by washing or terminating treatment. The therapist must work to keep her from avoiding. By being required to remain in the presence of such stimuli, Mrs. C. would be flooded with fear, but soon the anxiety would begin to extinguish since there is no shock, no primary punishment, to reinforce the conditioned fear. The pinworms are gone; her parents will no longer hurt her. All she has to fear is conditioned fear itself, and that can be extinguished rapidly if she does not run.

Mrs. C. would first be asked to imagine symptom stimuli, such as scenes related to pinworms. Without regard to reality, she would be instructed to picture as vividly as possible that she is at home and is determined to conquer her compulsions. She enters the basement to do the laundry for the first time in years. As she gathers the filthy underwear, she smears a bit of feces on her hands and arms. She also feels something crawling on her arms. She is getting more and more anxious. She feels a desperate need to wash, so she drops the clothes and runs to the sink. As she turns on the faucet, there is no water. Instead, out pour pinworms: all over her hands and her arms, and she cannot wash them off. The worms begin burrowing into her skin; they are crawling in her ears; eating away at her eyes. Soon they cover her body, consuming her flesh. Looking like a Swiss cheese with worms, she weakens and passes out on the pile of dirty underwear.

After this first scene, Mrs. C. is ready for a scene that combines symptom and dynamic cues. She is ready for an anal picnic. In this session she is with her husband and her parents on a picnic at a park. As she is preparing the table, Mrs. C. feels the need to defecate. She walks to the outhouse, and as she goes to sit down, she notices that the hole is huge and she could fall in backwards. The thought panics her and she becomes light-headed, beginning to pass out. She indeed falls backward and tumbles down into the deep, dark dung. As she struggles to the surface, she looks up in time to see her mother preparing to defecate on her. She yells out, and her mother is shocked to see her daughter playing in such filth. Her mother's scolding angers Mrs. C., so she throws a handful of dung into her mother's face, causing her to lose her balance and fall in. A similar thing happens with her father, but when her husband discovers that he is being left out, he grabs the paper plates and jumps in, exclaiming that they are not going to have a picnic without him.

To her disgust Mrs. C. finds herself unable to resist selecting the tidiest turds for herself. As she bites into a tidbit, she can feel it crunching in her teeth and feels hair in her mouth. As the stuff sticks to her throat, she swallows some warm, yellow urine to wash it all down. Disgusting, but evocative!

Progressing in the series of avoidance cues, Mrs. C. is ready to attend to her anger and aggression. While some of her anger would be elicited toward her children, her father was the original stimulus that evoked both anger and anxiety over expressing anger. Therefore, a scene involving aggression toward her father should elicit maximum anger and extinguish maximum anxiety. Imagining herself as a 17-year-old, she arrives home 15 minutes late from a date. Her father is waiting up in his pajamas. He insists on knowing where she had been. When she tries to explain that they were delayed in the restaurant, he yells at her to shut up. She wants to explain that she did nothing wrong, but he smacks her and tells her to get in the kitchen and make him a sandwich. Anger begins to swell up within, as she tells herself, "Oh, I'd love to get even with him." In the kitchen she notices a hatchet near the basement door. She has the urge to pick it up, to really fix him this time. She puts a butcher knife in her belt and grabs the hatchet.

Her father is yelling for her to hurry up with his sandwich, and as she slowly approaches him saying, "Yes, Daddy dear, coming Daddy dear," she begins to raise the hatchet over her head. Her father's back is to her, and she can see the light glancing off of his bald head. With the insults and the indignities of her childhood running through her mind, she raises the hatchet higher and, with all her might, buries it in his scalp. With blood gushing down his face, her huge father somehow rises and starts coming toward her with his hands aimed at her throat. Backed into a corner, she pulls out the knife and jams it into his belly.

As she stands over him, he begs her to help him. "Like hell I will," she says. "You've bullied me long enough." She notices that his pajamas are open, and he is dying with a huge erection. So she pulls the hatchet out of his scalp and begins chopping away at the base of his penis, shouting, "You dirty bastard, you. I'll fix you good. You'll never rule me again." As he moans in pain, she pulls on his penis, stretching the last piece of skin until it snaps. Then, as if it were a bat, she takes his penis and smashes him in the face, saying, "That's for all the times you ridiculed me. That's for making me so afraid." And she ends by shoving the penis into his bloody mouth.

These imposive scenes, and others like them, are designed to evoke maximum anxiety and anger. As Mrs. C. becomes fully involved in the scenes, considerations for realistic detail fade into the background, like in an effective horror movie. What are real are her fears and fantasies of pinworms, dirt, and the danger of anger. As the imaginary stimuli elicit increasing anxiety and anger, she becomes flooded with such emotions. She wants to avoid them, but the therapist is there to break through her defenses, to urge her to feel as fully as she can, to not run but rather to face what she fears most. In facing her fantasies and feelings, Mrs. C. discovers that the shock is indeed off, the external danger is gone. And with the cathartic release and extinction of anxiety, the internal danger is also disappearing. The anxiety that has both stimulated and reinforced her constant washing is being extinguished. Mrs. C. will no longer have the motivation to avoid thoughts of pinworms, anger, or hands that are a little dirty. After all, what is a little dirt on her hands after a picnic in a cesspool?

BEHAVIOR THERAPY

SUSAN WAS A PROFOUNDLY RETARDED YOUNGSTER like most of the children at her special school. But she stood out because of her unnerving habit of smacking herself in the face with her fist. Four to five times a minute, 3,000 times a day, 1 million times a year, she hit herself. Susan's head banging had begun when she was around age three. At first anticonvulsants and tranquilizers had reduced her head banging. But at age seven she began to cry frequently. Her neurologist thought that perhaps her medication was excessive so he reduced it on a trial basis. Unfortunately, her head banging intensified, and the crying remained the same. Increasing the medication and trying new drugs proved to be of no help. Other methods were just as fruitless, and out of a sense of desperation, the neurologist referred Susan to our clinic.

My colleagues and I (Prochaska, Smith, Marzilli, Donovan, & Colby, 1974) went through Susan's school records to see what techniques other psychologists had tried in treating her head banging. Unfortunately, most of our ideas had already been tested and had failed, such as reinforcing an incompatible response like piano playing or trying to extinguish her head banging by paying no attention to it, while giving considerable attention to constructive behaviors. We also felt limited by the fact that baseline records indicated that Susan's rate of head banging seemed to remain quite stable across situations, including in an isolation room where she was unaware of being observed through a one-way mirror.

We decided to experiment with aversive conditioning. After wiring electrodes to Susan's legs and taking 15-minute baseline readings, we gave Susan a 2.5-milliamp shock each time she hit herself. It soon became apparent that the contingent shock was reducing the rate of head banging in the clinic. Systematic recordings even indicated some generalization to her school. Before long, however, we realized that Susan had begun to discriminate the stimulus that set the occasion for the shock. She would hit herself until the electrodes were attached, then she would stop. After awhile she even learned that she could hit herself without receiving a shock as long as her therapist wasn't watching her. Now there was no generalization outside of the clinic. We had been outsmarted by this supposedly profoundly retarded nine-year-old!

Realizing that a punishment paradigm of aversive conditioning could be really effective only if given on a continuous schedule, we decided to purchase a remote-control shocking apparatus that would allow us to shock Susan any time of the day in any setting without her being able to discriminate where, when, or by whom she was getting shocked. Our therapy plan was interrupted, however, by the director of mental retardation, who had strong feelings against using aversive techniques in a state-supported school. Only after writing a detailed document defending the ethics and possible effectiveness of our proposed plan were we able to continue.

On the first day of the remote conditioning Susan hit herself 45 times compared to the usual 3,000 times. The next day it dropped to 17 hits, followed by 6 hits. Then the apparatus malfunctioned and began giving noncontingent shocks. Following repairs, it took only two days with a total of 12 shocks to bring Susan's head banging down to zero. For months she didn't hit herself. So we decided to take the apparatus off her arm, and to our surprise she came over to us and wanted it back on. But we kept the apparatus off and she would go for months without hitting herself. In fact, for the past five years she has hit herself approximately 250 times compared with the 5 million hits she might have delivered without the aversive conditioning.

A SKETCH OF BEHAVIOR THERAPY

No one figure dominates behavioral approaches to therapy the way Freud dominates psychoanalysis or Rogers reflects client-centered therapy. Behavior therapists are tremendously varied in both theory and technique. Traditionally learning theory was seen as the ideological foundation for behavior therapy, even though there never was agreement as to which learning theory (e.g., Pavlov's, Hull's, Skinner's, Mowrer's, or others) was the core of behavior therapy. Today there is even disagreement over whether or not behavioral techniques should be grounded in any theory, let alone one of the learning theories (Lazarus, 1971; London, 1972; Yates, 1975). In spite of theoretical disagreements, the assumption generally remains that maladaptive behaviors are to a considerable degree acquired through learning and can be modified through additional learning.

Traditionally behavior therapists also tended to agree that the maladaptive behavior itself was the problem and needed to be changed, rather than focusing on some underlying causes. No longer was troubled behavior seen as a symptom of some underlying disorder, but rather this medical notion was rejected in favor of assuming that the symptom was the problem and was the appropriate target for therapy. Even on this assumption, however, there has been disagreement as some operant therapists criticized practitioners of desensitization for focusing on the hypothetical construct of anxiety as the underlying cause of phobias. In spite of such disagreements, behaviorists have continued to assume that so-called symptoms can be targeted as the behaviors to be changed without fear that some underlying causes will result in the substitution of new symptoms or the return of old symptoms.

What tends to unify behavior therapists most is the assumption that therapy is an empirical endeavor that must be tested and validated by the same rigorous, experimental procedures used in investigating any scientific question. Techniques cannot be assumed to be valid because they are derived from a favored theory. They must be validated under controlled conditions that utilize reliable and valid measures. Such validations of the effects of therapy require that the goals of therapy be clearly articulated in behavioral terms that can be observed and measured. Baseline levels of target behaviors need to be established prior to therapy in order to determine whether or not the therapy is producing any change in the rate or intensity of responding. While behaviorists agree upon approaching therapy as a data-based, experimental method, they disagree about just what the data or the experimental method should look like. Should the data be only overt responses that the experimenter-therapist can observe, for example, or are self-reports of subjective units of distress acceptable measures of anxiety? Should the experimental designs be based on small-n procedures in which a few clients are studied rigorously, or should techniques be validated through multigroup designs that include placebo and no-treatment control groups?

The point is that behavior therapy includes rather divergent views about techniques, theories, and even empirical methods for testing therapy. While such divergence can be a source of confusion and ambiguity for students, the fact is that it is also the source of some of the most creative work currently being carried out in therapy. Appreciating the importance of divergence among behavior therapists, we will nevertheless attempt to impose some clarity on this complex system by emphasizing three major thrusts within behavior therapy.

The first point of view we shall survey is best represented by Joseph Wolpe's *reciprocal inhibition* or counter-conditioning approaches to therapy. Wolpe's approach has been based primarily upon a respondent conditioning explanation of anxiety-related behavior problems. Therapists utilizing counter-conditioning techniques, such as systematic desensitization or assertiveness training, have been most comfortable with being called *behavior therapists*.

The second emphasis has traditionally been labeled *behavior modification* and has focused on an operant conditioning approach to behavior disorders that is especially concerned with changing the contingencies that control behavior. With Skinner as a model, behavior modifiers have been particularly rigorous in validating interventions through well-controlled, small-n designs, while being less concerned with theoretical explanations for effective techniques. In part because of the negative connotations that some politicians and some of the public have ascribed to the term *behavior modification*, the name *behavior analysis* is more often attached to this approach to therapy.

The third thrust has a less clear heritage and a less clear leadership but nevertheless represents those behaviorists who are most willing to use cognitive explanations and cognitive techniques for producing behavior change. *Cognitive behaviorists* draw upon a diversity of procedures, including thought stopping, systematic rational restructuring, systematic problem solving, and techniques based upon attribution theory.

While the complex system of behavior therapy is presented as three separate branches for simplicity's sake, it should be recognized that many contemporary behavior therapists work with techniques and theories from each of the three major viewpoints. Many behavior therapists are not particularly concerned with being technically or theoretically pure but rather are concerned with applying whatever methods are most effective and efficient in changing troubled behavior. The multimodal schema of Lazarus (1971) will serve as an example of how behavior therapists can use methods from each of the three major thrusts in practicing a more complex but also more complete form of behavior therapy. Even though Lazarus himself (1977) has moved toward his own brand of eclecticism, his multimodal model can still serve as an effective guide for a more comprehensive approach to behavior therapy.

In an attempt to provide a more integrative view of the behavior therapies, we will modify the standard outline we have been following. First of all, behaviorists have generally believed that environmental conditions or situations are of much greater influence in controlling behavior than are internal personality traits (Mischel, 1968). While it is true that many behavior therapists, especially those in England, have at times talked in terms of traits, and while even Mischel (1973) has found empirical support for some personality variables, as a system behavior therapy has not been concerned with constructing a comprehensive theory of personality. Consequently, we shall omit the section on personality theory. Furthermore, since the emphasis of behavior therapy has been upon the processes of change rather than the content to be changed, we shall also omit the section on the theory of therapeutic content. We shall first present the core of psychopathology and therapy of each of the three major orientations within behavior therapy. Then we shall examine one of the major views of the therapeutic relationship—a modeling view. The outcome research on each of the behavioral techniques will be presented in the section on evaluation, followed by criticisms of behavior therapy. Finally, Mrs. C. will be analyzed from a more comprehensive, multimodal approach to behavior therapy.

COUNTER-CONDITIONING TECHNIQUES

Joseph Wolpe's (1915–) work on *Psychotherapy by Reciprocal Inhibition* (1958) is the most comprehensive approach to behavioral techniques based on counter-conditioning processes. Wolpe came to a learning-based theory of therapy in a rather indirect manner. As a Jew raised in South Africa, he was influenced by his grandmother, who took on the responsibility of trying to make him into a pious believer. He read many Jewish writers, especially Maimonides. In his early 20s he began investigating other philosophers, beginning with Kant, moving to Hume, and progressing through several other thinkers to Bertrand Russell. By the time his own intellectual journey was completed, his theistic beliefs were replaced by a physical monism.

Since he views Freud as a rigorous materialist, Wolpe's view of humanity became increasingly more psychoanalytic during his middle 20s. He might have developed into a psychoanalytic psychiatrist except that he began reading the studies by Malinowski and others suggesting that Freud's theory did not fit some important facts. He was also struck by the fact that Russia, with a materialistic ideology, had rejected Freud in favor of Pavlov. Wolpe was impressed by Pavlov's research but found that he preferred the theoretical interpretations of conditioning that he found in Hull's *Principles of Behavior* (1943).

In 1947 he began research on animal neuroses for his M.D. thesis at the University of Witwaterstrand in Johannesburg. Working with cats, he paired a buzzer with a shock and classically conditioned anxiety to the buzzer. When the buzzer was on, the cats were inhibited from eating. Wolpe reasoned that if conditioned anxiety could inhibit eating, then maybe under the right conditions, the eating response could be used to inhibit anxiety. Since the troubled cats would not eat in their home cages, he began to feed them in dissimilar cages where their fear was much less. Wolpe thus began to counter-condition the animals' anxiety by substituting an eating response for the anxiety response. By gradually feeding the cats in cages that were more and more similar to their home cage, he reduced their anxiety until they could eventually eat in their home cage. In a similar manner he was able to use the eating response to inhibit the anxiety to the buzzer.

Wolpe was now convinced that the use of such counter-conditioning procedures could serve as the basis for a radically new approach to therapy. He began looking for responses in humans that could be used to successfully inhibit and eventually counter-condition anxiety. As we shall see, the use of deep relaxation to inhibit anxiety became the basis for systematic desensitization; the use of assertive responses to inhibit anxiety became the basis for assertiveness training, and the use of sexual arousal to inhibit anxiety became the basis for new approaches to sex therapy.

Wolpe surveyed the effectiveness of his counter-conditioning approaches to treating human problems and reported success with 90 percent of more than 200 clients. His research with animals and his success with humans were reported in his book on *Psychotherapy by Reciprocal Inhibition* (1958), which he wrote while at the Center for Advanced Study in the Behavioral Sciences at Stanford. His work received considerable attention from clinical psychologists who had been trained in learning theory during their graduate education.

Wolpe continued his therapy and research at the University of Virginia. Later he moved to the Temple Medical School and the Eastern Pennsylvania Psychiatric Institute as a professor of psychiatry. He has been a key figure in helping to establish behavior therapy as a major movement in mental health through his writings, workshops, leadership in such groups as the Association for the Advancement of Behavior Therapy, and through establishing and editing the *Journal of Behavior Therapy and Experimental Psychiatry*.

Theory of Psychopathology

Anxiety is the key to most behavior disorders. It is primarily a pattern of responses of the sympathetic nervous system when an individual is exposed to a threatening stimulus. Physiological changes include increased blood pressure and pulse rate, increased muscle tension, decreased blood circulation to the stomach and genitals, increased blood circulation to the large voluntary muscles, pupil dilation, and dryness of the mouth. These bodily changes are the basis of anxiety and can be elicited by such unconditioned stimuli as shock, a startling noise, or a physical beating.

Anxiety can also be learned. Learning is said to occur if "a response has been evoked in temporal contiguity with a given stimulus and it is subsequently found that the stimulus can evoke the response although it could not have done so before. If the stimulus could have evoked the response before but subsequently evokes it more strongly, then, too, learning may be said to have occurred" (Wolpe, 1973, p. 5). Thus people can learn to respond with anxiety to any stimuli, including buzzers, dogs, people, sex, elevators, and dirt, even though such stimuli previously had not evoked anxiety. Through classical or respondent conditioning a neutral stimulus, such as a dog, can be paired contiguously with a threatening stimulus, such as being bitten. The anxiety evoked by being bitten is associated with the sight of the dog, and the sight of the dog can become conditioned to evoke anxiety. Similarly being threatened for sex play can lead to sex as a conditioned stimulus that evokes anxiety, or being spanked for playing with dirt can result in dirt being able to evoke intense anxiety. Even the thoughts associated with threatening stimuli, such as sexual thoughts, can become conditioned to elicit anxiety.

Through the process of *primary stimulus generalization*, stimuli that are physically similar to the original conditioned stimulus, such as other dogs, can also evoke anxiety. The more dissimilar a stimulus is to the original conditioned stimulus, the less anxiety the dissimilar stimulus will evoke, such as a puppy eliciting minimal anxiety because it is very dissimilar from the original large dog that bit the individual. Stimuli can be ranked on a gradient of similarity that constitutes a generalization gradient or a hierarchy that goes from the original stimulus that evokes maximum anxiety to a very dissimilar but related stimulus that evokes minimal anxiety. Human beings can also form hierarchies based upon similarities of internal effects through the process of secondary or mediated generalization. Thus situations that are physically dissimilar, such as being turned down on a date, being made to wait, and missing a bus, can form a hierarchy or generalization gradient based on the internal response of feeling rejected. As a result of either stimulus or mediated generalization, most patients will report that their anxiety levels vary depending on the stimulus situations they are in. A person conditioned to fear authority figures may complain of physical upset at work where the boss is, for example, but report less anxiety at home, except when a spouse or child becomes bossy. People who complain of constant, pervasive, or freefloating anxiety seem to be responding independently of any specific elicitor. Anxiety, however, is always the consequence of the elicitor, and the problem for these patients is that they have been conditioned to fear stimuli that are omnipresent. One example was a client of mine who was constantly anxious, even when trying to sleep or shower, because apparently he had been conditioned by severe parents to respond with anxiety to his own body, which is obviously omnipresent.

Anxiety is the primary learning problem in psychopathology. Once anxiety is established as a habitual response to specific stimuli, however, it may undermine or impair other aspects of behavior and lead to secondary symptoms.

Sexual performance may be disrupted through an inhibition of sexual arousal; sleep may be disrupted through muscle tension; tension headaches or stomach upsets may occur; irritability may increase; concentration, thinking, and memory may be impaired; or embarrassing tremors or sweating may occur. Over time the chronic physiological reactions of anxiety may impair bodily functions and result in psychosomatic symptoms, such as ulcers and colitis. These secondary symptoms themselves may elicit anxiety because of their painfulness, their association with learned fears of physical illness or mental illness, or just their embarrassing social consequences. If these secondary problems produce additional anxiety, then new learning may be acquired, and a "vicious circle" is created that leads to more complicated symptoms.

Conditioned anxiety can lead to responses that are acquired in order to avoid or terminate anxiety. Physical avoidance, such as phobias, may be learned because such avoidance leads to the automatic consequence of terminating anxiety. Thus, some patients complain of having to avoid doctors, airplanes, elevators, or social gatherings. Other patients learn to terminate anxiety through consuming alcohol, barbiturates, narcotics, or other drugs. Over time the primary complaint is no longer anxiety but the drug habits patients have developed in order to avoid anxiety. Of course, the drug habit itself can produce anxiety and can lead to further drug abuse in order to reduce the new anxiety, and the vicious circle goes on.

The symptoms of patients are highly varied, ranging from sexual dysfunctions, to phobias, to psychosomatic complaints, to interpersonal difficulties, to drug abuse. The same patient may have several complaints that are not necessarily related in some supposed dynamic pattern. Thus, a patient may have an elevator phobia and insomnia without the two problems being related, just as a medical patient may have a tremor that is entirely unrelated to a cold. The successful treatment of a phobia may have no effect whatsoever on the insomnia. Specific symptoms are the result of specific anxieties elicited by specific stimuli. Therefore, the successful elimination of a specific anxiety and a specific secondary symptom will not lead to new symptoms. Symptom substitution or symptom return is a theoretical myth of those who see all behavior as being interrelated by some common underlying dynamic pattern. What is common to most behavior problems is the presence of conditioned anxiety that is highly specific in both the stimuli that elicit it and the consequences that result from it. Successful treatment thus calls for successful and at times successive elimination of specific anxiety responses.

Theory of Therapeutic Processes

Since anxiety is learned through conditioning, it can be unlearned through counter-conditioning. As Wolpe discovered with "neurotic cats," there are two critical issues in effective counter-conditioning. The first is finding a response that is incompatible with anxiety and can be paired with the stimuli that evoke anxiety. The principle of *reciprocal inhibition* states that "if a response inhibiting anxiety can be made to occur in the presence of anxiety-evoking stimuli, it will weaken the bond between these stimuli and anxiety" (Wolpe, 1973, p. 17). With enough pairings of the anxiety-inhibiting response with the anxiety-evoking stimuli, the new, more adaptive response is eventually substituted for the maladaptive anxiety response. While there are many responses that can inhibit anxiety, the ones that have been most frequently used by behavior therapists are relaxation, assertion, and sexual arousal, all of which are associated with a predominance of parasympathetic nervous activity. The second important issue is that a strong sympathetic anxiety response is very likely to disrupt relaxation, assertion, or sexual arousal. Therefore, it is critical that counter-conditioning begin with stimuli low on a generalization gradient or hierarchy. Stimuli low on a heirarchy, such as a small puppy versus a large German shepard, will elicit much lower intensities of anxiety. With stimuli low on a hierarchy, deep relaxation, strong assertion, or strong sexual arousal will be able to clearly inhibit the anxiety response. By repeating such pairings with stimuli low on a hierarchy, the anxiety at each level is deconditioned. With the anxiety level receding, such pairings can proceed to stimuli higher in the hierarchy, until eventually the anxiety responses to the entire stimulus hierarchy can be deconditioned.

The principles of counter-conditioning will first be illustrated by describing the techniques of *systematic desensitization*. Here progressive, deep-muscle relaxation is the predominantly parasympathetic response that is incompatible with anxiety. Borrowing from Jacobson (1938), clients are first taught how to relax the muscles throughout their bodies. While behavior therapists vary their relaxation training to some extent, they do include teaching clients how to clearly discriminate between when their muslces are tensely contracted and when they are fully relaxed. The therapist might begin by having clients grip the chair and focus on the tension in their forearms. Clients are then encouraged to relax their arms and to feel the contrast between the tension and the relaxation. Clients are encouraged to actively let go of the tension in their forearms until each fiber in their arms is relaxing. Clients are to learn that relaxing is an activity that can come under their control as they tightly tense each muscle group and then actively let their muscles relax. Some therapists encourage clients to relax a tensed arm, for example, by acting as if it were lead and letting the arm fall rapidly to their lap. Others encourage clients to relax slowly, feeling the sensations of tension gradually but fully leave the fibers of their muscles. Usually muscles are tensed for 10–20 seconds, followed by 10–20 seconds of relaxation. Each important muscle group in the body is tensed and relaxed, usually beginning with the hands and forearms, and then moving to the biceps and triceps. Next the muscles in the head, beginning with the forehead and moving down to the eyes, nose, mouth, and tongue, are tensed and relaxed. By moving step by step through each of the muscle groups in the body, clients become more and more relaxed. While Wolpe takes six sessions to train clients in progressive relaxation, most research reports have used only one or two sessions for teaching relaxation. The relaxation instructions can be taped while the therapist is taking the client through each muscle group, and then the client can practice relaxing at home for 20–30 minutes a day.

The next step in desensitization is to construct an anxiety hierarchy that ranks stimuli from the most anxiety-arousing to the least anxiety-arousing. Frequently the hierarchy is constructed along some stimulus dimension, such as time or space, as the stimulus situations move closer and closer in time to an anxiety-arousing situation, such as a job interview, or closer in space to a feared object, such as an elevator. The stimulus situations are imagined by the client and ranked from the least to the most anxiety-arousing. A typical hierarchy will have 10–20 stimulus scenes, spaced relatively equally along a 10-point scale from practically no anxiety elicited to intense anxiety elicited. The scenes included in a hierarchy are usually realistic, concrete situations related to the client's problem. Frequently clinical patients will have more than one hierarchy to work on, although the greater number of specific anxieties they have, the less likely that desensitization will be effective.

Once the hierarchies are constructed, clients are asked to think of one or two relaxing scenes, such as lying on the beach on a sunny, summer day, which can be used to facilitate relaxation during the presentation of items in the hierarchy. Now the clients are ready to begin the actual desensitization. Once they are deeply relaxed, they are told that they will be asked to imagine a scene and that they should imagine it as clearly as possible and imagine only the scene that is presented. They are told that if they experience any anxiety at all, they should signal immediately by lifting their right index finger. The client signals once the scene is being clearly pictured and continues imagining the scene for 10 seconds, if no anxiety is elicited. If anxiety is elicited, then the clients are instructed to stop imagining the hierarchy scene and to go back to imagining the relaxing scene. Once clients report being clearly relaxed again, they are instructed to imagine the scene again. If a scene fails to elicit anxiety, then it is repeated at least once again before moving to the next item in the hierarchy. When a scene repeatedly elicits anxiety, the therapist can move back to the anxiety-arousing scene. If the scene continues to elicit anxiety, then clients need to be asked if they are adding stimuli to the scene. If they are not, then new items may need to be added to the hierarchy in order to allow the client to continue to progress. Usually a therapy session is ended by having the client successfully complete a scene. The next session usually begins with the client imagining the last item that was successfully completed. Typically a desensitization session lasts 15–30 minutes, with most clients finding it difficult to sustain both concentration and relaxation for more than 30 minutes. For clients with more than one hierarchy, a session will include scenes from each hierarchy rather than treating the separate hierarchies sequentially.

Once systematic desensitization is completed, clients are encouraged to test its effectiveness in a gradual manner. They frequently are instructed to use in vivo desensitization, in which they approach previously feared stimuli in a gradual manner. They approach stimuli in the environment that were low on their hierarchies before confronting stimuli of greater intensity.

While desensitization is the therapy of choice for phobias of nonhuman objects and situations and for anxieties evoked by the mere presence of people, *assertiveness training* is the choice for most anxieties related to interpersonal interactions. Candidates for assertiveness training include people who are afraid of complaining about poor service in a restaurant because of anxiety over hurting the waiter's feelings, people who are unable to leave a social situation when it is boring for fear of looking ungrateful, people who are unable to express differences of opinion because they are afraid others will not like them, people who are afraid to tell professors or authority figures that they do not like being left waiting or treated inconsiderately because they are afraid the authority figures might get angry with them, people who are unable to ask for a raise or for a better grade because they feel inferior, and people who are unable to participate in competitive games for fear of losing. The meek will not inherit the earth. The meek and the shy will frequently find that all they inherit is bad feelings because they are inhibited by anxiety from standing up for their rights.

Assertiveness training is not just for the meek and shy, however. People who respond too often with inappropriate anger can frequently be helped by assertiveness training as they learn to have more effective control over social situations instead of feeling constantly frustrated and angry over not being able to influence others. Also, people who keep from expressing admiration, praise, or positive feelings because they might feel embarrassed can learn to be more positive through being more assertive. *Assertive behavior* is defined by Wolpe (1973, p. 81) as "the proper expression of any emotions other than anxiety toward another person."

Assertion and anxiety are to a considerable degree incompatible. Actively expressing admiration, irritation, and appropriate anger can inhibit anxieties over rejection, embarrassment, and possible failure. By learning to assert themselves in stimulus situations that previously evoked anxiety, patients begin to decondition anxiety by substituting an assertive response. As patients become more active and effective in their assertive behaviors, they are reinforced not only by the reduction of anxiety but also by their increased abilities to be more successful in social situations. Individuals who have been inhibited by anxiety gradually become more effective as they remove anxiety through the counter-conditioning effects of assertive responses.

The techniques of assertiveness training include teaching clients direct and effective verbal responses for specific social situations. Clients who, for example, feel irritated but are unable to say anything when people cut in front of them in line, are taught such responses as "This is a line, please go to the back of it," or "I and others here would appreciate you respecting the rules of waiting in line." Clients are also taught more assertive nonverbal expressions that can inhibit anxiety. Salter (1949) discusses facial talk that displays appropriate emotion when asserting, such as smiling when telling a spouse, "You look so lovely this evening!" Looking directly in the eyes when insisting that a person be on time for meetings communicates nonverbally a greater determination that others will not be allowed to violate one's right to be respected. Appropriate smiling, eye contact, and voice volume are nonverbal responses that can inhibit anxiety in social interactions.

Clients are encouraged to rehearse such new assertive responses both covertly and overtly. Covertly, the clients imagine being more assertive in situations in which they previously were inhibited. Overtly, the clients are encouraged to rehearse being assertive through role playing interactions with the therapist. The therapist may play a waiter or waitress and the client practices insisting both verbally and nonverbally that a steak be taken back because it was improperly prepared. The therapist can provide resistance to the client's assertions, such as saying, "I know the steak isn't quite right, but if I take it back the chef will be angry." Clients can then practice thinking on their feet, such as saying, "That's a problem for you and the chef to resolve. My concern is that I get what I ordered." The behavior rehearsals provide deconditioning of anxiety as well as preparation for clients to deal more effectively with adversaries that previously would have inhibited them.

As anxiety is reduced through role playing of assertive interactions, clients become more confident about their abilities to face real-life situations. Therapists then give graduated homework assignments, beginning with situations that are least frightening and are most likely to lead to successes for the client. Beginning with situations that are less anxiety-arousing is like starting at the bottom of an anxiety hierarchy in desensitization. As the anxiety in these less threatening situations is effectively deconditioned through assertion, the person will usually experience less anxiety when preparing to assert in a more stressful situation. Beginning with too threatening a situation is likely to lead to failure, which will punish rather than reinforce the client's attempts to be more assertive.

Special care is needed when clients desire to be assertive in situations where assertion may lead to punishment. In the past many behavior therapists frequently used the rule of never encouraging assertive behavior when punishment is likely to follow. As Goldfried and Davison (1976) point out, however, such a rule encourages maintenance of the status quo for many people, such as women who traditionally have been derided for being aggressive when they were being assertive. Nevertheless, most clients and therapists do want to minimize the risk that the assertiveness of clients will evoke punishment, especially hostility or violence.

Rimm and Masters (1974) suggest that the rule of using the minimally effective response helps reduce the probability that assertion will be met with hostility or other potentially punishing responses. Thus, in expressing feelings such as hurt or anger clients should express the minimum negative emotion that is required to attain a desired goal. Thus, if the client's goal is not to be kept waiting by a professor, the client can knock on the door and with minimal irritation inform the professor that it is 2:00 and they have an appointment. A minimally effective response is less likely to evoke anger in the other person, and thus punishing consequences are less likely to occur. If a minimally effective response does not lead to the desired goal, then clients can be prepared to escalate their assertiveness and express more emotion and more determination to have their rights respected.

While Wolpe's theory is still one of the leading explanations for the effectiveness of assertiveness training, current assertiveness trainers use techniques that involve more than just counter-conditioning. Many clients need to first reevaluate their attitudes toward what it means to be an effectively assertive person. For some clients this involves value clarification techniques as they reexamine such goals as trying always to be a nice, polite person. Smith (1975), for example, presents clients a personal bill of rights that challenges values suggesting that clients cannot be decent human beings while also being effectively assertive. For other clients it is important to distinguish between being aggressive and being assertive. The therapist may role play aggressive regimens in which part of the goal is to hurt the other person's feelings and contrast that with assertive behavior aimed at keeping others from violating one's personal rights.

Assertive training techniques also include operant conditioning as therapists reinforce clients for each attempt that is made to become more effectively assertive. Using a successive approximation paradigm, the therapist reinforces each step in the client's practice of becoming more assertive, such as reinforcing just an increase in eye contact or an increase in voice volume. Most assertiveness trainers also prefer doing assertiveness training in groups so that group members can provide additional reinforcement for each other. The very process of giving effective reinforcement allows clients to practice being more effective in expressing positive emotions toward others.

Assertiveness training also involves a great deal of feedback, as clients are encouraged to become more cognizant of the verbal and nonverbal responses that fail to communicate assertiveness. Some therapists use videotapes, which allow clients to get direct feedback concerning such behaviors as failure to make eye contact or crouching over in a nonassertive manner. Other therapists rely on feedback from themselves or from group members to increase the client's awareness of what changes are needed to be more assertive. Once again, the practice of group members giving feedback allows for direct practice in being more assertive. Thus, the therapist can give group members feedback on how effective they were in providing direct feedback to another group member.

Modeling is another important technique used in assertiveness training. Either through role playing or through direct interaction with clients, the therapist is able to provide a model for more effective assertion. Most behavior therapists would agree that a minimal requirement for doing assertiveness training is that assertiveness trainers themselves be effectively assertive individuals.

The final counter-conditioning behavioral technique that we shall consider involves the use of sexual arousal to inhibit anxiety. Most of the new forms of sex therapy (Kaplan, 1974; Masters & Johnson, 1970) either implicitly or explicitly use counter-conditioning as an integral part of treating sexual dysfunctions. Wolpe (1958) was one of the first to report that sexual dysfunctions, such as impotence and frigidity, could be successfully treated with counter-conditioning techniques. Sexual arousal is primarily a parasympathetic response that can readily be inhibited by anxiety, which is primarily a sympathetic nervous system response. Given the negative attitudes toward sex that have traditionally prevailed in our society, it is not surprising that many people have been conditioned to respond to sexual situations with anxiety. If their conditional anxiety is intense enough, it will inhibit their sexual arousal. Reciprocally, sexual arousal can be used to inhibit the anxiety response, and through counter-conditioning the sexual response can be substituted for the disrupting anxiety response.

Wolpe's (1958, 1973) approach to sex therapy is quite similar to his approach to in vivo desensitization. Clients are first asked to identify when in their approach to a sexual encounter they first feel anxiety. They are instructed to limit their sexual approaches to that point where anxiety begins. Obviously the spouse's cooperation is important, since it can be extremely frustrating to have to stop just when genital caressing begins, or just after penetration occurs. Actually, in most cases anxiety is evoked when intercourse is about to begin, so the cooperative spouse can still be provided a reasonable degree of sexual gratification through manual stimulation. It is essential, however, that the partner not mock or goad the inhibited spouse into progressing beyond the point at which anxiety begins. By stopping and just lying still or talking, the anxiety can subside and sexual arousal can increase. Gradually the anxious person will find that more and more anxiety is being inhibited and counter-conditioned by sexual arousal. Gradually the couple is able to move from lying in bed naked together, to caressing the nonerogenous areas of the body, to caressing genitals, to beginning intercourse, and continuing with intercourse to orgasm without anxiety.

Wolpe (1973) reports that his in vivo approach to sex therapy works best for impotency cases. For many women who are more inhibited in their sexual response, he tends to begin with systematic desensitization and gradually reduces their anxiety to sexual images before proceeding to the in vivo form of sex therapy.

While sex therapists like Masters and Johnson (1970) and Kaplan (1974) include techniques that involve counter-conditioning of anxiety, they would think it naive to hold that counter-conditioning is the only process involved in effective sex therapy. The technique that these sex therapists use for reducing anxiety involves a series of sensate-focusing exercises. In these exercises partners take turns pleasuring each other, beginning with sessions in which the genitals and breasts are avoided and the rest of the body is caressed. The person being pleasured gives verbal or nonverbal feedback about what does and does not feel good. Once the couple is able to enjoy nonerogenous stimulation without anxiety, they give each other sensate pleasuring that includes genital caressing but with no demands to reach orgasm. If this step goes well, the couple is then able to proceed with sensate pleasuring that includes intercourse, but with no concern over reaching orgasm. With the gradual decrease in anxiety and marked increase in sexual arousal, couples are eventually able to participate in relatively free and gratifying sexual experiences.

While Kaplan explicitly accepts the importance of counter-conditioning processes in sex therapy, Masters and Johnson (1970) seem to accept counter-conditioning only implicitly. Both Kaplan and Masters and Johnson, however, argue that other processes are of equal importance in effective sex therapy. Increasing consciousness through educational techniques that involve giving clients the latest and most accurate sex information is important with many uninformed or underinformed clients. Increasing consciousness through communicating feedback about what each partner needs in order to be more fully aroused and to be orgasmic is also critical, such as the wife giving the husband feedback by guiding his hand as he gives her clitoral stimulation. Helping clients to reevaluate their attitudes toward goal-oriented sex is important in helping them become free of performance anxiety. Just being free to enjoy the pleasure of the moment without worrying about whether intercourse or orgasm will follow allows for more spontaneous and uninhibited enjoyment of all that sexual pleasuring can mean, rather than reducing sex to just intercourse or just orgasm.

Most modern sex therapists also realize that relationship issues and not just conditioned anxiety are important aspects of sexual problems for many couples. Kaplan, for example, integrates a psychoanalytic interpretative approach with a behavioral approach so that relationship problems, such as indirect expressions of anger through sexual nonresponsiveness, can be interpreted and resolved in therapy. Masters and Johnson disapprove of psychoanalytic interpretations but do focus on relationship issues. They encourage couples to be more intimate by giving each other feedback about their feelings and about what they would like improved in their relationship.

CONTINGENCY MANAGEMENT TECHNIQUES

Theory of Psychopathology

Human behavior, including maladaptive behavior, is largely controlled by its consequences. People are continually labeled pathological as if they are some strange breed of organism, when in fact their behavior can be explained by the same operant principles that account for most human behavior. Thus, maladaptive responses, such as painful head banging, are likely to increase in frequency if they are followed by reinforcements, such as special attention given only when head banging occurs. Conversely, maladaptive responses are likely to decrease in occurrence if they are followed by punishments, such as a remote-control shock. Maladaptive behaviors are also likely to decrease in frequency when they are consistently unrewarded, and they will eventually extinguish if no reinforcement occurs.

Reinforcements and punishments that are made contingent upon particular responses will not only affect the probabilities of maladaptive behavior patterns that already exist but are also critical in affecting the development of new responses. To illustrate the development of a new maladaptive response, let me relate an experience I had as an undergraduate out to have fun at a carnival. Walking along with a female friend, I was spotted by a barker who wanted me to try my luck at his gambling game. If he had told me that the eventual response he wanted was for me to plunk down my money as fast as I could get it from my wallet, I would have kept on walking. Over the years, however, he had learned something about the process of *shaping* behavior. Thus he began with a *prompt*, which included challenging me to win a big, furry $50 stuffed animal for my female friend. Responding to his prompt, I asked what I had to do to win, and he said just put 50 cents down and spin the wheel. When the wheel stopped, I had gained 450 points, which was more than half of the 800 points I needed for a prize. Winning points also gave me the opportunity to spin again, and this time I earned 100 additional points. The next spin was reinforced by 25 more points. When I failed to get any points on the next spin, he again used a prompt to encourage me to put down another 50 cents. After all, 675 points on one bet was certainly worth another try. This time my spin was followed by 50 points and then 10 points, and there was no way I could lose, he said. He had been *fading* out such prompts, as my tendency to spin the wheel was becoming more reliable. Soon I was reaching for more money and winning five points here and five points there. My money, however, was going out faster than points were coming in. He indeed had shaped me into responding with rather rapid bets. Soon I lost the $19 in my wallet, and all I had to show for it was 785 points. As a psychology major, I went away shaking my head, thinking that Skinner had nothing on this carnival man and Skinner's pigeons had nothing on me. No wonder compulsive gamblers have the saying that if you lose the first time out the Lord is on your side, and if you win big the first time out the Devil is on your side.

Maladaptive behavior does not take place in a vacuum. Some environment or stimulus situation sets the occasion for the behavior. A male patient beats up his wife at home almost every weekend but apparently treats her politely when in public. A woman client stole only in fancy stores and never in a discount store. The control that environmental stimuli can have over maladaptive behavior is in part the result of the fact that certain stimuli serve as signals that reinforcement is likely to follow a response when the response is emitted in that particular stimulus situation. These are called *discriminative stimuli* (S^D). Other stimuli (S^Δ) serve to signal that reinforcement will not follow a response when made under these particular stimulus conditions. Thus clients learn that aggressive behavior or stealing may be reinforced in one situation and not reinforced or even punished under a different stimulus situation. An analysis of a behavioral problem involves specifying the stimulus situation that sets the occasion for the maladaptive behavior, as well as specifying the behavior itself and the reinforcement contingencies that control it.

An analysis of behavioral problems indicates three categories that occur most often. First, there are problems that involve an excess in responding, such as washing one's hands 30 times a day. The washing of hands per se is not maladaptive, but the washing of hands excessively can become maladaptive. There are also problems that involve a deficit in responding, such as rarely interacting with people. Often with deficits the problem is a lack of learning, such as a failure of the social environment to teach the appropriate skills required for effective social interaction. Traditionally, therapists have focused on reducing maladaptive behaviors rather than increasing positive, effective behaviors.

The third type of problem involves responses that are inappropriate to a particular stimulus situation, such as a patient of mine who occasionally drops his drawers in public. The problem here is not the rate or skill of disrobing but the fact that the particular response is inappropriate to the particular situation. Frequently what is meant by inappropriate is that for most of us, we would expect that under this particular stimulus situation the behavior would not lead to a reinforcement and might even be followed by punishment. For the person with such maladaptive behavior, however, the same situation seems to signal that reinforcement is likely to occur. Either the person has failed to discriminate the stimulus situation accurately, such as a person who is drunk or profoundly retarded, or there is indeed a powerful reinforcement occurring that is not readily apparent to the observer. What we frequently forget as observers is that what is a reinforcement is entirely an individual matter determined by an individual's particular reinforcement history. Thus, a consequence that might be neutral or even aversive for us might be a reinforcement for another person. A consequence can be judged to be a reinforcement only if it increases the probability that a response will be repeated and not on the basis of whether the consequence appears to be pleasant. Inappropriate behavior usually is surprising and unexpected until we begin to analyze the problem on an individual basis and discover what is in fact a reinforcement for this individual or determine the person's ability to discriminate across situations.

Theory of Therapeutic Processes

Environmental contingencies are forever shaping, maintaining, and extinguishing our behavior and the behavior of clients. Behavior modification attempts to systematically control contingencies in order to shape and maintain adaptive behavior and extinguish maladaptive behavior. Theoretically, the therapeutic process is straightforward: change the contingencies and maladaptive behavior will change. Technically effective contingency management involves the following six steps (Sherman, 1973):

1. Stating the general problem in behavioral terms, including the maladaptive responses and the situations in which they occur.
2. Identifying behavioral objectives, which includes specifying target behaviors and whether the behaviors should be increased, decreased, or reinforced only when emitted in more appropriate situations, and what the acceptable level of performance of each target behavior is.
3. Developing behavioral measures and taking baseline measures in order to be able to determine if treatment is being effective. Baseline measures show the rate of responses prior to beginning therapy. Frequently multiple baselines are taken, including measures of behaviors that are not targeted for change, in order to determine if the changes in contingencies are specific to changes in the target behaviors.
4. Naturalistic observations, which involve observing patients in their natural environments in order to determine what the existing contingencies are and thus what are effective reinforcements for a particular patient.
5. Changing existing contingencies, which involves specifying the conditions under which reinforcements are or are not to be given, what reinforcements shall be, and who shall administer them.
6. Monitoring the results by continuing to chart the rate of responses and comparing the results to baseline measures in order to determine the effectiveness of present interventions. Changes in treatment can then be made when necessary, and treatment can be terminated or stabilized when the behavioral objectives have been met.

The application of contingency management procedures varies somewhat according to who is most effectively able to control contingencies and what type of consequence is being controlled. Contingency management procedures can thus be categorized according to (1) institutional control, (2) self-control, (3) mutual control or contracting, (4) therapist's control, and (5) aversive control.

Institutional control indicates that the managers of institutions are most effectively able to change the appropriate contingencies. In the past institutions like mental hospitals, training schools for delinquents, schools for retarded, and classrooms for troubled students frequently provided too few reinforcements. The reinforcements that were provided were frequently given noncontingently. Thus, meals, television watching, recreation time, and field trips were given independently of the resident's daily behavior. Some reinforcements, such as special attention of the staff, often were given for maladaptive responses, such as self-abusive behavior or aggressive acting out.

There was little incentive for residents to improve their living conditions, their hygienic habits, or their social behaviors, since most reinforcements were given independently of any effort the clients might make.

As operant principles began to be applied to maladaptive behavior, therapists in charge of wards or troubled classrooms began to make reinforcements contingent on particular behaviors through the use of *token economies*. Tokens are symbolic reinforcers, such as poker chips or points on a tally sheet, which can be exchanged for items that constitute more direct forms of reinforcement, such as cigarettes or recreational activities. An economy involves an exchange system that determines exactly what the tokens can be exchanged for and the rate of exchange, or how many tokens it takes to get particular items or privileges. The economy also specifies the target behaviors that can earn tokens and the rate of responding that is required to earn a particular number of tokens, such as making one bed can earn one token, and one token can be exchanged for one cigarette.

While establishing a token economy may sound simple, such economies are truly complicated. Ayllon and Azrin (1968) articulate the many rules that must be followed for an effective economy to work. Some of the more important considerations include staff cooperation and coordination, since the staff must be more observant and more systematic in their responses to clients than in a noncontingent system. A variety of attempts at establishing token economies have failed because the staff did not cooperate adequately in monitoring the behavior of residents. Effective token economies must also have adequate control over reinforcements, since an economy becomes ineffective if residents have access to reinforcements by having money from home or being able to bum a cigarette from a less cooperative staff member. Problems must be clearly defined in terms of specific behaviors to be changed in order to avoid conflicts among staff or patients. Improving personal hygiene, for example, is too open to interpretation by individuals, and patients may insist that they are improving their hygiene even though staff members may disagree. There is much less room for misunderstandings if personal hygiene is defined as clean fingernails, no evidence of body odor, clean underwear, and other clear-cut rules. Specifying behaviors that are positive alternatives to problem behavior is very critical in teaching residents what positive actions they can take to help themselves, rather than relying on just a negative set of eliminating responses. Perhaps most important for more lasting effectiveness of token economies is that they be gradually faded out as problem behaviors are reduced and more adaptive responses become well established. Obviously the outside world does not run according to an institution's internal economy, and it is important that clients be prepared to make the transition to the larger society. Using an abundance of social reinforcers along with token reinforcers helps prepare clients for the fading out of tokens, so that positive behaviors can be maintained by praise or recognition rather than by tokens. Also encouraging patients to reinforce themselves, such as by learning to take pride in their appearance, is an important step in fading out tokens. Some institutions use traditional wards where clients go from token economies and learn to maintain adaptive behaviors through more naturalistic contingencies, such as praise from a fellow patient. In such transitional settings, backup reinforcers are available if needed, but they are used much more sparingly than in the token economies. Without the use of fading, token economies can become nothing more than hospital management procedures that make the care of patients more efficient without preparing patients to live effectively in the larger society.

At the opposite extreme of institutional control is *self-control*. In order to serve as their own therapists, clients must first be taught the fundamentals of the experimental analysis of behavior. They need to realize that self-control problems are not due to a lack of some mystical willpower or moral character but rather involve an inadequate appreciation of how a systematic manipulation of antecedent stimuli and response consequences can change behavior. Clients must appreciate fundamental rules of behavior, such as immediate consequences have much greater control over behavior than do delayed consequences. Self-control problems, such as obesity, smoking, alcohol abuse, and not studying, generally involve behaviors that have immediate positive consequences but long-term negative consequences.

Following an adequate baseline period that includes charting the stimulus situations that set the occasion for the maladaptive responses, clients can begin to redesign their environments. Obese patients, for example, can be taught Stuart's (1971) principle of self-control of eating behavior, which includes narrowing the stimulus situations for eating from TV watching, newspaper reading, and visiting with friends, to eating only at the table with the TV off. In beginning to narrow their eating responses to the table, clients reduce the number of occasions for overeating. Clients are also informed of the empirical findings of Schachter (1971), which demonstrate that for obese people the presence of food rather than hunger is the more important stimulus for eating. Clients can then restrict the availability of high-caloric foods in their environment.

Clients can also work to increase behaviors that are incompatible with eating, such as hiking, biking, or lovemaking. The more hiking or lovemaking, the less likely they are to be eating. To increase their biking or hiking, they may make reinforcing activities, such as TV watching, contingent on an increase in hiking behavior. Clients should also reinforce themselves for avoiding fattening foods, such as allowing themselves to call a friend if they limit their calories at dinner. They can also inform their friends of their changes in eating behaviors so that friends or family can provide social reinforcement for avoiding overeating.

Appreciating the importance of shaping principles, clients should be careful to provide reinforcement for just improving, such as studying for 10 minutes, rather than withholding reinforcement until their ideal goal is attained. Immediate reinforcement for studying should also be provided, such as going for a Coke or playing cards for 15 minutes, since the positive consequences of studying are quite delayed. It is also important for clients to intervene early in the fairly long sequence or chain of responses that is terminated by the problem response, such as intervening when beginning to approach the refrigerator rather than trying to stop eating after the potato chip is gone. Rather than testing their willpower by seeing if they can win the bet that they can eat just one, clients should realize that so-called willpower usually means intervening early rather than late in a chain of events that lead to trouble.

Mutual control techniques are required when two people in a relationship share control over the consequences that each wants. Couples, for example, share control over many of the interpersonal consequences that each would like from the relationship. The most common form of mutual control of contingencies involves contracting. To form a contract, each person in a relationship must specify the consequences that he or she would like to have increased. Each can then begin to negotiate what he or she would want in exchange for giving the consequences the partner desires. For example, Stuart (1969) worked with four married couples who were in family court to get divorced. The couples shared the rather common complaint that the wife wanted more intimate talking while the husband wanted more frequent lovemaking. The couples then worked out contracts in which the husband would get a poker chip for each quarter hour of active talking that he engaged in with his wife. Once he had earned eight poker chips he would trade them in for a sexual encounter. Needless to say, the rate of talking increased dramatically. At the same time the wives were much more responsive to lovemaking. Some of the wives even acted out their fantasies of hustling by charging for sex, and the husbands would try to bargain them down to five or six chips when they were short on tokens. While some people might find such contracting artificial and unromantic, the couples in fact seemed to enjoy their talking and lovemaking more than ever, and each of the four couples was able to avoid divorce. What some people tend to dislike is that contracting makes explicit the exchange theory of interpersonal relationships, which holds that we interact in order to exhange reinforcements. As long as there is a fair exchange of reinforcements, people are likely to continue in a relationship and to feel relatively satisfied with the relationship.

For outpatients there can usually be very little *therapist control* over the environmental contingencies affecting clients. Therapists can, however, control social reinforcers, such as attention, recognition, and praise, that occur in therapy. Therapists can take care to make their social reinforcers contingent upon improvement in the client's behavior. Greenspoon (1955) was one of the first to demonstrate that verbal reinforcers can influence the types of responses emitted by clients, such as the number of "I" messages increasing as a fuction of verbal reinforcement from the therapist. Effective therapists make a point of managing their own verbal and nonverbal reinforcements to make sure they are encouraging adaptive behaviors. All too often therapists give special attention to only maladaptive responses, such as leaning forward and listening carefully when clients begin to express self-hatred.

Therapists can gain greater control over contingencies by forming contracts with clients. The therapist can, for example, require the client to deposit $100 and allow the client to earn the money back through making appropriate responses, such as losing weight each week. Harris and Bruner (1971) found that a contingency contract in which the client earned 50 cents to $1 for each pound of weight loss added to the effectiveness of a self-control package. The contract between client and therapist can also include a provision for response cost, such as the client losing $1 for each pound gained. Even better, the $1 can be donated to the client's least favorite organization, such as the John Birch Society, the American Communist Party, or the CIA.

Of course, there is no reason why therapists must remain in their offices. There usually is no reason why outpatient therapists cannot go out into the client's natural environment. Within the natural setting therapists can help clients restructure the stimuli and consequences that are controlling their troubled responses. Working right in the natural environment has the decided advantage of not having to worry about generalization from the office to the client's home. There need be no concern with transfer of training, since the training is done right in the troubled environment. When working with children, for example, the therapist can go into the home and train parents to function as therapist surrogates. Parents may be trained to manage contingencies more effectively through instituting a token economy, through contracting with their children, or through a more subtle use of social reinforcements made contingent on positive responses from the child, while avoiding reinforcement of negative behaviors.

There are cases in which the control of discriminating stimuli and the appropriate management of reinforcements fail to change the troubled behavior, and the therapist must consider the use of *aversive controls*. Maladaptive behaviors that have traditionally been labeled *impulse-control* problems, such as sexual deviations, alcoholism, obesity, smoking, and repetitive self-abuse, may respond to aversive controls even when more positive techniques have failed. Aversive techniques are tried only after more positive alternatives have failed. When aversive controls are applied within a contingency management paradigm, the emphasis is generally on the contingent use of punishment.

Punishment, in which an aversive consequence follows a particular response, has been minimized as a useful way of modifying behavior ever since Estes (1944) reported his research on punishment. Estes's studies indicated that punishment led to the suppression of the performance of a response but not to its unlearning. His research also indicated that noncontingent punishment was just as effective in suppressing a response as was contingent punishment. The general conclusion was that a response could not be eliminated by punishment alone. Twenty years later Solomon (1964) reviewed the laboratory work on punishment and concluded that punishment alone could indeed lead to new learning. Organisms can learn to avoid punishment through either *active* or *passive* conditioning. In active learning, the organism learns to do something, to make some alternative responses that will lead to the avoidance of punishment, such as a child learning to stop and look both ways before crossing a street in order to avoid punishment from a parent. Likewise the organism can learn to just passively avoid by not making a response that leads to punishment, such as a child learning not to cross the street at all in order to avoid punishment.

Azrin and Holz (1966) have summarized the conditions in which punishment can be most effective in producing powerful and lasting effects upon behavior. The rules of effective punishment include: (1) the more immediate the punishment the more effective, (2) the more aversive the punishment the more effective, (3) the more consistent the punishment the more effective, so the punishment should be delivered on a continuous schedule; otherwise the undesirable behavior will be reinforced on a partial reinforcement schedule and be even more resistant to extinction, (4) if the maladaptive response needs to be extinguished entirely, such as child molesting, the response must be punished across all stimulus situations, otherwise the person learns to avoid responding in punished situations but not in unpunished situations, and

(5) adaptive behaviors that can provide the same reinforcements as the punished behavior should be taught, such as teaching a child molester the social and assertive skills required for developing a sexual relationship with an adult.

The sample of rules for effective punishment is enough to indicate why the punishment paradigm can become practically unworkable. With a 27-year-old exhibitionist, for example, it might be impossible to have a therapist available whenever the client might come across a school bus. In the case of Susan, it was possible to have someone available under all situations, but it obviously would become a highly expensive treatment if the parents had had to hire someone to follow her with a remote-control device throughout her waking hours. One alternative with some patients is to train them to deliver their own shock immediately following a maladaptive response. The use of painful punishers also raises important ethical and legal issues for the therapist. In Susan's case we spent two months convincing the Department of Mental Retardation that contingent shock was the best alternative available for treating Susan's self-abuse. In many cases, such as with prisoners, the use of aversive paradigms has been ruled illegal and is thus not available as an alternative. Thus, while we now know that the contingent application of aversive stimuli can be a powerful modifier of behavior, much needs to be done to resolve the practical, ethical, and legal issues involved in its use.

The use of *covert sensitization* as an aversive technique has raised fewer objections, in part because it has frequently been conceptualized as a self-control approach to modifying behavior. In covert sensitization (Cautela, 1967) conditioning is done through the use of covert stimuli and responses, such as thoughts and images. The client is usually first taught deep-muscle relaxation and then encouraged to imagine a scene that the therapist describes. A 30-year-old pedophiliac was asked to imagine approaching a 10-year-old boy to whom he was attracted. As he approaches the boy to ask him to come up to his apartment, he feels his stomach becoming nauseated. He feels his lunch coming up into his esophagus, and just as he goes to speak to the boy he vomits all over himself and the boy. People on the street are staring at him, and he turns away from the boy and immediately begins to feel better. He begins walking back to his apartment feeling better and better with each step he takes. He gets back to his apartment, washes up, and feels great. After teaching this man the covert scene we had him practice it overtly, including making vomiting noises and gestures. To make the scene even more vivid we had him sit in his apartment window, and when he saw a boy on the street that he would like to approach sexually, we had him go to the bathroom and stick his fingers down his throat and vomit as he imagined propositioning the young boy. Within two months this chronic offender was no longer feeling the urge to approach young boys, and he had followed through on our assertiveness techniques for forming adult homosexual relationships.

Covert sensitization is usually conceptualized as a punishment paradigm in which an aversive scene follows the first responses in a maladaptive chain of responses. Since the first response in a maladaptive chain is often a coverant or covert operant response, such as thinking about approaching a stimulus, punishment rather than reinforcement of the coverant can lead to an increase in self-control over an impulsive chain of responses. Imagining turning away from a desired but maladaptive stimulus is a new coverant that gets reinforced.

With practice the punishment of a maladaptive coverant and the reinforcement of more adaptive thoughts and images can break up the automatic chain of responses that eventually leads to problems for the individual. Since covert sensitization works with thoughts and images, it could just as readily have been categorized with the cognitive behavior therapies considered next.

COGNITIVE TECHNIQUES

Cognitive approaches to behavior have been the most controversial alternatives for behavior therapists. For more radical behaviorists, cognitive techniques are by definition incompatible with the traditional principles of behaviorism. Behaviorism was established as a radical alternative to mentalistic theories of psychology, which attempted to account for all human behavior in terms of cognitive constructs. Conditioning replaced cognition as the critical determinant of human behavior. Cognitive processes were not denied; they were just not seen as relevant to an effective analysis of behavior disorders. Thus, in some books on behavior therapy (Liberman, 1972; Sherman, 1973; Ullmann & Krasner, 1965), cognitive approaches have been omitted.

As experimental psychologists began to do more rigorous research on cognitive processes, cognitive conceptualizations of behavior became respectable again. More comprehensive surveys of behavior therapy began to include coverage of cognitive techniques (Bandura, 1969; Kanfer & Phillips, 1970; Rimm & Masters, 1974), although frequently cognitive approaches were reserved to the last chapter and given the least coverage. Some behavior therapists, such as Lazarus (1971) and Goldfried and Davison (1976), have begun to give a much more prominent place to cognitive approaches. They argue that once we go beyond treating children and retarded and psychotic individuals, we must take into account the cognitive processes that are critical in maintaining and changing much of adult behavior. Estes (1971), a prominent learning theorist, states emphatically:

For the lower animals, for very young children, and to some extent for human beings of all ages who are mentally retarded or subject to severe neurological or behavior disorders, behavior from moment to moment is largely describable and predictable in terms of responses to particular stimuli and the rewarding or punishing outcomes of previous stimulus-response sequences. In more mature human beings, much instrumental behavior and more especially a great part of verbal behavior is organized into high-order routines and is, in many instances, better understood in terms of the operations of rules, principles, strategies, and the like than in terms of successions of responses to particular stimuli. Thus, in many situations an individual's behavior from moment to moment may be governed by a relatively broad strategy which, once adopted, dictates response sequences rather than by anticipated consequences of specific actions. In these situations it is the selection of strategies rather than the selection of particular reactions to stimuli which is modified by past experience with rewarding or punishing consequences. (p. 23)

Theory of Psychopathology

Since cognitive approaches are still becoming established as respectable alternatives for many behaviorists, it is not surprising that cognitive theories of psychopathology and therapy are the least developed of the behavioral alternatives. Frequently behaviorists, such as Rimm and Masters (1974) and Goldfried and Davison (1976), borrow theories and techniques developed outside of the behavioral tradition, especially from the work of Albert Ellis.

Lacking an adequate cognitive theory of pathology that is unique to behaviorists, we shall adopt a cognitive model of maladaptive behavior that parallels the contingency model of maladaptive behavior. Thus, there are maladaptive behaviors that reflect a deficit in cognitive activity. Autonomic nervous system disorders, such as essential hypertension, migraine and tension headaches, and chronic anxiety, were traditionally assumed to be outside of cognitive control because there is an inherent deficiency in psychological information available to the individual trying to control autonomic responses. With little or no feedback available, individuals are unable to use cognitive processes to gain voluntary control over disruptive autonomic responses.

There are other problems characterized by an excess in particular cognitive responses, such as in the case of a client who was constantly ruminating over the possibility of having cancer. Here the problem is that the same cognitive activity is occurring repeatedly and interfering with the client's ability to use cognitive processes to solve other problems and to relate effectively with the environment. In such cases, what is needed is a decrease in particular cognitive responses, such as a decrease in the frequency of thinking about cancer.

Perhaps the most common problem is the use of inappropriate or ineffective cognitive responses. For some clients this involves inappropriate labeling, such as a client who mislabels sex as dirty and then responds to a sexual encounter with disgust. Other clients develop cognitive expectancies that are mistaken, such as a graduate student who expected all people in authority to be harsh, cold, and condemning and thus had extreme difficulty in dealing with professors and supervisors on even the most routine matters. From a cognitive perspective, such clients are having trouble because they are not responding to the actual stimuli and consequences that occur in their environments. Instead the clients are responding primarily to the labels and expectancies that are used to process environmental events. If their labels and expectancies are sufficiently inaccurate, then their behaviors are bound to be maladaptive.

At a more complex level, there are clients who have developed ineffective strategies for solving problems. In a rapidly changing society it can be extremely important to be cognizant of the most effective methods for attacking such common problems as dealing with an upsetting boss, handling one's budget in a time of inflation, solving the inevitable conflicts that emerge in marriage, and living with the anxieties of adolescents facing an uncertain future. If people learn ineffective strategies for approaching such problems, they are likely to make serious mistakes that will lead to frustration, depression, and other emotional upsets. Clients, for example, who adopt a strategy of trying not to think about problems in hopes that they will go away, frequently wait until the problem is out of control before taking action. Other clients, who are frequently labeled overly dependent, may have adopted a strategy that involves rushing to an authority for the best solution. Such clients may be unable to cope with even such minor problems as what style of clothes to wear, what courses to take each semester, or how to study for an exam. Such clients may do well when therapists give them specific directions on how to solve a particular problem, but the clients are also being reinforced for relying on a strategy that calls for running to an authority whenever any problem arises. What such clients frequently need is more detailed information regarding the basic principles of effective problem solving.

Theory of Therapeutic Processes

If a client's problem is the result of a deficit in information that precludes cognitive control over maladaptive responses, then the solution is to increase the client's awareness by providing the information necessary for cognitive control. If clients are not aware, for example, that their blood pressure is increasing, then there is obviously no way they can consciously prevent such an increase. In the case of maladaptive responses within the autonomic nervous system, the necessary information could not be given to clients until an adequate technology was developed. With the development of instrumentation over the past 20 years, it has become possible to give clients ongoing feedback about specific physiological activity occurring within their body. Such *biofeedback* techniques allow clients to become conscious of each change that occurs in their blood pressure, pulse rate, brain waves, dilations of blood vessels, and other functions. When clients are wired to a biofeedback apparatus they can receive the physiological information or biological feedback that provides the possibility of an increase in cognitive control over autonomic responses. At this point in its development, however, the clinical applications of biofeedback are so problematic and limited that we shall not analyze it further as a clinical treatment.

Cognitive techniques for reducing the frequency of particular cognitions are still rather primitive. Perhaps the most developed alternative has been the use of *thought stopping* (Rimm & Masters, 1974; Wolpe, 1973). This technique begins with clients verbalizing aloud their repetitive thoughts. At the beginning of the chain of thoughts, the therapist shouts, "Stop," thereby breaking up the chain. Next the clients do not verbalize their thoughts, but signal with their hands when they are beginning to think their troubling thoughts. Again the therapist shouts, "Stop!"

Once the thought-stopping technique is clear to clients, they again verbalize to themselves but now yell "Stop" when they begin to repeat their troubling chain of thoughts. Once the overt shouting is effective in stopping the repetitive chain of thoughts, clients begin to practice saying "stop" to themselves whenever their excessive thoughts begin.

Thought stopping may prove to be more effective when combined with *covert assertion* (Rimm & Masters, 1974). With covert assertion clients are taught to assert to themselves some thought that directly challenges their obsessive thoughts. A 22-year-old man who was obsessed with going crazy was taught that immediately after stopping his troubling thoughts, he was to assert himself, "Screw it, I'm perfectly normal." First, clients assert aloud with considerable affect, and then they are encouraged to assert to themselves constructive thoughts that challenge their repetitious ideas.

Several explanations can be given for the possible effectiveness of the combination of thought stopping and covert assertion. The thought stopping itself may follow a punishment paradigm in which the shouting and covert verbalizing of the word *stop* serves to suppress the repetitive chain of thoughts. The covert assertion may function as a counter-conditioning technique by which anxiety that is assumed to motivate the excessive thinking can be inhibited by a covert assertive response. The most cognitive explanation holds that both the thought stopping and the covert assertions serve as distractors. With these distractors available, clients are taught to consciously switch their attention from troubling, repetitive thoughts to more constructive thoughts.

When confronted with trying to change mistaken labels and expectancies, behaviorists frequently rely on techniques derived from rational-emotive therapy (Goldfried & Davison, 1976; Kanfer & Phillips, 1970; Rimm & Masters, 1974). Such emotionally upsetting labels as *awful* and *terrible* are challenged through the basic rational-emotive therapy techniques outlined in Chapter 7. So too are catastrophic expectations challenged, not only for the realistically low probability of their occurrence, but also for the exaggerated negative consequences that they are assumed to bring. In adopting Ellis's basic techniques, some of the behaviorists have made important changes. Goldfried and Davison, for example, describe *systematic rational restructuring*, which parallels systematic desensitization. In this approach a hierarchy is constructed of increasingly more difficult situations with which a client is having trouble coping. Clients imagine the situations and imagine how they would normally cope with the upsetting situation. Then they are asked to rationally reevaluate their responses in order to discover a more effective cognitive response to the situation. Successful coping with an imaginary situation at one level leads to the client progressing in therapy to dealing with situations further up the hierarchy. Systematic rational restructuring gives clients considerable practice in challenging their own upsetting labels and expectancies before having to face the greater stress that comes with in vivo situations. Goldfried and Davison also report that with some clients it is critical that the therapist not try to change the client's cognition, since research indicates that some people will actively resist attempts by others to change them. They recommend that therapists encourage clients to be as active as possible in challenging their own disruptive thinking rather than follow Ellis's model of the therapist being such an active debater with clients.

In his self-instructional training, Meichenbaum (1977) has also made important modifications to an approach heavily influenced by Ellis. Besides working to reduce self-statements that produce maladaptive emotional responses, Meichenbaum also works with individuals to develop self-statements that facilitate self-control of overt verbal and motor behavior. Impulsive and aggressive children have been of special concern for Meichenbaum and his associates (Meichenbaum and Goodman, 1969; 1971; Meichenbaum, 1977).

To help impulsive children develop more adaptive cognitive controls, Meichenbaum draws on the theorizing of Russian investigators, such as Luria (1961) and Vygotsky (1962). Luria postulates three stages in children developing voluntary control over their behavior. In Stage 1 control is exercised by the verbal behavior of others, such as parents. In Stage 2 children repeat the overt speech patterns of parents to control their own behavior. Finally, in Stage 3 the child's behavior becomes increasingly under the control of covert self-speech. As Meichenbaum (1977) points out, self-statements thus exert control over the individual's behavior in much the same way as statements coming from another person.

To help children develop better self-control through self-instruction, the therapist performs a task while talking out loud to him or herself. The child then performs the task with guidance from the therapist. Next, the child performs the task while giving self-instructions aloud. The child then whispers the self-instructions while going through the task. Finally, the child carries out the task employing covert self-instructions.

Meichenbaum and Goodman (1971) illustrate what the therapist might say aloud at Step 1 while copying live patterns.

Okay, what is it I have to do? You want me to copy the picture with the different lines. I have to go slowly and carefully. Okay, draw the line down, down, good; then to the right, that's it; now down some more and to the left. Good, I'm doing fine so far. Remember, go slowly. Now back up again. No, I was supposed to go down. That's okay. Just erase the line carefully. . . . . Good. Even if I make an error I can go on slowly and carefully. I have to go down now. Finished. I did it! (p. 117)

By internalizing such self-statements impulsive children can learn to instruct themselves to slow down when doing a task and to correct themselves without becoming angry or upset. Not only do these self-instructions replace irrational ideas that can lead to emotional upset, but they also provide cognitive coping skills for directing children in more adaptive behaviors.

Another alternative to challenging mistaken cognitions has emerged from the social psychological research on attribution theory. An attribution is an explanation for an observed event or an account of what caused something to happen. In their classic research on attributions, Schachter and Singer (1962) gave subjects injections of epinephrine and told one group that the emotional arousal they would experience could be attributed to the drug they were given. Other subjects were not informed of the effects of the drug and were placed in situations designed to evoke particular emotions, such as with a stooge modeling anger toward the experiment. Subjects who were able to attribute their arousal to the drug demonstrated less emotional responding than those who were not aware of the effects of the drug.

Misattributions can have devastating effects on clients. One couple came in complaining that the husband had been impotent for the first three years of their marriage. The problem began on their wedding night. There had been the usual tensions and conflicts. At the reception the groom's friends insisted on buying him drinks. By the time the couple was in their hotel room, they were tired and tense, and he was more than a little tipsy. When they climbed into bed and he couldn't get an erection, the bride blurted out, "Oh, my God, I married a queer." Needless to say, her attributing his lack of arousal to homosexuality was devastating to their sexual relationship. If they had been able to attribute his lack of arousal to situational stresses, they might have been able to avoid a very troubled start to their marriage.

Working from attribution theory, Goldfried and Davison (1976) suggested several ways in which clients can be helped through more accurate or more benign attributions. Clinical assessments, for example, are attributions made by clinicians, and the assessments can vary in the emotional upset they evoke. A client who attributes impotence, for example, to unconscious conflicts over possible homosexual impulses may be relieved of considerable anxiety to learn that situational tension combined with alcohol can produce impotence. Clients with physical symptoms, such as a man with chronic headaches who is highly anxious because he attributes his headaches to a brain tumor, may be helped immensely if he learns that the accurate attribution is that the headaches are due to anxiety over health. The expectations that clients have for future events can be dramatically changed if their attributions over past or present events are significantly altered. Goldfried and Davison (1976) and Rimm and Masters (1974) are careful to point out, however, that it might be a mistake to attribute too much power to attributions. Since therapy techniques based on changing attributions are in their infancy, a cautious, experimental attitude is clearly advised.

Although there is considerable variation in how individuals solve problems, D'Zurilla and Goldfried (1971) report a remarkable degree of agreement among various theorists and investigators about the operations involved in effective problem solving. Goldfried and Davison (1976) expand on the five stages of effective problem solving, which can be taught to clients who need more effective strategies for approaching problems. They first educate clients in a philosophy that encourages independent problem solving. Their general *orientation* stage includes teaching clients that problems are a normal part of life with which they can cope. Clients are also encouraged to learn to identify problems early and to inhibit the tendency to respond to one's first impulse to a problem. Emotional upsets, for example, can be identified not as a sign of pathology but rather as *cues* to shift attention to the problem situation that is producing the upset.

Defining and formulating the problem is the next stage, with clients being taught to define problems operationally in terms of the stimuli, responses, and consequences involved. Once all aspects of the problem situation are defined concretely, clients are able to formulate the problem more abstractly, such as a conflict betwen two or more goals or between a goal and the available means to the goal. A student came to me, for example, for advice about whether she should drop out of school. She had just found out that her father was having an affair and that her parents were going to get a divorce. She was having trouble studying and was thinking about dropping out. In formulating her problem, it became evident that her major conflict right now was between her goal to advance herself and her desire to help her mother and younger siblings.

With the problem formulated, the next step is to generate alternatives. The client is encouraged to generate a range of possible responses to the situation. Osborn's (1963) principles of brainstorming are encouraged during this stage, including: (1) withholding criticism of any alternative, (2) freewheeling is welcomed, and the wilder the idea the better, (3) the more alternatives the better, since the probability of effective ideas occurring increases, and (4) combining and improving alternatives into better ideas.

With a variety of alternatives generated, the problem then moves into the stage of decision making. Obviously, the person is trying to choose the best alternative from those available. Goldfried and Davison recommend two criteria: (1) the likelihood that the chosen alternative will indeed resolve the major issues of the problem, and (2) the likelihood that the person can indeed carry out the chosen strategy. The student, for example, might choose to stay in school while taking out a loan and thereby help herself educationally and her family financially, but a loan might not be available. She may then decide that another of her alternatives, to live at home, work, and go to school part time, might both resolve her conflict and be able to be carried out.

Many people get bogged down in decision making when they should realize that very few decisions are irreversible. They need to make their best bet on one alternative and then move to the stage of verification, in which they begin to test the validity of their alternative. In taking action, such as moving home while continuing in college, the individual observes the consequences of her decision in order to verify its effectiveness. If the consequences of her action seem to match her expectation, then she has exited (Miller, Galanter, & Pribram, 1960) from her problem. If the consequences do not adequately match her expectations, then she can always return to an earlier stage, such as generating new alterntives or deciding on a previously discarded alternative. An awareness of the verification stage can be extremely helpful in moving people from decision making to action, since it assumes that if mistakes are made they can be corrected by reversing the problem-solving strategy.

A MODELING THEORY OF THE THERAPEUTIC RELATIONSHIP

The importance of the therapeutic relationship has usually been assumed to vary according to the particular behavioral techniques used. With systematic desensitization, for example, the relationship may be inconsequential, since Lang, Melamed, and Hart (1970) have demonstrated that effective desensitization can be carried out by a computer. With some of the reinforcement techniques, however, the relationship can be of more consequence, especially if the therapist is using social reinforcement. Under such conditions, the more valuable the therapist is to the client, the more effective a social reinforcer the therapist can be.

If there is any general value to the relationship, it is certainly not in terms of the criteria that Rogers suggested. The therapist would do clients an injustice to pretend to be unconditional in positive regard, since social reinforcements, including positive regard, are in reality contingent. The therapist is not concerned with accurate empathy, since accurate observation is most critical in determinng both the rate of responding and whether therapy is in fact being effective. Nor is the therapist particularly concerned with being genuine, since what clients need is a competent therapist, not one who is preoccupied with being authentic.

If there is any general value to a therapeutic relationship, it is most likely to be the result of the *modeling* that the therapist does for clients. In assertiveness training, for example, the therapist serves very directly as a model who teaches clients to observe more effective methods of being assertive. Modeling is such a critical part of assertiveness training that therapists who are not genuinely assertive would probably not be competent as assertive trainers. Modeling effects probably occur with most other forms of behavior therapy as well. A desensitizer, for example, models a fearless approach toward phobic stimuli, teaching clients that such stimuli can be mastered if approached in a gradual and relaxed manner. The contingency contractor models a positive approach toward problem solving and teaches clients that conflicts can best be solved through compromise and positive reinforcement rather than through criticism and other forms of punishment.

If modeling is going to be made a more systematic part of therapeutic relationships, then we should take into account what is presently known about effective modeling. We know, for example, that a model who is perceived as more competent will be imitated more than a less competent model. A more powerful model, one who has control over important reinforcements, will be a more effective model. A model of higher status and greater age is usually a more effective modifier of behavior. Multiple models of diverse characteristics will tend to increase the chances of generalization outside the modeling situation, since observers are less likely to attribute the model's success to any particular characteristics of the model (Bandura, 1969). Thus, multiple therapists or group therapy with clients serving as models may increase the generalization of observational learning.

We also know that modeling can serve many important functions in changing behavior (Rimm & Masters, 1974). Through observation clients can *acquire* new behaviors, such as clients observing a really competent asserter for the first time and then beginning to acquire the essentials of effective assertion. Modeling can *facilitate* appropriate behaviors by inducing clients to perform behaviors that they are capable of performing but have not been performing in appropriate ways, such as expressing positive feelings toward a spouse because the therapist has been observed to express such positive feelings. Modeling can *disinhibit* behaviors that were previously avoided because of anxiety, such as clients learning to talk openly about sex because the therapist has been direct about sex. Finally, modeling can lead to *vicarious and direct extinction* of anxiety associated with a stimulus, such as children extinguishing fear of dogs because they have observed the therapist's children having fun with dogs.

The important point is that considerable research (Bandura, 1969) has been done to demonstrate the effects that modeling can have and also how modeling can be most effective. If therapists are to make therapeutic relationships a part of the process of change, they would do well to ask themselves just what it is that they are modeling and how effective a model they are becoming.

PRACTICALITIES OF BEHAVIOR THERAPY

Behavior therapists show considerable variation in the practical aspects of their work. Therapists using counter-conditioning and cognitive techniques are most likely to work in a traditional office setting. Therapy is usually done on an individual basis, although many of the techniques, including desensitization, can be done in groups. Therapists working with contingency management techniques are likely to work in office settings when they are doing contracting work with individuals or couples. Some behavior analysts are critical of therapists staying in their offices and suggest that intervention done in the natural environment is not plagued with the same generalization or transfer of training problems as therapy done in the office. Certainly when behavior therapists are managing contingencies on a larger scale, such as with token economics, they work right in the environment of clients. Unfortunately, because of exaggerated fears of brave new world phenomena, behavior modification has been officially banned from some environments, the most noteworthy being prisons under the influence of the federal government's Law Enforcement Assistance Agency.

Behavior therapists are perhaps most open to using technology as part of therapy. The equipment can vary from a simple rocker-recliner chair for relaxation to remote-control aversive stimulators to complex biofeedback equipment.

Behavior therapists are continuing to test the limits of their techniques and consequently have worked with a wide range of clients. Counter-conditioning techniques have been used most often with verbal adults who would traditionally be labeled neurotic, psychosomatic, and character disordered. Cognitive techniques are most often used with adults, although problem-solving approaches are also advocated for adolescents (Goldfried & Davison, 1976), and self-instruction is used most often with children (Meichenbaum, 1977). Contingency management techniques have been applied to problems that have been most difficult for verbal therapies, such as impulse-control problems, children's problems, and the problems of severely retarded and psychotically regressed individuals.

Behavior therapists represent the full range of mental health professions, with psychologists being the largest group since they are more likely to have been trained in learning theories. Especially noteworthy is the role that experimental psychologists have played in the development of behavior therapy, since they traditionally have not been a direct part of any therapy systems. The Association for Advancement of Behavior Therapy welcomes people from a diversity of backgrounds, although it encourages the independent practice of behavior therapy only for individuals with advanced degrees and special training in behavioral techniques. At the present time, however, there are no special restrictions on who can practice behavior therapy other than state laws governing mental health practice. In private practice the fees of behavior therapists tend to parallel the $35–$60 an hour fees of most therapies. Behavior therapies are intended to be short-term treatments, although the needs of particular clients can lead to a more extensive treatment.

EFFECTIVENESS OF BEHAVIOR THERAPY

Some behavior therapists have argued persuasively that there are legitimate research alternatives to the traditional multigroup design that uses placebo and/or no-treatment control groups. They argue that well-controlled case studies or studies with a small n can yield valid data when techniques like the multiple baseline of ABAB designs are used. In the multiple baseline design several of the subject's behaviors are measured initially instead of just one. The therapeutic intervention is then introduced for one of the behaviors at the same time as all the behaviors are measured. If the intervention produces improvement in the target behavior but not in the other behaviors, it is argued that there is something about the specific relation between the target behavior and the environmental modification that has produced the improvement. The assumption is that other behaviors would have been equally subject to non-specific effects, such as the passing of time, and the relationship with the therapist. While there is much to recommend this design, one problem with it is that we cannot say just what changes in the environment produced the changes. Was it changes in concrete contingencies, for example, or was it the result of experimenter demands or expectations?

A similar problem arises with ABAB types of designs. In the ABAB design, the person receiving the treatment is measured repeatedly: (A) prior to intervention, (B) during the time when the intervention is in effect, (A) during a subsequent period while the intervention is briefly terminated, and (B) then again under the influence of the therapeutic intervention. The rationale behind this design is that if the subject's behavior improves during the periods when therapy is being administered and is worse during the initial period and at any other time when therapy is withdrawn, the therapist's intervention is presumed to be responsible for the change. One problem again is that we cannot say just what in the therapeutic intervention produced the change. Was it the therapist's expectations, demands, or special attention? Another problem is that the therapy might produce an irreversible effect, such as with the punishment of the retarded girl's head banging. If the therapy is withdrawn and the behavior does not revert back to baseline levels, are we to say the change was not due to the therapeutic intervention? Furthermore, most clients and therapists are looking for lasting changes from therapy, not for ephemeral effects that can be reversed as soon as treatment is removed.

The point is that there are excellent aspects to these small-n designs, and they can serve as a model for doing clinical research when only a small number of subjects are available. Hersen and Barlow (1976) describe many of the advantages of these designs. At the same time, however, there are important control issues that must be worked out by advocates of these designs. In our review we will include some of the hundreds of small-n studies that have used these research designs, but we will concentrate mainly on studies that have included traditional control groups.

Desensitization

While hundreds of studies have been done on desensitization, the vast majority have been done with college students rather than with clinical populations. Furthermore, the majority of the studies have been done with relatively mild rat, mouse, snake, or spider phobias, which are not everyday problems for most people and which are also very susceptible to change through non-specific factors such as experimenter demands (Bernstein & Paul, 1971; Borkovec, 1973). While mild animal phobias can be appropriate targets for testing particular theoretical issues, they are not the most appropriate problems for evaluating the clinical effectiveness of a therapy. In this section, therefore, we shall limit our review primarily to research with clinical populations. Classic studies will be presented in more detail, while other research will be summarized to give a flavor of the type of problems on which the effectiveness of desensitization has been tested.

One of the classic studies was done by Lazarus (1961), who compared group desensitization with interpretative group therapy and interpretative group therapy plus relaxation. Subjects were volunteers with phobias that severely interfered with their functioning. The three treatment groups were matched for severity and nature of symptoms, sex, and age. The desensitization treatment was run with small groups who had the same symptoms. Stimulus hierarchies were organized around common themes taken from questionnaires filled out by the subjects. The groups moved at a pace determined by the most anxious subject in the group. The interpretative group was described as insight-oriented along reeducative lines in the style of Wolberg (1954). The third group was the same with the addition of relaxation training.

Success in treatment was determined mainly by rather stringent behavioral criteria, such as acrophobics climbing to the third landing of a fire escape, then traveling from an elevator to the eighth-floor roof garden, where passing cars were counted for two minutes. Subjects also had to be rated as having the appearance of neutrality after the test. Thirteen out of 18 in the desensitization group succeeded, zero out of nine in the interpretative group, and two out of eight in the group with relaxation plus interpretation. The 15 failures in the latter two groups were then treated by desensitization, and 10 succeeded. A nine-month follow-up by questionniare indicated that 19 of 25 recoveries were sustained, for a total success rate of 54 percent. A drawback of this study is that Lazarus did both the therapies and the assessments, and the results may have been influenced by experimenter bias.

Paul's (1966) study is recognized as the classic outcome research with desensitization, since it was outstanding in design. The major problem with Paul's study was that the subjects were college students enrolled in public-speaking courses who were recruited for the study rather than regular clinic or counseling center clients. Because of its recognized importance, however, we shall include the study in our review.

The subjects were 96 university students enrolled in required public-speaking courses who reported and were rated as high on public-speaking anxiety and related interpersonal anxiety. Subjects were assigned to one of five treatment groups:

1. Desensitization (n=15).
2. Insight-oriented therapy with neo-Freudian and Rogerian therapists (n=15).
3. Attention placebo group given an inert drug described as a fast-acting tranquilizer and then asked to perform tasks designed to help them think under stress (n=15).
4. Waiting-list controls who had one telephone contact, a short interview, and two test speeches (n=29).
5. No-contact control group (n=22).

A unique feature of Paul's study was that the insight-oriented therapists were trained by Paul and ran the desensitization subjects as well as the attention placebo treatment. Subjects were seen individually in five 50-minute sessions over six weeks. The length of therapy was selected on the basis of what the insight-oriented therapists said would be sufficient for the insight therapies to successfully treat the subjects.

Outcome was measured by self-report, physiological measures of anxiety, and observer ratings during a four-minute speech in front of an unfamiliar audience. Success rates on all three types of measures were 100 percent for desensitization, 47 percent for insight and attention placebo, and 17 percent for controls. A six-week follow-up produced equivalent results. A two-year follow-up by Paul (1967) indicated that all groups reported somewhat lower mean anxiety scores, but the desensitization group continued to show a clear superiority over the other groups. A careful check on symptom substitution after six weeks and after two years failed to reveal any evidence of symptom substitution.

Gelder and Marks (1966) and Gelder, Marks, and Wolff (1967) compared the effectiveness of desensitization and psychoanalytically oriented therapy for treating severe phobias. While there was significant improvement in the majority of phobic patients, there were no signficant differences in the effectiveness of the various therapies.

In Munich, Germany, Kockott, Dittmar, and Nasselt (1975) compared systematic desensitization, routine psychiatric treatment, and a waiting-list control with erectile impotence. Twenty-four males unable to maintain erections to allow intromission to occur were matched on several variables and assigned to one of the three groups. The desensitization group was treated for 14 sessions, while the men in "routine" therapy were seen once a month for four sessions. Only two men in each of the treatment groups and one in the waiting list group were able to have intercourse to orgasm following treatment. The only significant gain from desensitization was less subjective anxiety following therapy but no significant gains on physiological measures or clinical ratings of improvement.

Krisch and Henry (1979) randomly assigned 38 speech anxious students to the following self-administered treatment conditions: (1) systematic densensitization, (2) desensitization with meditation replacing progressive relaxation, (3) meditation alone, and (4) no treatment. All three treatment manuals included coping skills instructions. The three treatments were equally effective in reducing public speaking anxiety. Reliable changes in physiological measures were found only in subjects who rated the treatment rationale as highly credible. High credibility ratings were also associated with significantly greater reductions in self-rated anxiety.

Moore (1965) found desensitization more effective than relaxation alone or relaxation plus suggestion in reducing some of the symptoms of asthma in children and adults. Zeisset (1968) reported that the interview anxiety of hospitalized psychotic patients was reduced significantly more by both desensitization and relaxation alone than by placebo treatment or no treatment. Rimm, DeGroots, Boord, Heiman, and Dillon (1971) attempted to desensitize anger in college students but on a two-week follow-up found no differences between placebo, no-treatment, and desensitization subjects. There have also been a variety of studies done on the desensitization of debilitating test anxiety in college students. The results have been mixed, with some studies reporting reductions on self-report but not performance measures (e.g., Emery & Krumboltz, 1967); others finding the reverse (e.g., Johnson & Sechrest, 1968); some finding reductions on both types of measures (e.g., Hancur & Prochaska, 1977); and at least one study (Osterhouse, 1972) finding that on a final exam untreated subjects outperformed desensitized students and students who were in a study skills treatment.

Finally, it should be pointed out that there has been considerable research to challenge Wolpe's theory that desensitization is primarily a counter-conditioning process (Meichenbaum, 1977; Wilkins, 1971). The most popular alternative has been that desensitization is a cognitive process, such as changing patients' expectancies that approaching phobic stimuli will lead to dire consequences. However, since such research is not aimed directly at evaluating the effectiveness of desensitization, it will not be reviewed here. While the underlying processes of desensitization remain to be documented by further research, the practicing therapist may still find it useful to follow the traditional assumption that conceptualizes desensitization as a counter-conditioning process.

Relaxation Training

Lick and Heffler (1977) compared the effectiveness of progressive relaxation training with and without a relaxation tape for use at home against a placebo treatment and no treatment for severe insomnia. There were 40 adult insomniacs who responded to newspaper ads seeking people who took at least 50 minutes to fall asleep. Subjects were treated individually for six weekly sessions. Both relaxation treatments were significantly more effective than placebo or no treatment in reducing the time it takes to fall asleep, the consumption of sleeping medications, and anxiety. The relaxation training cut in half the time it took subjects to fall asleep and markedly increased the quality of their sleep.

Blanchard and his colleagues (1982) used 10 sessions of progressive relaxation as the initial treatment for three types of headaches: (1) tension ($n=33$), (2) migraine ($n=30$), and (3) combined ($n=28$). Patients who did not show substantial improvement were then given biofeedback training. Relaxation therapy alone led to significant improvement for all three headache groups. Biofeedback therapy led to further significant reduction for all three types of headaches for those subjects who were not successful with relaxation training.

Turner and Ascher (1979) compared the effectiveness of progressive relaxation, stimulus control, and paradoxical intention procedures with insomnia problems. There were 25 men and 25 women randomly assigned to one of the three treatment groups, a placebo group, or a waiting list. The stimulus control treatment involved: (1) going to bed only when sleepy, (2) getting out of bed after 10 minutes if not able to sleep, and returning when sleepy, (3) getting up at same time every morning whether rested or not, and (4) no naps. The paradoxical intention groups were requested to try to remain awake at night. However, subjects were told not to move around or engage in any activity designed to prevent sleep. The relaxation group were taught to relax during the first session and were to told to practice relaxation twice a day for 20 minutes. Most of the four weekly sessions for all treatments were spent on discussing how the treatments were progressing.

The results indicated that each of the three therapy procedures were effective in reducing sleep problems, and there were no differences between the therapies. The average latency to sleep was reduced from about 60 minutes to 30 minutes in each of the therapy groups. Quality of sleep also increased, and drug consumption decreased in the treatment groups.

Assertiveness Training

Lazarus (1966) randomly assigned 75 outpatients with interpersonal problems to: (1) behavior rehearsal of assertiveness, (2) direct advice, or (3) nondirective reflection-interpretation. With only four half-hour sessions, 92 percent of those in behavior rehearsal improved, compared with 44 percent of the group given advice and 32 percent of those in nondirective therapy. Twenty-seven of the patients who failed to improve with advice or with reflection and interpretation were given assertiveness training, and 86 percent of these patients improved.

Wagner (1967) found that with female outpatients assertiveness training could increase the ability to express anger only when assertive role playing of anger was reinforced by the group. Rimm, Keyson, and Hunziker (1971) reported that group assertiveness training was more effective than placebo therapy in increasing the assertiveness and decreasing the agressiveness of male inpatients with a history of antisocial aggressiveness. Lomont, Gilner, Spector, and Skinner (1969) indicated that with nonpsychotic inpatients there were no significant differences between group assertiveness training and group insight therapy in lowering the clinical scales of the MMPI. Delali (1968) found that with adult stutterers assertiveness training did not add significantly to the role playing therapy already used in a speech clinic.

Hersen, Eislen, Johnson, and Pinkston (1973) compared the components of assertiveness training in treating alcohol, neurotic, and psychotic patients. Ten subjects were assigned to one of five groups: (1) assertiveness modeling and instructions, (2) instructions alone, (3) modeling alone, (4) practice control, and (5) no treatment. Watching a videotaped model of assertiveness combined with assertiveness instructions facilitated assertiveness more than did any of the other treatments. Practice asserting, without modeling or instructions, was no better than no treatment at all.

Goldsmith and McFall (1975) compared assertive training with placebo and no treatment for hospitalized psychiatric patients. Assertive situations and appropriate responses were empirically derived from hospital staff ratings of situations that were particularly difficult for this population. Treatment involved three one-hour sessions. Following treatment, subjects interacted with a confederate of the experimenters. In terms of self-ratings, comfort, and skill in interpersonal interactions, assertive training was far superior to the control conditions. Generalization to nontreated situations, however, was rather weak, with the magnitude of change being only one third as great as the treated situations.

Thelen, Fry, Dallinger, and Paul (1976) had made resident delinquents observe videotaped models and role play increasing mastery of group, home, and school situations. In terms of behavioral ratings at home (but not in school), treatment subjects showed significant gains. Surprisingly, improvement was not maintained at two-week follow-up.

Christensen, Arkowitz, and Anderson (1975) had dating shy males and females exchange written feedback after each date. Feedback involved two aspects of appearance and behavior that were liked and one aspect of behavior they wished changed. Contrary to the experimenters' predictions, practice dating without feedback was generally superior, apparently because the feedback made some of the subjects more anxious.

Yulis (1976) compared the Seaman squeeze technique (Masters & Johnson, 1970) for treating premature ejaculation with the same treatment combined with assertiveness training. All 23 men in the study reported significant improvements in ejaculating control with the female partners who participated in the Seaman squeeze procedure. Significant generalizations of ejaculatory control to relations with other females, however, occurred only with the group who also received assertiveness training.

Sex Therapy

Masters and Johnson's (1970) research is impressive in the sheer numbers of patients treated but is still a patient study rather than a controlled experiment. As ground-breaking research, however, it does suggest that sex therapy may be highly successful with particular sexual dysfunctions. The Seaman squeeze technique for premature ejaculation, for example, was successful with 98 percent of the men five years after treatment. The sensate-focusing approach to impotency was successful with 74 percent of men having secondary impotence, i.e., those who once could maintain erections until orgasm was achieved during intercourse. For the males with primary impotence, who had never maintained erections until orgasm during intercourse, however, the therapy was only 60 percent successful. Eighty percent of the nonorgasmic females reported freedom to be orgasmic. Of the 29 women with vaginismus, an involuntary spasmodic contraction of the circumvaginal muscles that makes penetration impossible, 100 percent were able to enjoy intercourse. Overall, Masters and Johnson write that 80 percent of their patients were reporting successful sexual relations when followed up five years after treatment.

Prochaska and Marzilli (1973) reported a similar 80 percent success rate in their modifications of Masters and Johnson's approach in an outpatient clinic. Of special interest was the fact that nearly half of their successful patients reported improvements following the marital therapy phase of treatment, which occurred before the actual sex therapy had begun. This finding suggests that an important part of the effectiveness of Masters and Johnson's program may be the result of such variables as communicating more effectively and resolving conflicts rather than just the more behavioral aspects of sex therapy. An identification of the critical variables in sex therapy can only be made, however, after the appropriately controlled research is completed.

In a controlled study on male and female sexual dysfunctions, Obler (1973) compared desensitization with 10 weeks of psychoanalytic group therapy and no treatment. Approximately 80 percent of the desensitized patients reported being sexually functional a year and a half after treatment, compared with none functional in the other groups. Unfortunately, Obler does not report the rate of sucess for each of the specific sexual dysfunctions, although his treatment did appear to be somewhat more successful with men.

In 1976 Mathews and his colleagues compared systematic desensitization plus counseling, Masters and Johnson's approach plus counseling, and a self-help manual based on Masters and Johnson's approach with a variety of sexual inadequacy problems. There were 36 couples, with half classified as primarily male problems. Of the 18 male complaints, 13 had erectile failure, 12 had some degree of premature ejaculation, and 8 had both. Thirteen of the females were nonagressive, 1 had vaginismus, and 17 out of 18 had low sexual arousal. The desensitization treatment involved imaginal desensitization for both partners followed by in vivo desensitization of scenes that were successfully completed. Half of the couples in each treatment were seen by a single therapist and half by a dual-sex therapist team.

No significant differences between the treatments were found either at posttreatment or 4-month follow-up on client's, therapist's or independent assessor's ratings of the couples' sexual or general relationship. There also were no significant differences between single or dual therapists or between male and female problems. Overall the couples showed only modest improvements in their sexual relationships, improving on a 5-point rating scale from a mean of 4 to a mean of 3 at posttreatment and follow-up.

Zeiss (1978) randomly assigned 18 couples with problems of premature ejaculation to one of three treatments: (1) totally self-administered treatment, (2) self-administered treatment with minimal therapist contact, and (3) standard therapist-administered treatment. All treatments were based on Masters and Johnson's approach to premature ejaculation. Couples working on their own with no therapist contact failed to complete treatment successfully. The other two treatments led to significant improvement. While there was some deterioration at three-month follow-up, the two therapist-treated groups were still significantly improved. Latencies to ejaculation increased from about 1½ minutes to 10 minutes at posttreatment for the two therapist-assisted groups. At follow-up, however, the mean latencies were down to four and five minutes.

Anderson (1981) randomly assigned 30 women with primary orgasm dysfunction to one of three conditions: (1) systematic desensitization, (2) directed masturbation, and (3) a waiting list. Five-person treatment groups met for 1½ hours twice a week for five weeks. Both treatments were equally effective in improving subjects' sexual self-acceptance and increasing sexual pleasure. Changes in sexual anxiety were negligible. At the conclusion of therapy, 10 percent of the desensitization group, 20 percent of the directed-masturbation group, and 10 percent of the waiting-list group were orgasmic. At six-week follow-up an additional 20 percent of the directed-masturbation group had become orgasmic. Surprisingly, when the waiting-list group was given the directed-masturbation treatment, 60 percent became orgasmic, suggesting that waiting might somehow enhance the effectiveness of this treatment.

Institutional Contingency Management

In a classic study, Fairweather and his colleagues (1960, 1964) designed a program to increase the competency of chronic inpatients. Money and pass privileges were used as reinforcements for improving social and self-management behaviors. The program also included two hours a day of decision making in which the entire group could be reinforced or penalized for the appropriateness of the group's decision-making behaviors. After 27 months, the patients in the contingency program showed much less pathological behavior, more social interaction, and more verbal activity in meetings than patients in a regular program comparison group. Patients in the special program remained hospital-free longer and worked and socialized more when out of the hospital. While the concrete reinforcements seemed to be important early in treatment, patients came to rely much more on intrinsic reinforcements, like pride, and on social reinforcements, like approval.

In one of the first token economies, Ayllon and Azrin (1968) demonstrated that contingent reinforcement was a powerful determinant of time spent on rehabilitative work activities. The 44 patients in the program spent 45 hours a week on work activities when there was contingent reinforcement, compared with only 10 hours a week when reinforcement was withdrawn.

A major concern with institutional control over contingencies is the generalization of such treatment from the hospital to the community. To aid in generalization, Fairweather, Sanders, Maynard, and Cressler (1969) turned a motel into a lodge where patients could be transferred after achieving a minimum level of social competence in the hospital. The lodge was not a halfway house, since patients were responsible for their own behavior, including taking medication. The patients ran an independent custodial business and earned $52,000 in three years. Each week the group allocated funds to members contingent upon the extent of personal responsibility and productivity of each member. As long as the lodge was in operation, 100 percent of the lodge patients were active in the community, while only 20–30 percent of a matched control group remained in the community. During the seven months after the lodge closed, 80 percent of the former lodge patients remained in the community, compared with less than 20 percent of the controls. Furthermore, after the lodge had closed, nearly 40 percent of the lodge patients were employed full time, compared with fewer than 3 percent of the control patients.

Token economy systems have been reported to be effective in increasing the prosocial behaviors of predelinquent adolescents living in Achievement Place, a family-style residential center (Phillips, 1968; Phillips, Phillips, Fixen, & Wolf, 1971). In regular schools as well, token economies have been found to improve the behavior of elementary school children (O'Leary & Becker, 1967; O'Leary, Becker, Evans, & Saudargas, 1969). Bolstead and Johnson (1972) found that with elementary school children behavior improved more when the children were taught to evaluate and reinforce their own behavior than when the tokens were regulated only by the teacher.

Contingency management programs have been applied to a wide range of other problems in children, such as extreme passivity (Johnson, Kelley, Harris, and Wolf, 1966), extreme withdrawal (Allen, Hart, Briell, Harris, & Wolf, 1969;

Brawley, Harris, Allen, Fleming, & Peterson, 1969), social disruption (MacPherson, Candee, & Hohman, 1974; Sanders & Glynn, 1977), hyperactivity (Ayllon, Layman, & Kendel, 1975; Wulbert & Dries, 1977), obesity (Epstein, Parker, McCoy, & McGee, 1976), constipation (Wright & Busch, 1971), enuresis (Finley, Wansley, & Blenkarn, 1977; Popler, 1976), fire setting (Stawar, 1976), and school phobias (Patterson, 1965). With adult clients contingency management programs have been applied to such problems as public masturbation (Mellstrom & Gelsomino, 1976), frequent urination (Masur, 1976), writers block (Passman, 1976), anxiety and depression (Reisinger, 1972; Vasta, 1975), phobias (Marshall, Boutilier, & Minnes, 1974), conversion reactions (Kallman, Hersen, & O'Toole, 1975), and psychogenic pain (Cautela, 1977).

A variety of investigators have found contingency programs extremely useful in working with profoundly retarded individuals. Such skills as toilet training (Giles & Wolf, 1966) and self-help skills such as dressing, dining, and attending to verbal instructions (e.g., Bensberg, Colwell, & Cassel, 1965) have been effectively taught with contingency techniques. Bostow and Bailey (1969) report that aggressive and destructive behavior of retarded individuals could be effectively controlled through the use of time-out periods for destructive behavior and positive reinforcements for constructive behaviors.

Self-Control Procedures

Most of the research evaluating the effectiveness of self-control techniques has focused on the control of overeating and smoking. Stuart (1967) did the classic work on weight reduction. Eight obese women were taught learning principles and given specific self-control assignments, beginning with merely interrupting a meal for five minutes. Over a 12-month period the women showed a linear decrease in weight, losing between 26 and 47 pounds. Stuart (1971) then studied a more complete program that included exercise and specific diet selection. A year after treatment had begun, one group of obese women had lost an average of 35 pounds, and a second lost an average of 21 pounds.

Wollersheim (1970) worked with 79 overweight women to compare the effectiveness of self-control procedures with a social pressure group, an insight group, and no treatment. At the end of 10 weeks of therapy the self-control group had lost the most weight, but by the end of an 8-week follow-up all groups regained one to two pounds. Hall (1977) compared self-control with contingency control, in which money could be earned if the women met their goals after five weeks. An average of one pound a week was lost with contingency control, compared with 0.6 pounds with self-control.

Mahoney (1974) assigned 49 obese women to one of four conditions: (1) self-reward for weight loss, (2) self-reward for habit improvement, (3) self-monitoring of weight and eating habits, and (4) delayed treatment control. All three experimental groups achieved substantial weight loss during the two-week self-monitoring baseline period. Those on the self-reward for improved habits treatment lost the most weight at the end of eight weeks. At a one-year follow-up, 70 percent of this group maintained or improved their losses, compared with only 40 percent of the other groups.

Heckerman and Prochaska (1977) assigned 40 obese subjects from a health maintenance organization to one of four treatments: (1) standard self-control, (2) self-control plus contingency control, (3) self-control plus cognitive control, and (4) no treatment. Each of the treatment groups lost significantly more than the no-treatment group, but there were no differences between treatment groups. The average weight loss was approximately 10 pounds after 10 weeks of therapy. Subjects maintained their losses over three months but lost no further weight. The authors point out that if self-control techniques are indeed under the control of clients, then the obese subjects should have continued to lose weight until their goals were attained, even though weekly contact with the therapist and the group had stopped. If the weight loss occurs mainly during the formal treatment time when there is regular contact with the therapist and the group, the techniques might better be described as social control rather self-control.

Hall (1977) and her associates compared insight psychotherapy, self-management of reinforcements, self-management plus external reinforcement, external reinforcements alone, and delayed treatment with obese subjects in the TOPS program (Take Off Pounds Sensibly). There were 74 TOPS members randomly assigned to one of the five groups, and the four treatment groups met once a week for 10 weeks. The three contingency control groups did not differ from each other at posttreatment but were significantly more improved than the insight therapy and the delayed therapy groups. At three- and six-month follow-up there were no significant differences between the five groups.

Smoking has been one of the problems most resistant to formal therapeutic interventions. Working with 35 college students who smoked at least a pack a day for over a year, Ober (1968) compared three treatments: (1) self-control, (2) aversive control in which subjects self-administered a shock as soon as a cigarette was desired, and (3) transactional analysis. All treatments led to a significant decrease in smoking, but there was no difference between treatments. A four-week follow-up indicated the beginnings of recidivism.

Sachs, Bean, and Morrow (1970) assigned 27 college-age smokers to one of three treatments: (1) self-control, (2) covert sensitization, and (3) an attention placebo. Subjects receiving covert sensitization showed an initial advantage at the end of three weeks of therapy, but after a one-month follow-up all groups were indicating a trend toward recidivism.

In reviewing the literature, Bernstein (1969) has concluded that when different treatments are compared, including self-control procedures, they all tend to lead to a significant initial reduction in smoking. Bernstein suggests that smoking habits are susceptible to an initial placebo effect followed by a high rate of relapse on long-term follow-ups. Nevertheless, most of the research on smoking, including self-control studies, has used only short-term follow-ups.

Fuchs and Rehm (1977) compared a self-control behavioral therapy for depression to a nonspecific therapy and no treatment. The self-control therapy involved training in self-monitoring, self-reevaluation, and self-reinforcement. The nonspecific therapy involved discussion of past and present problems and reflection of feelings. Thirty-six depressed women responded to ads and were randomly assigned to one of the three groups. The self-control subjects showed significantly greater reduction in depression on self-report and behavioral measures and greater improvement in overall pathology on the MMPI. A six-week follow-up generally confirmed maintenance of improvement.

Roth, Bielski, Jones, Packer, and Osborn (1982) compared Rehm's (1977) self-control therapy for depression with a combination of self-control therapy and antidepressant medication. Thirty-two depressed men and women participated in group therapy sessions for 12 weeks. Both treatment conditions evidenced marked decreases in depressive symptoms. The combined treatment resulted in significantly more rapid improvement. Three-month follow-up indicated that treatment gains were maintained in both groups.

Contingency Contracting

Stuart's (1969) classic work on contingency contracting with married couples has already been described. Stuart was also one of the first advocates of contracting with delinquents for more positive behaviors. Upon the completion of four years of research, Stuart and Lott (1972) reported on work with 79 delinquents and their families. The families were involved in time-limited treatments of 15, 45, or 90 days, with the major focus on negotiating effective contracts. Fifteen families that declined initial therapy served as a comparison group.

An analysis of the process of therapy indicated that (1) contracts tend to depend more upon the therapist's interventions than upon characteristics of the clients and (2) the characteristics of contracts appear unrelated to treatment outcome. The authors suggest that the effectiveness of treatment may be more a function of developing communication skills or learning the general process of negotiating contingency contracts, rather than being determined by the exact nature of the contracts.

Alexander and Parsons (1973) reported a much better controlled study on delinquency in which they compared (1) contingency contracting-based family therapy ($n=46$), (2) client-centered family therapy ($n=19$), (3) psychodynamic family therapy ($n=11$), and (4) no treatment ($n=10$). Results indicated that at a 6–18-month follow-up the contingency contracting group had a 26 percent recidivism rate, compared with 47 percent for client-centered, 50 percent for no treatment, and 73 percent for dynamic family therapy. Tests of family interactions at the end of therapy indicated that the behavioral group talked more, showed more equality in terms of who talked, and were more willing to interrupt each other.

Harris and Bruner (1971) compared contracting procedures for weight loss with self-control procedures. At the end of eight weeks of therapy, the self-control subjects had lost an average of 7.4 pounds, compared with 13.4 pounds for the contract group. The initial difference was significant, but at the end of a 10-month follow-up, the self-control group had a weight loss of 3.5 pounds, while the contract group had actually gained 2.8 pounds.

Baucom (1982) randomly assigned 72 distressed couples to one of four treatments: (1) contingency contracting, (2) contingency contracting plus problem-solving/communications training, (3) problem solving/communications training alone, and (4) waiting list. Each couple was seen in 1 to 1½ hour conjoint sessions weekly for 10 weeks. All of the behavior marital therapy treatments were more effective than the waiting list condition. There were no significant differences between the three treatments. All gains were maintained at three-month follow-up.

Murphy and his colleagues (1982) examined the effect of spouse involvement upon weight loss and maintenance for 75 obese adults. Subjects were randomly assigned to one of the following conditions: (1) one-party contingency contract with spouse present or (2) without spouse present, (3) two-party contingency contract with spouse present or (4) without spouse present, (5) attention placebo or (6) waiting list. One-party contracts were basically self-control procedures emphasizing self-reinforcement and self-punishment. Two-party contracts involved spouse monitoring compliance and controlling rewards and punishments. Subjects attended 11 weekly group sessions and 8 maintenance sessions over a two-year follow-up period. Each of the treatment conditions were effective in producing weight loss, and the greatest weight loss occurred during therapy and prior to the 12 week follow-up. At the one- and two-year follow-ups, subjects who had attended sessions with their spouses had lost significantly more weight than subjects who had attended without their spouses.

Aversive Control

A review of over 300 articles on aversive conditioning found that only 14 of the studies included appropriate control groups. The focus here will be primarily on the studies using a punishment paradigm.

A diversity of aversive controls have been tried with smokers, including: (1) putting quinine on smokers' tongues whenever they lit a cigarette (Whitman, 1972), (2) punishing themselves with a shock after imagining smoking (Berecz, 1972), (3) blowing smoky air in their faces as contingent punishment (Grimaldi & Lichtenstein, 1969), (4) holding their breath until painful after desiring a cigarette (Keutzer, 1968), and (5) punishing themselves by smoking extremely rapidly (Lichtenstein, Harris, Bircher, Wahl, & Schmahi, 1973). Regardless of the aversive controls that have been tried, the same pattern emerges: initial reduction in smoking followed by rapid relapse.

Curlee and Perkins (1968) investigated the effects of aversive controls upon stuttering. Twelve male stutterers were assigned to one of three groups: (1) an aversive group who were shocked when they signaled that they expected to stutter, (2) a control group who received the same number of shocks but not contingently, and (3) a no-treatment control. Those in the aversive group were found to stutter significantly less following the termination of treatment compared with baseline levels, while neither of the other two groups showed improvement.

Weingaertner (1971) informed 45 schizophrenic patients that electric shock had been found to cure patients of hearing voices. He then assigned them to one of three groups: (1) a self-shocking group, (2) a placebo group told that some people feel the shock more than others and to shock themselves even if they don't feel it, and (3) a no-treatment group told that the therapist wanted to see if there were any changes in voices over the next few weeks. Results indicated significant decreases in hallucinations in all three groups. There were no differences among treatments, and the effects were attributed by the author to changes in expectancies.

Lovaas and Simmons (1969) used shock in a punishment paradigm to reduce self-destructive behavior in three children. After baseline levels were established, shocks were administered whenever self-destructive behavior occurred. With the first child, 12 shocks were spread over four sessions, and the self-destructive behavior rapidly approached zero. This reduction did not generalize to other experimenters until shock was administered by a different experimenter. The shock effects did generalize to other behaviors, lowering the rate of whining and increasing the avoidance of adults. The shock effects did not generalize to other areas of the hospital until five shocks were administered in other areas. Virtually identical results were replicated with the other two youngsters.

Stollack (1967) designed a study to evaluate the effectiveness of aversive control of obesity. He assigned 190 subjects to one of five groups: (1) a no-contact group, (2) a no-contact/diary group told to keep a daily diary of food intake to help in self-regulation, (3) a contact/diary group who kept the diary and also met twice a week, (4) a contact/diary/noncontingent shock group given shocks at specified times during the discussions, and (5) a contact/diary/contingent shock group given shocks when vividly imagining eating fattening foods. Only the contact/diary group showed significant weight loss at the end of eight weeks. After 10 more weeks, the weight loss was not sustained.

Birk, Huddleston, Millers, and Cohler (1971) used aversive conditioning not only to alter the sexual patterns of 18 male homosexuals but also to affect a whole range of human feelings. They compared aversive conditioning with a placebo treatment in which a light comes on instead of a shock. There were 20–25 half-hour sessions over six weeks. The aversive conditioning was given at the halfway mark of a two-year group therapy program. The aversive conditioning primarily followed an avoidance paradigm—like that described in Chapter 9 on implosive therapy—rather than a punishment paradigm. Subjects were conditioned to avoid their favorite pictures of men and to approach their favorite pictures of women.

Using the frequencies of homosexual caressing, petting, and orgasm one year after therapy, the treated group reported less homosexual activity. The men also rated themselves and were rated by two outside psychiatrists on general happiness and comfort with themselves as human beings. There were no significant differences between the groups on these ratings.

McConaghy (1975) compared aversive therapy to a positive conditioning treatment for homosexuals. The aversive therapy involved shocks being paired with pictures of nude men. The positive conditioning technique involved the pairing of pictures of nude women first with pictures of nude men and then with pictures of heterosexual relations. Thirty-one homosexual patients were randomly assigned to five days of one of the two treatments. Pretest, posttest, and one-year follow-up measures were taken of penile blood flow during films that included segments of nude women or men. Patients reported significantly greater reduction in homosexual feelings and behavior following aversive conditioning. There were no differences between the treatments in terms of penile responses to nude pictures. It was concluded that aversive therapy reduced the secondary reinforcement value of homosexual stimuli but did not alter sexual orientation.

Cannon, Baker, and Wehl (1981) randomly assigned 20 male alcoholics to (1) a multifaceted inpatient alcoholism program alone, (2) emetic aversion therapy plus the program, or (3) shock aversion therapy plus the inpatient program. Aversion therapies involved 11 sessions, including 30 escape trials. At the six-month follow-up emetic aversion exerted a modest beneficial effect, but emetic and hospital program alone subjects did not differ at 12-month follow-up. Shock aversion subjects had fewer days of abstinence than either of the other two groups at both 6- and 12-month follow-up.

Covert Sensitization

Research on covert sensitization with smoking has produced rather conflicting results. In terms of initial success, Gerson (1971) reports covert sensitization to be more effective than either a placebo or a comparative treatment. Fuhrer (1972) and Painter (1972), on the other hand, conclude that covert sensitization has no greater initial effect than placebo treatments. Wagner and Bragg (1970) report covert sensitization alone to have no greater effect than regular counseling; but covert sensitization combined with desensitization appears to produce a more lasting effect than previous treatments. Gerson also reports maintenance occurring after five weeks, but Fuhrer, Painter, and Wagner and Bragg report the typical pattern of rapid relapse when covert sensitization is used alone.

Janda and Rimm (1972) applied covert sensitization to the problem of losing weight and compared it with an attention placebo and no treatment. Initial analysis indicated no significant weight losses for any group. A correlation of $r=.53$ was found, however, between subjective discomfort during covert sensitization and weight loss. Groups were then compared using only the three subjects in the covert sensitization treatment who were most aroused by the aversive scenes, and a significant treatment effect was found. The authors suggest that for covert sensitization to be effective, subjects must be able to vividly imagine the aversive scenes.

Maletzky (1980) tested the effectiveness of covert sensitization with four groups of sexual offenders: (1) court-referred pedophiliacs, (2) self-referred pedophiliacs, (3) court-referred exhibitionists, and (4) self-referred exhibitionists. A total of 100 male patients were included in the study, with 38 homosexual pedophiliacs and 62 exhibitionists. Covert sensitization involved pairing a nauseating odor when sexual pleasure is aroused to a deviant scene. Though covert sensitization was the major treatment, a variety of adjunctive therapies were also used. The basic treatment involved 24 weekly sessions, followed by booster sessions every 3 months for 3 years. Three deviant scenes were usually presented during each office visit, and tape recordings were made for home practice. Treatment was effective across all four groups, with no significant differences between self- and court-referred clients at 6-, 12-, 18-, 24-, and 30-month follow-ups. Using an arbitrary criterion of improvement, such as 75 percent reduction in covert and overt deviant behavior, revealed the following percentages of each group that reach criterion: self-referred pedophiliacs,

89 percent; court-referred pedophiliacs, 73 percent; self-referred exhibitionists, 91 percent; court-referred exhibitionists, 89 percent. The results indicate that covert sensitization can be effective with involuntary patients as well as with voluntary patients.

Thought Stopping

Wisocki and Rooney (1971) compared thought stopping, covert sensitization, and an attention placebo on the modification of smoking. Treatment lasted five weeks, with two 20-minute sessions a week. There were significant reductions in the two therapy groups but not in the placebo and no-treatment groups. There were no differences among therapies, and no long-term follow-up reported.

Attribution Therapy

Storms and Nisbett (1970) provided insomniacs with a placebo drug and told some subjects to expect arousal from the drug and another group to expect a reduction in arousal. The prediction was that subjects in the arousal condition would attribute their emotional state to the drug rather than to personal anxiety or worries. Subjects in the relaxation condition were expected to focus even more on their sleep problems because the drug was clearly not working. As expected, subjects who attributed arousal to the drug did get to sleep earlier than subjects who attributed arousal to personal problems. Neither group reported a significant decrease in personal discomfort.

In their classic study, Valins and Ray (1967) gave a treatment group false feedback about their heart rate, indicating that they were less fearful of snakes than of electric shock. Another group heard the same feedback but were told it was irrelevant to their fear of snakes. Subjects who were deceived into believing they were less afraid of snakes did show a significantly greater ability to approach snakes following the false feedback. Though Valins and Ray's study has been cited many times in support of cognitive approaches to treatment of fears, it should be pointed out that their initial finding was quite weak. Even more importantly, several investigators have been unable to replicate their results (Kent, Wilson, & Nelson, 1972; Sushinsky & Bootzin, 1970).

Self-Instruction Training

Girodo and Ruehl (1978) compared self-instructional training to preparatory information treatment, a combination of the two treatments, and a placebo control with female undergraduates who reported a fear of flying. The 56 subjects were randomly assigned to group treatments that involved 2½ hours of training. They were then taken on a flight, with half the subjects flying in a plane with the cockpit door open. All subjects also experienced a planned, unexpected missed landing. There were no significant differences between the four groups in terms of anxiety levels during the ongoing stress of flying. Under serious threat, however, of the unexpected missed landing with the door open, the self-instruction group and the combined group coped better than the other two groups. With the door closed all groups increased in anxiety. There were no differences between the three treatment groups in flight apprehension at 4½ month follow-up.

Kaplan, McCordick, and Twitchell (1979) analyzed the desensitization and cognitive components of Meichenbaum's therapy with test anxiety. The 24 college students were randomly assigned to one of the following groups: desensitization only, cognitive component only, both combined, and waiting-list control. On a variety of test anxiety and self-rating measures, the combined treatment and desensitization-only treatments were less effective than the cognitive-only treatment. These results suggest that the cognitive component of Meichenbaum's therapy is most effective in treating test anxiety.

Kendall and Finch (1978) tested the effectiveness of cognitive-behavioral treatment that emphasized self-instructions with 20 impulsive children. Therapy involved six 20-minute sessions using training materials related to attention to detail, conceptual thinking, and other cognitive skills. The therapy subjects received the training along with self-instructions and contingent rewards for performance. The controls received the training without self-instructions and were rewarded noncontingently. Two self-report measures on impulse control and teachers' ratings of locus of conflict (internal with impulses or external with others) did not reveal any treatment effects. However, performance on a cognitive task and teachers' ratings of impulsive classroom behavior revealed positive effects due to therapy. These treatment effects remained evident at three-month follow-up.

Kendell and Braswell (1982) compared self-instructional training via modeling and behavioral contingencies, to modeling and behavioral contingencies without instructions, and to an attention placebo. Twenty-seven impulsive children (8–12 years old) were randomly assigned to receive 12 sessions of individual contact under one of the three conditions. The self-instruction treatment improved teachers' blind ratings of self-control, and both treatments were better than placebo on teachers' ratings of hyperactivity. Parents' ratings did not show any treatment effects. Several cognitive and academic performance measures showed improvement for both therapy groups. Self concept changes were evident only for the self-instruction group. Naturalistic observations in the classroom suggested positive effects for both therapies. While 10-week follow up indicated treatment effectiveness, there were no differences between the three groups at one-year follow-up.

Kendrick, Craig, Lawson, and Davidson (1982) compared the efficacy of cognitive-behavior therapy emphasizing self-instructions and attention-focusing techniques with behavior rehearsal and a waiting-list control in the treatment of debilitating musical performance anxiety. There were 53 pianists randomly assigned to one of the three conditions. The therapy subjects met in small groups for 1½ to 2 hours for three weeks. Although there were no differences between the three groups at treatment termination, the two therapy groups were out-performing the control group at a five-week follow-up. The self-instruction group was superior to the behavior rehearsal group on two of five measures at follow-up.

Problem Solving

Apparently no controlled outcome research with clinical populations has been done on the systematic approach to problem solving suggested by Goldfried and Davison (1976).

Modeling

Although hundreds of studies have been done on modeling as a basic learning process, relatively few controlled outcome studies have been done with clinical populations. One of the classic studies was done by Chittenden (1942), who used symbolic modeling to modify children's hyperaggressive and domineering reponses to frustration. A group of hyperaggressive nursery school children observed and discussed eleven 15-minute plays involving dolls. The dolls represented preschool children involved in common interpersonal conflicts, such as a dispute over who gets to play with a wagon. Each play demonstrated an aggressive and a nonaggressive solution to the conflict. The aggressive solution led to unpleasant consequences, such as the wagon being broken, while the cooperative solution resulted in rewards. Children who observed the models displayed a significant decrease in domination and an increase in cooperativeness in the nursery school, as observed immediately after treatment and one month later.

Lovaas and colleagues (1966; 1967) carried out a series of studies with autistic children that included the use of modeling procedures. One of his dramatic effects was to develop language functions in profoundly autistic children. The therapist displays progressively more complex forms of verbal behavior and reinforces the child for imitating, at first reinforcing any imitation and then gradually shaping the child's responses to more and more accurate imitations. The use of extrinsic reinforcements, such as praise and food, is especially important in the early phases of treatment but becomes less critical once imitative behavior is established. It frequently takes a few days to establish the first word, but subsequent imitative learning generally proceeds at a rapid rate.

After the children learn to speak and to label objects, they are trained in abstract linguistic functions, such as the rules of grammar. To overcome the problem of the children remaining too dependent on imitation for use of language, they are taught to imitate and maintain interactions. The treatment progresses into more natural interactions with naturalistic models; verbal approval and a sense of accomplishment replace primary rewards as the major controlling consequences. Lovaas, Freitas, Nelson, and Whalen (1967) also demonstrated how self-care skills, play patterns, appropriate sex role behaviors, intellectual skills, and interpersonal skills can be established even more rapidly than language skills when the appropriate combination of modeling and reinforcement is used.

Bandura, Grusec, and Menlove (1967) treated dog-phobic children in one of four conditions: (1) a fearless model at a party who gradually demonstrates more fear-provoking interactions with a dog, (2) modeling alone, (3) a party alone, and (4) observing a dog at a party. In the two modeling groups 67 percent of the children were able to remain alone with the dog after treatment, compared with very few of the children in the two control groups. The party contributed little to treatment.

In a related study Bandura and Menlove (1968) used movies to compare the effects of multiple models with a variety of dogs against a single model with one dog. The multiple-models approach was more effective in eliminating dog phobias. The single-model treatment reduced but did not eliminate the fear of dogs. The use of a live model was more effective than the use of symbolic models.

Comprehensive Behavior Therapy

As indicated in Chapter 2, the major study of Sloane, Staples, Cristol, Yorkston, and Whipple (1975) compared a comprehensive approach to behavior therapy with brief psychoanalytic therapy and found no significant differences between the therapies in effectiveness with outpatients. The results were sobering in part because two of the top behavior therapists in the country were included in the study.

Besides the outcome data, there were also interesting results based on Truax's measures of an effective therapeutic relationship. From tape recordings, analytic therapists and behavior therapists were not found to differ on degree of warmth or positive regard. There were significant differences, however, on accurate empathy, genuineness, and depth of interpersonal contact. The behavior therapists were surprisingly rated higher on each of these variables.

CRITICISMS OF BEHAVIOR THERAPY

From a Psychoanalytic Perspective

For a system priding itself on its empiricism, behavior therapy certainly is disappointing. In place of quality research, we get quantity. If numbers are good, then more numbers must be better. But what about the conceptual foundations of a problem that determine whether a study is even worth doing? So what if desensitization can reduce a college coed's fear of white rats? Does that have anything to do with the devastating problems that therapists are confronted with daily in their clinical practices? Whoever sees a snake phobic in a clinic? Most behaviorists would do themselves justice when planning a study if they asked the key clinical question for any outcome research—the so-what question. So what if having college students imagine vomiting in their lunches leads to a loss of a pound a week? So what if some of the loss lasts for four months? There is plenty of evidence that 85 percent of the people who lose weight through any means regain it within two years. How come only a tiny fraction of their studies use a two-year follow-up? Are the authors more concerned with completing a thesis quickly or rushing to publish than with establishing a really useful therapy? Perhaps many of the researchers could use a little insight into the motives that lead to such shoddy research.

Behavior therapists would like us to believe that somewhere there are data that demonstrate the superiority of behavior therapy. But where are the data? Are they to be found in Paul's (1966) study using five sessions of insight therapy to treat the anxiety of students in a required speaking class? Send such students to Dale Carnegie! Certainly Sloane et al. (1975) provide little solace. Even with short-term, time-limited therapy, the analysts held their own. What evidence is there of lasting recovery of truly troubled people as the result of behavior therapy? There are a few fascinating case studies, of course, but that's nothing new.

What most of the behavior therapy research demonstrates is not the superiority but the superficiality of the behavioral view of humanity. Only such superficial theoretical thinking could account for hundreds of researchers wasting their time trying to substantiate clinically relevant therapies with normal college sophomores as clients. Researchers from other systems may at times be naive about methodology, but that is nothing compared to the behaviorists' naivete about psychopathology.

From a Humanistic Perspective

Examine the criteria for success in almost all the behavior therapy studies and it is apparent what is missing. Only one study (Birk et al., 1971) clearly included the patients' feelings of general happiness and harmony as criteria for successful therapy, and the shocking in that study did not help homosexuals find happiness. What is missing from behavior therapy and behavior theory is a humane sense of values that can help us to decide what is a significant outcome for therapy. Significance in life is not determined by a .05 level of probability of changing symptoms. In a time when people are suffering from a collapse in a sense of significance, behavior therapy strives only for symptom relief.

What behavior therapy offers to people seeking happiness and harmony in an alienating and dehumanizing world is a bunch of gimmicks and techniques. Do people who have been manipulated all their lives to believe that cigarettes can make them cool and attractive need to have hot smoke blown in their faces? Do people who overeat need to chart each bite of food to rid themselves of the boredom or the anxiety that gnaws away at them? Can thought stopping prevent middle-aged people from thinking that life is passing them by? Do we need people who are desensitized of all their anxiety, or do we need people who are anxious about all the insensitivity that surrounds them? Do we need to teach people to exchange poker chips to encourage talking, or should we learn how to help people find the intrinsic meaning that comes in sharing their most basic feelings? Alpha waves will not cure alienation. A gimmick a day will not keep the doctor away.

The dehumanizing technology of Western society that has played such a role in removing people from their roots is no longer seen as a problem—it is now seen as part of the therapy. Does it not make us shudder to realize how readily patients and therapists alike can reduce themselves to fit a hollow and mechanical model of human beings? Have we become so alienated that we no longer realize that having smoke blown in our face or poker chips given in exchange for love is part of a much larger process of dehumanization? We create our cures to match the image of who we think we are and what we believe plagues us. The rise of behavior therapy reflects an image of humanity as being directed by conditions outside of our control. Is the solution to our contemporary problems to be found in submitting ourselves to even more mindless conditioning?

From an Eclectic Perspective

Welcome to the club, behaviorists! Most people who are in this business long enough come to accept that no one therapy or single theory is complete enough to match the complexities of our clients. Certainly there is no unifying theory behind what is called *behavior therapy*. There are just a series of techniques and a unifying commitment to determine which approaches work best with which types of problems. This sounds like classical eclecticism rather than classical conditioning. Even though prominent behavior therapists like Cyril Franks (1974) have criticized eclectics for muddying the therapeutic waters, the rapid proliferation of new behavioral techniques with no integrating theory is cerainly adding more to our complexity than to our clarity. But eclectics have never had trouble living with ambiguity, even the ambiguity of a system of therapy that is supposedly united yet includes as much diversity as desensitization, covert sensitization, biofeedback, rational restructuring, token economies, self-control, and conscious problem solving. These techniques are about as alike as an eclectic's bag of tricks. Of course, there is really no criticism intended here. We don't mind being called behaviorists if you don't mind being called eclectics.

A BEHAVIORAL ANALYSIS OF MRS. C.

Complex cases like Mrs. C. require a comprehensive approach to behavior therapy. Her multitude of problems will be analyzed according to Lazarus's (1971) multimodal approach to behavior therapy. Mrs. C.'s maladaptive responses can be conceptualized within the following modalities:

1. Behavior.
2. Affect.
3. Sensation.
4. Imagery.
5. Cognition.
6. Interpersonal relations.
7. Drugs.

The BASIC ID of Lazarus is an ironic acronym that is intended to counteract the traditional view of problems being due to unconscious forces, such as anal impulses to be messy or to destroy. Mrs. C.'s problems are not with such irrational wishes but rather with maladaptive conditioning of most of her modes of responding.

In the *behavior* mode, for example, Mrs. C. has problems with conditioned avoidance of dirt and disease. Her particular mode of avoiding is to wash excessively whenever she feels she has been in contact with such conditioned stimuli as pinworms or dirt. Avoidance of these stimuli has also led to such behavioral problems as avoiding cooking and caring for her children. Behaviorally, Mrs. C. also avoids sexual relations, which may in part be related to her avoidance of dirt and disease, but is probably more related to having learned in childhood to model her mother's responses toward sex.

Mrs. C.'s *affect* is dominated by anxiety that is rather pervasive, perhaps because it is elicited by stimuli like dirt, which are to some extent always present in the environment. Mrs. C. learned an excessive fear of dirt and disease early in life from modeling her mother, as well as from the dangers that her mother associated with such stimuli. As an adult Mrs. C. was further conditioned to be anxious about dirt because of the excessive dangers that both she and her physician apparently attributed to pinworms. Mrs. C. also has problems with directly expressing her anger and with the considerable depression she is currently experiencing.

In the mode of *sensations*, Mrs. C. is out of touch with all sensual sensations. Her *imagery* is dominated by fantasies of pinworms contaminating her environment.

Mrs. C.'s *cognitive* problems include those outlined by Ellis in Chapter 7. Besides her irrational beliefs, however, Mrs. C. seems unable to control the excessive recurrence of thoughts of pinworms. She is mistaken in attributing her problems to the possibility of getting pinworms rather than to her conditioned anxieties over pinworms. We might also suspect that after years of insight therapy, Mrs. C. might attribute her problems to "evil" forces within herself, such as hostility. Part of Mrs. C.'s problems may be sheer misinformation both about the reality of pinworms and about sexual issues.

Mrs. C.'s *interpersonal relations* are characterized by excessive control, especially control of her family in order to prevent a plague of pinworms. Mrs. C. probably also receives considerable reinforcement by being the sick center of attention within the family.

When a client like Mrs. C. has problems in almost all modalities, the more modes of therapy we use, the greater impact we are likely to have. It is doubtful with such deeply entrenched disorders that Mrs. C. would recover to her previous level of functioning without a broad-based behavioral intervention program.

Her *affect, imagery,* and *behavior* problems evoked by pinworms and dirt could best be treated with systematic desensitization followed by in vivo desensitization. Training in deep relaxation would be followed by hierarchies made up of stimuli related to dirt and pinworms. Part of a hierarchy would include, for example, imagining buying brand-new underwear wrapped in cellophane, followed by touching brand-new underwear, then approaching freshly laundered underwear, and moving toward picking up underwear that are basically clean though worn. Mrs. C. would be able to actually approach such stimuli as dirty underwear only after the automatic and uncontrollable response of anxiety is no longer elicited because it has been counter-conditioned by desensitization.

The lack of sensual *sensations* and the avoidance of sex would best be treated with sensate focusing, followed by the progressive steps of sexual therapy. It may also be necessary to provide Mrs. C. with more accurate information regarding sexuality to counteract some of the myths she probably learned from her parents.

Some of Mrs. C.'s *cognitive* problems would best be treated by systematic rational restructuring. Her obsessive thoughts of pinworms may have to include thought stopping and covert assertion techniques as means of reducing the frequency of such thoughts. The thought-stopping procedures could be made part of a larger self-control package that would include self-reinforcements for thinking more positive thoughts, such as sensual thoughts or thoughts of caring for her family. After years of insight therapy, we may have to help Mrs. C. attribute her problems to her learning history instead of to unconscious forces that are threatening to overwhelm her.

Changing Mrs. C.'s *interpersonal relations* would involve the whole family, since they have gone along with her tendencies to dominate the family's interactions. We could experiment with family assertiveness training to help them to stand up to Mrs. C.'s unreasonable demands and also to help her express her frustrations more directly. It would be important, of course, to include complimentary assertions as part of the training, since this family seems to rely heavily on negative rather than on positive means of mutual control.

It would also be critical to teach the family reinforcement principles in order to help them reinforce Mrs. C. for constructive behaviors, such as cooking and playing with the kids, and to help them not to reinforce her maladaptive behaviors. Since Mrs. C. has spent so much of her time in washing, it would not be adequate to just reduce her washing through desensitization. She could be left with a rather empty day, which could increase her depression. Thus, it is necessary that both the therapist and the family begin prompting and reinforcing constructive alternative responses that could replace the washing.

While Mrs. C. currently is not using any *drugs*, medication should be considered, especially if she is not able to learn deep relaxation. Medication might also be indicated for her depression, since there is some evidence that conditioning techniques are less effective with depressed individuals.

The aim of a multimodal behavioral approach with Mrs. C. is to help her learn a variety of constructive modes of responding. The assumption is that the more new alternatives she learns in therapy, the more likely she is to recover and the less likely she is to relapse. If she can learn to calm herself in the presence of dirt, assert herself when angry, pleasure herself and her husband, use self-control with her pinworm preoccupations, and earn reinforcements from her family for caring rather than cleaning, then Mrs. C. will have a chance to return to modes of responding that have some semblance of sanity. As it now stands, without an intensive and extensive program of behavior modification, Mrs. C. is in high risk of being punished for her failures by being sent to the state hospital.

SYSTEMS THERAPIES

KATHY AND DAN were from very prominent extended families. Historically, Kathy's family had been influential in government, while Dan's family were financiers. Kathy and Dan, however, were from branches of the family that were in decline. Dan's parents were plagued by alcohol abuse, as was Dan. Kathy's family was multiproblemed, with alcohol and drug abuse, divorce, depression, and physical abuse among the family problems. Kathy herself was troubled by depression and passivity. Though they were in their late 30s, both Kathy and Dan were stuck in their career development, unable to complete their graduate degrees. Their modest inheritances were rapidly disappearing. They seemed to be stuck in a family system that was steadily deteriorating.

With the help of marital therapy, Kathy and Dan were able to communicate more openly about how they were repeating patterns from their families of origin. Dan was having to deal with rules against succeeding. Kathy was struggling with rules against being active and assertive. As part of therapy Kathy traveled to different parts of the country to meet with her mother, sister, and brother. Instead of stepping into blame games, Kathy tried to communicate in a more objective and understanding manner. She was trying to complete the process of differentiating herself from her family of origin while remaining emotionally connected to family members.

Kathy was not surprised that she was becoming more active, less depressed, and more successful. She was surprised, however, that her brother took dramatic steps to get off drugs; her sister entered family therapy to work on physical and emotional abuse of her children; and her mother began to feel her long standing depression lifting. From her graduate studies, Kathy knew how family members can deteriorate as one member improves in therapy. She was pleasantly surprised to discover that an entire family system could begin to improve as one member began to restructure her relationship to her family of origin.

THE CONTEXT IN WHICH SYSTEMS THERAPIES DEVELOPED

Systems therapies maintain that individuals can only be understood in the social context in which they exist. Systems therapies, themselves, can best be understood within the context in which they emerged. The decades of the 50s and 60s were seminal years for the development of systems therapies. These decades also witnessed the emergence of general systems theory in biology and cybernetics in computer science. Rather than follow the traditional scientific method of analyzing and reducing phenomena to their simplest elements, such as electrons, neutrons, and protons, general systems theory advocated studying the biological processes that lead to increasing complexity of organization of whole organisms (von Bertalanffy, 1968). Cybernetics advocated studying the methods of communication and control that are common to living organisms and machines, especially computer systems. First we shall look at how systems are understood from these two perspectives and then see how this understanding has been applied to the study and treatment of troubled individuals, couples, and families.

To understand the functioning of whole organisms we must study not only the separate parts of the organism but also the relationships between the separate elements. A *system* is defined as a set of units or elements that stand in some consistent relationship with each other. A system is composed not only of elements but of elements that are organized by the consistent nature of the relationships between the individual family members. Even the labels that we give to the individual members, such as parent and child, suggest consistent relationships between them.

Organization and system are virtually synonymous. A system is a set of organized units or elements. Principles of organization suggest that once elements are combined in a consistent pattern, an entity is produced that is greater than the additive sums of each of the separate parts. This is the concept of *wholeness*. A marital system, for example, cannot be broken down just into two separate individuals. Not only are there two individual subsystems but there is also a consistent relationship between the individuals that creates a marital subsystem. In this case 1 plus 1 equals 3.

Systems are also organized in such a way that relationships between elements create boundaries around the system and each of its subsystems. In biological systems the boundaries may be easily identifiable like a cell membrane or animals' skin that delineates the system. In human systems, boundaries are frequently more abstract. The rules of relationships delineate boundaries, such as the rules of monogamy help identify the boundaries of a traditional marriage. The spouse who is having an affair would be considered to be "out of bounds" or acting outside the rules of the relationship. Boundaries may be too permeable and create unclear rules about who can interact with whom and how. In incestuous families, for example, the boundaries between the parental subsystem and the child subsystem are unclear and permeable to the point of being pathological. Rules about incest are important in part because they help define healthy boundaries in family systems. Boundaries may also be too rigid and prevent adequate interactions between individuals in a system or between systems. Families with child abuse, for example, may be rigidly bound off from the larger social system and be unable to accept social support that could help prevent such abuse.

Systems are most often conceptualized as being hierarchically organized. Systems themselves are organized one to another according to a series of hierarchic levels. Each system is envisioned as composed of component subsystems of smaller scale, and in turn, each system is a component part of a larger subsystem. A family system, for example, is composed of individual subsystems, a marital subsystem, a sibling subsystem, and a parental subsystem. The family system, in turn, is a component part of a larger neighborhood system which is hierarchically related to even larger social systems.

In order to function effectively, systems require methods for controlling or maintaining organization. Living systems have been characterized as dynamic steady states. Steady states reflect the condition of a system not changing over time. Systems theory has emphasized balance or stabilization within systems. Often this is mistakenly understood as rigidity—a sort of forced and inflexible structuring of behavior. Systems theory actually emphasizes controlled change which allows the development of highly complex interactional patterns that increase rather than decrease options for the system. Control mechanisms allow elements to remain in dynamic interaction. These elements are able to relate meaningfully to each other because of an intricate and delicate series of control mechanisms. The control mechanisms keep the individual elements within an acceptable set of limits but also permit adaptation to occur. Controlled adaptation is the key to meaningful change. Controlled growth leads to differentiation and development of tissues, organs, and individuals. Uncontrolled growth, like cancer, leads to the disorganization and even death of a living system.

The concept of *homeostasis* or balance has been used to explain how living systems control or maintain a steady state. Walter Cannon (1939), the physiologist, first described a set of mechanisms within the neuroendocrine system whose function was to maintain consistency of the internal environment of the organism, such as constant blood pressure, temperature, and water content. If changes in the organism start to exceed a set of safe limits, then control mechanisms in the hormonal and autonomic nervous system will be activated to help bring the system back into balance.

Family systems are seen as having a set of mechanisms whose primary purpose is the maintenance of an acceptable behavioral balance within the family. Families have been found, for example, to maintain surprisingly stable rates of speech interaction (Reiss, 1977). High-interaction families maintain a high rate of speaking across sessions, even though individual members vary a great deal in speaking across sessions.

The mechanisms that contribute to self-regulatory processes within marriage or the family have been conceptualized as analogous to servomechanisms in cybernetics (Wiener, 1962). Servomechanisms are automatic devices used to correct the performance of a mechanism by means of an error-sensing feedback. Feedback loops are seen as the most important control mechanisms. Instead of assuming that two events can only be related in a cause-and-effect fashion, two events can be related in a circular fashion, characterized as either a positive or a negative feedback loop.

In the positive feedback loop an increase in any component part of the loop will, in turn, increase the next event in the circular sequence. Deviations from the norm actually get amplified in such a situation, so that positive feedback loops increase deviations and serve as a self-destructing mechanism. Positive feedback loops set up a runaway situation that eventually drives the system beyond the limits or range within which it can function. Violent arguments in families, for example, can get out of control as anger in one spouse increases anger in the other, which in turn increases anger in a circular fashion. Runaway rage can disrupt or even destroy a family's ability to function.

Negative feedback loops, in contrast, establish a balance between the deviations of different events within the loop. Negative feedback loops decrease deviations from the system's rules of relating and help maintain stability of marriage and family. If a family member becomes angry, another may become sick. If the two deviations balance each other, the family can maintain a stable level of hostility in the system.

Living systems are characterized as open systems, which means that energy can be freely transported within and out of the system. Information is the most important type of energy in living systems, since it is an energy that reduces uncertainty. Increases in information allow systems to be organized in more complex patterns. When information is packaged or programmed appropriately and efficiently it has a powerful effect on a system's ability to function in a highly complex and well-organized manner. Communication involves the process by which information is either changed from one state to another, or moved from one point to another in space. Cybernetics serves as a model for how information can be transformed or transmitted effectively within marital and family systems.

These core concepts from general systems theory and cybernetics have served as the intellectual inspiration for innovative approaches to systems therapy. Three major approaches, the communications, the structural, and the Bowenian family systems approach, will be presented, since there is no one unifying approach to systems therapy. Since these systems therapies have focused on patterns of relationships within systems rather than on individual personalities, the sections on theories of personality will be omitted. Each of the systems therapies do, however, have important things to say about the development and/or maintenance of psychopathology and how psychopathology in human systems can best be changed.

COMMUNICATIONS SYSTEMS THERAPY

The communications approach to therapy emerged from two interrelated organizations rather than from a single individual. The first organization was the Double Bind Communications Project begun in 1952 by Gregory Bateson, with Jay Haley and John Weakland as members of the project and Donald Jackson as consultant. The second organization was the Mental Research Institute (MRI) founded by Jackson in 1958, with Virginia Satir and Paul Watzlawick as two important members of the institute. The two organizations had unclear boundaries, since Jackson participated in both projects; the Double Bind Project was located at MRI; and when the Double Bind Project terminated in 1962, Haley and Weakland joined MRI. It is not surprising that both of these organizations were founded in Palo Alto, California, which is part of Silicon Valley, one of the foremost centers of computer science in the world.

What these individuals shared in common was the assumption that communication is the key to understanding human behavior. The MRI group went so far as to assume that all behavior is communication. Just as we cannot not behave, so too, we cannot not commmunicate. Communication then involves both verbal and nonverbal behaviors.

The Double Bind Project originally focused on how conflicting communications could produce symptoms of schizophrenia. Initial research on double bind communications revealed important relationships between family dynamics and schizophrenic communications. In 1959 the project was divided into an experimental approach and a family therapy project. Family interactions were videotaped, and attempts made to differentiate "schizophrenic" from "normal" communications. In the family therapy project, observations were made in natural settings, and various techniques based in part on communications theory were introduced. Over the 10-year period that the project existed, there were some 70 publications produced, reflecting the creative work emerging from this research and therapy group (Sluzki & Ransom, 1976).

The staff at MRI was even more productive, with 130 articles and 9 books being published just during the period fom 1965 to 1974. In these writings a format was described that focused on analysis of communication between individuals and subsequently between family members. Then interventions were designed to change communication patterns between one individual and another and between all members of a family (Greenberg, 1977).

Gradually the organization of these two groups began to change. Bateson's project ended in 1962, and he went on to advance a systems perspective to a broad range of human concerns. Jackson died in 1968 in the midst of a young but very creative career. Satir left to contribute to the human potential movement that began in California and rapidly became a worldwide phenomenon. Haley relocated to the East Coast at the Philadephia Child Guidance Clinic to participate with Salvador Minuchin in creating a vital center for systems therapy. Such a creative group of individuals would not be expected to leave behind a single, coherent theory of therapy. They did, however, create an innovative set of concepts for understanding psychopathology in systems and a set of therapeutic principals for helping systems change.

Theory of Psychopathology

Systems therapists have frequently observed that decreases in psychopathology in one family member are often accompanied by increases in symptoms in another family member. Jackson, for example, treated a woman for depression and as her depression subsided, her husband began phoning to complain that his wife's emotional condition was worsening (Greenberg, 1977). The continued improvement by the wife finally resulted in the husband's loss of his job and subsequent suicide.

Psychopathology is fundamentally an interactional process between family members rather than an intrapersonal problem within one member. Psychopathology serves as a homeostatic mechanism to help families maintain an internal balance for family functioning. When a family is threatened, it can move toward balance through puzzling, psychotic, or other pathological behaviors. A family's status quo may be one in which the parents fight infrequently. When they do fight, if violence threatens to run out of control, a child can communicate concern by becoming symptomatic. These symptoms serve as a negative feedback loop that results in a halt in hostilities as the family develops a new-found concern with the identified patient. But the system should be the patient and not the individual who has developed symptoms to help save the system.

A breakdown in family functioning occurs when the rules of relating become ambiguous. The rules of relationships provide a stable organization for family functioning. If the rules become ambiguous, the system becomes disorganized and symptoms are likely to develop to restore order to the family. If the rules are clear, such as the rule that family members will not relate violently, then an argument between parents need not threaten the family's functioning and a child would not have to develop symptoms to control a threat of violence.

The rules of relating in a family are best observed through the patterns of communication in the family. Who communicates to who, how, and about what define the patterns of relationships that make up a family. Most families, for example, have a clear rule that when parents are communicating with each other in an angry manner, the children stay out of it. The spouse subsystem has clear boundaries or rules that prohibit children from becoming part of intimate arguments.

When communication patterns in families are unclear, then rules become more ambiguous and psychopathology is likely to develop. Double bind communications are one of the most troublesome patterns of communicating since they involve two incompatible messages. A classic example of a double bind situation is presented by Bateson and his colleagues:

A young man who had fairly well recovered from an acute schizophrenic episode was visited in the hospital by his mother. He was glad to see her and impulsively put his arm around her shoulders, whereupon she stiffened. He withdrew his arm, and she asked, "Don't you love me anymore?" He then blushed, and she said, "Dear, you must not be so easily embarrassed and afraid of your feelings." The patient was able to stay with her only a few minutes more and, following her departure, he assaulted an aide and was put in the tubs. (1956, p.259)

Verbally the mother is communicating a wish to be close to her son, but nonverbally her tightening communicates a wish to be distant. So the son withdraws, and the mother contradicts her nonverbal message by saying, "Don't you still love me?" The rules for relating are being communicated as ambiguous at best. Are mother and son supposed to have a close or a distant relationship? The son clearly cannot win. If he relates closely, his mother tightens up. If he pulls back, she becomes upset. No wonder the son becomes confused, frustrated, and hostile.

Communication is a complex pattern of interactions that is frequently misunderstood by therapists, let alone clients. In the book, *Pragmatics of Human Communication*, Watzlavick, Beavin, and Jackson (1967) conceptualize communication by five axioms. First is the axiom already stated that it is impossible to not communicate. Silence is obviously communication, though it is frequently ambiguous communication open to interpretation and to misunderstanding.

Besides transmiting information, communication also implies a commitment and defines the nature of the relationship. Communication contains both a report, which is the content of the message, and a command, which defines how the communicators are to relate. Satir (1967) emphasizes that if the content and the command are congruous, then the relationship is defined as harmonious. If the two levels of communication are incongruous, such as the mother reporting a wish to be close and a tightening that commands distance, the relationship is likely to be characterized by disharmony and pathology.

The third axiom states that the nature of a relationship is contingent upon how a communication sequence is punctuated. If a communication response cannot end with a period until the same person always has the last word, then such punctuation defines the person with the last word as having greater power in the relationship.

The fourth axiom states that human beings communicate verbally and nonverbally. Verbal communication is most clear for content being sent but does not provide much information about the relationship between the communicators. Nonverbal communication tells us more about the relationship but is still ambiguous about the nature of the relationship. For example, tears can be a source of joy. The more families rely on nonverbal messages, the more ambiguous their relationships are likely to be and the more problems are likely to arise.

The final axiom states that all communication exchanges are either symmetrical or complementary, depending upon the type of relationship that exists. If equality exists and either party is free to take the lead, a symmetrical relationship exists. If one leads and the other follows, the relationship is complementary. Psychopathology can occur in either type of relationship. In symmetrical relationships competition can escalate, and a runaway occurs in the communication as each struggles to have the last word in defining the nature of the relationship. Arguments can become endless. Pathology in symmetrical relationships is characterized by more or less open warfare, or schism, as Lidz (1963) calls it. Marital schism is defined as a state of severe chronic disequilibrium, discord, and recurrent threats of separation. There is constant undercutting of one parent by the other. The competition leads to parents vying for the love of the children and the children in rivalry for the parents' affection. The rule that is being communicated in families with marital schism is mutual distrust and angry competition instead of cooperation.

Complementary relationships can rigidify and prevent adequate growth of family members. A parent who insists that a young adult relate as a child can disconfirm the young adult's sense of self as a person who should be able to relate more equally. Such disconfirmation can lead to symptoms of depersonalization, confusion, or aggressive acting out. In marital systems that have become rigidly complementary, one partner must always be in overt control and dominate the family. There is a lack of reciprocity, or give and take, between the partners, and the marriage and the family is skewed in the direction of the controlling partner (Lidz, 1963). The weak partner allows the domination so that continuation of the marital and family system is not constantly threatened. The domination is allowed even if it is domination by irrational or pathological ways of behaving. The rule of these families is accommodation, even if it means compromising one's self away.

Theory of Therapeutic Processes

If psychotherapy is primarily a function of unclear communication that results in ambiguous rules for relating, then psychopathology can best be changed by helping individuals in systems to communicate more clearly about the rules of their relationship. The emphasis in communication therapy is not on the content of the communication but rather on the relationship defining aspects of communication. The emphasis is not so much on what people communicate about but rather on how people communicate. Since people can only relate through communication, if they change how they communicate they also change how they relate. Homeostatic mechanisms in families, however, make family systems very resistant to change. If therapists are to be effective in changing the family's rules for communicating and relating, they will need interventions that are powerful enough to disrupt the family's rigid resistance to change.

CONSCIOUSNESS RAISING

Among the communication therapists, Jackson has placed greatest emphasis on the importance of family members becoming more aware of how dysfunctional are their current rules for communicating and relating. Jackson assumes that before change is possible, the family must understand rule functioning. His emphasis on knowledge of family functioning has resulted in Jackson being labeled a cognitive communication therapist (Foley, 1974).

The Client's Work. The client's task is not to develop historical insight into their rules of relating and communicating. The family is not to focus on the historical reasons for why they relate as they do. The family's work is simply to relate in the here and now. Then by either following the therapist's directives or by resisting such directives, they can begin to see how dysfunctional are their communication patterns and their rules for relating.

The Therapist's Work. The first task for the therapist is to not get blinded by the content of communications. Focusing on a family history, for example, can be one of the quickest ways to miss how the family is interacting in the here and now. Since rules for relating are enacted in the present, the therapist's first task is to become more aware of who communicates to who, about what, and how. In the initial sessions the therapist will try to clarify the family's rules for functioning by asking about the family's expectations for each parent and about the role that each child plays in the family system. The therapist tries to open these areas up for more clear communication and, hopefully, for change.

Relabeling is a technique that is designed to make explicit the rules by which a family operates. Jackson (1967) gives the example of a mother and a daughter talking, and the mother begins to cry. Because the daughter has been labeled as aggressive, she is assumed to be the cause of her mother's crying. The daughter even confirms this unwritten assumption by stating that she did not mean to hurt her mother. The therapist intervenes by seeing the hurt as a "touching closeness." Such a technique takes away the negative motivation of an act and labels it in a positive way. From the family's rules of communication, the daughter is perceived only as aggressive and hurtful rather than trying to touch her mother in a close way. Family members may define a relationship between two people in a negative way for years so that all communications between them are interpreted negatively. If the therapist can suddenly define the communication in a more positive way, the family can begin to see itself in a new way.

Another means of making the family aware of dysfunctional rules is to produce a runaway in the system by prescribing the symptom. If the problem is that the parents are being too punitive, the therapist would recommend that they be even more punitive as a means of regaining control. The parents then have the opportunity to discover just how they are relating to their children. As their punitive communications increase, they threaten to produce a runaway or breakdown in the system. The parents then have the opportunity to gain genuine insight into how dysfunctional their punitiveness is for the family's well-being.

A technique similar to prescribing the symptom is that of reduction ad absurdum. This technique reduces the complaint to the absurd so that a client can become aware of how dysfunctional it is to relate in a such a manner. With a mother who is complaining about her daughter's aggressiveness, the therapist could commiserate with the mother regarding the daughter's acting out, talk with her about the cross she has had to bear and the fact that anyone else would have been completely crushed by it, so that finally the mother has to say, "I didn't say it was *that* bad." The mother and the family can become aware that she is not as vulnerable to her daughter's acting out as she seems.

Choosing

Clients experience symptoms as being outside of their personal control. Clients do not experience themselves as having any choice when it comes to symptomatic behavior. They are helpless when it comes to choosing whether to be free from symptoms or not.

Symptoms are especially likely to emerge in family systems characterized by double bind communication patterns. Double binds cause individuals to develop a sense of having no choice. They are damned if they do or damned if they don't respond. Double bind communications contain rules to relate in two incompatible ways. "Come close but don't touch!" Double bind communications help to create symptoms in part because they leave the receiver with no choices for resolving incompatible or paradoxical communications. Communications therapists have been ingenious in liberating clients from double bind situations and from symptoms by creating therapeutic double binds. When constructed correctly these paradoxical techniques liberate clients by giving them two choices: to cooperate with the therapist's communications or to refuse to cooperate.

THE CLIENT'S WORK.   The client's work is simple: to choose to follow the therapist's instructions or to choose to rebel.

THE THERAPIST'S WORK.   The therapist's task is more challenging. The therapist must create a paradox that will help liberate clients whether they chose to cooperate or refuse to cooperate with the therapist's directives. A therapeutic double bind presupposes an intense relationship, the therapeutic relationship, which has a high degree of survival value and expectation for the patient (Watzlawick et al., 1967). In this context, a directive is given which is structured so that it:

1.   Recommends continuing the very behavior the patient expects to change.
2.   Implies that acting out the symptomatic behavior will produce change.
3.   Thereby creates paradox because the patient is told to change by remaining unchanged. Patients are put in an untenable situation regarding their symptoms. If they cooperate and choose to carry out their symptoms, they no longer have the experience of "can't help it." The behavior becomes choice behavior rather than symptomatic or helpless behavior. If the clients resist the directive, they can do so only by not behaving symptomatically, which is the goal of therapy. Therapeutic double binds give clients two choices, both of which liberate them from symptomatic or helpless behavior.

The therapeutic double bind must, however, be communicated in such a convincing manner that the client cannot dissolve the paradox by commenting on it. If the client says, for example, "you're trying to trick me," the paradox is dissolved.

In the case of a couple who argued constantly, Jackson told them that their arguing was a sign of emotional involvement and that this apparent discord only proved how much they love each other. He recommended that they continue their fighting in order to express their love. No matter how ridiculous the couple may consider this interpretation—or perhaps because it was so ridiculous to them—they set about to prove to the therapist how wrong he was. This was best done by stopping their arguing, just to show that they were not in love. The moment they chose to stop their arguing, they found they were getting along much better (Watzlawick et al., 1967).

In another case, Jackson was trying to interview a bearded young man who believed he was God and remained completely aloof from other patients and the staff. The patient deliberately remained across the room from Jackson and ignored any questions or remarks. Jackson told the patient that his belief that he was God could be dangerous because he might let down his guard and neglect to check what was going on around him. But if he wanted to take this kind of chance, the therapist would go along with it. During this structuring of a therapeutic double bind, the patient became increasingly nervous and at the same time interested in what was going on. Should he choose to take the chance of being treated like God or not? The therapist then got down on his knees and presented the patient with a key to the hospital, saying that since he was God he would have no need for a key, but if he was indeed God, he deserved to have the key more than the therapist. The patient dropped his stony demeanor, came over to Jackson, and said, "Man, one of us is crazy."

Catharsis

Virginia Satir was unique amongst her Palo Alto colleagues in that she placed much more emphasis on feelings than did the others. She actually combined a symptoms approach with an ego psychology and gestalt therapy perspective. Satir agreed with the assumption that troubled families need to communicate clearly. Most troubled families, however, have difficulty in communicating their feelings directly. If they cannot be clear about their feelings toward each other, they certainly would be more likely to have ambiguous rules for relating. Satir's (1967; 1972) approach to systems therapy then would place much more emphasis on helping families express their emotions and thereby change rules that prohibit relating on a feeling level.

The Client's Work. The client's task is to begin to take the risk of communicating feelings more directly rather than indirectly through nonverbal actions. Clients first try to gain insight into which feelings they usually omit from their communications. Blamers ususally omit feelings about the other person; placaters omit feelings about themselves; super reasonable communicators omit feelings about the subject being discussed; and irrelevant communicators omit everything. Once aware of the pattern of communication they tend to use, clients then need to struggle to become more congruent communicators by expressing the emotions they usually eliminate.

The Therapist's Work. The therapist first uses consciousness raising processes to help clients become more aware of which of the four patterns of dysfunctional communication they typically use. Through feedback and interpretations, the therapist helps clients become aware of the meanings contained in both their verbal and nonverbal communications. As clients start to become aware of the deeper feelings that they are communicating only indirectly, the therapist encourages them to express their feelings more directly. Rather than communicating secondary feelings, like anger or envy, the therapist would encourage clients to express the primary feeling of hurt. Secondary feelings like anger can be dysfunctional for families, while expressions of hurt almost always help families to create more supportive and caring rules for relating.

Theory of the Therapeutic Relationship

Even though Satir would be active and directive with families, she would emphasize the importance of accurate empathy, positive regard, and genuineness in family systems. The therapist needs to relate in such a way as to help develop an atmosphere that is conducive to more congruent and functional communication. Functional communication requires an atmosphere in which anything can be discussed, anything can be raised, and there is nothing to hold a person back. This type of therapeutic context can best be developed in families when the therapist is able to relate to each family member in a caring, empathic, and congruent manner. Rather than be nondirective, however, the therapist needs to jump right in with the family and help direct them to the feelings that have been omitted from their incongruent communications.

Jay Haley (1973) would place greatest emphasis on the command or power aspect of communications. The most obvious theme between two human beings centers on who is in charge. The issue is which person is to govern the behavior of the other and so set the conditions for what sort of relationship they will have together. Since the issue of who is in charge is critical to any relationship, it is also the central issue in a therapeutic relationship. In troubled systems individuals avoid taking responsibility for defining the nature of their relationships. In a therapeutic system it is necessary for the therapist to be responsible for defining the nature of the therapeutic relationship. The rule for relating is clear. The therapeutic relationship is organized hierarchally, with the therapist in charge. Haley (1973a) posits a strategic therapy in which it is necessary for the therapist to be in charge of the relationship. To be successful, the therapist must be in control. A major strategy of therapy, therefore, consists of the therapist communicating directives to the client.

Giving directives is the means by which therapists can change the rules of relating and communicating in families. If a mother keeps intruding when a father and son are communicating, the therapist can directly change this pattern by giving the mother a directive to stop intruding. Directives also serve to intensify the relationship between the therapist and the family. By telling people what to do, the therapist becomes involved in the action and becomes important to the clients. When the family follows directives at home, the therapist remains in their lives throughout the week.

But the therapist doesn't always want clients to follow the directives. Paradoxical strategies are directives that the therapist would want the family to resist. Family members can attempt to regain control of the therapeutic relationship by resisting the therapist's suggestions. By resisting, however, they are actually doing what the therapist prefers. Haley (1973b) was impressed with how an uncommon therapist like Milton Erikson could use direct and indirect hypnotic techniques to control the therapeutic relationship. This is beautifully illustrated in the classic case of a bedwetting couple treated by Erikson.

Erikson told the couple that the absolute requisite for therapeutic benefits would be in their unquestioning and unfailing obedience to the instructions given to them. Erikson then commanded the bedwetting couple to deliberately wet the bed before getting into it each night for a period of two weeks. At the end of this time they would be given one night off and would sleep in a dry bed on Sunday night. On the following Monday morning they were to throw back the covers when they saw a wet bed, then and only then, would they realize that they would face another three weeks of kneeling and wetting the bed. There was to be no discussion or debate, only silence and obedience.

The outcome was that each night the couple, with considerable distress, wet the bed. However, two weeks later when they awoke on Monday morning, the bed was dry! They started to speak but remembered the order to be silent. That night without speaking they "sneaked" into a dry bed and did so for the next three weeks.

Did the couple choose to change their behavior or were they following the injunctions of the therapist? Were they conscious of the use of paradox or did the therapist have an indirect hypnotic control over their behavior? In Haley's view of therapy as a power struggle, the processes of change are not really important. What is important is the outcome, who won the battle.

Practicalities of Communications Therapy

Communication patterns can best be observed when a full family system is present. Communication therapists are flexible, however, and will work with marital subsystems or even an individual subsystem if necessary. While therapy sessions usually last only one to two hours, the therapist expects therapy to continue at home as the members struggle with the suggestions or directives of the therapist.

Communications therapy was originally developed with schizophrenic families and has probably been most applied with such families. Therapy with such families would typically be longer-term, lasting a year or two. More recently Haley (1976) has advocated a problem-solving approach where the goal of systems therapy is to solve the presenting problems or symptoms of the family. With this approach therapy can be much more of a short term endeavor, lasting just a few weeks or months.

Because so much of communication is nonverbal behavior, communications therapists can find it very helpful to videotape sessions, especially for training of novice therapists. Videotaping also permits the sessions to be used for research on communication patterns in families.

Fees have at times been a tricky issue for system therapists. Most insurance policies are individual health programs that cover treatment for individual psychopathology but not marital or family problems. Family or marital therapists can be forced to go along with the ideology of an identified patient for insurance purposes. Families also wonder if fees will be greater because more people are being seen in therapy. Typically, systems therapists charge a standard fee per session regardless of whether a family, a couple, or an individual are being seen.

Effectiveness of Communications Therapy

Most of the communication therapists have not been involved in systematic assessments of their treatments. In a recent evaluation of her approach to therapy, for example, Satir (1982) reported that she had treated close to 5,000 families in nearly every shape, form, nationality, race, income group, religious orientation, and political persuasion. While she believes that her approach has been generally useful to her clients, she indicates that she has done no formal research on her effectiveness.

The closest thing to an evaluation of therapy from the Mental Research Institute group are the clinical surveys of Weakland, Fisch, Watzlawick, and Bodin (1974) and Segal (1982). These researchers evaluated the effectiveness of their particular form of communications therapy that they label *brief therapy*. While this approach is based on communications theory as presented by Watzlawick et al., (1967), there are some important changes in practice. Brief therapy is time-limited, with clients being seen for a maximum of 10 sessions. Treatment is oriented toward solving specific problems and changing symptoms rather than necessarily changing systems. While case formulation is based on a systems perspective, treatment often involves a single individual. Finally, communication changes are made primarily by changing behavioral interactions between members of a family system.

The clinical surveys of brief therapy use relatively subjective measures given by researchers other than the therapist. The researchers do attempt to assess symptom substitution as well as improvements in areas other than the primary complaint. In short-term follow-ups of 97 cases seen for an average of seven sessions, Weakland et al., (1974) found that: (1) 40 percent reported complete relief of the presenting complaint, (2) 32 percent reported significant improvement, and (3) 28 percent failed to improve. The authors also report that in none of the success cases was there any report of new problems arising, and in many of these cases there were improvements in additional areas as well. In a more recent follow-up that apparently included the previous 77 cases, Segal (1982) reported similar results with 148 cases. Thirty-six percent reported maximum improvement, 26 percent showed significant improvement, and 38 percent did not improve. None of the cases got worse with therapy.

A couple of outcome studies include important aspects of communications therapy. Langsley, Flomenhaft, and Machotka (1969) randomly assigned 150 patients to an outpatient family crisis therapy and 150 controls to the normal hospitalization program. Most of the patients were experiencing acute schizophrenic episodes. The purpose of the study was to determine if family crisis therapy could prevent or reduce the need for future hospitalizations. The family therapy cases received an average of 4.2 office visits, 1.3 hour visits, 8.4 telephone calls, and 1.2 collateral contacts with social agencies. Treatment lasted a mean of 24.2 days. The hospitalized control group received individual and group therapy, mileau therapy, and pharmacotherapy. The average length of stay was 28.6 days.

At six-month follow-up, 39 percent of the hospital cases were readmitted, while only 19 percent of the family therapy clients were hospitalized during that period. In addition the average length of stay for the control group was three times as long as the family therapy group.

At 12- and 18- month follow-up the differences in hospitalization rates gradually declined, going from a ratio of 39:19 at 6 months, 22:17 at 12 months, and 17:15 at 18 months (Langsley, Machotka, & Flomenhaft, 1971). Nevertheless, over an 18-month period, the 150 clients who were seen in the much less costly outpatient family therapy were doing as well as the patients who were hospitalized. It is important to remember that at the time this study was conducted hospitalization was the routine treatment of choice for such patients.

A communications-oriented family therapy was also found to be more effective than long-term individual therapy for clients suffering from work phobias (Pittman, Langsley, & DeYoung, 1968). Of the 11 clients seen for work phobias, 9 had a history of school phobias. Subsequently, the family therapy was based on family treatments that had been found to be effective with school phobias. Treatment focused on the symbiotic dependencies between the mother figure who stayed home alone and the child figure who had to go to work alone.

The 11 cases were randomly assigned to one of two treatments. Of the five clients seen in family therapy, all were able to return to work relatively comfortably. Of the six seen in individual therapy, the only one who returned to work was the client who had not been school phobic.

Structural Therapy

Salvador Minuchin (1922–   ) learned about the diversity and adaptability of families while growing up in a Jewish family in rural Argentina and while living in Israel, where families from all over the world converged to help build a new nation. He didn't learn about the power that families have over psychopathology, however, until the early 1960s when he was doing therapy and research with delinquent youths at the Wiltwyck School in New York. Minuchin had been trained as a psychiatrist in traditional psychotherapeutic techniques that were developed to fulfill the needs of verbally articulate, middle-class patients burdened by intrapsychic conflicts. The boys he was working with, however, were from disorganized, multiproblem, and poor families. Improvements achieved through the use of traditional techniques in the residential setting of the school tended to disappear as soon as the children returned to their families.

Minuchin and others were looking for more effective alternatives with delinquents at a time when psychotherapy was becoming liberated from its almost exclusive preoccupation with individual psychopathology. Family therapy emerged in the 1950s and was developing a new perspective on psychopathology. Minuchin and others at Wiltwyck began applying this perspective to *Families of the Slums* (Minuchin, Montalvo, Guerney, Rosman, & Schumer, 1967). Approaching delinquency as a family issue proved more helpful than defining it as a problem of the individual. But Minuchin and his colleagues recognized that they had not discovered a panacea for delinquency, since psychotherapy does not have the answers to poverty and other social problems (Malcolm, 1978).

In 1965 Minuchin became director of the Philadelphia Child Guidance Clinic, where he was able to develop structural family therapy with a wider cross-section of families. His approach had considerable impact with diabetic and asthmatic children who were having an unusually high rate of emotional stress-related emergency hospitalizations. Minuchin, however, knew he could not cure diabetes or asthma through family therapy, because these problems had a physical etiology. He believed that his model could best be tested with anorexia nervosa, because this condition of an individual not eating could be construed as entirely due to emotional factors (Minuchin, 1970). By working to change the structure of families, Minuchin demonstrated that he was able to cure more than 80 percent of children with anorexia nervosa, a syndrome that traditionally was attributed to individual psychopathology.

Theory of Psychopathology

Structural theory is more concerned with what maintains psychopathology rather than what causes psychopathology. By the time therapists see clients with symptoms, the causes of the problems are part of history. These historical causes frequently cannot be empirically determined and certainly cannot be changed. What can be changed are the contemporary factors that maintain psychopathology. Rather than being maintained by the intrapsychic dynamics of the individual, psychopathology is maintained by the interpersonal dynamics of the family. We should be focusing on pathological family structures rather than searching for pathological intrapsychic structures.

Pathological family systems can best be understood in contrast with healthy family systems (Minuchin, 1972). An appropriately organized family will have clearly marked boundaries. The marital subsystem will have closed boundaries to protect the privacy of the spouses. The parental subsystem will have clear boundaries between it and the children, but not so impenetrable as to limit the access necessary for good parenting. The sibling subsystem will have its own boundaries and will be organized hierarchally, so that children are given responsibilities and privileges consistent with age and gender as determined by the family's culture. Each family member is also an individual subsystem with a boundary that needs to be respected. Finally, the boundary around the nuclear family will also be respected, although the extent to which kin are allowed in varies greatly with cultural, social, and economic factors.

The boundaries of a subsystem are the rules defining who participates in the subsystem and how. The boundary of a parental subsystem is defined, for example, when a mother tells her older child, "You aren't your brother's parent. If he is playing with matches, tell me and I will stop him." Healthy development requires that subsystems in a family be relatively free from interference by other subsystems. For example, the development of skills for negotiating with peers, learned among siblings, requires noninterference from parents. Clear boundaries or rules help maintain freedom from outside interference.

The rules that govern transactions within a family, though not usually explicitly stated or recognized, form a whole—the structure of the family. In order for a family to change its structure, it must change some of its fundamental rules for interacting.

Two major types of family structures are pathological and need changing. The first is the disengaged family that has excessively rigid boundaries. In the disengaged family there is little or no contact between family members. There is a relative absence of healthy structure, order, or authority. Ties between family members are weak or nonexistent (Minuchin et al., 1967). The overall impression of this type of family is one of an atomistic field. Family members have long moments in which they move as in isolated orbits, unrelated to each other. The family is disconnected. The mother in this group tends to be passive and immobile. She feels overwhelmed, has a derogatory self-image, experiences herself as exploited, and almost always develops psychosomatic and depressive symptomatology. The children in such families are at risk of developing antisocial symptomatology.

The second type of troubled family is the enmeshed family that has diffuse boundaries. The most distinguishing quality of such families is a "tight interlocking" of its members. This quality of connectedness is such that attempts on the part of one member to change elicits fast complementary resistance on the part of others (Minuchin et al., 1967). Enmeshment is essentially a weakening of the boundaries that allow family subsystems to function. The boundary between nuclear family and families of origin is not well maintained, so in-law problems are likely to develop. The boundary separating the parents from their children is crossed frequently in improper ways, such as in incestuous families. The roles of spouse and parent are insufficiently differentiated so that neither the spouse subsystem nor the parental subsystem can operate. The children are not differentiated on the basis of age or instructional level, so that the sibling subsystem cannot contribute properly to the socialization process. Finally, individual boundaries are not respected, so that individual subsystems are not able to develop adequate autonomy and identity. An anorectic adolescent, for example, may be able to assert autonomy only by saying no to the family's demands to eat.

Families are open systems that continually face demands for change. The demands may come from changes in the larger environment, such as the death of a family friend. The demands may also come from developmental changes in the family, such as the birth of a baby or a child attaining adolescence. Healthy families respond to such demands for change by growth on the part of each individual in the family, each subsystem within the family, and the family as a unit. Dysfunctional families respond to demands for change in pathological ways, such as a mother in a disengaged family becoming more depressed or a child acting out. Usually one family member develops symptoms and becomes the identified patient, even though the basic problem is the family's inability to grow and adapt to change.

Theory of Therapeutic Processes

Since symptoms emerge and are maintained in family structures that are unable to adapt to environmental or developmental demands, the goal of therapy is to restructure families in order to free the members to grow and relate in nonpathological patterns. Since the structure of a family reflects the rules for interacting that govern a family, then changing a family's structure involves changing a family's rules for relating.

CONSCIOUSNESS RAISING

Minuchin (1974) shares a view of consciousness that is rather unique to systems theorists. Consciousness is not just an intracerebral process but also includes the extracerebral events that are occurring within the individual's context. Individuals think and feel and exist within social contexts, such as families, and the events they experience in the family are important aspects of consciousness. If the family context changes to a higher level of development, then the individual's consciousness will also be raised. Members of disengaged families, for example, are likely to perceive the social world as structured like an atomistic field, with disconnected people revolving in their individual orbits. To conceive of people as interrelated and interdependent is against the family rules. By participating in a family context that begins to change and become more engaged, the individual becomes mindful of how people are inherently related.

The Client's Work. The client's work in this process is relatively simple: to attend the family sessions and be attentive in the sessions; to give feedback to the therapist when asked about changes that might be desired;

and to perceive changes in relationship patterns as they occur in the family context. In a classic case with an anorectic girl, Minuchin (1974) asked the attentive adolescent about the family's rule against closed doors. Would she like to close her door in order to have more privacy? The girl gave feedback that indeed she would. She was thus helping the therapist to become more aware of the need to develop more clear boundaries around individual subsystems in this enmeshed family. By perceiving others in the family context beginning to close their doors, including the parents closing their bedroom door for the first time, the clients could begin to see how a family can function better by having better boundaries.

The Therapist's Work. In structural therapy, the therapist does much of the work. The therapist is active and directive. In order to direct actions in an appropriate way, however, the therapist must become conscious of the structure and the rules that govern a particular family. The therapist's attention is focused on the here and now, since family rules can best be perceived by observing who interacts with who and how. Some of this increased awareness the therapist shares overtly with clients, while other aspects are best perceived by changing the family context. The therapist will, for example, almost routinely reframe a presenting problem, so that the family members can become more conscious of how symptoms are system events rather than individual events. Minuchin (1974, p. 1) illustrates reframing in an opening session with Mr. Smith, who has been hospitalized twice for agitated depression, his wife, 12-year-old son, and father-in-law. Minuchin asks, "What is the problem?", and Mr. Smith says, "I think it's my problem." "Don't be so sure. Never be so sure," Minuchin says. "Well, I'm the one that was in the hospital," Mr. Smith responds. "Yeah, that still doesn't tell me it is your problem," says Minuchin. "Okay, go ahead. What is your problem?" Minuchin asks. "Just nervous, upset all the time . . . seem to be never relaxed," Mr. Smith responds. "Do you think you are the problem?" asks Minuchin. "Oh, I kind of think so. I don't know if it is caused by anybody, but I'm the one that has the problem," says Mr. Smith. "Let's follow your line of thinking. If it would be caused by somebody or something outside of yourself, what would you say your problem is?" asks Minuchin. "You know, I'd be very surprised," says Mr. Smith. "Let's think who in the family makes you upset?" asks Minuchin. "I don't think anybody in the family makes me upset," says Mr. Smith. "Let me ask your wife, Ok?" Minuchin replies.

Instead of focusing on the individual, Minuchin focuses on the person within his family context. He is beginning to help the family become aware of how symptoms are system issues rather than individual problems. Reframing the problem in this way will help the family members to raise their consciousness based on a strictly individualistic ideology to an awareness based on a systems perspective.

Frequently, reframing is used to interpret the role that symptoms play in maintaining homeostasis, or balance, within a family. With the parents of a girl who had been hospitalized for a psychotic break, Minuchin told the parents that he was concerned that when they return home with the daughter, she would go crazy again (Malcolm, 1978). The reason she would go crazy was to save their marriage. The psychotic symptoms then are interpreted as the means by which a good daughter can help her family stay together rather than as a weakness of a bad daughter who falls apart. Interpretations through reframing help each of the family members to become more aware of how symptoms are an integral part of the family's functioning.

The therapist will encourage a family to enact family transactions rather than to describe them. The therapist would give explicit directions, such as, "Discuss with your mother your curfew time and try to come to a decision." More dramatically the therapist may arrange an anorectic lunch and have food brought to the session so the family can enact how they dine with an anorectic in their midst. Enacting transactional patterns help family members to experience their own reactions with heightened awareness. Enactment also allows therapists to see family members in action, and it is through such observations that the therapist becomes aware of the family structure.

Choosing

Structural therapy is relatively unique in that it emphasizes the process that we have labeled *social liberation*. Social liberation is the process by which a social system is changed in such a way as to create more alternatives for responding. The more alternatives there are in a system the greater freedom individuals have to choose responses that are conducive to their own growth as healthy human beings. Structural therapists emphasize restructuring of family subsystems as the means by which subsystems in the family can be freer to respond and relate in healthier patterns. Families are liberated from rules of relating that foster pathology and are freer to create patterns of transaction that foster growth throughout the family system.

The Client's Work.   The client's commitment to help liberate the family system from pathogenic rules begins with a formal or informal contract to participate in therapy. The contract includes rules of how often the family will meet, who will attend, how long sessions will last, and the initial goals for therapy. Implicitly the family is also choosing to let an outsider, the therapist, join their system. Once therapy is underway, clients need to find the courage to try alternative ways of relating that the therapist recommends. Restructuring assignments in the session and for homework can produce stress, because the assignments transgress rules that have bound the family together. By cooperating with such assignments, however, the family members actively participate in creating a new set of rules that permit them to relate in a family that can foster growth rather than illness.

The Therapist's Work.   It would not be too farfetched to characterize the structural therapist as a freedom fighter committed to helping liberate a social system from patterns of relating that are destructive to members of the system. As with the freedom fighters of the 1960s, the first task is to join the system in order to change it from within. But that is no small task, because family systems have boundaries designed to exclude outsiders. The therapist must learn to speak the language of the family, such as learning the metaphors and idioms of the family. The therapist must also take care to join each of the subsystems in the family, lest the therapist be seen as the parents' agent or the children's agent. When joining with the parents, the therapist will speak the language of responsibility, but when joining the sibling subsystem, the therapist will speak the language of rights.

Like anthropologists who join new social systems, family therapists must initially accommodate themselves to the rules of the system. If the family is hierarchically structured across four generations, the therapist might address the great-grandmother first. This type of accommodation involves maintenance of the family subsystems through planned support of the family structure. The therapist also accommodates to the family through tracking the context of the family's communication and behavior, by asking questions for clarification, making approving statements, or asking for amplification of certain points. Another accommodation technique is *mimesis,* which involves imitating or miming important aspects of the family. In a jovial family, for example, the therapist becomes jovial; in a family with a restricted communication style, the therapist's communication becomes sparce.

Once the therapist and the family have joined, they have in fact created a new therapeutic system. The therapist is the leader of this system, as expressed through the therapist becoming more active and directive. The therapist's use of reframing, for example, communicates that the family will function at a systems level rather than focus on one identified patient. In the process of joining the family, the therapist would not be as confrontive, lest the therapist risk being excluded by powerful subsystems of the family. Once all parties are joined, however, the therapist can risk confronting and challenging the patterns and rules of the system.

Marking boundaries is one of the techniques the therapist uses to restructure the family. Like a good leader, the therapist has created a psychopolitical map of the family terrain. The therapist needs to have an accurate idea of who relates to who and how. Then the therapist can begin to give assignments that will redraw the boundaries along healthier lines. If mother and daughter relate like siblings, for example, the therapist may put mother in charge of the daughter's activities for a week. If the boundary that delineates an individual is not respected, the structural therapist may ask each person to think and speak only for her or himself. If a clear boundary does not exist around a couple who spend all their time parenting, the therapist may ask them to go away together for a weekend without children.

The therapist can keep the therapeutic system functioning at home by assigning tasks for homework. The mother who follows through on her homework of supervising her daughter's activities for a week is responding at home to the healthier therapeutic system rather than to the old rules of relating that defined mother and daughter as sisters.

The use of enactment in the sessions not only increases consciousness about current patterns of relating, but it also permits the therapist to change patterns of relating in the here and now. The therapist may, for example, use a blocking technique that breaks up the usual communication patterns. Daughter may be blocked from communicating to father via mother and may have to learn to relate to father directly. If mother and father consistently avoid clear boundaries around them by having a child sit between them, the therapist can block such transactions by directing the child to change seats with mother or father.

The therapist may use an exaggerated imitation of the family's actual style in order to point out a dysfunctional pattern. In a family with an overcontrolling mother who yells at her adolescent daughter, the therapist might yell louder. Manipulating such moods can force the mother to soften her interactions and thereby give the daughter more autonomy.

The therapist may also utilize symptoms to promote changes. Minuchin gives the example of a family where the apparent problem is the child's stealing. The stealing is interpreted as a reaction to ineffective control by the parental subsystem, and thus the child is instructed to steal from his father. This technique relocates the symptoms in an immediate situation that mobilizes the parents to set better controls (Minuchin, 1974).

By accommodating and joining and then confirming, blocking, and challenging the family's patterns of interacting, the therapist is liberating the family from destructive rules of relating. In the process of helping a family restructure itself, the therapist frees them from transactions that have created symptoms of psychopathology.

Theory of the Therapeutic Relationship

The structural therapist obviously has a rather unique way of relating to clients. The joining process would certainly include accurate empathy, warmth, and caring. But once a therapeutic system is created, the therapist clearly relates as an authoritative leader. The leader is like a psychopolitician who is advocating for the benefit of each of the family members against a social system that has developed a destructive structure. The therapist joins with each of the family subsystems to overthrow a set of rules that prevent the members from relating within and across clear and healthy boundaries. Without a therapeutic relationship based on joining techniques, the therapist would be impotent in trying to help families liberate themselves from enmeshed or disengaged transaction patterns. The relationship alone, however, cannot produce structural changes in family systems. The therapist must be willing to challenge, confront, and block and disrupt a homeostatic system. Only by using techniques that cause disequilibrium can the family therapist give troubled families greater freedom to restructure themselves along healthier lines.

Practicalities of Structural Therapy

The structure of therapy should be consistent with the current goals of therapy. If the goal is to observe how a family structures itself in space, then the whole family should be present. The room should be large and flexible enough to allow family members to initially sit wherever they choose, thereby revealing the family's rules for siblings. The therapist must also be flexible enough to restructure the seating as a means of restructuring the family. The practicalities of many therapies, such as the seating arrangements of clients, are part of the process of understanding and changing the structure of families.

If the therapist is trying to strengthen the boundaries of the spouse subsystem, then the therapist may request to see only the parents for a session or two. If a therapist is trying to restructure a multigenerational family, then it is most practical to have all generations present, rather than have the clients just talk about the grandparents. In practice, structural therapy has been used most often with families in which a child is the identified patient. Such families are usually more willing to come in as a full family than when one adult in the family is identified as the patient.

Structural therapy is generally designed to be a shorter-term therapy that initiates the processes that help families to become restructured. By releasing family members from their stereotyped positions, this restructuralization enables the system to mobilize its underutilized resources and to improve its ability to cope with stress and conflict. The structural therapist is encouraged to limit participation to the minimum necessary to set in motion the family's natural helping resources.

It may happen that as a result of the therapist's intervention the family is helped not only to change but also to metachange—that in addition to the overcoming of its current crisis, the family will also improve its ability to deal with future events without external help (Colapinto, 1982). This high level of achievement is of course desirable, but more modest and practical accomplishments are still valuable. Families may well need to come back for help at times of future crises. This prospect, however, is more practical, natural, and economic than the protracted presence of a therapist accompanying the family for years.

Effectiveness of Structural Therapy

During the 1970s, Minuchin and his colleagues published a series of clinical survey studies on four disorders in children: labile diabetes, anorexia nervosa, chronic asthma, and psychogenic abdominal pains. These surveys are generally accumulative, with later reports including cases from previous surveys. These surveys have the benefit of including relatively objective outcome measures.

In one of their most complete reports, they summarized information on 20 cases of labile diabetes (Rosman, Minuchin, Liebman, & Baker, 1978). These children, aged 10 to 18 years, suffered from an unusually high number of emergency hospitalizations for acidosis and/or instability in diabetic control. These problems failed to respond adequately to medical treatment or individual therapy and appeared to be related to stresses in the families of the children. The diabetic cases were in family therapy for periods ranging from 3 to 15 months, with a median of 8 months. They were followed up 2 to 9 years after treatment, with a median of 4½ years. At follow-up 88 percent of the children were judged to be recovered, meaning there were no hospital admissions for acidosis after treatment and/or diabetic control became stabilized within normal limits.

This same survey included outcome data on 53 anorectics, ranging in age from 9 to 21 (Rosman et al., 1978). Treatment lasted 2 to 16 months, with a median of 6 months; and follow-up was done between 1½ and 7 years, with a median of 2⅓ years. These children started treatment with a median weight loss of 30 percent. At follow-up, 86 percent of the children achieved normal eating patterns and a body weight stabilized within normal limits; 4 percent gained weight but showed signs of an eating disorder, such as borderline weight, obesity, and occasional vomiting; and 10 percent showed little or no change or relapsed.

In some reports (e.g., Minuchin, Baker, Rosman, Liebman, Milman, & Todd, 1975) it sounds as if these impressive effects with anorexia are due entirely to structural therapy. In other reports (e.g., Liebman, Minuchin, Baker, & Rosman, 1975), however, the treatment for anorexia nervosa is described as an integration of structural therapy and behavior modification. Contingency control processes are used in such a way that the anorectic children could earn activity privileges in the hospital or at home only by gaining weight. Because these are survey studies it is impossible to determine how much of the outcome is due to behavior therapy compared to structural therapy.

Rosman et al., (1978) also reported on 17 chronic asthmatics, suffering severe attacks with regular steroid therapy or an intractable condition with steroid dependency. The children, aged 7 to 17 years, were in therapy from 2 to 22 months, with a median of 8 months. Follow-up was completed one to seven years after treatment, with a median of three years. In 82 percent of the cases, recovery was achieved, meaning little or no school days lost, and moderate attacks with occasional or regular use of bronchodilator only. An additional 12 percent improved moderately, and 6 percent showed no improvement.

Once again reports are unclear as to whether these effects should be attributed to structural therapy (Minuchin et al., 1975) or to an integration of behavior therapy and structural therapy (Liebman, Minuchin, & Baker, 1974). Of course, the lack of placebo control groups, no-treatment groups, or an alternative family therapy make it even less clear as to what is producing these impressive results.

In the survey of 10 children suffering from psychogenic abdominal pain, treatment once again involved an integration of behavior therapy and structural therapy (Liebman, Horning, & Berger, 1976). There were seven boys and three girls, ranging in age from 6 to 14 years. All had been hospitalized at least once for medical evaluation and treatment. Therapy involving both individual and family sessions lasted from 5 to 11 months, with a median of 9 months. The treatment program was successful in enabling the patients to gain control of the abdominal pain and to develop more normal lifestyles manifested by normal school attendance, increased peer-group involvement, and increased physical activities. Two of the children had minor relapses and had to resume family therapy for one and two months.

In the only semicontrolled outcome study on structural therapy, Stanton and Todd (1979) compared different treatments with drug abusers. To qualify for family therapy, patients had to be males, under age 36, who were addicted to heroin for at least two years, and who continued to maintain contact with their families. Subjects and their families were randomly assigned to one of three family treatments: (1) paid family therapy ($n = 21$), in which each family member over age 12 was paid $5.00 for attending each structural therapy session, (2) unpaid structural therapy ($n = 25$), and (3) paid family movies treatment ($n = 19$), in which each member was paid to come in once a week for 10 weeks to view 10 different movies about people in different cultures. A nonfamily group ($n = 530$) did not qualify for the family treatments and received methadone and individual counseling.

Attempts were made to follow up each of the 118 experimental subjects 6 and 12 months after treatment. Outcome data included the number of days subjects were free from five different drugs, as well as employment and school records. There were no significant differences between the four groups on employment or school records. There were significant differences at the $p = .10$ level between the groups on days free from three of the five drugs. The nonfamily treatment group showed the fewest days drug-free. The paid family treatment group had the greatest attendance at therapy sessions and apparently had the most drug-free days following treatment. The term *apparently* is used since the significant differences seemed to be accounted for mainly by the greater drug use of the nonfamily treatment group. The size of this group makes significant differences more likely, but it must be remembered that this group was different to begin with rather than being randomly assigned.

BOWEN FAMILY SYSTEMS THERAPY

The audience was expecting Murray Bowen (1913–) to present a theoretical paper as part of a symposium at a professional convention. Instead Bowen (1972) presented a "convention shattering" procedure that he had used to change his own family of origin. Bowen was part of a large, extended kin group. His extended family had dominated a small Southern town for many generations. At the symposium in 1967, Bowen revealed how he had intruded into most of the dominant triangles of his immediate family by means of a surprising strategy. He sent off letters that told various relatives about the unpleasant gossip that others were circulating about them. He signed these letters with endearing salutations such as "Your Meddlesome Brother" or "Your Strategic Son." He also announced an impending visit.

Bowen then arrived as heralded, to deal with the predictably indignant reactions of his relatives. The effect on the family was dramatic. Many closed-off relationships were reopened. And once the initial fury against Bowen had subsided, his intervention created a warm climate of better feelings all around.

Bowen's intervention with his family of origin grew out of the family systems therapy he had been developing over the previous two decades. He had gone to Menninger's Clinic in Topeka, Kansas after serving as an Army physician in World War II. Like many of the early systems theorists he was particularly enthusiastic about trying to understand and treat schizophrenia. It was not new to conceptualize schizophrenia as having to do with an unresolved symbiosis between mother and child. It was a radical innovation in a psychoanalytic center like Menninger's, however, to actually bring the mother into the clinical picture as part of the investigation and treatment of schizophrenic patients.

His clinical work was followed by five years of family research, from 1954 to 1959, at the National Institute of Mental Health in Washington, D.C. Bowen began by having a small group of schizophrenic patients and their mothers live together on a hospital ward. After a year of individual therapy for both patients and mothers, fathers were included, and the family was treated as a single unit rather than treating individuals in the unit (Bowen, 1978).

After moving to the department of psychiatry at Georgetown University, Bowen (1978) completed detailed multigenerational research with a few families, including one case going back more than 300 years. Noting that one could spend a lifetime with only a few such family studies, Bowen made the seminal decision that his own family was most accessible for such a multigenerational study. From this study and the intervention with his own family, Bowen (1978) became convinced of the importance for both clients and therapists of differentiating themselves from their families of origin.

Theory of Psychopathology

Emotional illness arises when individuals are unable to adequately differentiate themselves from their families of origin. Differentiation of self is the ability to be emotionally controlled while remaining within the emotional intensity of one's family. Differentiation of self reflects the extent to which one can think objectively about emotionally loaded issues within the family. Fusion is the phenomenon that interferes with differentiation of self from family. Fusion refers to two aspects of immaturity. First, there is the fusion of feeling and thinking when objective thinking is overwhelmed by emotionality and becomes its servant. What results then is rationalization or intellectualization to justify the acting out of emotional immaturity. Fusion also refers to the absence of boundaries or the lack of individuality between two or more individuals, as in the case of symbiotic relationships.

Fusion in families results in an undifferentiated family-ego mass, which is a quality of "stuck togetherness." Fusion leads to a conglomerate emotional oneness that exists in all levels of intensity. The more threatened or insecure a family feels, the more they tend to fuse. The more stressed or distressed individuals feel, the more they seek the security of oneness that results from family fusion. Chronic distress can result in emotionally ill individuals who are unable to differentiate themselves from their family. They remain stuck forever in the family, and the family is stuck around them.

Fusion between any two people, such as a husband and wife, operates in such a way as to relieve tension by involving vulnerable third parties who take sides. Fusion thus gives rise to triangles. In marital conflicts the most common triangles lead to in-law problems, affairs, or child problems. Dyads are inherently unstable because they inevitably result in periods of insensitivity, abrasiveness, or withdrawal. The party who feels offended or rejected will attempt to triangle a parent, child, neighbor, or lover for support. Triangles are much more stable relationships. Triangles are the basic building blocks in any emotional system. Triangles can make differentiation from the family difficult because the parents need a child to maintain a stable system or because a child needs a parent for support against others. Families are made up of a series of interlocking triangles.

Triangles in a state of calm consist of a comfortable twosome and an outsider. One of the classic triangles of this type are the close mother and child with a passive, withdrawn father. The favored position is to be a member of the close twosome rather than be the odd one out. When tension mounts in the outsider, the predictable move is to try to form a twosome with one of the orignal members of the twosome, leaving the other one as an outsider. So the focuses within the triangle shift and move from moment to moment and over long periods of time. Each member is jockeying for a comfortable position. So if father tries to get close to his child, the mother is likely to react with upset, lest she be the odd one out.

When the triangle is in a state of tension, the outsider position becomes the preferred position. From this comfortable position the person can say, "You two fight and leave me out of it." In a state of tension, if it is not possible for the triangle to conveniently shift the focus within the triangle, two members of the original twosome will form another triangle with a convenient family person, such as another child. In periods of very high tension, a system will triangle in more and more outsiders. A common example is a family in crisis that uses the triangle system to involve neighbors, schools, police, and therapists as participants in the family problem. If the family is successful in getting others involved, then they can go back to a more comfortable homeostasis and let the outsiders fight.

Rather than resolve triangles through self-differentiation, most people use emotional cut-off mechanisms to cope with their unresolved attachments to their parents. The cut-off consists of denial and isolation of the problems when living close to the parents, or by physically running away, or a combination of the two. Whatever the pattern, the person yearns for emotional closeness but is allergic to it. People who use intrapsychic mechanisms to enable them to live closer to their parents generally function better. Those who put physical distance between self and parents tend to blame parents and act out immaturity impulsively in relationships. When problems develop in their own marriage or nuclear family, they tend to run from these as well. The emotional cut-offs keep triangles intact and block further differentiation, so that the more severe the cut-offs, the more severe pathology is likely to develop in new relationships.

Triangles tend to occur across generations, since a parent or child is often the most available and vulnerable person to be brought into a marital conflict. If a wife is experiencing considerable discomfort about her marriage, she can regain homeostasis or balance in her marriage by projecting her anxieties onto a child. A family projection process pulls the parents together by becoming preoccupied with a child's problem. The child who is most vulnerable to such projection is the child who is emotionally closest or most fused with the parents. This child will tend to be the person who develops symptoms for the family. This child will also have little chance of differentiating an adequate self, since the family needs a child to maintain homeostasis in the parents' relationship. If the child becomes unstuck and matures through the help of therapy, for example, then the parents' marriage will be at risk of falling apart.

Because triangles typically occur across generations, severe psychopathology can develop from a *multigenerational transmission process*. Because of having been triangled, a child can emerge from a family with a lower level of self-differentiation. This child is likely to marry someone of a similar differentiation level. Their children are likely to have even lower levels of differentiation. Finally, after several generations, a child can emerge who has such a low level of differentiation that a severe pathology,like schizophrenia, is almost inevitable. Rather than being an individual process, psychopathology is almost always a multigenerational transmission process.

Theory of Therapeutic Processes

Since emotional illnesses arise from an inadequate differentiation of self from the family emotional system, the goal of therapy is to increase differentiation of self. Since triangles are the phenomenon that interfere with differentiation of self, successful therapy will need to involve detriangulation of family members. Rather than have to work on all possible triangles in a family, the therapist has the advantage of knowing that a family is a system of interlocking triangles. Thus, if change can be produced in one triangle, it will cause change in all the triangles.

Since a nuclear family is formed as the result of the fusion of a husband and wife, they are the most important members who need to increase their differentiation of self, even if it is a child who is manifesting symptoms for the family. Bowen (1978) prefers then to work with the marital subsystem rather than to have the children present in therapy. Bowen, however, indicates that therapy can be successful just by working with one individual member who is motivated to mature. When there is finally one member of a troubled triangle who can control his or her emotional responsiveness, not take sides with the other two, and still stay in constant contact with the other two, the emotional intensity within the twosome will decrease and both will move to a higher level of differentiation. Unless the triangle person can remain in emotional contact, the twosome will triangle in someone else. By helping just one member to become more differentiated and detriangled, a therapist can help an entire family system to change.

CONSCIOUSNESS RAISING

The Client's Work.   Differentiation of self involves the ability to think ojectively about emotionally loaded issues in the family. Clients can begin to think more objectively about themselves and their families by developing more profoundly the powers of observation. Observation involves the ability to step back from an emotional interaction and perceive the events from an emotional distance. Observation helps control automatic and autonomic reactions.

When two or more members of a family system are present, such as spouses, the work of each client is to observe what the other person is communicating to the spouse. Observation can allow clients to become more objectively aware of what others are communicating rather than being busy building an emotional rejoinder. Even clients working alone can learn to use these same powers of observation as part of their homework. When they are home, their work is to observe the role they play in family triangles and to observe the typical emotional reactions they make in each triangle. Observation not only leads to an objective perspective but it also leads to the development of a unique perspective that is different from the perspective of family members who are too caught up in the family drama to see themselves and others clearly.

The Therapist's Work.   When two or more family members are present, the therapist's work includes keeping the emotional system sufficiently toned down to allow clients to process issues objectively without undue emotional reactions. The therapist is active with constant questions, first to one spouse and then to the other. The therapist will then ask the listening client to share his or her thoughts and observations about what was just communicated. Encouraging spouses to communicate directly to each other will just encourage them to react emotionally rather than objectively to each other.

The therapist also uses education to teach clients about how family systems function and dysfunction. This education begins by helping clients become more aware of each other's family history and the role each client played in the history of their family of origin. Often the therapist will create a genogram that illustrates the relationships of family members across three generations. The genogram will illustrate which family members were close, which were cut-off, and which were conflicted. This genogram can then be used to teach clients about triangles and how they interfere with differentiation of a more autonomous self.

Observations will be emphasized by the therapist as a means of teaching clients to be more objective. The therapist may observe, for example, that the husband is trying to convince the therapist that the husband is right and the wife is wrong. Such observations help both the therapist and the clients to become more conscious of how the spouses are trying to triangle the therapist into their relationship.

Family system therapists emphasize observations rather than interpretations as the means to a more objective and differentiated level of consciousness. Interpretations are directed more at the "why" of family interactions. Why people act the way they do is not open to direct observation, and interpretations about the motives of others tend to be subjective and more emotional. Observations focus on the who, what, when, and where of family relationships, which are more objective facts of the family.

CHOOSING

The Client's Work. Clients can liberate self from the family system by choosing to respond in a more autonomous fashion. Autonomy involves responding from an "I" position rather than reacting from a "We" position. The "I" position is developed in part from what "I" observe to be factual rather than what "We" as a family know to be true. It takes courage, however, to choose to respond differently from the family ideology; because the individual risks the wrath or rejection of family members, just as Bowen risked the fury of his family when he chose to respond differently.

Choosing to respond autonomously does not mean returning to the family of origin and blaming one's parents or siblings for personal problems. Such blaming is just another emotional reaction to the family system that will stimulate the blamed relative to triangle a third party for support. Autonomous responding is not intended to blame or to change the other person. The differentiating person chooses the "I" position to communicate "This is what I think or believe" and "This is what I will do or not do" without imposing my values or beliefs onto other family members. It is the "responsible I" which assumes responsibility for one's own experiences and comfort and leaves emotional and intellectual space for others to create their own happiness. A reasonably differentiated person is capable of genuine concern for others without expecting something in return. The togetherness forces of family fusion, however, treat differentiation as selfish and hostile.

The person who chooses to be different in significant ways from their family must be willing to respond reasonably rather than react emotionally to the predictable forces against differentiation. The predictable steps in the family reaction to differentiation are: (1) "You are wrong," (2) "Change back," or (3) "If you do not, you will be criticized, ostracized, or be guilty for driving your parent or partner crazy."

The Therapist's Work. The therapist's task is to respond autonomously to family forces rather than to react emotionally. The therapist chooses to remain differentiated rather than be triangled into the family system. The therapist is differentiated enough to respond reasonably to clients' attempts to make the therapist feel guilty, angry, anxious, or overresponsible. The therapist responds from a well-differentiated "I" position rather than a "We" or a "You" position.

When clients are ready to risk more autonomous responses in their families of origin, the therapist will function more like a coach or consultant. The therapist will help the client to clarify that the goal in such responding is to differentiate oneself, not to blame or change others. The goal is not to win in a confrontation or to impose an interpretation but simply to enhance one's differentiation. The clients can be reminded that they can choose to respond differently in their family regardless of whether others change or not. Responding differently can indeed liberate relatives to change; but that is their responsibility, not the client's. Like a good coach, the therapist will check on the progress clients have made between sessions in their relationships to their family of origin.

Theory of the Therapeutic Relationship

The therapeutic relationship is important as much for what the therapist does not do as for what the therapist does. Effective therapists do not allow themselves to be triangled into family relationships. Even though spouses will, for example, use all types of conscious and nonconscious maneuvers to triangle the therapist into reacting emotionally, the differentiated therapist consciously chooses to respond reasonably. Unlike some family therapists who dive right into the family system to create strong emotional transference reactions, the Bowenian therapist prevents a transference reaction by maintaining an objective "I" position. Entering a triangled relationship with spouses may indeed allow them to reestablish a homeostasis that removes symptoms, but it does nothing to help them establish differentiated selves that can prevent future symptoms.

By maintaining an "I" position the therapist does relate in a genuine manner, which allows clients to differentiate their own beliefs and actions from the therapist's. The therapist relates in a calm, relaxed, and interested style that communicates caring without trying to establish the unconditional positive regard that is more conducive to family fusion than self-differentiation. Finally, the Bowenian therapist would rely more on the powers of observation and objective thought rather than empathy for trying to understand what is going on in troubled families.

Practicalities of Bowen Family Systems Therapy

Bowen's family therapy is much more flexible than some system theories that insist on having all family members present. Actually, the more family members present the more difficult it is to detriangle the parents, since the energy and emotions can shift from one triangled child to the next. Thus, Bowen (1978) himself prefers to work with the spouses or with one motivated parent rather than with the children present. Other Bowenian therapists, however, will work with entire families as part of their practice. Robert Aylmer (1978), the past president of the Society for Family Therapy, estimates that about 25 percent of his family practice is with entire families, 25 percent with spouses, and 50 percent with individuals.

Family system therapists will usually see clients once a week for 45 to 60 minutes at the beginning of therapy. Once clients have become more conscious of their family's functioning and their role in the family, sessions will shift to alternate weeks or even monthly sessions. Spacing of sessions allows clients more adequate time for doing their homework of observing their family of origin and responding autonomously rather than reacting emotionally while in the context of their family. Differentiation of self is a process that takes years before people can become more autonomous adults in the presence of their parents. Therapy can certainly facilitate this process. It is recognized, however, that many clients are seeking just relief from symptoms rather than differentiation of a self. Therapy will thus be briefer with many clients but will take several years of well-spaced sessions to complete a genuine growth process. Because it is critical for therapists to avoid becoming triangulated by the togetherness forces within emotional systems, it is important for Bowenian therapists to participate in personal therapy designed to differentiate themselves more fully from their family of origin.

Effectiveness of Bowen Family Systems Therapy

In an evaluation of family systems therapy, Singleton (1982) reports that there were no controlled outcome studies on Bowen's approach to treatment. Singleton did report that a controlled study was to be completed in 1981 comparing Bowen's therapy, Haley's approach, Satir's approach, and a control group. Unfortunately, as of 1983, data were still not available from this study.

CRITICISMS OF SYSTEMS THERAPIES

From a Psychoanalytic Perspective

Structural therapy is another in a long series of attempts to construct simple solutions for complex problems. It is simplistic, for example, to assume that all of psychopathology is maintained by structured relationships in current family living. What about more severely disturbed adults, like many borderline personalities, who are living alone? What is the structural therapist going to do for a person who needs help in developing relationships, not restructuring relationships? Remember that the large majority of clients seek individual psychotherapy (Norcross & Prochaska, 1982; Prochaska & Norcross, 1983). What is structural therapy going to offer to the majority of clients? There are only so many ways that therapist and client can restructure their seating arrangements. What structural relationships is the therapist going to observe, map, and rearrange with individual clients?

Simplistic also is the assumption that there is a normative model for healthy family functioning that transcends all class, cultural, and ethnic differences. In a pluralistic society like the United States it is a constant struggle to help people appreciate that there is richness and strength in diversity, including diversity of family forms. After an intensive study of healthy families, the investigator decided to title his book, *No Single Thread* (Lewis, 1976), implying that he found no single structure in the ways these families functioned. Minuchin, nevertheless, would hold on to an Ozzie and Harriet model of the family that includes well-bonded spouses and parental, sibling, and individual subsystems. What about the large number of single-parent families in our society or the increasing number of child-free families (Prochaska & Coyle, 1979)? Are these alternative family forms going to be stereotyped as abnormal?

How comforting it must be to believe that the history of the family, the developmental history of the clients, and the internal processes of patients can simply be ignored. Just join the family and let the action begin. But the family never gets to become aware of how problems developed. Nor are they necessarily likely to understand how the problems disappeared. All that is clear is that they were joined by a benign parent figure who rearranged the furniture and used metaphors about open and closed doors to settle boundary disputes. It certainly can shake things up and probably even help. But what happens when the family faces its next developmental crisis? There has been no systematic attempt to help the family gain insight into either the causes or the cures of their problems. No wonder the family is likely to have to return for more restructuring (or is it reparenting) from an all-knowing therapist.

From a Behavioral Perspective

Bowen is pouring old wine into new bottles. The old wine is his psychoanalytic heritage, and the new bottles are multigenerational families. Key concepts have such a Freudian flavor. Differentiation of self from family fusion sounds like differentiation of ego from id. The goal of having intellect control emotions is like the goal of having the ego control the id. Triangles are seen as the source of psychopathology. This sounds similar to the oedipal conflict being the key to psychopathology, with mother, father, and child in conflict over each other. No wonder psychoanalytic theorists, like Meissner (1978), claim Bowen as one of their own.

In therapy, Bowen is prepared to continue the same type of archeological expedition that psychoanalysis favors. Psychoanalytic therapists, however, would only take the patient back to birth, while Bowen is prepared to dig back for generations for further clues to contemporary problems. Unlike communication and structural therapists, Bowenian family system therapists don't stop when symptoms go away. They continue to restructure multigenerational relationships in search of an autonomous self, just as psychoanalysts restructure the psychic in search of an automonous ego.

Like psychoanalysts, Bowenian therapists cannot serve as objective guides for such archeological expeditions unless they have also undergone the almost interminable training process of differentiating self from family of origin. Lest therapists be at risk of becoming triangulated in therapy (acting out the countertransference?), they need to undergo intensive therapy themselves.

Bowen tries to bridge two theoretical perspectives, psychoanalysis and systems therapy, without appreciating that neither theory has a solid foundation in scientific research. The result is a shaky structure that has not undergone the rigorous tests of controlled experimentation. The result is also a theory that is shaky as to whether it is grounded in principals and practices of individuals or of systems. Look, for example, at how Bowen prefers to work with individuals instead of having the whole family present. Even when Bowen works with couples, he doesn't focus on their communications or structural relationships but rather has each spouse communicate individually to the therapist. Furthermore, how can a true systems theorist believe in an autonomous self? Systems theorists are determinists who assume that an individual component is defined and controlled by the organized system of which it is a part. Bowen's thesis would seem to throw systems theory for a loop. Instead of the whole being greater than the sum of the individual parts, Bowen would have us believe that an individual can be greater and stronger than the sum of the whole family's forces.

From a Humanistic Perspective

Communication therapists present us with too many paradoxes. First, they create a theory based on how systems stay the same. Then, they recommend this theory to help people change. Concepts about wholes, hierarchies, homeostasis, and feedback loops explain how systems maintain a stable relationship, not how they change. This theory teaches therapists to expect resistance and encourages pessimism about the potential that families have for change. So families have to be tricked into changing rather than being treated responsibly. Parodoxically it may be the therapist's technique that encourages resistance rather than the system's rules. Who wouldn't resist being treated like God, being told to deliberately wet their bed, or having their complaints reduced to absurdities? Such therapists can produce the very resistance they have been taught to expect. When such tricks work, the therapist is so clever; when they fail, the family is at fault.

Why should we believe that marital and family systems are so stable, when marriages are breaking up at a unprecedented pace (Prochaska & Prochaska, 1978)? This theory may have been appropriate to the stable 50s but not the rapidly changing 80s. Change is the norm today, not stability. Future shock includes distress from two much change and too little stability in our social systems (Toffler, 1970). Do contemporary families need to be disrupted further, or do they need help in developing greater stability?

Do individuals matter in these families, or are they just mindless elements controlled by the rules of the system? But who is responsible for these rules—the system or the individuals in the system? And who will be responsible for changing the rules? Haley (1973) recognizes this paradox, but unfortunately he ends up advocating power to the therapist rather than power to the people in the system. In power struggles, processes of change don't matter, just the outcome—does the therapist win the struggle? This ethos sounds dangerously close to the ends justifying the means. But how else can you justify using such manipulative techniques as prescribing symptoms, placing patients in double binds, and reducing their complaints to absurdities? These techniques can make for good theater of the absurd, but they fail to create a humane system for the troubled individuals, couples, and families of our day.

From an Eclectic Perspective

Systems therapies can be very useful as long as they are kept within reasonable bounds. Communication therapists have, for example, created paradoxical interventions that can prove useful with highly resistant individuals, couples, or families. But there is no reason to assume that most clients cannot cooperate in therapy. Look, for example, at how cooperative Minuchin's families seemed to be with his restructuring techniques. Structural therapy lacks an adequate theory and technique for dealing with intense resistance but would appear to be helpful with families motivated to help a child in crisis with psychosomatic stress or anorexia. Bowenian therapy, on the other hand, would seem better suited for young adults who are experiencing problems in the process of separating from their families of origin. Within such bounds systems therapies can become part of the repertoire of a more comprehensive approach to change.

Systems therapies are out of bounds, however, when they try to construe every problem as a systems problem. It is true that, in some cases, improvement in one family member can be accompanied by a worsening in another family member. It is probably even more often the case that when one family member recovers from alcoholism, anxiety, depression, or other forms of psychopathology, the whole family system improves. Just as the spector of symptom substitution threatened therapists for generations, systems therapists would make us believe that patient substitution is the rule rather than the exception. Patient substitution occurs when symptoms shift from one family member to another. But there is no research to suggest that patient substitution is any more frequent than the old dread of symptom substitution.

A SYSTEMS ANALYSIS OF THE C. FAMILY

For six years individually oriented therapists attempted to treat Mrs. C. out of context. Mrs. C. was treated as an isolated event, even to the extent of being removed from the family for a year in a mental hospital. Blinded by the traditional ideological perspective that views psychopathology as an individual event, past therapists and theorists were unable to see how her symptoms were developed and maintained in a pathological family system.

The marital subsystem, for example, is characterized by a complementary relationship in which Mrs. C. speaks or acts and Mr. C. reacts. The entire family is skewed in the direction of Mrs. C.'s symptoms. Her obsession with cleanliness dominates the family's rules for relating. It is not surprising that Mrs. C.'s family of origin was skewed in the direction of her domineering father.

The family system is also characterized by enmeshment. Unclear boundaries abound, as Mrs. C. runs around with bare breasts in front of her teenage sons. The children have no space in their own home into which they can invite their friends. The boundaries between Mr. and Mrs. C. are lost when he partici-pates in the washing rituals. Mr. C. arises at 5:00 A.M. to yell out, "Right arm, Martha; Left arm, Martha." And yet only Mrs. C. has been identified as a pa-tient. Folie a deux! The entire family lets silverware and underwear lay around the house until it looks like a state dump. Yet only Mrs. C. is going to be dumped in the state hospital. Folie a family!

What threatened this family to the extent that it could regain balance only by the development of puzzling and pathological behaviors? The family history suggests that the family health care system was threatened by a runaway of pinworms, Asian flu, and a sixth pregnancy. Apparently the family was unable to grow and adapt to the changes imposed by this crisis. The family physician prescribed washing, and Mrs. C. washed and washed until she became the identified patient. But were other family members able to grow to help meet the tremendous demands on the family? Was Mr. C., for example, able to grow into a more complete parent to help with the burdens of five children, illness, and an infestation of pinworms?

The boundaries of this enmeshed family were becoming too permeable. The boundaries had already been permeated by pinworms and a foreign influ-enza. The systems' preoccupation with cleanliness seemed to communicate a need to establish more clear boundaries. Mrs. C., for example, was becoming entirely enmeshed in her children's health and hygienic concerns, just as her father had been enmeshed in her personal concerns. In a desperate attempt to clarify her personal boundaries, Mrs. C. would scrub her skin; Mrs. C. was trying to keep clean the skin which defines the physical boundaries of herself as an individual.

The C. family became organized around a set of compulsive rules for relat-ing. Perhaps because there were so many children in the family already, these rules forbid any neighbor children from crossing the literal boundaries of the home. Mr. and Mrs. C. were able to relate as a couple in the intimacy of their bedroom primarily around the compulsive shower. The shower also set limits on Mrs. C.'s availability for relating to her children in the morning. She also set limits on her concerns by communicating only about their health and hygiene and not about friends and feelings.

For 10 years the compulsive rules for relating served to cleanse and clarify many of the boundaries in the family. With the older children entering adoles-cence and adulthood, however, these rules were perhaps too rigid and con-strictive to respond to the children's increasing needs for autonomy, intimacy, and privacy. In trying to restructure itself, the family was threatening to remove Mrs. C. from the boundaries of the home. She, in return, threatened suicide.

The C. family is clearly in need of an authoritative agent from outside the system who can join with the family to help them restructure their communica-tion patterns and rules for relating. The entire family should be seen, including Mrs. C.'s parents, if necessary. The therapist would first have to join with each of the subsystems in the family. With the children, the therapist would speak the language of greater autonomy and responsibility. The therapist might help the children to communicate a goal of being able to invite a friend to visit within the bounds of their own room. The therapist would help open new areas of communicating, such as rules about dating, curfews, and working outside the home.

Once the therapist had joined the family to create a new therapeutic system, then the therapist would begin to liberate the family from dysfunctional rules and structures by producing disequilibrium. Of course, there is no rigid way of restructuring a family system. A rigid set of rules for relating in therapy could present the paradox of substituting one compulsive set of rules for another. The therapist would want to relate in a flexible manner, responding more freely to pathological communications or structures than the family members respond. If the family insists on defining the problem as Mrs. C.'s problem, for example, the therapist will be able to reframe the compulsive symptoms into systems language. The compulsive rules of cleanliness can be reframed as an expression of the family's desire to stay healthy together. Reframing the symptoms can produce cognitive disequilibrium that helps the family become more aware of how the symptoms have served the family.

The therapist can help liberate the family from compulsive rules by prescribing alternative ways of relating both in the sessions and at home. If Mrs. C., for example, keeps her physical distance from her children in the sessions, the therapist may take a younger child's hand and say, "Come on, let's give Mama a big hug to show her we love her." As part of the concern about staying healthy together, the therapist may give the parents a homework assignment to spend one evening together, cooking their children a big healthy meal. This assignment could help to create better boundaries around the parents and could help the children to perceive them as more equal rather than complementary.

If the family proves to be particularly resistant to restructuring, the systems therapist can always call on paradoxical techniques for liberating the family. The therapist may prescribe the symptom. The therapist may prescribe a two hour shower in the morning. The rationale would be that the shower is one of the best ways that Mrs. C. has for communicating her concern for staying clean for the good of her family. Also, the morning shower is one of the best ways that Mr. C. has for showing his concern for his wife. Since the shower is one of the best ways they have for cooperating together as a couple, a long, leisurely, and warm shower is just what the doctor ordered. Of course, prescribing a long morning shower would serve as a therapeutic double bind. This assignment would give Mr. and Mrs. C. two choices: to cooperate or not to cooperate with the assignment. If they choose to cooperate, then they are choosing to carry out their symptoms. The symptoms would no longer be out of control, since they would no longer have the experience of "I can't help it," "I must wash," or "I must keep track of my wife's washing." If they choose not to cooperate, then they are choosing to not carry out their symptomatic behavior. Either way they begin to liberate themselves from a pathologically structured way of relating.

COMPARATIVE CONCLUSIONS: TOWARD A TRANSTHEORETICAL THERAPY

AFTER SURVEYING such a diverse and conflicted discipline as psychotherapy, we are even more acutely confronted with the dilemma of how to choose what type of therapist we might become or what type of therapist we might consult. What further structure can we give to such a fragmented discipline?

We must realize that the way we structure the field of psychotherapy cannot at this time be a function of data that indicate what system or systems of therapy are superior. Nor can a rational analysis of the diversity of theories provide the answer. Yet students should strive to impose some structure on this diversity, lest they be left with total confusion. At this stage in development of knowledge, we should realize that the structure we impose on the diversity of therapy theories is in large part a function of the level of our own intellectual and ethical development.

DEVELOPMENTAL STAGES

As William Perry (1970) has so clearly articulated, given the pluralistic nature of knowledge, educated individuals will attempt to structure knowledge according to the particular forms and structures that characterize their current level of cognitive development. Let us examine Perry's model of intellectual and ethical development to see how it applies to the personal view that we are likely to take toward the diverse theories of psychotherapy.

Based upon longitudinal research on the development of Harvard undergraduates, Perry (1970) derived a cognitive stage theory of intellectual and ethical development. He identified nine different stages, each representing a qualitatively different mode of thinking about the nature of knowledge. Since several of Perry's stages are primarily transitional, we shall focus on only the four stages that represent the most contrasting structures that students impose onto knowledge. The diagram below represents these four stages of intellectual and ethical development:

DUALISTIC→MULTIPLISTIC→RELATIVISTIC→COMMITTED

Dualists

In the dualistic stage the world is seen in such polar terms as right-wrong, truth-error, good-bad. Right answers are assumed to exist for everything, and it is assumed that an authority in a field can provide the correct answer. Dualistic students are likely to expect that in this final chapter the author as authority will reveal which theory of therapy is correct. Dualistic students view themselves as receptacles eagerly waiting to receive the truth about therapy.

Dualistic therapists believe they have had the truth revealed to them. Dualistic therapists are the *true believers* among us who think that a particular system of therapy is correct and all others are in error. Data are of little concern since the true system of therapy is already assumed to be known and data would only document the obvious.

Dualistic therapists can be found in any system of psychotherapy. True-believing analysts, behaviorists, humanists, or eclectics are the result not of the structure of the system in which they believe, but rather of the structure of their own intellects.

Multiplistic Thinkers

As students develop they come to accept that diversity and uncertainty in an area such as psychotherapy do exist. At first such diversity is seen as unwarranted confusion that comes from poorly qualified authorities. "Psychotherapists or psychologists don't know what the hell they're doing," may be a common complaint of such students. Later, diversity and uncertainty are seen as legitimate. In the later multiplistic stage such diversity and uncertainty is seen as only a temporary level in the development of our knowledge about psychotherapy. The multiplistic therapist thinks that at some point in the future a particular theory of therapy will be proved correct. The multiplistic therapist is a *true bettor* who is convinced that betting his or her energies on a particular therapy will pay off in the future when that particular system is proven to be correct.

Relativists

Students in the relativistic stage of intellectual development view knowledge as disconnected from the concept of truth and absolute correctness. Diversity and uncertainty are not temporary. The very nature of knowledge is that it is contextual and relative. The truth about therapy is that it is pluralistic with a variety of valid alternatives. The relativistic therapist is the *true eclectic*. The validity of any particular system of therapy is relative to some particular issues. Some eclectics see the form of therapy as being relative to the particular problems or symptoms that patients have. Other therapists see the validity of therapy systems as relative to the personality of patients, while others assume that the value of any therapy is relative to the personality of the therapist. The system of choice for such eclectics is to pick the system of therapy that best fits their personality. Other eclectics see the choice of therapy as relative to the values of clients, so that a therapy should be selected to best match the clients' values.

Given the relativistic nature of knowledge, the eclectic thinks that no one theory of therapy will ever be found to be the best or the most correct. Some developing therapists find the relativism of therapy to be tremendously disconcerting. The old guidelines of right-wrong and true-false are lost, and the developing therapist can be faced with an alienating experience of being lost and alone in a chaotic world of psychotherapy. Such therapists are usually judged to have a low tolerance for ambiguity, although more accurately they have a low tolerance for relativity. Given the existential anguish that can come from such a sense of alienation, the developing therapist can retreat or escape to the more secure stages of dualism or multiplicity.

While the relativism of eclecticism is a highly respectable, scholarly position, the problem is that the therapist is an activist, not only a scholar. Seeking to match symptoms with systems or personalities with psychotherapies is truly an important task of our time. But what does the relativistic therapist do when confronted with a particular patient in need of assistance? The data are not in on which therapies work best with which types of problems or patients, except perhaps that desensitization is the therapy of choice for isolated phobias (Luborsky, Singer, & Luborsky, 1975). For now the eclectic is left with acting on the basis of clinical folklore, much of which might well be fact but some of which is surely folly. For now we have inadequate data for distinguishing fact from folly.

The true eclectic is still confronted with the issue of deciding which of the available forms of treatment should be mastered. Thorne (1973), for one, advocates that the true eclectic is one who is skilled in all available forms of therapeutic intervention. He argues that only such highly skilled and experienced clinicians have the basis for making clinical judgments that will indeed be therapeutic for clients.

Given the knowledge explosion in the therapeutic domain, does anyone seriously believe that any therapist can expect to master all the available theories and techniques of psychotherapy? Many therapists who reach the stage of intellectual relativism begin to apprehend the necessity of becoming oriented in a relativistic world through some form of personal commitment.

Ethical Therapists

The dilemma for the ethical therapist is how to maintain intellectual integrity while making a commitment to a personal approach without the availability of adequate data. Realizing that the data are not in and that there is no consensus on a paradigm for studying or doing therapy, the individual therapist is free to make a commitment to a system of therapy that is based on an ethical position, a position of values. The ethical therapist moves beyond the realm of knowing to the realm of acting or being by affirming, "This is the approach to humanity that I would love to see valid, and I commit myself to trying to validate it." An ethical commitment brings with it a passion to master the particular approach, to improve it, and to evaluate it.

The ethical therapist is not a dogmatic absolutist. The commitment flows out of an undeniable relativism, and the ethical therapist maintains a humility that comes with knowing that other systems of therapy may be equally valid for other individuals. The ethical therapist is prepared then to refer clients to other approaches when it is apparent that the client is not going to make a commitment to the therapist's most valued alternative. In contrast, the dualistic therapist will work to convert the client in the name of truth and righteousness and all that is good.

The ethical therapist is aware that therapy is currently a question of values because there are inadequate data on which to make most therapeutic decisions. Whether therapy is fundamentally a question of values depends on whether or not intellectual relativism can be transcended by data or by higher-order theorizing.

Ethical therapists form a community of committed professionals who realize that at this point in our intellectual development the questions we share are more important than the answers we give. That is, an ethical therapist is centrally concerned with questions of what is the best way to be in therapy; what is the most valuable model we can provide for our clients, our colleagues, and our students; and how we can help our clients attain a better life. As intellectual relativists we know can we give no absolute answers to such questions. We value the fact that other colleagues are committed to actualizing other alternatives that we have given up for our personal values.

The problem for therapists is that we are committed to both knowing and doing. If we were pure scholars we could remain at the stage of intellectual relativism and share the sense of virtue of those who serve who only stand and wait. Our commitment to act, however, takes us beyond the realm of what is known and into the realm of ethical being—the realm of doing therapy on the basis of a commitment to what we believe is the most helpful way to be.

THE TRANSTHEORETICAL APPROACH

A transtheoretical therapist is one who strives to go beyond the relativism of eclecticism though a commitment to creating a higher-order theory of therapy. Transtheoretical therapists make an epistemological commitment more than an ethical commitment. Such a commitment is based on the belief that the current relativism can be transcended by discovery or creation of concepts and processes that cut across or transcend present theories of therapy. Obviously this book is committed to moving toward such a transtheoretical position.

The following are some suggestions for possible directions for those involved in transtheoretical thinking. After surveying what outstanding theoreticians have suggested is the essence of therapeutic change, we can begin to summarize their positions to determine where the major therapies converge and where they diverge. We have suggested in this book that the major systems of therapy diverge much more in terms of the content that is focused upon rather than the processes that are used to change content. Divergences in content are a function of the multitude of personality theories that are currently available rather than of a multitude of change processes that are the essence of the therapeutic endeavor.

A summary of the change processes advocated by the various theories of therapy begins to show more convergence than would appear when we are distracted by the content of therapy. Table 5 presents a summary of where each of the major therapeutic systems fits within the model of change that we have been using throughout this book.

One thing that becomes quickly apparent from Table 5 is that the change process that has yielded the greatest agreement is consciousness raising. Compared with other processes of change, three times as many therapies include an increase in consciousness as a central factor in therapeutic change. Unless major theorists have really missed the mark, Table 5 would suggest that considerable research needs to go into exploring just which specific techniques are most effective in helping people to process information that was previously outside their awareness. One strategy of research for therapists is to join forces with educators who are equally concerned with finding the most effective means of helping to increase the awareness of students.

Table 5 also suggests that the area that has been most overlooked by the major theories of therapy is the category of change due to nonspecific factors in therapy. If therapists are to increase their impact, they can no longer afford to leave such factors unspecified. Well-controlled studies that have included placebo treatments to control for nonspecific factors frequently find that such factors account for as much as 50 percent or more of the variance in therapy (Paul, 1966; Sloane, Staples, Cristol, Yorkston, & Whipple, 1975).

Therapists who have taken a close look at nonspecific factors suggest that such factors are indeed the essence of a transtheoretical process of therapy. Franks (1974), for example, affirms that all therapy systems provide an expectancy for change that gives clients a sense of hope that counteracts the demoralized or helpless state that has forced them to seek therapy.

My personal assumption is that the critical process of change in placebo groups is that clients have chosen to change. They have made a commitment to change, as affirmed by their continuing attendance at placebo sessions. The placebo sessions provide a public forum for them to make their commitment known, and it is generally believed that a public commitment is more likely to be lived up to than is a private decision. The probable reason that placebo groups improve more than a waiting-list control group is that the waiting-list clients have made either a covert or overt choice to wait until the therapist gets to them before they will use all of their resources to try to overcome their problems.

From this point of view, the critical question becomes just what techniques people use to solve their own personal problems. We therapists should not be so arrogant as to believe that people do not solve their psychological problems without our assistance. One strategy of research that we began in our labora-

TABLE 5
Summary of Theories of Therapy According to the Change Processes Assumed to be the Essence of Therapy

Consciousness Raising
1. Feedback:
   Psychoanalysis
   Ego analysis
   Psychoanalytically oriented
      psychotherapy
   Adlerian therapy
   Existential analysis
   Logotherapy
   Reality therapy
   Client-centered therapy
   Gestalt therapy
   Character analysis
   Bioenergetics
   Primal therapy
   Rational-emotive therapy
   Cognitive therapy
   Transactional analysis
   Assertiveness training
   Sex therapy
   Biofeedback
   Systematic problem solving
   Communications therapy
   Structural therapy
   Bowenian therapy
2. Education:
   Psychoanalysis
   Adlerian therapy
   Logotherapy
   Character analysis
   Transactional analysis
   Assertiveness training
   Sex therapy
   Modeling
   Self-control therapy
   Self-instructional training
   Bowenian therapy

Catharsis
1. Corrective emotional experiences:
   Psychoanalytically oriented
      psychotherapy
   Client-centered therapy
   Gestalt therapy
   Character analysis
   Bioenergetics
   Implosive therapy
   Primal therapy
   Satir's family therapy
2. Dramatic relief:
   Gestalt therapy

Conditional Stimuli
1. Counter-conditioning:
   Desensitization
   Assertiveness training
   Sex therapy
   Cognitive therapy
2. Stimulus control:
   Self-control therapy

Contingency Control
1. Reevaluation:
   Adlerian therapy
   Rational-emotive therapy
2. Contingency management:
   Rational-emotive therapy
   Token economies
   Contracting
   Self-control
   Aversive control
   Covert sensitization
   Assertiveness training
   Thought stopping

Choosing
1. Self-liberation:
   Adlerian therapy
   Existential analysis
   Logotherapy
   Reality therapy
   Transactional analysis
   Assertiveness training
   Self-control therapy
   Communications therapy
   Bowenian therapy
2. Social liberation:
   Adlerian therapy
   Character analysis
   Structural therapy

Nonspecific Processes
   Placebo therapy

*Therapeutic Relationship as Change
   Process*
   Psychoanalytically oriented
      psychotherapy
   Adlerian therapy
   Existential analysis
   Client-centered therapy
   Gestalt therapy
   Modeling
   Communications therapy
   Structural therapy

tory was to study people who successfully change their problem behaviors on their own. We shall now see how research on self-changers and therapy changers has provided data and concepts for developing a transtheoretical theory of therapy.

STAGES OF CHANGE

The initial study of self change involved a retrospective analysis of smokers who successfully stopped smoking on their own, compared to smokers participating in two well-known treatment programs (DiClemente & Prochaska, 1982). Smoking was selected as the problem behavior for both clinical and practical considerations. First of all, smoking is an addictive behavior that is difficult to overcome. Across a range of therapies, nearly 80 percent of clients resume smoking within a year of terminating treatment. These relapse rates are as high as those of alcoholics and heroin addicts (Hunt & Bespalec, 1974). Nevertheless, many people do successfully quit smoking on their own (Adult Use of Tobacco, 1975). This means there are adequate samples available for large-scale studies, and there are also objective measures available for assessing recovery.

Both the self-changers and the therapy changers in our study taught us that the change processes they used varied according to the stage of change they were in (DiClemente & Prochaska, 1982). Retrospectively, these subjects seemed able to differentiate four stages of change: (1) *contemplation*, (2) *decision*, (3) *action*, and (4) *maintenance*.

Our research shifted from smokers to a general outpatient population to determine if people presenting for therapy are in different stages of change (McConnaughy, Prochaska, & Velicer, 1983). We studied 155 outpatients with a broad range of clinical problems coming to an urban community mental health center. All clients were assessed on the stages of change test during their first week of therapy. The stages of change test contained 25 items for each of the four stages. There were also 25 items representing a precontemplation stage that had been identified from clinical work with more resistant clients. The *precontemplation stage* was conceptualized as involving people who are either unaware of having a problem or are not thinking seriously about changing. They may enter therapy because of pressure from others, but they are not seriously intending to change.

The results of this research indicated that the outpatients did discriminate four different stages of change: *precontemplation, contemplation, action, and maintenance*. The decision stage did not emerge as an independent component, but rather the items for this stage loaded on both the contemplation and the action stages. It is possible that decision making is such a transitory phenomenon that people can not be assessed when making important but relatively quick commitments. An alternative explanation is that decision making involves both contemplation and commitment to action. Profile analyses of the outpatient sample supported the latter interpretation and suggested that decisions to change are not realized until some action is taken.

The stages of change research resulted in a 32-item test that assesses four key stages of change in a highly reliable and statistically powerful manner. This test can be used to help assess which stage of change clients are in upon entering therapy. This test can also be used to assess whether clients are progressing from one stage to the next during the course of therapy.

Figure 1 presents a schematic representation of the four stages of change. Which stage of change clients are in at the beginning of therapy is an important determinant of the prognosis for particular clients. The further along in the stages of change that clients are in at the beginning of therapy, the more quickly clients can be predicted to progress. When therapy involves two or more clients working together, such as in marital therapy, then therapy can be expected to progress most smoothly when each of the clients are at the same stage of change. If one spouse is ready for action while the other has not contemplated what change will mean, then therapy will be difficult at best. The therapist is in the difficult position of being damned by one spouse for moving too slowly or being resisted by the other for moving too quickly. With family therapy it is almost axiomatic that some of the family members will be in different stages of change. Perhaps this is one reason why homeostasis as a source of resistance to change has been such a key concept in family therapy. Getting all family members to the same stage of change at about the same time is no small challenge. In a recent book on transtheoretical therapy, Prochaska and DiClemente (1984) present detailed descriptions of the clinical phenomena related to each stage of change and the clues to look for in interviews that can reveal which stage clients are in.

Termination of a problem does not occur until the person no longer experiences any temptation to return to troubled behaviors and no longer has to make any efforts to keep from relapsing. Obviously, termination of therapy and termination of a problem are not coincidental. Frequently therapy terminates before serious problems terminate. Consequently, it is expected that for many clinical problems clients will return for booster sessions, most often when they feel they may be slipping back from previous gains. Also, because therapy terminates before most problems have reached the termination stage, it is one of the reasons that clients tend to experience considerable anxiety and distress over therapy coming to a close. The clients have been in part dependent on the therapist for coping with problems that may have improved significantly but are by no means completely overcome.

Some clients move smoothly from contemplation to action to maintenance and to termination without complications. Most patients, however, follow a more complicated course of change. Patients can become stuck at any stage of change. Many precontemplators, for example, never admit to their personal problems and never seek therapy or alternative means of changing. Many troubled drinkers, overeaters, and smokers, for example, die from their unhealthy lifestyles without ever knowing what killed them. Some obsessives can contemplate a major life change without ever finding the courage to make a commitment to action. And some addicted people just keep taking action over

FIGURE 1
The Stages of Change

Precontemplation Stage → Contemplation Stage → Action Stage → Maintenance Stage

and over again, losing pounds in the process but never obtaining a fat-free, or smoke-free, or alcohol-free existence.

The more common course of change for many clinical problems is circular rather than linear. With addictive problems, for example, a revolving-door schema is a more accurate representation of the sequence that people pass through in their efforts to become free from addictions. Figure 2 presents a diagram of the revolving-door schema applied to addictive behaviors. The lower half of the figure represents the more static world of precontemplators, those who are not currently aware enough or motivated enough to contemplate changing. The center circle is the revolving-door world of people in transition. Precontemplators enter the realm of change when they are aware enough and motivated enough to begin to seriously contemplate changing their problem behaviors.

A commitment to change brings individuals into the relatively addictive-free world as they begin to actively change their behaviors and environment. Though individuals experience some of the satisfaction of being free from addictions for varying amounts of time, most of them cannot exit from the revolving door the first time around. They struggle to maintain their recent success,

FIGURE 2
The Revolving-Door Model of the Stages of Change

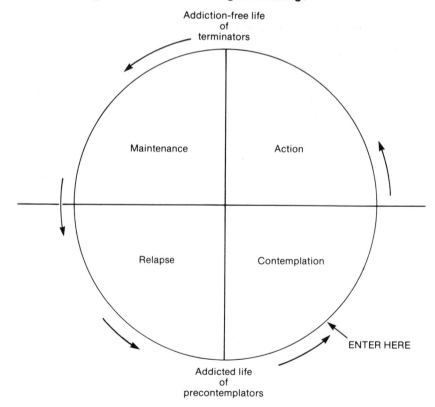

Addiction-free life
of
terminators

Maintenance   Action

Relapse   Contemplation

ENTER HERE

Addicted life
of
precontemplators

FIGURE 3
The Common Exits from the Stages of Change

but they soon find themselves relapsing back into an addictive lifestyle. They want to exit while they are in the realm of nonaddiction. Forces unknown to them, however, seem to hold them back, and the momentum of the revolving door seems to shove them back around into an addicted life again.

But relapsers don't stop there. Many individuals in transition move back into the contemplation stage again, as they prepare for another trip around the revolving door. However, some eventually exit from this circle of change. Figure 3 presents the most common exits used to leave the revolving door. Exit 1 is the quickest way out. People who have been contemplating change decide that they don't really want to change, even though they have been thinking about the hazards of the habit and the advantages of overcoming an addiction. Or they decide they can't change. Exit 1 is one of the common points at which many clients drop out of therapy.

Exit 2 is the truly successful way out of an addicted lifestyle. The person who exits here no longer experiences temptation or at a minimum experiences little, if any, difficulty in resisting their addictive behavior across all situations. The first three to six months of action appear to be the most difficult and dangerous time for relapse. The next six-month period requires active maintenance but is not as difficult. Temptations to smoke, for example, tend to decrease with each six-month period of successful maintenance over a three-year period of time (Prochaska & DiClemente, in press). Those individuals who continue to experience temptations to smoke remain in a prolonged maintenance stage in which specific strategies must be used to keep them from relapsing.

Unfortunately, Exit 2 doesn't appear to open up for most addicts prior to the second revolution of change. For successful former smokers it takes an average of three revolutions of change before they find their way to becoming fully free of the habit (Prochaska & DiClemente, in press). Even more unfortunate is the fact that some addicted individuals never find their way to become free of their habit. Some avoid the frustration of continued failure by leaving the revolving door through Exit 3 and try to resume the life of a satisfied substance abuser. Others continue to contemplate change, waiting for the right moment or the right method to come along to try again. Others decide they need a rest from struggling with the stresses of change. They tell themselves that someday in the future they will once again go back to struggling to succeed in overcoming their addiction.

Until recently it has been pretty much a mystery as to how and why some people successfully exit from the complicated circle of change, while others seem to find no exit. We shall now examine how people can apply particular processes of change to successfully negotiate each of the stages of change.

PROCESSES OF CHANGE

To assess the processes that are involved in successful self-change, we began with the 10 change processes applied throughout this book. In developing a processes of change questionnaire we tested some refinements in the processes. We were uncomfortable with the fact that the behavioral process of contingency control included both a cognitive process (reevaluation) and a behavioral process (contingency management). We decided to analyze these processes separately at both an experiential and an environmental level of intervention, yielding the following processes:

1. Cognitive restructuring.
   a. Self-reevaluation.
   b. Social-reevaluation.
2. Contingency management.
   a. Self-management.
   b. Social management.

It was also unclear whether the therapeutic relationship should be conceptualized as a process of change, the content to be changed, or a precondition for change. The helping relationship was included to determine if it would emerge as a separate process of change.

The study was designed, then, to analyze a total of 13 processes of change:

1. Feedback.
2. Education.
3. Corrective emotional experiences.

4. Dramatic relief.
5. Self-liberation.
6. Social liberation.
7. Counter-conditioning.
8. Stimulus control.
9. Self-management.
10. Social management.
11. Self-reevaluation.
12. Social reevaluation.
13. Helping relationship.

From previous interview studies (DiClemente & Prochaska, 1982; Prochaska, Crimi, Lapsanski, Martel, & Reid, 1982), test items were generated for each of the processes. Four trained judges selected five items to represent each of the processes. The test items were concrete behaviors or experiences, such as "I do something else instead of smoking when I need to relax" or "I look for information related to smoking." The self-changers responded in terms of how frequently and how helpful they experienced each item.

Principal component analyses were performed to determine how many independent processes of change were used by the self changers. It should be remembered that these analyses could have yielded any number of components. The analyses could have yielded two separate components, representing verbal and behavioral processes of change. They could have yielded three components, representing affective, behavioral, and cognitive processes of change.

These analyses, however, yielded 10 independent processes of change. Table 6 presents the 10 processes of change that were identified. Of the original 13 processes tested, 7 are clearly represented by a single component. In addition, the feedback and evaluation scales combined to form a single component. These two scales represented the experiential and environmental levels of the same process (consciousness raising), indicating that self-changers did not differentiate two levels for this process. The self-management and social management scales also combined into the single process of contingency management, indicating that self-changers did not discriminate two levels for this process. Self-reevaluation items and corrective emotional experience items combined into a process that involves both an affective and a cognitive reevaluation of self. The self-changers taught us that we were being too cogni-

TABLE 6
The 10 Change Processes of Transtheoretical Therapy

1. Consciousness raising
2. Self-reevaluation
3. Social reevaluation
4. Self-liberation
5. Social liberation
6. Counter-conditioning
7. Stimulus control
8. Contingency management
9. Dramatic relief
10. Helping relationship

tive in our conceptualization of the self-reevaluation process. Finally, the helping relationship emerged as a separate process of change occurring in the natural environment as well as in therapy.

The processes of change test was then cross-validated on a separate sample of 460 self-changers from Houston, Texas. Results from this sample yielded highly similar components for both current and past attempts at quitting smoking and for both frequency and helpfulness ratings. These results provided strong cross-validation for the processes of change (Prochaska & DiClemente, 1983).

Further validating data on the change processes have been and are being gathered in studies of therapists treating clients and themselves for psychic distress (Prochaska & Norcross, 1983), and for alcohol abuse (Prochaska & Norcross, in preparation); self-changers coping with psychic distress (Prochaska, Norcross, & DiClemente, in press), and with obesity (Prochaska & DiClemente, in press); alcoholics in a hospital-based therapy program; obese individuals in two therapy programs compared to self-changers; and a variety of outpatients at community mental health centers.

INTEGRATION OF STAGES AND PROCESSES OF CHANGE

One of the most helpful findings to emerge from our research with self changers and therapy changers is that particular processes of change are emphasized during particular stages of change. The integration of stages and processes of change can serve as an important guide for therapists. Once it is clear what stage of change a client is in, the therapist would then know which processes to apply in order to help the client progress to the next stage of change. Rather than apply the processes of change in a haphazard or trial-and-error approach, therapists can begin to use change processes in a much more systematic style. We shall first see how the integration of stages and processes of change emerged from research and then examine how this integration can serve as a more systematic guide to helping people progress.

In a cross-sectional study we assessed 866 smokers and former smokers who were in one of the following stages of change: precontemplation, contemplation, action, maintenance, or relapse (Prochaska & DiClemente, 1982). The cross-sectional study was the first phase of a two-year longitudinal investigation of how people change their own behavior. The participants were assessed every six months with a battery of tests that included the processes of change questionnaire.

In the cross-sectional study the participants indicated how frequently they were currently using each of 10 processes of change. Table 7 indicates that, as predicted, there were highly significant differences between the groups in terms of how much they were currently using each of the 10 change processes. Table 7 also indicates that with 8 of the 10 processes there was less than 1 chance in 10,000 that the findings could be due to chance. The problem is that Table 7 indicates that there are highly significant differences between some of the groups but does not indicate which of the particular groups differed.

TABLE 7
T Scores of the 10 Processes of Change for the 5 Stages of Change Groups

	Group					*F*
Process	*P*	*C*	*A*	*M*	*RL*	
Consciousness raising	45.3	53.1	48.5	48.6	52.2	15.64‡
Self-liberation	41.3	48.2	55.9	51.3	50.8	40.82‡
Social liberation	51.0	51.4	46.6	50.3	50.1	5.19†
Self-reevaluation	41.5	52.4	51.9	47.8	53.7	38.13‡
Environmental reevaluation	44.3	50.8	48.9	51.4	51.4	12.22‡
Counter-conditioning	42.6	49.3	52.6	52.0	50.4	21.48‡
Stimulus control	45.6	48.3	52.5	51.3	50.7	10.28‡
Reinforcement management	45.2	29.4	53.8	49.6	51.0	12.41‡
Dramatic relief	46.6	51.3	49.0	50.6	51.1	7.21‡
Helping relationship	48.5	49.6	51.4	49.2	51.2	2.50*

*p < .05
†p < .001
‡p < .0001

Legend: P = Precontemplators; C = Contemplators; A = Actors; M = Maintainers; RL = Relapsers.

TABLE 8
Group Comparisons on Each of the Processes of Change

Process	*Comparisons of Stage of Change Groups*
Consciousness raising	P < A, M < RL, C
Self-liberation	P < C, RL < M < A
Social liberation	A < P, C, M, RL
Self-reevaluation	P < M < C, A, RL
Environmental reevaluation	P < C, A, M, RL
Counter-conditioning	P < C, RL < A, M
Stimulus control	P < C < A, M, RL
Reinforcement management	P < C < M, RL < A
Helping relationship	P, C, M < RL, A

Note: < =p < .05, using Newman-Keuls tests.

Legend: P = Precontemplators; C = Contemplators; A = Actors; M = Maintainers; RL = Relapsers.

Further analyses were needed to compare each of the separate stages to determine just how a group in one stage differed from a group in the next stage in terms of the change processes being used. Table 8 presents the results of these analyses. Table 8 shows where there were significant differences between stages on each of the processes.

The reader may find Table 8 as confusing as did the investigators. In fact, Table 8 at first represented one of the lowest points in our efforts to develop an empirically supported integrative model of change. Up to this point our data had been extremely supportive of our model. We had been able to successfully identify and assess 4 different stages of change and 10 independent processes of change. But we couldn't make sense out of Table 8. Our data analyst said we finally struck out. The data were a mess. But in research, as in therapy, we at times need to hit bottom before we can find the inspiration to jump ahead.

It was about one o'clock in the morning when I was pouring over the data, trying to synthesize a mess. Suddenly I had a eureka reaction. The relapsers were messing up the data, as they so often tend to do. But relapse was not part of the original transtheoretical model, so we didn't really have any basis for predicting how they would respond. What if we ignored the relapsers for a while? Suddenly the data made sense. Table 9 presents a diagram showing the integration that was revealed between the stages and the processes of change. Specifically, the diagram in Table 9 shows the stages in which particular processes of change are emphasized the most and the least. Table 9 indicates that subjects in the precontemplation stage use 8 of 10 processes significantly less than any other group. As predicted from the transtheoretical model, consciousness raising is emphasized the most by individuals in the contemplation stages.

Self-reevaluation bridges contemplation and action, since it is emphasized in both stages. An earlier study suggested that corrective emotional experiences appeared to move people from contemplation into action (Prochaska & DiClemente, 1982). Remember, however, that corrective emotional experiences are an integral part of the self-reevaluation process.

As predicted, self-liberation is emphasized when subjects take action, as are counter-conditioning, contingency control, and stimulus control. The helping relationship is also emphasized the most during times of action. Table 9 also indicates that counter-conditioning and stimulus control bridge action and maintenance, since those two processes are emphasized in both stages.

Let's examine in more depth what these data suggest about how change comes about and then look at the implications for helping our clients change in therapy. During the precontemplation stage, individuals use the change processes significantly less than people in any other stage. Precontemplators process less information about their problem; they spend less time and energy reevaluating themselves; they experience fewer emotional reactions to the

TABLE 9
The Stages of Change in Which Particular Processes of Change Are Emphasized the Most and the Least

Precontemplation	Contemplation	Action	Maintenance
Eight processes used the least			
	Consciousness raising		
	Self-reevaluation		
		Self-liberation	
		Helping relationship	
		Reinforcement management	
		Counter-conditioning	
			Stimulus control

negative aspects of their problems; they are less open with significant others about their problems; and they do little to shift their attention or their environment in the direction of overcoming their problems.

What moves people from precontemplation into the contemplation stage of change? What facilitates or forces people to become aware that previously acceptable patterns of behavior are now problematical or pathological? To respond to these important issues, we must be willing to go beyond research data and rely more on clinical experience and clinical theory.

Progress from precontemplation into the contemplation stage appears to be due to either developmental changes or environmental changes that occur in people's lives. Many individuals begin to contemplate changing particular aspects of their lives because of developmental processes that move them into a new stage in life. As Levinson, Dorrow, Klein, Levinson, and McKee suggest in their work on *The Seasons of a Man's Life* (1978) many men find themselves quite satisfied with a particular spouse during their twenties. When they enter the transition into the thirties, however, they begin to contemplate radical changes in their marriages. Similarly, many smokers begin to seriously contemplate stopping smoking as they approach age 40 and feel pressured to face the finiteness of their lives. It is not coincidental that the self-changers in our research who have been most successful in quitting smoking took action at a mean age of 39. And 39 is a mean age. Developmentally, facing 40 is a key time for many people to reevaluate their lives to determine where changes are needed.

Other individuals appear ready for change, not because of internal developmental changes, but because their external environment has changed. Perhaps a spouse or a child has reached a new developmental stage and asks or insists that they stop drinking or smoking. Or they may begin to realize that their environment no longer reinforces their drinking or smoking like it once did but now responds with subtle and not-so-subtle punishments to their old habits. Other changes occur in the environment that may or may not be related to people's personal behavior, and yet these events can cause them to seriously contemplate changing their behavior. A poignant example of such an environmental event occurred with a married couple who participated in our self-change research. Both spouses were heavy smokers for over 20 years. Then their dog died from lung cancer. The husband quit smoking. The wife bought a new dog.

The important theoretical issue here is that intentional change, such as occurs in therapy or self-directed change, is only one type of change that can move people. Developmental changes and environmental changes are other events that can cause people to alter their lives. Transtheoretical therapy focuses primarily on facilitating intentional change, but it recognizes and at times relies on other types of change when working with clients. It is assumed, however, that unless developmental or environmental changes produce intentional change as well, then clients will feel coerced and are likely to revert to previous patterns once the coercion is removed. It is obvious, for example, that a pedophiliac can be prevented from sexual activities with children by being imprisoned. Unless such change in environments also produces intentional change, the pedophiliac is likely to revert to molesting children once the coercion of imprisonment is completed.

As clients become increasingly more conscious about themselves and the nature of their problems, they are free to reevaluate themselves both affectively and cognitively. Self-reevaluation includes an assessment of which values clients will try to actualize, to act upon, and to make real. Clients need to also assess which values they will let die. The more central their problem behaviors are to the core of themselves, the more will their reevaluation involve changes in their sense of self. Clients ask, "Will I like myself better as a nondrinker or nonsmoker? Will others I care about like me better? What if I am a more anxious and irritable person after I change? If my shared community is primarily with drinkers or smokers, will I risk rejection? If I fail to change, will I feel coerced, guilty, or weak?"

As clients enter the action stage, the therapist realizes that the reevaluation process continues at a relatively high level. Actual changes in behavior and in the environment may affect their sense of self differently from what they had contemplated. A self-changer realized soon after quitting smoking that she became much more agitated and irritated than she had imagined. She felt that as a nonsmoker she was in risk of abusing her toddler, even though she had not worried about this as a smoker. Taking action on her smoking had caused her to have to begin reevaluating herself as a mother and not just as a smoker.

Our research with self-changers indicates that the more individuals continue to reevaluate themselves after taking action, the more likely they are to relapse (Prochaska & DiClemente, in press). Our interpretation of these data is that the more accurately and openly people reevaluate themselves prior to taking action, the less they will need to continue to reevaluate themselves after taking action. The sense of self they experience after taking action is more likely to match what they had imagined during the contemplation stage. They are less likely to be surprised or confused by how they experience themselves after changing their behavior. Thus, they will have less need to continue reevaluating whether they should stick with their new action or relapse to their old way of being. The importance of being adequately prepared for action cannot be overemphasized, especially for problems where relapse is the norm.

During the action stage it is important that clients act from a sense of self-liberation. They need to believe that they have the autonomy to change their lives in key ways. Yet they also need to accept that coercion is as much a part of life as is autonomy. Thus, if they slip during action and attribute it all to a lack of willpower, they can experience considerable guilt or shame that can keep them from trying to take action again. On the other hand, if clients attribute all of their success to the therapist or to other helping relationships, they risk becoming unduly dependent on the therapist.

Self-liberation is based in part on a sense of self-efficacy (Bandura, 1977; 1982), the belief that one's own efforts play a significant role in succeeding in the face of difficult situations. Self-liberation, however, cannot just have an affective and cognitive foundation. Clients must also be effective enough with behavioral processes, such as counter-conditioning and stimulus control, to modify the conditional stimuli that can coerce them into relapsing. Therapists can assess how adequately clients are able to apply processes such as contingency control and stimulus control. Therapists can provide training, if necessary, in the behavioral processes to increase the probability that clients will be successful when they do take action. As action proceeds, therapists can serve as consultants to the clients as self-changers to help clients identify any errors they may be making in their attempts to modify their behavior and environment in a freer and healthier direction.

Since action is a particularly stressful stage of change that involves considerable opportunities for experiencing, coercion, guilt, failure, and the limits of personal freedom, clients are particularly in need of support and understanding from helping relationships. For clients, taking action tends to mean taking risks with rejection. Knowing that there is at least one person who cares and is committed to helping serves to ease some of the distress and dread of taking life-changing actions.

Just as preparation for action is essential for success, so too is preparation for maintenance. Successful maintenance builds on each of the processes that has come before. Specific preparation for maintenance, however, involves an open assessment of the conditions under which a person is likely to be coerced into relapsing. Clients need to assess the alternatives they have for coping with such coercive conditions without resorting to self-defeating defenses and pathological patterns of response. Perhaps most important is the sense that one is becoming more of the kind of person one wants to be. Continuing to apply counter-conditioning and stimulus control is most effective when it is based on the belief that maintaining change maintains a sense of self that is highly valued by oneself and at least one significant other.

LEVELS OF CHANGE

We have discussed the processes that produce change in psychotherapy and the stages through which change progresses. We have identified the processes and stages of change and their interactions. But *what* is it that we are attempting to change? We shall now analyze the *content* of change from a transtheoretical perspective.

In transtheoretical therapy psychological problems are hierarchically organized across five different levels:

1. Symptom/Situational.
2. Maladaptive cognitions.
3. Current interpersonal conflicts.
4. Family/Systems conflicts.
5. Intrapersonal conflicts.

Historically, systems of psychotherapy have generally attributed psychological problems to one or two levels. Traditional behavior therapists, for example, focus on situational determinants and analyze the stimuli that immediately precede and follow a problem behavior. Cognitive behavior therapists recognize both situational and cognitive causes of problems. Marital and family therapists are examples of therapists who intervene at the current interpersonal and/or family/systems levels. Meanwhile, orthodox psychoanalytic therapists have worked primarily at the intrapersonal level of psychopathology.

What is the key level of content for psychotherapy? The answer obviously depends on the therapist's preferred theory of personality and psychopathology and/or the client's preferred theory of problems. As an eclectic approach, transtheoretical therapy appreciates the validity of each level of problems. How critical each level is can vary for different clients even when they are presenting the same symptoms.

With three cases of vaginismus reported by Prochaska and DiClemente (1984), for example, Case A recovered just by focusing on the symptom/situational level and changing the situations under which the couple had sexual encounters. Case B, a difficult success, clearly had current interpersonal problems of communication and control that contributed to the maintenance of vaginismus. Case C, a failure, appeared to have critical involvement of family/ systems conflicts, with the young woman experiencing her sexuality as still under the control of her mother's rules.

While therapists of different theoretical persuasions can present a case for attributing problems to at least five different levels, is it not the case that clients attribute problems to only one or two levels of causality? Research based on attribution theory, for example, suggests that the naive psychology of the public attributes behavior to either situational or dispositional causes (Jones & Nisbett, 1972). Similarly, locus of control research reports people attributing both effective and ineffective behavior to variables under either external or internal locus of control (Rotter, 1970).

The problem is that attribution research and locus of control research limit their search to only two levels. These theories artificially dichotomize the causal world of clients. The fact is that people perceive their problems in much more complex ways than suggested by most theories of behavior, including theories of troubled behavior. In research with college students with such problems as depression, anxiety, and academic difficulties, we found that students did indeed attribute problems to the five different levels emphasized in transtheoretical therapy (Norcross, Prochaska, & Hambrecht, in press).

Given five different levels of change, how can therapists proceed systematically across the different levels? In transtheoretical therapy we prefer to intervene initially at the symptom/situational level because change tends to occur more quickly at this more conscious and contemporary level of problems. The further down the hierarchy we focus, the further removed from awareness the determinants of the problem are likely to be. Also, the deeper the level, the further back in history are the determinants of the problem. Thus, we predict from the transtheoretical model that the deeper the level that needs to be changed, the longer and more complex therapy is likely to be. Furthermore, the further removed in history are the determinants of the problem, the greater resistance there will be to trying to change those determinants. One of the reasons for greater resistance is that deeper attributions tend to be more threatening to self esteem than are more surface attributions. It is more threatening, for example, to believe that vaginismus is due to hostility toward men and a desire to emasculate men than to believe that the anticipation of painful intercourse elicits fear and involuntary circumvaginal muscle contractions. One of the rules of transtheoretical therapy is to use the least threatening attributions that can be justified, since our clinical formulations have the potential for producing damage in their own right.

Unfortunately, it all too frequently is the case that problems are not resolved just by focusing on symptom and situational variables. At the same time, however, we frequently cannot predict beforehand that therapy cannot be an easy success. Thus, when in doubt we recommend starting at the symptom and situational level of problems.

At other times, both clients and therapists agree in their attributions that presenting complaints are due to more than the immediate situational variables. If they agree on which level needs to be changed, then therapy can begin at a deeper level with minimal resistance. A couple, for example, can present for therapy with a shared attribution that a sexual problem is being maintained by struggles for control and unresolved resentments in their current interpersonal life. Resolution of these problems may result in resolution of the sexual problem. Prochaska and Marzilli (1973) reported that in approximately half of their cases first treated for interpersonal conflicts, the sexual dysfunctions improved as the relationship improved. On the other hand, improvement of interpersonal conflicts could free the couple to cooperate more effectively to produce rapid change at the symptom and situational level. The transtheoretical therapist is prepared, then, to intervene at any of the five levels of change, though the preference is to begin at the highest level that clinical assessment and clinical judgment can justify.

LEVELS×STAGES×PROCESSES OF CHANGE

Integrating the levels with the stages and processes of change provides a model for intervening hierarchically and systematically across a broad range of therapeutic content. Table 10 presents an overview of the integration of levels, stages, and processes of change. There are three basic strategies for intervening across multiple levels of change. The first is the *shifting levels* strategy. Therapy would typically focus first on the client's symptoms and the situations supporting the symptoms. If the processes could be applied effectively at the first level and the client could progress through each stage of change, therapy could be completed without shifting to a deeper level of analysis. If treating just the symptoms was not effective enough, then therapy would shift to a focus on maladaptive cognitions that are supporting the symptoms. The processes of change would be applied to cognitive content with the goal of progressing through each stage of change. If progress was not sufficient at the cognitive level, then therapy would shift to current interpersonal conflicts. The processes would now be applied at an interpersonal level, with the goal of progressing through each stage of change. The same pattern of successfully progressing through the stages or shifting levels would be followed until the client has sufficiently improved or until the deepest, least conscious, and most resistant intrapersonal conflicts are analyzed. The strategy of shifting from a higher to a deeper level is illustrated in Table 10 by the arrows moving first across one level and then down to the next level.

The second approach is the *key level* strategy. There are more clear-cut cases where a high degree of consensual validation would emerge across clinicians as to the causes of a client's problems. If the available evidence is unambiguous and points to one key level of causality, then the therapist would work first and foremost at this key level of intervention. These cases are relatively easy to formulate once the data are in, though that does not mean that they are necessarily easy to treat.

TABLE 10
Levels×Stages×Processes of Change

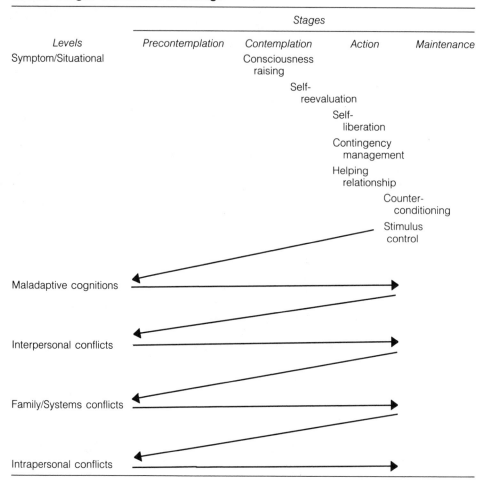

	Stages			
Levels	*Precontemplation*	*Contemplation*	*Action*	*Maintenance*
Symptom/Situational		Consciousness raising		
		Self-reevaluation		
		Self-liberation		
		Contingency management		
		Helping relationship		
			Counter-conditioning	
			Stimulus control	
Maladaptive cognitions				
Interpersonal conflicts				
Family/Systems conflicts				
Intrapersonal conflicts				

Hopefully, therapy research will progress to the point where we will know that a specific level of intervention is most effective with particular types of patients having particular types of problems. Research already suggests that about half of the patients with circumscribed phobias can be effectively helped by modifying the situational determinants of their phobias. Research does not suggest, however, what to do with the 50 percent of phobic patients who drop out or fail to progress at the situational level (Barlow & Wolfe, 1982). Comparative therapy studies now underway may determine that nonpsychotic and unipolar depression is most effectively treated at either the cognitive or the interpersonal levels. Until more clear-cut research is available for guiding therapeutic interventions with particular problems, the transtheoretical model provides a guide that is intended to be as efficient and effective as possible for clients who can make rapid progress and still provides alternatives for clients who are failing to progress at key levels of change.

The third alternative is the *maximum impact* strategy. With complex clinical cases it is at times clear that variables at every level are involved as a cause, an effect, or a maintainer of the client's problems. For maximum impact, interventions can be created that affect clients at each and every level of change. This is a synergistic approach that assumes that maximum impact in therapy occurs when our interventions affect clients at every level of change. The maximum impact strategy will be illustrated in the case of Mrs. C.

EFFECTIVENESS OF TRANSTHEORETICAL THERAPY

At this point in its development, the transtheoretical approach provides an integrative model for eclectic therapists. The core constructs of processes, stages, and levels of change have been based on research with both self-changers and therapy changers. Transtheoretical therapy is being used in a variety of clinical settings with a full range of clinical problems. However, transtheoretical therapy is just beginning to be tested under controlled conditions. The transtheoretical approach is being tested to determine not only its effectiveness as a therapy but also its effectiveness in creating self-help materials for maximizing self-change.

THERAPY AND OUTCOME WITH MRS. C.

Mrs. C. is entering therapy stuck in the contemplation stage of change. The six years she spent in psychoanalytically oriented psychotherapy had helped increase her consciousness about her obsessive-compulsive patterns and personality. She has spent considerable time reevaluating her life. Intellectually, she appreciates how much her life has gotten out of control; but emotionally, it still feels right to protect herself and her family from dirt and disease. As is often the case with obsessive-compulsive clients, Mrs. C. isolated much of her affect from her intellect when reevaluating her self and her symptoms.

Obsessive-compulsive patients are especially prone to getting stuck in the contemplation stage of change (Prochaska & DiClemente, 1982). They prefer to believe that if they keep thinking enough about an issue that eventually the problem will be resolved or enough information will be found that points to a perfect solution to a perplexing problem. They are seeking certainty as to the causes of their symptoms, when probability is the best that can be provided. Obsessives, like Mrs. C., hate to admit that there can be serious limits to thinking and that many personal problems can only be changed by commitments that go beyond reason. The fear of facing the irrational can keep obsessives seeking sufficient information for years, as they shift from one theory to another or from one therapist to another. Of course, some therapists are also afraid of making commitments to action without an obsessive understanding of their clients' problems.

Mrs. C. was feeling coerced into action. Her environment was changing and was threatening to force changes on her. Her therapist, for example, had given up and had decided to terminate therapy. Her family was also giving up on her. Mrs. C. took an overdose of aspirins to express the depression and anger she felt over the rejection that would come with the alternative of being placed in a state hospital.

Her alternatives for action then were to work with me, to go the state hospital, or to follow through on suicide. Hopefully, Mrs. C. would be able to identify with our efforts as potentially the most liberating alternative rather than feeling entirely coerced into cooperating. The fact is that if she felt entirely coerced, she really couldn't be able to cooperate and would resist being changed by someone trying to control her.

At what level should we try to help Mrs. C. change? Mrs. C. is clearly a complex case. At the symptom and situational level, it is clear that situations related to dirt and disease evoke compulsive handwashing that is apparently reinforced by reduction in anxiety. At the cognitive level, Mrs. C. believes that she needs to be perfectly clean in order to be perfectly safe and secure. Her maladaptive cognitions include perseverating about pinworms and magnifying the dangers of pinworms entirely out of realistic proportions. She seems to believe that even thoughts or images of dirt or pinworms are awful and unbearable. She also seems to believe that things around her would go out of control if she does not keep up her compulsive rituals.

At the interpersonal level, Mrs. C. has ambivalent relationships at best. She relates ambivalently to her children, as she struggles to protect them from dirt and disease and also avoids them as sources of dirt and disease. Her relationship to her husband has deteriorated to the point where it lacks intimacy or sexuality. Their only significant interaction involves Mr. C. participating in her morning shower ritual. Mrs. C. is in conflict over caring for her family or controlling her family.

At the family/systems level, Mrs. C. is still heavily influenced by her mother's rules to be ultraclean and careful about dirt and disease. She comes from a family in which she was dominated by her parents but was not free to acknowledge any anger or resentment toward their coercive control.

At the intrapersonal level, she appears to be defending against classic anal impulses. Any urges to play with her anus or its products have to be defended against by reaction formation defenses that include being perfectly clean. She has trouble letting go, as she hoards cheap jewelry and other junk. She lives a highly constricted life, as she overcontrols her feelings, her sexual urges, and her aggression. To let go of her defenses in the slightest would threaten to drive Mrs. C. crazy, as her impulses threaten to go out of control.

From a transtheoretical approach we have the options of beginning therapy at the symptom and situational level and shifting to deeper levels, if necessary. We could also intervene at a key level of change if one of the levels is clearly the key to her problems. Or we could use a maximum impact strategy and attempt to produce changes at each level. With a complex case like Mrs. C., where there are multilevel problems, preference is given to a maximum impact strategy.

Even though I treated Mrs. C. as a psychology intern long before transtheoretical therapy was developed, it is intriguing to realize how much my early eclectic style anticipated my later theorizing. With Mrs. C., for example, therapy involved multilevel interventions. Therapy also included a range of change processes that were appropriate for a client moving into action.

At the symptom and situational level, treating Mrs. C. as an inpatient can enable the therapist to have greater influence over stimulus situations that control her symptoms. Since her handwashing at home was so immediate and automatic, she had little voluntary control over washing. As an inpatient she would have to sign in at the nurses' station before she could wash and sign in again after completing her washing. The signing in gave an accurate count of her compulsive washing and would serve as feedback about the effectiveness of our treatment. The signing in also served as a delay during which the nurses could use counter-conditioning to help Mrs. C. cope with her anxiety, such as talking about it or encouraging her to relax by playing cards, knitting, or watching TV. The delays also allowed Mrs. C. to begin to use self-liberation and make more conscious decisions to wash or to resist washing. If she resisted washing, the staff could then use contingency management and reinforce Mrs. C. for not washing. As therapy progressed, the signing in also served as a stimulus control procedure that controlled how often and how long Mrs. C. could remain in washing situations.

A helping relationship was enhanced by meeting twice a week in more client-centered, supportive sessions. In these sessions Mrs. C. could share the many thoughts and feelings that were being generated by her hospitalization and treatment. These sessions also helped Mrs. C. identify with therapy, as she experienced her therapist as caring rather than coercive. The more Mrs. C. identified with therapy, the more she relied on self-liberation as she committed herself more fully to taking action to overcome her chronic compulsions.

Therapy also included implosive sessions three times a week. The implosive scenes described in Chapter 9 impacted upon almost every level of Mrs. C.'s problems. The first scene, for example, encouraged Mrs. C. to face such scary situations as dirty underwear filled with pinworms. The anal picnic scene would impact on several levels simultaneously, ranging from symptom stimuli of dirt and disease to intrapersonal desires to act out anal impulses. Also included were challenges to maladaptive cognitions of having to be perfectly clean in order to be safe and secure. Also introduced were family/systems themes related to rebellion against parental dominance over toilet training.

The third scene impacted upon interpersonal conflicts, especially Mrs. C.'s ambivalence toward her children. She imagined her children being infected by pinworms due to her carelessness. In the middle of the night, she heard her children crying to her for help, as they were being devoured by pinworms. Mrs. C. rejected their pleas and went to bed feeling free at last from having to care for her children.

The interpersonal level was also addressed by the therapist meeting with the family for biweekly sessions. The family members needed to express the considerable anger and resentment toward Mrs. C. that had accumulated over the years. For a while it looked like Mrs. C. might not be able to return home, since four of her children were adamant about not wanting her back. As the anger dissipated, however, Mr. C. and the older children could help the younger children to reevaluate their mother, as they shared happy memories of how Mrs. C. was before she became obsessed with pinworms. Individual sessions with Mr. C. also helped him to remember the warm feelings that had been buried under all the frustration and resentment.

The family/systems conflicts of Mrs. C. were most intensely impacted by the fourth scene, in which she imagined sinking an axe in her father's bald head. Besides the scenes described in Chapter 9, Mrs. C. also confronted oedipal conflicts with a father who waited up for her after dates. Of course, these scenes could also impact upon intrapersonal conflicts, as Mrs. C. imagined releasing some of her most taboo impulses of sex and aggression.

Another scene was directed at intrapersonal conflicts over losing control and going crazy. In this scene Mrs. C. imagined leaving the hospital, returning home, and going crazy. She imagined running around the house nude, grabbing her son's genitals, wrecking the house, and then being shipped back to the clinic for disposition. At the clinic a full staff meeting was held with the family members present. After discussing all the terrible things that Mrs. C. had done, the director asked if anyone from the clinic or the family had anything good to say about her. Silence was the only response. Again the question was asked, and again no one spoke. Finally, Mrs. C. was sent to the state hospital in a panel truck and placed in an isolated room with a sign on her door: "Hopeless Case: No Visitors Allowed." This scene also helped Mrs. C. confront some of her situational anxieties that she might relapse after returning home from the hospital. The final implosive sessions involved real unwashed underwear that Mr. C. had brought from home. Mrs. C. had to reach into the bag with her eyes closed and handle the dirty underwear. This session helped Mrs. C. confront not only situational stimuli but also her maladaptive cognitions that magnified out of all proportions the dangers of dirty underwear.

By the end of Mrs. C.'s six-week stay in the clinic, the sign-in sheets indicated a dramatic decrease in the frequency and duration of her washing compulsion. The biggest change came after the fourth implosive scene, in which Mrs. C. was to imagine sinking a hatchet into her father's head. During this session Mrs. C. was in a psychophysiological lab and was wired to seven different channels for measuring aspects of anxiety. As the session progressed, Mrs. C. reported that she was having trouble with the scene. She could imagine the scene all right, but she was not able to feel emotions like she had in previous scenes. Recognizing her reaction as a form of defensive isolation, I told her to really let go, to strike out with her hands and tell him what a bastard he was, to tell the son of a bitch she was glad he was suffering as he had made her suffer. Suddenly she began hacking away at the table and swearing, sobbing, and shaking. The seven anxiety channels all went off the recording paper, as Mrs. C. opened up for the last 15 or 20 minutes of the session. She then went up to her room and, with a nurse present, continued to relive the scene for over an hour with considerable affect expressed. The next morning she again relived the scene until she felt emotionally drained.

After that Mrs. C. looked and felt considerably better. She now reported being able to pick up such things as a ball of yarn off the floor. She could accept a drink of soda from the same can from which a hippie-type youngster had been drinking, where previously she would not even get near such an unclean person. Her showers and handwashing responses were down to normal times, and Mrs. C. was ready to go home.

Fortunately Mrs. C.'s family had been willing to use stimulus control to change their environmental conditions both for their own sakes and for the sake of Mrs. C. They had been painting, repairing, and redecorating the house, which had come to look like a state dump. On her first weekend home Mrs. C. joined right in and directed the throwing out of all the junk she had held onto for years. Her children and their friends formed a long line, as Mrs. C. handed them boxes of dresses, towels, and assorted things to be picked up by the trash truck. Mrs. C. really enjoyed the sense of freedom of being able to let go.

To our surprise she was also able to let go sexually with her husband more than she ever had in her life. The first day home they went up to their bedroom in the daytime, which they had never done before, and really enjoyed making love. Mr. C. blurted out spontaneously, "This isn't the girl I married!" A few months later, Mrs. C. experienced her first orgasm at the age of 47.

The family was amazed at Mrs. C.'s new-found freedom. The kids reported her doing things they could never imagine, such as getting down on the floor and playing with them or picking up a cookie off the new rug, brushing it off, and eating it. She was cooking special meals, helping with the cleaning, and allowing her children to have their friends over.

Mr. C. said that he was amazed by his wife's improvement but also troubled because he had always thought of himself as better adjusted then she was, whereas now she seemed to be better adjusted. I offered him some implosive sessions, but he declined with a smile, saying he could learn to adjust all right.

After the initial enthusiasm at being home and feeling good, there were some setbacks. Mrs. C. was generally more tense at home than in the clinic. Part of her anxiety came from trying to give to six children after having been withdrawn from them for so long. She was especially troubled by the guilt she felt over the emotional problems she believed she had helped cause in her second son. Even though her son was getting help in therapy, Mrs. C. still felt that her guilt was authentic and all she could do was continue her commitment of trying to be available emotionally to her children when they needed her.

Mrs. C. also reported that she was having trouble limiting her morning shower to five minutes. She felt much more anxious in her shower at home, which had been the scene of so many repetitions of her irrational ritual. So I went to the house and imploded Mrs. C. in her shower (while fully clothed, of course).

Mrs. C. also went through a mild depressive reaction when I left the clinic and our therapeutic relationship was terminated. My supervisor, who continued to see her on a monthly basis, half-jokingly suggested to me that her dramatic improvement seemed to him to be the result of her having fallen for me and thus trying very hard to please me. I told him that his explanation sounded an awful lot like a "transference cure" explanation for a behaviorist like himself!

The last I heard of Mrs. C. was two years after termination. Apparently she was continuing to function much more autonomously. Her morning shower was occasionally giving her problems, but that seemed to be helped most when she got a new job that would not tolerate her being late for work. There was no denying that Mrs. C. could still best be characterized as an obsessive-compulsive personality, but her needs for cleanliness and neatness were more under her control. She apparently had regained enough autonomy to continue with the commitment she had made many years before—to share her life with her children and her spouse rather than wasting it in her compulsion to wash.

REFERENCES

Abraham, K. The influence of oral eroticism on character formation. In K. Abraham (Ed.), *Selected papers*. London: Institute for Psychoanalysis and Hogarth Press, 1927.

Adler, A. *Study of organ inferiority and its physical compensation*. New York: Nervous and Mental Diseases Publishing Co., 1917.

Adler, A. *Problems of neurosis*. London: Kegan Paul, 1929.

Adler, A. Compulsion neurosis. *International Journal of Individual Psychology*, 1931, *9*, 1–16. Reprinted in H. L. Ansbacher & R. R. Ansbacher (Eds.), *Superiority and social interest*. New York: Viking Press, 1964.

Adler, A. The neurotic's picture of the world: A case study. *International Journal of Individual Psychology*, 1936, *3*, 3–13. Reprinted in H. L. Ansbacher & R. R. Ansbacher (Eds.), *Superiority and social interest*. New York: Viking Press, 1964.

Adult use of tobacco, 1975 (U.S. Department of Health, Education, and Welfare Publication). Washington, D.C.: U.S. Government Printing Office, 1976.

Alexander, F., & French, T. M. *Psychoanalytic therapy*. New York: Ronald Press, 1946.

Alexander, J., & Parsons, B. Short-term behavioral intervention with delinquent families: Impact on family process and recidivism. *Journal of Abnormal Psychology*, 1973, *81*, 219–225.

Allen, K., Hart, B., Briell, J., Harris, F., & Wolf, M. Effects of social reinforcement on isolate behavior of a nursery school child. *Child Development*, 1969, *35*, 511–518.

Anderson, B. A comparison of systematic desensitization and directed masturbation in the treatment of primary orgasmic dysfunction in females. *Journal of Consulting and Clinical Psychology*, 1981, *49*, 568–570.

Anderson, W. Personal growth and client-centered therapy: An information-processing view. In D. Wexler & L. Rice (Eds.), *Innovations in client-centered therapy.* New York: John Wiley & Sons, 1974.

Arbuckle, D., & Boy, A. Client-centered therapy in counseling students with behavioral problems. *Journal of Counseling Psychology,* 1961, *8,* 136–139.

Atayas, V. *Psychology and education of beyond adjustment.* Unpublished manuscript, University of Rhode Island Counseling Center, 1977.

Ayllon, T., & Azrin, N. *The token enconomy: A motivational system for therapy and rehabilitation.* New York: Appleton-Century-Crofts, 1968.

Ayllon, T., Layman, D., and Kendel, H. A behavioral-educational alternative to drug control of hyperactive children. *Journal of Applied Behavior Analysis,* 1975, *8,* 137–146.

Aylmer, R. Family systems therapy. Workshop presented at the University of Rhode Island, Kingston, Spring, 1978.

Azrin, N., & Holz, W. Punishment. In W. Honig (Ed.), *Operant behavior: Areas of research and application.* New York: Appleton-Century-Crofts, 1966.

Baehr, G. Comparative effectiveness of individual psychotherapy, group psychotherapy, and a combination of these methods. *Journal of Consulting Psychology,* 1954, *18,* 179–183.

Bandura, A. *Principles of behavior modification.* New York: Holt, Rinehart & Winston, 1969.

Bandura, A. Self-efficacy: Toward a unifying theory of behavior change. *Psychological Review,* 1977, *84,* 191–215.

Bandura, A. Self-efficacy mechanism in human agency. *American Psychologist,* 1982, *37,* 122–147.

Bandura, A., Grusec, J., & Menlove, F. Vicarious extinction of avoidance behavior. *Journal of Personality and Social Psychology,* 1967, *5,* 16–23.

Bandura, A., & Menlove, F. Factors determining vicarious extinction of avoidance behavior through symbolic modeling. *Journal of Personality and Social Psychology,* 1968, *8,* 99–108.

Barendregt, J. T., Bastians, A. W., & Vermeul-Van Mullem, A. A psychological investigation of the effects of psychoanalysis and psychotherapy. In J. T. Barendregt (Ed.), *Research in psychodiagnostics.* Paris: Mouton, 1961.

Barlow, D., & Wolfe, B. Behavioral approaches to anxiety disorders: A report on the NIMH-SUNY, Albany, research conference. *Journal of Consulting and Clinical Psychology,* 1981, *49,* 448–454.

Barth, J. *The end of the road.* New York: Doubleday Publishing, 1967.

Barton, A. *Three worlds of therapy.* Palo Alto, Calif.: National Press Books, 1974.

Bateson, G., Jackson, D., Haley, J., & Weakland, J. Toward a theory of schizophrenia. *Behavioral Science,* 1956, *1,* 251–264.

Baucom, D. A comparison of behavioral contracting and problem-solving, communications training in behavioral marital therapy. *Behavior Therapy,* 1982, *13,* 162–174.

Baum, M. Extinction of avoidance responding through response prevention (flooding). *Psychological Bulletin,* 1970, *74,* 276–284.

Beck, A. *Depression: Clinical, experimental, and theoretical aspects.* New York: Harper & Row, 1967.

Beck, A. The core problem in depression: The cognitive triad. In J. Masserman (Ed.), *Depression: Theories and therapies.* New York: Grune & Stratton, 1970.

Beck, A. *Cognitive therapy and the emotional disorders.* New York: International Universities Press, 1976.

Bellis, J. Emotional flooding and bioenergetic analysis. In P. Olsen (Ed.), *Emotional flooding.* New York: Human Sciences Press, 1976.

Bensberg, G., Colwell, C., & Cassel, R. Teaching the profoundly retarded self-help activities by behavior shaping techniques. *American Journal of Mental Deficiency*, 1965, *69*, 674–679.

Berecz, J. Modification of smoking behavior through self-administered punishment of imagined behavior: A new approach to aversion therapy. *Journal of Consulting and Clinical Psychology*, 1972, *38*, 244–250.

Berne, E. *Games people play.* New York: Grove Press, 1964.

Berne, E. *Principles of group treatment.* New York: Oxford University Press, 1966.

Berne, E. *Sex in human loving.* New York: Simon & Schuster, 1970.

Berne, E. *What do you say after you say hello?* New York: Grove Press, 1972.

Berne, E., Steiner, C., & Dusay, J. Transactional analysis. In R. Jurjevich (Ed.), *Direct psychotherapy* (Vol.1). Coral Gables, Fla.: University of Miami Press, 1973.

Bernstein, D. Modification of smoking behavior: An evaluative review. *Psychological Bulletin*, 1969, *7l*, 418–440.

Bernstein, D., & Paul, G. Some comments on therapy analogue research with small-animal phobias. *Journal of Behavior Therapy and Experimental Psychiatry*, 1971, *2*, 225–237.

Bibring, E. Psychoanalysis and the dynamic psychotherapies. *Journal of the American Psychoanalytic Association*, 1954, *2*, 745–770.

Binswanger, L. The case of Ellen West. In R. May, E. Angel, & H. Ellenberger (Eds.), *Existence.* New York: Basic Books, 1958.(a)

Binswanger. L. The existential analysis school of thought. In R. May, E. Angel, & H. Ellenberger (Eds.), *Existence.* New York: Basic Books, 1958.(b)

Binswanger, L. Insanity as life-historical phenomenon and as mental disease: The case of Ilse. In R. May, E. Angel, & H. Ellenberger (Eds.), *Existence.* New York: Basic Books, 1958.(c)

Binswanger, L. *Being-in-the world: Selected papers of Ludwig Binswanger.* New York: Basic Books, 1963.

Birk, L., Huddleston, W., Millers, E., & Cohler, B. Avoidance conditioning for homosexuality. *Archives of General Psychiatry*, 1971, *25*, 314–323.

Black, A. The extinction of avoidance responses under curare. *Journal of Comparative and Physiological Psychology*, 1958, *51*, 519–525.

Blanchard, E., Andrasik, F., Neff, D., Arena, J., Ahles, T., Jurrish, S., Pallmeyer, T., Saunders, N., Teders, S., Barron, K., & Radichok, I. Biofeedback and relaxation training with three kinds of headache: Treatment effects and their predictions. *Journal of Consulting and Clinical Psychology*, 1982, *50*, 562–575.

Bolstead, O., & Johnson, S. Self-regulation in the modification of disruptive behavior. *Journal of Applied Behavior Analysis*, 1972, *5*, 143–154.

Bordella, D. *Wilhelm Reich: The evaluation of his work.* London: Vision Press, 1973.

Borkovec, T. The role of expectancy and physiological feedback in fear research: A review with special reference to subject characteristics. *Behavior Therapy*, 1973, *4*, 491–505.

Boss, M. *Daseinsanalysis and psychoanalysis.* New York: Basic Books, 1963.

Bostow, D., & Bailey, J. Modification of severe disruptive and aggressive behavior using time-out and reinforcement procedures. *Journal of Applied Behavior Analysis*, 1969, *2*, 31–37.

Boudewyns, P., & Wilson, A. Implosive therapy and desensitization therapy using free association in the treatment of inpatients. *Journal of Abnormal Psychology*, 1972, *79*, 259–268.

Boulougouris, J., Marks, I., & Marset, P. Superiority of flooding (implosion) to desensitization for reducing pathological fears. *Behavior Research and Therapy*, 1971, *9*, 7–16.

Bowen, M. On the differentiation of self. In J. Framo (Ed.), *Family interaction: A dia-*

logue between family researchers and family therapists. New York: Springer, 1972.

Bowen, M. *Family therapy in clinical practice.* New York: Jason Aronsen, 1978.

Bowlby, J. *Attachment and loss, Vol. 1: Attachment.* New York: Basic Books, 1969.

Bowlby, J. *Attachment and loss, Vol. II: Separation: Anxiety and anger.* New York: Basic Books, 1973.

Brawley, E., Harris, F., Allen, K., Fleming, R., & Peterson, R. Behavior modification of an autistic child. *Behavioral Science,* 1969, *14,* 87–97.

Brill, N. Q., Koegler, R. R., Epstein, L. J., & Forgy, E. W. Controlled study of psychiatric outpatient treatment. *Archives of General Psychiatry,* 1964, *10,* 581–595.

Bronowski, J. *Science and human values.* New York: Harper & Row, 1959.

Brown, M. The new body psychotherapies. *Psychotherapy: Theory, Research and Practice,* 1973, *10,* 98–116.

Brown, N.O. *Life against death.* Middletown, Conn.: Wesleyan University Press, 1959.

Buber, M. *I and thou.* New York: Charles Scribner's Sons, 1958.

Bugental, J. *The search for authenticity.* New York: Holt, Rinehart & Winston, 1965.

Camus, A. *The rebel: An essay on man in revolt.* New York: Alfred A. Knopf, 1956.

Cannon, W. *The wisdom of the body.* New York: W. W. Norton, 1939.

Cannon, D., Baker, T., & Wehl, C. Emetic and electric-shock alcohol aversion therapy: Six and twelve-month follow-up. *Journal of Consulting and Clinical Psychology,* 1981, *49,* 360–368.

Carkhuff, R. *Helping and human relations: A primer for lay and professional helpers* (Vols. 1 & 2). New York: Holt, Rinehart & Winston, 1969.

Cartwright, R. The effects of psychotherapy on self-consistency: A replication and extension. *Journal of Consulting Psychology,* 1961, *29,* 376–382.

Cartwright, R., & Vogel, J. A comparison of changes in psychoneurotic patients during matched periods of therapy and no therapy. *Journal of Consulting and Clinical Psychology,* 1960, *28,* 121–127.

Cattier, M. *The life and work of Wilhelm Reich.* New York: Horizon Press, 1971.

Cautela, J. Covert sensitization. *Psychological Reports,* 1967, *74,* 459–468.

Cautela, J. The use of covert conditioning in modifying pain behavior. *Journal of Behavior Therapy and Experimental Psychiatry,* 1977, *8,* 45–52.

Chittenden, G. An experimental study in measuring and modifying assertive behavior in young children. *Monographs of the Society for Research in Child Development,* 1942, 7 (Whole No. 31).

Christensen, A., Arkowitz, A., & Anderson, J. Practice dating as a treatment for college dating inhibitions. *Behavior Research and Therapy,* 1975, *13,* 321–331.

Colapinto, J. Structural family therapy. In A. Horne & M. Ohlsen (Eds.), *Family counseling and therapy.* Itasca, Ill.: F.E. Peacock Publishers, 1982.

Colby, K. On the disagreement between Freud and Adler. *American Imago,* 1951, *8,* 229–238.

Comes-Diaz, L. Effects of cognitive and behavioral group treatment on the depressive symptomatology of Puerto Rican women. *Journal of Consulting and Clinical Psychology,* 1981, *49,* 627–632.

Cross, D., Sheehan, P., & Khan, J. Short- and long-term follow-up of clients receiving insight-oriented therapy and behavior therapy. *Journal of Consulting and Clinical Psychology,* 1982, *50,* 103–112.

Crumbaugh, J. C. Changes in Frankl's existential vacuum as a measure of therapeutic outcome. *Newsletter for Research in Psychology,* 1972, *14,* 33–37.

Curlee, R., & Perkins, W. The effect of punishment of expectancy to stutter on the frequencies of subsequent expectancies and stuttering. *Journal of Speech and Hearing Research,* 1968, *11,* 787–795.

Delali, I. The effect of active-assertion and feeling-clarification training on factor-analyzed measures of assertion. *Dissertation Abstracts International*, 1968, *29*, 4844–4845.

Denes-Radomisli, M. Existential-gestalt therapy. In P. Olson (Ed.), *Emotional flooding*. New York: Human Sciences Press, 1976.

DiClemente, C., & Prochaska, J. Self-change and therapy change of smoking behavior: A comparison of processes of change in cessation and maintenance. *Addictive Behavior*, 1982, *7*, 133–142.

DiLoreto, A. O. *Comparative psychotherapy: An experimental analysis*. Chicago: Aldine-Atherton, 1971.

Dollard, J. & Miller, N. *Personality and psychotherapy*. New York: McGraw-Hill, 1950.

Dorfman, E. Personality outcomes of client-centered child therapy. *Psychological Monographs*, 1958, *72* (Whole No. 46).

Dostoevski, F. *Crime and punishment*. New York: Dodd, Mead, 1963.

Dreikurs, R. The four goals of children's misbehavior. *Nervous Child*, 1947, *6*, 3–11.

Dreikurs, R. *The challenge of parenthood*. New York: Duell, Sloan, & Pearce, 1948.

Dreikurs, R. Techniques and dynamics of multiple psychotherapy. *Psychiatric Quarterly*, 1950, *24*, 788–799.

Dreikurs, R. Early experiments with group psychotherapy. *American Journal of Psychotherapy*, 1959, *13*, 882–891.

Dublin, J. Gestalt therapy, existential-gestalt therapy, and/versus "Perls-ism." In E. Smith (Ed.), *The growing edge of gestalt therapy*. New York: Bruner/Mazel, 1975.

DuPont, N. *Effects of induced expectancy and systematic desensitization on test anxiety in therapy, pseudo-desensitization, and control group subjects*. Unpublished doctoral dissertation, University of Rhode Island, 1975.

Dusay, J. Script rehearsal. *Transactional Analysis Bulletin*, 1970, *9*, 117–121.

D'Zurilla, T., & Goldfried, M. Problem solving and behavior modification. *Journal of Abnormal Psychology*, 1971, *78*, 107–126.

Ellenberger, H. A clinical introduction to psychiatric phenomenology and existential analysis. In R. May, E. Angel, & H. Ellenberger (Eds.), *Existence*. New York: Basic Books, 1958.

Ellis, A. *How to live with a neurotic*. New York: Crown Publishers, 1957.(a)

Ellis, A. Outcome of employing three techniques of psychotherapy. *Journal of Clinical Psychology*, 1957, *13*, 344–350.(b)

Ellis, A. *Sex without guilt*. New York: Grove Press, 1958.

Ellis, A. Rational-emotive therapy. In R. Jurjevich (Ed.), *Direct psychotherapy: 28 American originals* (Vol. 1). Coral Gables, Fla.: University of Miami Press, 1972.

Ellis, A. Rational-emotive therapy: Theory and practice. A two-day workshop at Church of the Mediator, Providence, R.I., Spring, 1973.(a)

Ellis, A. *Humanistic psychotherapy: The rational-emotive approach*. New York: McGraw-Hill, 1973.(b)

Ellis, A. Rational-emotive therapy. In R. Corsini (Ed.), *Current psychotherapies*. Itasca, Ill.: F. E. Peacock, 1973.(c)

Ellis, A., & Harper, R. *A guide to successful marriage*. Hollywood: Wilshire, 1972.

Emery, J., & Krumboltz, J. Standard versus individualized hierarchies in desensitization to reduce test anxiety. *Journal of Consulting Psychology*, 1967, *14*, 204–209.

Ends, E., & Page, C. A study of three types of group psychotherapy with hospitalized male inebriates. *Quarterly Journal of Studies of Alcohol*, 1957, *18*, 263–277.

Ends, E., & Page, C. Group therapy and concomitant psychological change. *Psychological Monographs*, 1959(Whole No. 480).

English, J. *The effects of reality therapy on elementary-age children*. Paper presented at the 21st Annual Conference of the California Association for School Psychologists and Psychometrists. Los Angeles, March 1970.

Epstein, L., Parker, L., McCoy, J., & McGee, G. Descriptive analysis of eating regulation in obese and nonobese children. *Journal of Applied Behavior Analysis*, 1976, *9*, 407–415.

Erikson, E. H. *Childhood and society*. New York: W. W. Norton, 1950.

Estes, W. An experimental study of punishment. *Psychological Monographs*, 1944, *57*(Whole No. 263).

Estes, W. Reward in human learning: Theoretical issues and strategic choice points. In R. Glaser (Ed.), *The nature of reinforcement*. New York: Academic Press, 1971.

Fairbairn, W. *An object-relations theory of the personality*. New York: Basic Books, 1952.

Fairweather, G. *Social psychology in treating mental illness: An experimental approach*. New York: John Wiley & Sons, 1964.

Fairweather, G., Sanders, D., Maynard, H., & Cressler, D. *Community life for the mentally ill: An alternative to institutional care*. Hawthorne, N.Y.: Aldine Publishing, 1969.

Fairweather, G., Simon, R., Gebhard, M., Weingarten, F., Holland, J., Sanders, R., Stone, G., & Reahl, J. Relative effectiveness of psychotherapeutic programs: A multicriteria comparison of four programs for three different patient groups. *Psychological Monographs*, 1960, *74*(Whole No. 492).

Fenichel, O. Problems of psychoanalytic techniques. Albany, N.Y.: *Psychoanalytic Quarterly*, 1941.

Fenichel, O. *The psychoanalytic theory of neurosis*. New York: W. W. Norton, 1945.

Finley, W., Wansley, R., & Blenkarn, M. Conditioning treatment of enuresis using a 70 percent intermittent reinforcement schedule. *Behavior Research and Therapy*, 1977, *15*, 419–427.

Foley, V. *An introduction to family therapy*. New York: Grune & Stratton, 1974.

Foulds, M. Measured changes in self-actualization as a result of a growth group experience. *Psychotherapy: Theory, Research and Practice*, 1971, *4*, 338–341.

Frankl, V. *Man's search for meaning*. New York: Washington Square Press, 1963.

Frankl, V. *Psychotherapy and existentialism: Selected papers on logotherapy*. New York: Washington Square Press, 1967.

Franks, C. Can behavior therapy find peace and fulfillment in a school of professional psychology? *The Clinical Psychologist*, 1974, *28*, 11–15.

Freud, S. *The ego and the id*. London: Hogarth Press, 1923.

Freud, S. Character and anal eroticism. In S. Freud (Ed.), *Collected papers*. London: Institute for Psychoanalysis and Hogarth Press, 1925.

Freud, S. *Civilization and its discontents*. New York: W. W. Norton, 1930.

Freud, S. The question of lay analysis. In J. Strachey (Ed.), *The standard edition of the complete psychological works of Sigmund Freud* (Vol. 20). London: Hogarth Press, 1959.

Fuchs, C., & Rehm, L. A self-control behavior therapy program for depression. *Journal of Consulting and Clinical Psychology*, 1977, *45*, 206–215.

Fuhrer, R. The effects of covert sensitization with relaxation induction, covert sensitization without relaxation induction, and attention placebo with the reduction of cigarette smoking. *Dissertation Abstracts International*, May 1972, *11-B*, 6644.

Gannon, W. *The effects of the gestalt-oriented group approach on the interpersonal contact attitudes of selected high school students*. Unpublished doctoral dissertation, Case Western Reserve University, 1972.

Gelder, M., Bancroft, J., Gath, D., Johnston, D., Mathews, A., & Shaw, P. Specific and nonspecific factors in behavior therapy. *British Journal of Psychiatry*, 1973, *123*, 445–462.

Gelder, M., & Marks, I. Severe agoraphobia: A controlled prospective trial of behavior therapy. *British Journal of Psychiatry*, 1966, *112*, 309–319.

Gelder, M., Marks, I., & Wolff, J. Desensitization and psychotherapy in the treatment of phobic states: A controlled inquiry. *British Journal of Psychiatry,* 1967, *113,* 53–73.

Gerson, P. The effect of covert sensitization and modeling in treating maladaptive behavior. *Dissertation Abstracts International,* September 1971, *32, 3–B,* 1841.

Giles, D., & Wolf, M. Toilet training in institutionalized, severe retardates: An application of operant behavior modification techniques. *American Journal of Mental Deficiency,* 1966, *70,* 766–780.

Girodo, M., & Ruehl, J. Cognitive preparation and coping self-talk: Anxiety management during the stress of flying. *Journal of Consulting and Clinical Psychology,* 1978, *46,* 978–989.

Glasser, W. *Reality therapy.* New York: Harper & Row, 1965.

Glasser, W. *Schools without failure.* New York: Harper & Row, 1969.

Glasser, W., & Zunin, L. Reality therapy. In R. Corsini (Ed.), *Current psychotherapies.* Itasca, Ill.: F. E. Peacock, 1973.

Glover, E. Notes on oral character formation. *International Journal of Psychoanalysis,* 1925, *6,* 131–154.

Goldfried, M., & Davison, G. *Clinical behavior therapy.* New York: Holt, Rinehart & Winston, 1976.

Goldsmith, J., & McFall, R. Development and evaluation of an interpersonal-skill training program for psychiatric inpatients. *Journal of Abnormal Psychology,* 1975, *85,* 51–58.

Goodstein, M. A comparison of gestalt and transactional analysis therapies in marathons. *Dissertation Abstracts International,* 1972, *33, 3–B,* 1283.

Gordon, T. *Parent effectiveness training.* New York: Peter Wyden, 1970.

Gordon, T. *Teacher effectiveness training.* New York: Peter Wyden, 1974.

Greenberg, G. The family interactional perspective: A study and examination of the work of Don D. Jackson. *Family Process,* 1977, *16,* 385–412.

Greenson, R. R. *The technique and practice of psychoanalysis* (Vol. 1). New York: International Universities Press, 1967.

Greenspoon, J. The reinforcing effect of two spoken sounds on the frequency of two responses. *American Journal of Psychology,* 1955, *68,* 409–416.

Grimaldi, K., & Lichtenstein, E. Hot, smoky air as an aversive stimulus in the treatment of smoking. *Behavior Research and Therapy,* 1969, *7,* 275–282.

Haley, J. Control in psychotherapy with schizophrenics. In D. Jackson (Ed.), *Therapy communication and change.* Palo Alto, Calif.: Science and Behavior Books, 1973.(a)

Haley, J. *Uncommon therapies: The psychiatric techniques of Milton Erickson, M.D.* New York: W. W. Norton, 1973.(b)

Haley, J. *Problem-solving therapy: New strategies for effective family therapy.* San Francisco: Jossey-Bass, 1976.

Hall, C., & Lindzey, G. *Theories of personality.* New York: John Wiley & Sons, 1970.

Hall, S. Self-control and therapist control in the behavioral treatment of overweight women. *Behavior Research and Therapy,* 1977, *10,* 59–68.

Hall, S., Hall, R., DeBoer, G., & O'Kalitchs, P. Self- and external management compared with psychotherapy in the control of obesity. *Behavior Research and Therapy,* 1977, *15,* 89–95.

Hancur, W., & Prochaska, J. *Symptom and dynamic stimuli in the desensitization of test anxiety.* Unpublished manuscript, University of Rhode Island, 1977.

Harris, A. A. A comparative study of results of neurotic patients treated by two different methods. *Journal of Mental Sciences,* 1954, *100,* 718–721.

Harris, H., & Bruner, C. A comparison of a self-control and a contract procedure for weight control. *Behavior Research and Therapy,* 1971, *9,* 347–354.

Harris, T. A. *I'm OK—you're OK.* New York: Harper & Row, 1967.

Hartmann, H. *Ego psychology and the problem of adaptation.* New York: International Universities Press, 1958.

Hartmann, H., Kris, E., & Loewenstein, R. M. Comments on the formation of psychic structure. In A. Freud, et al. (Eds.), *The psychoanalytic study of the child.* New York: International Universities Press, 1947.

Hawes, R. Reality therapy in the classroom. *Dissertation Abstracts International,* University of the Pacific, 1971, *32A,* 2483.

Hebb, D. O., Held, R., Riesent, A., & Teuber, H. Sensory deprivation: Facts in search of a theory. *Journal of Nervous and Mental Disorders,* 1961, *132,* 17–43.

Heckerman, C., & Prochaska, J. Development and evaluation of weight-reduction procedures in a health maintenance organization. In R. Stuart (Ed.), *Behavioral self-management.* New York: Brunner/Mazel, 1977.

Heidegger, M. *Being and time.* New York: Harper & Row, 1962.

Heilbrunn, G. Results with psychoanalytic therapy and professional commitment. *American Journal of Psychotherapy,* 1966, *20,* 89–99.

Heine, R. W. A comparison of patients' reports on psychotherapeutic experience with psychoanalytic, nondirective, and Adlerian therapists. *American Journal of Psychotherapy,* 1953, *7,* 16–22.

Hendricks, I. The discussion of the "instinct to master." *Psychoanalytic Quarterly,* 1943, *12,* 561–565.

Hersen, M., & Barlow, D. *Single-case experimental designs: Strategies for studying behavior change.* Elmsford, N.Y.: Pergamon Press, 1976.

Hersen, M., Eislen, R., Johnson, M., & Pinkston, S. Effects of practice, instructions, and modeling on components of assertive behavior. *Behavior Research and Therapy,* 1973, *11,* 443–451.

Hogan, R. Implosive therapy in the short-term treatment of psychotics. *Psychotherapy: Theory, Research and Practice,* 1966, *3,* 25–32.

Holden, E. The primal questionnaire: Patients' reports on changes during primal therapy. In A. Janov & E. Holden (Eds.), *The primal man.* New York: Crowell, 1975.

Holland, G. Transactional analysis. In R. Corsini (Ed.), *Current psychotherapies.* Itasca, Ill.: F. E. Peacock, 1973.

Horner, A. *Object relations and the developing ego in therapy.* New York: Jason Aronsen, 1979.

Hull, C. *Principles of behavior.* New York: Appleton-Century-Crofts, 1943.

Hunt, W., & Bespalec, D. An evaluation of current methods of modifying smoker behavior. *Journal of Clinical Psychology,* 1974, *30,* 431–438.

Jackson, D. The eternal triangle. In J. Haley & L. Hoffman (Eds.), *Techniques of family therapy.* New York: Basic Books, 1967.

Jacobson, E. *Progressive relaxation.* Chicago: University of Chicago Press, 1938.

James, M., & Jongeward, D. *Born to win.* Reading, Mass.: Addison-Wesley Publishing, 1971.

Janda, L., & Rimm, D. Covert sensitization in the treatment of obesity. *Journal of Abnormal Psychology,* 1972, *80,* 37–42.

Janov, A. *The primal scream.* New York: G. P. Putnam's & Sons, 1970.

Janov, A. *The anatomy of mental illness: The scientific basis of primal therapy.* New York: G. P. Putnam's & Sons, 1971.

Janov, A., & Holden, E. (Eds.). *The primal man.* New York: Crowell, 1975.

Johnson, S., & Sechrest, L. Comparison of desensitization and progressive relaxation in treating test anxiety. *Journal of Consulting and Clinical Psychology,* 1968, *32,* 280–286.

Jesness, C. Comparative effectiveness of behavior modification and transactional analysis programs for delinquents. *Journal of Consulting and Clinical Psychology,* 1975, *43,* 758–779.

Johnson, M., Kelley, C., Harris, F., & Wolf, M. An application of reinforcement principles to development of motor skills of a young child. *Child Development*, 1966, *37*, 379–387.

Jones, E. *The life and works of Sigmund Freud* (Vol. 2). New York: Basic Books, 1955.

Jones, E. *The life and works of Sigmund Freud* (Vol. 3). New York: Basic Books, 1957.

Jones, E., & Nisbett, R. The actor and the observer: Divergent perceptions of the causes of behavior. In E. Jones, D. Kanouse, H. Kelley, R. Nisbett, S. Violins, & B. Weiner (Eds.), *Attribution: Perceiving the causes of behavior*. Morristown, N.J.: General Learning Press, 1972.

Kallman, W., Hersen, M., & O'Toole, D. The use of social reinforcement in a case of conversion reaction. *Behavior Therapy*, 1975, *6*, 411–413.

Kanfer, F., & Phillips, J. *Learning foundations of behavior therapy*. New York: John Wiley & Sons, 1970.

Kanter, N. *A comparison of self-control desensitization and systematic rational restructuring for the reduction of interpersonal anxiety*. Unpublished doctoral dissertation, SUNY at Stoneybrook, 1975, 3611–B.

Kaplan, H. *The new sex therapy*. New York: Brunner/Mazel, 1974.

Kaplan, R., McCordick, S., & Twitchell, M. Is it the cognitive or the behavioral component which makes cognitive-behavior modification effective in test anxiety? *Journal of Counseling Psychology*, 1979, *26*, 371–377.

Karle, W., Corriere, R., & Hart, J. Psychophysiological changes in abreactive therapy—Study 1: Primal therapy. *Psychotherapy: Theory, Research and Practice*, 1973, *10*, 117–122.

Karpman, S. Script drama analysis. *Transactional Analysis Bulletin*, 1968, 7, 39–43.

Karst, T., & Trexler, L. Initial study using fixed-role and rational-emotive therapy in treating public-speaking anxiety. *Journal of Consulting and Clinical Psychology*, 1970, *34*, 360–366.

Keen, E. *Three faces of being: Toward an existential clinical psychology*. 1970 by The Meredith Corporation. Reprinted by permission of Irvington Publishers.

Keleman, S. *Sexuality, self, and survival*. San Francisco: Lodestar Press, 1971.

Keleman. S. We do have bodies and we are our bodies. *Psychology Today*, 1973, 7, 64–70.

Keller, J., Bookling, J., & Croake, J. Effects of a program in rational thinking on anxieties in older persons. *Journal of Counseling Psychology*, 1975, *22*, 54–57.

Kempler, W. Gestalt therapy. In R. Corsini (Ed.), *Current psychotherapies*. Itasca, Ill.: F. E. Peacock, 1973.

Kendall, P., & Braswell, L. Cognitive-behavioral self-control therapy for children: A components analysis. *Journal of Consulting and Clinical Psychology*, 1982, *50*, 672–689.

Kendall, P., & Finch, A. A cognitive behavioral treatment for impulsivity: A group comparison study. *Journal of Consulting and Clinical Psychology*, 1978, *46*, 110–118.

Kendrick, M., Craig, K., Lawson, D., & Davidson, P. Cognitive and behavioral therapy for musical-performance anxiety. *Journal of Consulting and Clinical Psychology*, 1982, *50*, 353–362.

Kent, R., Wilson, T., & Nelson, R. Effects of false heart-rate feedback on avoidance behavior: An investigation of cognitive desensitization. *Behavior Therapy*, 1972, *3*, 1–6.

Kernberg, O. Summary and conclusion of "Psychotherapy and psychoanalysis: Final report of the Menninger Foundation's Psychotherapy Research Project." *International Journal of Psychiatry*, 1973, *11*, 62–77.

Kernberg, O. *Borderline conditions and pathological narcissism*. New York: Jason Aronsen, 1975.

Kernberg, O. *Object-relations theory and clinical psychoanalysis.* New York: Jason Aronsen, 1976.

Kernberg, O. Some implications of object-relations theory for psychoanalytic technique. *Journal of American Psychoanalytic Association,* 1979, *70,* 207–239.

Keutzer, C. Behavior modification of smoking: The experimental investigation of diverse techniques. *Behavior Research and Therapy,* 1968, *6,* 137–157.

Kierkegaard, S. *Fear and trembling.* New York: Doubleday Publishing, 1954. (a)

Kierkegaard, S. *The sickness unto death.* New York: Doubleday Publishing, 1954. (b)

Knight, R. P. Evaluation of the results of psychoanalytic therapy. *American Journal of Psychiatry,* 1941, *98,* 434–436.

Kockott, G., Dittmar, F., & Nasselt, L. Systematic desensitization of erectile impotence: A controlled study. *Archives of Sexual Behavior,* 1975, *4,* 493–500.

Kohut, H. *The analysis of the self.* New York: International Universities Press, 1971.

Kohut, H. *The restoration of the self.* New York: International Universties Press, 1977.

Krippner, S. Relationship between reading improvement and 10 variables. *Perceptual and Motor Skills,* 1964, *16,* 15–20.

Krisch, I., & Henry, D. Self-desensitization and meditation in the reduction of public-speaking anxiety. *Journal of Consulting and Clinical Psychology,* 1979, *47,* 536–541.

Lang, P., Melamed, B., & Hart, J. A psychophysiological analysis of fear modification using an automated desensitization procedure. *Journal of Abnormal Psychology,* 1970, *76,* 220–234.

Langsley, D., Flomenhaft, K., & Machotka, P. Follow-up evelation of family crisis therapy. *American Journal of Orthopsychiatry,* 1969, *39,* 753–759.

Langsley, D., Machotka, P., & Flomenhaft, K. Avoiding mental hospital admission: A follow-up study. *American Journal of Psychiatry,* 1971, *127,* 127–130.

LaPointe, K., & Rimm, D. Cognitive, assertive, and insight-oriented group therapies in the treatment of reactive depression in women. *Psychotherapy: Theory, Research and Practice,* Fall 1980, *17,* 312–321.

Lazarus, A. Group therapy of phobic disorders by systematic desensitization. *Journal of Abnormal and Social Psychology,* 1961, *63,* 504–510.

Lazarus, A. Behavior rehearsal versus nondirected therapy versus advice in affecting behavior change. *Behavior Research and Therapy,* 1966, *4,* 209–212.

Lazarus, A. *Behavior therapy and beyond.* New York: McGraw-Hill, 1971.

Lazarus, A. Has behavior therapy outlived its usefulness? *American Psychologist,* 1977, *32,* 550–555.

Levinson, D., Dorrow, C., Klein, E., Levinson, M., & McKee, B. *The seasons of a man's life.* New York: Alfred A. Knopf, 1978.

Levis, D. Effects of serial CS presentation and other characteristics of the CS on the conditioned avoidance response. *Psychological Reports,* 1966, *18,* 755–766.

Levis, D., Bouska, S., Eron, J., & McIlhon, M. Serial CS presentation and one-way avoidance conditioning: A noticeable lack of delayed responding. *Psychonomic Science,* 1970, *20,* 147–149.

Levis, D., & Carrera, R. Effects of 10 hours of implosive therapy in the treatment of outpatients. *Journal of Abnormal Psychology,* 1967, *72,* 504–508.

Levis, D., & Stampfl, T. Effects of serial CS presentation on shuttlebox avoidance responding. *Learning and Motivation,* 1972, *3,* 73–90.

Levitsky, A., & Perls, F. The rules and games of gestalt therapy. In J. Fagan & I. Shepherd (Eds.), *Gestalt therapy now.* Palo Alto, Calif.: Science and Behavior Books, 1970.

Lewinsohn, P. A behavioral approach to depression. In R. M. Fredman & M. M. Katz (Eds.), *The psychology of depression: Contemporary theory and research.* Washington, D.C.: V. H. Winston, 1974.

Lewis, J. *No single thread.* New York: Bruner/Mazel, 1976.

Liberman, R. *A guide to behavioral analysis and therapy.* Elmsford, N.Y.: Pergamon Press, 1972.

Lichtenstein, E., Harris, D., Bircher, G., Wahl, J., & Schmahi, D. Rapid smoking: Warm, smoky air, and attention placebo in the modification of smoking behavior. *Journal of Consulting and Clinical Psychology,* 1973, *40,* 92–98.

Lick, J., & Heffler, D. Relaxation training and attention placebo in the treatment of severe insomnia. *Journal of Consulting and Clinical Psychology,* 1977, *45,* 153–161.

Lidz, T. *The family and human adaption.* New York: International Universities Press, 1963.

Lieberman, M., Yalom, I., & Miles, M. *Encounter groups: First facts.* New York: Basic Books, 1973.

Liebman, R., Horning, P., & Berger, H. An integrated treatment program for psychogenic pain. *Family Process,* 1976, *15,* 397–405.

Liebman, R., Minuchin, S., & Baker, L. The use of structural family therapy on the treatment of intractable asthma. *American Journal of Psychiatry,* 1974, *131,* 535–540.

Liebman, R., Minuchin, S., Baker, L., & Rosman, B. The treatment of anorexia nervosa. *Current Psychiatric Therapies,* 1975, *15,* 51–57.

Lipsky, M., Kassinove, H., & Muller, N. Effects of rational-emotive therapy, rational role reversal, and rational-emotive imagery on the emotional adjustment of community mental health center patients. *Journal of Consulting and Clinical Psychology,* 1980, *48,* 366–374.

Loevinger, J. *Ego development.* San Francisco: Jossey-Bass, 1976.

Lomont, J., Gilner, F., Spector, N., & Skinner, K. Group assertion training and group insight therapies. *Psychological Reports,* 1969, *25,* 463–470.

London, P. *The modes and morals of psychotherapy.* New York: Holt, Rinehart & Winston, 1964.

London, P. The end of ideology in behavior modification. *American Psychologist,* 1972, *27,* 913–920.

Lorenz, K. *On aggression.* New York: Harcourt Brace Jovanovich, 1963.

Lovaas, O., Berberich, J., Perloff, B., & Schaeffer, B. Acquisition of imitative speech by schizophrenic children. *Science,* 1966, *151,* 705–707.

Lovaas, O., Freitas, L., Nelson, K., & Whalen, L. The establishment of imitation and its uses for the development of complex behavior in schizophrenic children. *Behavior Research and Therapy,* 1967, *5,* 171–181.

Lovass, O., & Simmons, J. Manipulaton of self-destruction in three retarded children. *Journal of Applied Behavioral Analysis,* 1969, *2,* 143–157.

Lowen, A. *Physical dynamics of character structure.* New York: Grune & Stratton, 1958.

Lowen, A. *Love and orgasm.* New York: Macmillan, 1965.

Lowen, A. *The betrayal of the body.* New York: Collier, 1967.

Lowen, A. Bioenergetic analysis: A development of Reichian therapy. In G. Goldman & D. Milman (Eds.), *Innovations in psychotherapy.* Springfield, Ill.: Charles C Thomas, 1972.

Luborsky, L., Singer, B., & Luborsky, L. Comparative studies of psychotherapies. *Archives of General Psychiatry,* 1975, *32,* 995–1008.

Luria, A. *The role of speech in the regulation of normal and abnormal behaviors.* New York: Liveright, 1961.

Luthe, W. *Autogenic therapy* (Vols. 1–4). New York: Grune & Stratton, 1969–1973.

Luthman, S. *Intimacy: The essence of male and female.* Los Angeles: Nash Publishing, 1972.

MacPherson, E., Candee, B., & Hohman, R. A comparison of three methods for eliminating disruptive lunchroom behavior. *Journal of Applied Behavior Analysis,* 1974, *7,* 287–297.

Maddi, S. *Personality theories: A comparative analysis.* Homewood, Ill.: Dorsey Press, 1972.

Mahler, M. S. *On human symbiosis of the vicissitudes of individuation.* New York: International Universities Press, 1968.

Mahoney, M. Self-reward and self-monitoring techniques for weight control. *Behavior Therapy,* 1974, *1,* 48–57.

Malan, D. H. *The frontier of brief psychotherapy.* New York: Plenum Press, 1976. (a)

Malan, D. H. *Toward the validation of dynamic psychotherapy: A replication.* New York: Plenum Press, 1976. (b)

Malcolm, J. A reporter at large: The one-way mirror. *The New Yorker,* May 15, 1978, 39–114.

Maletsky, B. Self-referred versus court-referred sexually deviant patients: Success with assisted covert sensitization. *Behavior Therapy,* 1980, *11,* 306–314.

Malleson, N. Panic and phobia. *Lancet,* 1959, *1,* 225–227.

Marshall, W., Boutilier, J., & Minnes, P. The modification of phobic behavior by covert reinforcement. *Behavior Therapy,* 1974, *5,* 469–480.

Martin, D. *Learning-based client-centered therapy.* Monterey, Calif.: Brooks/Cole Publishing, 1972.

Maslow, A. Existential psychology—What's in it for us? In R. May (Ed.), *Existential psychology.* New York: Random House, 1960.

Masters, W., & Johnson, V. *Human sexual response.* Boston: Little, Brown, 1966.

Masters, W., & Johnson, V. *Human sexual inadequacy.* Boston: Little, Brown, 1970.

Masur, F. Behavior therapy in a case of Pollakiuria. *Journal of Behavior Therapy and Experimental Psychiatry,* 1976, *7,* 175–178.

Mathews, A., Bancroft, J., Whitehead, A., Hackman, A., Julier, D., Bancroft, J., Goth, D., & Shaw, P. The behavioral treatment of sexual inadequacy: A comparative study. *Behavior Research and Therapy,* 1976, *14,* 427–436.

May, P. R., & Tuma, A. H. Treatment of schizophrenia: An experimental study of five treatment methods. *British Journal of Psychiatry,* 1965, *111,* 503–510.

May, R. Contributions of existential psychotherapy. In R. May, E. Angel, & H. Ellenberger (Eds.), *Existence.* New York: Basic Books, 1958. (a)

May, R. The origins and significance of the existential movement in psychology. In R. May, E. Angel, & H. Ellenberger (Eds.), *Existence.* New York: Basic Books, 1958. (b)

May. R. *Psychology and the human dilemma.* New York: Van Nostrand Reinhold, 1967.

May. R. *Love and will.* New York: Dell Publishing, 1969.

McConaghy, N. Aversive and positive conditioning treatments of homosexuality. *Behavior Research and Therapy,* 1975, *13,* 309–319.

McConnaughy, E., Prochaska, J., & Velicer, W. Stages of change in psychotherapy; Measurement and sample profiles. *Psychotherapy: Theory, Research and Practice,* Fall 1983, *20,* 368–375.

McInerny, B. Research with primal patients. In A. Janov & E. Holden (Eds.), *The primal man.* New York: Crowell, 1975.

Meador, B., & Rogers, C. Client-centered therapy. In R. Corsini (Ed.), *Current psychotherapies.* Itasca, Ill.: F. E. Peacock, 1973.

Meichenbaum, D. *Cognitive-behavior modification.* New York: Plenum Press, 1977.

Meichenbaum, D., & Goodman, J. Reflection-impulsivity and verbal control of motor behavior. *Child Development,* 1969, *40,* 785–797.

Meichenbaum, D., & Goodman, J. Training impulsive children to talk to themselves: A means of developing self-control. *Journal of Abnormal Psychology,* 1971, *77,* 115–126.

Meissner, W. The conceptualization of marriage and family dynamics from a psychoanalytic perspective. In T. Paolino & B. McCrady (Eds.), *Marriage and marital therapy.* New York: Bruner/Mazel, 1978.

Mellström, M., & Gelsomino, J. Contingency management of an adult's inappropriate urination and masturbation in a family context. *Journal of Behavior Therapy and Experimental Psychiatry*, 1976, *7*, 89–90.

Meltzoff, J., & Kornreich, M. *Research in psychotherapy.* New York: Atherton, 1970.

Miller, G., Galanter, E., & Pribram, K. *Plans and the structure of behavior.* New York: Holt, Rinehart & Winston, 1960.

Minuchin, S. The use of an ecological framework in child psychiatry. In J. Anthony & C. Kaupernik (Eds.), *The child in his family.* New York:John Wiley & Sons, 1970.

Minuchin, S. Structural family therapy. In G. Caplan (Ed.), *American Handbook of Psychiatry* (Vol. 2). New York: Basic Books, 1972.

Minuchin, S. *Families and family therapy.* Cambridge, Mass.: Harvard University Press, 1974.

Minuchin, S., Baker, L., Rosman, B., Liebman, R., Milman, L., & Todd, T. A conceptual model of psychosomatic illness in children. *The Archives of General Psychiatry*, 1975, *32*, 1031–1038.

Minuchin, S., Montalvo, B., Guerney, B., Rosman, B., & Schumer, F. *Families of the slums.* New York: Basic Books, 1967.

Mischel, W. *Personality and assessment.* New York: John Wiley & Sons, 1968.

Mischel, W. Toward a cognitive social learning reconceptualization of personality. *Psychological Review*, 1973, *80*, 252–283.

Moleski, R., & Tosi, D. Comparative psychotherapy: Rational-emotive therapy versus systematic desensitization in the treatment of stuttering. *Journal of Clinical and Consulting Psychology*, 1976, *44*, 309–311.

Moore, N. Behavior therapy in bronchial asthma: A controlled study. *Journal of Psychosomatic Research*, 1965, *9*, 257–276.

Morganstern, K. Implosive therapy and flooding procedures: A critical review. *Psychological Bulletin*, 1973, *79*, 318–334.

Mosak, H., & Dreikurs, R. Adlerian psychotherapy. In R. Corsini (Ed.), *Current psychotherapies.* Itasca, Ill.: F. E. Peacock, 1973.

Mowrer, O. H. On the dual nature of learning—A reinterpretation of "conditioning" and "problem-solving." *Harvard Education Review,* 1947, *17*, 102–148.

Mowrer, O. H. *The crisis in psychiatry and religion.* New York: Van Nostrand Reinhold, 1961.

Murphy, J., Williamson, D., Buxton, A., Moody, S., Asher, N., & Warner, M. The long-term effects of spouse involvement upon weight loss and maintenance. *Behavior Therapy*, 1982, *13*, 681–693.

Murphy, R., & Ellis, A. *Rational-emotive psychotherapy outcome studies: A bibliography.* Unpublished manuscript, Institute for Rational Living, New York, 1976.

Neill, A. The man Reich. In P. Ritter (Ed.), *Wilhelm Reich memorial volume.* Nottingham, England: Ritter Press, 1958.

Nelson, M. O., & Haberer, M. H. Effectiveness of Adlerian counseling with low-achieving students. *Journal of Individual Psychology*, 1966, *22*, 222–227.

Nichols, M., & Zax, M. *Catharsis in psychotherapy.* New York: Gardner Press, 1977.

Norcross, J., & Prochaska, J. A national survey of clinical psychologists: Affiliations and orientations. *The Clinical Psychologist*, 1982, *39*, 1–6.

Norcross, J., Prochaska, J., & Hambrecht, M. Levels of attribution and change scale: Development, validation, and measurement. *Journal of Clinical Psychology*, in press.

Ober, D. Modification of smoking behavior. *Journal of Consulting and Clinical Psychology*, 1968, *32*, 543–549.

Obler, M. Systematic desensitization in sexual disorders. *Journal of Behavior Therapy and Experimental Psychiatry*, 1973, *4*, 93–101.

O'Connor, J.F., Daniels, G., Flood, C., Karush, A., Moses, L., & Stern, L. The effects of psychotherapy on the course of ulcerative colitis: A preliminary report. *American Journal of Psychiatry*, 1964, *120*, 738–742.

O'Leary, K., & Becker, W. Behavior modification of an adjustment class: A token reinforcement program. *Exceptional Children*, 1967, *33*, 637–642.

O'Leary, K., Becker, W., Evans, M., & Saudargas, R. A token reinforcement program in a public school: A replication and systematic analysis. *Journal of Applied Behavior Analysis*, 1969, *2*, 3–13.

Olsen, P. *Emotional flooding.* New York: Human Sciences Press, 1976.

Olson, P., Ganley, R., Devine, V., & Dorsey, G. Long-term effects of behavioral versus insight-oriented therapy with inpatient alcoholics. *Journal of Consulting and Clinical Psychology*, 1981, *49*, 866–877.

Orgel, S.Z. Effect of psychoanalysis on the course of peptic ulcer. *Psychosomatic Medicine*, 1958, *20*, 117–125.

Osborn, A. *Applied imagination.* New York: Charles Scribner's Sons, 1963.

Osterhouse, R. Desensitization and study skills training as treatment for two types of test-anxious students. *Journal of Counseling Psychology*, 1972, *19*, 301–307.

Otto, H., & Otto, R. *Total sex.* New York: New American Library, 1972.

Painter, J. The modification of smoking behavior in a controlled public clinic. *Dissertation Abstracts International*, February 1972, *8–B*, 4867.

Parloff, M. Shopping for the right therapy. *Saturday Review*, February 21, 1976, 14–16.

Passman, R. A procedure for eliminating writer's block in a college student. *Journal of Behavior Therapy and Experimental Psychiatry*, 1976, *7*, 297–298.

Patterson, G. R. A learning-theory approach to the treatment of the school-phobia child. In L. P. Ullmann & L. Krasner (Eds.), *Case studies in behavior modification.* New York: Holt, Rinehart & Winston, 1965.

Paul, G. *Insight versus desensitization in psychotherapy: An experiment in anxiety reduction.* Stanford: Stanford University Press, 1966.

Paul, G. Insight versus desensitization in psychotherapy two years after termination. *Journal of Consulting Psychology*, 1967, *31*, 333–348.

Penfield, W. *The excitable cortex in conscious man.* Springfield, Ill.: Charles C Thomas, 1958.

Perls, F. *Ego, hunger and agression: A revision of Freud's theory and method.* Winchester, Mass.: Allen & Unwin, 1947.

Perls, F. *Gestalt therapy verbatim.* Lafayette, Calif.: Real People Press, 1969. (a)

Perls, F. *In and out of the garbage pail.* Lafayette, Calif.: Real People Press, 1969. (b)

Perls, F. Four lectures. In J. Fagan & I. Shepherd (Eds.), *Gestalt therapy now.* Palo Alto, Calif.: Science and Behavior Books, 1970.

Perls, F., Hefferline, R., & Goodman, P. *Gestalt therapy: Excitement and growth in personality.* New York: Dell Publishing, 1951.

Perry, W. *Forms of intellectual and ethical development in the college years: A scheme.* New York: Holt, Rinehart & Winston, 1970.

Phillips, E. Achievement Place: Token reinforcement procedures in a home-style rehabilitation setting for pre-delinquent boys. *Journal of Applied Behavior Analysis*, 1968, *1*, 213–223.

Phillips, E. L., Phillips, E. A., Fixen, D., & Wolf, M. Achievement Place: Modification of the behaviors of pre-delinquent boys with a token economy. *Journal of Applied Behavior Analysis*, 1971, *4*, 45–59.

Piaget, J. *The origins of intelligence in children.* New York: International Universities Press, 1952.

Pittman, F., Langsley, D., & DeYoung, C. Work and school phobias: A family approach to treatment. *American Journal of Psychiatry*, 1968, *124*, 1535–1541.

Popler, K. Token reinforcement in the treatment of nocturnal enuresis: A case study and six-month follow-up. *Journal of Behavior Therapy and Experimental Psychiatry*, 1976, 7, 83–84.

Polster, E., & Polster, M. *Gestalt therapy integrated.* New York: Vintage Books, 1973.

Prochaska, J. *Implosive therapy with a severe obsessive compulsive patient.* Paper presented at the University of Michigan Clinical Colloquium, May 1968.

Prochaska, J. Symptom and dynamic cues in the implosive treatment of test anxiety. *Journal of Abnormal Psychology*, 1971, 77, 133–142.

Prochaska, J., Crimi, P., Lapsanski, D., Martel, L., & Reid, P. Self-change processes, self-efficacy, and self-concept in relapse and maintenance of smoking cessation. *Psychological Reports*, 1982, 51, 983–990.

Prochaska, J., & DiClemente, C. Transtheoretical therapy: Toward a more integrative model of change. *Psychotherapy: Theory, Research and Practice*, 1982, 19, 276–288.

Prochaska, J., & DiClemente, C. Stages and processes of self-change of smoking: Toward an integrative model of change. *Journal of Consulting and Clinical Psychology*, 1983, 51, 390–395.

Prochaska, J., & DiClemente, C. *The transtheoretical approach: Crossing the traditional boundaries of therapy.* Homewood, Illinois: Dow Jones-Irwin, 1984.

Prochaska, J., & DiClemente, C. Self-change processes, self-efficacy, and decisional balance across five stages of smoking cessation. In *Advances in Cancer Control—1983*, New York: Alan R. Liss, in press.

Prochaska, J., & DiClemente, C. Processes of self-change with smoking, obesity, and psychic distress. In S. Shiffman & T. Wills (Eds.), *Coping and substance abuse.* New York: Academic Press, in press.

Prochaska, J., & Marzilli, R. Adaptation of Masters and Johnson's therapy for sexual problems to an outpatient clinic. *Psychotherapy: Theory, Research and Practice*, Winter 1973, 10, 301–306.

Prochaska, J., & Norcross, J. Contemporary psychotherapists: A national survey of characteristics, practices, orientations, and attitudes. *Psychotherapy: Theory, Research and Practice*, Summer 1983, 20, 161–173.

Prochaska, J., & Norcross, J. Psychotherapist's perspectives on treating themselves and their clients for psychic distress. *Professional Psychology*, 1983, 14, 642–655.

Prochaska, J., & Norcross, J. Treating ourselves versus treating our clients: A replication and extension. Manuscript in preparation, University of Rhode Island.

Prochaska, J., Norcross, J., & DiClemente, C. Psychotherapists' self-change versus laypersons' self-change: A comparative analysis of treatment strategies. *Psychotherapy: Theory, Research and Practice*, in press.

Prochaska, J., & Prochaska, Janice. Twentieth-century trends in marriage and marital therapy. In T. Paolino & B. McCrady (Eds.), *Marriage and marital therapy.* New York: Bruner/Mazel, 1978.

Prochaska, J., Smith, N., Marzilli, R., Donovan, W., & Colby, J. Demonstration of the advantages of remote-control aversive stimulation in the control of headbanging in a retarded child. *Journal of Behavior Therapy and Experimental Psychiatry*, 1974, 5, 285–389.

Prochaska, Janice. Sex information service expands. *The China News*, August 24, 1972, 1. Also cited in *New York Times*, August 24, 1972.

Prochaska, Janice, & Coyle, J. Choosing parenthood: A needed family life education group. *Social Casework*, 1979, 60, 289–295.

Psychology Today. Letter to the editor, May 1972.

Rank, O. *Will therapy.* New York: Alfred A. Knopf, 1936.

Rapaport, D. The theory of ego autonomy: A generalization. *Bulletin of Menninger Clinic*, 1958, 22, 13–35.

Rehm, L. A self-control model of depression. *Behavior Therapy*, 1977, *8*, 787–804.

Reich, W. *The function of the orgasm*. New York: Orgone Institute, 1942.

Reich, W. *Character analysis*. New York: Orgone Institute, 1945.

Reich, W. *Selected writings*. New York: Farrar, Straus & Giroux, 1951.

Reich, W. *People in trouble*. New York: Orgone Institute, 1953.

Reich, W. *Reich speaks of Freud*. Edited by M. Higgins & C. Higgins. New York: Farrar, Straus & Giroux, 1967.

Reich, W. *The mass psychology of facism*. New York: Farrar, Straus & Giroux, 1970.

Reik, T. *Listening with the third ear*. New York: Farrar, Straus & Giroux, 1948.

Reisinger, J. The treatment of "anxiety-depression" via positive reinforcement and response cost. *Journal of Applied Behavior Analysis*, 1972, *5*, 125–130.

Reisman, D. *The lonely crowd*. New Haven, Conn.: Yale University Press, 1961.

Reiss, D. The multiple family group as a small society: Family regulation of interaction with nonmembers. *American Journal of Psychiatry*, 1977, *134*, 21–24.

Riess, B. F. Changes in patient income concomitant with psychotherapy. *Journal of Consulting Psychology*, 1967, *31*, 430.

Rimm, D., DeGrost, J., Boord, P., Heiman, J., & Dillon, P. Systematic desensitization of an anger response. *Behavior Research and Therapy*, 1971, *9*, 273–280.

Rimm, D., Keyson, M., & Hunziker, J. *Group assertive training in the treatment of antisocial aggression*. Unpublished manuscript, Arizona State University, 1971.

Rimm, D., & Masters, J. *Behavior therapy*. New York: Academic Press, 1974.

Robinson, D. *The Freudian left: Wilhelm Reich, Geza Roheim, Herbert Marcuse*. New York: Harper & Row, 1969.

Roethlisberger, F., & Dickson, W. *Management and the worker*. Cambridge, Mass.: Harvard University Press, 1939.

Rogers, C. *The clinical treatment of the problem child*. Boston: Houghton Mifflin, 1939.

Rogers, C. *Counseling and psychotherapy*. Boston: Houghton Mifflin, 1942.

Rogers, C. *Client-centered therapy*. Boston: Houghton Mifflin, 1951.

Rogers, C. The necessary and sufficient conditions of therapeutic personality change. *Journal of Consulting Psychology*, 1957, *21*, 95–103.

Rogers, C. A theory of therapy, personality, and interpersonal relationships, as developed in the client-centered framework. In S. Koch (Ed.), *Psychology: A study of a science, Vol. III: Formulations of the person and the social context*. New York: McGraw-Hill, 1959.

Rogers, C. *On becoming a person*. Boston: Houghton Mifflin, 1961.

Rogers, C. *On encounter groups*. New York: Harper & Row, 1970.

Rogers, C. *On becoming partners: Marriage and its alternatives*. New York: Delacourte, 1972.

Rogers, C., & Dymond, R. *Psychotherapy and personality change*. Chicago: University of Chicago Press, 1954.

Rogers, C., Gendlin, E., Kiesler, D., & Truax, C. *The therapeutic relationship and its impact: A study of psychotherapy with schizophrenics*. Madison: University of Wisconsin Press, 1967.

Rogers, C., & Rablen, R. *A scale of process in psychotherapy*. Unpublished manuscript, University of Wisconsin, 1958.

Rokeach, M. Faith, hope, and bigotry. *Psychology Today*, April 1970, *3*, 33–38.

Rose, S. Intense feeling therapy. In P. Olsen (Ed.), *Emotional flooding*. New York: Human Sciences Press, 1976.

Rosenberg, J. *Total orgasm*. New York: Random House, 1973.

Rosman, B., Minuchin, S., Liebman, R., & Baker, L. *Family therapy for psychosomatic children*. Paper presented at the annual meeting of the American Academy of Psychosomatic Medicine, Atlanta, November, 1978.

Roth, D., Bielski, R., Jones. M., Packer, W., & Osborn, G. A comparison of self-control therapy and combined self-control therapy and antidepressant medication in the treatment of depression. *Behavior Therapy*, 1982, *13*, 133–144.

Rotter, J. *Social learning and clinical psychology*. Englewood Cliffs, N.J.: Prentice-Hall, 1954.

Rotter, J. Some implications of a social learning theory for the practice of psychotherapy. In D. Levis (Ed.), *Learning approaches to behavior change*. Hawthorne, N.Y.: Aldine Publishing, 1970.

Rush, A., Beck, A., Kovacs, M., & Hallan, S. Comparative efficacy of cognitive therapy and pharmacotherapy in the treatment of depressed outpatients. *Cognitive Therapy and Research*, 1977, *1*, 17–37.

Sachs, L., Bean, H., & Morrow, J. Comparison of smoking treatments. *Behavior Therapy*, 1970, *1*, 465–472.

Salmon, S. *The relationship between a counselor training program in gestalt self-awareness exercises and two measures of counseling effectiveness*. Unpublished doctoral dissertation, Indiana State University, 1972.

Salter, A. *Conditioned reflex therapy*. New York: Farrar, Straus & Giroux, 1949.

Sanders, M., & Glynn, T. Functional analysis of a program for training high- and low-preference peers to modify disruptive classroom behavior. *Journal of Applied Behavior Analysis*, 1977, *10*, 503.

Sartre, J. P. *No exit and three other plays*. New York: Vintage Books, 1955.

Sartre, J. P. *Being and nothingness*. New York: Philosophical Library, 1956.

Satir, V. *Conjoint family therapy*. Palo Alto, Calif.: Science and Behavior Books, 1967.

Satir, V. *Peoplemaking*. Palo Alto, Calif.: Science and Behavior Books, 1972.

Satir, V. The therapist and family therapy: Process model. In A. Horne & M. Ohlsen (Eds.), *Family counseling and therapy*. Itasca, Ill.: F. E. Peacock, 1982.

Satz, P., & Baraff, A. Changes in relation between self-concepts and ideal self-concepts of psychotics consequent upon therapy. *Journal of General Psychology*, 1962, *67*, 191–198.

Schachter, S. Some extraordinary facts about obese humans and rats. *American Psychologist*, 1971, *26*, 129–149.

Schachter, S., & Singer, J. Cognitive, social, and physiological determinants of emotional state. *Psychological Review*, 1962, *69*, 379–399.

Schiff, R., Smith, N., & Prochaska, J. Extinction of avoidance in rats as a function of duration and number of blocked trials. *Journal of Comparative and Physiological Psychology*, 1972, *81*, 356–369.

Schutz, W. *Here comes everybody*. New York: Harper & Row, 1971.

Segal, L. Brief family therapy. In A. Horne & M. Ohlsen (Eds.), *Family counseling and therapy*. Itasca, Ill.: F. E. Peacock, 1982.

Semon, R., & Goldstein, N. The effectiveness of group psychotherapy with chronic schizophrenic patients and an evaluation of different therapeutic methods. *Journal of Consulting Psychology*, 1957, *21*, 317–322.

Shaw, B. Comparison of cognitive therapy and behavior therapy in the treatment of depression. *Journal of Consulting and Clinical Psychology*, 1977, *45*, 543–551.

Sherman, A. *Behavior modification: Theory and practice*. Monterey, Calif.: Brooks/Cole Publishing, 1973.

Shlien, J. M., Mosak, H. H., & Dreikurs, R. Effect of time limits: A comparison of two psychotherapies. *Journal of Counseling Psychology*, 1962, *9*, 31–34.

Singleton, G. Bowen family systems therapy. In A. Horne & M. Ohlsen (Eds.), *Family counseling and therapy*. Itasca, Ill.: F. E. Peacock, 1982.

Skinner, B. F. *Beyond freedom and dignity*. New York: Vintage Books, 1971.

Sloane, R.B., Staples, F., Cristol, A., Yorkston, N., & Whipple, K. *Psychotherapy versus behavior therapy*. Cambridge, Mass.: Harvard University Press, 1975.

Sluzki, C. & Ransom, D. (Eds.) *Double bind: The foundations of the communicational approach to the family.* New York: Grune & Stratton, 1976.

Smith, M. *When I say no I feel guilty.* New York: Dial Press, 1975.

Solomon, P., Kubzansky, P., Leiderman, P., Menderson, J., Trumbull, R., & Wexler, D. (Eds.). *Sensory deprivation.* Cambridge, Mass.: Harvard University Press, 1961.

Solomon, R. Punishment. *American Psychologist,* 1964, *19,* 239–253.

Solomon, R., Kamin, L., & Wynne, L. Traumatic avoidance learning: The outcomes of several extinction procedures with dogs. *Journal of Abnormal and Social Psychology,* 1953, *48,* 291–302.

Solomon, R., & Wynne, L. Traumatic avoidance learning: The principle of anxiety conservation and partial irreversibility. *Psychological Review,* 1954, *61,* 353–385.

Spitz, R. Hospitalism, genesis of psychiatric conditions in early childhood. *Psychoanalytic Study of the Child,* 1945, *1,* 53–74.

Spring, D., Prochaska, J., & Smith, N. Fear reduction in rats through avoidance blocking. *Behavior Research and Therapy,* 1974, *12,* 29–34.

Stampfl, T. Implosive therapy: An emphasis on covert stimulation. In D. Levis (Ed.), *Learning approaches to therapeutic behavior change.* Hawthorne, N.Y.: Aldine Publishing, 1970.

Stampfl, T. Implosive therapy. In P. Olsen (Ed.), *Emotional flooding.* New York: Human Sciences Press, 1976.

Stampfl, T., & Levis, D. The essentials of implosive therapy: A learning-theory based psychodynamic behavioral therapy. *Journal of Abnormal Psychology,* 1967, *72,* 496–503.

Stampfl, T., & Levis, D. *Implosive therapy: Theory and technique.* Morristown, N.J.: General Learning Press, 1973.

Standal, S. *The need for positive regard: A contribution to client-centered theory.* Unpublished doctoral dissertation, University of Chicago, 1954.

Stanton, M., & Todd, T. Structural family therapy with drug addicts. In E. Kaufman & P. Kaufman (Eds.), *The family therapy of drug and alcohol abuse.* New York: Gardner Press, 1979.

Stawar T. Fable mod: Operantly structured fantasies as an adjunct in the modification of fire-setting behavior, *Journal of Behavior Therapy and Experimental Psychiatry,* 1976, *7,* 785–788.

Steiner, C. A script checklist. *Transactional Analysis Bulletin,* 1967, *6,* 38–39.

Steiner, C. *Scripts people live.* New York: Grove Press, 1974.

Stephenson, W. *The study of behavior.* Chicago: University of Chicago Press, 1953.

Stollack, G. Weight loss under different experimental procedures. *Psychotherapy: Theory, Research and Practice,* 1967, *4,* 61–64.

Storms, M., & Nisbett, R. Insomnia and the attribution process. *Journal of Personality and Social Psychology,* 1970, *16,* 319–328.

Straatmeyer, A., & Watkins, J. Rational-emotive therapy and the reduction of speech anxiety. *Rational Living,* 1974, *9,* 33–37.

Strupp, H. *Psychotherapy and the modification of abnormal behavior.* New York: McGraw-Hill, 1971.

Stuart, R. Behavioral control over eating. *Behavior Research and Therapy,* 1967, *5,* 357–365.

Stuart, R. Token reinforcement in marital treatment. In R. Robin & C. Franks (Eds.), *Advances in behavior therapy.* New York: Academic Press, 1969.

Stuart, R. A three-dimensional program for the treatment of obesity. *Behavior Research and Therapy,* 1971, *9,* 177–186.

Stuart, R., & Lott, L. Behavior contracting with delinquents: A cautionary note. *Journal of Behavior Therapy and Experimental Psychiatry,* 1972, *3,* 1–11.

Sushinsky, L., & Bootzin, R. Cognitive desensitization as a model of systematic desensitization. *Behavior Research and Therapy*, 1970, *8*, 29–34.

Thelen, M., Fry, R., Dallinger, S., & Paul, S. Use of videotaped models to improve the interpersonal adjustments of delinquents. *Journal of Consulting and Clinical Psychology*, 1976, *44*, 492.

Thorne, F. Eclectic psychotherapy. In R. Corsini (Ed.), *Current psychotherapies*. Itasca, Ill.: F. E. Peacock, 1973.

Tillich, P. *The courage to be*. New Haven, Conn.: Yale University Press, 1952.

Tinbergen, N. *The study of instinct*. Oxford: Clarendon, 1951.

Toffler, A. *Future shock*. New York: Bantam Books, 1970.

Truax, C. Reinforcement and nonreinforcement in Rogerian psychotherapy. *Journal of Abnormal Psychology*, 1966, *71*, 1–9.

Truax, C. Effects of client-centered psychotherapy with schizophrenic patients: Nine years pretherapy and nine years posttherapy hospitalization. *Journal of Consulting and Clinical Psychology*, 1970, *34*, 417–422.

Truax, C., & Carkhuff, R. *Toward effective counseling and psychotherapy: Training and practice*. Hawthorne, N.Y.: Aldine Publishing, 1967.

Truax, C., Wargo, P., & Silber, L. Effects of group psychotherapy with high accurate empathy and nonpossessive warmth upon institutionalized female delinquents. *Journal of Abnormal Psychology*, 1966, *71*, 267–274.

Turner, R., & Ascher, M. Controlled comparison of progressive relaxation, stimulus control, and paradoxical-intention therapies for insomnia. *Journal of Consulting and Clinical Psychology*, 1979, *47*, 500–508.

Ullmann, L, & Krasner, L. (Eds.). *Case studies in behavior modification*. New York: Holt, Rinehart & Winston, 1965.

Valins, S., & Ray, A. Effects of cognitive desensitization on avoidance behavior. *Journal of Personality and Social Psychology*, 1967, *7*, 345–350.

Vasta, R. Coverant control of self-evaluations through temporal cueing. *Journal of Behavior Therapy and Experimental Psychiatry*, 1975, *7*, 35–3.

von Bertonloffy, L. *General systems theory*. New York: George Braziller, 1968.

vonGebsattez, V.E. The world of the compulsive. In R. May, E. Angel, & H. Ellenberger (Eds.), *Existence*. New York: Basic Books, 1958.

Vygotsky, L. *Thought and language*. New York: John Wiley & Sons, 1962.

Wagner, M. Reinforcement of the expression of anger through role-playing. *Behavior Research and Therapy*, 1967, *6*, 91–95.

Wagner, M., & Bragg, R. Comparing behavior modification approaches to habit decrement-smoking. *Journal of Consulting and Clinical Psychology*, 1970, *34*, 258–263.

Walker, P.L. The effect of two counseling strategies with black disadvantaged clients. *Dissertation Abstracts International*, 1973, *33*, 8–A, 4106–4107.

Warren, N., & Rice, L. Structuring and stabilizing of psychotherapy for low-prognosis clients. *Journal of Consulting and Clinical Psychology*, 1972, *39*, 173–181.

Watzlawick, P., Beavin, J., & Jackson, D. *Pragmatics of human communication*. New York: W. W. Norton, 1967.

Weakland, J., Fisch, R., Watzlawick, P., & Bodin, A. Brief therapy: Focused problem resolution. *Family Process*, 1974, *13*, 141–168.

Weingaertner, A. Self-administered aversive stimulation with hallucinating hospitalized schizophrenics. *Journal of Consulting and Clinical Psychology*, 1971, *36*, 422–429.

Wexler, D. A cognitive theory of experiencing, self-actualization, and therapeutic process. In D. Wexler & L. Rice (Eds.), *Innovations in client-centered therapy*. New York: John Wiley & Sons, 1974.

White, R. W. Motivation reconsidered: The concept of competence. *Psychological Review*, 1959, *66*, 297–333.

White, R. W. Competence and the psychosexual stages of development. In M. R.

Jones (Ed.), *Nebraska symposium on motivation*. Lincoln: University of Nebraska Press, 1960.

Whitman, T. Aversive control of smoking behavior in a group context. *Behavior Research and Therapy*, 1972, *10*, 97–104.

Wiener, N. *Cybernetics, or control and communication in the animal and the machine*. Cambridge, Mass.: MIT Press, 1962.

Wilkins, W. Desensitization: Social and cognitive factors underlying the effectiveness of Wolpe's procedure. *Psychological Bulletin*, 1971, *76*, 311–317.

Wisocki, P., & Rooney, E. *A comparison of thought-stopping and covert-sensitization techniques in the treatment of smoking*. Paper presented to the annual meeting of the Association for Advancement of Behavior Therapy, Washington, D.C., September 1971.

Wittgenstein, L. *Philosophical investigations*. New York: Macmillan, 1953.

Wittgenstein, L. *The blue and brown books*. New York: Harper & Row, 1958.

Wolberg, L. *Technique of psychotherapy*. New York: Grune & Stratton, 1954.

Wollersheim, J. Effectiveness of group therapy based upon learning principles in the treatment of overweight women. *Journal of Abnormal Psychology*, 1970, *76*, 462–474.

Wolpe, J. *Psychotherapy by reciprocal inhibition*. Stanford: Stanford University Press, 1958.

Wolpe, J. *The practice of behavior therapy* (2nd ed.). Elmsford, N.Y.: Pergamon Press, 1973.

Wright, D., & Busch, G. Parental intervention in the treatment of chronic constipation. *Journal of Behavior Therapy and Experimental Psychiatry*, 1977, *8*, 93–95.

Wulbert, M., & Dries, R. The relative efficacy of melhylphenidate (retalin) and behavior modification techniques in the treatment of a hyperactive child. *Journal of Applied Behavior Analysis*, 1977, *10*, 21–311.

Yates, A. *Theory and practice in behavior therapy*. New York: John Wiley & Sons, 1975.

Yulis, S. Generalization of therapeutic gain in the treatment of premature ejaculation. *Behavior Therapy*, 1976, *7*, 355–358.

Zeiss, R. Self-directed treatment for premature ejaculation. *Journal of Consulting and Clinical Psychology*, 1978, *46*, 1234–1241.

Zeisset, R. Desensitization and relaxation in the modification of psychiatric patients' interview behavior. *Journal of Abnormal Psychology*, 1968, *73*, 18–24.

Zimring, F. Theory and practice of client-centered therapy: A cognitive view. In D. Wexler & L. Rice (Eds.), *Innovations in client-centered therapy*. New York: John Wiley & Sons, 1974.

AUTHOR INDEX

SUBJECT INDEX

*This book has been set Linotron 202 in 9 and 8 point Hel-
vetica Light, leaded 2 points. Chapter numbers are
Typositor Outline Helvetica Medium and chapter titles are
24 point Helvetica Black. The size of the type page is 30
by 47 picas.*